D1211082

# Guided Imagery and Music:

## The Bonny Method and Beyond

Edited by:
Kenneth E. Bruscia
& Denise E. Grocke

ISBN 1-891278-12-6

2 4 6 8 9 7 5 3 1

Distributed throughout the world by

Barcelona Publishers
4 White Brook Road - Lower Village
Gilsum NH 03448
Tel: 603-357-0236 Fax: 603-357-2073
SAN 298-6299

Cover illustration and design:
© 2002 Frank McShane

Cover photograph: "Rainbow Waves"
© 1995 Beth Kingsley Hawkins

This book is dedicated to

*Helen Lindquist Bonny*

*A courageous pioneer*
*in the uncharted territories of*
*music and consciousness,*
*and an inspiration to all who travel there*
*through the method she created:*
*Guided Imagery and Music*

# TABLE OF CONTENTS

## Part One: Overview

# Part Two: Applications

# Part Three: Orientations

# Part Four: Developments

# Part Five: Theory and Research

# Part Six: Professional Issues

# List of Appendices

# CONTRIBUTORS

Brian Abrams, PhD, MT-BC, FAMI
      Assistant Professor of Music Therapy
      Logan State University
      Logan, UT

James Borling, MM, MT-BC, FAMI
      Primary Trainer in the Bonny Method/Private Practice
      Director of Music Therapy
      Radford University
      Radford, VA

Joanna Booth, BSc, BM, LTCL, AIRMT, FAMI
      Private Practice in the Bonny Method
      Auckland, New Zealand

Darlene M. Brooks, PhD, MT-BC, FAMI, Reiki Master
      Associate Professor of Music Therapy: Temple University
      Private Practice in the Bonny Method
      Philadelphia, PA

Kenneth E. Bruscia, PhD, MT-BC, FAMI
      Professor of Music Therapy: Temple University
      Primary Trainer in the Bonny Method
      Philadelphia, PA

Debra S. Burns, PhD, MT-BC, FAMI
      Post-doctoral Fellow: Walther Cancer Institute
      Research Scientist: Indiana University School of Nursing
      Indianapolis, IN

Jill Carlisle, FAMI
      Private Practice in the Bonny Method
      Albemarle Gate, Cheltenham Glos., United Kingdom

Marilyn F. Clark, MA, LCPC, NCC, FAMI
    Primary Trainer in the Bonny Method
    Pastoral psychotherapist using the Bonny Method:
    Private Practice, Center for Health Enhancement,
    St. Joseph Medical Center. Baltimore, MD
Ginger Clarkson, MA, MT-BC, FAMI
    Primary Trainer & Private Practice in the Bonny Method
    Adjunct Professor of Music Therapy:
    La Universidad de las Americas – Puebla Cholula
    Puebla, Mexico
Nicki S. Cohen, PhD, MT-BC, FAMI
    Private Practice: GIM Services of North Texas
    Associate Professor, Music Therapy and Voice
    Texas Woman's University
    Denton, TX
Frances Smith Goldberg, MA, MT-BC, MFI, FAMI
    Primary Trainer in the Bonny Method
    Psychotherapist in Private Practice
    San Francisco, CA
Denise E. Grocke, RMT, MT-BC, FAMI
    Primary Trainer in the Bonny Method
    Associate Professor and Head of Music Therapy
    University of Melbourne
    Melbourne, Victoria, Australia
Florence Holligan, SJG, RMT, FAMI
    Primary Trainer in the Bonny Method
    Private Practice
    East Bentleigh, Victoria, Australia
Roseanne Kasayka, DA, MT-BC, FAMI; Reiki Master
    Primary Trainer in the Bonny Method; Vice-President
    Dementia Services & Integrative Therapies
    Heather Hill Hospital and Health Partnership
    Painesville, OH

Dag Körlin, MD (Psychiatry), FAMI
Certified psychodynamic psychotherapist
Head of Creative Arts Group Program for
Trauma Related Disorders: Stockholm County Council
Stockholm, Sweden

Kirstie Lewis, PhD, FAMI
Primary Trainer in the Bonny Method
Private Counseling Practice using the Bonny Method
Director of Irlen Center Northwest
Bellevue, WA

Carola Maack, MA, HPG, FAMI
Private Practice in the Bonny Method
Bucholz, Germany

Linda Keiser Mardis, MA, CST, FAMI, Reiki Master
Primary Trainer in the Bonny Method
Private Practice
Olney, MD

Anthony  Meadows, PhD, MT-BC, FAMI
Private Practice in the Bonny Method
Philadelphia, PA

Cathy McKinney, PhD, MT-BC, FAMI
Associate Professor/Director of Music Therapy
Appalachian State University
Private Practice using the Bonny Method
Boone, NC

Torben Moe, Music Therapist,  PhD., FAMI
Primary Trainer in the Bonny Method
Private Practice
Roskilde, Denmark

Elizabeth Moffitt, MA, MTA, RCC, FAMI
Primary Trainer in the Bonny Method
Private Practice
N. Vancouver, BC, Canada

Gabriella Giordanella Perilli, PhD, FAMI
> Cognitive-behavioral Psychotherapist
> Private Practice in the Bonny Method
> Rome, Italy

Eugenia Pickett, MA, FAMI, LCSW-C
> Certifications in group psychotherapy, medical psycho-
> therapy, clinical hypnotherapy, and addictions counseling.
> Private Psychotherapy Practice using the Bonny Method.
> Baltimore, MD

Alison E. Short, MA, RMT, MT-BC, RGIMT, FAMI
> Primary Trainer in the Bonny Method
> Private Practice; Prince of Wales Hospital;
> Sacred Heart Hospice; Ozanam Villa Aged Care Hostel
> Sydney, NSW, Australia

Ruth Skaggs, MA, LPC
> Director:
> Southeastern Institute for Music-Centered Psychotherapy
> Atlanta, GA

Sierra Stokes-Stearns, PhD, MT-BC, FAMI
> Primary Trainer in the Bonny Method
> Founder and Director, Mid-Atlantic Institute
> Severna Park, MD

Lisa Summer, MCAT, MT-BC, FAMI
> Primary Trainer in the Bonny Method
> Associate Professor/Director of Music Therapy
> Anna Maria College
> Paxton, MA

Lisabeth Toomey
> Private Practice in the Bonny Method
> Auckland, New Zealand

Madelaine Ventre, MS, MT-BC, FAMI
    Primary Trainer & Private Practice in the Bonny Method
    Certified Mandala Assessment Teacher
    Private Practice in the Bonny Method
    Director: Center for Creative Therapies and the Arts
    Forestburgh, NY
Karlyn Ward, PhD, LCSW, FAMI
    Certified Jungian Analyst
    Private practice in psychotherapy and the Bonny Method
    Mill Valley, CA
Margareta Wärja
    Primary Trainer in the Bonny Method
    Private Practice
    Stockholm, Sweden
Susan B. Wesley, PhD, MT-BC, LCPC, FAMI
    Private Practice in Jungian-oriented music psychotherapy.
    Bangor, Maine

# *Preface*

# AN OPENING METAPHOR

# Kenneth E. Bruscia

Helen Bonny is a truly great pioneer. She opened up new vistas for listening to music, charted new territories of consciousness, forged new paths for human development, created new possibilities for healing, and discovered new doors to spirituality. Her pioneering idea was simple but astounding: Open yourself to music, and it will take you beyond yourself.

Like other great pioneers, Bonny painted her "canvas" with broad strokes. Her "painting" gives possibility, it does not define reality; the images are suggestive and open to interpretation, they are not definitions of detail. Her work is a painting of and for the imagination; it invites the experiencer's imagination to go beyond it. And so, Bonny's full vision does not easily fit within the confines of her picture frame. Much of it resides in the imagination of those who have experienced it. It is no wonder that it is difficult to give her painting just the right title. Exactly where does its essence lie?

On the other hand, like other pioneers, Bonny also concerned herself with ritual and form. She learned how to begin a musical journey into consciousness, she learned how to proceed through this uncharted terrain, and she learned how to bring the journey to an end. And through these simple rituals and forms, she crafted a method, broadly entitled "Guided Imagery and Music" (GIM).

Metaphorically, GIM is a canvas of images that Bonny carefully selected and placed in relation to one another. This book, then, is a journey into the paradoxes of those images: the form and formlessness of GIM—its craft and its vision, its limits and its possibilities, its clarity and its vagaries. The purpose of the book is to examine the images that Bonny herself painted, and then to explore how these images have been further expanded by her "fellow" painters. The book has thus been entitled: "Guided Imagery and Music: The Bonny Method and Beyond."

The book was designed to look at the paintings and images of GIM from many different perspectives. The first perspective is an historical one. It is important to know how the images and paintings developed along with the painters. And so, several chapters of the book trace the evolution of GIM. In the Introduction, Eugenia Pickett details the history of writings in GIM—all the canvases in the collection by Bonny and her proponents—and this places the present book into historical perspective. Then immediately in the first chapter, Marilyn Clark traces how the defining features of Bonny's work evolved—how each image in Bonny's paintings was selected, shaped, colored, and located—and this places the entire method within an unfolding narrative of Bonny's professional life. History is also the focus of other chapters. Denise Grocke describes how Bonny's library of music programs was born, and how it grew in maturity and application. Later, the present writer gives an historical account of how Bonny's programs have been modified over the years, and how her followers have designed programs of their own. Most, if not all of the music programs known can be found in the Appendices of the book. Another historical thread is examined by Kirstie Lewis, who recounts how a very unique model of training evolved in GIM, starting from the experimental and exciting days of the Institute for Consciousness and Music, and ending with the formal endorsement procedures of the Association for Music and Imagery. Finally, at the end, Denise Grocke surveys how the seeds of GIM have spread to other countries, and bloomed beyond expectations. It seems fitting that history be important in a storytelling method such as GIM, and so accounts of the past are evenly distributed throughout the book.

Another perspective provided in the book emerges from the boundaries that authors have so carefully laid out for GIM and the "Bonny Method"—one must know which paintings are by Bonny and which are by her followers. Chapters by Marilyn Clark, Madelaine Ventre, Anthony Meadows, and the present writer all inspect the Bonny paintings, and try to identify her indelible marks. What defines the individual form of GIM and its basic premises? What defines the group form? How are these forms different from imagery techniques in psychotherapy, and music techniques in music therapy? Did Bonny really put all those things on her canvas, or was she much more selective? Seeing the boundaries of GIM is not only a perspective in itself, but also puts GIM in perspective.

Later, in Part Four, the reader will see how Bonny's followers are moving out in different directions to further develop GIM. The first chapter, by the present writer, proposes various approaches to client assessment in GIM, a topic that has not been addressed in Bonny's writings or in the GIM literature. Lisa Summer presents her own method of Group Music and Imagery Therapy (GMIT), going significantly beyond the kind of group work done by Bonny. Summer also introduces ideas to help systematize how and when to make appropriate adaptations in GIM. Another area of development is in methods of analysis of music programs. Brian Abrams surveys the myriad methods of analyses that have been developed by Bonny and her followers to understand the music programs used in GIM.

The applications of GIM create another very interesting perspective on the Bonny method—when a GIM painting is created in a different setting, what happens? What remains from Bonny's original images? What had to be removed or altered in some way? Is it still a GIM painting? In Part Two, applications with children and adolescents are described by Susan Wesley, and psychotherapeutic applications are presented by Anthony Meadows. Alison Short and Debra Burns look at GIM in medical settings Notice in these chapters the subtle variations that can be made to tailor GIM to the special needs of different populations. Also notice, how far these variations go from Bonny's original method, almost testing where the boundaries are.

One thing will become quite clear while reading this book—the nomenclature that has evolved in GIM is complicated and confusing indeed, despite the valiant efforts of both authors and editors! And there seems to be no easy or simple solution. As Bonny's work has been expanded and modified to accommodate different client needs and myriad styles of practice, significant boundary questions have arisen, which in turn have created considerable confusion in knowing what to call the various practices that were spawned by Bonny, but were significantly different from her work. This problem in nomenclature was then further exacerbated when GIM—which was already being used to refer to Bonny's work as well as modifications made by her followers—was renamed the "Bonny Method." Now the question became whether the title "Bonny Method" subsumes all related but significantly different practices developed by her followers. If so, then the "Bonny Method" should be used as the umbrella term; if not, then "GIM" is more appropriate. For a variety of reasons that will be offered throughout the book, and for the sake of clarity given current understandings of these terms, the editors have decided that "GIM" should be used as the generic or umbrella term, and that the "Bonny Method" should be used to refer only to the specific forms developed by Bonny. Thus, in this book, the following terminology is used as defined below.

- "Guided Imagery and Music" or "GIM" refers to all forms of music-imaging in an expanded state of consciousness, including not only the specific individual and group forms that Bonny developed, but also all variations and modifications in those forms created by her followers. GIM is therefore the umbrella title that subsumes all practices involving imaging to music in an altered state of consciousness, including work done in individual or group settings, for purposes of therapy, healing, self-development, or spiritual growth, whether the images are guided or unguided, whether classical or non-classical music is used, and notwithstanding variations in the form of the session itself. As will be discussed later however,

GIM does have boundaries; it does not include a host of related techniques that belong to music therapy.
- The "Bonny Method" refers to all of Bonny's original work. Logically, this includes *both* the individual and group forms that she developed; however, because of the important differences between these forms (e.g., therapy versus growth goals, and dialogue versus no dialogue with a guide), throughout the book, the acronym "BMGIM" is used to refer to her individual form, and either "Group GIM" or "Music and Imagery" is used to refer to her group form.

Because there is no uniformity in the GIM literature on how these terms have been used in the past, and because at present, there is no consensus within the GIM community on their definition, readers must still take note of how each author uses and defines these terms, despite efforts of the editors to be as consistent as possible. Also, readers will quickly discover that when authors are discussing any combinations of these practices, or making any comparisons (e.g., Bonny's work and the work of her followers, individual and group practices), any or all of these terms might be used within the same sentence or paragraph, and it can become quite difficult to write and confusing to read. One can even notice that the chapter titles themselves speak to the subtleties of trying to accurately name the complex expanse of practices spawned by Bonny.

Moving to another perspective on GIM provided in this book, Bonny has always been a person of deep belief. She identified with the ideas of Abraham Maslow and the humanistic school of psychology, and when transpersonal theories began to evolve, she found herself moving quite comfortably from third force psychology to fourth force spirituality. But in art, as in life, all painters and all viewers cannot have the same belief systems, nor can they look at paintings in the same way and derive the same meanings. One's orientation and position in relation to the work is the only perspective one has, and in GIM there are many. A person in second force psychology looks at a GIM painting and immediately sees twos; a person in third force sees threes, and a person in fourth force goes beyond number. But be not mistaken, the fact that GIM can be practiced within these various orientations does not mean that Bonny's belief systems or method change to accommodate them all. This does not give due credit to the care that Bonny took in laying down the theoretical foundations for her work.

Certainly, it is exciting to consider GIM from all the orientations presented in this book. Ginger Clarkson carefully crafts an amalgam of BMGIM and Gestalt therapy, selecting those elements that seem most related to one another. Karlyn Ward shows how many of Jung's constructs can be fruitfully applied to understanding all GIM work. Perhaps, of all orientations, a Jungian one is most closely allied to Bonny's combination of humanistic and transpersonal approaches. Then, the present writer examines how and when a psychodynamic orientation is applicable to BMGIM work, pointing out how easily resistance and transference can be detected in BMGIM work. Finally, Roseanne Kasayka removes GIM from the realm of traditional therapies, and takes it into the spiritual domain, an area of great dedication for Bonny.

Of course, the dilemma of possibility is choice. When is one orientation more fruitful for the client than another? As any practitioner of GIM quickly discovers when seeing a broad range of clientele, it is naïve to assume that a humanistic orientation can be taken with everyone, and at all times during the GIM process—notwithstanding the fact that this was Bonny's preferred orientation. Similarly, one cannot use psychodynamic, Jungian, Gestalt, or transpersonal orientations with every client through every stage of the work. To do so gives greater significance to the therapist's beliefs than the client's needs. Believing in a particular theory does not make it the best for every client. Ken Wilber offers very clear guidelines for choosing the orientation most effective in meeting client needs: It depends on the nature of the client's problem, and the developmental stage in which it originated. GIM practitioners who only use the humanistic orientation will need to understand the indications and contraindications involved, and then select and refer clients accordingly. It is not acceptable, and especially in a sensitive method like GIM, to simply say that everyone uses the same canvas and paints. And the same goes for those practitioners who use other orientations.

In Part Five, GIM is considered from the perspectives of theory and research. In looking at all the paintings in the GIM collection, what do they mean? Why do they have the effect that they do? How can we understand them? Four important and quite different theories are put forth. Brian Abrams presents an overview of transpersonal theories that have influenced our thinking in GIM, and then presents the results of his own theoretical research on what defines transpersonal within a GIM experience. Frances Goldberg, in an expansion of an earlier theory, lays out a very broad theoretical concept of the psychospiritual and holographic nature of GIM. Then, Dag Körlin takes the reader back into the body, as he seeks neuropsychological explanations for how GIM heals traumatic imagery. Lastly, Gabriella Perilli delves into the metaphoric aspects of GIM work, providing a psychological theory on the importance of metaphor in life, therapy, and GIM.

Following these chapters on theory, two chapters are presented on research. Cathy McKinney surveys the quantitative research done on GIM to date, and Denise Grocke surveys the qualitative research.

The final section of the book, Part Six, deals with professional issues. In our painting metaphor, this section is about the painters. How do they govern their conduct? How do they train and supervise one another in the work? And where have they taken GIM? Nicki Cohen begins with an examination of central ethical issues that arise in GIM practice and research. Kirstie Lewis outlines the important principles guiding training in GIM by presenting an historical account. Darlene Brooks contributes the first writing on supervisory practices in GIM, an area deserving much more attention in the literature, not only because of the importance of supervision, but also because of the unique approaches to supervision that come quite naturally out of the GIM process. In the final chapter, Denise Grocke collates information provided by GIM practitioners around the world describing the status of GIM practice and training throughout various countries.

Welcome to the first textbook on GIM! It is a tribute to Bonny and to the inspired and dedicated group of painters that have worked in her studio that the collection of paintings in GIM is so large, diverse, and interesting. And it is a tribute to the collection itself that this textbook is even possible.

There can be no better advice to the reader than to allow each painting to present itself without preconception. Then, when coming to the end of the collection, the openness and coherence of Bonny's paintings will be apprehended in their entirety, and the variations in images made by her followers will be fully appreciated.

# Introduction

# A HISTORY OF THE LITERATURE
# ON GUIDED IMAGERY AND MUSIC (GIM)

## Eugenia Pickett

This is the first published textbook on "Guided Imagery and Music" (GIM), a method developed by Helen Bonny for working with individuals and groups using music, imagery, and altered states of consciousness. The individual form which has very specific features has recently been renamed the "Bonny Method of Guided Imagery and Music" (BMGIM), while the various other forms of individual and group work inspired by Bonny are herein subsumed under the generic name of GIM.

Experienced practitioners who were trained by Bonny herself or by her students have authored this book. All of the authors are proponents of Bonny and her method. To understand the significance of this compilation, one can benefit by looking back on the history of writings and publications in the field.

## THE EARLY BEGINNING

GIM reaches the deeper layers of the psyche and brings that material to conscious awareness for examination and resolution. The individual form (BMGIM) had its early development at the Psychiatric Research Center in Baltimore, Maryland where Bonny developed music–listening programs to investigate altered states of conscious in a psychotherapeutic manner. The method was first discussed in a copyrighted version of her doctoral dissertation, *Music and Psychotherapy* (1976), where she presented the effects of music on the imaginative process and reported on this research, which began in 1969. In this very first writing on the individual form (BMGIM), Bonny described the therapist or guide as secondary to the music, a witness and facilitator to the experience, while the listener's drive toward his or her own healing and growth fulfilled itself through the music. She said that with proper caution, BMGIM could be an effective treatment for most types of psychiatric problems with persons seeking deeper self-knowledge. Unfortunately, *Music and Psychotherapy* only reached the reading audience of her academic committee and her students.

## THE SEVENTIES

Bonny's first publication to reach a wider audience, the general public, was published by Harper and Row. Co-authored with Louis Savary, *Music and Your Mind: Listening with a New Consciousness* (Bonny & Savary, 1973) is filled with exercises for individuals and groups to explore levels of creativity, insight, self-realization, deep memory, the unconscious, the transpersonal, and the religions. The authors suggested ways that music might be used in more than a superficial way and generated techniques for going beyond ordinary listening to conscious or heightened awareness listening. It is in this publication that Group GIM was introduced, along with other ways of working with related techniques both alone and with a guide. The basic format introduced consisted of a relaxation, focus, and induction into a deep music-listening experience followed by a return to one's usual awareness and further reflection on the experience. The group form was presented as a way of working toward a variety of educational, developmental, and spiritual goals; as such, it did not always involve clinical or therapeutic goals. Also, unlike the individual form of BMGIM, Group GIM did not involve an ongoing interaction with the guide during the music imaging experience. The book emphasizes the many intricacies in the interplay between music, imagery, and consciousness, and in the appendix, suggestions are given on how to choose the most effective music.

Bonny's work at the Psychiatric Research Center attracted many professionals interested in learning how to practice her method of using music in altered states of consciousness. As a result, in 1973, Bonny founded The Institute for Consciousness and Music (ICM) in Baltimore, and began to offer workshops and courses to train facilitators in GIM. Bonny also initiated and distributed a newsletter for all those interested in her work. The newsletters served as a vehicle of communication to all professionals interested in music and imagery. The ICM Newsletter was published from 1973 to 1981, and then when ICM moved to Port Townsend, Washington, the newsletter for "ICM West" continued for another four years.

Meanwhile, the ICM training seminars and workshops pointed to a need for more in-depth reading materials for her students. As a result, Bonny wrote three monographs based on her dissertation. The first monograph, *Facilitating*

*GIM Sessions* (1978a) contains five chapters that explored the qualities of a guide, handling a session, guiding techniques, working with the process, and the populations that BMGIM could benefit. It was here that one learned about setting up a preliminary interview, taking a history, how to explain the process to a client, and carrying out a music session. This monograph was the only textbook for how to manage a preliminary conversation with a client, types of inductions, how to handle the music listening process, and post-session integration. In a chapter, "How to Work with GIM Phenomena," the student-facilitator can learn how to use their own sense faculties to assist clients in the exploring and managing sensory representations of their own inner experiences.

In the second monograph, *The Role of Taped Music Programs in the GIM Process* (1978b), Bonny explored states of consciousness, the psychological effects of music, how the music programs were structured, and specific music programs that were available at that time. In this document, readers are introduced to consciousness as a means of providing ways for talking about the content and availability of accumulated perceptions. Bonny discussed how music could access and retrieve unconscious material to a discrete level of consciousness where it can be evaluated and integrated. She then discussed the qualities of music with regard to pitch, rhythm, mode, melody, and timbre and how they affect human consciousness. Bonny also explained how she selected music to contour the earlier music programs: *Death–Rebirth, Peak Experience, Comforting–Anaclytic, Affect–Release*, and *Imagery*.

In *GIM Therapy: Past, Present and Future Implications* (1980), Bonny gave the history of GIM and described it as radical and innovative in psychotherapy. She summarized the manner in which her research led to the creation of therapeutic music programs and presented a then current design for short-term psychotherapy using GIM. Bonny concluded the monograph with the need for continued investigation. A bibliography relevant to music and psychotherapy was included in this monograph and the music programs *Cosmic Astral, Positive–Affect* and *Beginners Group Experience* were added. These three monographs were not widely distributed but were created and used mainly for training.

Also in the 1970s Dr. Bonny collaborated with other therapists in the professional literature. She discussed the use of music in psychedelic (LSD) psychotherapy with Walter Pahnke in *The Journal of Music Therapy* (Bonny & Pahnke, 1972). In the *American Journal of Art Therapy,* Bonny and Kellogg (1977) explained how to combine music and art in "Mandalas as a Measure of Change in Psychotherapy," and Bonny and Tansill (1977) reported on the use of GIM in addictions recovery. One article that discussed music as a healing medium for enhancing and actualizing the self was published by Bonny (1975) in *The Journal of Music Therapy.*

# THE EIGHTIES

Bonny's center, the Institute for Consciousness and Music, was created in 1973, carried forward by Marilyn Clark and Linda Keiser Mardis in the 1980s and eventually renamed the Institute for Music and Imagery (IMI). This continuation generated additional literature on music listening and therapist training. Separately, Clark (1987) authored *The Institute for Music and Imagery Training Program for Guided Imagery and Music* and Keiser published *Conscious Listening* (1986), a book of tips on how to listen deeply to the Bonny music programs. Clark and Keiser (1989) together contributed a much needed training manual that included both conceptual and specific treatment of the nature of the training program that had emerged from the 1970s and which they promoted and carried out in the 1980s. This manual for GIM included teaching content, case studies, and appendices of resources, forms, and outlines. It served as a useful point of departure for the various other training programs, which began when IMI closed its doors in September 1988.

Further literature generated by Keiser and Clark included a continuation of the ICM newsletters by IMI, under a new name, *Crescendo.* This newsletter was distributed from 1986 to 1988 when IMI ceased to function. Initially, *Crescendo* included two ongoing columns. In the one named "Musings," Keiser presented thoughts about the GIM process itself and suggestions for choosing and using music; in the other, "In The Mind's Eye," Clark looked into the imaginative process itself. These newsletters provided the increasing number of trained GIM facilitators with edification in the GIM process and the ongoing sense of being part of a larger body.

Later newsletter editions included the columns "Image-scape" and "Grace Notes." These columns presented a more in-depth exploration of the key elements of imagery and music than the earlier editions of *Crescendo.* The newsletter at this point was providing the growing number of trained GIM facilitators both with instruction in the GIM process and an ongoing sense of being a part of a larger body.

Music and GIM have been used with many populations. Prior to the inception of a professional journal devoted solely to GIM, most documentation about its use and effectiveness was published in other professional journals and books. Summer (1985) in *The Journal of Mental Imagery* said that music facilitates imagery and healing. Bonny (1987) referred to music has an immediately available language in *The Arts in Psychotherapy.* Pickett (1987–1988), in *The Journal of Imagination, Cognition and Personality,* discussed two different types of healing using GIM for fibroid tumors. Keiser's *Light Search* (1988) is a personal journal account of the use of music in the healing process of breast cancer. Summer (1988), in a monograph geared to music therapists using various forms of music relaxation and imagery, discussed how she used GIM in an institutional group setting. In the *Journal of Music Therapy,* Summer (1981) described the use of GIM with the elderly, Nolan (1983) explored its usage in forensic psychiatry, and Kovach (1985) compared GIM with Shamanism. Kenny (1985) discussed GIM as a whole systems approach. In the publication *Music Therapy Perspectives,* Wylie and Blum (1986) described the use of GIM in hospice, Goldberg (1988) reported on GIM and head trauma, while Jarvis (1988) presented GIM as a primary therapy.

    Almost all of the earlier contributions are anecdotal records of successful therapeutic interventions. Some refer to GIM as a form of psychotherapy, some as an adjunct to psychotherapy, some as a spiritual process, and some as a vehicle for personal growth.

## THE NINETIES

More and more published material on GIM became available to both the public and the professional reader in this next decade. Bruscia (1991), in a collection of case studies in music therapy, included five that used GIM. Covering a range of therapeutic issues for both therapist and client, the various chapters discussed how GIM was used with a wounded healer, an emergent self, a physical disability, addiction, and AIDS.

    McKinney (1990) discussed the use of GIM in obstetrics in *Music Therapy Perspectives,* And Toomey (1991), in the *Journal of the New Zealand Society of Music Therapy,* discussed the parallels of GIM and music with the immediacy of improvisation. That same year in *Head Trauma,* Pickett (1991) discussed the imagery aspects of GIM as they can be applied in Head Trauma Rehabilitation. Additional clinical applications of GIM were discussed in *The Australian Journal of Music Therapy* by Erdonmez (1992).

    At that same time, several articles on GIM were published in the Journal *Music Therapy.* Short (1991) discussed how GIM can be used diagnostically in physical illness and trauma, Jacobiwitz (1992) described how GIM could be used with the elderly, Short (1992) presented GIM with the disabled; and Ventre (1993) discussed how mandala and music could be interwoven with the Mother archetype.

    In 1994 and 1995, Bonny and Keiser Mardis produced two discographies of the then current Core and Specialized Music Programs. These, and a later paper by Bruscia (1996), served as comprehensive guides for both the existing and Bruscia's newer music programs. The papers were distributed only to GIM trainers and practitioners. All are shown in the Appendices.

Meanwhile, Carol Bush, who had offered seminars to GIM students in dreamwork in the late 1970s, had also been working on a manuscript, which was later published in 1995 under the title, *Healing Imagery and Music*. This popular book served as both a text for GIM students and a resource for psychotherapists. Bush's own clinical work and teaching employed the use of bodywork. She encouraged GIM practitioners to understand how music and sound allowed for both an exploration of the deeper mind and for an examination of the mind-body connection. In her book she explored how GIM not only can be used as a primary therapy but also as a method for personal growth and "spiritual unfoldment." The book contains three sections. The first describes the music imagery experience with regard to her personal questions and resolutions. She then continues with the theoretical underpinnings and discusses how GIM works initially with personal agendas and then can expand to a more universal encounter with something larger than the self. The second section of her book is filled with stories of healing involving the mind and the body. The third section includes instructions for taking one's own journey, and music selections that relate to the both to the elements and to the processes of deepening.

In the popular self-help literature, Merritt (1996), in *Mind, Music and Imagery*, interwove the use of music and GIM in a guide that discussed how to increase learning and memory, stimulate creativity, help with conflict resolution, and relax. This book was marketed as one with instructions for unlocking one's creative potential and included forty exercises using classical music to find deeper feelings, build greater awareness, and to bring healing to both to the whole self.

Also in 1996, Keiser Mardis published *Program 33: A New Program and a New Programming Concept*, an in-depth discussion of music for experienced guides.

In 1998, Bruscia published an edited book entitled *The Dynamics of Music Psychotherapy*, containing six chapters, which explore transference and countertransference dynamics in GIM. The authors were Lisa Summer ("The Pure Music Transference"), John Pelliteri ("A Self Analysis of Transference in GIM"), and Kenneth Bruscia ("Modes of Consciousness," "Manifestations of Transference," and "Re-imaging Client Images").

In 1999, Hibben presented another edited book, entitled *Inside Music Therapy: Client Experiences*. This book contains nine chapters on GIM, all written from the client's point of view.

## A PROFESSIONAL JOURNAL

The inspiration for a professional journal, to lend voice to the GIM method, began in 1991 at the annual meeting of the Association for Music and Imagery

(AMI). The AMI had been formed in 1986 for the purpose of upholding the integrity of GIM, while also supporting those trained in the method. At the 1991 meeting, the present author requested the AMI membership to approve and fund a publication that would present GIM as a viable technique for growth in areas recognized by analytic psychology, consciousness and spirituality, psycho-neuroimmunology, musicology, imagery, and psychotherapy. This was approved, and so the *Journal of the Association for Music and Imagery* (JAMI) was founded. The present author spearheaded the effort and Carol Bush, Frances Goldberg, Beth Hawkins, Susan Hale and Stephanie Merritt were named as members of the first editorial board. The first volume was published in 1992, with an introduction by Helen Bonny. To date, JAMI has included articles in all areas of practice, including: addiction, cross-cultural issues, emotional and sexual abuse, mental illness and health, music, personal growth and healing, physical illness and healing, the body-mind connection, pregnancy and childbirth, professional issues, training, and research.

*Volume 1* (JAMI, 1992) explored the use of music as it elicits emotion and affect, as an aesthetic elixir and as co-therapist. It identified GIM as a therapeutic process capable of working with addiction and abuse. This issue included an article on the use of mandalas with GIM and an analysis of one of the GIM music programs.

*Volume 2* (JAMI, 1993) included articles that discussed GIM specifically with regard to physiology, change, and healing, and included an affective-intuitive music program analysis, an accounting of a body/mind healing and several case studies that addressed innovative uses of GIM. One article addressed how to use GIM within a fifty-minute hour.

*Volume 3* (JAMI, 1994) was made up of articles that discussed the application of GIM in institutional, private, and spiritual settings and included another music program analysis.

*Volume 4* (JAMI, 1995) presented a two-part discussion of transference and how it manifests in the GIM process. Also included were discussions of melding musical and psychological processes and how the hero's myth appears and develops in the GIM process. GIM was shown, in this issue, to be useful in working through PTSD symptoms, the transgenerational effects of the Nazi Holocaust, and in autism. There were two research studies: one found that GIM effects ß–endorphin levels and in healthy subjects may lower depression levels. Unfortunately the sample size was too small to determine statistically significant results. The other study indicated that GIM appears to lower depression and significantly increases the experience of a more meaningful and manageable life.

*Volume 5* (JAMI, 1996–1997) included four articles on the efficacy of GIM as therapy. One explored the use of GIM in the classroom for personal growth and a phenomenological study that indicated the necessity for GIM therapists to have worked therapeutically with the process themselves before using it with others. It was in this issue of the Journal that Toomey (pp.75–103) contributed the first comprehensive review of the GIM literature.

*Volume 6* (JAMI, 1998–1999) was focused entirely on the exploration of various spiritual experiences that were elicited by GIM.

*Volume 7* (JAMI, 2000) presented six articles that focused on evaluating the various aspects or the components of GIM and discussed how the process fosters integration and transformation of the psyche.

## CONCLUSION

The growth of Bonny's method has been inextricably linked with the evolution of scholarly literature devoted solely to practice, theory, and research on GIM. Considering what a short history GIM has (it was less than thirty years ago that Bonny developed and named her method), and considering the relatively small number of GIM facilitators (there are less than 150 listed in the current AMI registry), the literature on GIM is impressive indeed. With several books by Bonny and her proponents, numerous articles in important journals in the USA and abroad, a continuous newsletter, a professional journal, and now with this first edited textbook, GIM has become an important "keyword" in the literatures on music therapy, psychotherapy, and spirituality, to name a few. This attests not only to the devotion of Bonny's followers, but also to their passionate belief in the healing powers of the GIM process itself. One has to share the intricate beauty of the GIM experience, one has to document its effects, one has to wonder how and why it works—and because of this, the future of GIM and the continuation of an already rich legacy of writings is certainly ensured.

## *References*

Association for Music and Imagery (1992-2000), *Journal of the Association for Music and Imagery* (Volumes 1–7). Blaine, WA: Author.

Bonny, H. (1972–1980). *Newsletter for the Institute for Music and Imagery.* Salina, KS: Bonny Foundation.

Bonny, H. (1975). Mind and Consciousness. *Journal of Music Therapy,* 12 (3), 121–135.

Bonny, H. (1976). *Music and Psychotherapy.* Unpublished doctoral dissertation, Union Graduate School.

Bonny, H. (1978a). *GIM Monograph #1: Facilitating GIM Sessions*. Salina, KS: Bonny Foundation.

Bonny H. (1978b). *GIM Monograph #2: The Role of Tape Music Programs in the GIM Process*. Salina, KS: Bonny Foundation.

Bonny, H. (1980). *GIM Monograph #3: Past, Present and Future Implications*. Salina, KS: Bonny Foundation.

Bonny, H. (1987). Reflections: Music: The language of immediacy. *The Arts in Psychotherapy*, 14 (3), 255–262.

Bonny, H., & Savary, L. (1973). *Music and Your Mind: Listening with a New Consciousness*. New York: Harper & Row.

Bonny, H. & Kellogg, J. (1977). Mandalas as a measure of change in psychotherapy. *American Journal of Art Therapy*, 16, 126–130.

Bonny, H., & Tansill, R. (1977). Music therapy: A legal high. In G. Waldorf (ed.), *Counseling Therapies and the Addictive Client*, 113–130.

Bonny, H. & Keiser Mardis, L. (1994). *Music Resources for GIM Facilitators: A Discography of Core Programs*. Olney, MD: Archedigm Publications.

Bonny, H., & Keiser Mardis, L. (1995). *Music Resources for GIM Facilitators: A Discography of Specialized Programs*. Olney, MD: Archedigm Publications.

Bonny, H. & Pahnke, W. (1972). The use of music in psychedelic (LSD) Psychotherapy. *Journal of Music Therapy, 9* (2), 64–83.

Bruscia, K. (1991). *Case Studies in Music Therapy*. Gilsum, NH: Barcelona Publishers.

Bruscia, K. (1996). *Music for the Imagination: Rationale, Implications, and Guidelines for its Use in Guided Imagery and Music*. Blaine, WA: Association for Music and Imagery.

Bruscia, K. (1998). *The Dynamics of Music Psychotherapy*. Gilsum, NH: Barcelona Publishers.

Bush, C. (1995). *Healing Imagery and Music*. Portland OR: Rudra Press.

Clark, M. (1987). The Institute for Music and Imagery training program for Guided Imagery and Music. In C. Maranto and K. Bruscia (eds.), *Perspectives on Music Therapy Education and Training*. Philadelphia, PA: Temple University.

Clark, M., & Keiser, L. (1989). *Teaching Guided Imagery and Music: An Experiential-Didactic Approach*. Olney, MD: Archedigm Publications.

Erdonmez, D. (1992). Clinical applications of Guided Imagery and Music. *Australian Journal of Music Therapy*, 3, 37–44.

Goldberg, F. (1988). Music and imagery as psychotherapy with a brain damaged patient: A case study. *Music Therapy Perspectives, 5*, 41–45.

Hibben, J. (1999). *Inside Music Therapy: Client Experiences*. Gilsum, NH: Barcelona Publishers.

Institute for Music and Imagery (IMI) (1986–1988). *Crescendo: The Newsletter for the IMI: Transposing Images into Life Through Music*. Savage, MD: Author.

Jacobiwitz, R. (1992). Music and imagery with a physically disabled elderly resident: A GIM adaptation. *Music Therapy,* 11 (1), 65–98.

Jarvis, J. (1988). Guided Imagery and Music (GIM) as a primary psychotherapeutic approach. *Music Therapy Perspectives*, 5, 69–72.

Keiser, L. (1986). *Conscious Listening: An Annotated Guide to the ICM Taped Music Programs*. Olney, MD: Archedigm Publications.

Keiser, L. (1988). *Light Search*. Olney, MD: Archedigm Publications.

Keiser Mardis, L. (1996). *Program 33: A New Program and A New Programming Concept*. Olney, MD: Archedigm Publications.

Kenny, C. (1985). Music: A whole systems approach. *Music Therapy*, 5 (1), 3–11.

Korlin, D., Nyback, H., & Goldberg, F. (2000). Creative arts groups in psychiatric care: Development and evaluation of a therapeutic alternative. *Nordic Journal of Psychiatry, 54,* 333–340.

Kovach, A. (1985). Shamanism and Guided Imagery and Music. *Journal of Music Therapy*, 22 (3), 154.

McKinney, C. (1990). Music therapy in obstetrics. *Music Therapy Perspectives*, 8, 50–58.

Merritt, S. (1996). *Mind, Music and Imagery: Unlocking the Treasures of Your Mind*. Santa Rosa, CA: Aslan Publishing.

Nolan, P. (1983). Insight therapy: Guided Imagery and Music in a forensic psychiatric setting. *Music Therapy*, 3 (1), 43–51.

Pickett, E. (1987–88). Fibroid tumors and response to Guided Imagery and Music: Two case studies. *Imagination, Cognition and Personality*, 7, 165–176.

Pickett, E. (1992). Imagery Psychotherapy in Head Trauma Rehabilitation.

Short, A. (1991). The role of Guided Imagery and Music in diagnosing physical illness or trauma. *Music Therapy*, 10 (1), 22–45.

Short, A. (1992). Music and imagery with physically disabled elderly residents: A GIM adaptation. *Music Therapy*, 11(1), 65–98.

Summer, L. (1981). Guided Imagery and Music with the elderly. *Music Therapy*, 1, 39–42.

Summer, L. (1985). Imagery and music. *Journal of Mental Imagery*, 9 (4), 83–90.

Summer, L. (1988). *Guided Imagery and Music in the Institutional Setting*. St. Louis: MMB Music.

Toomey, L (1991). Musical improvisation and GIM: A comparative study. *Journal of the New Zealand Society of Music Therapy*, 13, 1.

Ventre, M. (1993). Guided Imagery and Music in process: The interweaving of the archetype of the mother, mandala, and music. *Music Therapy*, 12 (2), 19–38.

Wylie, M. & Blum, R. (1986). Guided Imagery and Music with hospice patients. *Music Therapy Perspectives*, 3, 25–28.

Music remained at the core of her personal spiritual search. She knew that what she had experienced could somehow be of service to others. With these understandings, she entered into the music therapy program at the University of Kansas where she received a master's degree with an emphasis in music therapy research.

> I had come to the realization that most people listen to music in a surface way, that emotions touched by music rarely reach the deeper layers of consciousness. My premise was that the magic could happen to others, as it had for me, if a way might be found to enter and uncover the creative potential in each person through the use of carefully chosen music. And further, I was determined through research, if that was possible, to discover how this might be done (Bonny, 1999, p. 7).

Bonny was studying with the father of music therapy, E. Thayer Gaston, at the University of Kansas. Research for her master's degree took place at the Veterans Hospital in Topeka, Kansas, where she met Dr. Kenneth Godfrey who was involved in LSD research. Among the visitors to the research program were Walter Pahnke, John Lilly, and Stanislov Grof who were all pioneers in the new field of consciousness exploration. This field piqued her interest because of her own experiences with meditative states and personal mysticism. Both Pahnke and Grof were interested in Bonny's ideas about music's ability to facilitate mystical experiences. She was invited to join them in LSD research at the Maryland Psychiatric Research Center at Spring Grove State Hospital in Catonsville, Maryland. It was her extensive experience with meditation, prayer, mysticism, and non-ordinary states of consciousness which was her primary qualification for the job. As a research associate, Bonny attended drug sessions, consulted with other researchers, and helped choose music for lengthy LSD sessions as part of her duties.

## EVOLUTION OF THE BONNY METHOD

### The Spring Grove Research

The researchers at Spring Grove were very interested in the mystical experiences that they witnessed in the carefully facilitated single high-dose LSD sessions administered at the research center. Prior to the LSD session there were several

Ventre, M. (1993). Guided Imagery and Music in process: The interweaving of the archetype of the mother, mandala, and music. *Music Therapy*, 12 (2), 19–38.

Wylie, M. & Blum, R. (1986). Guided Imagery and Music with hospice patients. *Music Therapy Perspectives*, 3, 25–28.

# Guided Imagery and Music:
## The Bonny Method
## and Beyond

# Part One:

# An Overview

*Chapter One*


# EVOLUTION OF THE BONNY METHOD
# OF
# GUIDED IMAGERY AND MUSIC
# (BMGIM)


## Marilyn F. Clark


This chapter traces the emergence and development of the Bonny Method of Guided Imagery and Music (BMGIM). It begins with a biographical retrospective of Helen Bonny with particular attention paid to the stepping-stones in her life that led to the development of her method. The next section focuses on the evolution of the method from the Spring Grove research through the first training programs. The last section looks at the movement toward professionalism as the method is renamed and training programs diversified to reflect the growing interests and expertise of practitioners.


## BIOGRAPHICAL RETROSPECTIVE


Early impressions in Bonny's life came from the gentle folds of lullabies and fairy tales. Comforting piano pieces played by her mother at bedtime instilled from an early age the sense of relaxing into music as a bridge to dreams and rest. The imaginary worlds painted in fairy tales and stories opened the way to her own imaginings. The family's life together encouraged artistic and musical pursuits. Bonny's mother read stories of operas to the children and then they would listen to the operas on the radio. With her brother playing cello, her sister playing flute, and her playing violin:

> We formed our own entertainment evenings around the piano as each
> in my family played or sang simple melodies from the masters'

repertoire. Enjoying my father's deep voice singing Schubert's *Erl King*; listening to Saturday operas on Texaco radio programs; attending concerts of great artists of the day; studying violin at the University of Kansas with Karl Kuersteiner. The school years, the recital years, the contests, orchestras, tutors, teachers—all led to the decision to let music become my life work (Bonny, 1999, p. 2).

Excelling at her musical endeavors led to the opportunity to pursue a degree at the Oberlin Conservatory. Helen Lindquist graduated with a major in violin and a minor in voice. She met Oscar Bonny, a minister with a liberal theological bent and similar religious beliefs. She fell in love with him and after she graduated they got married. Relatively comfortable with the role as preacher's wife, she felt personally shy in providing spoken prayer for others. Memorizing or reading prayers seemed to be the solution until she read a book about prayer by Frank Laubach, a well-known mystic and missionary. When she was twenty-eight, she took advantage of the opportunity to hear Frank Laubach talk at a women's retreat. It was a decision to take her violin to the retreat to get some extra practicing hours that led to an experience that changed her life.

The quality of the experience is as fresh and real today as when it happened over 50 years ago. Its inspiration has continued to periodically reawaken any flagging zeal that overtakes me as I share my work with others. Although the experience occurred in response to music, and my performing of it, the depth of its impact has affected every aspect of my life—philosophy, belief systems, and professional motivation—and is the creative force behind the development of the Guided Imagery and Music procedure. September 21, 1948 was the date. A church women's meeting was held in a distant city, which required an overnight stay. At the time I was preparing for a music performance. My accompanist was in my traveling group so I tucked my violin and music in the car along with the hope of some extra time for rehearsal. Dr. Laubach (the featured speaker at the meeting) heard me practicing and invited me to play at the evening session. I chose the simple but beautiful "Swan" from Saint-Saen's *Carnival of Animals*. Midway through the short piece a radical and inexplicable event occurred. Suddenly the tone quality issuing from my violin changed in volume and texture. It was of incredible beauty. Although I have often prized myself on the quality and warmth of my tone, this was different. Far surpassing my best efforts, the tones soared with an ease and purity beyond the boundaries of remembered sound. My first shocked impulse was to stop playing. My second, which overcame it, was an intense desire to remain connected with this ongoing beauty. To do so, I methodically placed my fingers on the strings and drew the bow taking care not to vibrato or impress any interpretation of the continuing melodic line. Unimpeded, the marvelous flow of music continued despite my clumsy, wooden efforts. I was trembling when I finished, and as I sat down, began to shake even more violently. Then I heard the speaker, Dr. Laubach's words. "That violin music was so beautiful, I cannot speak. Let us meditate for awhile." At the end of a short talk, he turned to me and said, "Would the young woman play for us again?" I was still shaking uncontrollably and knew that controlling the bow and fingers would be impossible. I hoped for a repeat of the marvelous music saying to myself, "If it happened once it can happen again." And after the first few shaky notes of Bach-Gounod's *Ave Maria*, it did. If anything, it was even more beautiful and expressive than before (Bonny, 1999, pp. 3–4).

She was not able to sleep that night. The numinous state continued for about two weeks as she experienced a deep sense of peace and joy as well as a visual experience of clarity and beauty in everything that she saw. She spoke with Dr. Laubach who advised simply that she pray regularly, get a prayer group together, and read the Bible. Laubach also recommended that Bonny attend the Gettysburg Camp Farthest Out (CFO) meeting where he was going to be speaking.

The CFO movement, begun in the 1930s, fostered creativity and discovery for persons seeking normal spiritual expression through active prayer. Bonny felt she was coming home to a family who understood her. It provided training for her prayer group and for life. She especially enjoyed the use of art and movement in expressing prayer. She also learned about non-ordinary states of consciousness experienced in prayer and hypnosis.

The mystical experience led to the opening of Bonny's inner life where she found both beauty and pain. There was a need for psychological healing and therapy in areas of unfinished business, especially childhood pain related to the death of her older brother when they were both stricken with pneumonia. Behaviorism and Freudian analysis were primary modes of psychological therapy at that time. However, the approach of Abraham Maslow attracted Bonny. She found a therapist who worked with Maslow's humanistic perspectives as well as with hypnotherapy. The effectiveness of self-understanding and insight-focused therapy enabled her to work through early trauma and a lengthy depression. Furthermore the use of hypnotherapy introduced her to the potential of relaxation and imagery in therapeutic use.

Music remained at the core of her personal spiritual search. She knew that what she had experienced could somehow be of service to others. With these understandings, she entered into the music therapy program at the University of Kansas where she received a master's degree with an emphasis in music therapy research.

> I had come to the realization that most people listen to music in a surface way, that emotions touched by music rarely reach the deeper layers of consciousness. My premise was that the magic could happen to others, as it had for me, if a way might be found to enter and uncover the creative potential in each person through the use of carefully chosen music. And further, I was determined through research, if that was possible, to discover how this might be done (Bonny, 1999, p. 7).

Bonny was studying with the father of music therapy, E. Thayer Gaston, at the University of Kansas. Research for her master's degree took place at the Veterans Hospital in Topeka, Kansas, where she met Dr. Kenneth Godfrey who was involved in LSD research. Among the visitors to the research program were Walter Pahnke, John Lilly, and Stanislov Grof who were all pioneers in the new field of consciousness exploration. This field piqued her interest because of her own experiences with meditative states and personal mysticism. Both Pahnke and Grof were interested in Bonny's ideas about music's ability to facilitate mystical experiences. She was invited to join them in LSD research at the Maryland Psychiatric Research Center at Spring Grove State Hospital in Catonsville, Maryland. It was her extensive experience with meditation, prayer, mysticism, and non-ordinary states of consciousness which was her primary qualification for the job. As a research associate, Bonny attended drug sessions, consulted with other researchers, and helped choose music for lengthy LSD sessions as part of her duties.

## EVOLUTION OF THE BONNY METHOD

### The Spring Grove Research

The researchers at Spring Grove were very interested in the mystical experiences that they witnessed in the carefully facilitated single high-dose LSD sessions administered at the research center. Prior to the LSD session there were several sessions with the therapist in which developing rapport and preparation for the drug session were the goals. The LSD sessions were administered with a high dose of the drug whose effects could last up to sixteen hours. There were always a male and a female therapist present. The environment was carefully set up with attention to beauty and comfort. The patient would recline on a couch, wear eyeshades, and listen to music under stereophonic headphones. The intention was to block out external visual stimuli so that a contemplative inner focus could be attained. After the LSD session, there would be several talk sessions for the purpose of integrating the experience into ordinary life. This discussion would use the patient's written account of the session as the primary focus (Grof, 1976; Yensen & Dryer, 2000).

The phenomena of the peak experience, which Abraham Maslow had researched, were commonly noted in these sessions. Walter Pahnke and William Richards (1966) reported research findings from an empirical study designed to investigate in a systematic and scientific way the similarities and differences between experiences described by mystics and those facilitated by psychedelic drugs. A description of the mystical experience was divided into nine categories. The sources for this typology came from the writings of mystics and scholars such as William James who had endeavored to characterize mystical experience.

These nine categories are of interest to the BMGIM student because the peak experience was emphasized in the early development of the Bonny Method. These categories are as follows: 1) unity, 2) transcendence of time and space, 3) deeply felt positive mood, 4) sense of sacredness, 5) objectivity and reality, 6) paradoxicality, 7) alleged ineffability, 8) transiency, and 9) persisting positive changes in attitude and behavior.

One of the researchers referred to the therapeutic milieu at Spring Grove to be close to ideal. The enthusiasm of the research team was fueled by the consistent positive results and mystical experiences of the subjects in the study. The research team felt they had something to offer the hopeless, the addicted, and the terminally ill patients that was life-changing (Yensen & Dryer, 2000).

Stanislov Grof, who came to the Maryland Psychiatric Center in 1967, had worked in Czechoslovakia with LSD for several years. He saw the therapeutic relationship evolve from a traditional psychoanalytic approach to one where the element of trust was the single most important therapeutic characteristic for the patient (Grof, 1976).

An article written about the use of music in LSD sessions was coauthored by Helen Bonny and Walter Pahnke (1972) and was published in the *Journal of Music Therapy*. The authors stated that music is a crucial "extra-drug variable" affecting both the patient's response to the experience as well as an important part of the psychological atmosphere. They further stated that music complemented several therapeutic objectives:

- By helping the patient relinquish usual controls and enter more fully into his inner world of experience. (Carefully selected music enhanced, not detracted from, the internal experience).
- By facilitating the release of intense emotionality. (Music evoked emotions because it sounded like emotions and gave expression to internal tension and release).
- By contributing toward a peak experience. (Unitive feeling states evoked by the music could provide optimum conditions from which a peak experience might evolve).
- By providing continuity in an experience of timelessness. (The rhythmic elements provided stability and predictability enabling the listener to relax and to feel secure).
- By directing and structuring the experience. (The wordless meaning of music provided its power of direction and emotional structure).

They also stated that the choice of music is crucial to support and facilitate the various psychological states that were reached and expressed in the LSD session.

> The extreme vulnerability of this state requires a sensitive and responsible use of the medium. The therapist chooses the records which will be played at various phases of the drug action because he has, through repeated experience, found that some selections are much more effective than others. His choice is further determined by the reaction of the patient to the evolving session material. At critical times during a session the therapist may variously use the music to communicate a reassurance, to deepen an experience, or to lead the patient into an area of therapeutic confrontation (Bonny & Pahnke, 1972, p. 76).

The phases of the LSD session followed a pattern having to do with the activity of the drug in the system and its effect on the psychological and emotional states of the patient. These phases are basic to the understanding of how Bonny's later designs of the programs used in the Bonny Method evolved. These phases were as follows:

- Pre-onset (0 to 1.5 hours), was when the effects of the drug were almost imperceptible. The music used was of a light, popular type or was that chosen by the patient.

- Onset (.5 to 1.5 hours) was when the drug began to have an effect and the patient's excitation level increased. Music of a quiet and positive nature was used to make the entry into the more active states a smooth one. Usually the client was encouraged at this point to recline on the couch and was given eyeshades and earphones to enable an inward focus.

- Building toward peak intensity (1.5 to 3.5 hours) which could be marked by a collage of many different feelings from resistance and fear to excitement. The music could draw the patient into the swiftly expanding experience and enable him to be fully aware of his emotions.

- Peak intensity of drug action (3 to 4.5 hours) was the time when the psychedelic peak experience was most likely to occur. All music choices were made toward that possibility during this phase. Careful choice of music in this stage was imperative.

- Reentry (4.5 to 7 hours) was a less active state during which integration of the experience began. Quiet and peaceful music helped maintain the positive feelings. Using music to assist in further working through of more difficult emotions might mean returning to music used in an earlier phase of the experience. Toward the end of this phase music of a lighter nature was used.

- Return to normal consciousness (7 to 12 hours) was often supported by music of the patient's choosing (Bonny & Pahnke, 1972, pp. 77–79).

Conclusions drawn by the authors suggested that the quality of the performance and of the recording were important, as the heightened sensory awareness of the patient would be acute and the deeply aesthetic possibilities of the music more able to be heard and absorbed. The close rapport between client and therapist which developed through this process created an unusual interpersonal connection which may have resulted in the client becoming aware of how the therapist felt about the music chosen. Sensory overload was to be guarded against. Persons' musical preferences could change after the deep peak experiences had been integrated (Bonny & Pahnke, 1972, pp. 82–83).

## A New Method Begins to Form

Bonny's first adaptations of the techniques learned in the Spring Grove research began in 1972 and were in group settings. She chose non-patient populations who were healthy, functioning adults. She was hoping to find that people could have some of the depth experiences she had witnessed in the psychedelic therapy but without the use of drugs. She worked with groups at retreats, conferences, and informally at her house. These experimental group sessions provided useful input as she saw the varieties of experiences which could be had (Bonny, 1978c).

By 1973 things began to develop quickly. Helen Bonny did not anticipate the immediate interest in her experimentation and in a sense found herself riding the crest of a wave before she had time to build the boat.

## Music and Your Mind

As word spread about these music and consciousness experiences, she was contacted by Lou Savary and Trinitas Bochini who were interested in learning more about what she was developing. Lou Savary, a priest and author of some popular personal growth books, invited Helen Bonny to write a book including her concepts on the effect of music on consciousness and several suggestions for explorations of consciousness for groups and individuals. This popular press book was put together quickly and was available to the public in 1973. It preceded the naming of the methodology and the one-on-one application. The authors discuss the "approach" as follows:

> In work at the Maryland Psychiatric Research Center, it was rediscovered that there was a new way to music, an approach that brings music into special focus and uses its powers to uncover and enrich one's listening patterns. This book invites you to learn to listen in this new way—with a new awareness, with heightened consciousness. Not only can this new way to music deepen your normal listening experience, but you will learn to let the music take you to places in your mind that you perhaps never knew existed. It can lead you to ineffable experiences of grandeur and beauty. (Bonny & Savary, 1973, pp. 16–17)

## Hanscarl Leuner's Guided Affective Imagery

Dr. Hanscarl Leuner, a respected psychiatrist doing research in altered states in Germany, traveled to Maryland to visit the research center. Dr. Leuner encouraged Helen Bonny to work with his prescribed imagery scenes setting them to appropriate music. She experimented with this by using music that was intended to evoke Leuner's imagery scenes. She gave a group of friends and relatives a deep relaxation exercise and then played the musical selections. They easily imaged with the music and often had images similar in nature to the Leuner scenes although Bonny had not suggested any particular images (Bonny,

1978c, p. 26). At this point, she decided to name this approach. She considered the title "Guided Affective Imagery and Music." She wanted music to be of equal importance to the imagery so she chose to drop "affective" and named the approach "Guided Imagery and Music" or GIM (Bonny, 2000).

Further experimentation with groups led to the following conclusions:

- Length of the music program varied according to the population's needs and length of preliminary relaxation.
- Healthy populations which were primed for personal growth and exploration were more amenable to unstructured experiences of a spontaneous nature. A structured approach was useful for the populations with pathologies or disabilities.
- Response to music deepened with more exposure thus enabling personal exploration to deepen (Bonny, 1978c, pp. 29–30).

## Collaboration with Daniel Brown

Daniel Brown was director of a drug crisis intervention center in Massachusetts. Bonny's work with him helped to focus the music programs and to develop the one-on-one dialogue thus strengthening the dyad approach. Brown had found that there were five areas where the use of music in drug crisis intervention was useful: to establish rapport, to generate guided imagery, to encourage affective expression and release, to process through the terminal stages of a session, and to facilitate positive experiences (Bonny, 1978c, p. 32).

With these themes in mind, music programs were created. These programs were entitled *Beginner's Group Experience* (based on Leuner environmental situations with an aim to rapport building); *Affect–Release* (for release of affect), *Comforting–Anaclytic* (for return to childhood), *Imagery* (for the terminal stages of a session [and for people who had difficulty imaging]), and *Music for Crisis Intervention* (for building toward peak and positive experiences).

Each program was about ninety minutes in length. They would be used by the therapist working with clients who were having "bad trips" or "flashbacks" to help them work through their emotions and fears to come to resolution and integration (Bonny, 1978c, pp. 32–33).

Brown further suggested that a dialogue during the playing of the music between the facilitator and the client could be very productive in deepening the experience and in keeping it moving. Brown understood from his extensive work with persons in a drug crisis that the unconscious could regulate itself. He suggested that the "guide" not direct the experience but rather operate with permissiveness and support of the client's unconscious process. The work was best facilitated by the guide exercising active empathy (Bonny, 1978c, p. 34).

The speaking out of the imagery experiences helped the client commit attention to the imagery whereas for persons in group settings where no verbalization occurred during the playing of the music, individuals often complained of forgetting what they had just experienced. The guide's function also gave the client the possibility of releasing vigilance for the sake of ego safety thus making deeper relaxation and deeper process possible.

By the time Bonny had completed her doctoral dissertation in 1976, the individual form of BMGIM had been developed. The following characteristics gleaned from the life, career, and research influences define the method.

- Music is central to the process as a powerful bridge to healing and spirituality (Bonny & Pahnke, 1972).
- Musical selections should match the needs and readiness of the client for internally focused therapy and personal growth work (Bonny, 1978c).
- Music can create an environment in which one may release intense emotions, regress to primary process states, express creativity and imaginativeness, and contribute toward the peak experience (Bonny & Pahnke, 1972).
- Attention is given to the environment and to the quality of musical recordings and players so that the best quality sound in a beautiful environment can enhance the experience (Grof, 1976; Yensen & Dryer, 1997).
- The therapist is called a "guide" and is actively empathic contributing to a deep level of trust and positive regard between the client, called the "traveler" or "subject," and the guide (Grof, 1976; Bonny, 1978c).
- The guide has extensive training in the helping professions as well as in BMGIM. Didactic and experiential training are necessary to understand how to perform the role of guide (Bonny, 1978a).
- The traveler who may find this process useful will have an interest in understanding herself more. With adaptations, it is a process that could be of use to many populations (Bonny, 1978a).
- The individual session will begin with background of the traveler including life history, goals, philosophical and religious attitudes, and perhaps musical preferences. The guide's initial function is to build rapport, help the traveler understand the process, and encourage openness to a new experience (Bonny, 1978a).
- After completing this introduction, the guide will encourage the traveler to recline and will offer the option of eyeshades and earphones if available. Relaxation instruction takes place using

appropriately chosen suggestions for the traveler based on prior experience, readiness, and therapeutic needs (Bonny, 1978a).

- With the introduction of music, the guide allows spontaneous imaging processes to ensue. A nondirective stance is preferable so that the unconscious can respond to music in whatever way is natural and necessary for the traveler. Dialogue is useful and is open-ended. The guide encourages, supports, suggests, repeats, engages, observes, and records. A physical touch, which could range from holding the hand of the client to bioenergetic pressure points, may be used to help release emotion (Bonny, 1978a).

- The guide remains open to the traveler's variety of experiences, trusting the traveler's unconscious process, the music, and her own training and experiences. While the peak experience is a hoped-for outcome, readiness for this experience will not be prematurely pushed by the guide (Bonny & Pahnke, 1972).

- Upon completion of the music listening period, the guide helps the traveler to return to waking consciousness and to integrate the experience. She may encourage the traveler to draw a mandala and to write down the experience to further integrate it (Bonny & Pahnke, 1972; Bonny, 1978a).

## Formation of the Institute for Consciousness and Music

In the development of BMGIM, Bonny had found a way to provide to people the possibility of experiencing a music-enhanced peak experience. Her life journey, enriched and guided by music, spiritual development, and personal growth, reached an important nexus with the evolution of this method.

Training and dissemination of materials became the next phase of development with the founding of the Institute for Consciousness and Music (ICM) in 1973. Bonny was eager to share this new approach to music and consciousness. She had a very open training program with her primary concern being the stability and readiness of the potential guide rather than the attainment of professional credentials. Therefore, persons from many walks of life were welcomed to study her method. By 1975 the training program was focused on the individual form of BMGIM.

As persons became trained in the method, new awarenesses and emphasis evolved. It became clear to Bonny and the newly trained guides that an individual's engagement with the method led to the unfolding of a process. Anecdotal sharing supported that a series of BMGIM sessions offered depth work, which for the appropriate client, could be more effective than traditional verbal therapies. A minimum series of six was recommended in the training program. In learning to work with non-ordinary states, the unconscious, imagery processes, and deep affect, the trainees were encouraged by Bonny to trust their intuition as well as to do their own personal therapeutic work through the GIM process (Clark, 1975).

Bonny's first co-trainer was Sara Jane Stokes-Stearns, who emphasized the role of the therapist as being a co-creator in the process. As co-creator, the therapist was in a relationship that was like a dance with the choices for action, inaction, response, and engagement encouraged by the therapist but ultimately under the control of the client. Stokes-Stearns (2000) described this relationship as a "team approach" in the style of Carl Rogers' client-centered therapy.

Stokes-Stearns shared Bonny's interest in the spiritual possibilities of the GIM process. She reported that after working with someone over a six-week period, spirituality usually came up spontaneously by at least the fifth or sixth session, even with people who did not have any prior experience (Stokes-Stearns, 1975). She also believed that these spiritual experiences were touching the very center where the healing process is activated.

In 1979 it became necessary for Bonny to take a less active role with ICM due to health reasons. She moved to Washington State to take a lengthy convalescence. The training program was turned over to Marilyn Clark, an educator and one of the first graduates of the ICM training program, and Linda Keiser Mardis, a professional musician, educator, and graduate of the training. While coming from very different backgrounds, they shared a similar commitment to the work begun by Bonny. Their styles were complementary as each concentrated on their area of interest and expertise. Clark's fascination was with the inner imagery processes and their correlation to Jung's concept of the collective unconscious. Mardis' passion was music and its use as a means of facilitating entry into altered states of consciousness. Both were interested in the dynamics of creativity, healing, and spirituality, as made available through the BMGIM process, and in the development of an adequate training curriculum to enable persons to become facilitators of this process.

## First Published Definition of Guided Imagery and Music

Helen Bonny referred to the process as an exploration of consciousness. An ongoing challenge for the directors of ICM was to try to write an adequate definition that would incorporate both the potential clinical aspects of the method and the spiritual possibilities inherent in combining beautiful music and non-ordinary states of consciousness. Clark and Mardis collaborated on the publication of a descriptive definition of Guided Imagery and Music which was made available in brochure form in 1986 (Clark and Keiser). This brochure constituted the first thorough definition of Guided Imagery (now called the

Bonny Method), and included sections entitled: the method, the session, the imagery, the music, and the possibilities. Under the method section, the following definition was offered:

> Guided Imagery and Music (GIM) is a method of self-exploration in which classical music is used to access the imagination. It includes listening to classical music in a relaxed state, allowing the imagination to come to conscious awareness and sharing these awarenesses with a guide. The interaction among listener, music and guide is what makes GIM unique. The GIM experience can lead to the development of self- understanding, the ordering of the psyche and the achievement of spiritual insight (Clark and Keiser, 1986, p 1).

The importance of the music was underscored as trainees were taught that music was co-therapist in the process. All guides worked with a common repertoire of music programs. Bonny (1978b) designed *Group Experience, Imagery, Quiet Music, Relationships, Comforting/Anaclytic, Nurturing, Mostly Bach, Emotional Expression I, Peak Experience, Positive Affect, Transitions, Affect Release, Death/Rebirth*. Linda Keiser Mardis designed *Creativity I, Creativity II, Grieving,* and *Expanded Awareness* (Mardis, 1986).

The primary application of Guided Imagery and Music as taught by Clark and Keiser Mardis was the individual form. Emphasis in training was the development of technique and expertise in working with the healthy, functioning adult through a session series. This definition would pertain to many people who would be seeking therapy or personal growth work. Adaptations of the method were encouraged for those who had training and expertise in working with specific populations such as children, adolescents, geriatrics, addictions, inpatient psychiatric, and the terminally ill. Group applications were seen of use primarily in workshop settings to introduce persons to the basic concept that music can evoke imagery.

## SECONDARY APPLICATIONS OF GUIDED IMAGERY AND MUSIC

### Training Application

There are two secondary applications of the BMGIM process. These are the training model and the group application model. The training model described

Lewis' chapter has its roots in the vision of Helen Bonny as well. Beginning from her mystical experience at age twenty-eight, her journey included spiritual retreats where artistic expression, dance and movement, and personal reflection were common. The flavors of these experiences were folded into the earliest intensive seminars and have remained as a part of the total experience of a BMGIM training. Further, the emphasis on the transformative, peak experience has been a part of training programs with the understanding that the psychodynamic work must proceed as well. This approach is the same as was emphasized in the Spring Grove Research (Grof, 1976; Yensen & Dryer, 2000).

It could be said that the training experience itself constitutes an application of the BMGIM process. Personal growth, catharsis, peak experience and spiritual awareness are all possible outcomes of the training program. Trainees are expected to experience each music program, to engage in their own "hero's journey", to become imaginative and musical. They also engage in a study of transpersonal psychology, music, mythology, archetypes and symbols. The outcome is personally transformative. Clark and Keiser Mardis (1989) suggest a comparison between the individual BMGIM session process and the intensive setting process:

> As the cycle of the Intensive Seminar gets underway, the trainers are aware of how the process of a GIM training seminar mirrors personal process work with GIM. The first goal is to establish trust and bonding. The deeper and clearer the trust, the more open the group and the individuals become. . . . The openness of the group is respected by the trainers as is the vulnerability of the individual participants. The group's sensitivity to stimulus will increase day by day, experience by experience. The trainers are careful in their music selections for the group music and imagery experiences and the individual GIM sessions that take place during the training seminars. The choices need to match the participants' readiness to experience the method. The trainers must be aware that any experience may trigger deeper process due to the gradual letting down of defenses that is likely to occur for the participant.
>
> As the Intensive Seminar comes to a close the participants are reminded that they will soon return to their life routines. They are taught simple techniques for grounding and for integrating new learnings from the Intensive Seminar. The trainers keep alert to help anyone who may have difficulty preparing to leave the safe container of the seminar and the training site.
>
> The experiential strands of the training become woven together with the didactic strands. They blend, they contrast, they provide

patterns. As one stands back and takes a look at the training, one can see something like the GIM process itself. There is the initial time of developing trust and rapport; then the testing of the method; the moving to the heart of the process; then the integration and return to the world (p. 4-5).

## Group Application

Bonny's early investigations took place in group settings. Before there was a named or defined technique, she was experimenting with a "new way to listen" to music in group settings. As the Bonny Method evolved, the group work was less emphasized. Training programs focused on the individual form and process. Introductory experiential workshops would often include group music and listening experiences, but they were generally considered introductory to the deeper processes available in the individual session.

The impetus to develop a group adaptation came from music therapists who worked with the Bonny Method. These adaptations evolved out of the interest of music therapists who work in psychiatric facilities with groups. In keeping with the basic steps of the Bonny Method, these adaptations begin with a time of rapport building, then move to relaxation and image focus, music listening, and integration to normal waking states. Variations have been made to fit the settings and the needs of patients in groups as well as to introduce the dynamic of group therapy.

During the 1980s Frances Goldberg worked with small groups in an acute psychiatric facility and developed an adapted form of Guided Imagery and Music for crisis intervention groups. Creative modifications to methodology and goals included shortening the entire experience and including all steps of the procedure within the music listening. Also the use of journaling during the imaging period helped to contain the experience. Careful choice of music was essential and was chosen "to stimulate a narrowing of the focus of attention, and a heightening of concentration on a reduced segment of available stimulation. . . . The     music choice must also be one which allows the therapist's voice to be entrained, with no competition between the music and the voice" (Goldberg, 1994, p. 27).

Lisa Summer's book (1988), *Guided Imagery and Music in the Institutional Setting*, further developed clinical applications of BMGIM in group and individual therapy. Her description of group work compares to the individual Bonny Method therapy in important areas such as the role of the music to evoke and develop an internal imagistic response which can lead to integration and wholeness. Summer says of the group GIM:

When doing GIM on a group basis it is not desirable to eliminate the defenses and all references to reality. This is the reason for a brief and superficial relaxation technique and for specific and restricted guidelines used during the inductions for the visual image and goal setting. . . .

Most importantly, there is no guiding during the music/synergy portion of the GIM session for group, where there is guiding of the individual because, contrary to expectations, guiding during the music/ imagery synergy actually increases the depth of the experience. With a guide present during the music the client feels safer to explore the subconscious and will do so. In the absence of the guide, as in the group sessions, the clients will not be able to venture into territory better left for healthy individuals to explore (Summer, 1988, 18–19).

In the early 1990s, Kenneth Bruscia began experimenting with variations on the basic protocol of the Bonny Method, by having a group image interactively while listening to the music. His technique varied from Summer's group work in that the facilitator/guide encourages verbal interaction of the group members during the music listening, leading to their co-creation of the imagery experience. This is facilitated by setting a common image focus and by encouraging all members of the group to see themselves and the members of the group within the image focus. Thus, Bruscia brought into the group setting the powerful dynamic of interaction within the imagery during the music itself. This interaction does in fact deepen the experience as Summer suggested. For a group of healthy, functioning adults, working with a trained facilitator, this technique can have positive results. The present author presented this form of group work in 1995 at the annual meeting of the Association for Music and Imagery (AMI) noting that the interactive format helped the individuals stay focused on the experience as well as provided a unique and expansive experience for all involved. Screening of members, a thorough understanding of the possible responses, and carefully constructed contracts among all members are important (Clark, 1995).

There have been numerous adaptations of the Bonny Method of Guided Imagery and Music which have led to confusion as to what the method is, how it is defined, and how persons are trained to become facilitators of it. In the mid-1980s, facilitators of the Bonny Method began to gather annually to share expertise and to develop a professional organization to support those who practice the method. They formed the Association for Music and Imagery (AMI) in 1986. This organization has attempted to bring unity of agreement in the definition of the method and set standards in training, ethics, and practice.

# MOVEMENT TOWARD PROFESSIONALISM

In 1988 several events occurred which had important consequences in the dissemination of BMGIM. The AMI was in its second year of existence and was providing continuing education and support for BMGIM facilitators and students. The primary training program, the Institute for Music and Imagery (previously named ICM), closed due to financial and organizational challenges. Helen Bonny, whose health had improved after several years of difficulty, had begun a new organization, The Bonny Foundation, which was focused toward training music therapists in BMGIM and other music therapy modalities. Temple University's music therapy program was laying the groundwork to bring BMGIM training into its master's program. Similar training programs had already begun in the music therapy departments at Montclair State University and New York University and were expanding. Several other BMGIM practitioners were ready to start their own training programs. There was a growing interest in Bonny's work in the music therapy profession both in the United States and internationally.

The AMI was challenged to become a centralized organization with many important functions, such as providing support to facilitators of the method and graduates of the various training programs, setting standards for the training programs, establishing a code of ethical conduct, founding a journal, and reaching agreement as to a comprehensive definition of the method. By 1990 these tasks were largely completed, though debate on details of training requirements continued for several years. In the 1990s literature about BMGIM began to be published. The AMI journals contained articles about work with particular populations, adaptations of the method, case studies, and research projects. New books were published and Bonny's first book, *Music and Your Mind*, was reissued.

A topic of discussion that often surfaced among the AMI membership was whether to change the name of the method. It was decided at the annual meeting of the AMI in 1990 to add Bonny's name to the generic title "Guided Imagery and Music." Thus, the present name, "The Bonny Method of Guided Imagery and Music" was established. This renaming was an attempt to differentiate the unique form and process of Bonny's method from a variety of other techniques that rely upon music and imagery, including those commonly used in mental health and retreat settings in the United States. This renaming also distinguished the traditional individual form of BMGIM from the various adaptations that have evolved over the years that are geared more toward group work and therapy for special populations. Unfortunately, many of these adaptations have also been referred to as Guided Imagery and Music or GIM, which has caused, and continues to cause, lack of clarity in publications and presentations.

With the renaming in 1990, came a refined definition of the method:

> The Bonny Method of GIM is a music-centered, transformational therapy, which uses specifically programmed classical music to stimulate and support a dynamic unfolding of inner experiences in service of physical, psychological and spiritual wholeness. The GIM therapist/guide maintains an active dialogue with the listener throughout the session, providing encouragement and focus for the emotions, images, physical sensations, memories and thoughts which occur (Association for Music and Imagery, 1990, p. 4).

In 1998, Bonny outlined for teaching purposes what she called "The Basic Premises of BMGIM," an unpublished document that she presented in various venues. Following this, in 1999, faced with the proliferation of adaptations and interpretations of name and methodology, several trainers of BMGIM convened to revisit the foundations of Bonny's work and to discover where their agreements and differences could be found as proponents of her method. Starting from the premises that Bonny had already outlined (Bonny, 1998), these trainers crafted a joint statement entitled "The Fundamentals of the Bonny Method" (Bush et al., 1999). The framers of these statements found that there was easy agreement on these points and that the fundamental work to which each ascribed bore a strong resemblance to the original qualities and characteristics of the method as originally developed by Bonny. Of particular significance in the trainer's document was the addition of a section that specifies the procedural components that define BMGIM. Upon completion of the document, these trainers asked Bonny to read and respond to their document, and in a communication to all trainers, Bonny supported their statements as "grounding principles," which can be used for "purposes of communication and interpretation," and as "the keystone to our shared mission" (Bonny, April, 1999).

What follows is a synthesis of the two documents, with citations indicating whether the statement or section was taken from Bonny's document or the trainers' document.

## Basic Premises of BMGIM

The Bonny Method is a music-centered exploration of consciousness leading toward integration and wholeness (Bonny, 1998; Bush et al., 1999).

- All healing comes from within (Bonny, 1998; Bush et al., 1999). This is consistent with client-centered therapy and Jungian theory (Bonny, 1998).
- The flow or directionality of the movement of healing is toward self-actualization, full humanhood, and exploration of human potential. Movement within the psyche creates a holistic orientation, and is consonant with Maslow's hierarchy of needs (Bonny, 1998). Movement within the psyche creates the impetus for change and transformation (Bush et al., 1999). The movement is that of spiraling in, and spiraling out (Bonny, 1998).
- In an expanded state of consciousness, the psyche is able to have a holistic view of itself and the universe (Bush et. al., 1999). The view is specific as well as holistic; the process looks at the past, the present, and the future as integrated (Bonny, 1998; Bush et. al.).
- Human life and growth are on a continuum from person-ego needs to transpersonal and spiritual concerns and realizations (Bonny, 1998; Bush et al, 1999). There is a gradual opening of focus, and thus, sensitivity from self to others, to world, to universe (but not necessarily in linear or orderly procession!) (Bonny, 1998).
- Each entrance into an altered state of consciousness is begun at a different growth place within each person; therefore, each music session is different within and between travelers (Bonny, 1998).
- All human experience is of value and is interconnected; therefore, both positive and problematic aspects of the person are valued and allowed to emerge (Bonny, 1998; Bush et al., 1999).
- Images may come in many forms and guises, and within each is contained valuable messages from the unconscious (Bonny, 1998);
- The guiding principle in BMGIM is the music: our co-therapist, generator of images, integrator of experiences, supportive structure for abreaction, entrance into the realm of higher consciousness, and facilitator of inner dialogue (Bonny, 1998). Music is able to initiate movement in the psyche, reveal realms of consciousness, evoke imagery, and promote integration of mind, body, and spirit (Bush et al., 1999).
- BMGIM is a self-limiting exploration of the self; one in which the client has the control. The client can decide whether to enter or not enter a difficult and challenging image sequence (Bonny, 1998).
- BMGIM is seen as a process; a step-by-step gathering of personal threads, a therapy, an integrative healing mode.
- Principles for the BMGIM facilitator:

- Accept persons as they are, wherever they are in their life process.
- Make no attempt to solve problems for the client but allow and guide whatever arises, trusting that the evoked material supplies grist for the healing.
- Discourage interpretation and analysis during the music/imagic experience. The image has a life of its own. It will instruct and ameliorate not only at the time of the session but with the passage of time.
- Keep your beliefs and reactions to yourself. Be an open receptacle for the client.
- Trust the music. Don't get in the way. Music superimposes its structure upon the unfolding experience.
- Do not analyze too soon, within the session, or outside it. Take time to get the whole picture of what the psyche is trying to say in all its fullness (Bonny, 1998).

- The process identifying the Bonny Method is: the presentation of specially sequenced classical music programs within a one-to-one modality conducted by a facilitator who is formally trained in The Bonny Method (Bush, et. al., 1999).
- The components of a session in the Bonny Method are:
  - Preparation
    - The facilitator and the client engage in an initial discussion.
    - The facilitator provides relaxation and focusing suggestions to assist the client's entry into an expanded state of consciousness.
  - Interactive Music Listening Experience
    - The client receives the music and describes the experiences evoked by the music.
    - The facilitator enters the musical space, observes the client's responses to it, and helps to focus and support these experiences in a variety of ways.
  - Closure
    - The facilitator assists the client's return from the expanded state of consciousness.
    - The facilitator helps the client integrate the experiences evoked by the music (Bush et al., 1999).

# CONCLUSIONS

The above premises serve to reiterate the basic concepts that describe BMGIM. As more and more people learn about BMGIM and various other forms of GIM, the flavor of Bonny's vision and intention will hopefully remain strong. The method can easily be adapted, modified, and combined with other techniques. The risk in these adaptations is that the method will become so broadly defined with so many exceptions to the original protocol that there will no longer be a clear sense of purpose or form of the method. To clarify these differences, it would be helpful if those who have made viable applications would name them rather than to call them "the Bonny Method," "GIM", or "Guided Imagery and Music." Dr. Bonny has repeatedly said of the method she developed that "its most powerful and effective form is one-to-one in private practice" (Bonny, 1989, p. 7; Bonny, 2000).

For more than twenty-five years, BMGIM has flourished as a process of exploration into the inner realms of consciousness. Throughout these years trends come and go, but some inspirations, such as the Bonny Method, grow into useful techniques. Research follows and articles are written.

The exploration of consciousness has been legitimized by transpersonal psychology which incorporates Eastern philosophy and Western psychology into a growing field of study and therapeutic application. Alternative therapies have become complementary medicine, and science is looking at consciousness, healing, vibration, the power of positive thought and prayer. Interest in myth and symbols of all cultures makes our own inner worlds less frightening. Music remains a constant with its ability to cut through defenses and preconceived patterns and take us to the core of beauty and vibration.

Bonny's mystical experience at age twenty-eight required her to search for an understanding of the unique gift which music can bring to humankind. In her address to the World Congress of music therapists in November 1999, Bonny spoke about the "divine collaboration" among composer, musician-interpreter, and listener.

> If the performer is able to get inside the music, to reach the heart of the composer's intent while adding the depth of his own spirit and sensitivity, the music will speak to the listener in ways that words cannot. . . . This deep intentionality which an individual musician or group of musicians arrives at, at the behest of a conductor, is what touches long held emotions and evokes holistic responses in us (Bonny, November 1999, p. 5).

It is the challenge of the facilitator and client to learn how to listen. Bonny's earliest writings focus on an approach to listening to music (Bonny & Savary, 1973). This approach is the element which all of the adaptations share. Depending on the individual's developmental level, psychological health, and openness to a positive outcome, this "new way of listening" can take the individual through an experience of expanded awareness and ineffable beauty to a place of renewed hope, transformation, and healing.

## *References*

Association for Music and Imagery (AMI) (1990). Minutes from business meeting, Blue Mountain Lakes, NY.

Bonny, H. (1978a). *Facilitating GIM Sessions.* Baltimore: ICM Publications.

Bonny, H. (1978b). *The Role of Taped Music Programs in the GIM Process.* Baltimore: ICM Publications.

Bonny, H. (1978c). *GIM Therapy: Past, Present and Future Implications.* Baltimore: ICM Publications.

Bonny, H. (1998). *Basic Premises of GIM.* Unpublished manuscript. Salina, KS: Bonny Foundation.

Bonny, H. (personal communication, April 1999).

Bonny, H. (personal communication, November 2000).

Bonny, H. (1999, November). Five International Models of Music Therapy: Founders Panel: Helen Lindquist Bonny. Paper presented at the World Congress of Music Therapy, Washington DC. Available from The Bonny Foundation, Salina, KS and Baltimore, MD).

Bonny, H., & Pahnke, W. (1972). The use of music in psychedelic (LSD) psychotherapy. *Journal of Music Therapy.* 9, ( 2), 64–83.

Bonny, H., & Savary, L. (1973). Music and Your Mind. New York: Harper and Row.

Bush, C., Clark, M., Clarkson, G., Goldberg, F., Lewis, K., Mardis, L., Merritt, S., and Stokes-Stearns, S. (1999). *The Fundamentals of the Bonny Method,* Unpublished manuscript.

Clark, M. (1975). *Training Notes for the Institute for Consciousness and Music.* Unpublished manuscript.

Clark, M. (1995, June). *Imaging Together.* Presentation at the annual meeting of the Association for Music and Imagery. Little Switzerland, NC.

Clark, M. and Keiser, L. (1986). *Guided Imagery and Music* (Brochure). Savage, MD: Institute for Music and Imagery.

Clark, M. and Keiser, L. (1989). *Teaching Guided Imagery and Music: An Experiential/didactic Approach.* Garrett Park, MD: Archedigm Publications.

Goldberg, F. (1994). The Bonny Method of Guided Imagery and Music as individual and group treatment in a short-term acute psychiatric hospital. *Journal of the Association for Music and Imagery*, 3, 18–35.

Grof, S., (1976). *Realms of the Human Unconscious: Observations from LSD Research.* New York: E.P. Dutton and Company.

Keiser, L. (1986). *Conscious Listening: An Annotative Guide to the ICM Taped Music Programs.* Olney, MD: Archedigm Publications.

Pahnke, W., and Richards, W. (1966). Implication of LSD and experimental mysticism. *Journal of Religion and Health,* 5, 175–208.

Stokes-Stearns, S. J. (personal communication August 9, 2000).

Stokes-Stearns, S. J. (1975, July). *The GIM dyad.* Unpublished lecture. Baltimore: Marriotsville Spiritual Center.

Summer, L. (1988). *Guided Imagery and Music in the Institutional Setting.* St. Louis: MMB Music, Inc.

Yensen, R., & Dryer, D. (2000). Rediscovering a lost psychedelic therapy: Did social taboo crush good science? *Shared Visions,* July, 28–32.

*Chapter Two*


# THE INDIVIDUAL FORM
# OF THE BONNY METHOD OF
# GUIDED IMAGERY AND MUSIC (BMGIM)


## Madelaine Ventre


The Bonny Method of Guided Imagery and Music (BMGIM) is a source of joy and wonder; in many ways it is indescribable. The best way to fully appreciate what BMGIM is and what it has to offer is to experience it. Unfortunately, this forum cannot provide the experience. Hopefully, the following explanation and description of this process will convey the excitement and privilege this author feels when engaged in a BMGIM session, either as client or therapist.

As a point of reference, a working definition of BMGIM is that it is a process that involves: a client who is willing and able to explore his/her inner process, through carefully selected music, in an altered state of consciousness, with a trained BMGIM therapist.

Classical BMGIM is a dyadic process, one in which the client and therapist are finely attuned to one another in individual sessions for the purpose of the client's internal growth and expansion of life choices. Exploration may involve *intra*personal, *inter*personal and/or *trans*personal relationships. It is a holistic process that allows a person to tap into his/her rich inner world of imagery to explore all that (s)he was, is and can be. It encourages the exploration of problems, issues, and strengths as well as hopes, fantasies and desires for the future. It is a multidimensional, integrative process in that the imagery and symbols that arise may be experienced on many levels at once, from the concrete to the abstract and from the very personal to the transpersonal. It is still amazing, after many years of working in BMGIM, how strong, creative, unique, and vibrant people are. BMGIM enables people to use all of these wonderful strengths to lead more creative, fulfilling lives.

In its individual form the BMGIM session takes approximately two hours. There is a natural flow of session components so that the whole session is experienced as a complete cycle that ebbs and flows according to the client's needs. What follows is a description of each component of a classical session.

## THE INTAKE INTERVIEW

As with most therapeutic processes, a BMGIM series begins with an intake session. This provides opportunities for therapist and client to become acquainted, and to see if there is sufficient rapport and trust to begin a therapeutic relationship. It also affords opportunities for the therapist to explain the BMGIM process, and for the client to experience it.

In this initial session, the therapist takes a full history. Typically, this would include: name; contact information (address, phone, e-mail); date and place of birth; medical history; information about family of origin; present family; significant others and friends; spiritual and religious beliefs; education and styles of learning; hobbies; previous and /or current therapy experience; life issues and goals; reasons for engaging in BMGIM; experience and knowledge of music and altered states of consciousness. In addition to the verbal intake, the therapist would make note of how the client reacts to inductions, altered states, music, their imagery process, interventions made by the therapist, and processing techniques.

A description of the BMGIM session and experience helps the client know what to expect and gives the client the opportunity to ask questions. The therapist would introduce or review simple explanations of altered states of consciousness and imagery as experienced in BMGIM. The description of the session would include brief definitions of the preliminary conversation, induction, music listening period, and post-session integration.

In explaining a typical BMGIM experience, Bonny (1978) recommends giving the following suggestions (pp. 12–14):

- Your inner self likes repetition.
- Music in a BMGIM session is programmatic.
- Try not to listen to music in an intellectual way.
- Feel free with your emotions.
- Feel free at any time to move your body to a more comfortable position.
- Commit yourself to any symbol or feeling that presents itself.
- Allow the movement and feeling of the music to take you from one scene to another.
- Finally, and of most importance, enjoy, enjoy.

As described by Bonny (1978), BMGIM was originally conceived as a contractual series of sessions, with six being the number initially proposed, with additional contracts made as needed. This is not always done in current BMGIM practice. Many therapists will suggest an initial session to "test the waters," and then, if the client and therapist agree to continue, therapy work begins in earnest. While most therapists would agree that periodic check-in sessions to evaluate progress are necessary, specific numbers of sessions are not always suggested.

## PRELIMINARY CONVERSATION

Bonny (1978) describes this preliminary conversation as "an introductory dialogue which serves as a rapport function, (and) happens at each session when the client first enters the room" (p. 16). This is the time in which the client can relate to the therapist what has been going on since the last session, what issues are most pressing, and how she or he is feeling. The client may share dreams and artwork or writings that have been done. The therapist uses this portion of the session to assess what issues are most likely to come up in the music, and in what way or awareness level. Energy level of the client is carefully noted. The therapist is also assisting the client in focusing internally on the major themes to be addressed in the music. This is done verbally through the interventions (questions and statements) made by the therapist, and non-verbally through the therapist's body language and mirroring of the client's affect and vocal patterns. All of these elements impact on the final statement of the induction and the choice of the music. This portion of the session may take approximately thirty minutes.

## THE INDUCTION

The induction, as Bonny (1978) conceived it, contained a physical relaxation of the musculature and a psychological concentration or focus on one stimulus to the exclusion of all other stimuli. Thus, the purpose of an induction is to help the client to screen out the external environment in order to give a greater focus and attention to the client's inner environment or process. This shift in focus is commonly known as an altered or alternative state of consciousness or ASC. It is important to note that there is not just one ordinary state and one altered state but many levels and gradations of alternative states of consciousness or awareness. They are qualitative and quantitative shifts in the perceptions of time, space, and energy. We all enter these states throughout a day and a lifetime. Some examples of ASCs are daydreaming, intense concentration, prayer, meditation, chemically induced ASCs (as with alcohol or drugs), sleep, dreaming, sensory deprivation or overload, creativity, unity, collective unconscious, and nirvana. The induction helps to induce or enhance the ASC and is also a very important introduction and link to the music.

Often, this internal focusing actually begins long before the client reaches the therapy room. When many people first become aware that they have an appointment (for therapy), they start to focus more and more on what will occur there. Questions arise like, "What shall I wear?", "When should I leave to get there on time?", "What will I talk about and deal with today?", "How do I feel about going?" The qualitative and quantitative shifts have already begun. They are screening out more of the external environment and becoming more aware of what they are experiencing internally. By the time they arrive for the session, they are already somewhat "altered." The therapist continues to facilitate this internal focusing throughout the preliminary conversation, as well as the induction.

The final step in the induction is the fine-tuning of the preliminary information, the energy level in which it was presented, and the level of ASC in which the work will be done to the music selected for the session. The therapist uses the information, affect, energy level, and knowledge of the client's issues, imagery languaging, and induction preferences to compose the "induction." Often, if the focusing has been accomplished in the preliminary conversation, not much more is required. The move into the music should flow naturally with the therapist's voice serving as the first musical sound of the music.

## THE MUSIC LISTENING PERIOD

"The music listening period involves three levels of experience: a prelude, a bridge and a heart or message" ( Bonny, 1978, p. 24). This part of the session may take from thirty to fifty minutes. The "prelude" is characterized by surface imagery that allows the client to make the necessary adjustments while entering altered states in relationship to the music, and to the personal issues that may be emerging as this happens. The "bridge" is characterized by imagery or inner experiences that enable the client to ascend or descend into deeper states of consciousness. The "heart" or message of the session contains the major themes and issues of the day's internal work (Bonny, 1978).

## POST-SESSION INTEGRATION
## OR POSTLUDE

When the client has completed the work with the music, the therapist assists the client in returning to a more externally oriented state. Some sessions lead to complete closure of an issue, but more often, the client comes to a comfortable stopping place knowing that more work with the issue(s) will continue.

The client now has the opportunity to review or creatively process the session. Awakening and learning to listen to and understand the creative spirit's symbolic language is one of the benefits of BMGIM. Therefore, processing is done most often in a creative modality. Some examples are artwork (mandala, clay, collage, etc.), writing (journaling, poetry, etc.), and verbal sharing, all of which may be used by the client between sessions as well as in the postlude.

The process of change continues even if the client does not use any of the techniques mentioned above, but many clients find them beneficial, enjoyable, and healing. The postlude also serves the very important function of continuing to assist the client to a more externally focused state. Payment and scheduling of the next session are usually conducted at the end of the postlude. The postlude takes approximately one half hour.

## GUIDING

The author believes that BMGIM is the use of music *as therapy* and that the music is actually the primary therapist. The human co-therapist serves as facilitator for the client-music relationship. This does not mean that the human therapist is unimportant. In a session, it is the human therapist who chooses the music and makes verbal and nonverbal interventions. Some people describe BMGIM as a nondirective form of therapy, but this may not be entirely true. The music chosen has traditionally been Western classical music, which in the author's opinion is directive in nature. The music can push or pull, comfort or stimulate. Certainly the interventions are directive, no matter how non-directive they can be in wording. Even the blandest "uh-huh" is timed and spoken for a reason and in response to a particular image. This does impact on how the client receives both the music and the intervention. What is important to note is that the therapist is not actively guiding the client (choosing where to go, how long to stay, or what to do), but facilitating the client's interaction with the music and his/her own imagery.

During the music portion of the session, the client is lying on a couch or mat and is relating verbally and nonverbally what she or he is experiencing. The therapist, sitting next to the client, maintains contact through his/her presence and verbal interventions. The verbal interventions are intended to facilitate, support, and/or deepen the experiences evoked and shaped by the music in interaction with the client's imagination. Thus, well-timed, verbal interventions are an integral part of the session, but generally less formative or transformative than the music itself. This process of verbally interacting with the client while relating to the music has been called "guiding"; perhaps "facilitating" might be a more appropriate word.

Some of the techniques Bonny (1978) recommended to be used in guiding are to support and encourage the client to: 1) act or react to the images, 2) encounter and work through images of resistances; 3) have emotional or feeling responses; and 4) have body responses.

Occasionally, physical interventions are warranted. When they are, care must be taken to ask the client's permission or inform the client before doing so (Bonny, 1978). Eyeshades and earphones were originally suggested, and may still be used.

The therapist chooses music that will allow, support, and deepen the client's work. Some BMGIM therapists are more inclined to present an entire program of music, that is, a program that has been predesigned and contains a number of selections. The objective here is to facilitate the client's exploration of a particular given musical environment. Other therapists choose to follow the client wherever the client goes, thus making music choices as the client progresses through the session. An entire predesigned program may be used if it is supportive of the work, or a new individualized program may be created in the moment. In both cases, the music is the environment, the catalyst and a dynamic partner in the client's work. Each client and indeed the same client on different days will approach and interact with the music differently. The client may relate to any number of the musical elements and in different states or levels of awareness. In effect, as the client changes, the music changes and vice versa.

In order for a client to move deeply into an ASC and his or her inner process, the therapist must be comfortable with and knowledgeable about the issues raised. The therapist must be able to maintain his focus on the client while "simultaneously and continually evaluating the effectiveness of the many elements in the situation: the musical selection being played, the music's mood; the client's physical and emotional reactions, what the client is verbally reporting; what is being communicated physically and emotionally in the moments between the client's verbal reports; what has led up to this point in the music session; how current BMGIM material relates to former sessions; how it relates to the goals of treatment" (Bonny, 1978, p. 41). And the therapist must do all this while taking a written transcript of the session!

"No interpretation of imagery is given by the guide during the session, or afterward. Essentially, the healing of the personality proceeds through the music as catalyst, and through the allowing, persuasive attitude of the guide". (Bonny, 1978, p. 20).

## SUMMARY AND CONCLUSIONS

BMGIM was originally conceived as a process to enable normal, healthy, ego intact individuals to experience, explore, and expand inner reality. As Bonny (1978) stated, "The best GIM subjects are persons well-motivated for treatment, whose belief system allows for a new and innovative approach" (p. 43). As individual BMGIM grew, in addition to touching expansive and transpersonal states, clients entered into areas of concern and trauma. The wonder and joy of BMGIM is that it is a truly holistic process that allows for integration of the traumas and the ecstasies. It supports the integration of mind, body, and spirit and teaches a new way of using the creativity inherent in us all. "In this, GIM is consonant with Humanistic Psychology as espoused by Maslow (1971), Rogers (1961), and Rollo May (1967), and with transpersonal aspects of the total person (Assagioli, 1965)" (Bonny, 1978, p.46).

Most BMGIM therapists come to this process with professional experience in some healing or therapy work. It is advisable and recommended that the therapist first learn and practice the BMGIM process as it applies to the "normal, healthy, and/or neurotic" adult populations. Then adaptations may be tried with other populations or in settings in which the therapist has experience.

## *References*

Bonny, H. (1978). Facilitating GIM sessions: GIM Monograph #1. Baltimore: ICM Books.

*Chapter Three*


# THE BOUNDARIES OF
# GUIDED IMAGERY AND MUSIC (GIM)
# AND THE BONNY METHOD


# Kenneth E. Bruscia


Over the last few decades, considerable confusion has arisen over the names and definitions for the various practices inspired by Helen Bonny involving spontaneous imaging to music while in an expanded state of consciousness. At first, every practice that met this description was called "Guided Imagery and Music" or GIM; then distinctions began to emerge between the individual form (which had evolved into a more in-depth therapy), and the group form (which was originally developed for non-therapeutic purposes) (Bonny & Savary, 1973). As a result, the individual form was dubbed "GIM," and all non-therapeutic uses of the group form were dubbed "Music and Imagery." Meanwhile, therapeutic applications of the group form were being developed in institutional and clinical settings by various music therapists (Summer, 1988). Because these applications were therapeutic, the group form was also dubbed "GIM." At that point, then, "GIM" was being used to refer to both individual and group forms that were therapeutic in intent, irrespective of whether the practice was developed by Bonny herself; while the term "Music and Imagery" remained a catch-all for a myriad of group practices that were not therapeutic.

Meanwhile, confusion was also brewing in psychotherapy-related fields. With the explosion of imagery techniques in the late 1970s and 1980s, the term "Guided Imagery" was used pervasively in the literature for any variety of therapeutic practices involving the imagination, some including music and others not—none developed by Bonny, and many not even remotely related to GIM.

During these same years and into the 1990s, the applications of "GIM" and "Music and Imagery" continued to grow, and more and more modifications were being made to accommodate the needs of different clientele, and the working styles of diverse practitioners.

Then in the mid 1990s, in an apparent attempt to clarify the situation, Bonny added her name to the method, and GIM became the "Bonny Method of GIM" or "BMGIM." While this created a clearer boundary for differentiating forms of music-imaging that she inspired from unrelated imaging practices in other fields, the name change did not provide a means of differentiating all the adaptations that had been made to her method by this time. The most obvious question that emerged was whether "BMGIM" include both the individual and group forms that Bonny herself developed. And this question quite naturally led to many more: Should all modifications and adaptations to Bonny's method be called the "Bonny Method?" If so, then exactly where are the boundaries of the Bonny Method? Exactly what did Bonny develop, and exactly what have others done to advance or expand upon her work? Should Bonny be identified with all the work done in her name, even if it is antithetical to what she intended?

Unfortunately, no consensus has been reached on these questions within the GIM community. At present, some practitioners use the "Bonny Method" as an umbrella term for all practices inspired by Bonny, including both the individual and group form that she herself developed, as well as modifications and adaptations to them. Others use "GIM" as the umbrella term for all practices inspired by Bonny, but then distinguish between those forms developed by Bonny herself (which are most accurately called the "Bonny Method"), and modifications and adaptations developed by her followers.

The stance taken in this chapter is the latter one. Specifically, the following terms are used as defined below.

- "Guided Imagery and Music" or "GIM" refers to all forms of music-imaging in an expanded state of consciousness, including not only the specific individual and group forms that Bonny developed, but also all variations and modifications in those forms created by her followers. GIM is therefore the umbrella title that subsumes all practices involving imaging to music in an altered state of consciousness, including work done in individual or group settings, for purposes of therapy, healing, self-development, or spiritual growth, whether the images are guided or unguided, whether classical or non-classical music is used, and notwithstanding variations in the form of the session itself. As will be discussed later however, GIM does have boundaries; it does not include a host of related techniques that belong to music therapy.

- The "Bonny Method" refers to all of Bonny's original work. Logically, this includes *both* the individual and group forms that she developed; however, because of the important differences between these forms (e.g., therapy versus growth goals, and dialogue versus no dialogue with guide), some writers (including the present author) reserve the acronym "BMGIM" for only individual work, and then refer to her group form as either "Group GIM" or "Music and Imagery." Because there is no uniformity in the GIM literature, and because there is no consensus within the GIM community, readers must take note of how each author uses and defines these terms. Perhaps, in a future publication, after there is more consensus on these matters, confusion might be avoided if "I" and "G" were inserted in the acronym to specify the individual or group form respectively. Thus we would use BMIGIM for the individual Bonny form, and BMGGIM for the group Bonny form.

- The Bonny Method does not include any adaptations or modifications in the individual or group form as originally developed by her. These variations may be referred to as "Modified BMGIM" or more generically as "GIM."

In short: GIM is all forms of music imaging within an expanded state of consciousness; the "Bonny Method" refers to all of Bonny's work; BMGIM is Bonny's individual form; and Group GIM or Music and Imagery refer to Bonny's group form.

As will become evident, a wide array of techniques and practices can be subsumed under the generic category called GIM—some clearly falling within the boundaries of the Bonny Method, and others going outside them. In addition, there are a host of music therapy techniques that involve music, relaxation, and/or imagery that developed quite independently from the work of Bonny and her followers, and clearly fall outside the boundaries of GIM and the Bonny Method. All of these techniques and practices vary considerably in goal, technique, orientation, and process; yet, they are often confused with one another, causing lack of conceptual clarity in the work itself, as well as misunderstandings about the competence requirements for practitioners. This in turn raises serious issues about the ethics of safe practice in GIM. Who is competent to do what kinds of work, and what kinds of training are necessary to practice the various techniques combining music, expanded states of consciousness, and imagery?

The purpose of this chapter, then, is to establish boundaries for what is GIM and what is not, and within that generic category, what is Bonny's Method and what is not. In doing this, distinctions will also be made between the various adaptations to GIM and the Bonny Method when compared to related music therapy techniques. Hopefully, these boundaries and distinctions will ensure the integrity of Bonny's Method, preventing unworthy identifications with it, while also freeing her proponents to develop their own concepts and styles of working. Such clarification may also help to define competency requirements for ethical practice of all forms of GIM.

To identify these boundaries, several questions must be answered: 1) Does Bonny's work have the theoretical, empirical, and procedural integrity needed to qualify as a method in its own right? 2) What is Bonny's work a method of? Is it a form of music therapy, psychotherapy, pastoral counseling, spiritual direction, or education? 3) What features define the Bonny Method as originally conceived? 4) What variables have been manipulated to vary, adapt, or expand upon the Bonny Method? 5) How do the various forms of GIM compare to music therapy techniques?

## DID BONNY CREATE A METHOD?

In surveying any field, a fundamental question that eventually arises is: what constitutes a distinct method of practice? For without an answer to that question, the various methods within a field cannot be accurately identified, defined, and differentiated, which in turn renders them useless in guiding practice. If all the methods are essentially the same, then one way of practicing is essentially no better or more appropriate than another, and variations in method are serendipitous rather than purposeful. So it is important to ask: Does Bonny's work constitute a method in its own right? Does it have the distinct-ness and clarity needed to guide practice in a consistent way?

A method can be defined as a complete system of practice, consisting of: theoretical principles, goals, indications and contraindications, methodological procedures and techniques, guidelines for relationships within the practice, expectations for the process of development, and competency or training requirements (Bruscia, 1987). Developing such a complete system requires that: 1) the originator has worked with the method in an in-depth and focused way for a sufficient length of time, and that 2) based upon this prolonged experimentation, the originator has identified a set of principles, methods, and techniques that fit together coherently (Bruscia, 1987).

When considered in terms of these criteria, Bonny's work certainly qualifies as a method. For over three decades, Bonny devoted her attention to the development of two forms, one for work in an individual setting, and the other for group work. In the process, she discovered indications and contraindications, created all the musical materials required (i.e., discographies, taped music programs), and developed very specific techniques for implementing each method. Bonny also applied principles from humanistic and transpersonal theories to define the goals and processes of her individual and group forms, and the nature of the client-therapist relationship. Thus, without reservation, GIM as originally developed by Bonny is truly a method of practice.

Going one step further, because methods are defined by their uniqueness and originality, it is important to look at what is unique and original about Bonny's method. While Bonny was certainly not the first to use music for changing consciousness or for evoking imagery, she was the first to devise a procedure that put both of these processes together. That is, based on her work with music in LSD therapy (Bonny & Pahnke, 1972), Bonny discovered that helping a person enter into an expanded state of consciousness before listening to the music greatly enhanced the person's responsiveness to the music, and in doing so, also gave the person greater access to his/her imaginal world. What she also discovered was that as a person listens to the music for an extended period, his/her consciousness continues to deepen, shift, and expand as a result (Bonny, 1999). Thus, one can certainly say that Bonny's strategy for working simultaneously with consciousness, music, and imagery is uniquely and originally her own, and thus defines her method.

Another important innovation by Bonny was her use of specifically designed classical music programs to guide the person's imagery experience. No other form of imagery work, within music therapy or related fields, has relied upon a library of music programs, pre-designed with general purposes and applications in mind. (While the programs are used primarily in Bonny's individual form, they also form the basis for selecting and sequencing music for her group form, where there is less need for an entire program because of the shorter music listening period).

Finally, Bonny's discovery of how to verbally interact with a person while in an expanded state of consciousness is also unique and original. What Bonny found out after years of experience working in LSD therapy and her own method is that when guiding an individual, there are some verbal interventions that facilitate the experience, and there are some that are intrusive and disturbing. The most effective interventions are: 1) nondirective (the guide allows the imager to direct and control his/her own experience), 2) non-analytical (the guide refrains from asking questions that would lead the imager into intellectualizing about the ongoing experience), and 3) music-based (the guide contextualizes all interventions according to what is happening in the music) (Bonny, 1978). Interestingly, these guiding approaches are very consistent with her humanistic orientation to therapy, and her basic premises about the process, thus bringing considerable coherence to the method (Bonny, 1999).

## WHAT KIND OF METHOD IS IT?

Because Bonny was employed as a music therapist when she originated her method, and because most of her early publications appeared in the music therapy literature, one might likely assume that the Bonny Method quite naturally belongs within the discipline of music therapy; yet, a cursory look at the *Journal of the Association for Music and Imagery* quickly reveals that GIM (generically defined) is practiced within a variety of other treatment modalities, including psychotherapy, counseling, psychiatry, medicine, healing traditions, nursing, spiritual direction, and education, to achieve quite varied goals. Moreover, practitioners have quite varied educational backgrounds and areas of expertise. As a result of this diversity, GIM is conceived in a variety of ways. Some see GIM as rooted in the field of music therapy, some see it as a method of verbal psychotherapy or counseling that uses music and imagery; some see the music as the healing and transformative agent; some see music as supportive of the healing and transformation that takes place within other aspects of the work (e.g., imagery, relationship, etc.).

To understand where GIM fits, it is first necessary to see how it relates and overlaps with music therapy. Music therapy is the use of music experiences (e.g., improvising, listening, composing, performing), within the context of an interpersonal relationship, for purposes of therapy, healing, and self-actualization (Bruscia, 1998a). Thus, to the extent that GIM uses music listening, within an interpersonal context for the same purposes, it can be seen as a form of music therapy.

Another fundamental similarity between GIM and music therapy is that their boundaries are both defined by the method that they use (i.e., music) rather than by the outcomes they induce (e.g., insight, healing, behavior change). Music therapy does not become another discipline merely because it leads to outcomes that are psychotherapeutic, or spiritual, or medical rather than musical. Music therapy is defined by the use of music as its core method—not by its goal, not by the context or setting in which the method is applied, and not by the expertise of the practitioner. In this regard, music therapy and GIM are similar to art, dance, drama, and poetry therapies. All of these modalities are defined solely by the fact that they use an art form as the *method* for producing any variety of *outcomes*. As such, GIM and the arts therapies are defined quite differently from psychotherapy, medicine, education, spiritual direction—all of which are defined by the nature of the outcome, rather than the specific method used. For example, psychotherapy is defined by the psychological nature of its outcomes, rather than by the methods used to achieve that outcome. Similarly, medicine, education, and spiritual direction are defined by the specificity of their outcomes rather than the diversity of methods that may be used to achieve the outcomes.

The implications for GIM are clear: GIM does not become a form of medicine when the goal is medical, nor does it become a method of nursing when it brings comfort to a hospitalized patient; moreover, GIM does not become a form of counseling simply because it has been used by someone trained in counseling, nor does it become psychotherapy or counseling simply because verbal discussion is used in tandem with the music listening. GIM, like the other arts therapies, is defined by the fact that music is used as the chief method.

But then, how does one explain why, in the literature, GIM is conceived as method of psychotherapy, healing, spiritual direction and so forth, rather than as a form of music therapy. What determines whether GIM is being practiced as a form of music therapy or as part of another modality? The shortest and most direct answer to this question is: it all depends upon how the music is used.

Presently, there are myriad ways that music is conceived and used in GIM, some relying more on the actual music experience than others. How music is used may vary from one session to another, one client or population to another, and one practitioner to another. Sometimes the work focuses and relies entirely on the music experience, and sometimes it focuses and relies more on other elements of the work. More specifically, sometimes the session, client, or practitioner focus and rely upon the music listening as the core experience in GIM, and sometimes the session, client, or practitioner focus and rely upon the imagery, the expanded state of consciousness, the verbal discourse, body work, or work done in other art modalities. Similarly, sometimes the actual change or transformation is causally linked to the music, and sometimes it is not.

All of these variations in how music is used have significant implications for whether GIM belongs to the discipline of music therapy or another treatment modality. When considering music as a central variable in practice, GIM can be seen along a continuum, ranging from music therapy on one end, to other modalities on the other. On the music therapy end of the continuum, music is used *as* therapy or *as* the transformational agent; on the other end of the continuum, music is used *in* therapy, or as one of many agents of transformation. (Bruscia, 1987). With specific reference to GIM, when the work consistently relies primarily on the music listening experience as the main agent of therapy or transformation—regardless of the nature of the desired change—it clearly falls within the boundaries of music therapy; however, when the GIM work relies variously on the imagery, the verbal discussion, relationship, the expanded state, the music, or other arts, it falls within the boundaries of other treatment modalities, depending on whether the desired change is emotional, spiritual, medical, and so forth. Let us know look at how these two ends of the continuum are manifested in the actual work itself.

## Music as Transformation:
## GIM is Music Therapy

When music is consistently used in GIM *as* the transformative agent, the client's change process is evoked, worked through, and completed through the music listening experience, with very little reliance on other modalities (verbal discourse, art work, movement, etc.) to shape the change process. This complete and focused experiencing of the music is commonly observed in GIM sessions when the imager opens up to the music and enters into the transformational processes unfolding in the music itself (Bunt, 2000) When this happens, the imager steps into the structures and processes unfolding in the music from moment to moment, and begins to live within them, generating images and inner experiences that arise directly out of the music. And by living in these musical structures and processes as they continually transform themselves, the experiencer and the experience are similarly transformed. The entire phenomenon is intrinsically musical in nature, and similarly ineffable; and this seems to hold true, even when the imager tries to describe the experience verbally, using nonmusical referents (e.g, images of an animal, person, situation, etc.). In fact, often the nonmusical images and the verbal reports of them seem like mere artifacts of an essentially *musical* experience. Bush (1995) shared one of her own personal experiences as a traveler that provides a perfect example of music *as* transformation. During the experience, her guide suggested that she let the music take her. This is how Bush described what happened:

> I shifted positions and refocused my attention on the implicit feeling in the music. As I did the sounds began to take on substance, totally absorbing me in their melodic flow. I began breathing in sync with the rhythms, entering what felt like hyperspace in the intervals between the sounds. My body forgotten, I became living harmony. All parts of my consciousness were in attunement with the music. I was being played. I had become a musical force field. Time and space were nonexistent. The music and I were one (pp. 8–9).

It is important to realize that these transformational music experiences may arise spontaneously, initiated by the client, or they may be evoked purposely by the guide; they may also be an entire approach to GIM work, or an occasional happening. Much depends on how the guide conceptualizes GIM, and how it works. Nevertheless, when GIM is consistently practiced, conceptualized, or experienced in this way, it clearly falls within the boundary of pure music therapy.

## Music in Transformation:
## GIM is Adjunct to Another Modality

On the opposite pole of the continuum is when music is used to facilitate transformations taking place in other media. This occurs in GIM when the client's change process is evoked, worked through, and completed in the imagery experience, the body work, the art work, or the verbal discourse, all with the help of music as the background stimulus. Here the focus is not on experiencing the music as an intrinsically transformational experience in itself, instead, the focus is on generating nonmusical images and experiences with the help of the music. Practitioners here regard GIM as the use of music-evoked *imagery*, rather than the use of *music* per se, and consequently tend to guide, explore, and discuss the meaning of the imagery rather than the trans-formations experienced in the music. Here verbal segments of the GIM session take on more importance than the music-listening segment, and the insights gained are more verbal than ineffable (musical). This approach to GIM moves away from music therapy and into another treatment modality, as defined by the goals or desired outcomes established for or with the imager.

In summarizing the above continuum, practitioners who typically "guide to the music" and who rely upon the music as the primary transformation agent are using GIM as a form of music therapy. In contrast, those who guide, explore, and discuss the imagery and experiences that arise out of the music are using GIM as a form of psychotherapy, counseling, medicine, body-work, and so forth, depending upon the purpose or outcome. In short, when GIM is method-centered, that is, when music is relied upon as the chief agent of transformation, it belongs to the discipline of music therapy; when it is outcome centered, that is when music is used to facilitate transformations in other modalities, it belongs to another discipline, depending on the nature of the outcome.

# WHAT DEFINES THE BONNY METHOD?

Bonny developed two forms of GIM, which for purpose of this book have been given two names. The individual form is called the "Bonny Method of Guided Imagery and Music" (BMGIM), and the group form is called "Group GIM."

## Individual Form

Based on a synthesis of Bonny's writings (2002), BMGIM may be defined as: 1) an individual form 2) of exploring consciousness (e.g., in healing, psychotherapy, self-development, spiritual work), 3) which involves spontaneous imaging 4) in an expanded state of consciousness 5) to pre-designed (taped) programs of classical music, 6) while interacting with a guide, 7) who uses nondirective, non-analytical, music-based interventions, 8) within a client-centered orientation, 9) all within a session that has the following components: preliminary conversation relaxation/induction, guided music-imaging experience, return, and postlude discussion. These nine characteristics define the method, and all must be present to be considered the pure form of BMGIM, as originally developed by Bonny. Thus, if any of these characteristics are missing or significantly different from what has been described above, the method should not be regarded or labeled as BMGIM; rather it should be considered: an adaptation of Bonny's method which, depending upon how many of the above defining features have been modified, may fall under the generic category of "GIM" or qualify as a different method altogether.

## Group Form

Based on a synthesis of Bonny's writings (2002), the Group GIM may be defined as: 1) a form of working with individuals in a group setting, 2) for purposes of exploring consciousness (e.g., in education, training, self-development or spiritual work), in which 3) each member images spontaneously, 4) while in an expanded state of consciousness 5) to one or more pieces of music (any style), 6) without ongoing direction or dialogue with the leader, 7) working in a client-centered orientation, 8) within a session form that includes: a preliminary conversation, relaxation/induction, music-imaging experience, and postlude discussion.

Here again, if any of these defining features are modified in any way, the practice must be considered an adaptation of the Bonny Method, that falls either within the boundary of GIM or outside of it.

# WHAT VARIABLES OF THE BONNY METHOD
# HAVE BEEN MODIFIED?

The variables used to define the Bonny forms of GIM can be modified in myriad ways to accommodate the client, the situation, the goal, or the practitioner. The discussion that follows explores these modifications and attempts to place them in relation to the boundaries for GIM and the Bonny Method.

## Goals

In comparing the individual and group forms, there seem to be no difference in goal—both are aimed at exploring and expanding consciousness. Yet, Bonny's writings, and the history of her work, suggest that she did very different kinds of consciousness work in individual versus group settings. Originally, she presented individual GIM as a form of music psychotherapy (Bonny 1976), and throughout her later writings (Bonny, 1999) and case studies (Bonny, 2002), she continually referred to her own individual work with clients as psychotherapeutic in nature. In contrast, the group form, which received much less attention in her professional writings, was originally presented as a way of working with "Music and Imagery" to pursue non-therapeutic goals, such as education, training, personal growth, spirituality, and so forth (Bonny & Savary, 1973). Bonny (1994) explains:

> With the discovery of the dyad as the primary and most effective mode of exploration into the deeper unconscious, the descriptions given of the technique in *Music and Your Mind* looked peripheral by comparison. They were part of the exploratory process and, as such, had value in certain situations (p. 72).

Notable examples of extending Bonny's group form into therapeutic arenas include the work of Summer (1988) who described clinical applications of Group GIM in various institutional settings, and who also developed Group Music and Imagery Therapy (see chapter in this book). Short (1992) also differentiated between ongoing "therapeutic groups using music and imagery" with a clinical population and Bonny's approach to groups.

Bonny's long-standing commitment to humanistic psychology is undoubtedly a factor that confounds whether her goals for the individual and group form were "therapeutic." In the humanistic orientation, health is emphasized over pathology, and the primary goal of all work, whether called therapy or not, is self-actualization (Bonny, 1999). Consequently, even when Bonny worked with individuals within a clear psychotherapeutic framework, the goals were characteristically holistic, growth-oriented, and transpersonal rather than pathology-driven and purely psychological (Bonny, 1999). Thus, while she followed this orientation in both individual and group forms of GIM, her goals certainly varied, and the nature of her relationship with clients varied as well.

When the previous criteria for a method are applied—that the originator must have worked with the practice in an in-depth and focused way for a sufficient length of time, and as a result identified a set of principles, methods, and techniques that fit together coherently—a clear boundary can be identified. Bonny did not work extensively with nor did she develop methodological principles for using the *individual form* for *non-therapeutic* purposes; likewise, she did not work extensively with nor did she develop sufficient methodological principles for using the *group form* for *therapeutic* purposes. Thus, technically speaking, though Bonny advocated the use of both forms for both therapeutic and non-therapeutic purposes, her own work included only *therapeutic* uses of the *individual form,* and *non-therapeutic* uses of the *group form.* All other uses or adaptations of GIM, though inspired by her, were not fully developed by her, and thus fall outside the boundary of the Bonny Method.

## State of Consciousness

An expanded state of consciousness is an integral part of all forms of GIM work (Bonny, 2002). Entering into such states helps the traveler to open up more fully to the music listening experience, which in turn leads to further exploration of expanded states. Thus, GIM uses expanded states of consciousness as a means to an end, and also fosters the exploration of these states as an end in itself. One might even say that the entire GIM session serves as an induction into expanded consciousness work.

Two boundaries must be drawn in reference to states of consciousness. The first is that only those music listening experiences that occur within an expanded state of consciousness fall within the boundaries of GIM. All other kinds of listening experiences do not. Thus, whenever the guide makes efforts to prevent, contain, or limit an expansion of consciousness before or during the music listening, the practice falls outside the GIM boundary. Two examples are projective listening and relaxation listening.

PROJECTIVE LISTENING. In this music therapy technique, the therapist presents music to clients who are in an upright position or ordinary state of consciousness, and then asks the client to react to it imaginatively. This includes free association to music, projective story-telling or dramatizing to music, projective drawing or moving to music, and so forth (Bruscia, 1998a). Thus, GIM is different from projective listening in that, in GIM, the therapist encourages the client to enter an expanded state of consciousness, whereas in projective listening, the therapist works to maintain ordinary levels of consciousness or limit the amount of expansion.

RELAXATION LISTENING. The second boundary is that the purpose of GIM is to *explore* consciousness, it is not to reach and maintain a state of relaxation. In GIM, the guide helps the client to enter a relaxed state so that it is easier to explore deeper states of consciousness with the help of the music. The aim of GIM is certainly not to hold the client in a relaxed state without any further exploration of that level of consciousness.

Music therapists often use music listening to help clients enter and maintain a relaxed state. These *relaxation listening* experiences are quite different in goal and outcome than GIM, though they typically involve the same elements of music, imagery, and relaxation. In relaxation listening, the music therapist narrates a relaxation induction (often employing images), using supportive music in the background. For example, the therapist may present a "ball of light" induction, wherein the client imagines the ball moving systematically through each part of the body, bringing warmth and relaxation, all while a very quiet music selection is heard in the background. In these experiences, the client is encouraged to follow the image presented by the therapist, rather than to allow additional personal images to arise. Most often, the background music is "New Age" in style because it has the repetition needed to support the repeated verbal suggestions in the induction, and because it is less likely to evoke additional imagery than classical music (Bonny, 1994).

Note that in *relaxation listening,* the image and music are used to induce and maintain an extended period of relaxation. In contrast, in GIM, the traveler undergoes a relaxation induction such as the "ball of light" before the music begins, in order to facilitate free imaging to the music. At this point, the image and music help the client to move beyond the "relaxed" feeling to a fuller exploration of more expanded states of consciousness, as they shift in depth and breadth from moment to moment. Thus, *relaxation listening* is a music therapy technique that is significantly different from GIM in goal and procedure, and therefore falls outside of its boundaries.

To summarize distinctions made with regard to states of consciousness: neither GIM, the generic method, nor the Bonny Method in particular, includes *projective listening* and *relaxation listening* techniques employed in music therapy. While projective listening engages the client's imaginative responses to music, it does not involve an expanded state of consciousness. Thus, though similar to GIM, projective listening is not a part of GIM or the Bonny method. While relaxation listening directs the client's imagination to use specific images to enter and maintain a relaxed state, it does not involve free exploration of the client's consciousness through spontaneous personal imagery and music listening. Thus, though similar to GIM in its components, relaxation listening is not part of GIM nor the Bonny method.

## Spontaneous Imaging

Both the individual and group forms of the Bonny Method involve *free, spontaneous imaging.* The traveler allows his or her imagination to unfold freely and extemporaneously, exploring whatever experiences emerge each moment in response to the music. The only direction the guide may give to the traveler is to suggest a starting image as the music begins, but even then, the traveler is free to follow or abandon this image at any time. Of course, there are also instances when a traveler may not be ready for such spontaneity in the imagination, when the goal of the imaging is somewhat different. The following types of imaging are examples.

CONTAINED SPONTANEOUS IMAGING. In this approach to imaging, the guide presents an image (e.g., a house), invites the traveler to explore one part of the image (the front door) for a few moments, then moves the traveler progressively along in the same image (into living room, dining room, etc.), so that the traveler images freely within a contained matrix, as presented throughout the imagery experience by the guide.

This contained spontaneous approach may be used in individual or group sessions. It is particularly helpful with healthy travelers who need preparation or practice before imaging completely spontaneously, or with psychiatric patients whose fragility necessitates a more structured approach to listening to music in a relaxed state (Moe, Roesen, & Raben, 2000). It is also highly recommended for travelers who have been traumatized and who need to contain the amount of unconscious material released at one time and thereby limit any accompanying cathartic reactions (Blake, 1994: Blake & Bishop, 1994).

While this type of contained imaging is not indigenous to the Bonny Method, in either the individual or group forms, it is an approach to imaging that requires the specific guiding skills of a GIM practitioner. Thus, though it is not an approach specifically developed by Bonny as part of her method, this modification, by merit of the nature of the guiding skills required, does belong within the boundaries of generic GIM practice.

DIRECTED MUSIC IMAGING. In contrast to spontaneous and contained spontaneous imaging, music therapists use a highly directed form of imaging, which falls outside the boundaries of GIM and the Bonny Method. The purpose of *directed music imaging* is to take the traveler step-by-step through an imagery experience that activates, reproduces, or rehearses a desired process or outcome, such as pain management (Rider, 1987; Steinke, 1991), enhancement of immune responses (Tsao, Gordon, Maranto, Lerman & Murasko, 1991), stress or anxiety reduction (Hammer, 1996), and healing of disease processes (Rider, 1987). Here, the image reenacts a sequence of physical or psychological events that are deemed to be therapeutic for the traveler.

Given the close relationship between the image and therapeutic outcome, it is important for the traveler to experience the image as directed, without any further expansion or development of the image. Thus, the guide directs the traveler in a very detailed way, specifying all aspects of the imagery experience from beginning to end, while managing the attention and consciousness of the traveler carefully to intensify his or her concentration on the image and its desired outcome. Notice that the aim of directed imaging is outcome-specific; it is not free exploration of outcomes that may arise in the traveler's imagination or consciousness.

REIMAGING. Yet another approach is called *reimaging* (Bruscia, 1998b). In re-imaging, one person has a short BMGIM session focused on exploring a previous imagery experience of another person. The technique is used in individual, couple, and group settings, for clinical or supervisory purposes. The sessions are guided in individual and couple settings, but unguided in group settings.

- *Group Reimaging (Unguided)*. After an induction, all members of the group enter into a previous image of one person, and participate in or observe what happens from his or her own perspective. The group images to a short excerpt of the same music heard by the person when creating the image originally. Usually the music is no more than five minutes in length. Each member images independently and silently, without dialoguing with other members or the guide. The guide assists the group in entering and leaving the person's imagery or dream, but does not dialogue with the group during the actual reimaging experience. The aim is to help one member benefit from the imaginal resources of the entire group. By all experiencing the same image from their own perspective, the group can gain new insights, or find new solutions or options to a particular problem that a member is confronting within his or her imagery.

- *Couple Reimaging (Guided):* After an induction, one partner in a relationship enters into a previous image of the other, and participates in or observes what happens from his or her own perspective. The person images to a short excerpt of the same music originally heard by the other partner. The guide maintains a dialogue with the traveler throughout the entire experience, using standard guiding techniques in

BMGIM. Both partners may be present, or each partner may work alone with the guide. The aim is to help partners empathize more fully with one another, while also sharing one another's insights and problem-solving resources.

- *Supervisory Reimaging (Guided).* After an induction, a trainee or practitioner enters into a previous image of a client who is being brought to supervision. The supervisee participates in or observes what happened in the client's image from his or her own perspective, while listening to a short excerpt of the same music heard by the client. The supervisor guides the supervisee throughout the entire reimaging experience, using standard BMGIM guiding techniques. The aims may be to: help the supervisee empathize more fully with the client; gain insights into the client's problems and possible solutions; bring into consciousness the supervisee's unconscious reactions to the client; and to explore options for working with the client more effectively. Two examples can be found in Bruscia (1998b).

Reimaging is a somewhat "contained" form of imaging, in that the experience of the other person provides a container for exploring his or her imaginal world. As such, like contained imaging, all forms of reimaging fall within the generic category of GIM, but go beyond the Bonny Method.

To summarize the three forms of imaging: *Free spontaneous imaging* is a defining feature of GIM as originally developed by Bonny; *contained spontaneous imaging* and *reimaging* are modified forms of GIM but are not within the boundaries of the Bonny Method; and *directed music imaging* is beyond the boundaries of both GIM and the Bonny Method, belonging to the discipline of music therapy. Thus, as the traveler moves from free exploration of consciousness to directed consciousness, the practice moves further away from Bonny's GIM.

## Dialoguing with Guide in Individual Work

The individual form of Bonny's Method always involves a dialogue between traveler and guide during the entire music-imaging experience. In the dialogue, the traveler reports his or her ongoing experiences, and the guide responds nondirectively and supportively. Thus, a defining feature of Bonny's individual form is an ongoing, nondirective dialogue between guide and therapist during the music listening. This creates a clear boundary for the individual form: Whenever there is no dialogue or whenever the dialogue is consistently directive, the practice should be considered a modified form of GIM or beyond its boundaries altogether, and in both cases, beyond the Bonny method. While this may seem unnecessary to point out, such clarification calls into question many practices assumed to be part of GIM or the Bonny Method that are actually beyond one or the other.

Three practices provide good examples. First, Marr (1998–99) and Clark (1999) both describe the use of short individual GIM sessions that are unguided. These types of sessions are clearly forms of GIM, but are nevertheless, modifications of the Bonny Method. A second example is directed music imaging (when the guide directs the traveler through a specific imagery sequence), which as established earlier, is beyond the boundaries of both GIM and the Bonny Method. The third example arises when directive interventions are used by the guide in response to spontaneous images being created by the traveler. Most often, such interventions are borrowed from another treatment method or orientation (e.g., Gestalt, cognitive, somatic, or energetic therapies). Invariably, the intervention is aimed at achieving a particular therapeutic outcome that is not occurring spontaneously in the traveler's imagery. For example, the guide may try to get the traveler to bring an empty chair into the scene for dialogue purposes (Gestalt), or the guide may ask the traveler to "reframe" a particular image (cognitive), or the guide may apply specific pressure points in the traveler's body in order to elicit a certain reaction. In all these examples, the practice falls within the boundaries of GIM, but certainly not the Bonny Method.

Throughout her writings, Bonny (2002) has consistently advocated that a nondirective stance be taken by the guide or therapist when dialoguing with the traveler during the music listening portion of the session, and that the entire session be approached within the humanistic or transpersonal traditions. Thus, whenever techniques are borrowed from other methods and orientations and introduced into a GIM session, two boundaries become necessary.

- When the guide approaches the work to be done in the prelude or postlude outside of the humanistic or transpersonal orientations, but maintains a nondirective approach when guiding the music experience, the work falls under the generic category of GIM, but remains outside the boundary of the Bonny Method. Thus, for example, when discussions before or after the music imaging are psychodynamic or cognitive in focus, or when Gestalt exercises are used (e.g., empty chair), the session should be considered a form of GIM that is beyond the Bonny Method. Though GIM certainly lends itself to such adaptations, and though these are certainly fruitful approaches to GIM therapy, they were not developed by Bonny.

- When the guide intervenes in a consistently directive way in the traveler's imagery, or when the guide dialogues with the traveler within a particular orientation (e.g., psychodynamic, cognitive, behavioral), the work falls within the boundaries of GIM but outside the boundaries of the Bonny Method. The Bonny Method is defined by a nondirective, humanistic approach to guiding.

## Dialoguing in Couple and Group Work

In contrast to individual work, Bonny's Group GIM does not involve a dialogue between each traveler and the guide. Instead, each traveler images without verbally reporting the images as they occur, and without verbal interventions by the guide.

An exception is the dialogue among group members that was reported in *Music and Your Mind* (Bonny & Savary, 1973, p. 109), but never further developed in any of Bonny's writings. In the "Group Fantasy," one group member begins to create an image, and when ready signals the next person to carry forward the image, who then signals the next person to continue, and so on until everyone in the group has contributed. Unfortunately, for some unknown reason, Bonny did not further develop or write about this form of group imaging, and therefore did not make it an integral part of her group form.

Many advancements have been made in the kinds of dialogues conducted in music-imaging sessions involving more than one person. In the early 1990's, the present writer began to study and experiment with how to guide several travelers as they spontaneously co-image to music together. As a result, the writer identified and worked with several, specific types of co-imaging, and began presenting these techniques in his training manual (Bruscia, 1992). The various types were defined according to whether the imaging is done by couples or groups, how the imaginal interactions are sequenced, and the extent to which the guide is involved.

PROGRESSIVE GROUP IMAGING: Each member takes a turn contributing to an evolving image or story. When one member finishes, he or she signals the next member to continue; members do not respond to one another image's out of turn. Other than preparing the group to begin, and perhaps providing a starting image, the guide's involvement is minimal. Thus, progressive group imaging is mostly unguided. As mentioned above, this type was used by Bonny, and termed a "group fantasy."

GROUP GO-ROUNDS ON INDIVIDUAL: Each member of the group takes turns imaging something about one person in the group; the person in focus may or may not react or respond to each group member's images. Group members usually follow a predetermined sequence, and do not participate out of turn. The guide always assists the group in entering and leaving the imagery experience, but during the actual imaging, may or may not enter into the dialogues between each dyad. Thus group go-rounds may be guided or unguided. Eventually, each member becomes the imagery focus of the group. An example is provided by Shorr (1986) who instructed a particular group as follows: "Imagine standing on Steve's shoulders. How would it feel and what do you imagine will happen?" (p. 173).

INDIVIDUAL GO-ROUNDS ON GROUP: This is the reverse of group go-rounds. Here one person is the main imager, who goes around imaging something about each member of the group. Each group member may or may not respond to the person imaging, but never out of turn. The guide always assists the group in entering and leaving the imagery experience, but during the actual imaging may or may not enter into the dialogue between each dyad. Thus, individual go-rounds may be guided or unguided. Shorr (1986) gives an example of asking a person to imagine being an animal, and then going around to each member of the group, one by one, and entering into a dialogue with each.

GROUP REIMAGING (GUIDED). After describing in detail a particularly significant image or dream with the group, a person selects members of the group to enter into the image or dream as participants or observers. The guide assists the person and co-imagers in entering and leaving the reimaging, and then plays an active but nondirective role in guiding the actual experience, using all the techniques belonging to individual BMGIM. The imagers dialogue with one another during the experience, and with the help of the guide, explore their own perspectives as well as unrealized options that the person may have within the image or dream. As the image or dream is continually reworked, new perspectives and action sequences are developed in the group interaction. Thus, ultimately, the image or dream is transformed.

COUPLE CO-IMAGING (GUIDED). Two partners in any kind of relationship have a joint GIM session, entering an expanded state, and then co-creating imagery to music while dialoguing with a guide. Merritt and Schulberg (1995) reported on such an approach in working through collective grief over the Holocaust. The partners were an American Jewish woman whose mother had been imprisoned in Auschwitz, and a German woman whose father had driven equipment into the camp as a soldier. The guide gave an induction and presented a starting image of looking into the stones the two women had picked up from the ground when they had visited Dachau together. The partners then explored the stone image from their own cultural and personal perspectives, dialoguing with one another and the guide.

GROUP CO-IMAGING (GUIDED). All members of the group spontaneously co-create the imagery experience while dialoguing with one another and the guide. The guide assists the group in entering and leaving the experience, and then plays an active but nondirective role in the dialogue, using all the techniques belonging to individual BMGIM. Two subtly different approaches have been taken, but very little has been written about either. In the present author's approach (Bruscia, 1992), the guide provides a starting image for the entire group, places each member in the imagery scene, and then invites them to begin interacting within the image. The guide holds the group within the imaginal space that continually evolves, using all of the nondirective guiding techniques of BMGIM. The second approach, as reported by Merritt and Schulberg (1995), was developed by Carol Bush and Sara Jane Stokes. In it, the guide provides a starting image, and invites members of the group to each go on their own separate journey, "relating aloud their experiences with the music as they feel moved to speak. The GIM facilitator guides the experience when direction or reinforcement seems appropriate. What begins as a separate journey ends in a joining together of each separate journey into one common experience" (Merritt & Schulberg, 1995, p. 106).

## Use of Classical Music Programs

One of the hallmarks of the Bonny individual form is the exclusive use of classical music (Bonny, 1978); whereas in the group form, various styles and genres of music may be used. She explains:

> Through trial and error, we have learned that for dyadic applications, classical selections are able to provide depth of experience, variety of color and form, harmonic and melodic complexity which are qualities needed for self-exploration. . . . Popular music, on the other hand, is more peripheral, simpler in form and less intrusive. Therefore popular music of the appropriate kind (usually instrumental) may serve as well in group GIM sessions (Bonny, 1999, p. 73).

Another hallmark of Bonny's individual form is the use of pre-designed programs, consisting of carefully selected and sequenced pieces of classical music. In fact, Bonny (1978) created an entire library of taped programs, with the clear intent that these programs be used in individual work. Bonny designed these programs with a particular intensity profile in mind. That is, each program was given its own affective contour, sensitively timed to lead the traveler into a particular state of consciousness and/or emotional space, hold the traveler there, and then provide a pathway out or back. Thus, these music programs, as designed by Bonny, are intended to shape the traveler's experience. As such, they are a core component of the individual session, and a defining feature of the method itself.

It is important to realize that, because the programs were presented on audiotape, there was little opportunity for guides to alter the program itself during the music imaging. The only options were to change midway within a program to another program, to add or omit a piece at the beginning or end of a program, or to present two or more complete programs in sequence (i.e., Death-Rebirth, Peak Experience) (Bonny, 1978). With the advent of CD technology, however, guides have gained much greater flexibility in selecting and sequencing the music for an individual session. Guides can now skip from one piece to the next within a program, or easily switch to any place within another program, thus opening up the possibility of completely spontaneous music programming.

When Bonny's original conception of classical music programs is considered in light of more recent developments, two important boundaries need to be drawn. First, only classical music is used in Bonny's individual form; thus, all uses of nonclassical music in individual "GIM" sessions go beyond the boundaries of the Bonny Method. Second, only pre-designed programs are used in Bonny's individual form; thus, all spontaneous music programming in individual "GIM" sessions goes beyond the boundaries of the Bonny Method.

In contrast, the boundaries for Bonny's group form are much larger; they include the use of nonclassical music, and there is no assumption that pre-designed programs be used.

## Length of Session and Music

As originally designed by Bonny, individual sessions usually last 1½ to 2 hours, and on rare occasions may even extend up to 3 hours, depending on the length of the music used, and a variety of other factors. These sessions can seem quite long when compared to the 50-minute hour that characterizes traditional psychotherapy practice. For this reason, Ritchey Vaux (1993) adapted the BMGIM session by using shorter music programs, and taking less time for prelude and postlude processing. She has found that even these shorter sessions, when adequately prepared, can "work at a level beyond the limits where brief psychotherapy is usually effective" (p. 29). Nevertheless, shortening the traditional individual GIM session goes beyond the Bonny Method. Two reasons can be given. First, full music programs of the usual length are rarely possible, and as established earlier, BMGIM is defined by the use of pre-designed programs, most of which exceed 30 minutes. Second, the depth of the work in a short session can rarely match the depth in a longer session, not only because the music continually deepens the traveler's experience as a full-length program unfolds, but also because, in a shorter session, the therapist must continuously monitor the depth of consciousness so the traveler can successfully negotiate the experience.

Group GIM sessions, on the other hand, can vary considerably in length, without going beyond the boundaries of the Bonny Method (see the length of music suggestions in Bonny and Savary [1973]). Much depends on the amount of music presented, and the needs and goals of the group in entering and leaving the imagery experience. For example, Moe, Roesen, and Raben (2000) describe the need to shorten the music-imaging portion of group sessions to accommodate psychiatric patients. They presented only 10 minutes of music in a 1½ hour session. Short (1992) found that when working with a physically disabled elderly group, the music imaging could last from 3 to 12 minutes, and that it is better to use two pieces instead of one for longer listening periods. In other group circumstances, the length of an unguided music-imaging experience may take anywhere from 5 to 20 minutes, with the prelude and postlude activities varying in length accordingly.

## SUMMARY

The purpose of this chapter has been to identify boundaries for the generic practice called GIM, as well as the individual and group forms originated by Bonny. First, it was established that GIM is truly a method in its own right, and that Bonny worked sufficiently with the method to develop a coherent set of principles and techniques that are uniquely and originally her own. Then, it was argued that GIM is a form of music therapy whenever it is method-centered, and that it becomes something else when it is outcome centered. Specifically, GIM is music therapy whenever the guide and traveler use the music as the primary agent or context for therapeutic change, regardless of whether the change is physical, emotional, mental, or spiritual.. GIM becomes a form of psychotherapy, healing, education, medicine, self-development, and so forth, whenever the guide and traveler focus on a particular outcome in these areas, and then use music as only one of the means of achieving it.

The individual and group forms of GIM as originated by Bonny were defined in terms of their essential features; then the myriad variations in each feature were examined and compared. Several practices were placed in relation to GIM and the Bonny Method. Three main categories emerged:

BONNY METHOD:

- Individual form: a modality of therapy involving spontaneous imaging, expanded states of consciousness, pre-designed classical music programs, ongoing dialogues during the music-imaging, and nondirective guiding techniques. This is most often referred to as "BMGIM."
- Group form: a modality for self-development involving spontaneous imaging, expanded states, various styles of music selected by the guide, and no dialogues or guiding during the music-imaging. This is most often referred to as "Group GIM" or "Music and Imagery."

GIM PRACTICES (OUTSIDE BONNY METHOD)

- Contained spontaneous imaging (as defined previously)
- Reimaging (unguided and guided work with couple, group, and supervisees)
- All GIM work done in orientations other than humanistic or transpersonal
- All directive approaches to guiding spontaneous imagery
- Group and individual go-rounds
- Co-imaging (guided work with couples and groups)
- All uses of nonclassical music in individual GIM sessions
- All spontaneous programming of music for individual GIM sessions
- All shortened individual GIM sessions

MUSIC THERAPY PRACTICES (NOT GIM OR BONNY METHOD)

- Projective listening
- Relaxation listening
- Directed music imaging

## *References*

Blake, R. (1994). Vietnam veterans with Post-Traumatic Stress Disorder (PTSD): Findings from a music and imagery project. *Journal of the Association for Music and Imagery,* 3, 5–17.

Blake, R., & Bishop, S. (1994). The Bonny Method of Guided Imagery and Music in the treatment of Post-Traumatic Stress Disorder (PTSD) with adults in a psychiatric setting. *Music Therapy Perspectives,* 12(2), 125–129.

Bonny, H. (1976). *Music and Psychotherapy.* Doctoral dissertation, Union Graduate School.

Bonny, H. (1978). *GIM Monograph #2: Facilitating GIM Sessions.* Salina, KS: The Bonny Foundation.

Bonny, H. (1980). GIM Monograph #3: *GIM Therapy: Past, Present and Future Implications.* Salina, KS: The Bonny Foundation.

Bonny, H. (1994). Twenty-one years later: A GIM update. *Music Therapy Perspectives,* 12(2), 70–74.

Bonny, H. (1999). *GIM Monograph #1: Facilitating GIM Sessions.(Revised Edition).* Salina, KS: The Bonny Foundation.

Bonny, H. (2002). *Music and Consciousness: The Evolution of Guided Imagery and Music.* Gilsum, NH: Barcelona Publishers.

Bonny, H., & Pahnke, W. (1972). The use of music in psychedelic (LSD) psychotherapy. *Journal of Music Therapy, 9*(2), 64–87.

Bonny, H., & Savary, L. (1973). *Music and Your Mind: Listening with a New Consciousness.* New York: Harper & Row Publishers.

Bruscia, K. (1987). *Improvisational Models of Music Therapy.* Springfield, IL: Charles C. Thomas.

Bruscia, K. (1992). *Level Three: GIM Training Manual.* Unpublished manuscript. Philadelphia, PA.

Bruscia, K. (1998a). *Defining Music Therapy (Second Edition).* Gilsum, NH: Barcelona Publishers.

Bruscia, K. (ed.) (1998b). *The Dynamics of Music Psychotherapy.* Gilsum, NH: Barcelona Publishers.

Bunt, L. (2000). Transformational processes in Guided Imagery and Music. *Journal of the Association for Music and Imagery, 7,* 44–58.

Bush, C. (1995). *Healing Imagery and Music: Pathways to the Inner Self.* Portland, OR: Rudra Press.

Clark, M. (1998–99). The Bonny Method of Guided Imagery and Music and spiritual development. *Journal of the Association for Music and Imagery, 6,* 55–62.

Clarkson, G. (1999). The spiritual insights of a Guided Imagery and Music client with autism. *Journal of the Association for Music and Imagery, 6,* 87–103.

Hammer, S. (1996). The effects of guided imagery through music on state and trait anxiety. *Journal of Music Therapy, 33* (1), 47–70.

Marr, J. (1998–99). GIM at the end of life: Case studies in palliative care. *Journal of the Association for Music and Imagery*, 6, 37–54.

Merritt, S., & Schulberg, C. (1995). GIM and collective grief. *Journal of the Association for Music and Imagery*, 4, 103–121.

Moe, T., Roesen, A., & Raben, H. (2000). Restitutional factors in group music therapy with psychiatric patients based on a modification of Guided Imagery and Music (GIM). *Nordic Journal of Music Therapy*, 9 (2), 36–50.

Rider, M. (1987). Treating chronic disease and pain with music-mediated imagery. *The Arts in Psychotherapy*, 14 (2), 113–120.

Ritchey Vaux, D. (1993). GIM applied to the 50-minute hour. *Journal of the Association for Music and Imagery,* 2, 29–34.

Shorr, J. (1986). Techniques in psycho–imagination therapy. In A. Sheikh (ed.), *Anthology of Imagery Techniques*. Milwaukee, WI: American Imagery Institute.

Short, A. (1992). Music and imagery with physically disabled elderly residents. *Music Therapy: Journal of the American Association for Music Therapy*, 11 (1), 65–98.

Steinke, W. (1991). The use of music, relaxation, and imagery in the management of postsurgical pain for scoliosis. In C. Maranto (ed.), *Applications of Music in Medicine*, 141–162. Silver Springs, MD: National Association for Music Therapy.

Summer, L. (1988). Guided Imagery and Music in the Institutional Setting. St. Louis, MO: MMB Music.

Tsao, C., Gordon, T., Maranto, C., Lerman, C, & Murasko, D. (1991). The effects of music and directed biological imagery on immune responses (S–IgA). In C. Maranto (ed.), *Applications of Music in Medicine*, 85–121. Silver Springs, MD: National Association for Music Therapy.

*Chapter Four*


# DISTINCTIONS BETWEEN
# THE BONNY METHOD OF GUIDED IMAGERY
# AND MUSIC (BMGIM) AND
# OTHER IMAGERY TECHNIQUES


## Anthony Meadows


Helen Bonny developed Guided Imagery and Music therapy (GIM) in the 1970s, at a time when there was a burgeoning of imagery methods in the United States (Sheikh, 1983; Singer & Pope, 1978). Grof's Holotropic Breathwork (Grof, 1985) was also developed in this period, and European imagery methods such as Jung's Active Imagination (Jung, 1916/1958) and Leuner's Guided Affect Imagery (Leuner, 1978) were gaining wider attention in the United States around this time as well (Sheikh & Jordan, 1983). In fact, Bonny worked with Stanislav Grof at the Maryland Psychiatric Center (Grof, 1985). She also met Hanscarl Leuner early in the development of GIM, and there was an exchange between these pioneers (Bonny, 1978b). Because of this exchange, and the range of imagery-based methods and techniques developed for use in therapy, the purpose of this chapter is to examine the relationship between GIM and these other methods, drawing distinctions between them in procedure, goal, and process. While a diverse range of imagery methods have been developed, only the following will be included, because of their historical significance, and/or because they are major imagery methods currently used in therapy: Freud's Free Association and Dream Analysis; Jung's Dream Analysis and Active Imagination; Leuner's Guided Affective Imagery; Grof's Holotropic Breathwork; Assagioli's Psychosynthesis; Ghendlin's Focusing Oriented Psychotherapy, and Hypnotherapy. It is important to note that these comparisons are based on writings of each method as it was originally developed. No attempt is made to incorporate adaptations or developments of these methods, unless made by the creator. It should also be noted that comparisons have been made only to the individual form of GIM, which is now referred to as the Bonny

Method of Guided Imagery and Music (BMGIM) as contrasted to Group GIM and various other adaptations.

# FREUD: FREE ASSOCIATION
# AND DREAM ANALYSIS

While Janet and Breuer were probably the first Europeans to employ imagery in therapeutic work in the 1880s and 1890s (Sheikh & Jordan, 1983; Singer & Pope, 1978), it was Sigmund Freud who became widely recognized for the use of imagery in psychoanalysis, and may be considered one of the first to develop a systematic approach to imagery work in his interpretation of dreams. In fact, he was probably aware in the early 1890s of the spontaneous images experienced by his clients and began to work with these extensively immediately prior to 1900. Freud developed an imagery technique where he would press on the patient's head and instruct him/her to observe the images that appeared when he released the pressure. Freud reported that patients saw, in rapid succession, various scenes related to core therapeutic issues.

However, Freud soon abandoned his focus on imagery in this form, as he came to regard images as a form of resistance (Sheikh & Jordan, 1983). He felt that imagery was more a primitive, primary process functioning associated with regressive features, and was "downplayed in favor of direct, logical thought" (Singer & Pope, 1978, p. 5). Instead, he focused on two techniques that have become synonymous with psychoanalysis: free association and dream interpretation (Wollheim, 1991), which he also used together (Freud, 1952). Both are techniques for accessing the unconscious, which Freud used extensively in psychoanalysis, but unlike his early use of imagery, they allowed both therapist and patient the opportunity to process verbally, in a direct and logical manner.

In free association, Freud instructed his patients to say whatever came into their minds, at times without further explanation, and on other occasions from a word, dream, or issue associated with a current therapeutic topic. Freud felt that at the point when the patient became stuck and could no longer freely associate, he had found a point of resistance that was important to therapy. It was at this point that he intervened verbally, to further explore and work through this resistance.

BMGIM is similar to free association in its focus on accessing material from the client's psyche, and on using a reclining restive state during therapy. Free association is different in that the purpose of the technique is to supplement verbal analysis, whereas in BMGIM the imagery experience is core to the client's therapy. In fact, free association may not use visual imagery at all; instead, it typically taps unconscious associations between words. In BMGIM the therapist enters into the experience with the client, engaging in the client's imagery (Bonny, 1978a), whereas in free association, the analyst remains detached from the patient, and offers no interventions during the period of associations. Here lies another subtle distinction. In psychoanalysis, the analysand is usually referred to as the patient, whereas in BMGIM, the term client is typically used. Both terms have different meanings, and may imply a difference in the client-therapist relationship. Further, in BMGIM the client usually receives a relaxation induction and starting image (Bonny, 1978a), while in free association there is little or no preparation for the patient. Finally, music is not used in free association.

A second approach developed by Freud was dream interpretation. He felt that dreams were the "royal road to the unconscious" and he never wavered in the importance he placed on them (Wollheim, 1991). During the course of a therapy session, Freud would have patients report dreams that had occurred since the last therapy session (Freud, 1952). He would listen to the retelling of the dream, and engage the patient in expanding upon the dream, revisiting a certain part, or engaging in free association with the dream. Freud would then work with the patient verbally to bring into conscious awareness the nature of the dream as it related to the patient's analysis. At the same time, Freud would analyze the dream according to his own interpretational system (Freud, 1952). He was very clear about the nature of dreams: "A dream is a (disguised) fulfillment of a (suppressed or repressed) wish" (Freud, 1935, p. 608, cited in Wollheim, 1991, p. 66). Thus, the purpose of dream analysis was to uncover the patient's wish, which he felt was always hidden (Wollheim, 1991).

BMGIM is similar to dream interpretation in its emphasis on images as an expression of the unconscious. Like Freud, Bonny felt that these images were a way for the psyche to communicate, and contained valuable information about the client's condition. However, Freud only processed dreams, whereas Bonny (1978a) worked with all kinds of imagery phenomena. Like Bonny, Freud encouraged the client to interact with the images in order to gain a deeper understanding of the images. However, Freud focused almost exclusively on verbal processing within his own interpretational system, whereas Bonny (1978a) focused more on helping the client to understand the meaning of the image within the client's own framework. In fact, Freud was primarily concerned with the content implications of images (Singer & Pope, 1978), whereas Bonny was at least as concerned with the lived experience of the images (Bonny, 1978a). And, as previously mentioned, Freud felt that dreams were always about "wish fulfillment," interpreting these according to his own analytic system, whereas Bonny uses a range of theories to understand the client's experiences (Bonny, 1978a). As such, this was a fundamental difference between the two methods. Further, while it is not completely clear, it appears that Freud did little to prepare patients for dream recall, whereas Bonny usually did prepare clients prior to the music-imagery experience.

Finally, Freud did not use music at all during dream recall and interpretation, although some parallels can be seen between BMGIM and psychoanalysis in eliciting the transference (Wrangsjo, 1994). According to Wrangsjo (1994), transference is the "process of the actualization of unconscious infantile wishes in relationship to the therapist" (p. 46). In psychoanalysis, the therapist evokes the transference through his/her neutral stance toward the client. In BMGIM, the transference can be evoked by both the therapist and/or the music (Bruscia, 1995; Summer, 1998). According to Wrangsjo (1994), however, transference phenomena are used and worked through differently in psychoanalysis, as the focus remains solely on the therapist.

# JUNG: DREAM ANALYSIS AND ACTIVE IMAGINATION

Shortly after his split with Freud, Carl Jung went through a period of intense inner personal work (1912–1917), in which he extensively explored his own unconscious. He had been deeply involved with imagery for many years, thus the importance of it was no stranger to him during this period. Unlike Freud, Jung regarded mental imagery as a creative process integral to the psyche, to be employed for attaining greater individual, interpersonal, and spiritual integration (Sheikh & Jordan, 1983). Jung stated, "The psyche consists essentially of images. It is a series of images in the truest sense, not an accidental juxtaposition or sequence but a structure that is throughout full of meaning and purpose" (Jung, 1960, pp. 325–326). Jung developed two methods for working with imagery material: dream analysis and active imagination.

Jung felt that dreams were the purest images of the psyche, and used them in two ways. First, dreams were brought to therapy by patients, and worked on over the course of analysis. For example, patients may be asked to return to the dream image, reimagining the dream so as to reconnect with some aspect of it. This would then be worked with verbally in the therapy session, although an emphasis is always placed on the experience of the dream. Further, Jung interpreted dreams according to his own understanding of the psyche and saw them as central to the analytic method (Jacobi, 1973). In clarifying the position of Jung on dreams and other imagery phenomena, Jacobi quotes Jung: "[dreams have their] own language and . . . laws, which we cannot approach subjectively with the psychology of consciousness. For 'one does not dream, one is dreamt. We "suffer" the dream, we are its objects.' One might almost say that in dreams we experience myths and fairytales, not as when we read them in a waking state, but as though they were really happening in our lives" (Jung, 1938–1939 cited in Jacobi, 1973, p. 73).

BMGIM is similar to Jung's dream interpretation in the values placed on the client's imagery and imagery experiences. In fact, Bonny (Bonny, 1978a, p. 46) refers to Jungian theory as being congruent with BMGIM in that both are interested in understanding and integrating all aspects of the human experience (psychological, physical, social, spiritual), along with experiences of the collective unconscious. While nothing more is said by Bonny of this relationship, this would also appear to imply that Bonny was referring to the imagery experience(s) as having these multiple layers of meaning; personal, cultural, and collective.

Bonny, like Jung, placed a value on the affective experiences of the imagery, and was not solely concerned with the verbal reflections of the imagery and/or imagery experience. In fact, both felt that the "healing" could take place within the actual experience or re-experience of the image(s). Regarding the imagery experience, where these methods appear to differ is in the role of the therapist. In BMGIM, the therapist supports the client in coming to his/her own understanding of their problems, whereas in Jungian analysis, the therapist uses a specific interpretational system to help the patient understand the dream and how is relates to his/her life. Again, another subtle distinction can be seen between the two methods. As previously mentioned, in GIM the *client* enters into relationship with the therapist, whereas in Jungian analysis, the analysand is referred to as the *patient*, who enters into relationship with the therapist or analyst. This subtle difference may imply a distinction in the relationship between client/patient and therapist/analyst in these methods.

Hand in hand with the differences between the nature of the imagery experience was a difference in the preparation for the imagery experience. In BMGIM clients are prepared with a relaxation induction and imagery focus by the therapist, whereas in dream analysis, the patient learns to still their mind and body on their own. Finally, whereas music listening was central to the BMGIM experience, no music was used at all in Jungian dream interpretation.

Jung also developed a method for accessing the unconscious known as active imagination. Jung coined the term to describe the client's conscious engagement with images from the unconscious. There are two important qualities to active imagination identified by Jung. The first is that the images develop a life of their own, that is, that the "story" of the images comes alive for the imager; and second that these symbolic events develop according to their own logic (Chodorow, 1997). Thus, Jung focused extensively on the experiences of the imager and the ways in which the imagery unfolded. These are important dimensions to understanding the client. Active imagination is central to Jung's approach to therapy, especially developed for use toward the end of therapy as a way for the patient to become more independent from the analyst. Various techniques were developed for facilitating active imagination (see Ward, chapter 13, in this volume). According to Much and Sheikh (1986) these included journal writing, free drawing, sand play, body movement, and clay work. Interestingly, creating songs with or without words are also included as techniques of active imagination, although little is said about this (p. 409). However, Much and Sheikh make it clear that listening to music during an active imagination experience is not advocated: "It can be convincingly argued that culturally conditioned music denies one a direct experience with his own unconscious contents" (p. 409).

BMGIM is similar to active imagination in emphasizing the client's spontaneous experience of images, where these images are understood to be a direct expression of the psyche, both conscious and unconscious. Further, both Bonny and Jung valued the lived experience of the images, rather than verbal processing of the imagery alone. However, BMGIM and active imagination differ in a number of ways. While the imagery experience is central to the BMGIM session, in active imagination, clients could conduct their own experiences outside sessions, as well as reimaging within a session. Thus, clients do not necessarily need the therapist for the imaging experience, whereas in BMGIM the therapist was integral to the imagery, engaging in the experience with the client. Further, while preparation was always offered to the BMGIM client prior to the imagery experience, little preparation was given prior to active imagination other than stilling the body and mind, and finding a quiet place (Sawyer, 1986). Further, while the BMGIM therapist always engaged with the imagery experience with the client, it is less clear how active the Jungian analyst is during active imagination. Certainly, when active imagination is conducted outside the therapy session, there is no therapist involvement, although it appears that therapists could be involved in the active imagination experience with the client. For example, Sawyer (1986) reports the technique of amplification, which means "enlarging upon the associations of the imager to the images" (p. 404), although this appears to be employed after the images have been reported. Finally, active imagination does not make use of music during the experience, although it may be used to process the experience, as previously mentioned.

# LEUNER: GUIDED AFFECTIVE IMAGERY

Hans Carl Leuner, a psychiatrist, began developing Guided Affective Imagery (GAI) in the 1950s, and subsequently developed it into a psychoanalytically-oriented method of psychotherapy (Leuner, 1978). GAI is a highly systematized and "graduated method and management model for the manipulation of the daydream" (Leuner, 1978, pp. 125–126). Leuner developed ten standardized imagery scenes (river; house; mountain; the woods; the name of a person of the same sex; awakening of a night dream; walking into the body of a vulcano; swamp; rosebush [for men]; couch [for women]), divided into three levels of difficulty. Each scene has a symbolic function that allows the therapist to understand something of the client's condition. For example, at the elementary level, the house scene is thought to be an image of one's personality. In line with Freudian theory, for example, the kitchen was thought to symbolize the oral sphere, and the bedroom and the contents of closets thought to hold information about the Oedipal conflict (Leuner, 1978, p. 135). Leuner would offer these scenes to clients to bring into awareness therapeutic issues to be worked through. These imagery scenes also had an assessment function in addition to being used to work through conflicts. Leuner was theoretically influenced by both Jung and Freud, and referred to Freud's theories of dream interpretation as being congruent with his own ideas of imagery interpretation (Leuner, 1978). He referred to Jung in terms of Jung's notions of the collective unconscious, although how Leuner used these concepts in therapy is unclear. Leuner felt that imagery was an important therapeutic vehicle because it allowed clients to project their core conflicts onto the imagery, and to be connected to these experientially. Thus, as with both Bonny and Jung, Leuner felt that imagery was synchronically transformational (Leuner, 1978, p. 130); that is, there could be a spontaneous transformation of the client's problems in the actual imagery experience, without the need for verbal processing. Leuner also spontaneously created imagery scenes for clients in response to therapeutic issues, and worked with these in the same style of intervention as the ten standard scenes.

BMGIM and GAI are similar in a number of ways. First, both place a similar value on the importance of imagery experience in therapy. Each understood that images have layers of meaning, both personal and collective. Both use relaxation inductions and imagery foci. Thus, they both rely upon altered states of consciousness, and their healing potential. In both, the therapist actively engages in the imagery with the clients. It is important to acknowledge that Bonny and Leuner met early in the development of BMGIM (Bonny, 1980). At this time, Leuner was experimenting with using music in the GAI process (Bonny, 2000). Bonny exchanged ideas with Leuner, as well as experimenting with six of the imagery scenes Leuner developed as part of assessing clients (Bonny, 1978b). In fact, Bonny's Beginners Group Experience program (Bonny, 1978b) was originally based on these imagery scenes. However, as Bonny developed the BMGIM method, she abandoned developing programs in this way.

However, both methods differ in important ways. While Bonny drew on a number of theoretical orientations, including psychodynamic, humanistic, and transpersonal (Bonny, 1978a), Leuner was specifically influenced by the dream theory of Freud, and to some extent by the archetypal concepts of Jung. Thus, while there was some overlap, the ways in which images were interpreted was different in each method.

In BMGIM, the therapist engages in the imagery experience with the client to support and facilitate the unfolding of the imagery experience according to the client's unique psychic structure. In GAI, the therapist takes on a similar role, tending however to engage in the imagery experience with the client by using questions, whereas in BMGIM, many forms of verbal intervention are used. Further, while Bonny developed starting images for clients, there was no attempt to systematize these, or to interpret them within a specific theoretical framework, whereas the ten standard images developed in GAI are interpreted in very specific ways (Leuner, 1978, pp. 132–139). In this way, BMGIM and GAI are fundamentally different. Finally, while music was central to the unfolding of the imagery experience, only passing references are made to the use of music in GAI (Leuner, 1978, p. 143), and it is unclear how music was employed.

## GROF: HOLOTROPIC BREATHWORK

Stanislav Grof, a psychiatrist, developed Holotropic Breathwork out of his work with LSD psychotherapy. Although specific dates for the genesis of this method are difficult to determine, it appears that Grof began using this method in the late 1960s as an adjunct to working in LSD sessions (Grof, 1985). Grof developed Holotropic Breathwork as an experiential psychotherapy, designed to tap the deepest recesses of the human psyche (Grof, 1985). As Grof describes, "the main objective of the techniques used in experiential psychotherapy is to activate the unconscious, unblock the energy bound in emotional and psychosomatic conditions, and convert a stationary energetic balance into a stream of experience" (Grof, 1985, p.380). Through his work with LSD and other pharmacological interventions, Grof mapped a cartography of the human psyche, which he felt existed in four interwoven layers, and to which clients connected or "traveled" in Holotropic Breathwork sessions: 1) abstract or aesthetic experiences; 2) psychodynamic, biographical or recollective experiences; 3) perinatal experiences; and 4) transpersonal experiences (Grof, 1985). Grof felt that it was important to understand these various levels of experience in order to comprehend the nature of the client's experience(s), and respond within the context of the experience.

Before a Holotropic Breathwork session, a facilitator gives an introductory talk describing the cartography, the process, and giving some examples of experiences that people might have (Taylor, 1994). Although Grof began using this process in individual sessions, he has since come to see the group setting as generally more valuable and safer as a container to hold this process. The sessions are done with participants working in pairs, one as a sitter and one as a breather, reversing roles in the following session. In the sessions, the facilitator suggests that the clients begin deep and fast breathing, so as to induce a state similar to hyperventilation. Typically, this takes around forty-five minutes (Taylor, 1994). Once energy has built in the body, the client begins to have experiences such as forms of imagery, or physical sensations or emotions, in an ongoing experience facilitated by the breathing. At the same time, the facilitator attends to the group, remaining present and responding as requested by the client, with physical interventions to accentuate those symptoms already happening as a result of the breathing. This intense experience may last a number of hours, depending on the client (Taylor, 1994). After the experience has come to a close, there is a sharing session with the group, in which each participant is encouraged to share what he/she feels has been important about the experience. This sharing is more in the spirit of amplification and support and is in no way analytical or judgmental of a person's experience (Taylor, 1994). Grof was very clear that verbal processing was of limited usefulness, and that the therapeutic value of Holotropic Breathwork lay in the experience itself (Grof, 1985). Grof uses music throughout the experience, commenting on the importance of music to induce and sustain non-ordinary states of consciousness (Grof, 1985, p. 385–386). Taylor (1994, p. 30) identifies the types of music typically used in sessions: drumming music; traditional ethnic spiritual music; new age music; parts of film soundtracks; and classical pieces. She further identifies two qualities that music usually has in sessions: "sonic driving," in that it facilitates accelerated breathing and harmonizes the participant's energies; and "music supports the experience" in that it evokes a full range of emotions. In so doing, it can lead the participant into an experience as well as follow the participant while they are in an experience.

Significantly, Grof and Bonny worked together at the Maryland Psychiatric Center during the LSD sessions, with Bonny providing music to support the LSD experience (Bonny & Pahnke, 1972; Grof, 1985). Both may therefore have been influenced by similar clinical experiences in the development of their methods. BMGIM and Holotropic Breathwork are also similar in a number of other ways. Both value the unfolding of the client's imagery according to the unique qualities of the client, and accept this non-judgmentally. Both place considerable importance on the imagery experience, moving in and out of this experience in similar ways; both employ a verbal prelude; both use inductions into non-ordinary states of consciousness; both facilitate non-ordinary states in order to access psychic material using music; in both the therapist plays an active role with the client; and in both there is a verbal postlude to sessions, which may employ mandalas or other materials to process the imagery material and bring the session to a close (Bonny & Kellogg, 1977; Grof, 1985). Like Bonny, Grof placed considerable importance on music in accessing the unconscious, and acknowledges the work of Bonny in this regard (Grof, 1985, p. 386). As Grof describes, "music tends to evoke powerful experiences and facilitates a deep emotional and psychosomatic release. It provides a meaningful dynamic structure for the experience and creates a continuous carrying wave that helps the subject move through difficult sequences and impasses, overcome psychological defenses, and surrender to the flow of the experience" (Grof, 1985, p. 386). These views seem very congruent with those of Bonny (Bonny 1978b, pp. 8–23).

BMGIM and Holotropic Breathwork are different in a number of ways. In BMGIM, individual sessions are more often scheduled at regular intervals, whereas Holotropic Breathwork sessions are usually conducted in intensive weekends, where a number of participants meet and work together (Grof, 1985). Further, while BMGIM can be conducted in groups, the most common and extensively discussed use of the method has been in individual therapy. Thus, there is a fundamental difference in the way clients experience BMGIM and Holotropic Breathwork sessions. Similarly, the role of the facilitator is different. In GIM, the therapist is nondirective, supportive, and reflective of the client's experience, actively engaging in the client's imagery experience (Bonny, 1978a, p. 5–9); whereas in Holotropic Breathwork, the role is that of facilitator, not therapist. The facilitator may provide physical interventions to magnify the client's experiences, and only periodically engages with the client's imagery (e.g., at the end of some sessions in working for integration or closure) (Taylor, 2000).

Further, it also appears that Grof and Bonny were working in somewhat different theoretical frameworks. While Bonny discusses theoretical influences that have a humanistic and transpersonal orientation (Bonny, 1978a, p. 46), it is unclear how these are enacted in therapy. Grof, in contrast, is quite clear about understanding experiences within the four levels of the human psyche previously discussed. In fact, Grof has written extensively about imagery experiences as they relate to the perinatal matrix (Grof, 1985; 1993). These four levels of imagery experience, based on his clinical observations, are his working theory of the psyche.

Finally, while music is integral to both methods, the way music is selected is very different. Bonny selected music for BMGIM according to both formal and intuitive processes (Bonny, 1980). She analyzed the music for its musical qualities, and used her own experiences of listening to music to formulate music programs for use in BMGIM (Bonny, 1980). In fact, based on her experiences working with clients in LSD therapy, Bonny designed programs to move through six stages: pre-onset; onset; build to peak; peak; stabilization; return (Bonny, 1980, p. 39); and only used "classical" music selections. She also designed these programs with specific therapeutic intent (Bonny, 1980, pp. 40–58). How Grof selected and used music is much less clear. According to Bonny (2000), Grof selected the music in order to move the client quickly and directly to deeper layers of imagery experience, particularly those concerned with the perinatal matrix. His musical selections are therefore more strident, selected from a broader range of genres. Grof appeared to be less concerned with form in the way Bonny was, and so the music selected does not appear to have the same levels of relationship found in the Bonny programs. Thus it appears that while Bonny and Grof shared the same basic understanding of music, they implemented this in fundamentally different ways.

## ASSAGIOLI: PSYCHOSYNTHESIS

Psychosynthesis was developed by Roberto Assagioli, an Italian psychiatrist who believed that Freudian psychoanalysis did not address and integrate all aspects of the human experience (Assagioli, 1965). He therefore developed an orientation to human growth that offers principles and practices for integrating the personality around a center of being and for accessing the energies of what he called "higher self." As defined by Parfitt (1990), the "essential aim of Psychosynthesis is to help people discover their true spiritual nature, [and] then to utilize this discovery effectively in everyday life" (p.1).

In developing Psychosynthesis, Assagioli has drawn on a diverse imagery background, including the principles of Jung (1954), Desoille (1965), and Leuner (1978) as well as conditioning and cognitive restructuring approaches (Sheikh & Jordan, 1983). In fact, Psychosynthesis incorporates a range of imagery techniques, including symbolic visualization (where the client meditates on religious/spiritual symbols in order to connect with the spiritual self), initiated symbol projection (where the client focuses on specific images offered by the therapist), guided daydreaming (where the therapist guides the client through an imagery experience), spontaneous imagery (where the client reports imagery as it occurs spontaneously in a session), active imagination (as developed by C. G. Jung), meditation on positive symbols (where the client meditates in positive images suggested by the therapist) and other transcendent techniques (Sheikh & Jordan, 1983). Assagioli took these various techniques and developed them into a method of therapy based on his own theory (Assagioli, 1965; Parfitt, 1990).

Psychosynthesis moves through two related stages (Parfitt, 1990). The first stage of therapy is concerned with "personal psychosynthesis" or "analysis, that gives the individual a thorough knowledge of the personality" (Parfitt, 1990, p. 7). Assagioli developed a number of imagery techniques to meet this end. These include techniques of visualization, where the client learns to work in the imaginal world, to techniques designed to enhance self-esteem, desired qualities, and relationships (Moleski, Ishii & Sheikh, 1986). The second stage of therapy is to explore the spiritual dimensions of the self, and this has been called "spiritual psychosynthesis," where "we find the source of all intuition and our sense of value and meaning in life" (Parfitt, 1990, pp. 7–8). Again, a series of imagery techniques have been designed to address transpersonal issues. Often there is an overlap between these two areas. These techniques are used in a relatively eclectic way to the meet the individual needs of the client.

Assagioli used music in two basic ways, both of which are exercises rather than a music-centered approach to therapy. First, he developed techniques of auditory evocation (Moleski, Ishii, & Sheikh, 1986) where the client would imagine hearing music. This was designed to enhance the client's ability to image, and was used in the early stages of therapy. Second, he also used this technique to develop concentration and will strength, suggesting to clients that they imagine hearing a specific piece of music. It was in the act of "hearing" the music that the client's concentration and will strength developed. It is important to note that in both these techniques music is not listened to, only imagined. However, Assagioli (1965) also recognized the profound healing properties of music, as well as its potential harmful effects, such as inducing depression or arousing excessive emotion, and therefore the need for careful application. On the positive side, he stated that music can be used as a powerful healing agent to induce calm, soothe pain, stimulate memory, awaken feelings, arouse the will and excite to action, and help eliminate repressions and resistances (Assagioli, 1965, pp. 237–266). However, how music was used by Assagioli is unclear.

BMGIM is similar to psychosynthesis in its basic understanding of imagery as an expression of the human psyche, and the synergistic nature of imagery experiences. In particular, both acknowledge the transpersonal dimensions of imagery experiences as imperative to psychological growth (Bonny, 1978a; Parfitt, 1990). Both structure sessions using the same basic format: a verbal discussion centered on current issues; an imagery experience; and, verbal processing of the experience (although not all psychosynthesis involves imagery). Both also use imagery foci to start the client's imagery experience. In both, the therapist focuses on connecting the client to his/her inner world of images and enabling these images to speak in everyday life. In this sense, both seek to move the client to a deeper and more enduring connection to their inner worlds so as to be more autonomous and "self-actualized."

However, BMGIM and psychosynthesis differ in a number of important ways. Whereas Bonny is eclectic in her theoretical orientation (Bonny, 1978a, p. 46), Assagioli developed his own theoretical framework, from which he interpreted client sessions. One important distinction between these two theoretical orientations is that while Bonny understood imagery to have multiple layers of meaning which were personal, interpersonal, and collective, Assagioli was quite clear that all imagery was a projection of the self (at various levels), no matter how distorted or displaced (Sheikh & Jordon, 1983). Second, while Bonny used starting images to orient the client's internal world and enter into the music-imagery experience, Assagioli was quite interpretive and prescriptive in his use of imagery, using these to achieve specific therapeutic goals.

Another difference lies in the role of the therapist. In BMGIM, the therapist is integral to the entire process, resonating, supporting and responding to the client's process. In psychosynthesis, the therapist's role is to help the client develop a range of techniques that they can use independently in their own therapeutic process.

Finally, music is used in a fundamentally different way in BMGIM. Music underpins the entire BMGIM experience, whereas in psychosynthesis, the role of music is far less clear. Certainly, the music-focused techniques Assagioli developed do not actually involve listening to music at all, and while Assagioli wrote about music, how music is applied in therapy is quite unclear.

# GENDLIN: FOCUSING-ORIENTED PSYCHOTHERAPY

Focusing-Oriented Psychotherapy (hereby referred to as Focusing) was developed by Eugene Gendlin in the 1960s (Gendlin, 1981). Defined as a "mode of inward *bodily* attention" (Gendlin, 1996, p. 1), the client attends to the inner experiences and voice of his/her physical body, and uses these experiences to work through and understand therapeutic problems. Focusing is an eclectic, experiential approach, drawing on a range of therapeutic traditions including

Freudian and Jungian psychoanalysis, Gestalt therapy (Perls, 1959), Client-Centered therapy (Rogers, 1961), and Psychosynthesis. Gendlin took various techniques from each of these methods and arranged them according to *avenues*, or similarities in therapeutic experience (e.g., imagery techniques) (Gendlin, 1996). The purpose of doing so was to have a range of therapeutic tools available in order to work with the *felt sense*. A felt sense is a core component of the client's therapy, being the bodily feeling associated with a therapeutic issue. "And, once there is a felt sense, all avenues are ways to carry it forward. From a felt sense the next step can come words, an image, an emotion, or an interpersonal interaction" (Gendlin, 1996, p. 171).

Focusing sessions are divided into six sequential steps, concerned with finding and working with the felt sense (Gendlin, 1986). Through these steps, the therapist guides the client into contact with the felt sense, and then works with this. The first stage, "clearing the space," involves taking time to be silent and attune inward. The second and third stages, "felt sense" and "handle," involve connecting with the felt sense and getting to know it. In third stage, Gendlin encourages the client to develop images or words to describe the felt sense and then bring the felt sense in relation to the word or image. The latter stages involve working through this relationship to come to a new understanding of the problem. It is in the "working through" that techniques from other therapeutic orientations are used. Imagery methods are central to Focusing, used extensively throughout the session. For example, "coming into contact with the felt sense" is achieved through imagery techniques, as are the methods for working with the "felt sense" and "handle." Gendlin continually emphasized that these imagery techniques were experiential, and not cognitive, and that the core of this method took place in the imagery experience.

BMGIM is similar to Focusing in emphasizing imagery as experience. For both, the imagery experience was core to the client's therapy. Both Bonny and Gendlin also emphasized the self-efficacy of imagery—for both, the solutions to the client's problems were always contained within the client. Both also used a transition from talk to the imagery experience. Bonny typically used a relaxation induction and imagery focus. Gendlin used a technique of inward focusing which he called "clearing the space" (Gendlin, 1981, p. 52). There are also a number of similarities in the basic stance and attitude of the therapist toward the client. In particular, both emphasize the therapist's presence (Bonny, 1978a; Gendlin, 1981) with the client as integral to the therapy experience.

However, both are different in a number of significant ways. First, both value and treat images differently. For Bonny, the spontaneous creation and experience of images in the music is central to the client's therapy. For Gendlin, the starting place is the client's body, and all therapeutic work begins there (1996, p. 212). If a client enters into a stream of images, Gendlin always connects these to the body, often placing the images metaphorically within the client's body, or allowing the client to do so themselves. For Gendlin, it is not until the client's body has "spoken" that the client is focused to begin work. Bonny was far less directive, allowing the natural flow of images to develop, only providing basic guidelines for working with and interpreting body imagery (1978a, pp. 34–39). Gendlin was also very structured in his six-step process of intervention. Bonny provided no such guidelines, preferring to respond to the client *in vivo* within the context of the basic structure of a session. Further, in BMGIM the therapist takes a nondirective role in the imagery, instead helping the client to connect with, expand upon, and deepen his/her own experiences. In Focusing, the therapist takes a very directive role, even suggesting solutions to problems encountered in the client's imagery (Gendlin, 1996, pp. 212–220) until the client has come to a new understanding of the problem. In this way, Focusing has a very cognitive orientation, although Gendlin is clear in distinguishing between these two methods (Gendlin, 1996, pp. 238–246). In BMGIM, a relaxed state is a way of opening to the dimensions of the imagery experience, whereas in Focusing, "clearing the space" is more a centering technique. While Bonny was interested in expanding the client's consciousness using the relaxation induction as a conduit, Gendlin did not share the same emphasis. Finally, in BMGIM, music is central to the experience, while Gendlin makes no references to the use of music.

## HYPNOTHERAPY

Unlike all the methods previously discussed in this chapter, Hypnotherapy cannot be identified with a single founder or tradition, although historically Jean Charcot, Sigmund Freud, and Milton Erickson are all recognized for their pioneering work in this area (Fromm & Shor, 1979; Heap, 1991a). In fact, there are a range of theories of hypnosis (Rowley, 1986), and diverse approaches to hypnotherapy (Heap, 1991b). Heap (1991a), however, has identified a number of elements of hypnosis that are congruent with many of these approaches: hypnosis involves selective attention (the client is focused on limited stimuli, usually internal); relaxation (of the client's mind and body); expectancy (where the client expects to feel, think, or respond in a particular way); imagination (the client may be absorbed in an imagery scene, under the direction of the hypnotist); conformity or compliance (to the hypnotist's wishes); and role-playing (behaving according to beliefs about how a hypnotized person should respond). Heap further identified "the role of suggestion" as central to the hypnotherapy experience. According to Heap, a "suggestion is a communication by the hypnotist to the subject . . . intended to alter the recipient's feelings, thoughts and behavior in a specific way" (Heap, 1991a, p. 3). As such, a client may respond in a voluntary or involuntary manner, or in a combination of both. Thus, in some models, the hypnotist makes suggestions directly to the client's unconscious, often with imagined rehearsal, to reinforce changes that are the focus of therapy. At the end of this process, the hypnotist may suggest that the client forget this experience so that the conscious mind cannot interfere. In other models, the hypnotic state is used to access unconscious material from the client and then bring this material into conscious awareness, sometimes for processing. Perhaps the most well known advocate of this method is Milton Erickson (Erickson, Rossi, & Rossi, 1976) who believed that clients always had the resources within to solve their own problems. Hypnosis provides a way of accessing this material, which can be then worked through in a multitude of ways.

Hypnotherapy sessions can be divided into a number of stages, although in practice these exist as a fluid whole. To begin, the context of the session is established, and the goals set. The client is then prepared for hypnosis, using a range of techniques congruent with the various models outlined by Heap (1991b). This can include describing the session format, connecting with previous hypnotic experiences, and reminding clients of everyday hypnotic states. At this point, a formal induction and deepening procedure is utilized, this again varying according to the specific model used. Heap has identified three characteristics indicative of deepening procedures: focusing the client's attention on a limited range or single stimulus in a particular modality (e.g., visual or auditory); repeating suggestions of relaxation, comfort, calmness "letting go" etc.; and coupling the previous two steps (e.g., with each breath, your body is becoming more and more relaxed). At this point, the specific hypnotic procedure is utilized. As previously mentioned, this may include direct communication with the unconscious, regression to traumatic events or specific experiences, or techniques such as ideomotor signaling, whereby the client's unconscious can communicate directly with the therapist by way of hand signaling. Imagery experiences may be a part of this process. These experiences can take various forms, including memories, metaphoric imagery suggested by the therapist, and visual rehearsal. While imagery can play an important role in the hypnotic experience, it is only one of many hypnotic techniques used. After the hypnotic experience, the client returns to a normal state of awareness with the assistance of the therapist. The client may or may not be instructed to forget the experience, depending on the approach of the therapist. There may be further discussion or processing of the experience prior to the completion of the session.

BMGIM and hypnotherapy are similar in a number of ways. Both have a preliminary discussion, leading to a focus for the session. Both use relaxed or altered states of consciousness for therapeutic purposes; both use inductions into these states; and both use procedures for returning to a normal state of awareness. Both also employ imagery as part of the therapeutic process, and in both the therapist engages in the imagery experience with the client.

However, both vary in important ways. While both employ relaxed or altered states of consciousness, the nature and purpose of these varies in each method. In BMGIM the purpose of the relaxed state is to aide entry into the music-imagery experience, whereas in hypnotherapy the purpose is to aide the client in relinquishing some control of his/her psyche. In BMGIM, the purpose of entering into this state is to facilitate the client's self-exploration of the psyche related to specific clinical goals, whereas in hypnotherapy the purpose is to communicate directly with the unconscious about a specific therapeutic issue (e.g., smoking cessation). While in BMGIM the music-imagery experience unfolds as a dialogue between therapist and client, in hypnotherapy other forms of dialogue, such as ideomotor signaling, can also take place. Further, in BMGIM the client takes a nondirective stance toward the client, facilitating the client's unfolding imagery experience, whereas in hypnotherapy, the therapist takes a very directive role, suggesting images (remembering a childhood experience), feelings, and behavioral rehearsal scripts (e.g., I will not crave cigarettes). Further, in BMGIM a nondirective stance is usually taken to the solutions found by the client to his/her problems, whereas in hypnotherapy, the therapist can be quite directive is suggesting a solution. While in BMGIM imagery is central to the client's therapeutic experience, in hypnotherapy imagery is only one method of working with the psyche. Further, while transpersonal issues and experiences are part of the BMGIM process, hypnotherapy does not appear to deal with that dimension of human experience. Finally, music is not typically used in hypnotherapy.

## SUMMARY

There are clear similarities and differences between BMGIM and these other imagery methods. These are important to recognize because they are assumptions about the nature of imagery-based therapy, and as such underpin the methods themselves, even though their founders may think about or describe these in different ways. The first and perhaps most important commonality of all the above methods is that imagery experiences have layers of meaning. That is, imagery can be interpreted in a number of ways, and from a number of different theoretical perspectives (e.g., Freudian or Jungian). For example, the image of a house may be a memory of a childhood home, or interpreted as a symbol of the client's personality structure (Leuner, 1978, p. 135). Thus, in some methods certain images have a specific meaning (e.g., Leuner and Assagioli), or are interpreted according to a specific theoretical framework, whereas in other methods the same image can be understood in a variety of ways (e.g., Bonny and Grof).

Second, imagery experiences allow access to both conscious and unconscious material. And, within the unconscious, there may be layers or levels of experience. By bringing imagery material into consciousness, important gains can be made therapeutically. Each, however, varies in the way inner experiences are understood, accessed, and worked through. And each places a different emphasis on the imagery experience within the therapeutic method. Freud, for example, only used dream analysis as an adjunct technique in his method of therapy, whereas for Bonny the imagery experience was core.

Third, each uses techniques for moving in and out of the imagery experience. These can include focusing techniques, where the therapist asks the client to attend to or focus on a specific image, or relaxation techniques, where the therapist helps the client relax physically in order to enter into the imagery experience. Some methods use a combination of both these techniques.

Fourth, in each method the therapist takes a role in relationship to the client, and the client's imagery experience. This can include suggesting images to clients to work with, engaging in the imagery experience with the client, and/or interpreting the client's imagery. Importantly, there is considerable variation in the role of the therapist in each of these methods.

Finally, each method has embraced music in a different way. In some methods, music is not advocated (even contraindicated), whereas in others it takes on a more central role. Again, there is considerable variation in the role of music in each of these methods, and this is perhaps the most important distinguishing feature of BMGIM in relation to these other methods.

## *Acknowledgments*

The author would like to thank Cheri Franklin (Assagioli), Annie Hart (hypnotherapy), Roseann Kasayka (Gendlin), Gina Kastele (Leuner), Kylea Taylor (Grof), and Karlyn Ward (Jung) for their helpful comments in earlier versions of this chapter.

# *References*

Assagioli, R. (1965). *Psychosynthesis: A Collection of Basic* Writings. New York: Viking Press.

Bonny, H. (1978a). *Facilitating GIM Sessions.* Salina, KS: The Bonny Foundation.

Bonny, H. (1978b). *The Role of Taped Music Programs in the GIM Process.* Salina, KS: The Bonny Foundation.

Bonny, H. (1980). *GIM Therapy: Past, Present and Future Implications.* Salina, KS: The Bonny Foundation.

Bonny, H. (2000). Personal communication. July.

Bonny, H., & Kellogg, J. (1977). Mandalas as a measure of change in psychotherapy. *Journal of Art Therapy*, 9(2), 64–87.

Bonny, H. L., & Pahnke, W. N. (1972). The use of music in psychedelic (LSD) psychotherapy. *Journal of Music Therapy,* 9, 64–87.

Bruscia, K. E. (1995). The many dimensions of transference. *Journal of the Association for Music and Imagery*, 4, 3–16.

Chodorow, J. (ed.) (1997). *Jung on Active Imagination.* Princeton, NJ: Princeton University Press.

Desoille, R. (1965). *The Directed Daydream.* New York: Psychosynthesis Research Foundation.

Erickson, M. H., Rossi, E. L., & Rossi, S. H. (1976). *Hypnotic Realities: The Induction of Clinical Hypnosis and the Indirect Forms of Suggestion.* New York: Irvington Press.

Freud, S. (1952). *On Dreams. The Standard Edition.* New York: W. W. Norton and Company.

Fromm, E. & Shor, R. (Eds.). *Hypnosis: Developments in Research and New Perspectives (Second Edition).* New York, NY: Aldine Publishing Company.

Gendlin, E. T. (1981). *Focusing* (second edition). New York: Bantam Books.

Gendlin, E. T. (1986). Focusing techniques. In A. A. Sheikh (ed.), *Anthology of Imagery Techniques*. Milwaukee, WI: American Imagery Institute.

Gendlin, E. T. (1996). *Focusing-Oriented Psychotherapy: A Manual of the Experiential Method.* New York: The Guilford Press.

Grof, S. (1985). *Beyond the Brain: Birth, Death and Transcendence in Psychotherapy.* Albany, New York: SUNY Press.

Grof, S. (1993). *The Holotropic Mind.* New York: HarperCollins Publishers.

Heap, M. (1991a). Introduction to hypnosis. In M. Heap & W. Dryden (eds.), *Hypnotherapy: A Handbook*. Bristol, PA: Open University Press.

Heap, M. (1991b). Role and uses of hypnosis in psychotherapy. In M. Heap & W. Dryden (eds.), *Hypnotherapy: A Handbook*. Bristol, PA: Open University Press.

Jacobi, J. (1973). *The Psychology of C.G. Jung*. New Haven, CT: Yale University Press.

Jung, C. G. (1916/1958). The transcendent function. *Collected Words, Volume 8*. Princeton, NJ: Princeton University Press.

Jung, C. G. (1954). The development of personality. *Collected Works, Volume 17*. Princeton, NJ: Princeton University Press.

Jung, C. G. (1960). The structure and dynamics of the psyche. *Collected Works, Volume 8*. Princeton, NJ: Princeton University Press.

Leuner, H. (1978). The basic principles of Guided Affective Imagery. In J. L. Singer & K. S. Pope (eds.) *The Power of the Human Imagination*. New York: Plenum Press.

Moleski, L. M., Ishii, M. M., & Sheikh, A. A. (1986). Imagery techniques in Psychosynthesis. In A. A. Sheikh (ed.), *Anthology of Imagery Techniques*. Milwaukee, WI: American Imagery Institute.

Much, N. C. & Sheikh, A. A. (1986). The oneirotherapies. In A. A. Sheikh (ed.), *Anthology of Imagery Techniques*. Milwaukee, WI: American Imagery Institute.

Parfitt, W. (1990). *The Elements of Psychosynthesis*. London: Element Books.

Perls, F.S. (1959). *Gestalt Therapy Verbatim*. Moab, Utah: Real People Press.

Rogers, C. R. (1961). *On Becoming a Person*. Boston: Houghton Mifflin.

Rowley, D. T. (1986). *Hypnosis and Hypnotherapy*. Philadelphia: Charles Press.

Sawyer, D. (1986). How Jungians work with images. In A. A. Sheikh (ed.), *Anthology of Imagery Techniques*. Milwaukee, WI: American Imagery Institute.

Sheikh, A. A. (ed.) (1983). *Imagery: Current theory, Research and Application*. New York: John Wiley and Sons.

Sheikh, A. A. & Jordan. C. S. (1983). Clinical uses of mental imagery. In Sheikh, A. A. (ed.) *Imagery: Current theory, Research and Application*. New York: John Wiley and Sons.

Singer, J. L. & Pope, K. S. (1978). The use of imagery and fantasy techniques in psychotherapy. In J. L. Singer & K. S. Pope (eds.) *The Power of the Human Imagination*. New York: Plenum Press.

Summer, L. (1998). The pure music transference in Guided Imagery and Music. In K. E. Bruscia (ed.) *The Dynamics of Music Psychotherapy*. Gilsum, NH: Barcelona Publishers.

Taylor, K. (1994). *The Breathwork Experience: Exploration and Healing in Nonordinary States of Consciousness*. Santa Cruz, CA: Hanford Mead Publishers.

Taylor, K. (2000). Personal communication. July.

Wollheim, R. (1991). *Freud (second edition)*. London: Harper Collins Publishers.

Wrangsjo, B. (1994). Psychoanalysis and GIM. *Journal of the Association for Music and Imagery*, 3, 35–48.

## Chapter Five

# THE EVOLUTION OF BONNY'S
# MUSIC PROGRAMS

## Denise E. Grocke

This chapter traces the evolution of the music programs used in the Bonny Method of Guided Imagery and Music (BMGIM). Bonny created eighteen music programs between 1973–1989. The early programs evolved from her work at the Baltimore Psychiatric Center and others were created for specific therapeutic purposes. Bonny categorized each program according to its appropriateness to issues being explored in therapy, and these categories are reproduced in this chapter. Bonny also wrote about the characteristics of music that she chose for the programs and these characteristics and musical elements are described. Some of the information reproduced in this chapter was obtained from interviews between Helen Bonny and the author.

## EARLY HISTORY OF
## THE MUSIC PROGRAMS

In 1968 Helen Bonny was appointed to the Maryland Psychiatric Research Center in Baltimore, as a music therapist and research associate. Her task was to develop music programs to be used in the LSD research program. There was a large collection of music recordings at the Center that had been collected by various staff members and Bonny's first task was to determine which music was thought to be the most effective for the LSD sessions.

The LSD session often lasted twelve hours, and Bonny identified six stages of the LSD experience and programmed music that was appropriate for each stage. The stages were:

1) pre-onset,
2) beginning, or onset of the effect of the LSD,
3) a building of the experience to a peak,
4) the "peak" experience
5) stabilization after the peak, and
6) return to normal consciousness (Bonny, 1978b, p. 39)

Bonny catalogued the music that was already being used by the therapists at the Center, and asked the therapists which music they thought was the most effective for each stage of the LSD therapy experience. There was a wide range of recordings at the Center, representing different styles and genres, and when Bonny catalogued the music most frequently used by the therapists, she found that classical music was most often requested (Bonny, 1995). She described the music that was effective for the LSD experience as:

> music that is structured, that has a harmonic background which people are acquainted with, not too "new" (i.e., unfamiliar), but with building crescendos and not too much resolution (Bonny, 1995).

At the Maryland Psychiatric Research Center each staff member was required to have a personal experience of a LSD session each year. The purpose of this was for staff to experience the effects of the drug, and therefore to have a better understanding of what the patients experienced during an LSD session. Bonny describes the experience of the drug and the role of the music to support the experience:

> In the early minutes there is gentle imagery, then all of a sudden the drug hits you. You go to a very high place, very ecstatic, then into some deep place where it's like a camera out of focus (and) the imagery changes very fast. It's like a roller coaster and you have to 'let go', more than you ever have in your own life. The therapists are reminding you to do that. The imagery goes up and down in waves (and) people can get stuck in a very unpleasant place. That's why you need to let go and not hang on to any image, but always go on to the next one. What the music does—the rhythm and regular harmonic structure—is to support you in that. You would be very lost if you didn't have the structure of the music (Bonny, 1995).

The LSD session that Bonny experienced in 1971 is of particular interest because of the sequence of music selections used. The following transcript of the music selections was made by the therapist during Bonny's session, and identifies a number of pieces that Bonny would use subsequently in devising the music programs for GIM. (Note: the transcript does not specify whether all or part of the bigger works were played in their entirety.)

*First Hour:*

- Mendelssohn: *Violin Concerto*, 2nd movement.
- Mozart: Laudate Dominum from the *Vesperae Solennes* (included on the *Positive Affect* music program).
- Smetana: *The Moldau.*

*Second Hour:*

- Bach: *St Matthew Passion.*
- Beethoven: *Leonore Overture.*
- Weber: *Der Freischutz* Overture.
- Bach: *Jesus, Dearest Master, Come, Come ye Saints, Oh, my Father.*
- Elgar: *Enigma Variations* (#8 & #9 included on the *Positive Affect* program).
- Vivaldi: *Gloria* ("Et in terra pax" from the *Gloria* included on the *Peak Experience* program).
- Stravinsky: *Firebird Suite.*
- Tschesnokoff: *Salvation is Created* (included on the *Beginner's/Group* program).
- Wagner: *Prelude* from *Lohengrin* (included on the *Peak Experience* program).
- Anon. Deep River (Spiritual).
- Brahms: *Violin Concerto* (slow movement included on the *Mostly Bach* program).
- Barber: *Adagio for Strings* (included on the *Positive Affect* program).

*Third Hour:*

- Gounod: Sanctus and Benedictus from the *St. Cecilia Mass* (the *Sanctus* is included on the *Positive Affect* program).
- Strauss: *Death and Transfiguration* (an excerpt of this work ends the *Positive Affect* program).

*Fourth Hour:*

- Palestrina: *Sabat Mater.*
- Gregorian chants.
- Mahler: *Symphony #4*, 3rd movement "Ruhevall" (included on the *Serenity* program).

*Fifth Hour:*

- Brahms: *Requiem* (Parts 1 and 5 are included on the *Emotional Expression 1* program).
- *Music for Zen meditation*
- Bach: *Concerto for Two Violins* (slow movement included on the *Mostly Bach* program).
- Bach: *Air on G String.*
- Holst: *The Planets:* "Neptune" (included on the *Cosmic Astral* program). "Venus" (included on the *Quiet Music* program).

*Sixth Hour*

- Canteloube (arranger): *Songs of the Auvergne*: Brezairola (included on the *Nurturing* program).
- Copland: *Appalachian Spring* (an excerpt included on the *Imagery* program).

Sixteen of the total thirty works played during Bonny's LSD session in 1971 were used subsequently for the GIM music programs, and all selections included on the *Positive Affect* program were played during the session. Her choice of these sixteen selections for the GIM programs was influenced by the fact that she had experienced the music under the influence of LSD, and knew how well the music selections worked in an altered state of consciousness.

## THE DEVELOPMENT OF
## SHORTER MUSIC PROGRAMS

In the early 1970s the LSD research work was terminated (Bonny, 1980, p. 18), and Bonny started exploring the use of music and imagery without the use of LSD. She believed that the music alone was powerful enough to stimulate imagery, without the need for the LSD drug. As she explored new ways of using only the music as stimulus, she found that people could recall the details of the imagery and the feelings they had experienced in far greater detail than if they had been under the influence of LSD.

At the same time, therapy programs were being devised to help those people who had become addicted to LSD, and in response to an initial request from Dan Brown at the psychology department of the University of Massachusetts, Bonny started to develop shorter music programs of approximately 30–40 minutes duration. From 1973–1989 Helen Bonny devised eighteen programs of this shorter length. The development of these programs spans three distinct periods of time. Eight programs had been developed by 1973, a further seven were developed between 1975–1983, and the final three programs date from 1987–1989.

When Bonny devised a music program she gave it a title, sometimes to depict the intent of the program, other times because the title described the affective quality of the music. In choosing music selections for the programs, Bonny first of all identified what she liked in the music based on her intuitive knowledge developed from years of experience as an orchestral musician, and from her experience with the music in the LSD sessions (Bonny, 1995). She recalls that her decision to include one piece over another was made by trial and error, viz. "I like the beginning of this . . . this fits in with the next one" (Bonny, 1978b, p. 25). Finally she put the selections together in a sequence she thought would follow the affective contour needed to stimulate imagery and to match the intention of the program. By 'trial and error' she developed the final version of the program. A comprehensive description of the music in all eighteen programs can be found in Chapter Six.

When a new program was created, it was announced in the *Newsletter* of the Institute for Consciousness and Music (ICM), an organization established by Helen Bonny and others in 1973. The *ICM Newsletter* gave a brief description of the intention of each music program These descriptions (in part) and the year in which each program was devised are presented below in three stages.

## Programs developed in 1973

*Positive Affect:* The program was created for a Humanistic Psychology
    conference, and selections relate to the six stages of the LSD session. Its
    purpose was to involve the client in psychodynamic issues with a possible
    peak experience if the client was adequately prepared.
*Beginner's Imagery:* The program was based on six of Leuner's ten Guided
    Affective Imagery scenarios. It was renamed *Beginner's Group* in 1976,

then *Group Experience* in 1982, and revised and renamed *Explorations* in 1994. Its purpose was to provide a diversity of music that enables a diagnostic map of possible areas to explore.

*Comforting/Anaclytic:* The program was devised for students at the University of Massachusetts, and its purpose was to encourage a return to childhood memories, and to explore the anima/animus.

*Cosmic-Astral:* The program was devised for experienced travelers. The music was demanding, complex, varied, and unpredictable (Bonny, 1995). The program was removed from distribution in June 1975, after feedback from therapists indicated that the program was too confronting (Bonny, 1995).

*Affect Release:* The program was devised for students at the University of Massachusetts, to encourage clients in the expression of anger, and for specific use in sessions where strong feelings of grief, fear, anger, or impotence occur.

*Imagery:* The program was devised as a diagnostic program, to encourage visual aspects of imagery and for a general exploration of the inner personality. The selections are exclusively instrumental.

*Death-Rebirth, and Peak Experience:* The original intention was that the two programs be used together. The Death-Rebirth program explores issues of death and separation, followed by rebirth opportunities. The Peak Experience program provides a healing mode for a variety of issues which often includes a peak experience.

## Programs Developed between 1975 and 1983

*Quiet Music (1975-1976):* The program was first listed in the ICM *Newsletter* Spring 1976, but versions of it were developed before that date. Its purpose was to carry listeners to far away places, to invite them to respond with dance or other movement, and to stimulate creative imagery or warm, interpersonal responses.

*Emotional Expression I (1976):* The purpose of the program was to encourage the client to explore, break open, and break up issues.

*Mostly Bach (1977:* The program was devised to encourage deeper and wider experiences, to loosen forces of resistance, and to provide supportive transference.

*Serenity (1978):* The program's basic theme was serenity, but it also delineates joy, gaiety, elevation, innocence and deep intention.

*Transitions (1978):* The program was created when ICM moved to a new residence. Its purpose was to view life, to approach transitions of death, new adventure, change, and challenge.

*Nurturing (1980):* The program was designed to uncover early experiences of nurturing (or lack of nurturing), feelings, and emotions in a non-confrontational manner.

*Relationships(1983):* The program was first listed in the ICM *Newsletter* in 1983, but it was developed prior to this date, under the title *Quiet Music 2*. Its purpose was to explore the animus/anima, sub-personalities, sexual identity, and adult marital relationships.

## Programs Developed between 1987-1989

*Inner Odyssey*
*Body Tape (Program)*
*Emotional Expression II*

The three programs were given their first trial conducted at a seminar at New York University in 1989. These programs were created after the closure of ICM and the purposes were not described in the *Newsletters*.

## CATEGORIES OF FUNCTIONAL USE

Bonny categorized the eighteen programs according to their primary function within a series of GIM sessions (Bonny, unpublished paper, no date):

- BASIC/BEGINNING: *Quiet, Peak, Imagery, Nurturing, Comforting/Anaclytic*, and *Group Experience.*
- SUSTAINING AFFECT: *Affect Release, Expanded Awareness* (programmed by Keiser), *Death/Rebirth, Nurturing,* and *Grieving* (programmed by Keiser).
- WORKING: *Comforting/Anaclytic, Group Experience, Relationships, Positive Affect, Grieving, Emotional Expression I, Mostly Bach, Transitions, Death/Rebirth, Conversations,* (programmed by Skaggs), and *Serenity.*
- EXPLORATION: *Group Experience, Cosmic/Astral, Transitions, Expanded Awareness,* and *Creativity 1* (programmed by Keiser).
- ADVANCED WORKING: *Body Program, Inner Odyssey,* and *Emotional Expression II.*

Bonny also categorized the music programs according to their appropriateness to clients' therapeutic issues (Bonny, unpublished paper, no date):

- ANGER: *Affect Release*, and *Emotional Expression I.*
- INTERPERSONAL RELATIONSHIPS: *Relationships, Comforting/Anaclytic, Conversations*, and *Nurturing.*
- GRIEVING: *Comforting Anaclytic*, and *Grieving.*
- LIFE ASSESSMENT, GROWTH, AND SPIRITUAL ORIENTATION: *Transitions, Expanded Awareness, Death-Rebirth, Positive Affect* and *Peak Experience.*
- RESISTANCE TO UNCOVERING PROCESSES: *Mostly Bach, Serenity*, and *Creativity I.*

## CHARACTERISTICS OF THE MUSIC
## CHOSEN FOR THE PROGRAMS

Over many years Bonny lectured to various audiences about the music programs used in GIM. In discussing the characteristics of music chosen for the programs, Bonny identified six distinctive characteristics of the music.

First, she draws on the theories of Leonard Meyer to explain music as a catalytic agent that creates tension and release. Meyer's theory rests on the dictum that "emotion is aroused when a tendency to respond is inhibited" (Meyer, 1956, p. 14), so that in the GIM experience, music that has an element of expectation and suspense may evoke more intense imagery responses. When the release or climax is heard in the music, there may be a concomitant resolution in the imagery sequence. The degree of resolution is based on the degree of uncertainty, "the greater the buildup of suspense, of tension, the greater the emotional release upon resolution" (Meyer, 1956, p 28).

Second, Bonny believes that the music in GIM acts as a "container" for the client's imagery experience. The concept of "music as container" emerged from the writings of Winnicott, who developed a theory of containment in relation to child development, and this theory has been applied to the practice of GIM (Bonny, 1989; Goldberg, 1992; Kasayka, 1988; Summer, 1992, 1995, 1998). The boundaries of the music container in GIM must be fluid and flexible, in that the music is ever changing and unfolding in time (Bonny, 1995). The music that underpins a transpersonal experience, for example, must allow a wide space for exploring the expansiveness of emotion, whereas for a client to express anger the music must provide a container with strong boundaries within which the client can express strong emotion (Bonny, 1995).

Third, Bonny believes that music stimulates the flow and movement of the imagery experience. Movement is suggested by the tempo of the music, and also by ornamentation (Bonny, 1996). For example, the use of pizzicato in the lower strings creates movement in the music itself, and may influence movement in the client's experience of imagery.

The fourth characteristic of the GIM music is its variability. Bonny asserts that minimalist music and so-called "New Age" music may not be effective in GIM programs because there is not sufficient variability to stimulate the client's imagery (Bonny, 1996). Variability may be provided by changes in timbre, melody, harmony, and dynamics. Too much variability in the music, however may be perceived by the client as disorganized (Bonny, 1996), and therefore a certain amount of redundancy is needed to provide a sense of musical stability.

The mood conveyed by the music selection is the fifth crucial characteristic in choosing a work for a program, and also in deciding its sequential place in the program. The mood may be determined by many factors: the melodic line, harmonic progressions, modulation points, and the timbral effects of certain instruments. Associations with particular instruments also influence the emotional substance of the music. The harp, for example, is usually associated with the higher aspects of self, the woodwinds with the medium, everyday experiences, and the bass instruments for aspects of sustaining rhythmic security (Bonny, 1978b. pp. 27–28; Bonny, 1996).

The sixth characteristic is that the music comes exclusively from the Western classical tradition. Bonny's extensive experience as an orchestral musician gave her a wide knowledge of classical music of all genres, and this is clearly evident in the choice of music for the GIM programs. She identified several features of classical music that makes this style effective in GIM:

- Classical music is multi-layered in that several melodic and harmonic lines are moving along simultaneously, thereby influencing the flow of imagery sequences. "The multi-dimension of music is in the complexity of layering. Harmonically this is evident in chords, and melodically this is represented in the canon and fugue" (Bonny, 1996).
- Classical music has a predictable structure, but with appropriate variability. There is a simplicity in classical form, for example certain selections have a solo line with accompaniment, and this may evoke dialogue between the client and a significant person in the imagery. There is also variability in classical music, such

as variability in timbre, provided by different instruments of the orchestra. The extent of this variability is not found in music of other traditions (Bonny, 1996).

- The dynamic change in classical music raises the potential for emotional content in the GIM experience, in that classical music is descriptive of human emotion. "Classical music is used because it is by great composers, our human geniuses. Their music lasts over centuries. It lives over time, like any great art" (Bonny, 1996).

- Some of the music selections on the GIM programs create a sense of ambiguity and suggestibility that provokes imagery. For example, the opening of *Siegfried's Funeral March*, by Wagner (featured on the *Death-Rebirth* program) features a slow beating of the drums. The client hearing the slow beat may have an immediate sense of foreboding, that the music speaks to the funeral dirge (Bonny, 1996). Similarly, the excerpt from Strauss' *Ein Heldenleben* (on the *Transitions* program) commences with a similar beating of the tympani, followed by a call motif. Such music creates expectation in the client, and may immediately evoke imagery of a journey (Bonny, 1996).

- Bonny comments that "when we are actively listening to music we are directly entering another person's (the composer's) creative imagination" (Bonny, 1996). The client's imagery therefore may reflect the intention or the emotions of the composer at the time of writing the musical work. This is borne out in a study of Hanks (1992). Her study explored transcultural experiences of people in the United States compared with those in Taiwan. She found for example that imagery associated with Brahms *First Symphony*, 3rd movement, was similar for both groups of people, and that both groups experienced imagery of tall mountains. The ontological connection was that Brahms composed the symphony following a holiday in the Alps where he was inspired by the grandeur of the mountains.

- The extent to which classical music is "familiar" to GIM clients may differ according to the music preferences of the clients, their musical background and cultural background. In addition, the client's perception of music alters according to the nature of the emergent imagery, and may be different each time the music program is used, depending on the therapeutic issue being explored and the client's mood on the day. Even if the music is, or becomes familiar, the client's perception of it will alter to fit the therapeutic need (Bonny, 1996).

- The quality of the performance is an important aspect in choosing a music selection for a GIM music program The differing timbral qualities of vocalists in particular can create certain associations. For example, Bonny's preferred recording of the Mozart *Laudate Dominum* (*Positive Affect* program) features Lucia Popp. Bonny explains that many other soprano soloists have recorded this work, but the quality of the voice may be dominated by vibrato, suggesting a more mature voice—an older woman, perhaps, in the imagery experience. Lucia Popp's voice, however, is clear and lyrical, suggesting a purer sound, which in turn may suggest a younger female figure in the client's imagery (Bonny, 1996).

## BONNY'S RETROSPECTIVE ANALYSIS OF THE MUSIC PROGRAMS

When Bonny was at the Maryland Psychiatric Research Center she conducted research into the effectiveness of the music programs (Bonny, 1978c). She conducted her own analysis of the music programs that she had devised. The process began "by the taking the final product (which I knew worked) back through an analysis as to *how* it worked and *why*" (Bonny, 1978b, p. 26).

The variables she found to be the strongest influences were:

1) pitch
2) rhythm and tempo,
3) vocal and/or instrumental mode,
4) melody (linear line) and harmony, and
5) timbre (color) (Bonny, 1978b, p. 26).

In her Second Monograph (1978b), Bonny provides examples of these aspects and how they influence the client's imagery.

## Pitch

The association of music elements with imagery responses is culturally laden in meaning. High pitch, for example, may signify going up, or "to be lifted up" in the Biblical sense. Bonny found that women's voices singing the high pitches in religious liturgical music most generally signified the "high" religious state, ". . . a transcendent experience" whereas "low pitches . . . are often associated with the ground or below ground—it can mean death, sadness, heaviness or something lowly" (Bonny, 1978b, p. 27). When sung with low timbre, a low pitch may evoke "very positive feelings of warmth, security and support" (Bonny, 1978b, p. 27), but when a music work moves from predominantly low pitch to high pitch, the listener may have a sense of an opening awareness to higher aspirations (Bonny, 1978b, p. 28).

## Rhythm and Tempo

Bonny quotes Gaston's dictum that "rhythm is the energizer and organizer of music" (Gaston, 1968, p. 17). Rhythm keeps music moving through time, giving the listener "a sense of ebb and flow, of activity and stability, of stimulation and release" (Bonny, 1978b, pp. 28-29). "A regular rhythm played at moderate tempo, say metronome 60 which is close to the heart beat, is a secure, quieting, universally acceptable beat. At a faster tempo, a regular rhythm might suggest dancing or a tapping of toe or finger in time with the music," whereas "diverse rhythmic patterns may be confusing, conflictual or exciting" (Bonny, 1978b, p. 29).

## Vocal and Instrumental Music

Bonny found that many people objected to the inclusion of vocal music on the music programs. They claimed that vocal music, choral or solo voice, interfered or interrupted the train of thought, imagery, or feeling states in which they were immersed (Bonny, 1978b, p. 30). Bonny argues that the listener's like-dislike of vocal music, may well be "an unconscious response to the influence of the human voice on their emotional reactions to life experience" (Bonny, 1978b, p. 31). For example male-female voices may evoke feelings associated with parental figures.

With regard to instrumental sounds, Bonny found that "a full orchestra, (with) many types of instruments playing together, offers infinite possibilities for complexities of tension-release; it presents a wide range of emotional tone, intricate rhythms, and varied structures in musical themes, textures, colors, and harmony-melody combinations (Bonny, 1978b, p 31).

In addition, "instrumental music provides underlying support and structure while vocal music often touches areas of deep relationships and tends to encourage feelings of closeness and humanness" (Bonny, 1978b, p. 32).

## Tonal Combinations

Bonny notes that melody and harmony may form a Gestalt figure-ground in music. She explains that in many GIM music selections a solo instrument plays with orchestral backing (e.g., in concertos for solo instrument and orchestra). The solo instrument carries the melody, the "figure" or "sense of self" against the full orchestra representing the "ground" or "sense of other." Thus a concerto movement allows the listener a choice to identify with self or others (Bonny, 1996).

Compositions where the melodic line in solo or duet form is passed from instrument to instrument provide a unique opportunity in GIM to use Gestalt techniques of dialogue and confrontation. Each distinct instrument may symbolize a significant person who has something to "tell" the listener. The content of the message usually has significant meaning for the client, to hear what the "deeper self" has to say (Bonny, 1978b, p. 36).

## Mood

When these elements are taken together, the sum of the parts creates a prevailing mood. Bonny comments that "selections with well-integrated and clearly focused moods seem to have a more pronounced effect upon the GIM listener" (Bonny, 1978b, p. 36).

## CONCLUSION

This chapter has traced the historical processes that led to the creation of the music programs used in GIM practice. Bonny's categories of function and her rationale for incorporating music of the western classical tradition, contribute to our knowledge of how and why these music programs work.

It is testimony to Bonny's expertise and intuitive depth of understanding that her eighteen programs have stood the test of time. For many GIM therapists these programs are the stalwarts of GIM practice, and although some modifications to these programs have been made over the years, and other GIM practitioners have developed new programs, Bonny's still stand as fundamental to GIM practice.

## *References*

Bonny, H. L. (1978a). *Facilitating GIM Sessions. GIM Monograph No. 1.* Baltimore, MD: ICM Books.

Bonny, H. L. (1978b). *The Role of Taped Music Programs in the GIM Process.* GIM Monograph no. 2. Baltimore, MD: ICM Books.

Bonny, H. L. (1980). *GIM Therapy: Past, Present and Future Implications. GIM Monograph Number 3.* Baltimore, MD: ICM Books.

Bonny, H. L. (1989). Sound as symbol: Guided Imagery and Music in clinical practice. *Music Therapy Perspectives*, 6, 7–11.

Bonny, H. (1995). Interview, October 15.

Bonny, H. (1996). Interview, January 16.

Gaston, E, Thayer (ed). (1968). *Music in Therapy.* New York: Macmillan.

Goldberg, F. S. (1992). Images of emotion: The role of emotion in Guided Imagery and Music. *Journal of the Association for Music and Imagery,* 1, 5–17.

Hanks, K. J. (1992). Music, affect and imagery: A cross-cultural exploration. *Journal of the Association for Music and Imagery,* 1, 19–31.

Kasayka, R. E. (1988). *To Meet and Match the Moment of Hope: Trans-personal Elements of the Guided Imagery and Music Experience.* Unpublished paper. Savage, MD: Institute for Music and Imagery.

Meyer, L. (1956). *Emotion and Meaning in Music.* University of Chicago Press.

Summer, L. (1992). Music: The aesthetic elixir. *Journal of the Association for Music and Imagery,* 1, 44–53.

Summer, L. (1995). Melding musical and psychological processes: The therapeutic musical space. *Journal of the Association for Music and Imagery,* 4, 37–51.

Summer, L. (1998). The pure music transference in Guided Imagery and Music. In K. E. Bruscia (ed.) *The Dynamics of Music Psychotherapy,* pp. 431–459. Gilsum, NH: Barcelona Publishers.

## Chapter Six

# THE BONNY MUSIC PROGRAMS

# Denise E. Grocke

Helen Bonny designed eighteen music programs for use in the BMGIM. These programs were developed over a sixteen-year period, with the earliest developed in 1973, and the last developed in 1989. They are at the core of GIM practice, and one of the challenges of trainees in GIM is to know the music on the programs. In this chapter, the eighteen programs will be outlined by using phenomenological descriptions that draw out the salient features of the music as it is heard. Further insights are provided from interviews between Helen Bonny and the author conducted in 1995 and 1996, and by other writings of Helen Bonny. Insights about the *Peak Experience* program come from an interview between Roseanne Kasayka and Helen Bonny (1989). Each program will be presented by giving the details of the selections and their duration. These indications of the selection length come from Helen Bonny's first discography, listing the recordings (LPs) from which the selections came (Bonny, no date), and from her *Advanced GIM Discography* (Bonny, 1995a). The duration of each selection is important because it indicates the tempo at which the selection was performed, and this is a key element in Helen Bonny's choice of performance.

## AFFECT RELEASE

| | |
|---|---:|
| Holst: *The Planets* (Mars) | 7:11 |
| Bach: *Toccata & Fugue in d minor* (orchestrated by Stokowski) | 9:32 |
| Orff: *Carmina Burana:* | 10:03 |
|     O Fortuna; Fortuna plango vulnera | |
|     Ave Formosissima; O Fortuna | |
| | Total: 26:46 |

The Holst commences at the outset with a strong dotted rhythm heard in the percussion, strings, and brass. The theme is introduced by the brass, and although the theme is played legato, it is punctuated by the incessant, driving rhythm that pushes the music ahead. There is a building to a climax point in high register, followed by a catastrophic plunge down to low register. Section A is repeated with a return to the driving dotted rhythm in full orchestra. The strings and brass play the theme in unison, amplified by the dotted rhythm in percussion with snare drum. The tension increases and the selection ends with strong dissonant, detached chords in the brass, and a final chord, held in low register. Throughout this selection clients can be supported in their expression of strong emotion, particularly anger and frustration.

Bach's *Toccata and Fugue in d minor* was originally written as a solo organ work. Structurally the work is of the Baroque era, with orchestration by Stokowski for large orchestra. The orchestration style is typical of the Romantic era, with large woodwind and brass sections. The opening to the *Toccata* is dramatic—an ornamented long held note followed by a descending phrase, which is repeated in lower register—and creates a sense of inconsistency and unpredictability. There is a contrasting section of fast movement, punctuated with pauses and silences. The rhythm throughout is unpredictable and the ornamentation of notes creates a dramatic effect.

The *Fugue* begins with violins—this is softer than the *Toccata*, and the rhythm is more consistent. The fugue theme is played in lower strings (basses), then in woodwinds, followed by interplay between the strings and woodwinds in the development of the theme. The strings move into a section with a glissandi motif, followed by a lighter section in the woodwinds. There is a long section, which leads to an interrupted cadence, leading into the cadenza (on strings). The climax is developed with full orchestra, and with the strings playing fast passages, punctuated with brass chords, and an overall feeling of large waves of sound pouring over the listener, and an encouragement of outpouring of emotion, and expansiveness.

Orff's *Carmina Burana* is a ritualistic work and highly repetitive. The voices are strong and male dominated (although female voices are included). O Fortuna commences fortissimo, followed by a quieter section in which the pizzicato bass and chant-like voices may conjure up a ritualistic scene. Suspense and tension build, and the voices explode in a fortissimo repeat of the first theme, with percussion and tympani punctuating the end of each phrase. There is a dramatic shift to a major chord and a resolution.

A male-voice chant in Latin introduces the next section (Fortuna plango vulnera—"I bemoan the wounds of fortune"). The voices become percussive, emphasizing the rhythmic, gutteral expression of the words. The female voices join in. There is an orchestral interlude of fast strings and woodwinds, creating a frenzied sound. This pattern is repeated twice as the voices chant in Latin. The predominant feature of this music is its predictability and rhythmic consistency. The voices create a primal song that can draw out primal feelings and imagery.

Ave Formosissima ("Hail most beautiful one") is a triumphant and celebratory song of praise to the virgins Blanchefleur (one of the medieval heroines), Helena, and Venus. Then a low gong announces the repeat of O Fortuna, continuing a sense of ritual celebration, and triumph. Male and female voices repeat against a rocking bass line. There is an expansive orchestral sound with full texture and the selection concludes with resolution on the major chord.

Bonny commented that the Affect Release Program "should not be used until proper preparation of the subject is complete . . . (and) must include the preliminary arousal of some of the above affective feelings. Care has been taken to secure the affect in a strongly rhythmic context; for . . . rhythm means security . . . listeners can then go further out in their experience of the usually forbidden expression of what we, in our culture, call negative emotion. This encouragement is in line with the theory of GIM which asserts that all healing comes from within and from the expression and exploration of all areas of one's being" (Bonny, 1978b, p. 54).

## BEGINNERS IMAGERY/GROUP EXPERIENCE/ EXPLORATIONS

| | |
|---|---:|
| Ravel: *Daphnis and Chloe Ballet* (excerpt) | 7:21 |
| Brahms: *Symphony #1* (Un poco Allegretto e grazioso) | 4:41 |
| Respighi: *The Pines of Rome* (Gianicola) | 6:15 |
| Debussy: *Nocturnes* (Sirenes) | 10:53 |
| Tschesnokoff: *Salvation is Created* | 5:02 |
| Pachelbel: *Canon in D* | 7:09 |
| | Total: 41:21 |

The *Daphnis and Chloe Ballet* score is in three movements, and is scored for orchestra and off-stage choir. The section that is included on the *Beginners/Group Experience* program is the *Introduction and Religious Dance*. The movement begins quietly with an ascending sequence of open fifth intervals, and the choir enters singing wordlessly on the sound "Ah." A solo flute floats above. There is a gentle rocking rhythm that creates a secure and supportive milieu. The horn and flute exchange the melody line, and there is a gradual build-up in the strings, voices, and full orchestra to a fortissimo. The volume decreases to lead into the Dance Religieuse. There is an interplay between the gentle movement of the strings and the wordless voices. A brief development of the first theme is heard on oboe, horn, and flute before a fade-out of the music at 7 minutes 21 seconds.

The Brahms is "more mundane . . . This is a relief to go from the less-specific Ravel to the more certain rhythms of the Brahms" (Bonny, 1996). The first theme is heard on the clarinet, and developed by the strings. The middle section has a stronger rhythmic motif and is more insistent, calling attention through the repeated motif. The first section is repeated with an embellished melodic line, and the movement ends quietly.

The Respighi begins with a solo piano cadenza passage, followed by a yearning, longing melody on clarinet while muted strings hum quietly in the background. The melody is repeated by strings with the celeste and harp creating a wash of sound, enhanced by the muted string accompaniment. A second theme is exchanged between flute and cello, then strings. Glissandi on harp and celeste continue the wash of sound, and the movement ends with solo clarinet, muted strings in high register playing tremolo, interspersed with bird calls. The overall image created throughout is one of a pastoral setting.

The wordless chorus returns in Debussy's Sirenes (part 3 of Debussy's *Nocturnes*). The chorus comprises women's voices only, but there is an alternation between the high soprano and lower mezzo soprano voices. The string accompaniment is based on a repeated rhythmic phrase that adds an insistence, and drives the music forward. Repetition is featured throughout so that there is constant movement. There is an alluring quality to the voices, typifying the mythical Sirenes. A more romantic theme is heard in the strings perhaps evoking images of the sea or flowing water.

Tschesnokoff's *Salvation is Created* is a beautifully mastered un-accompanied choral work for four-part choir. The work is perfectly shaped with a gradual build to a climax point and a gradual decrease in volume and tone. This is repeated. The low bass notes are a feature, as are the quality of the choir and the balance of male and female voices. The music is evocative of spiritual imagery and an expansiveness of feeling and emotion.

The Pachebel *Canon* is well known to most clients and provides a grounding to the lofty heights of the Tschesnekoff work. The performance recommended by Bonny is one of the slower recordings of this work. Musically the *Canon* is a two-measure sequence played by lower strings, repeated twenty-seven times with variations in the upper parts. The canon provides a fundamental structure of security, allowing the client to bring imagery to a close.

Bonny and Mardis revised the *Group Experience* program in 1994, substituting the vocal version of Ravel's *Dahnis and Chloe Ballet* excerpt with

Ravel's *Daphnis and Chloe Suite #2* (Lever du Jour and excerpt from the Pantomine) as the first selection. This program was then named *Explorations* (Bonny & Mardis, 1994).

## BODY TAPE (PROGRAM)

| | |
|---|---|
| Shostakovitch: *Quartet #3* (Allegretto) | 6:50 |
| Shostakovitch: *Quartet #8* (Allegretto) | 4:50 |
| Nielsen: *Symphony #5* (Andante un poco Tranquillo (excerpt) | 4:36 |
| Vierne: *The Chimes of Westminster* (for organ) | 6:26 |
| Beethoven: *Piano Concerto #3* (Largo) | 10:08 |
| Prokofieff: *Classical Symphony* (Larghetto) | 3:53 |
| | Total: 36:43 |

The *String Quartet #3*, Allegretto, blends conventional tonality with dissonance. The first theme, played by the first violin, is supported by staccato accompaniment. There is a sense of playfulness in the first section of the movement, although the dissonant intervals of the melody can also suggest something macabre. In contrast, the middle section is quieter and played legato. The repeat of the first section is written in fugue form, and gathers speed toward the end.

The *String Quartet #8*, Allegretto, starts with a dramatic statement played by the first violin. The predominant feature of the movement is the steady rocking 3/4 beat creating a persistent movement, and also the pizzicato bass line and staccato melody line.

The excerpt from Nielsen's *Symphony #5* blends in with the dissonant tonality of the Shostakovitch. It is quiet and muted, with a melancholic melody that develops, sounding more romantic as it fills out in texture and register. Bonny merges the Nielsen with the Vierne *Chimes of Westminster*, fading the Nielsen out after 4:36 minutes, and imperceptibly fading in the opening of the Vierne.

The *Chimes of Westminster* is the sixth piece of the Third Suite of *Pièces de Fantaisie for Grand Organ*. The central theme of the piece is the familiar sequence of chimes associated with Big Ben at Westminster, London. The variations on this theme are heard in the melody and pedal line. Throughout the piece the organ can sound like a domineering authority figure. This is achieved partly by the sheer size of the instrument (the registration calls for a 32' pedal stop), and by Vierne's indication for the swell pedal to create surges of sound.

This music may suggest images of the cathedral (religious experiences) or grotesque images (through associations with Dracula).

In stark contrast to the very loud ending of the Vierne, the Beethoven is quiet and restful. It commences with solo piano, introducing a slow lyrical melody. This is repeated by the orchestra. There is a gentle interplay between the piano and orchestra, providing a musical safe ground of respite. A repeat of the first section is followed by a brief piano cadenza leading to a quiet ending but a forte chord to conclude.

The *Body Program* concludes with the playful Larghetto from Prokofieff's *Classical Symphony*. The melody is supported by staccato accompaniment, reminiscent of the Shostakovitch *String Quartet* that began the program.

Bonny describes the program as combining dissonant music of the twentieth century with conventional tonalities. It was designed to assist clients into body experiences (Bonny, 1996), and this is achieved by the use of dance-like rhythms (in the Shostakovich works and Prokofieff), and the intrusive fullness of the Vierne work. Interspersed are selections that provide a quieter time of reflection (the Nielsen and Beethoven selections).

## COMFORTING/ANACLYTIC

| | |
|---|---:|
| Haydn: *Cello Concerto in C* (Adagio) | 9:45 |
| Sibelius: *The Swan of Tuonela* | 7:50 |
| Villa-Lobos: *Bachianas Brasileiras*, #5 | 5:53 |
| Boccherini: *Cello Concerto in B flat* (Adagio non troppo) | 6:57 |
| Glinka: *The Life for the Tzar*, Act IV (Susanin aria) | 5:20 |
| Schubert: *Die Schöne Mullerin* (Der Neugierige) | 4:15 |
| Debussy: *Prelude: The Girl with the Flaxen Hair* | 2:44 |
| | Total:  42:44 |

The Haydn is written in traditional concerto form, so that the main themes heard at the beginning of the movement are repeated in the middle (development section), and again in the recapitulation. The first theme is heard in the orchestra and is warm in tone. The bass line provides a steady unchanging pulse beneath the melody line of the violins. The solo cello comes in with a long sustained note, which can depict security and support (Bonny, 1995b). The melody is played in mid-register, creating a warm and nurturing tone. Throughout this movement the string sound is comforting and there is little change in rhythm or tempo, and therefore the client may be content to stay with the one image or feeling. Bonny had heard the recording of Jacqueline Du Pre playing this work and felt "this woman knows how to express womanhood through the cello. The recording is remarkable because Du Pre's breathing is audible, and it helps the traveler get into the music" (Bonny, 1995b).

The *Swan of Tuonela* was chosen to represent another aspect of parenting (Bonny, 1995b). The cor anglais creates a mournful musical timbre, and its reedy quality conjures up imagery of a dark lake, "a foreboding beginning" (Bonny, 1995b). The high notes of the strings tend to maintain tension, but the horn gives it depth and stability. The cor anglais sounds across the top of the strings, creating a lonely, distant melody supported by sparse orchestration. The cor anglais is often a voice of admonition, an authority figure, either suggesting to the client they "should" do something, or alternatively giving the client freedom, depending on their orientation (Bonny, 1995b). Throughout the entire piece the cor anglais is "the" voice, although others may come in. This selection may be depressing for some clients because of the funeral march quality of the music.

The *Bachianas Brasileiros #5* was originally written for soprano and cello ensemble, but Bonny preferred the guitar accompaniment version. The female voice is filled with emotion, and the imagery may reflect feelings about women in the client's life (Bonny, 1995b). The soloist "slides" into the sound. It is a strong voice, but not too operatic and there is opportunity to encourage conversation or dialogue in the client's imagery. The first section returns and repeats and the song finishes with a note in high register, pianissimo, held and sustained.

The Boccherini has a similar music structure to the Haydn cello concerto. The first theme commences with a long sustained note on cello, which may capture and pull together threads of imagery from the previous selections. There is a gentleness in the cadenza so that the client may travel deeper while the violins are supportive and give assurance (Bonny, 1995b).

The quality of the male voice in the Glinka can be a shock for a client in an altered state of consciousness. The aria comes from the opera "The Life for the Tzar." Some of the words might be upsetting to a client who understands the Russian language, in particular the words (translated) "My last dawn. My time has come. Oh, bitter hour. Oh, fearful hour. Oh, how frightening and hard to die under torture." Bonny wanted a strong male voice to bring out the experiences of the masculine and she liked the strength of the voice. The timbre of the basso is important—Bonny liked the fullness of emotion in the voice, depicting the Russian character of intensity, deep emotion, dark color, and a strong sense of masculinity (Bonny, 1995b). "The voice is more important than the accompaniment—he has so much color in his voice. The voice can represent the priest, as well as the father figure" (Bonny, 1995b). The tremolo in the strings, and the solo voice increase the intensity and a resonant low tone is sustained at the end.

The Schubert song *Der Neugierige* (The Question) depicts a different color in the timbre of the high, younger male voice asking the question "does she love me?" The music structure is simple and light and a contrast to the heaviness of the Glinka. It brings out another male characteristic (Bonny, 1995b).

The simple melody of the Debussy *Prelude* matches the Schubert song in simplicity and timbre. The *Prelude* oscillates between a single melody line and simple chordal accompaniment. It provides a secure and gentle finish to the program.

Bonny and Mardis revised the *Comforting/Anaclytic* program in 1994, and it is now known as *"Recollections"* (described at the end of this chapter).

## COSMIC–ASTRAL

| | |
|---|---:|
| Strauss, R: *Thus Spake Zarathustra* (excerpt) | 11:09 |
| Scriabin: *Poéme of Ecstasy* | 19:28 |
| Holst: *The Planets* (Neptune) | 7:00 |
| Total: | 37:37 |

The *Cosmic-Astral* program was devised by Bonny in 1973 for clients who were experienced with GIM and altered states of consciousness (ASC), and who wanted to "go to the outer rims of the cut-log, quickly" (Bonny, 1996). Bonny thought the Strauss tone poem *"Thus Spake Zarathustra"* would match that intention well. The Scriabin work *"Poéme of Ecstasy"* she felt would help the client stay at the outer rims of the ASC, likewise *Neptune* from Holst's *The Planets*.

Bonny removed the *Cosmic-Astral* program from circulation after feedback from GIM Fellows indicated that the program was too challenging for clients. There was a period of time when the program was not available, however it was remastered in 1989 and became available for a brief period of time up until the Bonny music tapes were no longer sold.

# DEATH–REBIRTH

| | |
|---|---|
| Wagner: *Götterdämmerung* (Siegfried's Funeral March) | 7:40 |
| Rachmaninoff: *The Isle of the Dead* | 17:00 |
| Bach: *B minor Mass* (Crucifixus) | 4:50 |
| Mahler: *Songs of the Earth* (Der Abschied) | 10:22 |
| Total: | 39:52 |

The program begins with Siegfried's Funeral March from *Götterdämmerung* ("The Twilight of the Gods," the fourth opera in *The Ring* cycle) by Richard Wagner. The selection commences with a solemn kettle drum roll, and threatening chromatic passages heard in the lower strings. Siegfried's motif is heard on the horns, and the overall color is dark and foreboding, like the archetypal funeral march. The middle section becomes more yearning, with solo fragments in cor anglais, clarinet, and oboe. Siegfried's motif is heard clearly on trumpet (an ascending pattern), and the mood lifts to a triumphal climax, punctuated by emphatic brass. The introduction of the harps briefly softens the tone, but there is a return to the intensity of the brass and the driving rhythmic patterns. The march fades out quietly, but maintains the insistent beat of the kettle drum.

The tone poem *The Isle of the Dead* was inspired by Böcklin's painting of the same name. The primary feature is the 5/8 meter. Initially the emphasis falls on the first and third beats of the measure, then changes to an emphasis on the first and fourth beats of the measure. This oscillation creates a sense of persistent movement, depicting the progression of the boat toward the isle. The work features various timbral colors, including the haunting muted brass, used with effect to create an eerie image of the death barge. The melodic line is based on the plainchant *Dies Irae* and is heard throughout in the strings, particularly on cellos and horns in the middle section of the work. A sense of churning is created by two-note slurs, and at the recapitulation point there is more turgid movement created by the incessant eighth-note patterns. The lyrical, yearning theme is heard on violins, and with increasing intensity the work soars to a climax point. A brief section of respite is followed by a chromatic rise of great intensity, and the brass "stab" out a rhythmic phrase. There follows a "death walk," in 4/4 time, with plucked pizzicato chords in the lower strings on the second and fourth beats, against violins playing tremolo. The combination evokes images of a macabre processional. There is a coda that repeats the opening measures of the work in modified form, and the work concludes with the eeriness and incessant movement of the boat returning from the Isle.

This is followed by the Crucifixus from Bach's *Mass in B minor*. The choral work provides a plateau after the lengthy *Isle of the Dead*, and a possibility for the client to either rest, or for imagery suggestive of spirituality or religious experience—of being "in peacefulness of death and the promise of new life" (Bonny, 1978b, p. 44). The main feature of the selection is the consistent pulse provided by the stepwise descending bass line, and similarly the descending line of the vocal parts. There is a layering of the voices as each enters and overlaps with another. The overall tone is quiet and sombre.

In the original version of the *Death-Rebirth* program, the Mahler *Der Abschied* (The Farewell), from the *Songs of the Earth*, is sung by a baritone, the warm tone of the voice providing a fitting finale to the program. A later version adopts the alto voice, which likewise produces a warm tone. *Der Abschied* is the sixth and last song in the cycle in which death is depicted as winter. It is written in a minor key, however toward the end of the movement, there is a dramatic modulation from the minor key to major, and a corresponding lift in emotional tone. The movement ends with a rocking motif aided by the celeste, providing an almost magical, childlike quality to the end of the program. "The hope and anticipation of a new being is expressed by the lingering, repetitive last two notes of the voice that seems to reach into infinity" (Bonny, 1978b, p. 45).

## EMOTIONAL EXPRESSION I

| | |
|---|---|
| Brahms: *Piano Concerto #2 in B flat* (Allegro non troppo) | 17:52 |
| Brahms: *A German Requiem* | 16:49 |
| Part 1: Selig sind, die da Leid tragen | |
| Part 5: Ihr habt nun Traurigkeit | |
| Brahms: *Symphony # 4* (Andante moderato) | 12:40 |
| Total: | 47:21 |

The French horn provides the opening statement of the *Piano Concerto*. The piano then commences in earnest with a strong rhythmical passage that sets the pace for the first part of the movement. There are short moments of rest, within strong rhythmical statements that build in intensity. Throughout the movement there are many sections that increase this intensity, however there are no noticeable climaxes that release the tension (Bonny, 1996). Therefore the entire movement demands a concentrated effort on the part of the client, who needs the emotional energy to sustain engagement with the music. Changes happen very fast throughout the movement, and the pounding of the piano can "loosen up the soil" (Bonny, 1996). The second theme of this movement has a sad yearning quality to it and provides moments of respite, but then the piano re-enters with driving energy. The movement is composed in strict concerto form, so that there is a middle development section before the recapitulation (repeat) of the first section. The movement finishes with flourishes from the solo piano, which can "hammer" home a message.

In contrast to the sustained energy of the *Piano Concerto*, the *Requiem*, parts 1 and 5 are quieter, slower and more lyrical in quality, "a reward for the hard work of the previous selection" (Bonny, 1996). Part 1 commences with a low note in the strings, followed by a layering of higher strings playing a melody of very simple line. The voices enter, with a beautifully balanced sound of the male and female parts. There is close harmony of the voices, chorale-style, which suggests integration. The orchestra and voices alternate in a section of dialogue. In the middle section, the voices separate out—male and female voices are heard separately and are differentiated. Then they are in dialogue—one phrase offered by the male voices "suggesting a message" (Bonny, 1996), answered by the female voices. There is a repetition of the first section and a chordal ending with gentle harp arpeggiated chords. Overall this movement is very supportive and the balance of male and female voices enhances the support.

The soprano solo in part 5 of the *Requiem* offers opportunity for a more personal experience (Bonny, 1996). Female clients may identify with the solo voice and what the soloist depicts in song. For others the solo female voice may be heard as singing especially to them. The phrase "as one whom his own mother comforteth" is thought to indicate that Brahms may have written this part of the *Requiem* in memory of his mother, who had died one year previous to the work being composed. The song can be comforting, the soloist suggesting a nurturing, caring mother figure, or healing image, and the chorus murmuring assent (Bonny, 1996).

There is more structure in the movement from *Symphony #4* than the previous sections from the *Requiem*. The regular rhythm suggests moving ahead in a walking or marching pace. In the middle section there is a beautiful melody heard first in the cellos. There is a return to the first section and repetition of the main themes. The second theme in particular is warm and emotionally filling. The ending of the movement trails off, providing a gentle close to the program.

Bonny (1996) recalls that Robert MacDonald, a GIM Fellow working with clients who were depressed, would reverse the order of the selections on the program by commencing with the *Symphony*, followed by the *Piano Concerto* and concluding with the two parts of the *Requiem*. In this order the *Symphony* provides more consistent movement in rhythmic structure and form than the *Piano Concerto*, and this was more suitable for depressed clients.

# EMOTIONAL EXPRESSION II

Menotti: *Piano Concerto in F* (Lento)                                    9:32
Shostakovitch: *Symphony # 5* (Moderato [excerpt] and Largo)             15:02
Mendelssohn: *Symphony # 3* (Adagio)                                     10:58
                                                                Total: 35:32

The Menotti commences with low tones on tympani, followed by solo oboe. It is a sad, melancholy melody (Bonny, 1987), a haunting sound that sets the scene for the selection as a whole. Muted trumpets add a sense of foreboding. The piano enters with a spacious melody accompanied by simple chords that provide some sense of security. Bonny comments that the music could be "disintegrating and frightening . . . (however) it becomes romantic and builds to the positive . . . could be an opportunity for affect release from negative to positive" (Bonny, 1987). Dissonant embellishments are heard throughout the selection and these can create an unsettling effect. The build to the climax is marked by a heavily accented "peal-like" sequence. The piano re-enters toward the end and there is a quiet finish.

The Shostakovitch begins quietly and is a welcome respite from the dissonance of the Menotti. A consistent rhythm on strings provides support. The melody is heard on flute in dialogue with the horn. Although the music is principally dissonant, the consistent rhythm is very secure. The middle section features woodwinds in dialogue. Brass play a role in heralding a new section of thin texture, and the melody is heard in the flute (and later solo violin), supported by the strings. The brass punctuate from time to time, and the celeste creates a sense of expectation with ascending scale passages.

The Largo movement begins pianissimo—and strings only. The primary feature is the dissonance of the melody and harmonic sequence, however the low strings create a sense of support. The middle section is introduced by harp. The flute plays a wandering melody supported by soft strings. There is a mistiness to this music—the way is not clear—but it builds to a climax where the melody line is stronger, and the bass gives more direction. The first section is repeated with solo clarinet and strings held in high register, creating a thin texture, but a quite beautiful sound. The next section gradually lowers in pitch as the brass and lower woodwinds descend. The build-up that follows is gradual, passionate, and insistent, and the full orchestra penetrates with punctuated, emphatic notes. The music quietens and the ending finishes with strings and harp resolving on a major chord.

The shift to consonant tonality in the Mendelssohn is marked after the dissonance of the Menotti and Shostakovitch. The strings play a very safe melody that is predictable and lyrical. A plucked accompaniment on the second violins and violas creates a sense of movement, or perhaps a resolution of what has gone before. There is warmth to this music, and repetition to give a sense of security. The first variation features muted brass, with a dotted rhythm that creates a martial effect. This might be an opportunity for the client to celebrate in a majestic scene. A return to the lyrical theme furthers the sense of security. The martial theme returns briefly in full orchestra, and the theme returns on the lower strings, creating a very positive ending. There is an extended coda, and the movement finishes softly and quietly.

## IMAGERY

| | |
|---|---|
| Ravel: *Introduction & Allegro* | 11:00 |
| Copland: *Appalachian Spring* (excerpt) | 9:00 |
| Tschaikovsky: *Symphony # 4* (Scherzo) | 5:17 |
| Respighi: *The Birds* (The Dove) | 4:35 |
| Turina: *La Oración del Torero* | 11:00 |
| Total: | 40:52 |

The main feature of the Ravel is the use of several themes throughout the work, which are dispersed throughout the orchestra giving a great variety of tone color. The flute and clarinet introduce the first theme that is completed by the strings. This theme is developed throughout the work. A change to 3/4 time starts a playful, joyous section that stimulates movement in the imagery. The cello melody in this section has long, sweeping lines that create a more lyrical mood. The Allegro section commences with the harp playing a variation of the first theme and this repetition increases the familiarity for the listener. The flute and clarinet introduce a second theme of the Allegro section, and the harp creates a sense of playfulness through the use of glissandi, "like waves of sound tumbling over and over" (Bonny, 1995b). The middle section of the work is warm and secure with the melody in the strings, and a sensuous ostinato pattern in the muted lower strings creating a lulled feeling. There is a bridge section in which a short phrase passes from violins to celli to flute to clarinet (each creating a different tone color). An expectation builds about what is about to happen. The solo harp enters with the second theme of the Allegro, which builds quickly to a peak, then just as quickly descends from it. Another bridge is structured with the same short phrase as before, over an ostinato, and this builds to another peak, more strident than before. The harp cadenza leads to the recapitulation and a restatement of the first melody. The harp picks out melodic notes while also creating a thin filigree of sound. There is a lot of repetition, of passing the melody from woodwinds to strings and harp. An accelerez (increase in speed) toward the end of the work brings it to a strong finish.

The excerpt from *Appalachian Spring* is based on a folk melody that is simple and familiar but also challenging because of the dramatic changes in the tempi of the music. There are four sections—the opening builds on a tonic chord, first in clarinet, then flute and horn. Each instrument enters over the last, creating a rich chord "like building blocks" (Bonny, 1995b). The solo violin and flute introduce the melody. The spaced notes give a feeling of rest, and there is an effective use of instrumental color. Then there is a very abrupt and unanticipated change. The second section is rhythmically disjointed and fast moving, but with rests that create a stop–go feeling. The dance movement (third section) is created by the strings alternating between pizzicato and legato over the piano's percussive arpeggios. There is a lot of interchange between instruments and this can be an incentive to the imagination. In the fourth section there is rhythmic contrast as the time meter changes (3/4 to 6/8, 4/4, 5/4) creating different rhythmic emphases. A comic character is introduced in the music and the bassoon introduces a waltz–like tune. Bonny comments that whenever another voice (instrument) comes in, another personality, or another image may emerge (Bonny, 1995b). A definite negative, strident voice comes in, followed by a definitely sad minor mode, perhaps suggesting some regret (Bonny, 1995b), and the section ends quietly.

The principal feature of the Tschaikovsky is the pizzicato in the strings, which can be perceived by the listener as light and jovial, or as pressure (Bonny, 1995b). The Trio provides a change of mood and there may be new imagery, and a relief from the fast tempo of the first section. The repeat of the first section is even faster than at the beginning, so that the whole movement is full of energy.

Bonny's intention in including the Respighi was to bring a plateau or rest from the previous frenetic selection. The solo oboe plays the first theme that can sound mournful, or peaceful and calming. The muted strings create an interesting effect, like the flapping of birds' wings. The second theme, also played on solo oboe, continues the wistful, almost melancholy sound with embellishments that add a sense of the shepherd's call, or a pastoral scene. The birds'-wing motif is used increasingly in the strings and woodwinds, and toward the end of the work the ascending strings create an impression of flight. "It is interesting what Respighi does with the violin to make a sound like birds—it is a fast/short tremolo . . . the strings 'flutter' through embellishments" (Bonny, 1995b).

The Turina is more complex, modal, and emotional than the previous selections. The strings in tremolo create a strange eerie sound, created by using the wood of the bow rather than the hair (Bonny, 1995b). The melody enters, low, and in a Spanish idiom. "It is very visceral music—the client will feel this in the body. The Toreador speaks from a very deep place inside" (Bonny, 1995b). In the Allegretto section the cellos have a singing quality and all instruments are muted. There is a return of the dance theme that is quite joyful. Toward the close there is a sense of resolution, a single voice, then a sense of peace. The work ends with a "luscious sequence of rich harmonies in the high register of the strings" (Bonny, 1995b).

## INNER ODYSSEY

| | |
|---|---:|
| Brahms: *Symphony #3* (Allegro con brio) | 10:23 |
| Nielsen: *Symphony #5* (Adagio) | 9:43 |
| Beethoven: *Violin Concerto* (Larghetto) | 10:15 |
| Corelli: *Concerto Grosso #8 in g minor* (Adagio-Allegro-Adagio) | 3:32 |
| Total: | 33:53 |

Two chords played on brass herald the start of the Brahms symphony. The first theme is strong rhythmically and is built on the chord of F major alternating with a diminished chord. It is an expansive sound, but harmonically ambiguous. It is a challenging start for the client as there is no gradual introduction to the work. Another element is introduced which is bright, with warm tone color. This is a quieter section and steady. The bridge features passages rising and falling on woodwinds, in dialogue with the strings. There is a pastoral quality to the second theme, heard on clarinet— the meter is 9/4, suggesting a waltz. A gentle pulse in pizzicato lower strings gives security and also a sense of movement. The tempo picks up, with an interweaving between strings and woodwinds and chromatic scale passages in an ascending pattern that increases the tension. The rhythm from the first statement heralds the development section. The second theme forms the basis of the development (heard in cellos and violas), then in violins, over an ostinato in the bass. A darker section emerges. Horns predominate with long drawn out tones, harmonically close with a rather haunting mood quality. The rhythm of the first theme forms the basis of the bridge passage to the recapitulation. The first theme is more fully orchestrated, giving a thicker texture. The pastoral passage is heard again, leading to the coda that is based on the opening theme. A second, quieter coda leads to a string restatement of the opening rhythmic phrase.

Initially the Nielsen is a quiet contrast to the Brahms. The time signature is 3/4, and the first theme is heard on the bassoon and violas in G major. The theme is plaintive, yet warm and rather restful despite the dissonance. The first theme is repeated in violins. A further repeat a 7th higher takes the violins into high register and an increase in tension and anticipation. There is a climax and fortissimo passage where horns dominate with a three-note ascending "fanfare," against descending violins. Brasses dominate throughout this section. The texture of the music changes markedly. Violins repeat the theme, but the woodwinds introduce a threatening motif, which punctuates the theme. The dissonance increases. The timpani enter with a fortissimo roll and tubas play a descending passage. The brasses take the melody, and the timpani continue the drum roll. The tension accelerates and grows. There is a layering of the instruments throughout this section and the three sections of the orchestra (timpani, brass, and strings/woodwinds) seem disconnected. A snare drum introduces a solo part against the orchestra (a fourth component). The instructions to the snare drum player are "to improvise, as if to disturb the music at all costs" (Fjeldsoe, 2000). The overall impression of this section is one of disintegration and fragmentation, each section of the orchestra focused on its own part with seemingly nothing to integrate the sections together. This disintegration continues at length and is very challenging for the client. It resolves at last with a wonderful climax that brings relief to the dissonance and fragmentation. The theme soars on woodwinds, strings, and brass, supported by rapid passages in the lower strings. A strong descending scale passage leads to a further climax point. There is an immediate decrescendo with strings playing tremolo. The work moves to a tranquillo section. The snare drum sounds its presence with an intermittent roll. The movement closes with a rhapsodic solo part for clarinet against a quiet chord held by strings and brass. The snare drum is directed to play diminuendo and to cease playing so that the clarinet alone holds the final note.

The Beethoven is a beautiful movement for solo violin and orchestra, providing a restful plateau in which the client can reflect on what has gone before. Bonny's preferred performer is Sophie Mutter, who provides a performance of great warmth, beauty, and authenticity. Set in G major, this movement carries the G tonality from the Nielsen piece. The opening phrases of the Beethoven are characterized by a simple rhythmic phrase featuring a dotted rhythm and two-note slur, followed by a beat rest. The overall effect is one of a deep breathing and resting. The harmonic structure is very simple and the consonance contrasts with the previous dissonance of the Nielsen. The horn heralds the violin solo. The solo line embellishes the melody and dialogues with the clarinet first, then the bassoon. The violin line extends to the upper register, creating a filigree of sound, while the lower strings provide tentative support. The warmth of the bassoon timbre fills the middle range. The orchestra enters and the bass line is strengthened, giving more support. Again the violin solo takes an embellished line, leading to the second theme in mid-register. The second theme is particularly beautiful in its simplicity. It is very spacious, as if time stands still, and there is a feeling of yearning. The strings provide support with long held notes. The solo violin develops the melody with an embellished variation, and the strings provide a pizzicato accompaniment. The second melody is repeated in the solo violin, with spacious chordal support from clarinet and bassoon, then the strings join with a quiet chordal accompaniment. The solo violin drifts into higher register and the sound floats away.

The Corelli excerpt is scored for two violins, cello, and string orchestra, in typical Baroque style, in which the melodic line is supported by a steady repetitive line in the bass. The melodic line shifts between first and second violin, then cello, yet the overall sense is an unbroken line. The harmonic structure follows a figured bass. It is predictable and steady. The Allegro section, although faster in tempo, is very consistent. This section ends with a brief cadenza on solo violin. The Adagio is repeated without change, but there is a coda of four measures, with a downward moving scale passage, to ensure that the client brings the imagery experience to a close.

## MOSTLY BACH

| | |
|---|---|
| *Bach: *Passacaglia & Fugue in c minor* | 14:37 |
| *Bach: *Come Sweet Death* | 5:50 |
| *Bach: *Partita in b minor* (Sarabande) | 4:30 |
| *Bach: *Fugue in g minor(The Shorter)* | 3:50 |
| Brahms: *Violin Concerto* (Adagio) | 8:38 |
| Bach: *Concerto for Two Violins* (Largo ma non  troppo) | 7:38 |
| | Total:  45:03 |

* Orchestral arrangements by Stokowski

The *Passacaglia* theme is an eight-measure statement heard from the outset on lower strings. It is a soft, gentle beginning and allows the client to settle into the program. There follows a series of twenty variations of the *Passacaglia* theme heard in different sections of the orchestra, sometimes in the bass line, other times in the melodic line. The essential quality is the repetition, and this provides the strong structure to the work. Clients sense that this structure gives a secure musical container in which they can explore major issues in their lives. The dynamics of the work also encourage the client to look at the focus issue from different perspectives, because of the relentless movement and changeable tone color. There is a contrast too between the full texture of the orchestra, and softer lighter variations. "It is like a thick tapestry of different things happening in different places" (Bonny, 1996). The climax occurs in variations 19 and 20, where the brasses carry the *Passacaglia* theme, against strings in high register and woodwinds adding intensity and emphasis.

The last chord carries immediately into the *Fugue*, so that the client has no respite. The *Passacaglia and Fugue* together constitute almost fifteen minutes of intense work, and for this reason the *Mostly Bach* program is one of the most effective "working" programs, allowing the client to explore an issue in depth, through a "loosening up of the soil" (Bonny, 1996). The fugue theme includes the first four measure of the *Passacaglia* theme, and therefore continues the repetitive nature of the work. There is a second and third fugue subject, and these three themes are developed throughout. Stokowski uses a similar formula heard in the *Passacaglia* to develop the fugue themes. There is contrast between the tone color of strings, woodwinds, and brass, and a contrast of intensity and lighter sections. The *Fugue* ends triumphantly, with the use of the trill to add emphasis and strength to the final climax and a loud ending.

The second selection, *Come Sweet Death* is extremely slow. "There is a liquid quality to the music, and also a sad quality . . . it is not always sad for the person, sometimes it is a blissful or positive place to be" (Bonny, 1996). It can be experienced by the client as gentle or lulling, but it can also draw out emotions of grieving, sometimes a grief for what has been loosened up during the *Passacaglia and Fugue*. There is a sense of this piece having two "verses," the first "verse" in strings only, and the repetition having much fuller orchestration that is "thick and condensed, almost like velvet" (Bonny, 1996). The harp adds a "healing" quality of the repetition.

The Sarabande comes from the *Sonata. #2 in b minor for Solo Violin* (although Stokowski's score states it is from *Partita #1 in b minor*). The harp plays a major role in sustaining the steady pulse of this work through arppegiated chords that add intensity to the work. There is some respite with the pure tone of the flute. It has some interesting climaxes, where the whole orchestra plays together in chords, and clients may have a peak experience.

The *Fugue in g minor* was originally written for organ. It is quite short, and has a lightness, and almost a jocular, comical quality at times. The first subject of the *Fugue* is played staccato by the oboe, and is then repeated eight times. Woodwinds give the subject theme its character, particularly the bassoon and contrabassoon. Stokowski uses the same structure heard in the *Passacaglia and*

*Fugue* to build to a climax—the fugue subject is played fortissimo in the lower brass, against high strings and woodwinds. The final chord is a "tierce de Picardie," that is, a resolution on to a major chord, giving a flash of light at the very end of the work.

After the sheer strength and loudness of what has gone before, the Brahms slow movement of the violin concerto is particularly beautiful. There is a classic structure to the music, with first and second themes, a development section and recapitulation. "It gives a soaring quality, a quality of peacefulness and rest, but also if an individual is ready for it, a peak experience" (Bonny, 1996). The second melody introduces a new aspect to the music, as if to offer a question and answer. There is anguish, intensity, and strength in the violin part, as it soars throughout this section, building emotion and intensity in a dramatic and declarative way. The ending is particularly beautiful as the horn and woodwinds hold a long chord, and the violin has the final say.

The Largo "is one of the most beautiful pieces written. It has a very beautiful melody with orchestral background and is a profound piece of music" (Bonny, 1996). Bonny's preferred recording is of David and Igor Oistrach, the father and son combination adding a significant quality to the performance. The principle feature of the music is the interweaving of the first and second violin parts. As one completes a phrase the other enters imperceptibly. Repetition is another key factor in this movement that helps the client bring a close to the imagery experienced during the program. It is a stabilizing piece of music and may often be used at the end of other GIM sessions where the client needs to integrate an experience further before finishing with the imagery.

## NURTURING

| | |
|---|---:|
| Britten: *Simple Symphony* (Sentimental Sarabande) | 7:10 |
| Vaughan Williams: *"Rhosymedre" Prelude* | 3:55 |
| Berlioz: *L'enfance du Christ* | 11:00 |
|     Overture to Part 2 | |
|     Shepherd's Farewell (Chorus) | |
| Puccini: *Madame Butterfly* (Humming Chorus) | 2:58 |
| Massenet: *Scènes Alsaciennes* (Sous le Tilleuls) | 4:02 |
| Canteloube (arr): *Songs of the Auvergne* (Brezairola) | 3:36 |
| | Total: 32:41 |

The *Sarabande* has a strong beginning, in the minor key. It has a certain intensity and demand that is engendered by the octave-leap ostinato (on the note G) in the bass line and also by the equal emphasis placed on each note of the melody. A second phrase, played by the violin, is softer and more reflective. The melodic line becomes more lyrical and sweeter, however as the first theme is repeated it becomes louder and more insistent again. Within the repeat there is a modulation to the major key, introducing a new color to the music. The second theme is heard on the cellos. This is a lulling melody supported gently by pizzicato bass, and later the violas. There is a brief pause and suddenly a strong broken chord in violins heralds a repeat of the first section. The bass line has an ascending scale to give it more emphasis, followed by a repeat with more urgency and emphasis. The strings in unison lead into a modulation and a series of strong statements. The second theme is repeated, with the strings muted, creating a sweet and very tender sound. The section of repeated three-note phrases is like an affirming tap-tap-tap (Bonny, 1995b). There is a brief restatement of the lyrical theme and the movement ends gently and quietly.

The *"Rhosymedre" Prelude* is based on the hymn tune of the same name, and was originally composed for organ. Vaughan Williams also arranged an orchestral version. The strings introduce the Prelude interweaving in a gentle consistent movement "like lacing themselves around each other" (Bonny, 1995b). The cellos in mid register introduce the hymn tune, creating a mellow tone, "a renewal of the goodness of life, a resting place" (Bonny, 1995b). The hymn tune often evokes spiritual and religious imagery, or a nurturing figure. The tune is repeated on violins but more defined than before. The melody is passed between the different string instruments and there is a slowing down to the end of the piece.

The Berlioz overture starts quietly, and is written in a minor mode. Initially it is fugue-like as the instruments overlap in their parts. The first section is repeated in the woodwinds and gradually it gains more volume and comes out into the open more. The melody is long and winding, like a journey is being undertaken. Even the last modal phrase leaves the listener uncertain what will follow.

The Berlioz chorus is introduced by a pastoral phrase on oboe and clarinet reminiscent of a shepherd's pipe call. The choir enters in a closely harmonized hymn-like tune that is lyrical and predictable. The tune is perfectly shaped with a climax point at the end of the third phrase, and beginning of the fourth. The oboe's shepherds call bridges into the subsequent second and third verses. Marked "pppp," the third verse creates a very tender, nurturing sound. The words of the third verse (in part) are ". . . nothing harm you, nothing alarm you, faithful pair and blessed child." A key feature is the beautiful blend of the male and female voices, providing a sense of very positive nurturing (or lack of it) in the listener. Some clients can be overwhelmed by the supportiveness of this work; others may experience sadness at having missed the tenderness in their lives.

The *Humming Chorus* follows smoothly from the Berlioz. It is scored for soprano and tenor voices, although the soprano line seems more evident in recordings. The voices hum throughout, well supported by a pizzicato bass line that gives stability, and a sense of being rocked.

The Massenet begins with a brief introduction, then the theme is introduced by cello solo. There is a slight swooping in the melody line that continues the sense of being rocked from side to side. A dialogue develops between cello and clarinet that may evoke dialogue within the imagery. The overall feeling is one of warmth and safety.

The *Songs of the Auvergne* are a collection of folk tunes from the Auvergne, and the Brezairola is a cradle song. The artist preferred by Bonny is Jill Gomez, who has a young, clear voice, free of vibrato. The slow movement of the bass line continues the secure lull of the song. There are three verses to the song—the first and third sung in a high register, while the middle verse is lower in pitch. The translation of the words (in part) are "sleep, sleep, come to the little one," (and in the last verse) "Ah, here it is at last—the child wants to sleep". (Notes, CD-EMX-9500).

## PEAK EXPERIENCE

| | |
|---|---|
| Beethoven: *Piano Concerto #5* (Adagio un poco mosso) | 6:36 |
| Vivaldi: *Gloria* (Et in Terra Pax) | 5:46 |
| *Bach: *Toccata, Adagio & Fugue in C* (Adagio), (titled Intermezzo by Ormandy) | 5:12 |
| Faure: *Requiem* (In Paradisum) | 2:56 |
| Wagner: *Lohengrin* (Prelude to Act 1) | 9:50 |
| | Total: 30:20 |

* orchestrated by Ormandy

The Beethoven is a beautiful selection to begin the program. It "gets the client into themselves in a very supportive way and is an introduction to transpersonal or positive aspects of the self" (Bonny, 1989). It commences with a gentle, muted, and sonorous string sound. The melody line rises and falls, and is supported by a pizzicato bass line. The piano enters but introduces a different theme. "When an individual instrument comes in, it is like another individual or our deeper selves speaking" (Bonny, 1989). The very light touch and pearl-like tones of the piano convey a sense of security and purity. Each phrase of the piano descends melodically, while the bass line of the piano provides support through a pattern of triplet eighth notes. In the middle section the piano part becomes more insistent with an ascending line in thirds and sixths. The piano then carries a section of ascending trills, as if transcending to a higher plane. The piano now makes a repeat of the first theme. The theme is filled out in a chordal sequence, creating more warmth. The clarinet, flute, and bassoon pick up the melody again, giving different timbral colors. There is a final section of great beauty as the piano descends slowly through a chromatic sequence of half tones, against a pizzicato string accompaniment. It is a filigree of sound barely audibly, yet superbly controlled. The movement finishes simply and quietly.

Commencing on the same note that ended the Beethoven, the Vivaldi goes into a minor key with the words "et in terra pax" (and on earth peace). There is an urgency here that is not on the first selection (Bonny, 1989). The voices are introduced in turn: bass, tenor, alto, and soprano. The accompaniment is quite sparse, with basso continuo providing a repeating pattern of the bass line, and the upper strings providing an obbligato line and middle line. The voices are in close harmony throughout, rising as the melody line dictates by stepwise movement. This section creates more intensity, but quickly reverts to the peaceful, stable pulse of the beginning. "This urgency is designed to take people more deeply into themselves or higher into themselves. This piece broadens and heightens the area of the unconscious. It can take the person deeper into material which has already been covered, or it can open up to those very positive levels, or in some people it can do both" (Bonny, 1995b).

The *Adagio* is the second movement of Bach's work for organ. The original recording Bonny used was an orchestral arrangement by Ormandy, and his score titles the selection "Intermezzo." The principal feature of the movement is the "rocking" bass sustained by the lower strings that provide security and continuity. The melody is introduced by oboe. The "reedy" quality of the oboe may evoke feelings of sadness, but the "earthy" quality also provides a grounding for the imagery experience. Throughout the movement there is a chordal accompaniment, similar to a hymn structure, and this maintains a steadiness. The coda section of the movement embodies the climax. It is announced by the strings, unison, in a dramatic falling sequence, which immediately implies a descent. The full orchestra increases in sustained intensity punctuated by the brass fortissimo, building toward a climactic point in both melody line and harmonic fullness. There is a further increase in volume on the last chord. "The coda is something of a surprise, like something from the depths comes up and says, 'look here, I want to be recognized, had you taken *this* into consideration,' The orchestra gives it all they've got. That's what we have to do in our lives—give it all we've got" (Bonny, 1989).

*In Paradisum* (may angels lead thee to Paradise) is the seventh and last section of Faure's *Requiem*. It is written for a four-part choir, accompanied by organ. The organ part has an uninterrupted flow of arpeggios, creating a sense of flowing water. Depending on the recording, there can be a child-like quality to the choral voices, suggesting an innocence. There is "an unmistakable association with church music, so it will usually bring up in the Western listener images of church, or of spirituality" (Bonny, 1989). Overall this piece has sustained tranquility and peacefulness.

The strings in high register that commence the Wagner selection blend well with the ending of the Faure. Wagner uses the high strings to set the scene for the opera *Lohengrin*, which is a story about the Holy Grail. "With the intensity of the strings he was emphasizing that it is so high, it is almost unreachable, yet he was calling to that aspect of the person as well. . . . Almost as though we *can* bring this down to earth. The Holy Grail *can* be discovered" (Bonny, 1989). Wagner himself said of the *Prelude* that it "represented the descent from heaven of a host of angels bearing the Grail, and their return to heaven" (Sadie, 2000).

The melody is first heard in the strings in high register, and is then repeated by woodwinds. With each successive repetition the register moves steadily downward. With the entry of the brass the melody is heard on cellos and string basses, giving the theme greater depth and resonance. As the trumpets take on the melody there is a building to climax point and gradual releasing from it. In the last measures of the work the strings ascend into high register again. Often the client is still in a bliss state, and Bonny (1978b) indicates that a period of silence is required at the end of this program to enable the client to integrate the experience and to return to the non-altered state of consciousness.

A further discussion can be found in Kasayka's (1988) excellent study of transpersonal experience and the *Peak Experience* music program.

## POSITIVE AFFECT

| | |
|---|---|
| Elgar: *Enigma Variations* (#8–W.N. & # 9–Nimrod) | 4:00 |
| Mozart: *Vesperae Solennes de Confessore* (Laudate Dominum) | 4:00 |
| Barber: *Adagio for Strings* | 6:21 |
| Gounod: *St. Cecilia Mass* (Offertoire and Sanctus) | 7:53 |
| Strauss, R.: *Death and Transfiguration* (excerpt) | 4:00 |
| Total: | 26:14 |

Elgar's *Variation #8* states a positive mood from the beginning. The melody line ascends, then falls back, and then ascends again. Bonny comments that "this music is pushing, then giving a little breath, as in expand-exhale-expand" (Bonny, 1995b). The woodwinds give a sense of playfulness, adding to the effectiveness of this variation as an introduction to the program.

*Variation #9, Nimrod,* commences with a slow, regal melody that is hymn-like and sustained. The strings create a full and secure tone and as the woodwinds and brass enter the sound expands, the melody and bass lines widening and building toward the peak. The tympani roll heralds the climax, and the orchestra opens out further with emphasis from trumpets to a full climactic peak that dies away quickly

In choosing the preferred soloist for Mozart's *Vesperae Solennes* Bonny liked the purity of Lucia Popp's voice. The string introduction is gentle and inviting. The soprano voice enters, almost as an extension to the strings, and with the same positive, sustaining mood. The stringed arpeggio accompaniment creates movement without overcoming the voice, so that the balance between the soloist and orchestral background is perfect. The choir enters with a harmonic version of the theme that gives a layering of support particularly with the lower voices. Each entry of the chorus is very smooth, as is the reentry of the soloist, with a long sustained note, gradually increasing in fullness, leading to the height of the phrase, then gently descending from it.

Bonny wanted to use Barber's *Adagio* as the central piece of the program and she placed the pieces on either side of it, knowing it would be the core of the program (Bonny, 1995b). The *Adagio* begins very quietly, with a meandering melody on first strings, accompanied by deep and sustained chords in the lower strings. It alternates between major and minor throughout the opening. Barber extends a long tone into the next measure as a form of syncopation, which creates anticipation and expectation (Bonny, 1995b). The basses and cellos are supportive and the second violins and violas use octave leaps to strengthen the tension. Then there is a leap of a minor tenth in the violin part, and the work has a brighter tone. The violas have a rich middle line and there is a passing back from one stringed instrument to another. A soft, gentle pulling open as celli go into deep tones is followed by an increase in tension and layering that encourages the client to open up psychologically. There is a steady crescendo, and the strings ascend into higher and higher register culminating in a series of four sustained chords, the last being held longer than one would expect (Bonny, 1995b). A long pause follows, and the strings re-enter pianissimo two octaves lower. The contrast at this point is very dramatic, from a build of sheer intensity, to a soft, beautiful sonority. There is a repeat of the opening and the work finishes with an emphasis on the final four notes.

The main characteristic of this selection is the intense build to the climax point, and the plummeting down of the strings following the climax. There are powerful dynamic changes, and the use of sustained tones creates tension but also holds the work together. The effect on the listener can be pivotal, "a catharsis-type experience, in which flood gates of feeling are opened and exposed" (Bonny, 1978b, p. 41). The listener cannot escape the intensity of the build-up to the climax, or the shrill tone of the strings in high register. The dramatic pause is full of anticipation, and with the re-entry of the strings, pianissimo, the listener may feel as if on a roller coaster. Certainly the listener is encouraged to open up.

The Gounod *Offertoire* is a respite after the intensity of Barber's *Adagio*. There is an Introduction, then the melody is heard. Each note is important, as if the melody is spoken. The tone is brighter than the *Adagio*, although the strings are muted. "There is a little push to go deeper, as if pulling back the curtains" (Bonny, 1995b).

"The *Sanctus* is probably one of the most intensely religious vocal pieces in Western music" (Bonny, 1978b, p. 41). The first chord is quite loud and may startle the client. The solo tenor enters and the strings in tremolo add tension and also support. The chorus enters providing a full, balanced tone adding another layer of support. The tenor states the second part of the theme. The chorus comes in with a layering of voices leading to the climax. Clients frequently have imagery of groups of supportive people here (Bonny, 1995b). The music stays in high register with a second peak in the violins. After the climax the intensity reduces quickly, with the flute having a final say.

The excerpt from *Death and Transfiguration* comes from the recapitulation section of the tone poem. This selection gives a final opportunity for a peak experience. It reaches "majestic and lofty heights and returns the listener to a quiet, restful ending" (Bonny, 1978b, p. 41). The selection commences with a low roll on tympani supported by long-held notes in trombone and contrabassoon. The horns build harmonically. The harp enters, making an interesting contrast. The ascending line gives a sense of climbing. The strings enter with a motif of an octave leap and stepwise progression descending (the "desire to live") theme. Descending scale passages create an interweaving that becomes more intense and there is a gradual crescendo, and a building toward a point of anticipation. The melody is heard in the full orchestra. It is the "Transfiguration" theme, a broad, sweeping line, with thick texture and rich harmonies. It builds to a climax through various repetitions—the strings sounding sweetly, and then the brass instruments enter, assisting the building to climax point. In the coda, the strings are sustained in high register, alternating with the horns and brass, and harp arpeggios, returning the client to a quiet ending.

## QUIET MUSIC

| | |
|---|---:|
| Debussy: *Danses Sacrée et Profane* | 10:30 |
| Debussy: *Prelude L'après midi d'un faune* | 11:15 |
| Holst: *The Planets* (Venus) | 8:55 |
| Vaughan Williams: *Fantasia on Greensleeves* | 4:08 |
| | Total:  34:48 |

The *Danse Sacrée* is written in a modality of d minor, and commences with a whole-tone scale theme in octaves in the strings. It immediately sets a scene of anticipation and expectation. The harp enters with the main theme also written in the whole-tone scale, and featuring parallel fifths and octaves. The atmosphere created is expansive and evocative of water and fluidity. The pizzicato in the bass line creates an ambiguity. Section 1 is more animated (en animant peu á peu), and contains a richer texture and increased dynamics, the harp part alternating between chords and running passages. Section 2 sees the return to the first theme, and the harp bridges the ending of *Danse Sacrée* into the *Danse Profane*.

There is a change in meter to waltz time (3/4) in the *Danse Profane* that may create surprise. The strings carry an interesting and pulsating rhythm in the first theme. This is repeated in the strings, then in the harp. A modification of the rhythm continues the sense of movement in a consistent manner. The harp then moves into a pattern of alternate downward and upward scale passages, against the consistent rhythm in the strings. The closing section returns to the first theme, embellished in the harp by runs and rich chords. The *Danse* ends in a flurry of movement on harp, with long drawn out chords in the strings, and finally a delicate pizzicato finish on the strings. It may depict fun and playfulness, and the two dances together are useful when demonstrating the evocative potential of music in stimulating imagery.

The *Prelude L'après midi d'un faune* (The Prelude to the Afternoon of the Faun) was inspired by Mellarme's poem, paraphrased as "a faun—a simple, sensuous, passionate being—wakens in the forest at daybreak and tries to recall his experience of the previous afternoon." The flute starts the work with a melismatic introduction that sets the pastoral, forest scene. The French horn, harp glissandi, and soft strings add to a very relaxing opening. The melody is repeated in flutes. A new section introduces a passionate theme, introduced first on the oboe, followed by a more urgent rhythmic phrase, leading to the first climax. A new theme on solo flute is supported by the woodwinds. In the middle section of the work the thematic structure is chromatic and this coupled with two-note slurs in the woodwinds increases the sense of movement and build-up of anticipation. This section shows the thickest orchestration texture of the piece. There is a return to the first theme, and a flurry of activity depicted by the oboe and later cor anglais, evoking playful imagery of the faun at the end of the day. The "cymbals antique" are introduced to provide a delicate and dreamlike quality to the music. The final section includes a short theme played by bassoons and horns together effectively, creating a nighttime atmosphere, and a quiet subsiding of energy to the end of the piece.

Holst's *Venus* (the Bringer of Peace) opens with a haunting horn-solo theme in high register. This rising theme gives a sense of hope and is developed against a descending line in the flutes. A gentle rocking pattern is developed in the horns, harps, flutes, and celeste. The opening is repeated briefly. A change in tempo (to Andante) heralds a theme in the solo violin, which is expanded by the strings against syncopated muted horns. A return to the steady secure rhythm in harps and horns is followed by a passage for solo violin, with dialogue between oboe and clarinet, and later, cello. The horn reintroduces the first theme and this is repeated by cello and muted first violins. There is a gradual increase in texture with woodwinds, harp, and horn. In the final section the celeste enhances the sense of rocking, and the piece finishes with the strings in high register, fading out. The overall effect of this piece is one of secure, steady rocking, which is deepened by the haunting themes, often on muted horn.

The Vaughan Williams arrangement of the familiar English folk tune "Greensleeves" is written in 6/8 in the Dorian mode on F. It maintains a gentle, lilting rhythm throughout. The flutes provide an introduction to the theme, creating a pastoral mood. The melody is then introduced on second violins and violas, providing a rich and secure sound. A middle section is introduced by a sforzando chord in the strings, and another folk tune, "Lovely Joan," is introduced. This melody is repeated by the flutes with plucked strings giving a sense of movement. The flute cadenza leads into a repeat of the first theme on violas and cellos (giving a deeper quality than at the start of the piece) and with harp accompaniment. The piece comes to a quiet close. The familiarity of the Greensleeves melody is useful in helping the client to bring imagery to a close. For some clients the Greensleeves melody can be a little trite.

# RELATIONSHIPS

| | |
|---|---:|
| Pierne: *Concertstück for Harp and Orchestra* | 14:15 |
| Rachmaninoff: *Symphony # 2* (Adagio) | 10:00 |
| Respighi: *The Fountains of Rome*: | 9:00 |
|     Valle Giulia at Dawn | |
|     Villa Medici at Sunset | |

Total:  33:15

The Pierne *Concertstück* features three different sections, and within each there are two themes. These themes are developed throughout the work, on solo harp and on different orchestral instruments, and with each repetition different colors are conveyed, and as such the work is typically Impressionistic. The first section, Allegro Moderato, is written in 12/8 time. There is an extended introduction in which violas and cellos introduce the first theme, repeated and interspersed with harp arpeggios. The harp introduces the second theme of this section, with a broad flowing line, and it is repeated on horns. Strings and woodwind introduce another expressive theme, which builds to a climax. There is dialogue between the different themes, heard on strings, harp, and cellos, and eventually a gradual accelerando and crescendo build to an impassioned climax. A harp cadenza (at approximately 5:10 minutes) is exceptionally quiet and in high register, creating a veiled sense of anticipation. A new section (Andante) is introduced in 3/4 time. The first theme of this section is an expansive romantic theme, and is repeated by harp, then developed by various sections of the orchestra. The second melody of the Andante section features dotted rhythms that suggests playfulness. The Allegretto scherzando section is introduced by a new melody (also featuring a dotted rhythm) accompanied by strings pizzicato. The strings and woodwinds take over and there is a building to a climax based on the romantic theme (at approximately 12:30 minutes). There is further development of the earlier themes and the harp re-enters to herald the finale. A harp cadenza follows, and this has greater flourish than before, but soon moves into quiet, fast arpeggio passages. The harp solo plays a quiet recapitulation of the romantic theme, and a final flourish leads into a loud ending.

The Rachmaninoff commences with a "ritornello," an introductory theme heard on the violins. The violas, carrying a relentless eighth-note accompaniment, provide the middle texture. The clarinet solo enters with a beautiful melody of twenty-three measures. It is a meandering theme but enhanced by the rich harmonies created by the strings. It is repeated with a countermelody in the bassoon. The melody continues on with two interrupted cadences, which forestall the ending of the melody. The strings develop the theme in a rich, tightly textured sound. In the middle section of the movement there are question/answer motifs, which are tossed between different woodwind instruments—particularly the bassoon and oboe—and answered by the orchestra. There is a gradual build toward a climax, increasing in intensity and emotion. The climax fades quickly, and after a brief moment of silence, the horn enters with the ritornello theme, repeated by clarinet. The strings restate the first theme with the countermelody in the horns. There is much repetition, as if to reassure the listener that everything will be fine. The movement is highly romantic in its harmonic sequences, and some listeners may recognize the popular song "Never going to fall in love again," which was inspired by the ritornello theme.

Respighi's *The Fountains of Rome* consists of four depictions of well-known fountains. The first and fourth are included to end the *Relationships* program. The main feature of the Valle Giulia is the muted strings in continual movement. The melody is heard on oboe, and developed by clarinet, and bird calls are heard on oboe. The strings continue to provide a wash of sound over which the clarinet and flutes carry the melody line. The overall sense is a pastoral scene, with the strings creating the sound of flapping wings of the birds, and woodwinds in a descending passage depict birds in flight. The selection ends with the strings in high register, tremolo, and the clarinet sounding the last of the melody.

The fountain of Villa Medici begins with the flute and clarinet playing the melody, and celeste and harp providing a shimmering accompaniment. The overall mood is one of peace and calm. Bells chime out softly, suggesting the end of the day. A warm melody heard in cellos is answered by celeste and strings, then bird calls are heard. The descending passage of woodwinds and strings helps bring the music back to the ground. The bells chime once more, the flute plays its final tune, and the movement ends very softly and very gently.

## SERENITY

| | |
|---|---|
| Vaughan Williams: *Fantasia on a Theme by Thomas Tallis* | 16:15 |
| Mahler: *Symphony #4* (Ruhevoll) | 23:10 |
| Total: | 39:25 |

The principal feature of the *Fantasia* is that it is written for three different groupings of string players—a string orchestra, a group of nine players who are seated at the front of the orchestra, and a quartet. Therefore the interchange between the three groups creates a sense of dialogue between the instruments, and this may be seen in the imagery experiences of clients. There is a tentative beginning as the strings start in high register and move down, against the lower string moving up, as if a very wide expansiveness is narrowing. The lower bass strings introduce the theme played pizzicato. On repetition the pizzicato notes sound like footsteps (Bonny, 1996). The strings playing in unison add emphasis and intentionality, like a statement is made, or a calling forth. The theme is repeated in the cellos, and its modal quality may evoke imagery of an ancient scene. There is a shift between major and minor and more intensity unfolds, broadening the view and culminating in a strong sense of grandeur and openness. There is a brief moment of reflection before a surprising minor chord and a modal melody is heard, moving between the various string groups (the string orchestra, the group of nine players, and the quartet). A hymn-like tune is introduced, followed by an introspective viola solo. Violin and viola dialogue, then the cello enters. A further section of dialogue and contrast is heard between the three groups of players, leading to the climax. There is a release of the tension, as the texture thins and soft phrases are contrasted with sharp chords. The melody returns on solo violin and other strings come in with repetition in the lower instruments. Another change is slower and mysterious, and the listener may sense the end is coming. The work ends on a major chord.

A pizzicato bass opens the Mahler, creating a sense of moving forward. This can be reassuring after the changeable uncertainty of the Vaughan Williams. There is a yearning quality to the melody heard in cellos, and repeated by oboe. The string sound is warm and secure, and there is an overall feeling of rest and calm. The harp adds a rocking rhythm, leading into a contrasting section with second theme heard on oboe solo. The violins introduce a tender melody created by a sliding between intervals. The tempo picks up with a brief melody on horns, and a repeat of the tender melody, followed by a more exaggerated sliding in strings and brass. A playful bridge section leads into the Allegretto grazioso section. There is a different quality to this section, like a dance movement and an interweaving of violins, cellos, and woodwinds that can help in integrating the imagery. The unusual blend of oboe, cor anglais, and horn introduce a section of contrasting color and tone. A return to the playful theme contrasts with the serious sections. The full orchestra with brass and tympani adds weight, and expansiveness. The minor chord resolves to the major, then back to minor, then back to major, suggesting that more is to come.

A new section is introduced. The strings return to the bright dance melody and playful trills in violins and flutes encourage the tempo faster and faster to a quick climax. The French horn gives a sober tone and the first theme is re-stated with long sustained notes drawing out the progression. There is a sense that the ending is coming, but instead, there is a surprising octave leap in strings, fortissimo, and matched by brass, with strong rhythmic beating on tympani. This is a triumphal celebratory statement, as if to receive a reward after a long struggle. A reflective statement of the melody is heard on strings, and suddenly there is a key change and the strings move into high register, "like moving into the clouds" (Bonny, 1996). There is long drawn out finish.

## TRANSITIONS

| | | |
|---|---|---:|
| Strauss, R.: *Ein Heldenleben* (excerpt part 6) | | 8:04 |
| Brahms: *Symphony #3* (Poco allegretto) | | 5:29 |
| Beethoven: *Symphony #9* (Adagio molto e cantabile) | | 14:47 |
| Brahms: *Piano Concerto #2* (Andante piu Adagio) | | 14:29 |
| | Total: | 42:49 |

The excerpt from Strauss' tone poem *"A Hero's Life"* begins with a steady, almost threatening drum beat, while the cor anglais plays a pastoral theme based on the Hero's Theme. There is a change of time signature (to 6/8), and the strings, together with the full complement of horns, introduce a serene melody depicting the Hero's Contentment. At section 103 of the score there is a brief reprisal of the Hero's Battle Theme, but Bonny made a cut in the music excluding sections 103-106. The cut is completely disguised in the mastering of the program, nevertheless the tremolo in the strings at section 103, lasting only three measures is sufficient for clients to image an emerging storm. At section 106 the solo violin, depicting the Hero's Helpmate, returns with a rather plaintive melody of consolation. A restatement of the love theme (from the Hero's Helpmate) is asserted on horns, and the work closes with the strings ascending against descending horns, giving a sense of opening out. A coda of eight measures increases the dynamics to a fortissimo ending.

    The first theme of the Brahms is introduced by cellos. This is repeated by the violins and later by the horns and woodwinds. The orchestration throughout is thick, with the strings providing triplet figures in middle register. The Trio section commences with a melody played by the woodwinds, and characterized by two-note slurs over the bar line. The cellos add a syncopated accompaniment, giving the effect of a gentle rocking. The strings then introduce a gentle second theme. Both themes are repeated and there is a bridge to the restatement of the Minuet. The first theme of the Minuet is heard this time on the horn, then by the oboe (over plucked string accompaniment). The remainder of this lyrical Minuet is a straightforward repetition with a short coda.

The first theme of the Beethoven is played by strings mezza voce, a gentle, still melody which creates a feeling of security and predictability. The second theme is introduced at the Andante moderato, in the key of D major. It is also played by strings, and as the melody unfolds the woodwinds punctuate and amplify the high points of the melody line. This theme produces a sense of movement, almost like a dance theme. A return to Tempo 1 and the key of Bb major introduces a long variation on the first theme played by first violins, with cellos playing pizzicato. A return to Andante sees the repeat of the second theme, this time in the key of G major. This section is characterized by very long phrases of sixteenth notes in the violins giving constant movement. A new section (Adagio) is introduced in the key of Eb major and the first theme is heard in the clarinet. A further change of tempo (Lo stesso tempo) and key change to Bb major introduces another long variation on the first theme, with the theme heard in the woodwinds and the strings providing an elaborate accompanying line in relentless sixteenth notes. There is a dramatic change in mood as the coda heralds a dotted rhythm passage on brass. There is a return to the variation pattern (woodwinds with the melody and strings accompanying), then a repetition of the dotted rhythm heralded by the brass. In what appears to be a third coda, the tympani sound out a consistent beat over which the strings and woodwind draw out the final bars.

The cello opens the third movement of the Brahms *Piano Concerto* with a beautiful melody in middle register, giving a deeply sonorous feel to the music. When the piano finally enters, it presents quite different material to the main theme—a piano solo lasting ten measures. The orchestra reenters and restates the first theme, the piano providing a dramatic interplay with characteristic thick chord sequences. Within the music structure, there is a solo instrument playing its own theme, and the orchestra as background. In the middle section, Piu Adagio, the clarinet introduces a second theme. The theme is carried by the strings, and then leads into the recapitulation with a return of the cello melody. The movement finishes with the piano elaborating on an ascending melodic line with long trills. Throughout this movement there is a beautiful blend of the sonorous cello and the piano as complementary instruments. The overall feeling of this music is of a quiet, still, contemplative mood.

## REVISIONS TO THE BONNY PROGRAMS

In 1994, Helen Bonny and Linda Keiser Mardis made revisions to the *Comforting/Anaclytic* and *Nurturing* programs, and created two new programs entitled *Caring* and *Recollections*.

## CARING

| | |
|---|---|
| Haydn: *Cello Concerto in C* (Adagio) | 9:43 |
| Puccini: *Madame Butterfly* (Humming Chorus) | 3:07 |
| Debussy: *String Quartet in g minor* (Andantino . . . ) | 7:41 |
| Bach: *Christmas Oratorio,* Sinfonia, Part II, BWV 248 | 9:30 |
| Dvorak: *Serenade in E major* (Larghetto) | 6:06 |
| Warlock: *Capriol Suite* (Pied-en-l'air) | 2:13 |

Total:  38:20

The Haydn and Puccini are described under *Comforting/Anaclytic* and *Nurturing* respectively. The new selections are the Debussy, Bach, Dvorak and Warlock.

The Debussy starts with a mournful but sweet melody, played on muted strings. A middle section is introduced with a viola solo, supported by open fifth chords on the other strings. A second theme on viola, and repeated on cello, is more impassioned and dissonant. As the middle section increases in tempo there is a build to a restatement of the theme as the quartet opens out. There is a quiet return to the opening section, ending "as quietly as possible."

The Bach *Sinfonia* is written in 12/8 time with a lilting melody that suggests a pastoral scene. A chorus of four oboes is featured in the middle section, giving a reedy quality that contrasts with the strings. The two timbres alternate throughout

The Dvorak has a descending melodic line, and a yearning romantic quality to the opening section. The middle section has more movement, with sudden sforzando chords, and pizzicato melodic line. The repeat of the first section is more fully harmonized and the pizzicato bass line adds more movement than at the beginning.

The Pied-en-l'air is a beautiful lullaby in 9/4 time. A very sweet melody is played by strings, with rich harmonizations provided by suspended cadences. The melody is repeated, but with variation through the use of chromatic harmonies. The overall feeling is of complete rest and comfort.

## RECOLLECTIONS

| | |
|---|---|
| Sibelius: The *Swan of Tuonela* | 7:50 |
| Villa-Lobos: *Bachianas Brasilieras #5* | 5:53 |

| | |
|---|---|
| Boccherini: *Cello Concerto in B* flat, Adagio | 6:57 |
| Glinka: *The Life for the Tzar*, Susanin Aria | 5:20 |
| Mussorgski: *The Spirit of Heaven* (song) | 3:15 |
| Canteloube (arr.): *Songs of the Auvergne*, Bailero | 5:19 |
| Britten: *Simple Symphony*, Sentimental Sarabande | 7:10 |
| | Total: 41:44 |

The Sibelius, Villa-Lobos, Boccherini, and Glinka are described under *Comforting/Anaclytic*, and the Britten is described under *Nurturing*. The new selections are the Mussorgski and Canteloube.

The Mussorgski song follows the Glinka aria, and offers a different male voice quality. Sung in Russian and accompanied by piano playing tremolo almost throughout, the song is a lament—a "silent passage of sorrow." The middle section of the song is filled with great emotion, followed by a repeat of the first section. Toward the ending of the song the sobbing in the voice carries even more emotion. Clients may experience a strong transference to the voice quality and the emotionally-laden performance.

The Bailero is a love song, sung to a shepherd boy across the water. There is a gentle lulling to the song, and the oboe may convey a pastoral scene. The piano plays an important role with ascending and descending rippling passages that depict the water. The Bailero provides a gentle and loving finish to the program.

## OTHER REVISIONS
## TO THE BONNY PROGRAMS

Other revisions to the Bonny music programs were made with the development of "*Music for the Imagination*," a collection of ten CDs compiled by Bruscia. The impetus for the CDs came from the problems associated with copyright laws, which prohibited the selling of the Bonny music programs on cassette tapes. Bruscia entered into an agreement with the recording label Naxos, and compiled the music programs using existing recordings made by Naxos. Inevitably not all the selections on Bonny's programs were available on Naxos, and Bruscia made substitutions for some selections thereby creating modified versions of the programs (Bruscia, 1996).

## ADDITIONAL ORIGINAL PROGRAMS

Over the sixteen-year period that Bonny developed her eighteen programs, GIM therapists designed other music programs for use in Guided Imagery and Music sessions. These programs are listed in Appendices at the end of the book.

## *References*

Bonny, H. L. (1978a). *Facilitating GIM sessions. GIM Monograph #1.* Baltimore, MD: ICM Books.

Bonny, H. L. (1978b). *The role of taped music programs in the GIM process. GIM Monograph #2.* Baltimore, MD: ICM Books.

Bonny, H. L. (1980). *GIM Therapy: Past, Present and Future Implications. GIM Monograph #3.* Baltimore, MD: ICM Books.

Bonny, H. B. (1987). Unpublished handwritten notes.

Bonny, H. B. (1989). Interview with Helen Bonny and Roseanne Kasayka.

Bonny, H. B. (1995a). *Advanced GIM Discography.* Unpublished paper.

Bonny, H. B. (1995b). Interview October 17.

Bonny, H. B. (1996). Interview, January 18.

Bonny, H. B. and Keiser Mardis, L. (1994). *Music Resources for GIM Facilitators.* Olney, MD. Archedigm Publications.

Bruscia, K. (1996). *Music for the Imagination: Rationale, Implications and Guidelines for Its Use in Guided Imagery and Music (GIM).* Santa Cruz, CA: Association for Music and Imagery.

Fjeldsoe, M. (2000). Notes. Dacapo CD 8.224156.

Institute for Consciousness and Music (ICM) (1976). *Newsletter,* 3, (2) Spring. Baltimore, MD: Author.

Institute for Consciousness and Music (ICM) (1979). *Newsletter,* 6, (3) Fall. Baltimore, MD: Author.

Kasayka, R. E. (1988). *To Meet and Match the Moment of Hope: Transpersonal Elements of the Guided Imagery and Music Experience.* Unpublished paper. Savage, MD: Institute for Music and Imagery.

Sadie, S. (ed.) (2000). *Wagner and His Operas.* The New Grove Composers Series, London. Macmillan.

# Part Two:

# Applications

*Chapter Seven*

# GUIDED IMAGERY AND MUSIC WITH CHILDREN AND ADOLESCENTS

## Susan B. Wesley

Since its inception, Guided Imagery and Music (GIM) has been used in individual and group settings, with diverse populations, and for a variety of therapeutic, educational, and developmental purposes. Central to the method are a preliminary conversation, a relaxation and induction, a music-imaging experience, a return to an alert state, and a closing conversation or processing of the images (Bonny, 1978). In the individual form, the traveler maintains an ongoing dialogue with the guide while imaging to the music, whereas in the traditional group form, the travelers image without such a dialogue.

While GIM is used predominately with adults, it may also be used quite effectively with children and adolescents. Certain modifications are necessary however, in both goal and method. The purpose of the present chapter is to examine how GIM has been used with children and adolescents, starting with the original model (Bonny & Savary, 1973), and then examining further expansions of that model. This will be accomplished by reviewing a small but growing collection of studies using GIM with children and adolescents, four to eighteen years old. Settings for these studies have included public and private schools, Head Start programs, special education units, and medical and psychiatric in-patient settings. All of the studies describe practical applications of GIM with this population. Within these studies is a select few which have attempted research applications for GIM with children/adolescents.

## THE ORIGINAL MODEL

The original model for using GIM with children was developed by Bonny and Savary (1973). The suggested setting was a school music appreciation classroom, which they felt was a natural place for children to learn new ways of listening to music. The purpose of the model was to help children foster a "heightened awareness and a fresh sense of reality" (p. 138). The model involves the same procedural components as the group GIM for adults, however, with the following suggestions and guidelines.

First, children need to be adequately prepared for the experience through a complete explanation of the process, followed by opportunities to ask whatever questions may arise. Second, the class period must be carefully planned so that there is sufficient time for the preliminary conversation, induction, music listening, return and processing of the experience. Third, the relaxation and induction should be appropriate to their attentional needs and interests. Sample induction themes suggested by the authors include a trip to a favorite place, an adventure in outer space, and scenes in nature. Finally, when selecting the music, the teacher should try out the music in a relaxed state prior to using it with children. The length of the music program should be geared to the age of the children. Shorter programs (five to ten minutes) are most appropriate for younger children. The music program should be consistent in mood. Music that may suggest negative moods should be avoided. The recordings should be of high quality.

The following are examples of music found effective with school-age children: Grofe, *Grand Canyon Suite*; Holst, *Planets* (all but Mars and Saturn); Dukas, *Sorcerer's Apprentice*; Prokofiev, *Peter and the Wolf*; Rimski-Korsakov, *Scheherezade*; Stravinsky, *Petrouchka*; Strauss, R., *Til Eulenspiegel*; Tchaikovsky, *Swan Lake* and *The Nutcracker;* Bizet, *Carmen*; Humperdinck, *Hansel and Gretel*; Menotti, *Amahl and the Night Visitors*; Verdi, *Aida*; Debussy, *Afternoon of a Faun*; Copland, *Appalachian Spring*

## BEYOND THE ORIGINAL MODEL

In the twenty-seven years since Bonny and Savary offered the first model of GIM with children, music appreciation classrooms have continued to be a venue. In addition to Head Start programs, special education units, correctional facilities, and medical and psychiatric in-patient hospitals. A literature search conducted electronically and by hand revealed eleven articles. Two may be considered as research-related, and the remaining nine are informational papers or applications reports. In addition, six recorded music programs also surfaced. Aside from their value as teacher resources, these programs provide insight into which music selections have remained as "standards" when using group GIM with children and what new music has been introduced. The review that follows is intended to provide the reader with basic information on the populations, settings, goals, formats, choices of music, outcomes, and modifications found in this literature.

## Regular School Classrooms

Summer (1981) developed a model for using GIM in regular classrooms. The goal was to help children engage the "whole brain." Citing the dangers of an exclusively left brain approach to education in the schools, Summer proposed an antidote of various right-brain activities such as free movement, deep breathing and fantasy, all within the context of GIM. She used a two-step tuning-up process. Step one is relaxation. Step two brings the class together through music and imagination using group drawing, free movement, movement prefaced with an induction, storytelling, and imagery. The imagery exercise Summer outlines is like that of the Bonny and Savary model (1973) where there is a relaxation, induction, music listening, and processing. She suggests the following music for Imagery: Debussy, *Danses Sacred and Profane*—forest; Beethoven, *Eighth Symphony* (Second movement)—meadow and brook; Debussy, *Prelude to the Afternoon of a Faun.*

Summer also provided suggestions for active physical imaginal work. In her "Free Movement" model, she suggests walking to the beat of the music and then considering what else the music might suggest for movement. Music suggested for this approach includes: Poulenc, *Piano Concerto*; Beethoven, *Third Symphony* (Fourth movement); Schubert, *Arpeggione Sonata* (First movement).

In the "Group Storytelling" model either a child or the teacher initiates an opening and then ask the others to continue the story based on how the music inspires their imaginations. Summer suggested the following music for group story telling: Bartok, *Concerto for Orchestra* (First and second movements); and Ponchielli, *La Gioconda* (Dance of the Hours).

The "Movement with Imagery" model is similar to the free movement model except that the teacher provides an induction appropriate to the music such as: a bud beginning to open in spring time for Wagner's, *Tristan and Isolde* (Love/Death); a nobleman or woman at a coronation for Wagner's, Prelude to *Der Meistersiger*; or an animal of the forest for Beethoven's, *Eighth Symphony* (First movement). Music selections for this model include: Berlioz, *Symphonie Fantastique* (Second movement); Beethoven, *Eighth Symphony* (Third movement) and the *Fifth Symphony* (First movement). She suggests asking the children to "close their eyes and let the music go through their ears and come out their crayons" (p. 49).

In a later publication Summer (1988) briefly mentions two actual settings for her work with GIM and disadvantaged but normal children. She comments on the use of subject appropriate inductions such as one with animals. She explained that by asking the children in her Head Start and settlement music school programs to draw an animal of their choice prior to the induction, it provided a necessary grounding to the music and imaging experience and facilitated their sharing of imagery through movement, acting, or storytelling. Summer also references the use of a GIM-related activity for which she used a "markedly shortened version of Wagner's *Ring of the Nibelungen*" (p.34).

Gregoire et al. (1989) used a modified form of GIM with eleven fourth-grade students who attended the resource room for gifted students at a public elementary school. Their aim was to assess the effect of "creative listening" and other Orff-based music activities on the self-concept of these students. Creative listening was defined as "a type of GIM experience in which a scene is suggested to begin imagery, followed by a musical selection for imagery development" (p. 25). The listening experiences began with a relaxation of breathing, yawning, and stretching followed by an induction related to a spaceman, inventor, nature, or zoo. Then a single music selection was played and the students wrote or drew in response to the music. The music selections and images were chosen from the Bonny and Savary recording *Creative Listening,* Volume I: They are:

- Spaceman's Message: Bach, *Sinfonia to Cantata 29*;
- Uncle Euler's Invention: Dukas, *The Sorcerer's Apprentic)*;
- Mother Nature: Grofe, *Grand Canyon* (Sunrise); and
- Zoo Safari: Holst, *The Planets* (Uranus).

The listening activity generated the material which was then the basis for the Orff activities. For example, after listening to the Bach, the children were asked to write down what they heard as the message from the spaceman. Based on the messages a chant was developed and also became the initial activity for the second session where additional Orff chants were developed. The only other reference to the creative listening experiences was a mention of the "Zoo Safari." In this experience, the authors explain that the "children drew the animal they brought back in their imagery, named it, and chose an instrument to make its sound" (p. 26).

Grindel (1989) described the use of GIM in exploring creativity in children, seven to nine years of age. The nine children selected for the project were identified as withdrawn or highly guarded. Her goals for the children were to demonstrate "an increased sense of self-worth through the sharing of their creative experiences with music and imagination through drawing, movement, constructions and discussion" (p. 152)

The GIM format was again like that of the Bonny and Savary model (1973), including: gathering talk; centering exercise of autogenic relaxation; induction with specific theme; imaging with a single selection of music from two to eight minutes in length; drawing, painting, constructing, or moving; and discussion. Grindel expanded the induction by using props such as colored scarves, shells, and stones. She also expanded the response to imagery by using various media such as oil and chalk pastels, water color paints (sessions 1–4), individual movement in fabric tubes, movement within specified space of thirty-six-inch hoops (sessions 5 & 6), and group construction where children selected group members to build a structure from the imagery (session 7). She also encouraged immediate active response to the music, having the children use scarves, hoops, fabric tubes, etc. to move about the room while the celebratory music played. Each session always concluded with a group discussion.

The music and inductions used by Grindel included:

- Holst, *Planets* (Venus): A flower growing in a field; landing a hot-air balloon and exploring the environment;
- Holst, *Planets* (Mercury): Using a colored scarf as magic carpet and exploring outer space; using a colorful scarf as a raft and exploring the sea;
- Mussorgsky, *Pictures at an Exhibition* (Ballet of the Unhatched Chicks): Using a polished stone to imagine a small creature who might live near or under it;
- Vaughan Williams, *Fantasy on Greensleeves*: Using a shell to explore what a creature might experience living in that environment;
- Vollenweider, *Down to the Moon* (Moon Dance, and Steam Forest): Landing on a planet and observing the constructions;
- Holst, *Planets* (Uranus): Celebration.

Roy (1996–1997) used GIM in a high school music appreciation class to foster personal growth, provide a creative outlet, provide stress reduction, and build self-esteem. Roy examined the imagery of nine participants chosen from among a pool of about seventy-five sophomores enrolled in a private all-girls school.

The session format included time for students to briefly describe their feeling state before the activity, then a relaxation exercise was provided. This was followed by the induction, music listening to a single selection, a written response to imagery, and an optional discussion about the imagery. The nine selected students were asked to provide a written autobiography; participate in an interview after the fifth session; and complete a set of questions six months post sessions.

The music chosen for the sessions included: Pachelbel, *Canon in D*; Copland, *Appalachian Spring*; Pierne, *Concertstucke*; Elgar, *Enigma Variations* 8 & 9; Brahms, *Second Piano Concerto* (Allegro non troppo); Britten, *Simple Symphony* (Sentimental Sarabande); Vaughan Williams, *Rhosymedre, Prelude*; Berlioz, *L'Enfance du Christ* (Shepherd's Farewell Chorus); Puccini, *Madama Butterfly* (Humming Chorus); Beethoven, *Fifth Piano Concerto* (Adagio); Vivaldi, *Gloria* (Et in Terra Pax); and Haydn, *Cello Concerto in C* (Adagio).

Roy gave detailed information on one of her student's experiences and then summarized follow-up evaluations of four additional students. She concluded that:

> GIM seemed to be a very good tool for these students in focusing their midway point in Sophomore year. Holidays, school life, personal experiences, the past, the present, and the future all combined to affect these GIM sessions in a school setting. GIM permits students to delve more deeply into themselves. If schools are to model learning and learning includes how to prioritize values, what better forum than to value one's self through GIM? While GIM unveils the discoveries of self, the trained educator/GIM guide can foster the growth process of the student, in a school system that looks to this kind of education" (p. 74).

## Special Education Classrooms

Ventre (1981) was one of the first to explore the therapeutic potential of GIM in a special education setting. Her purpose was to explore the effects of GIM on autistic children. Working in individual rather than group sessions, Ventre added improvisational music therapy to the GIM session, using the improvisation as a means of assessing feeling tone at the start of the session when verbal skills were unavailable. Relaxation techniques were expanded to include the option of physical massage of the limbs, neck, and back as well as a "tense-release" progression. When appropriate, Ventre asked the child to bring their identified feeling state "to the mat" and allow the music to help them explore it.

Because the physical space available for these sessions was often noisy, Ventre and the client used headphones to listen to the music. The music programs lasted ten to twenty minutes. The listening material was taken from the standard GIM repertoire based on the child's presented feeling-tone. Selections listed by Ventre include: Haydn, *Cello Concerto in C* (Adagio); Sibelius, *Swan of Tuonela*; Villa-Lobos, *Bachianas Brasileiras No. 5*; Boccherini, *Cello*

*Concerto in B* (Adagio); Britten, *Simple Symphony* (Sentimental Saraband); Vaughan Williams, *Rhosymedre Prelude*; Berlioz, *L'Enfance du Christ*, (Shepherd's Farewell Chorus); Puccini, *Madama Butterfly* (Humming Chorus); Massenet, *Scenes Alsacienne* (Sous les Tilleuls); Canteloube, *Songs of the Auvergne* (Brezairola); Ravel, *Daphnes and Chloe* (excerpt); Brahms, *First Symphony* (Allegretto): Brahms, *Third Symphony* (Poco Allegretto), Brahms, *Second Piano Concerto* (Allegro non troppo); Respighi, *Pines of Rome,* (Giancola); Elgar, *Enigma Variations, No. 8 & 9*; Mozart, *Vesperae Solmes*, (Laudate Dominum); Barber, *Adagio for Strings*; Gounod, *St. Cecilia Mass* (Offertoire, Sanctus); and Strauss, *The Hero's Life* (excerpt).

Ventre concluded that through the use of GIM with the six autistic boys ages eight to sixteen, there was a marked decrease in stereotypical behaviors and hyperactivity; increase in attention span; increase in ability to follow one-and two-step directions; increase in eye contact; increase in self-initiated meaningful nonverbal and verbal communications.

Ten years later, Elliot (1991) explored another use of GIM with ten students identified as having special needs. Her unpublished report includes an overview of fourteen sessions conducted with children who were identified as behaviorally disturbed and who received non-mainstreamed instruction at the local state hospital. Elliot's format was similar to that of the original Bonny and Savary model (1973). She used a check-in for identifying participant feeling states. Her relaxation activities included autogenic or tension-release exercises. For inductions, Elliot used fantasy settings such as a meadow or staircase as well as the Dr. Seuss book *Oh the Places You'll Go.* An induction often became a narrative accompanying the music selection. Elliot described her music listening selections as new age, jazz, or classical recordings from two to twenty minutes in length. Like Bonny and Savary, Elliot emphasized that knowing the music well was of great importance. The processing of imagery for Elliot was individual or group drawing. The last component of each session was a discussion. She also expanded student access to the in-class experiences by providing relaxation and induction tapes for out-of-session use.

Elliott's therapeutic intentions were to increase the success of the mainstreaming program measured by the number of hours a child could maintain in a regular classroom; increase student ability to identify and express underlying issues which affect success in the mainstreaming process; improve student introspective skills; increase ability to use verbal counseling; and decrease stress by increasing relaxation skills

Wager (1992) used GIM in a specialized classroom setting for emotionally disturbed children. Her therapeutic intention was to build skills that the children needed for healthy ego development. Wager emphasized the necessity of concrete explanations for the children and step-by-step instructions. She spent considerable time in teaching progressive muscle relaxation techniques using music with very little dynamic or timbre variation. Later she shifted to music selections with greater variety with the induction of imaging a "safe place." Music selections named in her article included Halpern, *Spectrum Suite*; Debussy, *Danses Sacred and Profane*, and Bonny's *Children's Imagery Tape*.

Wager also used the *Children's Imagery* tape for individual thirty-minute GIM sessions. These were offered to children who had good contact with reality, were responsive to music, and liked art. Again, Wager used progressive muscle relaxation or deep breathing, but the inductions were most often from the tape. She suggested that some children benefited from the prompt of a specific story scene even before the induction. The children used the music selection to draw or construct what they imaged from the music.

Wager concluded that GIM enabled children to express the emotional issues important to them, while also helping to reduce anxiety and increase trust in the adult teacher. It also provided an opportunity for the children to practice imaginative and creative play skills. Wager emphasized that GIM should not be used indiscriminately with children and that individual sessions, when effectively applied, could be a helpful process for assisting traumatized children to work through memories of past traumas.

## Institutional Settings

CORRECTIONAL CENTER. Skaggs (1997) used GIM with adolescent male sex offenders in a correctional institution and describes her approach as a group music-centered therapy that was provided once weekly for sixty minutes in addition to other therapies. She modified the individual GIM technique for group application and used only one short piece of music. A group processing time followed. Sometimes art materials were included for increased processing particularly when a patient's own victimization surfaced. Skaggs emphasized the need to build trust with the adolescents and she accomplished this by teaching relaxation techniques and assisting the boys to find an inner imaginal safe place. Two music selections were cited in the article. Vivaldi's, *Guitar Concerto in D*, RV 93 was identified as the piece which assisted the boys to identify their "safe place" and Saint-Saens, "The Swan" from *The Carnival of the Animals*, was used after a drawing exercise focused on personal victimization.

Skaggs (1997) concluded that "Although many approaches have been tried in the treatment of juvenile sex offenders, with varying degrees of success, music and other creative arts therapies have been underused. Preliminary empirical data indicate promising results from the use of these modalities" (p. 78).

MEDICAL HOSPITAL. There are only a few published studies which discuss various hospital settings for GIM work with children. Fagen (1982) suggested that GIM be used with terminally ill children along with other forms of music therapy. She felt that the use of music listening activities involving guided imagery could encourage the withdrawn or apathetic patient to personalize her/his thoughts by thinking of favorite places and remembering such special and positive feelings.

PSYCHIATRIC HOSPITAL. Wesley (2001) used GIM individually with three boys, aged six, seven and ten, on a locked unit of a psychiatric hospital. The sessions were twenty to thirty minutes, meeting weekdays for eight weeks. Each session, for the seven- and ten-year olds, began with singing a song identified as "my song". This served as a focus for usually high energy. The song was followed by a choice of colored scarf to be used as a cocoon, raft, balloon, tent, or magic carpet. A brief autogenic relaxation was provided and the induction choices revolved around sitting by a small pond, looking out from a mountaintop, feeling the sun on the cocooned caterpillar, or standing on a shore looking out to sea.

Each boy would often identify the preferred induction and that was paired with a particular music selection. The pairing was also done by the patient, since they would ask for a particular piece of music based on a previous experience with it. For example, Dexter and Bearns' *Cathedral Sunrise* and Harris and Mendietta's *Crystal Creek* were often selected if a pond or cocoon induction was requested. Respighi's *The Nightingale* and *Birth of Venus* were often chosen if the mountain or ocean induction were used. Grieg's *Cradle Song* became the fishing pond for the seven-year-old. The processing after imagery was often done through drawing and discussion.

The six-year-old chose to start his sessions most often by being a purple cloud and using the music as a breathing relaxation. His processing was with drawing and a brief story. The music selection used most often was Thompson, *Alert Relaxation*.

Wesley's goal for the GIM experience in this setting was not unlike that of Bonny and Savary (1973): to heighten awareness and provide a fresh sense of reality. For severely traumatized children a heightened sense of awareness of victimization is their sense of reality. By using GIM and expanding the repertoire of positive imagery through music these three boys acquired additional coping skills for daily living.

# RECORDED MUSIC PROGRAMS

Recorded music programs have been created to facilitate music and imagery experiences for children and adolescents. Some have narration and some do not. Generally, the focus for such programs may be relaxation, enhanced creativity and increased intelligence. What follows is a synopsis of six recorded music programs which specify the GIM process for children and/or adolescents.

## Creative Listening I-II

Bonny and Savary (1973) collaborated on creating recorded music programs for children, the result being a set called *Creative Listening I-II* (1973 &1974). The programs were available on LP through the Institute for Consciousness and Music (ICM). These recordings provided several music selections, each prefaced with a story or viable scene which were intended to provide new ways of listening to music. *Creative Listening I* included familiar classical music selections, coupled with specific imagery inductions:

- Spaceman's Message: Bach, *Sinfonia to Cantata 29*;
- Uncle Euler's Invention: Dukas, *The Sorcerer's Apprentice)*;
- Mother Nature: Grofe, *Grand Canyon* (Sunrise);
- On a Raft: Smetana, *Ma Vlast* (The Modau);
- Undersea Jourey: Sibelius, *Second Symphony* (Lento);
- Zoo Safari: Holst, *The Planets* (Uranus).

*Creative Listening II* provided a dance orientation to world cultures and also included a "surprise journey." Most music selections on volume two come from folk-song literature. The theme for side A was Dancing around the World with folk tunes from: the Caribbean Islands *(Mummies)*, Rhodesia *(Kumakudo)*, Ireland (Van Dam's *Hornpipe)*, Israel *(Debka)*, Yugoslavia *(Gaida Avasi)*, and Italy *(Tarentella Paesana)*. The theme for side B was a Surprise Journey and included music from: Brazil (Villa-Lobos' *The Little Train of Caipira); Czechoslavakia *(The Ragman's Signal)*; Afghanistan *(The Song of the Cricket)*; United States *(Lullaby to Martha)*; and Germany (Orff's *Rundadinella)*. Both recordings were complete with written instructions and suggestions for use with children and both are currently out of print.

In 1983, Ann Lindquist McClure revised the out-of-print *Creative Listening-I*, and renamed it *Children's Imagery*. The revision was made available as a cassette tape and most of the material was taken directly from the original tape including the same narration. Side A is narrated and includes Bach,

*Sinfonia to Cantata 29*; Smetana, *The Moldeau*; Dukas, *The Sorcerer's Apprentice*; Grofe, *Grand Canyon Suite* (Sunrise); Holst, *The Planets* (Uranus). Side B is not narrated and adds Vaughan Williams, *Fantasy on Greensleeves*; and Pachelbel, *Canon in D*, which did not appear on the original. In addition, a small guide titled *Guided Imagery and Music with Children* was printed which provided information on preparation for the tape inspired activities.

Then in 1989, Bonny re-released *Creative Listening I* under its original name, as a cassette tape. The tape was part of a series of GIM recordings called the "Bonnytapes." This was yet another version of the 1973 recording. Side A includes all selections of the LP and narration. Side B includes the same selections as side not narrated, as well as Vaughan Williams, *Fantasy on Greensleeves*.

## The Hero's Journey

Whereas the original LPs by Bonny and Savary were stand-alone themes or narrated scenarios accompanied by music selections, Lisa Summer and Joseph Summer (1989) created a tape program built on a sequence of five music selections each of which complements a stage in the cycle of a hero's journey. Side A uses a narrative and side B is music only. Summer and Summer suggest that "The selections are to be used singly based upon the needs of the listener or group." The instructions specify a short relaxation exercise before listening to the story/narration and then letting the music guide the adventure, after which one may verbalize, draw, write, and/or compose a song based on the experience.

Dvorak's *Ninth Symphony* (Second movement) is used for "The Departure of the Hero. Stravinsky's *Four Norwegian Moods* (Song) comes next as the "Meeting the Anima." Prokofiev's *Romeo and Juliet* (Morning Dance) was selected for "Meeting the Shadow." This is followed by Mahler's *First Symphony* (Fourth movement excerpt) for the "Dragon Fight." Finally Wagner, *Die Meistersinger* (Overture) for "The Return."

## Childhood Experiences

Bruscia's CD program entitled *Childhood Experiences* (See Appendix of this book) demonstrates yet another approach to children's imaginative music listening. Intended for individual GIM sessions with children (or with adults who want to revisit childhood), this program has no recorded narrative. The pieces were selected and sequenced to reflect the way a child daydreams. It consists entirely of classical pieces by well-known composers who were seeking to describe a children's world. Interestingly, these music selections are not among commonly featured titles in music appreciation classes for children.

These include: Ravel, *Mother Goose Suite,* (Pavane, Petite Poucet, and Le Jardin Feerique); Barber, *Allegretto*; Tschaikovsky, *Nanny*; Mompou, *Scenas d'Enfants* (Numbers 2 & 3); Saint-Saens *Carnival of the Animals* (Tortoises, Aquarium, and Cuckoo). Bruscia offers no suggestions for relaxation techniques, inductions, processing activities, or prescribed stories. The emphasis appears to be on the process of image making as prompted by the music, not by words.

## SUMMARY

This discussion of GIM with children and adolescents demonstrates both a sparseness and richness. Although this chapter is based on a very small number of available writings, it is important to recognize that, since the early 1970s, GIM has been used for many reasons with children and adolescents. From trauma intervention to creativity generation, in schools, correctional facilities, group homes, and hospitals as settings, GIM with children and adolescents continues today. The material presented here hopefully reflects only a few of the many possibilities of GIM with children and adolescents in the future.

## *References*

Bonny, H. (1978). *Facilitating GIM Sessions.* Baltimore: ICM Publications.

Bonny, H. (1989). *Creative Listening I.* Music Tape Program. Salina, KS: Bonnytapes.

Bonny, H. & Savary, L. (1973). *Music & Your Mind.* Barrytown, NY. Station Hill Press.

Clark, M. & Mardis, L. (1992). *The Bonny Method of Guided Imagery and Music.* Brochure. Olney, MD: Archedigm Publications.

Elliot, A. (1991). Guided Imagery and Music: An Affective Educational Tool. Unpublished paper submitted to the Capital City Schools. Topeka, KS.

Fagen, T. (1982). Music therapy in the treatment of anxiety and fear in terminal pediatric patients. *Music Therapy,* 2 (1), 13–23.

Gregoire, M., Hughes, J., Robbins, B., & Voorneveld, R., (1989) Music therapy with the gifted? A trial program. *Music Therapy Perspectives,* 7, 23–27.

Grindel, S. (1989). Imaging with music: An exploration in creativity for selected second grade students. *Southeastern Journal of Music Education*, 1, 151–159.

Lindquist (McClure), A. (1983). *Children's Imagery*. Music Tape. Port Townsend, WA: ICM.

Roy, M. (1996–1997). Guided Imagery and Music group experiences with adolescent girls in a high school setting. *Journal of the Association for Music and Imagery*, 5, 61–74.

Savary, L. & Bonny, H. (1973). *Creative Listening*, Vol. 1. Music LP. Baltimore: ICM.

Savary, L. & Bonny, H. (1974). *Creative Listening*, Vol. 2. Music LP. Baltimore: ICM.

Skaggs, R. (1997). Music-centered creative arts in a sex offender treatment program for male juveniles. *Music Therapy Perspectives*, 15, 73-78.

Summer, L. (1981). Tuning up in the classroom with music and relaxation. *Journal of the Society for Accelerative Learning and Teaching*, 6 (1), 46–50.

Summer, L. (1988). *Guided Imagery and Music in the Institutional Setting*. St. Louis: ICM.

Summer, L. & Summer, J. (1989). *The Hero's Journey*. Music Tape. Salina, KS: Bonnytapes.

Ventre, M. (1981). GIM and the Autistic Child: A Pilot Study and Two Case Excerpts. Unpublished manuscript.

Wager, K. (1992). Experiences, Thoughts and Reflections on the Use of GIM with Emotionally Disturbed Children. Unpublished manuscript.

Wesley, S. (2001). Within these walls: Auditory considerations in a psychiatric hospital for inpatient children. *Proceedings: Integrating Design and Care in Hospital Planning for the New Millennium*. Karolinska Institute.

*Chapter Eight*


# GUIDED IMAGERY AND MUSIC (GIM) IN MEDICAL CARE


## Alison Short


At a time when much is being said and written about the healing process in both the popular and professional literature, and where similarly a range of therapeutic techniques are being explored in a wide range of settings, it is pertinent to consider the place of Guided Imagery and Music (GIM) within this health care milieu. Throughout this chapter GIM is used as a generic term for various techniques which involve imaging to music in a relaxed state, either in individual or group settings; whereas the Bonny Method of GIM (BMGIM) refers specifically to the individual form of work as defined below:

> A music-centered, transformational therapy, which uses specifically programmed classical music to stimulate and support a dynamic unfolding of inner experiences in service of physical, psychological, and spiritual wholeness. The GIM therapist/guide maintains an active dialogue with the listener throughout the session, providing encouragement and focus for the emotions, images, physical sensations, memories, and thoughts which occur (Association for Music and Imagery, 1990).

The role that GIM may play as a treatment modality within the broad area of medical care has been investigated, both in formal literature and in informal anecdotal material. Such reports have often been individually treated as unusual, unique, even perhaps miraculous, and have not been substantially integrated into any particular theoretical framework within GIM practice. This chapter seeks to focus on GIM applications in health care, looking particularly at the relationship between imagery and the multifaceted issues and needs of medical patients.

# MEDICAL CARE

First, it is important to further define what is meant by medical care. Looking to a standard textbook, medical care may be defined as "the provision by a physician of services related to the maintenance of health, prevention of illness, and treatment of illness or injury". (Anderson, Anderson & Glanze, 1994, p. 967). A medical problem is therefore generally considered to be an illness or disease that affects the physiology of the person (Harkness & Dincher, 1999). The medical problem is delineated by a diagnosis that is based on a determination of the cause of a patient's illness or suffering by the combined use of physical examination, patient interview, laboratory tests, review of the patient's medical records, a knowledge of the observed cause of observed signs and symptoms, and a differential elimination of similar possible causes (Anderson et al., 1994). Thus, data are collected from the patient in various forms, based substantially on what the clinician observes and what the patient states with regard to his or her experience. Medical care and treatment may be directed at any and all health problems experienced by people, including trauma, disease, bodily imbalances, developmental changes, and so on. Emotional, psychological, and physical symptoms may be evident, and contribute essential information toward the full diagnosis.

Despite the earlier integrated views of the Greeks, the theoretical basis of established medical, or biomedical practice, has been strongly influenced in recent centuries by the work of Descartes, who proposed a philosophical viewpoint of separation of the mind and body. An advantage of this has been the development of modern technology with its associated lifesaving benefits. However, the resultant mechanistic view of the body has had important societal influences. Belief systems about health and illness are now being challenged by many in present-day society, and a more holistic view of the interaction of mind and body is now becoming increasingly popular.

As a response to this, alternative medicine has evolved out of a perceived need for a change to current medical practice, and for exploring new ways of conceptualizing health and illness. As an example of their popularity, a recent study published in the *New England Journal of Medicine* indicates that one in three Americans use therapies considered "unconventional" (Eisenberg, Kessler, Foster, Nortack, Calkins, and Delbanco, 1993, cited in Keegan, 2000). Alternative medicine has been described as "an unrelated group of non-orthodox therapeutic practices, often with explanatory systems that do not follow conventional biomedical explanations" (U.S. National Library of Medicine, Medical Subject Headings). An alternative therapy is therefore one that is used instead of conventional or mainstream therapy (Keegan, 2000). Alternative medicine often seeks to connect with traditional and ancient non-medical approaches, based on distinctive belief systems. In fact, the main reason people become involved with alternative medicine is their health-related values and beliefs (Siahpush, 1999). Such alternative therapies may make use of media such as the creative arts and techniques of multisensory input, with a view to engaging the emotions.

Among some thinkers in the field of alternative medicine, it has become popular to consider that Western biomedical care treats *only* the physical side of illness, trauma and the like. Such a clear-cut statement runs contrary to the author's almost twenty years of observation, interaction and experience as a team music therapist in clinical care. Many people would agree that good medical practice takes a great many factors about the person into account, and is as much an art as a science. This holistic nature of both nursing and medical practice has been noted by many authors (Owen & Holmes, 1993). As more moderate areas of alternative medicine have been researched and absorbed into the health care field in specific instances, so its name has begun to change to complementary medicine, reflecting a new partnership in health care. As Keegan (2000) points out, "a complementary therapy may be an alternative therapy, but becomes complementary when used in conjunction with conventional therapy. It helps to potentiate the effect of the conventional therapy" (Keegan, 2000, p.94).

And as Rankin-Box points out, "complementary therapies challenge western perceptions of health, but the premises on which many are based are not irrational, simply different" (Rankin-Box & Campbell, 2000). Furthermore, "the intent of complementary medicine is to support and encourage a state of physical, mental, and social well-being, as well as an absence of disease" (Freeman & Lawlis, 2001, p. 4). GIM has been recognized as a complementary therapy capable of having significant effects on the body, particularly in the way that working with emotions, music and imagery can impact on physiological measures (Freeman & Lawlis, 2001).

Not only is it helpful for medicine to work together with new approaches such as GIM, but also it is conversely important for GIM practitioners to recognize and acknowledge the contributions and importance of other health care professionals in the treatment of the medical patient. For example, if the current author had treated the cardiac patients of her study *only* with GIM, and with no cardiac surgery, medication, advice about diet, exercise, and the like provided by other professionals, it may perhaps have led to a very pleasant experience for the patient, but they would have been very much closer to dying—and the GIM therapist would have been ethically liable! So, in fact, this chapter does not focus on an "either/or" mentality, that is, medical or alternative interventions; rather, it seeks to understand how to harness and use the amazing, sometimes mind-boggling effects of GIM as it impacts on the body in a way that enhances clinical understandings. This, in turn, has the capacity to contribute to the treatment of people undergoing physical disease, disorders, or other situations requiring the promotion of physical health.

## CLINICAL PRACTICE
## IN MEDICAL CARE

Medical patients are generally very different from those attending self-help or encounter groups. They may not have had any prior psychotherapy treatment, or even had experiences with relaxation or imagery. This has been typical of those attending the author's cardiac research study, as discussed later. People with severe medical problems may have reduced defenses, and therefore any unresolved grief, other latent and undiagnosed difficulties, or previous traumatic stress may unexpectedly become evident. For this reason, practitioners undertaking clinical GIM sessions with people with medical conditions need to proceed with extreme care and caution, in line with advice from relevant practitioners. Such patients may be very vulnerable due to their physical problems, which can promote pain, confusion, anxiety, and depression related to the physical impact on the body. At a time when all their defenses may be down, it is essential that medical patients be treated with gentleness and consideration. The practitioner working in this area is expected to have a full understanding of the medical and physical condition(s) in question and its implications both physically and emotionally. It is also imperative to have an extensive report and referral system, and to exercise impeccable team-related and ethical principles and standards. Clearly, this is not a suitable area for an inexperienced GIM trainee or graduate!

Medical applications may require various approaches or modifications to GIM, due to the needs and constraints of particular hospitals, facilities, medical conditions, and patient groups. For example, in working with cardiac patients, the nature of their sternotomy led to their inability to lie down comfortably, and hence all sessions were conducted in a comfortably seated position (Short, 1999a).

In other GIM approaches, group work has been found effective where individual sessions may have been rejected by the clientele, especially with older residents receiving medical care in a nursing home (Short, 1992a). Some of the same guiding principles of BMGIM do apply to group work (Bonny & Savary, 1973), including the matching of induction to individual needs, careful choice of music, and opportunities for talking about the imagery experienced. Nevertheless, the effect of not "talking" the imagery as it occurs detracts from the therapeutic process, and the sense of immediacy and connection of specific imagery to specific music may be modified, due most likely to short-term memory difficulties.

The use of group GIM could be indicated in order to engage the patient, where individual BMGIM is not acceptable for a range of reasons. Being part of a group has the advantage of lessening anxiety and diffusing the intensity of the leader's attention. Individual BMGIM is often very intense in focus, and this may require too much energy and reserves of resilience for the medical patient. Fears about the nature of therapy may be better tolerated in a group, since medical patients typically have not had experiences of psychotherapy before. The ability to connect with others with similar medical problems in a group may enhance therapeutic development at this point. Nevertheless, individual work in standard BMGIM is also very important for medical patients, since the process can be tailored specifically to the person's needs, both in terms of relaxation process and music choices, in order to promote maximum benefits of relevancy and insight for that person.

## CONCEPTUAL FRAMEWORK FOR GIM IN MEDICAL CARE

How, then, may the occurrence of and the relationship between imagery and the multifaceted issues and needs of medical patients be understood from a conceptual point of view? Selected writers have addressed the use of imagery in health care, as potentially carrying information about the state of the body. For example, as early as 1933, by carefully interpreting the imaginal signs of a client's dream, Jung found that he could correctly diagnose a problem with blocked cerebrospinal fluid (Jung, 1968). More recently, Siegel (1986) has examined the pictorial imagery of cancer patients for clues about the progress of their disease. Clinical evaluation of spontaneously-generated imagery has also been pursued by Simonton, Matthews-Simonton & Creighton (1980), Achterberg (1985), and Lockhart (1983). All these examples suggest support for the notion that there is an inherent inner knowledge which connects body and mind, which can be accessed via imagery processes within the therapeutic context (Freeman & Lawlis, 2001; Sheikh, Kunzendorf, & Sheikh, 1989).

Combining theoretical understandings with clinical experience, the current author has put forward the model of a conglomerate of imagery produced by a physical event, as evidenced in BMGIM therapy sessions (Short, 1990). In line with total care and holistic concepts, this model proposes that any physical problem is likely to promote a range of reactions and responses in the person.

Such reactions may be evidenced through the data produced in the GIM session, that is to say, the reported imagery and accompanying discussion. This model is depicted diagrammatically in Figure 1. Individual aspects of the spontaneously generated imagery conglomerate may be considered separately, but are understood to form part of an integrated whole. These individual aspects may occur in the imagery as markers, in turn linked to the range of responses (psychological, social, etc.) experienced by the person as a reaction to the physical event. Markers may be a clue that delineates and carries further information about the physical and emotional status of the person.

Assuming that such imagery markers occur, it is important to consider how such markers may convey useful clinical information, capable of contributing to assessment and the diagnostic endeavor (Short, 1991), and in turn, provide opportunities for contributing to effective clinical practice, as part of the clinical team.

This theoretical model assists in the interpretation of clinical material. For example, one client's imagery segment was based on abstract colors, where a sense of power, smothering, and helplessness conveyed by the reported imagery immediately suggested a physically abusive situation. Later spontaneous discussion confirmed the client's memories of just such a traumatic incident some twenty years previously. Another client entered the GIM session with current and severe pain, but her fears of a return of cancer were not corroborated by the client's spontaneous imagery. Images involving color and light in relationship to the body occurred in a way which suggested no aberrations or unusual characteristics. Subsequent examination by her oncologist confirmed for the client what her imagery had already suggested — a continued cancer-free medical diagnosis. Yet another client saw and verbally described images of actual cancer cells and their interaction with her, and related them to her fight against cancer. Based on her reported imagery, it seemed to the GIM therapist that the fight did not seem to be entirely effective. In the imagery, she was undefended from some directions and experienced significant fear.

Figure 1.

Schematic of the Imagery Conglomerate
Generated by Physical Illness or Trauma

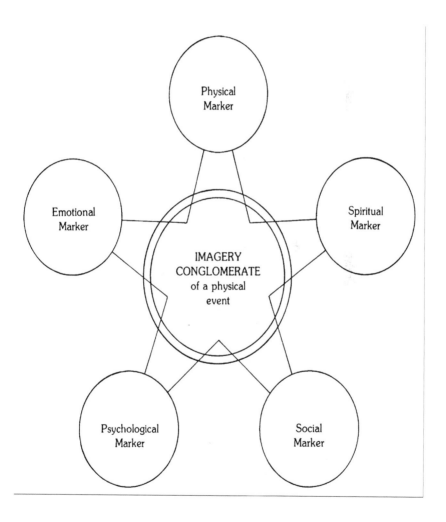

In later discussion, spontaneous statements by the client indicated medical statistical risk for the return of cancer of 50 percent over five years. This confirmed what the imagery had already been suggesting: an incomplete bodily defense. These brief examples show how imagery spontaneously produced by clients undergoing GIM sessions can be carefully examined for clinical and diagnostic information (Short, 1991). In deriving such information, significant factors include a) recognizing possible mind-body links via appropriate imagery, whether images of past or present situations, traumatic or rehabilitative processes, b) applying interventions to pinpoint processes in the imagery and screen out unnecessary data, and c) following through with discussion and validation of the imagery processes with the client in the postlude of the BMGIM session (Short, 1991).

## THE INCREASING LINK OF GIM
## TO MEDICAL CARE

Through exploring the relationship of imagery to medical problems or issues, early interest by the current author has focused on two areas: individual BMGIM related to pregnancy, and group GIM with elderly physically disabled residents. Such exploration has been aimed towards gaining further understandings of the significance of imagery to the person and how it interacts and integrates with their lives, particularly with regard to their physical problems. These early studies have suggested interesting features that will now be further explored.

Pregnancy is a unique physical condition requiring ongoing adjustment for continued physical and emotional health. Even in a "normal" pregnancy, emotional and physical difficulties are not uncommon, and both processes and outcomes can be unpredictable.

A client underwent eight BMGIM sessions over a period of thirteen weeks during middle and late pregnancy. Post-analysis by review of transcripts showed that this client used BMGIM to address the challenges of adjustment to pregnancy, both physically and emotionally (Short, 1993a, 1993b). Adaptation to pregnancy was evidenced in the imagery by the client considering and undertaking appropriate reactions as a pregnant woman, for example, in the choosing of nutritional (rather than "junk") food and in foregoing physically demanding or dangerous movement. Emotional connection with the new baby, the new physical being that she was carrying within her, was evident in imagery indicative of relationship and bonding. Significantly, this client also used the BMGIM setting to explore the trauma of loss from a previous ectopic pregnancy, spontaneously creating an image of a little boy, and, over several sessions, saying good-bye and finding resolution. This client also used the BMGIM sessions to practice and enhance deep relaxation, which she was subsequently able to maintain through the final labor and delivery. Interestingly, a BMGIM session some months later indicated this client's continued adaptation to the ongoing physical and emotional demands of motherhood. It suggested that she was responding positively and appropriately to a new view of herself, her body, and her new baby (Short, 1996–1997). Clearly, the spontaneous imagery generated in the session related to both physical and emotional aspects of the medical condition.

In another instance, elderly residents with physical problems in a long-term rehabilitation and nursing facility welcomed advanced and insightful activities to extend their cognitive and emotional options. The GIM technique was modified and implemented with a small group of residents with an average age of eighty-three years. The residents had a wide range of physical disabilities and most were wheelchair-bound. In the light of such physical problems, the entire music and imagery session was undertaken in an upright postural position, and relaxation procedures were modified to take into account physical disabilities and sensitivities. The length of session was reduced to one hour, to match attention span and health facility requirements. Residents were empowered to participate in the choice of relaxation procedures, sometimes even suggesting possible music choices.

This group form of GIM explored the way that elderly physically disabled residents used imagery to relate to physical and emotional aspects of their current condition. A simple qualitative research framework was implemented. Extensive field notes written after each session were substantially analyzed for themes after the completion of twenty-one sessions. Results suggested that elderly residents imaged vividly and effectively. Emergent themes related to disability, bereavement, sexuality, and the aging process, and in doing so, addressed a broad range of past, current, and impending issues (Short, 1992a).

For example, one resident reported imagery of Helen Keller, a person who had shown great courage and strength in surmounting blindness and deafness, and this became a vehicle not only to absorb strength and inspiration from the image but also to further discuss the resident's own fourteen-year blindness. This resident usually avoided such deep sharing via humor or topic changes, but in this instance the use of imagery with music led to the eliciting of deep and authentic feelings. The group responded with positive feedback about the way that this resident was coping with her disability, and thus offered further support toward ongoing adjustment to her visual disability.

In an extension of this initial group program, a subsequent set of twenty-three sessions (session numbers 28–50 inclusive) were reviewed, and similarly treated to a simple qualitative analysis. In this series, themes related especially to the experience of aging, finding meaning in life, sadness, loss and grief, coping with chronic illness, finding relaxation, coping with institutional life, relating to the extended family, reviewing life and memories, and dealing with approaching death (Short, 1992b).

For example, the music and imagery setting prompted one client to remember a poem from childhood. This poem brought increased meaning to her current difficulties that included current multiple leg ulcers and poor circulation as well as a history of osteoarthritis, cancer, and bilateral hip prostheses. The anonymous poem, shown below, expressed a sense of grappling with the difficulties of life and growing through these struggles. Symbolically, the image of the tree may be considered to represent the body, and hence the "broken branches" and "scars" in the poem may well represent the many operations and physical difficulties which the resident's body had experienced (Short, 1992b). Here, increased clinical information about the resident's experience of her body was being conveyed by this imagery.

A Remembered Poem
From Childhood

A tree that never had to fight
For sun and air and sky and light
Never became a forest king
But lived and died a scrubby thing

A man who never had to toil
Or win his share of light and air
Never became a manly man
But lived and died as he began

Where thickest lies the forest growth
We find the patriarchs of both
And they hold converse with the stars
Whose broken branches show the scars
Of many winds and much of strife
This is the common law of life.

Clearly, this group form of GIM was able to draw out and address the deep issues confronting these elderly participants in a way that was acceptable and meaningful for them. In fact, working with these physically disabled residents in this way suggested even more far-reaching implications for health care, as Marcus (1992) comments:

> [Alison Short] describes her use of Guided Imagery and Music-based techniques—relaxation and induction with the wheelchair-bound and physically disabled, imaging work with the visually impaired and legally blind, verbal processing with the aphasic—with a calm modesty that belies both the degree of her innovation and the far-reaching significance of her results. Surely the disabilities she is dealing with are not exclusive to the aging population in which she has encountered them. Her results may indicate that GIM-based techniques are more widely applicable than is the present practice and may also shed some light on the nature of music itself (p. x).

The relationship of music and imagery to physical conditions and medical issues has been addressed by selected writers (Erdonmez, 1992; Toomey, 1996–1997), with most reports in the form of anecdotal and case study material. Some authors have proceeded from an unsubstantiated and unclear theoretical base and belief system. Nevertheless, their interpreted view of the client's imagery may shed some light on imagery and healing within the GIM context.

Reviewing anecdotal and case reports, the current author suggests that spontaneous imagery leading toward physical or emotional healing of a medical condition typically may include ventilation of emotions, insight into often longstanding relational problems or negative patterns of behavior, emergence of an archetypal guide figure, symbolic transformation of body part(s), and increased feelings of physical and mental health or rejuvenation (Hale, 1992; Merritt, 1993; Pickett, 1987). Aspects of loss, related to physical trauma, may also appear spontaneously in imagery, which can then be addressed according to standard BMGIM practice (Goldberg, 1988; Pickett, 1996–1997), as is the case of emotional reactions related to self concept resulting from physical disability (Moffit, 1991). Recovery from the physical trauma of sexual abuse may require the addressing of images related to fear and the archetypal hero, in turn leading to empowerment and the development of inner strength by the client (Tasney, 1993).

Investigating the range of physical and emotional effects commonly suffered by Vietnam veterans, Blake (1994a, 1994b) looked at the role of GIM in relation to post-traumatic stress. Her study suggested that imagery was effective with regard to relaxation, ventilation of emotions, accessing of traumatic memories, and achievement of insight, with associated increased positive feelings and empowerment by clients. Somatic responses with regard to difficult emotional material are an interesting area requiring further research.

Such somatic responses may include headaches, body tension, pain, numbing of body parts, sweating, and temporary paralysis (Blake, 1994a).

McKinney (1995) has undertaken formal quantitative research aimed at examining GIM-induced changes to fundamental biological effects of the body, in the form of beta-endorphin levels. Her findings suggested that GIM may be effective in reducing depression. Elizabeth Jacobi has also substantially studied the effects of BMGIM on the management of arthritis, using questionnaires and quantitative measurements (personal communication, November, 1999).

## CARDIAC CARE

Current hospital-based research has deliberately set out to discover more about the use of GIM in recovery from a severe medical physical event, and the area of cardiac surgery was chosen as a focus for this chapter. There is little doubt that emotional and psychological factors, as well as physical and genetic factors, may have a strong impact on the health and well-being of people with cardiac disease (Cornett & Watson, 1984). Fundamental physiological responses to stress, such as increased heart rate, add support to the notion of emotional effects impacting on physical health. Programmed music listening in the Intensive Coronary Care Unit suggests that such an intervention using music may decrease heart rate, improve tolerance of pain and suffering, and lessen anxiety and depression (Bonny, 1983). Other research in related fields supports such findings (Bolwerk, 1990; Davis-Rollans & Cunningham, 1987; Guzzetta, 1989, 1994; White, 1992; Zimmerman, Pierson, & Marker, 1988).

Seeking to research the role of BMGIM in cardiac care, the current author selected a small group of participants aged 57 to 69 years who then underwent six individual BMGIM sessions, commencing at six to twelve weeks after coronary artery bypass grafting (CABG). This was good population to study, because of the well-defined recovery trajectory, potential for insight, and broad-based clinical focus in the rehabilitation program. Participants in this study were required to be progressing well in their recovery, speak English competently (two were from a non-English speaking background), and have no psychotic problems. BMGIM sessions were of standard length (approximately two hours) and took place in a quiet room in the hospital. Participants reported their imagery experience as it occurred with standard BMGIM music programs. The entire session was audiotaped, transcribed, and analyzed qualitatively according to textual and semiotic principles. The overall aim of the study was to clarify how meanings related to adjustment from a health crisis (such as cardiac surgery) were depicted in music-supported imagery.

Participants were surprised with and fascinated by their spontaneously emerging imagery, especially since several participants expressed beforehand the belief that they were unlikely to be able to produce imagery. Participants were naive in terms of psychotherapy, with the exception of one participant who suffered from longstanding chronic pain and had had therapy to help with related symptoms. One participant had undertaken yoga before, and another has used relaxation in childbirth, some forty or more years previously. Results suggested that all clients were able to relax deeply. One client spontaneously reported improved sleeping patterns as a result of the music therapy session. Patients also commented positively on the specific music used (BMGIM programs), and on the role of the music in promoting and enhancing the relaxation and imagery process.

## Ventilation of Feelings

Participants often connected strongly with the opportunity to discuss their emotional responses related to cardiac surgery and appeared to derive benefits from having these personal responses acknowledged and validated. For some, it seemed to be the first time that they had talked about some issues, and at times this produced a "flood" of words and feelings. For example, in the words of one participant, during the music and imagery:

> I just wish I could open it up a little bit . . . as I mentioned to you before, if I could just open it, pull the zip down an inch just to give my shoulders a bit more flexibility, because it does get a bit tight. But that will come with time . . . I quite often feel, yes, if I could just open that up a little bit. But it isn't like it all the time, but tends to be mostly when you're in bed, and I think that's more uncomfortable because of lying down (Music: Debussy's *Danse Sacree et Danse Profane*).

Here, the participant was referring particularly to her sternotomy, and comparing it to a zipper. The term sternotomy refers to the opening of the sternum by the surgeon to gain access to the cardiac area in order to perform surgery. It is subsequently secured with metal staples or metal wire after surgery. Clinically, many patients experience discomfort from their sternotomy in the recovery phase.

This participant used imagery concerning her sternotomy, which was still painful and uncomfortable, especially if lying down, to relate not only to her body but also increasingly in a broader sense to relate to her emotions. In fact, this participant burst into tears soon after the beginning of the music, and subsequently reflected (during the music and imagery) on her need to be strong and hold things in tightly. Thus, the imaginal experience of the sternotomy appeared to carry both physical and emotional connotations, of being "zipped too tight" compared with "opening up." For a more detailed discussion of this case, refer to Short (1999a).

## Pain Management

In this study, a number of participants spontaneously reported that the BMGIM sessions were helpful with regard to pain relief. This is not so surprising, if one looks to the Gate Control theory (Melzack & Wall, 1983), which suggests that the experience of pain is mediated by descending influences from the brain, for example, the higher CNS processes of attention, anxiety, anticipation and past experiences (Lanceley, 1995). Perception of pain is a major factor in undermining the rehabilitative process, and may further relate to a negative perception of oneself and one's body.

For example, one participant in the current study was subject to chronic pain and used an implant for pain relief. He was also from an Hispanic background, and had resided in Australia for 35 years. One of his problems, as he reported in the sessions, was that his increasingly arthritic body could not keep up with his increasingly energetic heart following bypass surgery. He was also being treated for depression, resulting from more than ten years of chronic pain, and presented as anxious and agitated.

In contrast, in his fifth session, he enjoyed imagining being at the beach. Upon being asked, "So what would you like to be doing now?" he responded:

> Oh, still, I will lie down on the sand. Because the music is very nice too. I lay down on my back now. It will be worse for me after, to move, but never mind. I will enjoy the moment. You know, I hear, I lay down on my back. I hear the sea. I see the sky, at the same time I feel the sand, and I feel the sun. What else can I ask for? I've got it all! Oh, it feels beautiful. It comes to my mind, that the best things in life are free. The sun is free, the sand is free. The sea is free. You don't need money to enjoy that. (Music: Faure's *Requiem* [In Paradisum])

And later . . .

> I feel so good, about everything. Life is beautiful. When you can enjoy all these things. It makes me feel so good about myself. I feel that I've got everything. At this moment, nothing will spoil my happiness. No pains, no worries, nothing. Just enjoying myself. (*Therapist: Mm. Let*

*yourself enjoy that).* I'm so lucky, to have all that. (Music: Wagner's *Lohengrin* [Excerpts from Preludes to Acts 1 and 3])

After the session, this participant spontaneously reported that he felt like a "new person." It is apparent from what he was saying that something had changed about the way he was thinking about himself and his body. His apparent anxiety and depression appeared reduced, and he now had increasingly positive experiences of his body. He reported an absence of pain after the music and imagery, and in the next session commented that he was deliberately using music to assist with his pain management at home.

## Rehearsal of Activities

For bypass patients, the change in physical capabilities due to revascularization is commonly quite dramatic; however, it can be accompanied by a reluctance to change from self-protective and compensatory behaviors to a more active lifestyle. This is one of the major problems of cardiac rehabilitation.

Interestingly, and unexpectedly, the reported imagery of many participants in the study suggested a transitioning of awareness from a pre-surgery to a post-surgery self-image, as evidenced by imagery of interests and activities. This imagery provided an apparent inner sense of rehearsal and realization of increasing health and abilities, reinforcing the recovery process. This is not the first time that imaginal rehearsal has been observed by the current author (Short, 1995; Short & William, 1999c). However, here it was being directly applied to the participants perceptions of their body and its activities, and indicated a change following surgery, related to the rehabilitative process.

For example, one participant imagined playing seven holes of golf during the music, in a typical social game with his brother and his son. Every event in the imaged game was reported, including club selection, shots, scores, and walking down the fairway. On further analysis, it became obvious that this was a very ordinary, normal game of golf for this person. But the normality of this session was deceptive. It could easily have not been normal. Last time he played golf, it was obviously not normal—he had angina. Physical exertion of this type was undoubtedly a problem to his health and well-being. During the music and imagery, in two separate instances, he commented on how it felt to be back playing this game of golf.

So now we join up together again, for the walk down the middle of the fairway. They both ask me what it's like to be back playing golf. And I say: "It's great!" "Are you feeling any pain?" "No, not like I used to." We comment about that, about no angina pain. And that's, that makes me feel, good, that's a good feeling. *(Therapist: Is there anything else you would like to say to them?)* No, not at the moment. (Music: Mendelssohn's *Scottish Symphony No. 3* [Vivace non troppo])

And later . . .

Well, I can't hit very far these days. *(Therapist: You can't?)* No, I think it's because of having my surgery, and I'm not strong enough yet. But I accept that. I'll get better. I'll get better. *(Mm. You'll get better).* When I do I'll have a harder swing. I don't want to swing too hard, anyway, in case it does upset things. Well, we're just walking down the fairway, together, chatting again. (Music: Excerpt from *Ravel's Daphnis and Chloe, Suite No.2)*

Such spontaneous imaginal rehearsal had not been expected in this study; however, on further reflection, it could be understood via the physical/imaginal rehearsal often used in other fields such as sports training (Hecker & Kaczor, 1988; Jowdy & Harris, 1990), stroke rehabilitation (Decety, 1993; Van Leeuwen & Inglis, 1998) and health care training (Bucher, 1993). This aspect of spontaneous imagery related to increasing health and well-being was a very positive result of the BMGIM sessions, and clearly links bodily, emotional and imaginal change (Short, 1999b).

## FINAL COMMENTS

Current literature and research indicates that there is an increasingly important role for GIM in medical and physical health care. One of the problems to date has been finding ways to move from anecdotal case studies to a more rigorous and credible, but at the same time sensitive, method of research. Qualitative research, with due attention to methodology, theoretical base and analysis procedures, seem to promise a bright future in this regard.

The imagery produced in group GIM and BMGIM sessions, in a range of settings and with a range of physical difficulties, indicates clear and unequivocal connections between physical and emotional material. It also gives insights into how such information may be used clinically to enhance the health and well-being of the person, particularly in relation to their body and their potential rehabilitation. Future research will no doubt continue to discover more about how such music-supported imaginal processes can be used to promote and enhance the broad spectrum of medical care and treatment, as we grow to understand more about this exciting field of Guided Imagery and Music.

## *Acknowledgements*

The author gratefully acknowledges the assistance of the hospitals, staff, and patients who have participated in her study and research projects. The author also acknowledges the significant support and direction of her doctoral supervisors, Professor Heather Gibb, Professor Colin Holmes, and Professor Michele Forinash.

## *References*

Achterberg, J. (1985). *Imagery and Healing: Shamanism and Modern Medicine.* Boston: Shambala Inc.

Anderson, K. N., Anderson, L. E. & Glanze, W. D. (eds.) (1994). *Mosby's Medical, Nursing,& Allied Health dictionary.* (4th ed.). St. Louis: MO: Mosby-Year Book Inc.

Association for Music and Imagery (1990). Definition of the Bonny Method of Guided Imagery and Music. Approved at the Annual Conference of AMI, Blue Mountain Lake, NY.

Blake, R. (1994a). Vietnam veterans with post-traumatic stress disorder: Findings from a music and imagery project. *Journal of the Association for Music and Imagery,* 3, 5–18.

Blake, R. (1994b). The Bonny Method of Guided Imagery and Music (GIM) in the treatment of post-traumatic stress disorder (PTSD) with adults in the psychiatric setting. *Music Therapy Perspectives,* 12 (2), 125–129.

Bolwerk, C. (1990). Effects of relaxing music on state anxiety in myocardial infarction patients. *Critical Care Nursing Quarterly,* 13 (2), 63–72.

Bonny, H. (1978). *The Role of Taped Music Programs in the Guided Imagery and Music process. (GIM Monograph No.2).* Baltimore, MD: ICM books.

Bonny, H. (1983). Music listening for intensive coronary care units: A pilot project. *Music Therapy,* 3 (1), 4–16.

Bonny, H. & Savary, L. (1973). *Music and Your Mind.* New York: Harper and Row.

Bucher, L. (1993). The effects of imagery abilities and mental rehearsal on learning a nursing skill. *Journal of Nursing Education,* 32 (7) 318–324.

Cornett, S. & Watson, J. (1984). *Cardiac Rehabilitation: An Interdisciplinary Team Approach.* New York: John Wiley and Sons.

Davis-Rollans, C., & Cunningham, S. (1987). Physiologic responses of coronary care patients to selected music. *Heart and Lung,* 16 (4), 370–378.

Decety, J. (1993). Should motor imagery be used in physiotherapy? Recent advances in cognitive neurosciences. *Physiotherapy Theory and Practice,* 9, 193–203.

Erdonmez, D. (1992). Clinical applications of Guided Imagery and Music. *Australian Journal of Music Therapy,* 3, 37–44.

Freeman, L. W. and Lawlis, G. F. (2001). *Complementary and Alternative Medicine: A Research based Approach.* St. Louis, MO: Mosby.

Goldberg, F. (1988). Music and imagery as psychotherapy with a brain injured patient: A case study. *Music Therapy Perspectives,* 5, 41–45.

Guzzetta, C. (1989). Effects of relaxation and music therapy on patients in a coronary care unit with presumptive acute myocardial infarction. *Heart and Lung,* 18 (6), 609–616.

Guzzetta, C. (1994). Research for practice: Soothing the ischemic heart. *American Journal of Nursing,* 94 (1), 24.

Hale, S. E. (1992). Wounded Woman: The use of Guided Imagery and Music in recovering from a mastectomy. *Journal of the Association for Music and Imagery,* 1, 99–106.

Harkness, G. A. & Dincher, J. R. (1999). *Medical Surgical Nursing: Total Patient Care.* (10th ed.). St Louis: Mosby Inc.

Hecker, J. E. and Kaczor, L. M. (1988) Application of imagery theory to Sport Psychology: Some preliminary findings. *Journal of Sport and Exercise Psychology,* 10, 363–373.

Jowdy, D. P. and Harris, D. V. (1990). Muscular responses during mental imagery as a function of motor skill level. *Journal of Sport and Exercise Psychology,* 12, 191–201.

Jung, C. G. (1968). *Analytical Psychology: Its Theory and Practice.* New York: Pantheon.

Keegan, L. (2000). Protocols for practice: Alternative and complementary modalities for managing stress and anxiety. *Critical Care Nurse,* 20 (3), 93–96.

Lanceley, A. (1995). Wider issues in pain management. *European Journal of Cancer Care,* 4, 153–157.

Lockhart, R. (1983). *Words as Eggs: Psyche in Language and Clinic.* Dallas: Spring Publications.

McKinney, C. (1995). The effects of Guided Imagery and Music on depression and beta-endorphin levels in healthy adults: A pilot study. *Journal of the Association for Music and Imagery.* 4, 67–78.

Marcus, D. (1992). Foreword. *Music Therapy, 11* (1), ix–xi.

Melzack, R.& Wall (1983). *The Challenge of Pain.* NY: Basic Books.

Merritt, S. (1993). The healing link: Guided Imagery and Music and the body/mind connection. *Journal of the Association for Music and Imagery,* 2, 11–28.

Moffit, E. (1991). Improvisation and Guided Imagery and Music (GIM) with a physically disabled woman: A Gestalt approach. In K. Bruscia (ed.) *Case Studies in Music Therapy.* (pp. 347–356). Gilsum, NH: Barcelona Publishers.

Owen, M. & Holmes, C. (1993). "Holism" in the discourse of nursing. *Journal of Advanced Nursing,* 18 (11) 1688–1695.

Pickett, E. (1987). Fibroid tumors and response to Guided Imagery and Music: Two case studies. *Imagination, Cognition and Personality, 7* (2), 1987–88.

Pickett, E. (1996–1997). Guided Imagery and Music in head trauma rehabilitation. *Journal of the Association for Music and Imagery,* 5, 51–60.

Rankin-Box, D. and Campbell, K. (2000). Is there a rational basis underlying alternative medicine? *Nursing Times,* 96 (23), 18.

Sheikh, A. A., Kunzendorf, R. G. & Sheikh, K. S. (1989). Healing images: From ancient wisdom to modern science. In A. A. Sheikh and K. S. Sheikh, (eds.) *Eastern and Western Approaches to Healing: Ancient Wisdom and Modern Knowledge.* (pp. 470–515). New York: Wiley and Sons.

Short, A. (1990). Physical illness in the process of Guided Imagery and Music. *Australian Journal of Music Therapy,* 1, 9–14.

Short, A. (1991). The role of Guided Imagery and Music in diagnosing physical illness or trauma. *Music Therapy,* 10 (1), 22–45.

Short, A. (1992a). Music and Imagery with physically disabled elderly residents: A GIM adaptation. *Music Therapy,* 11 (1), 65–98.

Short, A. (June, 1992b). Memories and inspiration: Music and imagery with elderly physically disabled residents. *Proceedings of 21st Conference of the American Association for Music Therapy,* (pp. 57–71). Cape Cod, MA: AAMT.

Short, A. (1993a). GIM during pregnancy: Anticipation and resolution. *Australian Journal of Music Therapy,* 4, 7–18.

Short, A. (1993b). GIM during pregnancy: Anticipation and resolution. *Journal of the Association for Music and Imagery,* 2, 73–86.

Short, A. (1995). Relationship issues as reflected in the music therapy process. *Conference Collection,* AMTA 21st Conference, 35–37.

Short, A. (1996–1997). Jungian archetypes in GIM therapy: Approaching the client's fairytale. *Journal of the Association for Music and Imagery,* 5, 37–49.

Short, A. (1999a). At the heart of the matter: Communicating underlying messages through music and imagery in cardiac care. In D. Erdonmez Grocke & Pratt, R. (eds.) *Music Medicine and Music Therapy: Expanding Horizons*. (pp. 313–325). Melbourne: Faculty of Music, University of Melbourne.

Short, A. (1999b, October). Enhancing the rehabilitative process using music therapy after cardiac surgery. *Cardiac Rehabilitation News*. Cardiac Rehabilitation Association of NSW.

Short, A. & William (1999c). Review of GIM Sessions: William's story. In J. Hibben. (ed.). *Inside Music Therapy: Client Experiences* (pp. 153–161). Gilsum, NH: Barcelona Press.

Siahpush, M. (1999). Why do people favour alternative medicine? *Aust. & N.Z.Public Health,* 23 (3), 266.

Siegel, B. (1986). *Love, Medicine and Miracles*. New York: Harper and Row.

Simonton, O. C., Matthews-Simonton, S. & Creighton, J. L. (1980). *Getting Well Again*. New York: Bantam.

Tasney, K. (1993). Beginning the healing of incest through Guided Imagery and Music: A Jungian perspective. *Journal of the Association for Music and Imagery,* 2, 35–47.

Toomey, L. (1996–1997). Literature Review: The Bonny Method of Guided Imagery and Music. *Journal of the Association for Music and Imagery,* 5, 75–103.

U.S. National Library of Medicine, Medical Subject Headings: Alternative medicine. http://www.nlm.nih.gov/mesh/meshhome.html.

Van Leeuwen, R. & Inglis, J. T. (1998). Mental practice and imagery: A potential role in stroke rehabilitation. *Physical Therapy Reviews,* 3, 47–52.

White, J. (1992). Music therapy: An intervention to reduce anxiety in the myocardial infarction patient. *Clinical Nurse Specialist,* 6 (2), 58–63.

Zimmerman, L., Pierson, M., & Marker, J. (1988). Effects of music on patient anxiety in coronary care units. *Heart and Lung,* 17 (5), 560–566.

*Chapter Nine*


# GUIDED IMAGERY AND MUSIC (GIM) IN THE TREATMENT OF INDIVIDUALS WITH CHRONIC ILLNESS


## Debra S. Burns


## QUALITY OF LIFE


Many diseases once thought terminal are now being treated as chronic, long-term diseases. Cancer, HIV/AIDS, diabetes, coronary heart disease, autoimmune diseases, and arthritis are only a few of the chronic diseases that were once thought terminal, but with advances in health care, are now long-term diseases. While we may be grateful for the advancements in health care, the fact that individuals can now live with these diseases for a considerable period of time brings new challenges. The diseases and interventions bring about concomitant changes in a person's well-being. This chapter will focus on the processes a person with a chronic disease faces and the contributions that GIM can make to a person's quality of life. While the topic of this chapter includes issues related to chronic illness, specific illnesses will not be individually addressed.

In order to understand the contributions that GIM can make toward an individual's treatment, it is important for the reader to have a conceptual basis of the impact psychosocial interventions can have within an individual person. There are many theories conceptualizing the interaction of mind and body; however, even this terminology is limiting. Useful models include both mind/body interactions and social interactions. Theorists and researchers include the relationships of a person's biological, psychological, and social processes to explain potential phenomena and interventions outcomes. Some models also include spiritual processes when describing a person's well-being.

# BIOBEHAVIORAL AND
# BIOPSYCHOSOCIAL MODELS
# OF ILLNESS

One common aspect between biobehavioral and biopsychosocial models include the impact stress has on aspects of human functioning. Andersen, Kiecolt-Glaser, and Glaser (1994) provide a biobehavioral model of cancer stress that describes how stress impacts disease course. Biobehavioral models assume that psychological distress contributes to a down regulation in immune function, which leaves the body vulnerable to disease. Indeed, research supports the notion that increases in stress negatively impact immune function. While not every stressful event contributes to decreased immune function, continuous, objective, negative events from treatment can produce chronic stress leading to decreases in immune function.

Chronic illnesses can be conceptualized as chronic stressors. High levels of the hormone cortisol have been implicated in chronic stress, breakdown in immune function, and depressive disorders. Chronic hypersecretion of cortisol dampens the body's immunological reactivity. High levels of corticosteroids inhibit immune function by decreasing levels of interferon, interleukin-1, and lymphocyte metabolism (Baum, Herberman, & Cohen, 1995; McDaniel et al., 1995); therefore, chronic increases in cortisol increase the body's vulnerability to disease. Patients with cancer exhibit a dysfunctional regulation of the hypothalamus-pituitary-adrenocortical axis (HPA) that is similar to those seen in depressed patients without cancer (McDaniel et al., 1995). Cancer patients with advanced disease and depressive symptoms exhibit significantly elevated cortisol levels and decreased levels of tryptophan and serotonin when compared to healthy controls (Iwagaki et al., 1997; Lechin et al., 1990). Tryptophan is the amino acid the body metabolizes into serotonin and melatonin through the indoleamine pathway.

Research by McKinney and colleagues has demonstrated that hormone levels, including cortisol and beta-endorphin, change as a result of a series of group GIM sessions (McKinney et al., 1995) and individual session employing the Bonny Method of Guided Imagery and Music (BMGIM) (McKinney et al, 1997). In one instance, the decreases in cortisol were predictive of improved mood (McKinney et al., 1997). Researchers are not confident regarding the level of change needed in cortisol or beta-endorphin to reach clinical significance; however, these data suggest that both group and individual forms of GIM could have promising effects on immune and endocrine function for those individuals with chronic illnesses.

In addition to biological pathways, behavioral pathways are included in the biobehavioral model of stress. In the biopsychosocial model, the behavioral component is divided into psychological and social aspects of a person's well-being. Behavioral pathways include health behaviors such as appetite disturbances, self-medication with alcohol or drugs, sleep disorders, and cigarette smoking. Social pathways include the way a person interacts within his/her environment.

Health behaviors may be negatively and/or positively affected by a diagnosis of chronic illness. For instance, an individual recently diagnosed with a chronic illness may choose to stop smoking to improve health or they may increase the number of cigarettes smoked per day as a way of coping with the emotional distress related to the diagnosis and side effects of the illness. Certainly, the first choice is more desirable. Treatment adherence is another health behavior at issue. The treatment for a particular chronic illness may be deleterious enough that an individual chooses not to complete the treatment regimen. This can be the case in cancer care, where the side effects of chemotherapy or radiation treatment can include fatigue, anxiety, depression, nausea, pain, and an overall lower quality of life.

Emotional distress is a large component of psychological well-being. Depression and anxiety are common among individuals with chronic illness. Forty-one percent of individuals with chronic illnesses report a concurrent psychiatric disorder (Katon & Sullivan, 1990). The co-occurrence of depression and cancer is as high as 50 percent, depending on whether the measurement includes depressed mood or a depressive syndrome. Depression may be the result of the disease process or it may be an individual's reaction to the disease and treatment. There are many overlapping symptoms between the chronic disease process and depression, such as appetite change, weight loss, and loss of energy. Historically, such an overlap of symptoms has lead to a problem of underdiagnosis of depression, although this problem is being dealt with through physicians' increasing recognition that a person's mental health can affect medical outcomes. Additionally, the increased recognition of complementary and alternative medicines and the recognition of mind and body interactions has decreased the occurrence of underdiagnosis. Of most concern to clinicians is the fact that lack of treatment for depression and anxiety can lead to decreases in quality of life and difficulty returning to optimum levels of functioning. Research in the areas of chronic illness and quality of life indicates that emotional distress also affects physical parameters and treatment outcomes.

Evidence from quantitative and qualitative studies suggest that the Bonny method is an effective way to treat the emotional distress related to chronic illness. Quantitative studies indicate that GIM sessions can bring about significant positive changes in both mood and quality of life in health and ill individuals (Burns, 1999; McKinney et al., 1995; McKinney et al., 1997). Specific significant changes in mood include anxiety, depression, anger, fatigue, and confusion (Burns, 1999; McKinney, Antoni, Kumar, Tims, & McCabe, 1997).

Qualitative reports indicate that the process in which psychological healing takes place depends on the premorbid condition of the client. If the individual was relatively psychologically healthy prior to the onset of the chronic illness, the psychological distress will be more related to the disease process and adapting to the disease than previous psychological trauma. However, if an individual has experienced a significant amount of pre-disease trauma (i.e., sexual, physical abuse), that individual will have difficulty dealing with the illness without addressing the premorbid issues (see Bruscia, 1991; Hale, 1992, for further information).

Fatigue, a physical symptom that is affected by increases in emotional distress, is a common side effect of chronic illness and treatment. Fatigue is characterized by perceptions of tiredness and weakness and can result from treatment or from the disease itself. Cancer-related fatigue is often associated with anemia related to the destruction of red blood cells during chemotherapy or during advanced disease. Cella (1998) describes fatigue as a multi-symptom syndrome that can include dizziness, headache, chest pain, shortness of breath, and decreased motivation. It is important to note that this increased fatigue and lack of motivation can also relate to elevated levels of depression. While anemia can cause elevated fatigue levels, an individual with chronic illness can experience fatigue unrelated to anemia. Studies by McKinney and colleagues (1997) and Burns (1999) indicate that a series of GIM sessions can decrease the perception of fatigue, which is maintained through a six-week follow-up.

The treatment of nausea and pain in chronic illness has steadily advanced over the past ten years. There are currently very effective antiemetics that reduce both the incidents of emesis and the perception of nausea. Pain treatment has also become increasingly more effective with the differentiation between addiction and dependence. There is no longer any excuse for an individual with a chronic illness to experience pain. However, elevated levels of emotional distress can exacerbate the experience of pain and nausea.

While medications dramatically impact a health care provider's ability to manage symptoms related to treatment and illness, patients also seek out complementary therapies to assist in managing symptoms. These psychosocial therapies intervene through cognitive and affective pathways associated with biopsychosocial models. Cognitive pathways involve the interaction between thoughts, emotional responses, and corresponding behavioral patterns. The cognitive consequences relating to a chronic illness can have a wide impact on other areas of functioning. Feelings and thoughts of hopelessness, helplessness, and corresponding loss of self-esteem can begin a cycle of self-defeating thoughts and behaviors, which can lead to affective disturbances. Cohen and Rodriguez (1995) explain that cognitive interpretations characterized as catastrophizing, perfectionism, dichotomous thinking, and blaming self and others can lead to inaccurate cognitive distortions. These distorted cognitions lead to negative psychological responses including increased stress perceptions, decreased locus of control, self-esteem, self-efficacy, and associated affective disturbances (Cohen & Rodriguez, 1995).

Finally, social pathways have an impact on the outcome of chronic illnesses. Decreased social functioning such as sexual activity or enjoyment, decreased social network, and the decreased ability to work due to illness are included within the biopsychosocial model of disease impact. Bruscia (1991) illustrates the isolation an individual with HIV can experience through social withdrawal and the negative thought patterns associated with a chronic illness and with an illness that has a social stigma attached. Decreases in a person's ability to engage in life negatively impact health-related quality of life.

The concept of health-related quality of life developed through health care professionals' realization that aspects outside of the medical treatment of illness impact outcomes. While there are a variety of definitions of quality of life throughout the research literature, it is generally accepted that the level of quality of life is determined by the patient's perspective. Quality of life is a multidimensional concept that includes the patient's evaluation of physical, emotional, and spiritual well-being (Cella, 1998). As stated previously, an individual's experience of physical attributes such as fatigue, pain, strength, and functional dependency can contribute to their perception of wellbeing and satisfaction with treatment and life. Elevated levels of emotional distress also negatively affect quality of life. Spiritual well being is identified in the literature about quality of life as being correlated with positive health outcomes and psychosocial adjustment to illness. Studies indicating the exact relationship between spiritual well-being and health outcomes are sparse. The available literature suggests that a belief in God or a higher power helps manage distress related to chronic illness, and that prayer is an important coping strategy within spiritual practice (Khouzam, 1996; Potts, 1996).

## CHRONIC ILLNESS DISEASE TRAJECTORY

Chronic illness and treatment can be divided into stages of disease trajectory that are delineated by psychosocial and physical issues and corresponding treatment interventions (Andersen, 1992; Caudell, 1996; Emmelkamp, 1996; Lewis,

1997). Illness phases and corresponding psychological and physical issues create a structure for psychosocial interventions and treatment goals.

## Diagnosis

The process of diagnosis and treatment is emotionally overwhelming due to the new information concerning diagnosis and the need to make treatment decisions. Psychological issues include anxiety and fear, shock, disbelief, anger, bitterness, hostility, depression, and self-pity (Zabora et al., 1997). Due to the nature of distress experienced during this time, emotional support, adaptive coping, and education about treatment are helpful intervention strategies (Caudell, 1996). Individuals benefit from disease treatment education and education regarding techniques to improve coping such as stress management or cognitive restructuring. Therefore, intervention strategies such as listening, encouraging emotional expression, providing reassurance, facilitated prayer, and spiritual exploration are very helpful during this period.

GIM includes a majority of intervention strategies that are useful during the diagnosis stage. The interaction between the facilitator and the traveler provides multiple opportunities for the facilitator to listen to issues and feelings that the traveler may be experiencing. Being a good listener is the first quality of a GIM guide that Bonny lists in the initial monograph (Bonny, 1978). She goes on to say that "A guide is a listener and a sharer—with more emphasis on listening" (Bonny, 1978, p. 7). During periods of medical testing and diagnosis, a patient receives an enormous amount of new information, without much opportunity to talk about the experience and corresponding feelings. GIM sessions provide an opportunity for an individual to begin to share information and bring meaning into what has been happening to them, an opportunity to share his or her personal story.

One of the essences of a GIM experience is the opportunity to express feelings, regardless of the quality. As described previously, the process of testing and diagnosis is a negative, stressful event that may elicit multiple feelings including fear, anxiety, anger, and confusion. GIM provides ample opportunity to express these feelings and resolve emotional conflicts. In fact, researchers are beginning to understand the value of emotional expression in coping with chronic illnesses. Data suggest that emotional expression enhances the immune function and decreases chronic stress responses. Pennebaker, Kiecolt-Glaser, and Glaser (1988) found that writing about traumatic events has a positive impact on immune measures. Epping-Jordan, Compas, and Howell (1994) also demonstrated that behavioral avoidance, or any active attempt to minimize the impact of cancer and its corresponding emotional impact was significantly predictive of cancer recurrence. Cancer patients have also experienced enhanced immune response after four monthly support groups utilizing guided imagery and emotional expression (Post-White, 1993).

Logan (1998) provides an outstanding example of the benefits of BMGIM during the diagnostic phase of a chronic illness. The author describes working with a middle-aged woman with a blood-borne illness. Medical tests required hospitalization until the physicians could determine an accurate diagnosis. During the initial BMGIM session, the woman was able to release tears and tension related to her medical condition. Logan describes this process as "a steam valve – letting off some emotional tension . . ." (p. 21). This session also allowed for education regarding the impact that stress has on the body and the corresponding importance of stress reduction exercises.

There is not much literature describing the processes travelers may experience with GIM during the diagnostic phase of a chronic illness. It is certainly possible for this method to also provide reassurance, and to facilitate prayer and spiritual exploration. The presence of the guide and the stability of the music provide the support and reassurance individuals may require during this time of unpredictability. The guide's choice of music during this time can provide a contrast to the tumultuous feelings and events, and provide the opportunity for calm, security, and rest. These periods of rest can provide the opportunity for spiritual reflection, exploration, and prayer.

## Treatment

During the treatment process the focus shifts from a primary emotional supportive component to a focus on symptom management. This includes management of both treatment-related symptoms and disease-related symptoms. Interventions to alleviate pain, nausea, and improve coping are useful in supporting the patient during the treatment phase. The patient may also experience elevated levels of emotional distress related to symptoms and treatment, including fear of procedures, fear of decreased self-control, and fear of decreased quality of life. The stress related to these issues can lead to elevated levels of physiological arousal, which in turn can lead to immunosuppression. Intervention strategies that have shown positive impact on symptom control include relaxation and guided imagery, coping skills training, and cognitive/attentional distraction (Post-White, 1993; Meyer & Mark, 1995; Richardson et al., 1997; Sloman, 1995).

Researchers have demonstrated that BMGIM is effective in positively impacting chronic pain in rheumatoid arthritis patients (Jacobi & Eisenberg, 1994). There are a variety of ways that issues of pain can be addressed during a Bonny method session; two include either experiencing healing images that alleviate pain perception or through the symbolic representation of the pain in an effort to find meaning.

While cancer patients rarely have to experience the intensity of pain that they did in the past, bone metastasis continues to be the most painful symptom of cancer disease progression. Logan (1998) describes BMGIM sessions of a gentleman who was undergoing radiation therapy for stage four lung cancer, with bone metastasis. During the fourth session of his series, the traveler chose to focus on the pain in his ribs, legs, and vertebra. During the music, the traveler experienced bodily sensations of warmth through those areas experiencing pain. The music's bass lines supported the warmth as some of the pain subsided.

Another example of healing images used to alleviate pain perception is described by Burns (1999). This particular session was the fifth of a series of ten with a thirty-three-year-old woman recovering from a unilateral mastectomy to treat a duet carcinoma in situ. While the actual mastectomy had been completed six months prior to the first session, the traveler was beginning the process of breast reconstruction, which also is very painful. This particular session occurred after the reconstruction surgery. The traveler described an image of herself being in a bubble bath surrounded with lit candles. The water felt very warm and healing against her body. When the music was over, she stated that the imagery was helpful in relieving the pain related to the surgery and that it was also helpful in improving her mood.

Finally, Logan (1998) provides an example of how relief in both physical and emotional tension can provide pain relief. She describes a session with a woman who was experiencing a high level of anxiety and pain. The music provided structure for breathing and relaxation, thus encouraging peaceful images and feelings. This modification of the Bonny method served as a simple intervention that the client could use even when the therapist was not available.

Nausea is a common experience for individuals undergoing radiation or chemotherapy. Current treatments for chemotherapy-induced nausea are very effective, but patients continue to struggle with anticipatory nausea. The anxiety related to treatment side effects is enough for some people to refuse treatment. Some patients seek out interventions like GIM in order to alleviate these fears and anxieties related to treatment. Logan (1998) describes such a client undergoing radiation therapy to shrink a brain tumor. While the treatment period was abbreviated, the traveler sought out BMGIM sessions in an attempt to relieve the fear and symptoms related to his illness and the treatment. Bruscia (1991) describes a client's insight into nausea related to anxiety as the consequence of not crying. This client was able to identify several physiological consequences of not addressing the emotional challenges related to his illness and to his past abuse.

Increased levels of fatigue are common during the treatment period of a chronic illness. Individuals being treated for HIV or AIDS often experience fatigue related to the prescriptions needed to fight the virus. Cancer patients experience fatigue from both radiation and chemotherapy treatments. Patients experiencing fatigue after chemotherapy may be suffering from a low red blood count. Chemotherapy-induced anemia is easily treated with medication; however, GIM can also have a positive impact on levels of fatigue (Burns, 1999). It is not clear why fatigue levels may diminish during a series of GIM sessions, however, the music provides the support for rest and then the encouragement for action when the traveler has enough energy to accept the challenge. The case studies described by Burns (1999) indicate that travelers with cancer use the beginning portion of the session to rest and gain energy from the music and imagery. Increases in imagery movement often translate to increased energy at the completion of the sessions. The second half of the session, and series, is spent expressing emotions related to the illness and finding meaning to the experience.

## Survivorship

When the response to treatment is evaluated, there can be several outcomes that bring about additional psychosocial issues. These include cure or remission, nonresponse to treatment, advanced disease, or cure with eventual relapse. Individuals who have experienced a remission or cure still face numerous psychosocial challenges as they live without evidence of disease. They may experience an increased vulnerability to illness and death and/or have difficulty making decisions. These difficulties can result in increased stress and an increased incidence of depression and anxiety, which negatively impact immune and endocrine function, decreasing quality of life. Treatment interventions to address the challenges of survivors include support groups and stress management classes to increase adaptive coping.

Hale (1992) describes a series of sessions with a breast cancer survivor. This woman was three years postmastectomy and continued to experience fears related to recurrence. Hale describes the woman's process beginning with negative images surrounding her surgically altered body to healing images of light coming into the mastectomy wounds. Burns (1999) also describes BMGIM sessions with a woman five years post double radical mastectomy, who also continued to experience a poor self-image. Her process evolved from allowing herself to be a victim and expecting to be rescued into a strong, confident woman willing to take risks and allow herself to live her life without the fear of recurrence.

Recurrence may be more stressful to a patient and his family than the initial diagnosis; however, they may also be more familiar with the health care system, and therefore not as anxious as during the previous treatment period. Anxiety is a predominant feature of an individual experiencing a recurrence. Stress management, opportunity to verbalize feelings, and symptom management are important issues to address during this period.

## PALLIATIVE CARE

Nonresponders often receive additional treatment if it is clinically warranted. These individuals experience a high level of stress due to the lack of treatment effectiveness. Nonresponders may eventually enter into hospice where the focus is on palliative care. Hospice focuses on providing relief from depression and symptoms such as pain and the fear of pain. Common feelings include sadness, grief, worry, and insecurity. Individuals who are dying need a caring environment in which needs can be met without suffering the fear of becoming a burden. They also need the time and opportunity to voice fears, come to terms with oneself and the illness, draw closer to loved ones, and finalize personal affairs. Programs for depression and anxiety, prayer or spiritual exploration facilitation, storytelling or life reviews, and stress management can provide opportunities for individuals who are dying to address personal issues and prepare for death.

Marr (1998–99) describes two case studies of individuals at the end of life. First, she describes working with a man with advanced AIDS. Marr indicates that the goals for BMGIM therapy for this individual included "to define his purpose and meaning in the light of his present physical limitations, and to regain a sense of his spiritual core and his creativity" (p. 41). Through two sessions, the traveler was able to rediscover his spiritual strength and identity through musical support and image transformation. Marr also describes working with a woman with advanced breast cancer and Parkinson's disease. The traveler, who was interested in other types of complementary and alternative medicine, sought out BMGIM for pain control and distraction from her cancer. Her process also unfolded as an effort to rediscover the self and focus on her quality of life.

## TREATMENT CONSIDERATIONS

When considering whether an individual is appropriate for group GIM or BMGIM, the practitioner must consider the type of distress the person is experiencing, functional status, transportation issues, personal interest and motivation, and religious beliefs (Caudell, 1996). First, the type of distress a person is experiencing will influence the structure of the beginning sessions and the goals of therapy. If an individual is distressed (depressed or anxious) appropriate goals for treatment may begin with psychological healing, as they are already in a vulnerable, emotionally raw state. In this way, music that is very nurturing, predictable, and supportive is useful to provide emotional grounding before advancing in the therapy process. Hale (1992) explained that in working with a woman recovering from a mastectomy that she needed to experience inner strength, trust, support, and protection. Bruscia (1991) also describes using an induction designed to encourage inner strength in a client diagnosed with HIV. These are all examples of how the GIM can provide a supportive framework for psychological work. If the therapist determines that the client has gained sufficient internal strength and support through the music, it may then be appropriate to advance the therapeutic process with the "working tapes." These tapes encourage emotional expressions, which as stated previously may improve psychological functioning and improve immune status.

In addition to emotional status, functional status is also an important consideration when determining an individual's ability to participate in the therapeutic process. Pain and fatigue are both considered within this category. If an individual is experiencing extreme pain and/or fatigue, the therapist must structure the intervention so the client can experience a successful session. Successful sessions may focus on increasing relaxation and providing a sense of comfort. Increased muscle tension can increase pain perception; therefore, increasing relaxation is a very valid therapeutic goal. It may be necessary to ensure that a person is first treated medically before GIM sessions. Acute pain makes it very difficult to proceed with the process.

GIM sessions can significantly impact the perception of fatigue (Burns, 1999). But, as stated before, the process may be slow and depend upon music and imagery that involves rest and healing. It is imperative to allow the client to have as much control as possible over these sessions, as one of the consequences of chronic illness is the loss of control. Allowing the client to work through these issues on a slower timetable than what a healthy person may do is to be expected.

Personal interest and motivation are always a consideration when a person decides to enter into any type of psychotherapeutic process. Individuals with chronic illnesses are no exception. Some will participate because of the increased knowledge and media regarding the benefits of complementary therapies on health outcomes. Other patients will be extremely skeptical but desperate to try anything that may relieve symptoms. The GIM therapist must be cognizant of this fact and be sensitive to the client's objectives prior to beginning therapy sessions. Additionally, the therapist should not guarantee success—this is unethical—especially considering the lack of research that can be generalized to chronic patient populations.

Finally, religious beliefs can also increase or decrease a person's likelihood of becoming involved in the GIM process. Stories of spiritual experiences during GIM sessions abound, and the frequency in which individuals experience spiritual images makes it very appropriate for chronic populations who often undergo a existential crisis; there is no quantitative research however that speaks directly to the benefits of spiritual experiences during the GIM process.

There are many considerations when assessing the appropriateness of an individual with chronic illness. Marr (1998–99) also describes contraindications to GIM in palliative care. She states that if concentration is limited due to symptoms, the client will have difficulty maintaining focus and will not have enough energy to fully engage in the process. The facilitator should then decide whether or not minimal engagement can bring about positive outcomes. The traditional contraindications regarding hallucinations, personality disorders, and suicidality also apply. The rate of suicide success in some chronic illness sufferers is extremely high.

This chapter has mainly focused on the issues those with chronic illness face. Some of the issues that GIM and BMGIM can address are fairly obvious. It is a flexible modality that can address issues regardless of treatment stage and treatment. The therapist needs to be very knowledgeable regarding individual illnesses in order to intervene most effectively. Additional quantitative and qualitative research will add to our current knowledge base and ensure best practice within this modality.

## *References*

Andersen, B. (1992). Psychological interventions for cancer patients to enhance the quality of life. *Journal of Consulting and Clinical Psychology, 60,* 552–568.

Andersen, B., Kiecolt-Glaser, J., and Glaser, R. (1994). A biobehavioral model of cancer stress and disease course. *American Psychologist, 49,* 389–404.

Baum, A., Herberman, H., & Cohen, L. (1995). Managing stress and managing illness: Survival and quality of life in chronic disease. *Journal of Clinical Psychology in Medical Settings, 2,* 309–333.

Bonny, H. (1978). *Facilitating Guided Imagery and Music Sessions.* (Monograph # 1). Baltimore: ICM Books.

Bruscia, K. (1991). Embracing life with AIDS: Psychotherapy through guided imagery and music (GIM). In K. Bruscia (ed.), *Case Studies in Music Therapy* (pp. 581–602). Philadelphia: Barcelona Publishers.

Burns, D. (1999). *The Effect of the Bonny Method of Guided Imagery and Music on the Quality of Life and Cortisol Levels of Cancer Patients.* Unpublished doctoral dissertation. The University of Kansas, Lawrence, KS.

Caudell, K. (1996). Psychoneuroimmunology and innovative behavioral interventions in patients with leukemia. *Oncology Nursing Forum,* 23, 493–502.

Cella, D. (1998). Factors influencing quality of life in cancer patients: Anemia and fatigue. *Seminars in Oncology, 25,* (Suppl. 7), 43–46.

Cohen, S., & Rodriguez, M. (1995). Pathways linking affective disturbances and physical disorders. *Health Psychology, 14*(5), 374–380.

Emmelkamp, P. (1996). Psychosocial factors in HIV-AIDS. *Psychotherapy and Psychosomatics, 65,* 225–228.

Epping-Jordan, J., Compas, B., & Howell, D. (1994). Predictors of cancer progression in young adult men and women: Avoidance, intrusive thoughts, and psychological symptoms. *Health Psychology, 13,* 539–547.

Hale, S. (1992). Wounded woman: The use of guided imagery and music in recovering from a mastectomy. *Journal of the Association for Music and Imagery, 1,* 99–106.

Iwagaki, H., Hizuta, A., Uomoto, M., Tekeuchi, Y., Saito, S., & Tanaka, N. (1997). Cancer cachexia and depressive states: A neuro-endocrine-immunological disease? *ACTA Medical Okayama, 51,* 233–236.

Jacobi, E., & Eisenberg., G. (1994). *The Efficacy of the Bonny Method of Guided Imagery and Music (GIM) as Experiential Therapy in the Primary Care of Persons with Rheumatoid Arthritis.* Paper presented at the Association for Music and Imagery Conference, Little Switzerland, NC.

Katon, W., & Sullivan, M. (1990). Depression and chronic medical illness. *Journal of Clinical Psychiatry, 51,* 3–11.

Khouzam, H. (1996). Prayer and the treatment of depression in a case of prostate cancer. *Clinical Gerontologist, 17,* 69–73.

Lechin, F., Van der Dijs, B., Vitelli-Florez, V., Lechin, Baez, S., Azocar, J., Cabrera, A., Lechin, A., Jara, H., Lechin, M., Gomez, F., & Rocha, L. (1990). Psychoneuroendocrinological and immunological parameters in cancer patients: Involvement of stress and depression. *Psychoneuro-endocrinology,* 25, 435–451.

Lewis, F. M. (1997). Behavioral research to enhance adjustment and quality of life among adults with cancer. *Preventive Medicine,* 26, S19–S29.

Logan, H. (1998). Applied music-evoked imagery for the oncology patient: Results and case studies of a three month music therapy pilot program. Unpublished manuscript.

Marr, J. (1998–99). GIM at the end of life: Case studies in palliative care. *Journal of the Association for Mental Imagery,* 6, 37–54.

McDaniel, J., Musselman, D., Porter, M., Reed, D., & Nemberoff, C. (1995). Depression in patients with cancer. *Archives of General Psychiatry,* 52, 89–99.

McKinney, C., Antoni, M., Kumar, A., & Kumar, M. (1995). Effects of guided imagery and music on depression and beta-endorphin levels in healthy adults: A pilot study. *Journal of the Association for Music and Imagery,* 4, 67-78.

McKinney, C., Antoni, M., Kumar, M., Tims, F., & McCabe, P. (1997). Effects of guided imagery and music (GIM) therapy on mood and cortisol in healthy adults. *Health Psychology,* 16, 390–400.

Meyer, T., & Mark, M. (1995). Effects of psychosocial interventions with adult cancer patients: A meta-analysis of randomized experiments. *Health Psychology,* 14, 101–108.

Pennebaker, J., Kiecolt-Glaser, J., & Glaser, R. (1988). Disclosure of traumas and immune function: Health implications for psychotherapy. *Journal of Consulting and Clinical Psychology,* 56, 239–245.

Post-White, J. (1993). The effects of imagery on emotions, immune function, and cancer outcome. *Mainlines,* 14(1), 18–20.

Potts, R. (1996). Spirituality and the experience of cancer in an African-American community: Implications for psychosocial oncology. *Journal of Psychosocial Oncology,* 14, 1–19.

Richardson, M., Post-White, J., Grimm, E., Moye, L., Singeltary, E., & Justice, B. (1997). Coping, life attitudes, and immune responses to imagery and group support after breast cancer treatment. *Alternative Therapies,* 3(5), 62–70.

Sloman, R. (1995). Relaxation and the relief of cancer pain. *Nursing Clinics of North America,* 30, 697–709.

Zabora, J., Blanchard, C., Smith, E., Roberts, C., Glajchen, M., Sharp, J., Brintzenhofeszoc, K., Locker, J., Carr. E., Best-Casterner,S., Smith, P., Dozier-Hall, D., Polinsky, M., Hedlund, S. (1997). Prevalence of psychological distress among cancer patients across the disease continuum. *Journal of Psychosocial Oncology,* 15, 73–87.

*Chapter Ten*

# PSYCHOTHERAPEUTIC APPLICATIONS OF THE BONNY METHOD

## Anthony Meadows

The Bonny Method of Guided Imagery and Music (BMGIM) (Bonny, 1978) has been used as a form of psychotherapy with a variety of clinical and non-clinical conditions. These clinical conditions include adults with psychiatric diagnoses (e.g. schizophrenia), Post Traumatic Stress Disorder (PTSD), trauma related to sexual abuse, autism, depression, and eating disorders. Nonclinical conditions include grief, relationship issues, and loss. The purpose of this chapter is to analyze the case-study literature with these various populations according to goal, method, role of the therapist, role of the music, and theoretical perspective.

## SEXUAL ABUSE

Five case studies describe the experiences of clients who have been sexually abused: three with female clients abused by their fathers (Borling, 1992; Tasney, 1993; Ventre, 1994), and two with male clients abused by a man (Bruscia, 1991; Pickett, 1995). In most cases, the sexual abuse was the core clinical issue; however, clients exhibited a range of clinical characteristics including post traumatic stress disorder (PTSD), depression, nervous breakdown, substance abuse (in recovery phase), poor body image, sexual dysfunction, and chaotic family life.

All clients worked with therapists in private practice settings. The length of therapy varied considerably, from fifty-six sessions completed over two years (Ventre, 1994), to ten sessions over a period of six months (Tasney, 1993).

The most common goal was to help the client work through and heal the trauma of sexual abuse. Depending on the client's circumstances, this may have involved: re-experiencing the trauma within the safe container of the BMGIM experience; releasing feelings of grief, anger, and stuckness; doing inner child work; and undergoing various kinds of corrective emotional experiences. Also important to the process was building the client's self esteem, restoring their sense of personal power and control, finding more adaptive solutions to stress and pain associated with the abuse, and helping the clients function more effectively in the world. In some cases, the therapist directed the client into specific memories of abuse (Borling, 1992), whereas in other cases the therapist directed the client to operate on the images in specific kinds of ways (Pickett, 1995). Important to all these cases was the sense of trust and safety established between client and therapist in order to deal with the abuse trauma. Ventre (1994) felt that this was important so that work related to memories of the sexual abuse could begin. Borling (1992) viewed trust in terms of a plateau effect, as he felt that there were limitations to the work that a female client could do with a male guide.

Both individual BMGIM and group GIM have been used, and these sessions were sometimes interspersed with verbal therapy. Various approaches have been taken to understanding the client's process. Pickett (1995) and Ventre (1994) described their client's processes as unfolding in three related stages, whereas other therapists linked materials from the sessions into a narrative (Borling, 1992; Bruscia, 1991) or according to a specific theoretical construct such as the *Shadow* (Tasney, 1993). All dealt with preparing the client for the intense work, helping the client change his/her relationship with the perpetrator, and helping the client look to life beyond the abuse.

In reflecting on their own experiences as BMGIM clients, Lilly (Ventre, 1999) and T. (T. & Caughman, 1999) identified a number of important elements in their own recovery from sexual abuse. BMGIM helped T. to remember, confront, and integrate feelings and images associated with sexual abuse as a child, particularly anger. Lilly found that BMGM enabled her to re-connect with her own wounded child, bring this child into relationship with her adult self, and find a new sense of courage to "be in the world."

A range of theoretical perspectives were taken in interpreting the client's processes. These included Jungian theory (Tasney, 1993), psychodynamic constructs (Bruscia, 1991), Bradshaw's Inner Child Work (Borling, 1992), Grof's Perinatal Matrices (Borling, 1992), Kellogg's Mandala Theory (Borling, 1992) and Herman's (1992) diagnostic category of complex posttraumatic stress disorder. Pickett (1995) framed her client's experiences according to their imagery experiences.

Most often, therapists used the taped programs of Bonny (1978) and other programmers; in contrast, Ventre (1994) took an improvisational approach, selecting each piece in-vivo according to the client's needs. While anecdotal, it is interesting to note the types of music programs that were used. *Mostly Bach,* and *Emotional Expression I* were used by Borling (1992), Tasney (1993), and Pickett (1995) at different stages of the client's process, most notably, at key moments in the client's healing. For example, both Tasney and Pickett used *Mostly Bach* to help structure and support work on anger felt by clients that was related to the abuse experience. Tasney used *Emotional Expression I* to help her client deal with direct memories of the abuse and to evaluate the resolution of the anger which had been expressed in the previous session (when *Mostly Bach* was used). Pickett used *Emotional Expression I* to help the client work through murderous fantasies related to his father, who had abandoned him as a child. Her client was then able to grieve the loss of his father.

## POST-TRAUMATIC STRESS DISORDER

Six cases describe BMGIM experiences of clients with post traumatic stress disorder (PTSD): two working with Vietnam veterans in a veteran's affairs medical center (Blake, 1994; Blake & Bishop, 1994), one with a woman admitted to a psychiatric hospital (Goldberg, 1994), and three with clients who were sexually abused as children (Blake & Bishop, 1994; Pickett, 1995; Ventre, 1994). In all cases, the PTSD was a core clinical issue, seen as emerging out of sexual abuse, war experiences, or a specific traumatic event. Clients exhibited a number of other clinical characteristics, including depression, alexithymia, and sexual dysfunction.

Four approaches can be seen in working with PTSD: 1) using the individual form of BMGIM as developed by Bonny (1978) (Blake, 1994; Pickett, 1995; Ventre, 1994); 2) using an adapted individual form of BMGIM, which usually involves less music and directive guiding (Goldberg, 1994), 3) using another adapted individual form of BMGIM known as Directed Imagery and Music (DIM) (Blake, 1994) developed to confront specific traumatic events, and 4) using a group form of GIM. The use of each of these methods is determined according to several variables: whether the client is in an inpatient or outpatient environment; the client's level of psychological health; the goals of therapy; and the anticipated length of therapy.

When the *original form* of BMGIM is used with clients who have PTSD, clients are seen in individual sessions, and each session consists of the standard components developed by Bonny (1978) (prelude, induction, imagery focus, music, postlude), sometimes alternating with verbal therapy sessions. The goals of therapy center on uncovering and working through events associated with PTSD symptoms. This involves a) bringing into awareness and working through memories of sexual abuse so that clients can heal the wounds of the trauma, b) learning how to live in the present, less encumbered by the past, and c) finding adaptive solutions to their PTSD symptoms (Blake & Bishop, 1994; Pickett, 1994; Ventre, 1994). When working with Vietnam veterans in an inpatient setting (Blake, 1994), the goals of therapy were different, and centered on a) exploring inner feelings and inner lives while maintaining a sense of control, b) expanding the capacity to feel emotions, c) increasing self- understanding, d) achieving relaxation, and d) heightening concentration. Note that these clients were seen for shorter series of sessions, typically three to four.

Various approaches were taken to understanding the client's process. Two case studies (Pickett, 1995; Ventre, 1994) described their client's processes as unfolding in three related stages, whereas in others, individual sessions were described and/or linked together in a narrative (Blake, 1994; Blake & Bishop, 1994).

An *adapted individual form* of GIM was used with adults in an inpatient psychiatric setting (Goldberg, 1994). Clients were usually only admitted for short periods of time, so that the central goal of treatment was to help clients to stabilize, deal with "here and now" issues, and develop sufficient ego strength to return to the community. Each session consisted of the standard components of BMGIM previously mentioned, with two major differences. The first concerned the amount of music used. Goldberg (1994) tended to use less music (15-30 minutes) and was likely to sequence music selections according to some aspect of the client's presenting symptoms and/or process rather then according to a music program. In fact, Goldberg described the role of the music as being supportive and structured, with a shorter musical phrase (p. 22). She felt that this, combined with active and sometimes directive guiding, enabled clients to use the music as a "transitional object," keep their anxiety at more manageable levels, and build ego strength.

A third approach to working with clients who have PTSD was developed by Blake (1994), in response to the needs of Vietnam veterans dealing with traumatic war experiences. Blake developed Directed Imagery and Music (DIM) to retrieve specific traumatic memories so as to reconnect with associated emotions. The structure of DIM is similar to the traditional form of BMGIM (Bonny, 1978) with three main differences. The first is that the therapist and client meet a week prior to the session to select a specific traumatic event that will be the focus of the DIM session, and to describe any details that are remembered. Second, on the day of the session, the purpose of the prelude is to have the veteran re-describe as much of the event as possible and connect with any associated feelings. Third, the therapist typically selects only three to four pieces of music to accompany the memory. In a brief case vignette, Blake described how her client was able to relive a forgotten combat experience, mourn the loss of a close friend in battle, and connect with emotions associated with the combat experience. Her client reported that the music helped him stay in the memory, rather than drifting through different memories. This in turn helped him to reconnect with important feelings, and bring some emotional relief.

A fourth approach, an adaptation of Bonny's Group GIM, has been described by a number of therapists (Blake & Bishop, 1994; Goldberg, 1994). While Goldberg (1994) did not specifically discuss group work with PTSD clients, the reader is led to assume that her approach to group work has been used with this population. Both Goldberg (1994) and Blake and Bishop (1994) describe the necessity to make certain adaptations. Blake and Bishop (1994) described the following adaptations: (a) a short relaxation induction (one to two minutes); (b) the client remaining in a sitting position; (c) a high level of specificity for both the goal and the session and the starting image; (d) short duration of the music (no more than ten minutes); (e) experiencing the music and imagery with eyes open, and supported by drawing or movement; (f) an emphasis on safety, validation, and reinforcement of efforts to create solutions to problems identified in the prelude (p. 128). Goldberg (1994) described a similar approach to group work; however, she used music throughout the induction (relaxation and focus) and imagery experience, and emphasized the role of the therapist in providing a clear verbal structure to the imagery so that images did not become frightening or overwhelming. Goldberg's approach to guiding differed from that of Blake and Bishop as they did not guide clients during the imagery experience. Instead, Blake and Bishop worked with client's images in the postlude.

While Blake and Bishop (1994) did not discuss the purpose of GIM group work, Goldberg (1994) identified a number of goals: a) to address individual client goals identified at the beginning of each session; b) to facilitative supportive relationships between clients; and c) to encourage clients to take responsibility for themselves by attempting to understand the reasons they were hospitalized, and thereby gain some control and mastery of themselves (pp. 25-26).

On reviewing these approaches with PTSD clients, various uses of the music can be seen. In some approaches, the role of the music was to uncover material from the client's unconscious. For example, Blake (1994), Ventre (1994), and Pickett (1995) all used music is help their clients explore their imaginal worlds, to confront traumatic experiences, and to facilitate healing, using complete music programs, or selecting music in-vivo to meet the client's needs. Thus, the purpose of the music was to help break down defenses, re-connect with past events and experiences, and deal directly with trauma related to PTSD. This approach was taken in both outpatient private practice and an inpatient veterans affairs facility. The inpatient veterans were long-term residents who received a broad range of therapeutic services that supported their BMGIM experiences.

While Goldberg (1994) also used music to explore the client's imaginal world, she took a very different approach. The purpose of uncovering was to help clients discover the resources to deal with their outer world. Thus, rather than breaking down defenses, the purpose was to develop "defensive maneuvers" that would help the client build ego strength to function in the community. In facilitating this process, the music selected was much shorter in length, and described by Goldberg as primarily supportive. This would appear to imply that the music was not confrontational, expansive, or complex, but rather supported the client's search for comforting, positive images. This approach was taken in a short-term, inpatient psychiatry.

In another approach, developed specifically for use in Directed Imagery and Music (DIM) (Blake, 1994), three to four pieces of music were selected to match a specific traumatic memory (i.e., war combat). The purpose of the music was to provide accompaniment to the experience, to match the anticipated emotions associated with the experience, and to build to a peak in line with the memory. Thus, the purpose of the music was not to facilitate the spontaneous development of imagery, but rather to work through a specific memory, to remember this as completely as possible, and to connect with and release associated feelings. Blake also used "new age" music in the postlude, to allow for separation from the emotions uncovered in the music-imagery experience, and this was sometimes a means of closing sessions.

Not surprisingly, the BMGIM therapists took on a number of different roles in relation to the client. In all cases it appeared essential that a sense of trust and safety be established between client and therapist in order to deal with the PTSD symptoms. Ventre (1994) and Goldberg (1994) specifically describe this in the first stage of their work with clients. Goldberg (1994) felt that establishing a sense of safety and trust would help clients to begin to find their own resources to deal with their therapeutic issues, and thereby improve the client's ego strength. Blake (1994) described how she adopted very directive guiding during DIM sessions to help her clients stay in the combat memory. Blake also found that some veterans required more directive questioning and encouragement in communicating their imagery experiences. Similarly, Goldberg (1994) tended to take a directive role in supporting her clients to find positive resources to deal with their immediate needs. Through her guiding, Goldberg helped the client move away from difficult images and find images that were comforting and supportive. It was only when the client was ready, and had explicitly stated this, that Goldberg entered into the difficult images with the client, to work through them together.

## ADDICTIONS

Two authors have described their work with clients who have addictions, one employing individual BMGIM (Pickett, 1992), and the other employing Group GIM (Skaggs, 1997).

Pickett (1992) presented a case study on BMGIM with a female client with food (bulimia), alcohol, and drug (prescription medications) addictions. While the addictions were central to the client's work, she was also obese, and had been sexually and physically abused in her marriage. In presenting the case, Pickett selected key images to demonstrate her client's process and linked these together in a narrative. These included "the wall," which represented the client's isolation; "the addict," in which the client was able to dialogue with the addict inside; "the talking loaf of bread," in which she was able to dialogue with and understand her dependence on food; "the dead tree," in which the client was able to see herself as a dying tree, attend to the tree, and see herself in a new way; and "judge, nasty, tender child," in which various parts of the client, which had been acting independently, came to be understood as addictive dimensions of the self. With this understanding came a reduction in their individual power and the beginnings of alternate and healthier ways of dealing with internal and external stressors.

Skaggs (1997) outlined a rationale for Group GIM with the chemically dependent. She felt that addicts are essentially addicted to meet unconscious needs, and as GIM is a method that taps into unconscious material, it is well suited for work with this population. Skaggs offered weekly group sessions for a three-week period as part of a residential program for addicts in the recovery phase (post detoxification). Sessions were in Bonny's Group GIM format: an opening discussion in which clients talk about current issues, feelings, and concerns; a relaxation induction and imagery focus; an unguided music and imagery experience typically using a single piece of music (five to seven minutes in duration); and a final period of discussion and reflection on the imagery experience.

Reflecting on her clinical experiences, and with the use of vignettes, Skaggs outlined the following benefits of Group GIM in aiding recovery from addiction(s): (a) it allowed the client to view life from different perspectives; (b) it accessed and built trust in an inner helper, thereby building a sense of autonomy and control; (c) it took a moral and personal inventory of the self; (d) it resolved internal conflicts, and healed old wounds; (e) it brought together fragmented pieces of the self, and (f) served as a mental model for healthy responses (e.g. behavioral rehearsal) (p. 28).

## DEPRESSION

The BMGIM experiences of clients with depression have been described in four case studies (Bush, 1992; Holligan, 1992; Walker, 1993; Weiss, 1994) and a number of vignettes (Summer, 1988). In three of the case studies (Bush, 1992; Walker, 1993, and Weiss, 1994), depression was a core therapeutic issue whereas in a fourth (Holligan, 1992), it was secondary to an acute anxiety disorder. Clients also exhibited other clinical characteristics, including anxiety (Weiss, 1994), suicidal ideation (Holligan, 1992), sexual abuse (Weiss, 1994), paranoia (Summer, 1988), and dysthymic disorder (Summer, 1988).

Clear differences can be seen in both the goals and processes of clients. In most cases, the purpose of BMGIM was to lessen defenses, and help the client enter into unconscious psychic material. When this approach was taken, the depression could be dealt with indirectly (Holligan, 1992; Walker, 1993; Weiss, 1994), so that symptoms were addressed, or directly (Bush, 1992) so that the client would create images of her depression. Summer (1988) took a different approach. Instead of focusing on lessening defenses and allowing the client to enter deeply into psychic material, she was simultaneously concerned with helping clients to develop sufficient ego strength to deal with their current situations and stabilize their psychotic symptoms. Only when these goals had been met did Summer carefully allow clients to enter into imagery material related to their depression.

Clients worked with BMGIM therapists in private practice, outpatient settings and inpatient mental health facilities. The length of therapy varied considerably, from approximately seventy-eight sessions over eighteen months (Bush, 1992) to five sessions over six months (Walker, 1993), although the length of therapy was not always clear.

Typically the original individual form of BMGIM was used, although this was often interspersed with verbal therapy sessions (Holligan, 1992), or it was used as an adjunct to verbal therapy (Walker, 1993). An adapted form of BMGIM was also used in inpatient psychiatry (Summer, 1988). In the adapted form, the client was given a very structured prelude, a relaxation induction, and guiding during the session (Summer, 1988). While Summer did not discuss this in further detail, she appears to imply that the purpose of this adaptation was to enter into the client's imagery world in a contained way, one that maintains clear boundaries and a sense of control.

Various approaches were taken to describing the client's process. Bush (1992) and Holligan (1992) outlined their client's sessions according to three related stages. Walker (1993) described a series of five sessions that were used in adjunct to verbal therapy, linking these together in a narrative. Weiss (1994) contextualized her client's processes around the notion of the inner family, and described how facilitating change in clients, including those with depression, could be understood in terms of dialoguing with parts of the unconscious such as childhood selves and dissociated parts of the self. Summer (1988) provided a number of clinical vignettes to describe her clients' processes in BMGIM. Weiss (1994) contextualized her case study around a theory.

## EATING DISORDERS

Only two references are made to work with clients who have an eating disorder. A single case study describes the BMGIM experiences of an obese client with a food addiction (Pickett, 1992). This case has previously been described in the "Addictions" section of this chapter.

Justice (1994) briefly describes a group form of GIM as "shortened and abbreviated to allow the inpatient to work with one aspect of herself at a time and not be overwhelmed" (p. 108). While the structure of group sessions were similar to Bonny's Group GIM, the following considerations are made: a) to tailor the length of the music to the needs of the group; and 2) to identify a specific issue that is the focus of the session. This group form has been used intensively, where patients receive several sessions a week throughout the course of their stay.

## INPATIENT MENTAL HEALTH

While case studies for inpatients in mental health facilities have been addressed in other sections of this paper (e.g., depression; sexual abuse; PTSD), a separate category has also been identified because of the specific adaptations to the Bonny Method that have been developed. In fact, four distinct approaches exist, and each of these will be outlined below.

Before examining each of these approaches, it is worthwhile noting some commonalities in the characteristics and goals of clients in these studies. Common to many was a sense of hopelessness, isolation, and demoralization associated with being hospitalized (Goldberg, 1994). Many clients also had impaired ego strength (Goldberg, 1994; Nolan, 1983; Summer, 1988) associated with clinical diagnoses such as schizophrenia, mania, personality disorder, or depression. The main goals of therapy were to develop ego strength, lessen symptoms, provide insight into current problems, and prepare for reentry into the community.

The first approach to working with inpatients involved the traditional individual form of the BMGIM, and was used with clients suffering from PTSD (Blake, 1994; Blake & Bishop, 1994), and mixed personality disorder (Nolan, 1983). In this form, the standard components of a session were used in the way that was originally developed by Bonny (1978), although sessions may be interspersed with verbal therapy. The goals of therapy include uncovering and working through material related to trauma and PTSD, healing old wounds, and understanding the relationship between present behavior and past experiences. The length of therapy varied from six sessions over two months (Nolan, 1983) to three sessions over an unknown period (Blake, 1994).

When the full form of the BMGIM was used, two approaches were taken to understanding the client's processes. Nolan (1983) outlined his client's process over six sessions in a narrative. Blake (1994) and Blake and Bishop (1994) provided clinical vignettes and contextualized these around issues facing Vietnam veterans with PTSD.

In both cases, the therapists took a directive role in sessions, establishing clear goals, modifying elements of sessions such as the length of music or relaxation induction, and approaching therapy by containing the client's process.

The second approach involves adapting the individual BMGIM experience (Blake, 1994; Goldberg, 1994; Goldberg, Hoss, & Chesna, 1988; Summer, 1988). This approach was discussed by nearly all therapists with a wide variety of clients, including those with PTSD, depression, schizophrenia, and mania. When sessions were adapted, considerable variation was made to the length of the relaxation induction, music, and/or goals of therapy. Rather than focusing on goals that uncovered deep psychic material, therapists focused much more on "here and now" issues such as helping the client a) gain control over her imagery and her mind (Goldberg, 1994), b) connect with feelings (Blake, 1994), c) reduce social isolation (Goldberg, Hoss, & Chesna, 1988) and d) address current life stressors (Goldberg, 1994; Goldberg, Hoss, & Chesna, 1988; Summer, 1988). The various adaptations that were made included a) selecting safe starting images, b) only using short pieces of music, c) taking a directive role during the imagery experience, and d) concretely relating the imagery experience to current life stressors.

The third approach involved an adapted individual form of the BMGIM known as Directed Imagery and Music (Blake, 1994) for Vietnam veterans dealing with traumatic combat experiences and PTSD. This has previously been described in the PTSD section of this chapter.

A fourth approach involved Group GIM (Blake & Bishop, 1994; Goldberg, 1994; Justice, 1994; Summer, 1988) which has been discussed in previous sections of this chapter. As identified by Goldberg (1994), the general goals of group work were: a) to address individual client goals identified at the beginning of each session; b) to facilitative supportive relationships between clients; and c) to encourage clients to take responsibility for themselves by attempting to understand the reasons they were hospitalized and thereby gain some control and mastery of themselves.

Group work varied according to the following: (a) the length of the relaxation induction; (b) the seating position; (c) the level of goal specificity for the session and the accompanying starting image; (d) the duration of the music; (e) whether the client's eyes were open or closed; and (f) whether the client was guided or sitting quietly, writing, drawing or moving during the imagery experience. Common to all groups was an emphasis on safety, validation, and reinforcement of efforts to create solutions to problems identified in the prelude.

## MULTIPLE PERSONALITY DISORDER

Pickett and Sonnen (1993) describe how the BMGIM can be applied to working with clients who have multiple personality disorders (MPD). The central purpose was to bring the client's fragmented ego states into relationship, and create a unified personality contained within a single ego. Typically, this was achieved through dialogue with an executive ego, who moderates all the client's ego states. Important to this process are positive and healing images, which help clients to see that they have the inner resources to deal with their problems.

Typically, MPD clients have experienced some kind of early childhood trauma that may have led to ego fragmentation. After establishing trust and working with the various ego states, many clients returned to, or bring into awareness, this traumatic event(s), usually in the imagery experience. Pickett and Sonnen felt that this was essential to the healing and integration of the fragmented ego, and developed a number of techniques to work with the trauma. These included:

1)  *Phantom anchor and reaching through time*, where the therapist holds the client's right arm and talks to the client so that he/she understands what is happening at that time. This may include suggesting to the client that he/she "reach through time" to the child and take him/her out of the trauma experience;

2)  *Visual and kinesthetic dissociation*, whereby the therapist stops the client imaging because it is emotionally overwhelming, stands the client up, and asks him/her to project the images onto a wall. This allows the client to work through the trauma in a more manageable way; and

3)  *Reframing*, where the therapist helps the client dialogue with a disturbed or violent ego state, and find alternate ways to express the feelings contained within that ego.

Pickett and Sonnen used music in very specific ways. For example, while the basic structure of BMGIM sessions appears to have been maintained, specific music selections were used during "reframing" sessions to help the clients work with different ego states. The authors also found that choral music was helpful in decreasing client's anxiety and facilitating a different quality of listening to the different ego states. Specifically, they found that the structure of certain choral works allowed clients to dialogue and find ways to integrate these egos into a coherent whole.

Finally, Pickett and Sonnen found that the imagery experience itself served a diagnostic function for clients with MPD, in the following ways: 1) their imagery tends to be fragmented and discontinuous, 2) there are shifts in ego states, and indications of multiple egos, 3) the imagery can be unreal and dissociated from the imager, and 4) the existence of confusing visual images and memories that may indicate early trauma related to MPD.

# AUTISM

Two published case studies were found describing the use of an adapted form of individual BMGIM with an autistic man (Clarkson, 1995; Clarkson 1998-1999). In addition to compulsive behavior typical of a person with autism, the client could also be physically aggressive to self and others.

The client had fifty-nine sessions over a period of approximately two and a half years. The central goal of therapy was to facilitate inner exploration, and specific goals grew out of this process. In summarizing the outcomes of the work, Clarkson identified the following themes: 1) reconnection and then separation from the client's father, which led to a clearer sense of an adult self; 2) a need for freedom, characterized by wanting to be "normal" and live independently; 3) reduction in stress and anxiety associated with his current residential and work situation; and, 4) the emergence of spiritual insights that give the client's life broader meaning. In addition, Clarkson commented that there was a marked improvement in his behavior at work and home.

The sessions had three important characteristics. The first involved various adaptations of BMGIM, including short and focused preludes concentrating on a single issue, a brief induction, and listening to no more than twelve minutes of music; no interaction during the music-imagery experience, drawing immediately after the music-imagery experience, and then a brief discussion of the drawing and imagery experience. Each session typically lasted no longer than one hour.

The second characteristic involved the method of communication used between client and therapist. Clarkson assisted the client to spell out letters on a computer using a method known as "Facilitated Communication" (Clarkson, 1995). This method was used during the prelude and postlude to frame and reflect upon the music-imagery experience.

The third characteristic lay in the selection of music. Clarkson mainly used music from taped programs used in GIM. However, she also used other selections of classical music along with "new age" music.

## PERSONAL DEVELOPMENT

This category is distinct from all other psychotherapeutic applications previously described because clients do not generally have a specific DSM-IV diagnosis. Rather, it represents a diverse group of people who wish to work through and resolve various psychological issues that impinge on their inner and outer lives. This includes increasing self-esteem (Clarkson, 1994; Hale, 1992; McKinney, 1993), improving relationships (Brooks, 2000; Clark, 1991; Clarkson, 1994; Lewis, 1993; McKinney, 1993), changing life goals (Clarkson, 1994), integrating different parts of the self (Brooks, 2000; Clark, 1991), increasing trust in self and others (Hale, 1992), expressing and working through grief and trauma (Lewis, 1993; Pickett, 1996–1997; Smith, 1996-1997), reducing symptoms (Clarkson, 1994; McKinney, Antoni, Kumar & Kumar, 1995; Wrangsjo & Korlin, 1995) and integrating archetypal and spiritual experiences (Clark, 1995; McKinney, 1993; Short, 1996–1997; Ventre, 1994). It is clear that in each of these case studies, the goals of therapy were interrelated.

The length of work varied, from twenty-six sessions over one and a half years (Hale, 1992), to several sessions over an unknown time period (Pickett, 1996–1997). Clients worked in both private practice and medical settings.

In most of these cases, the individual form of the BMGIM was used, although sessions may have been interspersed with verbal therapy. When adaptations were necessary, this usually involved decreasing the length of the music-imagery experience, and/or increasing the level of directiveness of the guide (Pickett, 1996–1997). Adaptations were made to address a specific therapeutic issue (e.g., retrieving the memory of a trauma) and/or in response to the client's condition (e.g., recovering from head trauma).

Various approaches were taken to understanding the client's process. Three case studies (Clark, 1991; Clarkson, 1994; Hale, 1992) linked session descriptions together in a narrative, four analyzed sessions according to a specific construct (Brooks, 2000; Clark, 1995; Short, 1996–1997; Ventre, 1994), two provided multiple vignettes as examples of a specific construct (Pickett, 1996–1997; Smith, 1996–1997) and one described the client's process according to the themes of therapy (McKinney, 1993).

Two experimental research studies also examined the effects of a series of BMGIM sessions on psychological health (McKinney, Antoni, Kumar & Kumar, 1995; Wrangsjo & Korlin, 1995). Rather than describe the clinical process with clients, each study took pre/post measures on variables such as mood state, health of interpersonal relationships, and meaningfulness of life. A significant increase in scores on each of these measures was found after the series of sessions, suggesting that BMGIM can positively affect these variables.

A broad range of theoretical perspectives were used in interpreting the client's process. Aspects of Jungian theory were commonly used, and these included the anima (Brooks, 2000), myths (Clark, 1995; Ventre, 1994) and archetypal images (Clark, 1991; Short, 1996–1997; Ventre, 1994), all of which were used to contextualize the client's imagery experiences. Other case studies used a single construct (Clarkson, 1994; McKinney, 1993; Smith, 1996–1997), such as disenfranchised grief (Smith, 1996–1997), to frame the client's process. One case study did not use a theory to describe their client's process (Hale, 1992), instead outlining the client's experiences according to their imagery experiences. Finally, Mandala theory (Kellogg, 1984) was also used to assess clients, and evaluate change throughout the course of GIM (Clarkson, 1994; Ventre, 1994).

# CONCLUSION

As a method of psychotherapy, the Bonny Method has been used with a variety of clinical and nonclinical conditions to address diverse goals. Four main forms of GIM have been used. These are 1) using the individual BMGIM form as originally developed by Bonny (1978), 2) using an adapted individual form, which usually involves less music and directed guiding, 3) using a specific individual adaptation known as Directed Imagery and Music (DIM) (Blake, 1994), and 4) using Group GIM. Each form varied in the length of relaxation induction, the type, purpose, and length of the music, and the role of therapist. The use of each of these forms is determined according to several variables: whether the client is in an inpatient or outpatient environment; the client's level of psychological health; the goals of therapy; and the anticipated length of therapy.

Another variable that distinguishes the various forms of BMGIM is the extent to which the method is an uncovering technique, and conversely the extent to which it is used to contain the client and build healthy ego strength and defenses. For those clients with healthy ego strength, the full form of BMGIM has typically been applied, and used as an uncovering and reconstructive method of psychotherapy. However, when a client's ego strength is impaired (especially for inpatient mental health populations), the method is adapted to varying degrees, and goals concentrate more on managing symptomatology, providing insight into current life circumstances, and using positive images to build a healthier sense of self.

## *References*

Blake, R. L. (1994). Vietnam veterans with posttraumatic stress disorder: Findings from a music and imagery project. *Journal of the Association for Music and Imagery*, 3, 5–17.

Blake, R. L. & Bishop, S. (1994). The Bonny Method of BMGIM in the treatment of Post-Traumatic Stress Disorder (PTSD) with adults in a psychiatric setting. *Music Therapy Perspectives*, 12(2), 125–129.

Bonny, H. (1978). *Facilitating GIM Sessions*. Baltimore: ICM Books.

Borling, J. E. (1992). Perspectives on growth with a victim of abuse: A guided imagery and music (BMGIM) case study. *Journal of the Association for Music and Imagery*, 1, 85–98.

Brooks, D. M. (2000). Anima manifestations of men using Guided Imagery and Music: A case study. *Journal of the Association for Music and Imagery*, 7, 77–87.

Bruscia, K. E. (1991). Embracing life with AIDS: Psychotherapy through Guided Imagery and Music (GIM). In K. Bruscia (ed.), *Case Studies in Music Therapy*. Phoenixville, PA: Barcelona Publishers.

Bush, C. (1992). Dreams, mandalas and music imagery: Therapeutic uses in a case study. *Journal of the Association for Music and Imagery*, 1, 33–42.

Clark, M. F. (1991). Emergence of adult self in Guided Imagery and Music (GIM) therapy. In K. E. Bruscia (ed.), *Case Studies in Music Therapy*. Phoenixville, PA: Barcelona Publishers.

Clark, M. (1995). The hero's myth in GIM. *Journal of the Association for Music and Imagery*, 4, 49–66.

Clarkson, G. (1994). Learning through mistakes: GIM with a student in a hypomanic episode. *Journal of the Association for Music and Imagery*, 3, 77–94.

Clarkson, G. (1995). Adapting a Guided Imagery and Music Series for a non-verbal man with Autism. *Journal of the Association for Music and Imagery*, 4, 121–138.

Clarkson, G. (1998–1999). The spiritual insights of a Guided Imagery and Music client with Autism. *Journal of the Association for Music and Imagery*, 6, 87–103.

Goldberg, F. S. (1994). The Bonny Method of Guided Imagery and Music as individual and group treatment in a short-term acute psychiatric hospital. *Journal of the Association for Music and Imagery*, 3, 18–34.

Goldberg, F. S., Hoss, T. & Chesna, T. (1988). Music and imagery as psychotherapy with a brain damaged patient. *Music Therapy Perspectives*, 5, 41–45.

Hale, S. E. (1992). Wounded women: The use of Guided Imagery and Music in recovering from mastectomy. *Journal of the Association for Music and Imagery*, 1, 99–106.

Herman, J. (1992). *Trauma and Recovery*. New York: Basic Books.

Holligan, F. (1992). Case study: Guided Imagery and Music. *The Australian Journal of Music Therapy*, 3, 27–36.

Kellogg, J. (1984). *Mandala: Path of Beauty*. Clearwater, FL: MARI.

Justice, R. W. (1994). Music therapy interventions for people with eating disorders in an inpatient setting. *Music Therapy Perspectives*, 12(2), 104–110.

Lewis, K. (1993). Using Guided Imagery and Music to support and clarify relationship changes: A case study. *Journal of the Association for Music and Imagery*, 2, 87–97.

McKinney, C. H. (1993). The case of Therese: Multidimensional growth through guided imagery and music. *Journal of the Association for Music and Imagery*, 2, 99–110.

McKinney, C. H., Antoni, M. H., Kumar, A., & Kumar, M. (1995). The effects of guided imagery and music on depression and beta-endorphin levels. *Journal of the Association for Music and Imagery*, 4, 67–78.

Nolan, P. (1983). Insight therapy: Guided Imagery and Music in a forensic psychiatric setting. *Music Therapy*, 3(1), 43–51.

Pickett, E. (1991). Guided Imagery and Music (BMGIM) with a dually diagnosed woman having multiple addictions. In K. Bruscia (ed.), *Case Studies in Music Therapy*. Phoenixville, PA: Barcelona Publishers.

Pickett, E. (1992). Guided imagery and music (GIM) with a dually diagnosed woman having multiple addictions. *Journal of the Association for Music and Imagery*, 1, 55–68.

Pickett, E. (1995). The Bonny Method of Guided Imagery and Music: A technique for healing trauma. *Journal of the Association for Music and Imagery*, 4, 93–102.

Pickett, E. (1996-1997). Guided imagery and music in head trauma rehabilitation. *Journal of the Association for Music and Imagery*, 5, 51–60.

Pickett, E., & Sonnen, C. (1993). Guided Imagery and Music: A music therapy approach to Multiple Personality Disorders. In E. S. Cluft (ed.), *Experiential and Functional Therapies in the Treatment of Multiple Personality Disorders*. Springfield, IL: Charles C. Thomas.

Short, A. E. (1996–1997). Jungian archetypes in GIM therapy: Approaching the client's fairytale. *Journal of the Association for Music and Imagery*, 5, 37–49.

Skaggs, R. (1997). *Finishing Strong: Treating Chemical Addictions with Music and Imagery*. St Louis: MMB Music.

Smith, B. (1996–1997). Uncovering and healing hidden wounds: Using GIM to resolve complicated and disenfranchised grief. *Journal of the Association for Music and Imagery*, 5, 1–23.

Summer, L. (1988). *Music Therapy in the Institutional Setting*. St. Louis: MMB.

T., & Caughman, J. M. (1999). Tools of rediscovery: A year of Guided Imagery and Music. In J. Hibben (ed.), *Inside Music Therapy: Client Experiences*. Gilsum, NH: Barcelona Publishers.

Tasney, K. (1993). Beginning the healing of incest through Guided Imagery and Music. *Journal of the Association for Music and Imagery*, 2, 35–48.

Ventre, M. (1994). Guided Imagery and Music in process: The interweaving of the archetype of the mother, Mandala and music. *Music Therapy*, 12(2), 19–38.

Ventre, M. (1994). Healing the wounds of childhood abuse: A Guided Imagery and Music case study. *Music Therapy Perspectives*, 12(2), 98–103.

Ventre, M. (1999). A tape from Lilly. In J. Hibben (ed.), *Inside Music Therapy: Client Experiences*. Gilsum, NH: Barcelona Publishers.

Walker, V. (1993). Integrating Guided Imagery and Music with verbal psychotherapy. *Journal of the Association for Music and Imagery*, 2, 111–121.

Weiss, L. (1994). Accessing the inner family through Guided Imagery and Music. *Journal of the Association for Music and Imagery*, 3, 49–58.

Wrangsjo, B., & Korlin, D. (1995). Guided Imagery and Music (GIM) as a psychotherapeutic method in psychiatry. *Journal of the Association for Music and Imagery*, 4, 79–92.

# Part Three:

# Orientations

*Chapter Eleven*

# A JUNGIAN ORIENTATION
# TO THE BONNY METHOD

## Karlyn M. Ward

The concepts and constructs of Jung's analytical psychology easily lend themselves to work with the Bonny Method of Guided Imagery and Music (BMGIM), in part because both are methods of working with the unconscious. Both kinds of therapy may include symbolic or regressive work, current clinical issues, and/or spiritual development. Unlike the "customary" practice of Jungian analysis (which, in fact, varies considerably from analyst to analyst), the environment of BMGIM includes classical music within the relationship with a carefully trained therapist. In the practice of BMGIM, the music and the therapist can be thought of as co-therapists, who contain and act as tethers, allowing the patient to have a depth experience which may provide entrée to material often not so readily available in any other way. Additionally, work with BMGIM appears to be a factor in stimulating direct access to the unconscious via dreams, when previously there was none. Sometimes, too, the transference is initially to the music, already known and trusted, before there is a transference to the therapist.

Practitioners who have an interest in the archetypal dimension that is so characteristic of work with BMGIM also should be aware that today there are a number of differences in emphasis in the theory and practice of analytical psychology. The limited space of one chapter does not allow for any thorough discussion of them, although *all* are relevant to the practice and understanding of BMGIM. However, for the sake of accuracy it is important to at least name them: 1) rapprochement with newer developments in psychoanalysis, 2) the importance of the role of the transference, 3) the development and use of Jung's theory of typology, 4) emphasis on individuation, 5) emphasis on the importance of personality development from childhood (causality), 6) emphasis on the importance of the analytic/alchemical container, and 7) emphasis on the importance of dreams. For a more thorough discussion, the interested reader can consult the new and valuable book *The Jungians* (Kirsch, 2000).

Another excellent source for a more thorough definition and discussion of the Jungian concepts and viewpoints discussed in this chapter, including how they have been adapted or amended over time, is *A Critical Dictionary of Jungian Analysis* (Samuels, Shorter, & Plaut, 1986). A brief list of other suggested sources will be found at the end of the chapter.

This chapter will discuss 1) Jung's own relationship to music and some of what he said about it theoretically, 2) the basic elements of the structure of the psyche, as discovered by Jung in his research, and their relevance to the practice of BMGIM, and 3) Jungian thought as applied to phases of the BMGIM session.

## JUNG'S RELATIONSHIP TO MUSIC

The legend grew up around Jung that he was unappreciative of music, insensitive to it, disliked it, and did not discuss it. Although it is true that Jung did not write much about music, the evidence from Jung himself and the biographers who were his contemporaries informs us that he was, in fact, deeply related and exquisitely sensitive to music. For example:

> I have just returned from the Ticino, in Italian Switzerland, where they love music. But when they turned on the radio in the restaurant I got so exasperated that I pulled out the plug. . . Jazz and all that sort of stuff is silly and stultifying. But it is even worse when they play classics in such a place. Bach, for instance. Bach talks to God. I am gripped by Bach. But I could slay a man who plays Bach in banal surroundings (McGuire, 1977, p. 249).

Jung was especially related to Bach's last, perhaps greatest, and most difficult to understand work, *The Art of the Fugue*. That he thought it could tell him more about the *nature* of music than any other piece of music suggests something of the quality of his depth of connection and appreciation of music.

In 1956 Jung invited Margaret Tilly, concert pianist and gifted music therapist at Langley Porter Psychiatric Institute in San Francisco, to visit him at his home in Küsnacht, just outside of Zürich. Jung acknowledged to her that he had never been very impressed with music therapy, but was interested in what she had written about it, and requested that she use her own (musical) language in demonstrating to him her work. But she first inquired about his own relationship with music. Jung replied

My mother was a fine singer, so was her sister, and my daughter is a fine pianist. I know the whole literature . . . but I never listen to music anymore, it exhausts and irritates me . . . because music is dealing with such deep archetypal material, and those who play don't realize this (McGuire, 1977, p. 273-275).

Of course Tilly realized at once that he cared too much, not too little. So she demonstrated, on Jung's grand piano, her work, and

When I turned round, he was obviously very moved, and said, "Go on, go on." And I played again. This second time he was far more deeply moved, saying, "I don't know *what* is happening to me; what are you doing?" And we started to talk. He fired question after question at me. "In such and such a case what would you try to accomplish, where would you expect to get, what would you do? Don't just tell me, *show* me, *show* me"; and gradually as we worked he said, "I begin to see what you are doing, show me more." And I told him many case histories and we worked on for over two hours. He was very excited and as easy and naive as a child to work with. Finally he burst out with, "This opens up whole new avenues of research I'd never even dreamed of. Because of what you've shown me this afternoon—not just what you've said, but what I have actually felt and experienced—I feel that from now on music should be an essential part of every analysis. This reaches the deep archetypal material that we can only sometimes reach in our analytical work with patients. This is most remarkable" (McGuire, 1977).

Jung's own daughter, present at the meeting, independently confirmed its importance (Watts, 1972).

The clear conclusion, then, is that Jung disliked not the music itself, but the magnitude and intensity of his own inner experience of hearing the music, after which he might be agitated for days. He apprehended music through the unconscious, which was so open that the music could immediately impact the deepest levels. At times his response must have been, as he himself said, "unbearable." Perhaps his only defense was the gruff and churlish behavior that led to the impression that he disliked the music itself.

One of his clearest statements about music was in a letter declining (because of age and ill health) to write an article on the archetypes and music for a Parisian music journal. However, in declining, he said the following:

Music certainly has to do with the collective unconscious. This is evident in Wagner for example ... . Music expresses in sounds what fantasies and visions express in visual images. I am not a musician and would not be able to develop these ideas for you in detail. I can only draw your attention to the fact that music represents the movement, development, and transformation of motifs of the collective unconscious. In Wagner this is very clear and also in Beethoven, but one finds it equally in *Kunst der Fuge* (C. G. Jung Letters, 1906–1950 1973, p. 542).

## GENERAL JUNGIAN THEORY
## AND THE BONNY METHOD

All Jungian theory is based on the *reality of the psyche* and the *reality of the unconscious.* In BMGIM, these concepts are honored in the work with our patients' responses to the music, which often come from the unconscious in deeply symbolic ways and in the form of affects that may arise from the depths of nonverbal and preverbal levels. Never can we dismiss imagery or dreams as "nothing but my imagination," or "just a dream." Dreams and images have their own reality, just as real as this book. But it is this *psychic* reality which some patients have to learn to take seriously. BMGIM, like Jungian analysis, is not an intellectual process, but rather a process that allows for the possibility of repeated *experiencing* of the joys and pain of one's own psychic reality, but now with a trusted witness (the guide or analyst) who can both accept the reality of the patient, and allow the patient to see, when ready and without judgment, his/her flaws (the shadow material). (Please note: the word "patient" is used here because of its etymological connection with "pathos," which is a part of everyone's personal story.)

Jungian theory is based on the *theory of opposites.* Both positive and negative images and emotions are found, or implied, in BMGIM imagery. Jung once said: "One does not become enlightened by imagining figures of light, but by making the darkness conscious" (*Collected Works Vol. 13, Alchemical Studies, The Philosophical Tree,* para. 335). Only when the individual takes responsibility for *both* light and dark is it possible to move toward *wholeness* which is what Jung considered to be the fullest knowledge and/or expression possible of all aspects of one's personality. Often people come to BMGIM for personal growth and spiritual development, which also might be understood as their desire to move toward wholeness. Moving toward psychological *wholeness* is what Jung termed the process of *individuation,* a key concept in personality development, and in any depth therapeutic work, such as BMGIM. In essence, individuation is the process of becoming who one uniquely is, separate from the collective, yet related to it.

Only when this has been done sufficiently is one grounded enough truly to move into the spiritual dimension, which Jung thought essential to human mental health and development, linking it with finding meaning in life.

In fact, one essential purpose for engaging in and (sometimes) enduring this work (which has both its "ah ha's" and its "oh no's") is to find meaning or value in life's experience and in the experience of psychic reality. "A psychoneurosis must be understood, ultimately, as the suffering of a soul which has not discovered its meaning" (C. G. Jung, *Collected Works,* Vol. 11, para. 497). Wesley (1998–1999) also amplifies this point of "making meaning with music."

One final general concept is that of *synchronicity,* included here because of its general use in the culture. Jung used this word in several ways, but most clearly in describing those situations in which we experience *meaningful coincidence between inner and outer events,* but in which the events *are not causally related.*

## THE STRUCTURE OF THE PSYCHE

### Personality Types

One of the first theories fully developed by Jung is that of the personality types (the Myers-Briggs test is based on Jung's concepts). The types are certain *inherent patterns of behavior, thought, or reaction,* found in everyone. The theory of types is based on the opposites, and is the only such theory that includes the unconscious, which makes it especially useful for BMGIM and its work with the unconscious. The discussion that follows is aimed at helping the BMGIM practitioner understand the patient in terms of psychological type.

Development of all four functions (see below), inasmuch as that is possible, is essential to the individuation process. It is important that the BMGIM practitioner know not only the theory and structure of how typology works, but also his/her own type. All information is filtered through one's own type, and one needs awareness of how one may differ from or be similar to the patient, with all the advantages and pitfalls of each. The same holds true in working with patients about problems they may experience in relationships. The imagery and the way one images may lead to an understanding of what the patient's type truly is, since sometimes in the process of one's growth and development the innate type may get modified in service of psychological survival. In addition, the BMGIM process can help one develop more conscious use of all four functions as a part of the individuation process, in part by helping clarify through imagery and experience one's own relationship to perceiving and evaluating.

*Introversion and extraversion* (terms in common usage, but originated by Jung) are called the *"psychological attitudes."* BMGIM is essentially an introverted process, at best leading one into the depths of one's own psyche. Introverts more naturally gravitate to the contents of the inner world (although they must always learn to ground those contents in outer reality). Extraverted energy flows more naturally to the outer world, so extraverts may initially be more awed by the power of the contact with the inner world, via BMGIM.

*The psychological functions* are two more pairs of opposites: *intuition and sensation* (two ways of perceiving the world, thus the "P" in the Myers-Briggs test; they are also called the "nonrational" functions), and *thinking and feeling* (two ways of evaluating or judging the world, thus the "J" in the Myers Briggs test, they are also called the "rational" functions). The functions are colored by the psychological attitudes (introversion and extraversion), e.g., an introverted feeling type may look and function quite differently from an extraverted feeling type.

*Intuition and sensation* are ways of *perceiving* the world; they involve no judgment or evaluation. *Sensation types* are most likely to rely on getting information through the five senses, including sometimes very subtle powers of observation. The *intuitive type* goes a bit beyond what the senses might indicate, dealing more casually with the senses, but relying more on "intuitions" or "hunches." It is therefore, by nature, closer to the unconscious.

*Thinking and feeling* are ways of *evaluating or judging* the world; they do not involve perceiving. *Thinking types* approach the world with logical, linear thought, ideas, and formulations. The nature of our school system requires us to learn to use this function, and in fact, emphasizes its importance. There is, however, a fair amount of confusion about "feeling" in the context of typology. As used by Jung in this context, the *feeling function* is about *judging, valuing, and evaluating*; it has nothing to do with emotions, and is not necessarily even emotional (emotions are connected with the autonomic nervous system). The first response of a feeling type may be "I like it" or "I don't like it," perhaps having nothing to do with the intrinsic value of the person or object in question, but everything to do with the *inner system of values* of the feeling type. That is, it may appear to be nonrational, but has its own rationale.

One always has some use of all four functions, but leads with one (the dominant function), and has the least use of another (the inferior function). These two are always opposites. If the superior function is perceptive (e.g., sensation), the inferior is its opposite (e.g., intuition) and vice versa.

The second and third functions are the opposite *set* of functions (e.g., if the superior and inferior functions are perceiving, the second and third will be evaluative (e.g., thinking or feeling). The second function is more accessible, while the third and fourth functions are in the unconscious and therefore more difficult to access. The fourth is most likely to be problematic because it is linked with the shadow (see later discussion).

The *judging/perceiving* preference (as seen in the Myers-Briggs test) *is not an independent axis, but is linked to the functions*, which are either judging (thinking/feeling) or perceiving (intuition/sensation). In the extravert, the judging/perceiving preference is linked to the dominant, or leading function. If one is an extraverted thinking or feeling type, one is linked, by definition, to the judging function. If one is an extraverted intuitive or sensation type, one is linked, by definition, to the perceiving function. However, it is more complicated for the introvert. For the introvert, because the superior function is quite introverted, the judging/perceiving preference is linked with the second function, which is the one the introvert tends to show the world.

## Ego

The ego is linked to our first function and is our sense of our own identity, the center of the conscious personality, and responsible for decision making. It develops out of our first sense of continuity of ourselves, and later our sense of being able to reflect about ourselves (the so-called observing ego). Its distinguishing characteristic is consciousness. BMGIM sessions are an excellent place to observe how the patient's ego is functioning, e.g., whether it behaves in imagery as the waking ego would, is weak or inflated, or is merely an observer. Thus BMGIM can help identify the ego strength of the patient, and build on it. Sometimes the ego seems to feel it is in charge of the personality. Then in the imagery or affect there may be a numinous or awesome experience, revealing to the ego that something larger is in charge.

One person, a musician, only after years of analysis was able to request a BMGIM session. She had always felt both attraction to and fear of BMGIM, probably realizing on some level she needed to develop enough ego strength to cope with what she knew was the potential power of the music to take her into scary places. (Work with music can be so powerful that it is wise to follow the lead of the patient's psyche, and let the interest in BMGIM, and the ensuing material, unfold organically.) After the music session she was both satisfied and relieved to have approached long-held frightening imagery and make some peace with it.

## Persona

The persona is the mask we show the world. It is essential because it mediates between ourselves and society's expectations, and shields from the world what is too intimate to share. BMGIM has the capacity to bypass persona and defenses because music itself has the capacity to move us that deeply. The bypassing of defenses calls forth ethical issues: with whom should one *not* do BMGIM? On the one hand, for some it may not be a safe method. On the other, sometimes patients can allow the persona to relax *only* in the safety and strength of the BMGIM session. One patient, whose persona (and probably underlying fear) had long-prevented from revealing herself, finally wanted a BMGIM session. In it she sobbed deeply and for the first time in therapy. Only then could she comment to the therapist with great satisfaction, "Now you really know me." So the first task for the BMGIM practitioner may be to cope with the persona in order to discover its opposite, the shadow.

## Shadow

The shadow, linked with the fourth function, consists of all the unacceptable (positive and negative) parts of ourselves which reside "in the shadows" of the psyche, that area about which our ego is "in the dark." It is usually experienced in projection onto a person or group to whom we have a strong (usually negative) reaction. In dreams and imagery the shadow is usually seen as the *same gender* as the dreamer. Work on the shadow is often difficult and humiliating, and therefore requires courage. It is the facing of one's own dragons and monsters, the introjected negative developmental aspects of one's psyche, which are not only one's own (though it may feel that way) but have a larger cultural and universal context. Clark (1995) discusses how the patient, in her imagery, found a witch in the basement of her house. This is classical shadow imagery, personalized in this experience.

But the shadow is universal. Witches and dark places are found in imagery of all cultures, and in fairy tales and legends. In alchemy, gold is found in the dung. In Egypt the scarab, or dung beetle, was sacred, implying that work with the shadow is sacred. Individuation requires work with the shadow. In fact, one cannot truly approach work with the spiritual in a grounded way unless significant parts of the shadow are already integrated. Sometimes people want to avoid the shadow when working with music, which may elicit and support positive, even ecstatic, experiences. But it is important to remember that even the most positive images and feelings have their shadow side. The therapist may need to "hold" the dark side for the patient until s/he is able to do so. Early BMGIM experiences often must be positive in order to strengthen and support the patient's ego's ability gradually to cope with the darker aspects of the psyche. But to avoid the dark side is to put the patient at risk for splitting off the dark side and becoming inflated. Thus, Clark's (1995) patient was required to cope with the witch in her own psyche. She had to understand the witch-nature in her own house (psyche) and not let her live there unknown, and not allow her to become dominant. She had to cope with her own dark side so it would not be damaging to herself or another.

## Masculine and Feminine Principles

The masculine and feminine *principles* espoused by Jung transcend gender. Rather, they are archetypal patterns, or qualities of consciousness, found *both* in men and women. They are associated with Logos and Eros, yang and yin, and may be the most fundamental archetypal patterns in all of life.

Traditionally the masculine principle is associated with, for example, focused awareness, the sun, light, the sky father, Logos, Doing, the creative, hunting, and clear differentiation. Traditionally the feminine principle is associated with, for example, diffuse awareness, the moon, the dark, the earth mother, Eros or relatedness, Being, the receptive, gathering, and things softened.

All of the above qualities and images are often found in BMGIM imagery and should be understood as manifestations of the masculine or feminine principles in that patient. For example, in one woman all feminine images had been veiled and unclear, suggesting that the patient was not well-related to her own feminine side. Suddenly she began having BMGIM experiences in which the atmosphere was softened, the earth emphasized, often bathed in soft moonlight. She felt it as something new and natural coming to her, and indeed, a new phase of development was heralded.

## Anima/Animus

Jung thought of the anima/animus as the contrasexual images in our psychic life, our subjective experience of the masculine and feminine *principles*, separate from our biological maleness or femaleness. The feminine element in a man's psychology is called the *anima*, while the masculine element in a woman's psychology is called the *animus*. Each could be thought of as the inner partner of the opposite gender, of the totally "other." In imagery, the anima usually appears as a woman, sometimes mythical or larger than life, while the animus may appear either as a single man or a group of men, since in its negative manifestation the animus is often associated with collective or group opinions. So male or female images in BMGIM often can be understood as ego, alter-ego, shadow (same gender as imager), or anima/us (opposite gender from imager).

Like the shadow, in the outer world the anima/us appear in projected form, e.g., the phenomenon of "falling in love," in which the love object usually carries the projected anima/us of the patient (but may or may not ever be able to live up to the projection). The therapeutic work is to help the patient find internally those qualities that are being projected outward. Only when the projections are withdrawn is it possible for a pair to begin a real psychological relationship, based on a greater awareness of the reality of each.

The *anima* is about emotion and being related to it. The negative anima (usually first noticed by a partner, or possibly the therapist) accounts for a man's behavior when he is bitchy, out of sorts, or moody. "She" accounts for a certain kind of restlessness, sentimentality, promiscuity, or unconscious emotionality, his being "seduced" by attachments which are not up to his usual or conscious standards. Experienced internally "she" accounts for a certain quality of anxiety, petulance, depression, or fears.

*Integration of the anima* involves the therapist facilitating the conscious development of receptivity (the feminine), and the necessity of the man learning to experience and *suffer* his emotions and involvements. Then there is the real possibility of a relationship with the inner muse, the feminine inspiration to creativity, e.g., the end of Faust, where the Eternal Feminine becomes the guide. Another good example of inferior anima involvement vs. the muse is in the opera *Tales of Hoffman.*

As the anima is about emotion, the *animus* is about the realm of meaning, natural order, and assertion or authority. Possession by the negative animus makes a woman opinionated, judgmental, hard-edged, strident. She may mouth collective opinions that she really hasn't thought through for herself. Others may see her as managerial (controlling), obstinate, ruthless, domineering, tactless, dogmatic, righteously indignant. In argument, her points often are *beside* the point. This is the urge to separation and non-relatedness, the abdication of the feminine principle. Sometimes the witch (as mentioned earlier, Clark, 1995) is seen as a merger of shadow and animus, since she is usually so unrelated, so disconnected from the feminine principle. Experienced internally, the negative animus is responsible for all the "shoulds" and "oughts," associated with second-rate thinking, or the inner prosecutor or critic or saboteur.

*Integration of the animus.* As a woman lays to rest the nonessential "shoulds" and "oughts," in her life, usually a part of the therapeutic process, it allows for the development of the positive animus, which can become a guide for self-development, and clear and critical but undefensive thinking. It is connected with creative spirit and all that is creative.

All of these qualities represented by the anima/us, when apprehended in our dreams and imagery and then processed in the context of therapy, can be used to help patients more fully understand themselves and be more of who they innately are, to be more fully responsible for themselves and their actions in the world.

## Archetypes of the Collective Unconscious

At the most profound level of each of us is the *collective unconscious* sometimes called the objective psyche, which is the repository of all of humankind's psychic heritage and possibilities. Just as our biological heritage is reflected in the growth and development of the human embryo, our psychic heritage is reflected in the collective unconscious, which is made up of the archetypes. The *archetypes* are instinctive psychological patterns of behavior, analogous to the patterns of biological instincts, a part of the tendency of the psyche to structure experience in certain ways, e.g., the Mother, the Dark Feminine, the Hero, the *Puer aeternus,* the Wise Old Man. In other words, the archetypes are universal symbolic representations of certain patterns of behavior which may be expressed in different ways in different cultures over time.

The archetypes themselves are *invisible.* That is, we do not know what the prototype of any of the above images looks like, but we do recognize their *images* in cultural figures such as (in the case of the Wise Old Man) Moses, Schweitzer, Lao Tse, Ghandi, various sages, gurus, or other male wisdom figures.

What is apparent to us are not the archetypes themselves, but rather certain culturally determined images, called *archetypal images.* Each is simply one way that particular archetype can be expressed. For example, Christ is not the only god to be put to death, to descend to hell and be resurrected, rather he is just the latest expression of that archetypal pattern, seen also in the myths of Osiris and Inanna. Personal issues, e.g., around the personal mother, can sometimes be put in the context of the *archetype* of the mother through the BMGIM or other therapeutic experience. At a certain point in the therapy, putting the personal into the larger archetypal, or universal, context may alleviate some of the loneliness of the arduous journey toward individuation.

Archetypal patterns may be expressed in our dreams, fantasies and imagery, often including BMGIM imagery, and they are also the basic content of myths, legends, fairy tales, and religions. Sometimes the patient can be helped to find his/her own myth (see Short 1996–1997).

Archetypal patterns in BMGIM imagery were also examined in a cross-cultural study by Hanks (1998). In this study involving very different cultures with radically different musical traditions, a large proportion of the imagery was archetypal, showing marked similarities across cultures in responses to both Chinese and Western classical music.

## Self

*The Self* is the *a priori* inner determinant of our lives, the element that regulates and guides the psyche. The ego evolves out of the Self, but the Self is supraordinate, although the two are dependent on each other, and the ego-Self axis is the vital connection between the two. The goal of any depth therapy is the establishment of a living connection between these two, whether by meditation, prayer, dreams, BMGIM imagery, or some other means of connecting with the unconscious. When this central force appears in dreams and imagery, it calls forth some degree of awe, wonder, even fear, and is an experience of tremendous and compelling force, which may be carried by *any* image if there's enough feeling to it. Usually it leaves the imager shaken and humbled. The danger is that the imager may become inflated with such imagery. Being grounded is critical. Mandalas, such as done after many BMGIM sessions, may be one expression of the Self, and help ground the patient.

## Complexes

Jung once thought of calling his psychology "complex psychology" because the notion of complexes is so crucial to his theory. A complex is a reaction out of proportion to the situation. It is what is activated when we say our "buttons are pushed." The ego is not in charge at this point; the complex has taken over, and later one may wonder, "What came over me?" At the core of every complex are both a personal experience and an archetype related to it. Complexes may arise in BMGIM sessions, in response to either the music (and what it means to the patient) or to an image, or a life situation. One person literally and repeatedly yelled (the activation of the complex) at a recurring archetypal image to get out of his imagery. Months later, after a gradual softening toward it, it occurred to him to ask whether the image might be a part of his own inner process, rather than "only" a remnant from childhood—a transformative moment in the work.

### Active Imagination and BMGIM

Active imagination is a technique developed by Jung for working with the unconscious in order to further develop or amplify dream or other imagery. In the process of active imagination, the ego both steps aside in order to experience the "other" from the unconscious, and also actively participates, in order to engage in real dialogue with these "other," sometimes archetypal, contents.

Unlike BMGIM, active imagination traditionally is a solitary process of working with the unconscious, meant to allow the patient autonomy and independence from the therapist in the later stages of analysis.

The dialogue with the unconscious may be in the form of inner conversation, art, writing, dance, the writing of music, sand play, etc. The point is to enrich or clarify some image or affect, bringing it nearer to consciousness, and hopefully to integration and transformation.

Active imagination is work, sometimes hard work. The whole of the person enters consciously (and sometimes with some difficulty) into the inner event, with an appropriate emotional response, appearing in the fantasy as him/herself. There is no preprogrammed goal or image; one simply takes the first image to present itself. The therapist, if present, does not intervene, but only takes a position on what is genuine or not.

While there are other "definitions" of the process (see Chodorow 1997), the following summary of von Franz's (1993) ideas serves to review them all.

- Emptying the mind of "ordinary" mental activity, or opening to the unconscious.
- Welcoming the first fantasy image that arises, and interacting with it.
- Giving form to the image: writing, drawing, painting, dance, etc.
- Moral confrontation with the material produced, that is, the whole ego must enter into the "dialogue" with utmost honesty and *all alone*. The analyst does not "guide" or offer helpful suggestions or participate beyond being a witness to the process (pp. 146-162).

One can readily see that although there is considerable similarity between active imagination and BMGIM, they are not the same.

In BMGIM, the therapist is present and participates (to a greater or lesser extent), forming part of the container for the experience. One style of practicing BMGIM is for the therapist to be fairly nondirective, with a minimum of participation, in order to allow a fuller expression of the patient's dialogue with the unconscious. In this style, intervention is usually the form of a question or comment meant to help the patient amplify the process, becoming quite participatory, even directive, only if necessary. One might call this a "witnessing," or analytic, style. At the other end of the continuum is the "guiding" style, in which the therapist is quite participatory.

In active imagination, there is nothing preprogrammed to influence the patient. Music by its very nature is structured (programmed), and may evoke or suggest its own response, at least on the archetypal level (although it is well-known that not all patients seem to relate to the character of the music, but seem to have their own experiences *independent* of the music). In addition, the music is usually selected by the BMGIM practitioner, which in itself suggests a kind of structure to the experience.

After the BMGIM process, the patient may decide to draw a picture. Usually a drawn circle is presented in which the patient makes a picture, and the picture is considered to be a mandala. Here again, the structure is a "given." However, this process is closely aligned with von Franz's third step, "giving form to the image." The pictures drawn by the patients usually represent the part of the imagery that was most alive for them. Often the picture is numinous for the patient, and becomes a meditation piece and reminder of the power of the experience. This is very like the "moral confrontation" with the unconscious and, after the BMGIM experience, is continued by the patient alone.

While active imagination usually happens toward the end of an analysis, thus fostering an independence as a part of termination of the work with the analyst, BMGIM may be done with those who have never experienced much or any confrontation with the unconscious, so there is a wisdom and a safety in having the therapist be more participatory, especially at the beginning. Also, although there is a structure to the music, music by its very nature has the capacity to bypass the defenses, and may require more participation by the therapist, at least until it is determined that the patient can listen in this special way more independently.

However, all of that being said, when well-done, the results of the BMGIM process can be remarkably like the results of the active imagination process.

# A JUNGIAN APPROACH TO
# PHASES OF A BMGIM SESSION

This section is meant to give some ideas about how to bring Jungian thought into the BMGIM session. It is difficult to generalize about any of this, but hopefully specific examples will help the reader understand the kind of thinking that may be present in each phase.

## Prelude

In the prelude, the therapist will be listening to the patient for evidence of such things as personality type, whether the ego is functioning well or perhaps subsumed by persona, shadow reactions, anima/us, or complex. What defenses are in evidence? One might also be listening for relationship to the feminine, or mothering, or the masculine, or fathering, or relationship to the personal parents. What about the personality is in balance, and what is out of balance? Are there archetypal images present? If so, what is the patient's relationship to them: awe, inflation, dissociation, etc? Diagnostic category is another major consideration. Through it all, one is listening for the patient's affect and whether it seems appropriate to the situation. All of these considerations are part of the therapeutic process, but are also in service of planning the best possible induction and music for the patient for that session.

## Induction

Perhaps an induction that involves getting in touch with the body (breathing, tension/relaxation) will help ground, contain, and promote entry into the inner world, or help bring balance. Or, on the contrary, it might be more important to allow release from the body. For example, in the cross-cultural study (Hanks, 1988), the Chinese seemed unable to respond to a simple stretching induction, planned because it is a universal instinct. Cultural inhibitions about expressing themselves seem to mitigate against this simple bodily expression. However, they responded well to an autogenic induction.

The *image* for the induction is best chosen from the patient's own imagery, which may have both literal and symbolic meaning. If none seems available, as may be the case in an initial session, one possibility is to begin symbolically with the mother, which is where our experiment with life begins. The image of a tree, sometimes seen as symbolic of the mother, might be suggested, with the patient filling in the details about the tree—alive, dead, young, old, dormant, evergreen, etc. One woman, generally impatient, was often in the grip of a cynical, judgmental, negative (animus) aspect of herself, giving her personality a one-sided quality. After having had imagery of a lake, moonlight, etc, in which she recognized a new (feminine) way of perception, she became fascinated with the image of a rose, a feminine image, which opens only at its own speed. All the impatience in the world does not hasten it. Once her fascination with the rose became known, it was used as the image in the induction, with favorable results.

## Selection of the Music

It is difficult to generalize about selection of the music. In general the selection is guided by experience (sensation), knowledge and study of the patient, the music, and the composers (thinking), and often considerable feeling and intuition.

However, exploratory research (Hanks, 1988), indicates that there exists an archetypal substratum in music. That substratum evokes predictable imagery, though always colored by personal and cultural aspects unique to that patient, *when the patient is open to that deepest level of the experience.* With further study of this phenomenon, the selection of the music for a session also may be based on additional knowledge about what archetypal imagery is evoked by specific music.

For example, Hanks found that major elements in the imagery in response to the Brahms *Symphony #1, Movement 3, poco allegretto e grazioso,* are joy, dancing by humans or animals, relationship to nature, movement, beautiful mountain forests—all suggesting the feminine principle. In using such information, one first can be aware of the underlying archetypal dynamics of the music, its appropriateness for specific patients, and then whether and how the patient's responses to the music are similar or different to the known response patterns evoked by that music, perhaps providing useful diagnostic information.

If mothering, or issues of the feminine, or animus, are observed, one might choose music that is warm, nurturing, perhaps with female voices, and an emphasis on a gentle, cradling feeling.

If the personality seems out of balance in some way, one might consider music, such as Bach, which is very balanced and symmetrical. When the imbalance is due to intellectualization, one might take care to use music that emphasizes feeling, and not, for example, fugal music, which may promote intellectualization.

Cultural considerations also obtain. Clark (AMI Journal, Vol. 4, 1995) and Hanks (AMI Journal, Vol. 1, 1992) both used the *Finale* to Stravinsky's *Firebird,* which seemed to work well with patients in the U.S. However, in her research in Taiwan, Hanks found that the full orchestration, brasses, and variant rhythmic patterns frightened the Chinese subjects. None of these elements are typical to Chinese music, and so produced a very different effect and affect than they did in the U.S. subjects.

## The Music-Imaging Experience

During the session it is important to listen not only to the manifest content, but to the underlying symbolic content. An example is the woman (mentioned earlier) whose imagery for the first time included elements that implied the feminine. Understanding the underlying content will aid the therapist in supporting new growth, in this instance, of the feminine side of the personality. Interestingly, when the very balanced music of Bach was used after the induction, which used the imagery of the rose, the patient was able for the first time to see and understand some of the imbalance in her own psyche. In another example, a man molested sexually by his mother had very intellectualized imagery of major universities. While on one level this imagery seemed to point to a life change in the direction of *academia* on another it can be understood as a very deep need to find the archetypal mother, the *alma mater*, or fostering mother, in order to replace the abusive mother.

## The Postlude

This is a time of returning to the level of ego functioning. Often in the BMGIM experience, elements of shadow, complex, or anima/us have abated, allowing the patient to experience a more natural way of being, sometimes more related to, or in dialogue with, the Self. Since the altered state generally is more pervasive than the ego has known, it is very important that the patient have sufficient time to remain "in" the material, and return only gradually to ego consciousness, rather than having interpretations made too soon. It is important to let the *experience* continue, whether internally, or in the more extroverted expression of the experience, in the formation of a mandala made by the patient. Often the mandala emphasizes in its images what has been most important in the music session. It is, as in active imagination, a way of giving form to the experience of the psyche.

## CONCLUSION

The concepts of analytical psychology are invaluable to the practice of BMGIM. They can be used to great advantage for an in-depth understanding of the psyche of BMGIM patients, their imagery, their defenses, their potential, and their relationship to the unconscious.

As stated at the beginning, this chapter has not been the place for a thorough discussion of analytical psychology. However, the following books are among the many that may be consulted for further information.

## *References*

Castillejo, de I. C. (1997). *Knowing Woman*. Originally published 1973. Boston: Shambhala Publications.

Clark, M. (1995). The Hero's Myth in BMGIM Therapy. *Journal of the Association for Music and Imagery, 4*, 49–65.

Chodorow, J. (1977). *Jung on Active Imagination*. Princeton, NJ: Princeton University Press.

Edinger, E. F. *Anatomy of the Psyche: Alchemical Symbolism in Psychotherapy*. LaSalle, IL: Open Court.

Franz, M. von (1993). *Psychotherapy*. Boston: Shambhala Publications.

Hanks, K. (1988). *Music, Affect and Imagery: A Cross-Cultural Exploration of Responses to Chinese and Western Classical Music*. Doctoral dissertation. Berkeley: The California Institute for Clinical Social Work.

Kirsch, T. B. (2000). *The Jungians*. London & Philadelphia: Routledge.

Jacoby, M. (1984). *The Analytic Encounter: Transference and Human Relationship*. Toronto: Inner City.

Jung, C. G. *Collected Works*. Edited by R. Herbert, M. Fordham, & G. Adler. Translated by R. Hull (20 volumes). Princeton, N.J.: Princeton University Press. Citations from: Volume 11 on Psychology and Religion, and Volume 13 on Alchemical Studies.

McGuire, W. (ed.) (1977). *C. G. Jung Speaking*. Princeton, NJ: Princeton University Press.

Myers, Isabel Briggs (1962). *The Myer-Briggs Type Indicator*. Palo Alto, CA. Consulting Psychologists Press.

Samuels, A. (1985). *Jung and the Post-Jungians*. London: Routledge & Kegan Paul.

Samuels, A., Shorter, B., & Plaut, F. (1986). *A Critical Dictionary of Jungian Analysis*. London: Routledge & Kegan Paul.

Short, A. (1996–1997). Jungian Archetypes in BMGIM Therapy. *Journal of the Association for Music and Imagery*, 5 (37–49).

Stein, M. (Ed). (1982). *Jungian Analysis*. LaSalle IL: Open Court.

Watts, A. (1972). *In My Own Way*. New York: Random House.

Whitmont, E. C. & Perrera, S. B. (1989). *Dreams, A Portal to the Source*. London: Routledge.

*Chapter Twelve*

# A PSYCHODYNAMIC ORIENTATION
# TO THE BONNY METHOD

# Kenneth E. Bruscia

As evidenced throughout this book, the Bonny Method of Guided Imagery and Music (BMGIM) has been practiced within many different theoretical orientations, including the psychotherapeutic approaches of Rogers, Maslow, Freud, Jung, and Perls, as well as various spiritual and transpersonal traditions. Bonny herself identified GIM with several streams of thought, and found each of them useful to varying degrees in the actual development of her method. In a speech on this topic, Bonny (1990) described GIM as "based on Maslow and Jung's work, but using the format of Freud's "relaxation-on-the-couch-and-let-come-whatever-needs-to come" approach. In a later speech, she described the four forces of psychology (psychoanalytic, behavioral, humanistic, and transpersonal), and then proposed that while GIM already "includes both Third and Fourth forces" (Bonny, N.D., p. 5), it also "may include each of the four forces in practice" (p. 9).

The practical question that naturally arises out of such theoretical flexibility is: When is it appropriate to use which orientation? Is there any practical reason to work in one orientation rather than another? And in specific reference to this chapter, when do client needs indicate that a psychodynamic approach would more efficacious than another?

According to Wilber (1986), each stage of human development is associated with its own type of pathology or problem, each requiring its own type of therapy. At the first stage are psychoses which require pharmacological intervention; at the second are the narcissistic and borderline personality disorders which require "structure-building" treatment approaches; at the third stage are the psychoneuroses which require uncovering approaches such as the psychodynamic therapies; at the fourth are role and script pathologies which require cognitive therapies; at the fifth are identity neuroses which require introspection and philosophical dialogue: at the sixth are existential pathologies which call for humanistic-existential therapy, and at the seventh through ninth stages are the transpersonal pathologies which call for various contemplative traditions.

Thus, for example, according to Wilber, when a client presents problems originating in the third stage of development (i.e., psychoneurotic), and when these problems are still unresolved and still obstructing the person's ongoing development at the time of therapy, the most appropriate orientation is psychodynamic; whereas when a client presents a problem originating in the fourth stage (constructs or attitudes), the preferred orientation is cognitive, and so forth. Moreover, as a client progresses in therapy and resolves problems originating in an earlier stage of development, the client's work will shift to challenges posed by later developmental stages and the orientation to therapy should shift accordingly.

In terms of this chapter, the next important question is what are the kinds of client issues and problems that typify stage three and thus call for a psychodynamic approach. Wilber (1996) describes stage three as that time in development, starting at two or three years of age, when the mental or conceptual self begins to emerge, along with language. "The self is now not just a bundle of sensations and impulses and emotions, it is also a set of symbols and concepts. It begins to enter the *linguistic* world . . . and this changes everything" (p. 169). It is the time when the early ego or persona "first begins to emerge and differentiate from the body and its impulses, feelings, and emotions, and attempts to integrate these feelings into its newly conceptual self (Wilber, 2000, p. 103–104).

He also distinguishes the third stage from the previous two in that it has a triadic structure:

> In the monadic structures, there is basically one player on the stage—the self is either oblivious of the "other" (autistic), merged with the other (symbiotic), or part of an omnipotent dual unity with the other (narcissistic). As the monadic structure differentiates, self and other emerge as two distinct, if sometimes tenuous units. There are now two players on the stage, self and (m)other, with all the joy and all the tragedy that that involves. . . . Starting around age 2 or 3, however, the self awakens to its own gender identity, and this introduces three players on the stage: self, female-mother, and male father. This development immensely enriches and complicates the situation. New capacities, new desires, new taboos, new object relationships, a whole new set of conflicts—all come crashing onto the stage, with far-reaching, immensely complex interactions (Wilber, 1986, p. 112).

The problems posed by the child developing satisfactory relationships with both parents are further represented in the intrapsychic triad of id, ego, and super-ego, where primary conflicts arise between libidinal instincts and the constraints of reality and morality. Repression is the primary defense of this stage, as it helps the conscious mind ward off the libidinous demands of the unconscious to avoid the anxiety and guilt created by the moral demands of both parents. Wilber (2000) summarizes the problems that result:

> Failure at this crucial fulcrum (often summarized as Oedipal/Electra) can contribute to a classic neurosis: anxiety, depression, phobias, obsessive-compulsive disorders, and excessive guilt at the hands of the newly internalized super-ego. The conceptual self is frightened of, and overwhelmed by, the feelings of the body (especially sex and aggression), and in its misguided attempt to defend itself against these feelings, merely ends up sending them underground (as impulsive subpersonalities), where they cause even more pain and terror than when faced with awareness (p. 104).

In summary then, primary candidates for a psychodynamic approach to BMGIM are those individuals who present problems stemming from this period of childhood (approximately 2–7 years), when the developmental challenges were: 1) forming satisfactory yet acceptable relationships with both parents, while also 2) integrating the physical, mental, and moral parts of self. A key indicator is whether repression has obstructed healthy psychological development, as evidenced by the number and intensity of defenses needed to survive, if not triumph over, the everyday vicissitudes of adult life.

## PREMISES OF A PSYCHODYNAMIC ORIENTATION

A problem that inheres in defining a psychodynamic orientation to therapy is that it encompasses so many different theories, all based upon Freud's original notions about "psychoanalysis." What follows is an attempt to identify the primary beliefs shared by classical psychoanalysis and more contemporary psychodynamic approaches.

A central premise in the psychodynamic orientation is that there are at least three layers of consciousness that create the dynamics of the psyche. The *unconscious* layer contains all memories, instincts and psychic forms of energy of the individual, and is structuralized in the psyche as the "id." It manifests as a "primary process" aimed at survival, self-gratification, and homeostasis. As later pointed out by Jung, the unconscious layer also contains the memories and instincts of the entire species, which are structuralized as "archetypes" within the "collective unconscious." The *preconscious* layer contains material from the unconscious that, though not in awareness, is readily accessible to the conscious mind with a little effort. The *conscious* layer contains all that is in awareness, structuralized as the "ego." It manifests as a "secondary process" aimed at mitigating between the demands of the unconscious, the demands of reality, standards of morality ("superego"), and the need for safety.

*Repression* is any effort the psyche makes to prevent unacceptable or threatening material in the unconscious layer from entering the conscious layer. *Defense mechanisms* are psychological maneuvers used by the individual to ensure that repressed material lodged in the unconscious does not reach the conscious layer. These maneuvers are used whenever an experience threatens to destroy the delicate balance between what is repressed and what is in awareness. Depending on the nature of the material being repressed, a defense can require considerable psychic energy. Energy is needed to "ward off the anxiety that repression might fail and that the conscious mind will have to deal with the disturbing contents of the unconscious" (Bruscia, 1998a, p. 14). Based on Priestley (1994), the most common defenses are:

- Denial: disavowing or disowning an unacceptable impulse, desire, or characteristic of self.
- Splitting: dividing oneself or others into irreconcilably different polarities (good or bad).
- Projection: attributing aspects of oneself to someone or something.
- Introjection: making an external object of person a part of oneself through mental representation.
- Displacement: directing one's feelings or actions at an inappropriate object, not the object toward which they belong.
- Sublimation: rechanneling instinctual energy toward more acceptable aims.
- Reaction-formation: acting the opposite of one's unconscious desires.
- Intellectualizing: explaining something in a way that eliminates the pain or emotion.
- Rationalizing: finding ways of justifying oneself.

As a client engages in the therapeutic process, repressed material inevitably begins to leak out of the unconscious into the conscious layer, causing considerable anxiety and psychic pain. In an automatic self-protective response, the person tries to resist the therapeutic process. *Resistance,* then, is any effort the client makes to avoid or impede the therapeutic process for fear that repressed material will be uncovered. Any or all of the defense mechanisms may be used in these resistance efforts.

Another central premise of the psychodynamic tradition is that the past influences the present. Individuals learn from every experience they have in gratifying basic needs while also meeting the demands of reality and conscience, and then generalize what they learn from previous situations to present ones. The past provides a template for the present, with both positive and deleterious effects; this is particularly true for childhood experiences.

Interactions with significant others during childhood are particularly salient in shaping the individual's character as well as his or her relationships with others later in life. As psychoanalytic theory has evolved, the way that early relationships shape the personality has been described in terms of the mechanism of introjection—the process by which a person makes an internal mental representation of self and other in each significant relationship (Bruscia, 1998c). The centrality of these mental representations is seen in the "object relation" theorists such as Winnicott.

These internal mental representations (i.e., introjects of oneself and significant others) contribute to the formation of the *transference* relationship between client and therapist.

> A transference occurs whenever the client interacts within an ongoing therapy situation in ways which resemble relationship patterns previously established with significant persons or things in real-life situations from the past. Implicit is a replication in the present of relationship patterns learned in the past, and a generalization of these patterns from significant persons or things and real-life situations to the therapist and the therapy situation. Essentially, the client re-experiences in the present the same or similar feelings, conflicts, impulses, drives, and fantasies as he or she did with significant persons or things in the past, while also repeating the same or similar ways of handling and avoiding these feelings, persons, and situations (Bruscia, 1998b, p. 18).

In addition to forming a transference relationship, the client and therapist also form a *working alliance,* which is an adult-to-adult relationship with the shared goal of helping the client achieve the goals of therapy. The transference and working alliance are crucial to the treatment process, as is *countertransference*—"whenever the therapist interacts with clients in ways that resemble relationship patterns in either the therapist's life or the client's life" (Bruscia, 1998d, p. 52).

With these premises now outlined, the two primary aims of psycho-dynamically oriented therapy can be stated: "(1) to bring into the client's conscious experience material from the past that has been repressed and kept in the unconscious through defenses and resistances and that exerts adverse psychological effects on the present and (2) to work through that material by using transference and countertransference to engage the client in corrective emotional experiences" (Bruscia, 1998a, p. 14). The treatment process within a psychodynamic orientation therefore involves:

- Uncovering: Projective techniques aimed at relaxing or bypassing the defenses enough to allow repressed material that is problematic to safely enter into consciousness.
- Catharsis: Techniques aimed at helping the client to release and express feelings associated with the repressed material, as well as psychic energy required to maintain unnecessary defenses.
- Clarification and interpretation: Verbal techniques aimed at helping the client gain insight into the nature of the repressed material, and the various defenses and resistances that he or she is using to keep it repressed.
- Corrective emotional experience: The process of working through the transference relationship, using both the working alliance and countertransference, in order to help the client re-experience problematic aspects of the past in a positive way.
- Integration: The process of helping the client integrate the insights and corrective emotional experiences of therapy into the self and into current relationships with others.
- Fulfillment: The process of helping the client find more adaptive and productive ways of leading a life that is both meaningful and fulfilling.

## GENERAL COMPARISONS OF PSYCHODYNAMIC THERAPY AND BMGIM

Wrangsjo (1994) made a comparison of psychoanalysis and BMGIM, and found that the two have much in common. "The lying down position, the analyst/therapist being out of sight and making his presence known mainly by sound, and the state of consciousness during the work, are common features in the process of both methods" (p. 37). Wrangsjo also likened their focus on "primary process" as very similar: in psychoanalysis, the therapist seeks to induce a dream like state in order to encourage regression and primary process thinking; similarly in BMGIM, the therapist helps the client to relax and allow images, feelings, and memories to emerge while listening to the music. During the session, the psychoanalyst and the BMGIM therapist use a similar holding process with the client, involving attunement, empathy, support, and containment, all reminiscent of the parent-child relationship in early childhood. In both approaches, the therapist also takes a nondirective stance, but perhaps in different aspects of the work, and in different ways. Additionally, the psychoanalyst may tend to interpret more than the BMGIM therapist.

Wrangsjo also points to major differences. In psychoanalysis, the view of humankind is more focused on pathology, while BMGIM emphasizes the potential for growth and self-actualization. In psychoanalysis, religious or spiritual experiences are not regarded as integral to the growth process, whereas in BMGIM, such experiences are central to the process. And finally, music is used as an integral part of BMGIM but not of psychoanalysis. This use of music creates an entirely different therapist-client relationship, shifts the dynamics of the session, and provides an additional source of energy motivating change.

Taking a more experiential approach to examining the relationship between BMGIM and psychoanalytic therapy, Clarkson and Geller (1996) reflected upon their own work together. Clarkson (a BMGIM therapist) guided Geller (a psychoanalytic therapist) in a series of ten BMGIM sessions, which served as the foundation for reflective discussions on the process of both guiding and traveling. They discovered many of the similarities and differences noted by Wrangsjo, but also went on to elaborate resistance and transference phenomena in greater detail. They also examined the relationship between creative and analytic processes, and identified the various ways in which music activates unconscious material, and stimulates enactive memories, transpersonal imagery, and verbalizations.

Aside from these general comparisons of the BMGIM process and psychoanalysis, two very practical questions warrant careful consideration. How is resistance—a key factor affecting all forms of psychodynamic therapy—manifested and handled in BMGIM? And, how are transference, countertransference, and working alliance—key parameters of the client-therapist relationship in psychodynamic therapy—identified and managed in BMGIM?

# RESISTANCE IN BMGIM

Resistance is any attempt of the client to keep repressed material out of consciousness by avoiding full participation in the therapeutic process. In BMGIM, resistance may be any avoidance or misuse by the client of altered states of consciousness, imagery, music, the guide, or the client-therapist relationship that serves to halt the undoing of repression, and thereby impair the therapeutic process. The client may avoid: relaxing fully, imaging fully and responsively to the music, being responsive to the guide's intervention, or entering into an authentic and full relationship with the therapist; or the client may use these aspects of BMGIM in other ways to impede therapeutic progress.

In psychodynamic theory, repression is present in every individual, and for this reason, there is a need in every individual to resist therapy when it threatens repression. Thus, in therapy, both repression and resistance are to be expected and respected, as natural defense mechanisms. Like defenses, resistance can be healthy when it protects the client from unnecessary psychological danger or harm, and it can be unhealthy when it prevents the client from benefiting from therapy and living a full life.

Resistance may occur sporadically (with no obvious reason), only under specific conditions (e.g., when certain images appear), only at certain stages of the therapy process, or pervasively and indiscriminately. Thus, just as repression and defense mechanisms are unique to each individual, so are styles of resistance. In BMGIM, individual styles of resistance may be composed of ploys related to: 1) the music-imaging experience itself; 2) the integration of the music-imaging experience and verbal insight; and 3) the client-therapist relationship.

## Resisting the Music-Imaging Experience

Goldberg (1992) described resistance to the music-imaging experience as a "defensive maneuver," the evaluative process that takes place consciously or unconsciously while the client is imaging to music in a relaxed state. Its function is "to reduce the threat or stress by deflecting, changing, or repressing the emotional response to music and the issue it represents," and thereby avoiding fragmentation or the disintegration of the ego (p. 12). A defensive maneuver may result in: a flat or irrelevant affective reaction to an emotionally laden image, a defensive image, fleeing or changing images, or negative reactions to the music or therapist.

When the various elements of the music-imaging experience are considered separately, there are many very specific forms of resistance, which may include any of the following, in various combinations:

- Inability or refusal to enter or sustain an altered state of consciousness or return to a normal state of consciousness;
- Inability or refusal to generate, develop, or sustain images;
- Any limitation in the kinds of images generated (e.g., visual, kinesthetic, personal, etc.), or generating only stereotypic or concrete images;
- Avoidance of physical, emotional, or behavioral involvement in the imagery experience, or exclusion of any aspect of the self from appearing in the images;
- Inauthentic, prepared, or fabricated images which are disconnected from the ongoing experience;
- Incomplete, hidden, clouded, or vague images;
- Images of resistance (e.g., being stuck, immobile, blocked, paralyzed);
- Diversionary or irrelevant interruptions in the imagery, or abrupt changes in the imagery experience;
- Avoidance of the music, or imaging independently of or incongruently to the music;
- Over-dependence on the music for generating imagery;
- Responding to the music or imagery experience analytically or intellectually;
- Attempts to limit or censor what is reported to the therapist while imaging.
- Attempts to avoid or limit verbal interventions by the therapist while imaging;

## Resisting Integration of the Experience

Sometimes the client does not resist the music-imaging experience itself, but rather resists gaining any verbal insight about the experience, or connecting the experience to his/her life. Priestley (1994) faced similar forms of resistance in a form of music therapy wherein the client and therapist improvise their own music to explore significant images brought in by the client. She found that sometimes the client resisted the music experience, but then emoted and gained insight in the verbal discussion afterward, and at other times, the opposite happened. When applied to BMGIM, Priestley's outline of resistance layers can be adapted as follows:

- The client resists the music-imaging experience, and afterward discusses its significance insightfully, but with little affect.
- The client resists the music-imaging experience, but in the subsequent verbal discussion has a flood of body sensations or emotions, but no awareness or insight about their connection to his/her life.
- The client experiences body sensations and emotions in the music-imaging experience, but afterward is unable to discuss their significance or gain any insight.
- The client experiences body sensations and emotions during the music, then upon returning to an alert state has a flood of sensations or emotions, but during the discussion is unable to understand their significance or gain any insight.

Obviously, the ideal pattern is for the client to have full experiences during the music-imaging, and then be able to process the experience in a way that provides insight about how the experience is connected to his/her life. As with all forms of resistance, timing can be a key factor, as what a client cannot experience and connect in one session can often be experienced and connected in another.

## Resisting the Relationship

Finally, there are myriad other opportunities for resistance that arise within the context of the client-therapist relationship. Since this type of resistance is directly related to the transference dynamic, it will be discussed later.

## TRANSFERENCE IN BMGIM

Given the diversity of practice in BMGIM, it is not surprising to find that conceptions of transference vary considerably. Summer (1998) places transference on a linear continuum, ranging from a *pure music transference* on one pole, to a *pure therapist transference* on the other pole, with a *split transference* in the middle. She defines a *pure music transference* as:

a therapeutic relationship in which the music serves the essential therapeutic functions in the therapeutic process, including serving as the primary transference relationship. The therapist's role is secondary: to establish and further the client's relationship with music while serving minimal therapeutic functions for the client (p. 434).

Summer (1998) provides a clinical example of a *pure music transference* in the case of Gina. In this example, the music holds the client in the "me" experience, presents new "not me" experiences, and then "handles" the experiences until they are integrated. As the music-listening began, Gina started with an image of a blob. "At first, the music reflected and held her in her internal state so that she could experience and describe it fully. The music's holding function also helped her to engage with the image of the blob. . . . This was Gina's 'me' experience" (p. 452). Then Gina experienced the music as stirring up something inside the blob, a trapped creature of some kind. The music then began to solidify the blob until it became a rock which would not allow the creature to escape. "Then, as the music developed, it moved her into a 'not me' experience . . . the melting of the rock into a puddle with dancing raindrops" (p. 452), which emanated directly from her relationship with the music. And in the end, the music also served the third integrative function. "The music engaged and transformed not only the visual image (sponge > blob> rock > rain puddle) but also her feelings, thoughts, and body sensations. When the client is fully activated in this way by the 'handling' of the music, it is especially effective therapeutically because all the senses are integrated into a deeply transformative change throughout the psyche" (p. 453).

In contrast to the *pure music transference*, Summer defines the *pure therapist transference* as:

> a relationship in which the therapist serves the essential therapeutic functions in the therapeutic process, including being the primary object of the transference, and the music is used to support the establishment and development of the client-therapist relationship (p. 435).

An example in the literature is the case of Heather (Bruscia, 1995), which the author described as follows:

> Heather's transferences were indeed challenging. With all of her family of origin deceased, she had to reconstitute in therapy each significant person in her life so that she could better understand and feel the bond of love that she shared with each of them. At one time or another, I became her mother, who loved her but who could not be

held back by her; her grandmother, who never left her and supported her by loving her and holding up her back; and her aunt, who loved her but held her back through criticism and demands to get ahead . . . . I also became an idealized father . . . guiding her through her struggles with life and death. . . [and] there was also a negative [father] transference projected toward me (p. 27).

The *split transference* occurs when the music and the therapist both serve as the object of the transference. This can also be referred to as the "triadic" or triangular relationship in BMGIM, because it involves the client, the therapist, and the music as participants in the process. Clarkson and Geller (1996) explain the *split transference* as occurring when the music "absorbs some of the energy of transference, acting as a co-therapist and an extension of the guide. It becomes symbolically associated with the guide so that, unlike in psychoanalysis, a triangular relationship is established from the onset" (p. 312).

Upon examining the implications of using music as a "co-therapist" in this triad, Izenberg-Grzeda (1998) identified another possibility: The client may direct a transference toward another part of him or herself that identifies with the therapist. This means that the triad offers at least three objects for transference rather than only two as described by Summer (1998). Isenberg-Grzeda explains:

> The view of music as co-therapist may strengthen the facilitating transference directed to the therapist, thereby helping the patient become a co-therapist. The music may free the patient to perceive the therapist as a therapeutic ally rather than as a transference figure, thereby reinforcing the therapeutic alliance and increasing . . . the patient's empathy for the therapist's working ego. The patient would then ally not only with the therapist but also with the therapist's functions (p. 468).

Yet another possibility for transference emerges when imagery is considered within total relationship configuration in BMGIM. Specifically, clients may also project their transferences onto characters or objects that they create in their imagery. These imagery transferences may or may not duplicate transferences toward music, therapist, or introject, and therefore must be regarded as yet another object of transference available in BMGIM.

Admittedly, sometimes these imagery transferences are manifestations of transferences evoked by the music. Summer (1998) argues that "in GIM, the transference is experienced in relation to the music, then expressed and worked through indirectly, in the imagery" (p. 442). Just as often, however, imagery transferences are evoked by or related to the therapist rather than the music.

Pelliteri (1998) described how his own imagery helped him to work through parental transferences related to his therapist. Two shadowy characters, symbolic of parental figures, had physical characteristics that belonged to the therapist but not the parental figures. Pelitteri concluded: "My parental figures were thus 'hidden' behind (or within) the therapist, and both parents and therapist were represented in this ambiguous image" (p. 484).

It is important to also recognize the imagery transferences may not duplicate or relate to transferences toward the music or the therapist, but instead may stand on their own as separate and unique projections of certain parental dynamics. This is most likely to occur when the client is resisting a transference relationship with the music and/or therapist, and finds it easier to project certain parental dynamics on characters within the imagery instead.

Altogether then, based on clinical evidence, the clients may develop transferences toward several objects: the music, the therapist, introjected parts of themselves identified with the therapist, characters in their images, and any combinations thereof. Thus, the transference dynamic seems to go beyond the triad of client-therapist-music (where there are two objects) (Summer, 1998), to include at least three objects (therapist-music-imagery) (Bruscia, 1995), and even a fourth (introjects of client) (Isenberg-Grzeda, 1998). Moreover, in all likelihood, given the tendency of the unconscious to equate these objects and to replicate the past repeatedly but with endless variation, transferences toward multiple objects may not occur independently or without relation to one another. Instead, clients in BMGIM may develop an interdependent transference configuration directed toward two, three, or four objects, with each object implicated to a varying degree, and with one in the foreground and the others in various background positions. When this is the case, a transference toward any one object cannot be completely understood without acknowledging transferences that may also be directed toward other objects at hand within the BMGIM process. In other words, transferences in BMGIM may always be split, but the split may go be between two, three or four objects.

An example of a three-object configuration is the case of Jack (Bruscia, 1995). Jack talked incessantly throughout every session, rarely allowing the therapist to ask questions or make comments. He seemed very afraid that, if allowed to talk, the therapist would disturb his defenses in some way. Thus, the safest thing to do was to control the therapist's talking. At the same time, Jack always tried to be the good client, reporting on how much progress he was making, and telling the therapist how wonderful the therapy process was. He also responded very sensitively to the music, and had very full imagery experiences. The therapist described the transference configuration as follows:

> He controlled me, I controlled the music, and the music controlled him and the imagery. He was afraid of me no matter what I did, but he trusted the music no matter what it did. Jack's imaging depended entirely on what happened in the music, and the content of his imagery always brought solutions to his problems. . . . What makes this dynamic transferential is that these patterns of interacting paralleled how Jack related to his mother for most of his life. Jack's mother tried to control him through incessant verbal criticism and nagging. Jack resisted by either not listening to her talk or by talking over her. Regardless of this resistance to her, however, Jack would always do whatever she wanted and then justify it to himself by saying that it was really what he had wanted to do all along (p. 19).

The possibility of developing a configuration of transferences rather than a single transference has myriad implications for understanding the nature of resistance, and how resistance and transference are integrally linked together. If a client develops a positive maternal transference toward the music, a negative paternal transference toward a character in the imagery, and no apparent transference toward the therapist or self-introject, what does this imply? Does it imply that the client had an easier time projecting a particular dynamic onto one object as compared to another because of the similarities (e.g., between music and mother, character and father). Or could it imply that the client is resisting a transference toward the therapist, and in so doing, impeding the therapeutic process of working through the difficult dynamic? This leads to the next topic: the relationship between transference and resistance.

## Transference Resistance

Isenberg-Grzeda (1998) has examined the relationship between transference and resistance with special reference to the unique relation configured between therapist and music in BMGIM. She proposed that there are three main ways that music is conceptualized in BMGIM (as co-therapist, extension, or gift), and that each way can reinforce three forms of transference resistance defined by Gill (1982): resistance to 1) awareness of, 2) involvement in, or 3) resolution of transferences.

When music is used as "co-therapist," the "music is the therapeutic other, available for displacement and splitting . . . The therapist provides the music as if introducing a third person into the therapeutic space, an alternate person with whom to work through deeper issues" (Isenberg-Grzeda, 1998, pp. 471–472). Here the process is triadic rather than dyadic. This allows the client to split negative and positive transferences toward the music and therapist, which in turn can promote a "resistance to awareness of the transference" (with the therapist). "The allusions to the transference to the therapist are not recognized and the resistance may be reinforced. The working through of the transference reactions occurs in relation to the music" (p. 471-472. In short, the client and therapist can easily shift the more shadowy aspects of their relationship away from the therapist transference toward the music transference.

When music is used as an "extension" of the therapist, the therapist's selection of a music program or spontaneous creation of a music program is viewed as the "therapist's expression of self, the therapist's vehicle" (p. 472). The therapist is inseparable from the music he or she presents to the client, so that the relationship configuration is dyadic rather than triadic. Thus, when the client perceives the therapist's choice of music as a good one, the therapist is experienced as a positive source of nourishment; and when the therapist's choice is perceived as confrontive, withholding, or lacking in empathy, the therapist is experienced negatively, as a source of frustration. This encourages the client to direct or project all feelings toward the music onto the therapist, which in turn makes the therapist the only available object for transference. This promotes client resistance to "awareness of the transference" with the music, as well as "resistance to involvement in the transference" with the music.

When used as a "therapist's gift" to the client, the music can serve as a means of gratifying the transference needs and wishes of the client. The music becomes the vehicle for the corrective emotional experience needed by the client. Here the therapist is promoting the client's "resistance to the resolution of the transference" because the client may be unable to work through the difficult feelings involved in the transference without attacking the therapist or the therapist's gift of music.

An important implication of Isenberg-Grzeda's study is that the client is not alone in how resistance and transference are built into the therapy process; the therapist, too, plays an active role. This leads to another important topic in any psychodynamic approach to therapy—countertransference.

## COUNTERTRANSFERENCE IN BMGIM

No discussion of transference or resistance is complete without looking at the contributions of countertransference. A definition of it that is consistent with how transference was defined earlier in this chapter is as follows:

> Countertransference occurs whenever a therapist interacts with a
> client in ways that resemble relationship patterns in either the

therapist's life or the client's life. Implicit is a replication in the present of relationships patterns in the past, a generalization of these patterns from one person to another, and from real-life situations to the therapy situation, the casting of the client and/or therapist within the past relationship, and a reexperiencing of the same or similar feelings, conflicts, impulses, drives, and fantasies through identification (Bruscia, 1998d, p. 52).

Countertransference phenomena have been differentiated and categorized in myriad ways (Bruscia, 1998d). An *empathic or concordant* countertransference occurs when the therapist identifies with the client's position, or experiences what the client was or is experiencing. A *complementary* countertransference occurs when the therapist identifies with the client's parent or significant other, or relates to the client in a similar way. A *positive* countertransference facilitates the therapeutic process, while a *negative* one impedes the process. An *intrasubjective* countertransference is an identification that stems from the therapist's own life experiences, not experiences in therapy with the client. An *intersubjective* countertransference is an identification that stems from the specific experiences with the client in the therapy situation.

In BMGIM, signs of countertransference may include (Bruscia, 1998e):

- Preferences for particular clientele
- Philosophical orientation to BMGIM
- Types of client-therapist relationships typically developed
- Ways of setting up and handling transferences
- Ways of dealing with resistance
- The relative importance given to imagery, music, and verbal discussion
- Somatic or emotional reactions to the client's work
- Ways of responding to the client's shadowy side
- Selection of music programs
- How music is used
- Styles of intervention

The psychoanalytic literature provides an abundance of suggestions on how to analyze and manage countertransference reactions. One approach that has been specifically designed for BMGIM is the re-imaging technique. This involves the therapist having a short BMGIM experience focused on an imagery scene created by a client. Working with another guide, the therapist revisits the client's image in an altered state of consciousness, while listening to the same music originally experienced by the client. The therapist steps into the scene and begins to interact within the image. A transcript is taken. After the experience, the therapist analyzes and compares his/her images with the client's, and uses the comparison to identify transference and counter-transference reactions. For a more complete discussion of the many steps involved, see Bruscia (1998f, 1998g).

In addition to transference and countertransference dynamics, both of which involve child-adult relationships, the client and therapist must form a *working alliance*. The working alliance is an adult-adult relationship, wherein client and therapist work together as equals to accomplish the goals of therapy. The working alliance is what keeps the client coming back to therapy, regardless of the difficulties encountered.

## SUMMARY

As conceived by Bonny, BMGIM can be implemented in a variety of theoretical orientations. Many aspects of the BMGIM approach resemble classic psychoanalysis (free association, focus on primary process, nondirective guide, etc.). A psychodynamic orientation to BMGIM is most appropriate when the client presents problems related to the Oedipal/Electra stage of development which essentially involves the establishment of child-parent relationships, and the need to repress libidinous energy to meet the demands of reality and morality. Basic constructs of the psychodynamic approach include: intrapsychic structures for levels of consciousness and for mind-body functions, repression, defense mechanisms, resistance, transference, countertransference, and working alliance. In BMGIM, resistance can be discerned in how fully the client engages in the music-imaging experience, how well the client integrates the somatic and emotional experiences in the music-imaging with verbal insights, and in developing and working through the transference. Although transferences are often described as triadic (client, therapist, music), clinical evidence suggests that they may also be directed toward introjects of the client and characters within the imagery which are not directly related to the therapist or music. The way a BMGIM therapist uses the music relationally can reinforce resistance to awareness of, involvement in, or resolution of the transference. Countertransference may be implicated in promoting such resistance, as well as in a variety of other areas of BMGIM work. It is the working alliance between client and therapist that mitigates the many challenges and difficulties that the client must face to lift the tyranny of repression and to embrace a fuller life.

# References

Bonny, H. (1990). *Augment Your Creative Chord.* Speech presented at the Great Lakes Regional Conference of the National Association for Music Therapy, Chicago. March 21. Page 5.

Bonny, H. (N.D) *Music and Change.* Unpublished notes.

Bruscia, K. (1995). Manifestations of transference in Guided Imagery and Music. *Journal of the Association for Music and Imagery,* 4, 16–35.

Bruscia, K. (1998a). An introduction to music psychotherapy. In K. Bruscia (ed.), *The Dynamics of Music Psychotherapy,* (pp.1–15). Gilsum, NH: Barcelona Publishers.

Bruscia, K. (1998b). The many dimensions of transference. In K. Bruscia (ed.), *The Dynamics of Music Psychotherapy,* (pp. 17-33). Gilsum NH: Barcelona Publishers.

Bruscia, K. (1998c). The Dynamics of Transference. In K. Bruscia (Ed.), *The Dynamics of Music Psychotherapy,* (pp. 35–50). Gilsum, NH: Barcelona Publishers.

Bruscia, K. (1998d). Understanding countertransference. In K. Bruscia (ed.), *The Dynamics of Music Psychotherapy,* (pp. 51–70). Gilsum, NH: Barcelona Publishers.

Bruscia, K (1998e). The signs of countertransference. In K. Bruscia (ed.), *The Dynamics of Music Psychotherapy,* (pp71–91). Gilsum, NH: Barcelona Publishers.

Bruscia, K. (1998f). Reimaging client images: A technique for exploring transference and countertransference in Guided Imagery and Music. In K. Bruscia (ed.), *The Dynamics of Music Psychotherapy,* (pp. 528–548). Gilsum, NH: Barcelona Publishers.

Bruscia, K. (1998g). Reimaging client images: A technique for uncovering projective identification. In K. Bruscia (ed.), *The Dynamics of Music Psychotherapy,* (pp. 549–560). Gilsum, NH: Barcelona Publishers.

Clarkson, G. & Geller, J. (1996). The Bonny Method from a psychoanalytic perspective: Insights from working with a psychoanalytic psychotherapist in a Guided Imagery and Music series. *The Arts in Psychotherapy* 23(4), 311–319.

Gill, M. (1982). *Analysis of Transference. Volume I: Theory and Technique.* Madison, CT: International Universities Press.

Goldberg, F. (1992). Images of emotion: The role of emotion in Guided Imagery and Music. *Journal of the Association for Music and Imagery,* 5–15.

Isenberg-Grzeda, C. (1998). Transference structures in Guided Imagery and Music. In K. Bruscia (ed.), *The Dynamics of Music Psychotherapy* (pp. 461–479). Gilsum, NH: Barcelona Publishers.

Pelliteri, J. (1999). A self-analysis of transference in Guided Imagery and Music. In K. Bruscia (ed.), *The Dynamics of Music Psychotherapy* (pp. 481–490). Gilsum, NH: Barcelona Publishers.

Priestley, M. (1994). *Essays on Analytical Music Therapy*. Gilsum, NH: Barcelona Publishers.

Summer, L. (1998). The pure music transference in Guided Imagery and Music. In K. Bruscia (ed.), *The Dynamics of Music Psychotherapy* (pp. 431-459). Gilsum, NH: Barcelona Publishers.

Wilber, K. (1986). Treatment modalities. In K. Wilber, J. Engler, & D. Brown (eds.), *Transformations of Consciousness* (pp. 127–159). Boston, MA: New Science Library.

Wilber, K. (1996) *A Brief History of Everything*. Boston, MA: Shambhala.

Wilber, K. (2000). *Integral Psychology: Consciousness, Spirit, Psychology, Therapy*. Boston, MA: Shambhala.

Wrangsjo, B. (1994). Psychoanalysis and Guided Imagery and Music: A comparison. *Journal of the Association for Music and Imagery* 3, 35-48.

*Chapter Thirteen*

# COMBINING GESTALT DREAMWORK AND THE BONNY METHOD

## Ginger Clarkson

The term "Gestalt" means "whole." Gestalt psychologists are interested in the act of perceiving, which they consider not so much the passive reception of sensory stimuli from the environment, as the active process of structuring and imposing order on constantly changing figures against backgrounds or contexts (Polster, 1973). At any moment that which is figural may fade into the background, and an aspect of the background may become a figure for attention (Polster, 1973). For instance, a girl may be concentrating so hard on completing a colorful painting inside her bedroom that she ignores potentially distracting noises. At that moment, her brother arrives with an invitation to join him and some friends in a baseball game in the backyard. With her artwork temporarily forgotten, the girl focuses on the sounds of children laughing and yelling outside; her energy shifts from calm introspection to excited preparation for active exercise and social interaction. Our whole life may be viewed as background for the present moment (Polster, 1973). For example, when we are introduced to a stranger, we are often reminded of one or more people from our past, and our prior positive or negative interactions may affect our present response to the newcomer.

A vital characteristic of perception is the perceiver's impetus to close gestalts. In actuality many human interactions remain pending, without clear closure. Individuals are often interrupted in the midst of receiving or processing input; incomplete actions, which are forced into the background while attending to new stimuli, remain unresolved and incomplete, interfering with present matters (Polster, 1973). For instance, while a man is fixing himself a sandwich to satisfy his hunger, his wife enters the kitchen to discuss a pressing concern about their marital relationship. Even as he attempts to focus on her words, the smell of the food and his hunger pangs distract him from being fully attentive.

Frustrated by her spouse's emotional detachment, the wife leaves, without accomplishing her objective.

While some gestalts can be resolved in short order, others may remain open-ended (and a potential source of anxiety) for many years. The goal of Gestalt therapy is to enable clients to reach and fully experience closure in the present, so that preoccupations with old, unfinished business are resolved; then the client feels more freedom to move on to current possibilities (Polster, 1973). For example, a woman has been acting promiscuous without realizing that her behavior stems from never having been hugged by her cold, distant father. Her childhood longing for her father's affection has been for decades an unclosed gestalt that can be resolved either in a role-play with the Gestalt therapist enacting an affectionate father or in a guided fantasy about receiving paternal nurturing in the present moment. The Gestalt approach treats an original childhood trauma, with all of its accompanying emotional responses, as if it were occurring right now. Once the woman has relived her feelings of abandonment, she is more self-aware and better able to change current self-destructive behavioral patterns that have been connected to those feelings.

Fritz Perls, father of Gestalt therapy, was an expatriate German psychoanalyst who was analyzed by Wilhelm Reich, a student of Sigmund Freud. Throughout several decades before his death in 1970, Perls developed his own spontaneous style of working in the "here and now." He attracted an enthusiastic following at the Esalen Institute in California in the 1950s and 1960s. Perls was deeply influenced by the Taoist practice of acting according to intuition instead of reason (Naranjo, 1993). In therapy sessions, he never followed a set plan or formula, but met each evolving situation creatively. Claudio Naranjo, a renowned Chilean musician and Gestalt therapist, states that the philosophy of Gestalt is to "trust in organismic self-regulation," so that patients learn the transpersonal disciplines of awareness and acting spontaneously and authentically in each moment (Naranjo, 1993, p. xxvi).

Instead of employing the psychoanalytic mode of exploring a patient's past and interpreting verbally reported unconscious material, Perls focused on the patient's immediate experiences, both nonverbal and verbal. Rather than encouraging regression and transference from the sidelines in the classic psychoanalytic manner, he interacted directly with each patient to learn from their actual relationship (Perls, Hefferline, and Goodman, 1951). In a typical session, he would ask a client to describe her body sensations or point out the instant that her tone of voice changed. Or, if she were complaining about an intrapersonal or interpersonal conflict, Perls would ask her to give voice to both sides of the issue; through establishing a dialogue between aspects of the self, and switching back and forth between two chairs, the client could progress toward integrating polarities and reconciling paradoxes and disputes in her life.

Such simple exercises in raising consciousness often lead to profound insights and emotional catharsis.

# GESTALT DREAMWORK

Characteristically noninterpretive, Gestalt dreamwork consists in helping the dreamer "enter" the dream to recognize its existential message and to take responsibility for these projected aspects of the Self (Naranjo, 1993). The emphasis is on increasing awareness rather than on provoking intellectual analysis. Gestalt practitioners regard all characters and features in dreams as projections of parts of the dreamer's own personality (Perls, Hefferline, and Goodman, 1951). The dreamer begins the session by narrating the dream in present tense, as if it were occurring at that moment. Some Gestalt therapists suggest that the narrator say before each sentence, "This is my existence" (Naranjo, 1993).

According to Fritz Perls, "Dreams are concrete, nonverbal, sensory— 'eidetic' [marked by extraordinarily accurate or vivid recall]" (Perls, Hefferline, and Goodman, 1951, p. 217). Compared to other types of spontaneous expression, such as vocal intonation, posture, gait, and gesture, the dream is more articulate, with visual images that are almost as explicit as concepts but more expressive (Naranjo, 1993). At times dreams can evoke so much sensory stimulation that the dreamer wakes aware of particular smells and tastes. The spontaneity of dreaming, however, can threaten the sanity and safety of the ego and the rational mind (Perls, Hefferline, and Goodman, 1951). Sometimes clients are extremely upset by a nightmare, and they seek their therapist's help in integrating the dream's message into their current life process.

What we call "reality" depends on our frame of reference. Otto Rank noted that members of the Iroquois tribe believe that dreams are the reality and that their task is to "interpret the waking in terms of the dream rather than the dream in terms of the waking" (Perls, Hefferline, and Goodman, 1951, p. 218). One of their credences is that the soul has hidden natural desires that it makes known by means of dreams, which are its language. According to the seventeenth-century Jesuit Father Rageneau, Huron Indians believed that to carry out the actions suggested by a dream satisfies the soul, and to ignore the messages causes the resentful soul to produce illness (Naranjo, 1993). Thus the concept of dream enactment is not new or limited to Gestalt therapy. In an updated form, enacting and reliving dream imagery in Gestalt sessions can help dreamers understand symbols and metaphors that relate to concrete issues and pragmatic concerns in daily life.

Apparently, Freud considered childhood the period of life most psychologically real, and he interpreted the dreams of his patients in terms of childhood situations (Perls, Hefferline, and Goodman, 1951). Carl Jung criticized Freudian dream analysis for interpreting and reducing dream symbols and related physical symptoms rather than viewing them as vibrant parts of reality and as essential elements of creative process (Perls, Hefferline, and Goodman, 1951). Gestalt therapists would concur with Jung's criticisms of classical dream analysis. Unlike the Jungian concentration on the transpersonal archetypal aspect of dreams, however, the Gestalt therapist focuses on their interpersonal dimension (Naranjo, 1993). The emphasis is on applying insights from dreamwork to clients' issues in the here and now.

Since everyone can relate to archetypal themes, an individual's dream imagery may be used in Gestalt group therapy sessions to enhance self-understanding among all the participants (Zinker, 1977). The dreamer may cast members of the group in various dream roles, and direct the action or take over one of the roles and enact it in detail (Zinker, 1977). This group process has much in common with psychodrama sessions.

## RELATING GESTALT DREAMWORK
## TO THE BONNY METHOD

Gestalt dreamwork techniques are compatible with the Bonny Method of Guided Imagery and Music (BMGIM)—although the latter is used primarily in individual therapy, and clients arrive at most of their insights while traveling to music in a non-ordinary state of consciousness. In fact, Helen Bonny, attended Gestalt workshops in the 1960s. She acknowledges their influence on her use of a noninterpretive orientation and dialogue techniques in her method (personal interview, June 1999). Like Gestalt therapists, BMGIM facilitators concentrate on what is happening in the present moment. In both theoretical approaches, the client reports body sensations, emotions, and images that become figural from a background context. Both Gestalt and BMGIM therapists have faith in the capacity of clients to draw on inner wisdom and creative resources to follow their unique path of development. BMGIM sessions are often called "waking dreams," so dreamwork has a natural and safe home with this form of transpersonal music-centered therapy. In fact, the music may enhance the potential for closing gestalts and freeing up energy.

# First Case Study: Frida

What follows are two examples of BMGIM sessions, adapted to include Gestalt techniques for enhancing clients' insights about disturbing dreams. In the first instance, following seven BMGIM sessions that dealt with her long-awaited divorce, Frida was contemplating a major life change. She had fallen in love with a former classmate, Gian, with whom she reconnected at their twenty-fifth high school reunion. Upon completing training in the Bonny Method, she was planning to move with her ten-year-old son from Mexico City, her home of more than forty years, to live with her lover and his equally young son from an ex-marriage, in a faraway town on the Yucatan peninsula. Frida brought to her eighth session a recurring dream that was haunting her.

At the start of the session (9/25/98), I asked her to recount the dream sequence slowly, in present tense. The images seemed to crystallize all her doubts and fears and hopes about the upcoming transition in her life. Frida's recount of her dream was as follows:

> It is a dark night with a clear sky.
> I can see the stars shining.
> I am in a place surrounded by mountains.
> I see a large mountain with an irregular form in front of me.
> It is arid and stretches up high.
> I feel very small in comparison.
> I can see a cave high up on the mountaintop.
> I see a path leading to the cave.
> From the cave I see the light of a fire that illuminates the path.
> Up there I see the figure of Gian observing me in silence, as if he is waiting.
> I am looking up from far below.
> I can feel the dry, parched earth.
> Next to me is a large clay vessel of water, full to the brim.
> On the other side of the water jug is Emil [Gian's son].
> He is ready to begin the climb, but nervous and restless.
> We both begin to walk, carrying the water jug.
> It is hard to climb without spilling water.
> The jug is heavy, and we double over under the weight.
> I feel very tired walking on such dry land.
> I can feel the weight in my hands, and my back hurts.
> I see Emil's face sweating.
> We continue to climb the mountain in spite of our heavy load.

After recounting her dream, Frida lay down on a mat and closed her eyes to listen to the relaxation induction and the subsequent BMGIM music program.

For the induction, I asked Frida to tense and release each body part from feet to head. I selected the Bonny music program, *Transitions,* because it is best suited for major life changes. During the music, I followed the sequence of key images from Frida's dream, and, according to Gestalt principles, suggested that she embody and give voice to each one. In the following transcript, translated from Spanish, my verbal interventions appear in parentheses; ellipses indicate pauses or lapses in time.

### *The Hero's Life* (Excerpt) by Richard Strauss (9:34):

(You are the stars.) I can shine by myself in the darkness. (Sense that.) I know all things, as I live my own life. There are so many of us stars, each one with its own light. We rotate in the darkness . . .

(You are the irregular mountain.) I am very large, majestic, solid and immobile, eternal. (How do you feel being eternal?) Strong. With great roots. Nothing can move me from here—neither rain nor earthquakes can move me. I am too big and solid. I may change a bit on the outside. But nobody can destroy me. Within me there is life . . .

### *Third Symphony* (Poco Allegro) by Johannes Brahms (5:55):

(You are the cave.) I am the heart of the mountain. There I can be protected. There I can live. There is heat and light. I am a space within what's solid. (How is it to be that space?) I can breathe and just *be*. The cold outside does not affect me. I am comfortable being apart from the outside world. Peace . . . (Peace) . . .

(You are the path.) I'm narrow and difficult and dangerous. I have deceptive holes. I'm steep and I make it hard for people to climb over me. I head upward. I am hard and very narrow. (How does that feel?) It feels necessary to be hard and inflexible with people . . .

### *Ninth Symphony* (Adagio Molto) by Ludwig van Beethoven (16:02):

(You are the fire.) I am light and energy. I am life and heat. I am death. People who come near me burn. I am movement. (How do you feel?) Like I am hope . . . (Aha!) . . . SIGH . . .

(You are Gian.) I am strong, tenacious, with equanimity. I think clearly. I am strong but kind. (What do you see down below?) The path. I can allow [Frida and my son] to climb. I can give them confidence and security. Without talking, I convey that I'm waiting for them. I will be here, because I know they can arrive. I'll give them strength with my love and peace. I'll make space to receive them . . .

(You are the clay vessel.) I hold water, which is also life. I am the means for carrying this life. I'm also fragile and, without careful attention, I can be left empty or broken. (Repeat that.) REPETITION . . . With water inside, I am also life. (You are life.) On the outside I appear insignificant, but I'm important. (Say that again.) REPETITION . . .

(You are Emil.) I am a fragile boy. I want to climb the mountain, but I am afraid. Everything is big outside. I have to climb and carry water. I don't have enough strength, but I have energy. I don't have the choice to stay here. I must climb. I don't want to be alone. I want someone to take care of me. [I incorporated a Gestalt technique, asking the client to speak from another person's point of view—in this case, Emil's—in order to transcend her limited, egotistic outlook:] (How do you feel with Frida?) Cared for . . . I also care for and accompany her. She needs me, and I need her. The two of us can climb with the water jug. I cannot do it alone . . .

### *Second Piano Concerto* (Andante) by Johannes Brahms (13:08):

(You are the weight.) SIGH . . . I am like an anchor, an obstacle, a dense ballast. (Do you have a purpose?) I try to prevent them from climbing. I pull them down, countering their strength, their wishes, their energy. I hang from them. (How do you feel?) I'm negative. (How is that for you?) I'm dark and tense and ugly. (Sense the tension.) I hang on to prevent them from advancing.

[Here I decided to employ a Gestalt intrapersonal dialogue technique], (What could you communicate to Frida?) "I'll make it hard for you to climb. I'll keep you nailed to one place. There you'll stay even if you struggle." Also Emil can't move without my consent. I am a nightmare, a shadow, something unpleasant. Like death, I terminate all that I love. I create tiredness, exhaustion, sickness . . . (You are yourself.) SIGHING . . . RELAXING . . . I want to climb despite the weight. It's very hard. I'm tired. (Feel all the elements in your dream.) GENTLY CRYING . . .

MUSIC ENDS: (The music has ended. Stay with your memories of the many parts of yourself.)

In the post-session dialogue, Frida commented: "The journey was like a complete self-portrait. I experienced my feminine, masculine, and child-like sides. I sensed my potential, including strength, love, tenderness, light, and tenacity; and I faced my weak points, including dark heaviness, self-limitation, sadism, inflexibility, and cruelty."

This was a key session that proved to be a turning point in Frida's decision to break with her past and to commit to moving, with self-confidence and belief in the goodness of her intimate relationship. The *Transitions* music program supported perfectly Frida's emotional journey, and it finished right on cue, as soon as she had explored to her satisfaction all the elements of her dream. Because I knew the program intimately, I felt completely in synchrony with the points of tension and release in each piece of music and with the traveler as she worked on her dream imagery. I imagine that it would be difficult to guide such a BMGIM dreamwork session if the facilitator were not fluently connected with the chosen music program.

## Second Case Study: Silvio

Silvio, who was participating in the same training in the Bonny Method as Frida, had an equally powerful session that revolved around a dream that had scared him. In his early fifties, he is a retired seaman whose back was injured during heavy work on oil rigs. Divorced, Silvio has custody of two nearly grown sons, and he has experienced the loss of both his marriage and his professional identity. He has taken refuge in reading about psychological theories and spiritual paths, and in singing and playing guitar, while enrolling in music therapy courses. After weathering a lonely and impoverished childhood, he is finally financially flush, with a healthy pension, and free to follow some of his unrealized goals. Since his retirement, he has been plunging passionately into his inner life.

Silvio began his third BMGIM session (9/11/98) with an account of a frightening dream whose significance he could not decipher. Using a Gestalt therapy format, I asked him to narrate the sequence of events in present tense, with eyes closed, and to report any emotional responses and physical sensations in the pauses following each sentence. Because he tends to hide his feelings behind intellectual analysis, I encouraged Silvio to sense his body fully. His reported reactions appear within brackets in the transcript. Silvio's recounted his dream as follows:

I am in front of an old, dark house with many columns.
[My hands are sweating.]
I can see through the door.
[I sense fear in my feet.]
Inside there is a reception room with antique chairs.
[My heart is beating rapidly.]
I see the silhouette of a person.
[My legs feel weak.]
When I approach fearfully, I see an old woman with a very wrinkled
face.
[I feel fear in my whole body.]
She raises her right arm and says, "What is your Shadow? I will tell
you."
[I feel scared and don't know whether to flee or to stay.]
I feel panic and I try to run away.

In the induction, I asked Silvio to sense the weight of each part of the body and
the support of the cushions. I used the music program entitled *Transitions* as
modified by Bruscia on the CD series, *Music for the Imagination*. This nervous
traveler appeared to need the sweetness and support of Borodin's first symphony
to enter into such scary imagery. I ended up omitting the final Brahms piece on
the program because Silvio had a profound insight near the end of the third
music selection, and I did not want to evoke different issues or images.

In a more directive manner than usual, I suggested that the journey begin
with Silvio's dream image of the old house, but unlike in Frida's session, I
followed his strongly kinesthetic responses instead of reminding him to identify
with key imagery from the dream:

### *First Symphony* (Andante) by Alexander Borodin (6:12):

.. . . (What do you notice?) I feel pulled by my chin. (What's the environment
like?) Dark . . . (How are you feeling?) Calm . . . I don't see anything. ARMS
AND LEGS TREMBLING . . . (What's happening in your body?) I'm cold . . .

### *Third Symphony* (Poco Allegretto) by Johannes Brahms (5:54):

(What are you aware of?) I perceive nothing. I feel nothing except cold in my
trembling arms. (Stay with nothing.) SHOULDERS AND HEAD
STRETCHING. (What's occurring with your head?) I am stretching my whole
body, and my head is joining in. I am turning around. There is a transparent
energy. (Follow it.) My head is revolving. BODY JERKING AND HEAD

TWISTING. The energy does not want to leave me. It is my strength. (How do you feel?) I am pushing it to leave. I want it to leave, but it is very strong. Something in my body does not allow the energy to leave. It's hurting me.

### *Ninth Symphony* (Adagio Molto) by Ludwig van Beethoven (16:02):

BODY JERKING. I want it to leave, but it won't. STARTING TO CRY. (Feel it.) CRYING HARD. It's staying. It is all that I am that I don't permit myself to be. It's very sad. It wants to be with me. (Connect with the sadness.) CRYING HARD. (Sense the support of the music.) I feel as if I am fully myself. I feel peace. I'm content. SIGHING . . . (Breathe in that peace.) SMILING. I am with myself in peace. (Enjoy that.) SMILING. HUGGING HIMSELF. BODY SHUDDERING GENTLY. (Sense your body's vibrations.) I am rising. I am flying. (Let the end of the music support your flying.) I am the old woman! (Aha!) MUSIC ENDS.

POST-SESSION: I feel free now that I've integrated the energy of the Shadow. (Draw her.)

As Silvio incorporated his missing feminine side, his face glowed with happiness. This session was vital in his shift from relying on rational defenses to allowing himself to feel and express his emotions. He admitted that he had not drawn a picture since he was a little boy, when his mother humiliated him by making fun of one of his childish drawings in front of some of her friends. It was useful for him to contemplate the concrete image of his Shadowy female aspect.

## CONCLUSION

Silvio and Frida had BMGIM sessions that involved different applications of Gestalt principles. Before traveling with the music, both clients benefited from narrating their dreams slowly in present tense. Silvio deepened his connection to each image by reporting his immediate physical and emotional reactions, so that by the time the music started he could enter fully into his dream world. By identifying with each symbol according to the sequence of her dream, Frida gained insights about her interior world that helped her commit to an intimate relationship and move to a new city.

In both cases, the music added emotional profundity to the Gestalt dreamwork. For example, in Frida's session, each of the four pieces in the Bonny program *Transitions* evoked rich associations that fleshed out the skeletal synopsis of her dream. As the Strauss piece summoned her to embark on a hero's journey, she dealt with impersonal elements of her dream such as the stars and the mountain. The romantic fullness of the first Brahms piece supported her exploration of more detailed and emotionally charged components such as the cave in the heart of the mountain and the steep path to the summit. With the combination of gentle lyricism and firm strength provided by the Adagio Molto from Beethoven's *Ninth Symphony*, Frida could relate profoundly to the more personal images of the fire in the cave, her waiting lover, the clay vessel containing life, and the little boy Emil. The closing Brahms piece offered enough energy for Frida to confront the negativity of the heavy weight, and then enough lightness and spaciousness to synthesize her dream's messages.

Likewise, in Silvio's session, Borodin's graceful Andante movement allowed him to sink gently into the darkness of his unconscious realms. The force of the Brahms provoked intense kinesthetic and emotional turmoil, and the prolonged, strong yet serene passages by Beethoven gave Silvio time to absorb his sadness and to surrender to his feminine side.

Consciously incorporating Gestalt techniques into each section of BMGIM sessions can enhance the immediacy and power of the work. During the preliminary discussion, for instance, guides might increase their clients' self-awareness by pointing out significant changes in tone of voice, posture, or facial expression, rather than focusing on the content of issues being raised. The therapist can exaggerate particular manners of speaking or breathing or act as a mirror to reflect dramatic gestures. Inductions can be adapted by including intonations, phrases, or images that have been used by the client immediately beforehand. The traveler might be asked to lie down in a position that expresses the attitude that he or she has been conveying. For example, reposing in a submissive posture implies a different approach to the music than reclining in a confident pose.

Within a Gestalt framework, the music selection for a BMGIM session might depend more on the client's attitude, mood, and rhythm of moving and speaking than on a stated intention. During the music session, the guide can employ verbal interventions drawn from various Gestalt techniques suggested long ago by Helen Bonny and be prepared to track whatever sensations, emotions, images or memories that the client reports in the "here and now." The therapist can engage the traveler in dialogues with any musical elements or instruments that evoke emotional reactions or body sensations. The client might be encouraged to give voice to polarized body parts such as head versus heart or to the right versus left sides of the body. Likewise the traveler can express two opposing tendencies or desires in his/her personal or professional life. If the client reports the experience of regressing or advancing in age, the therapist might propose speaking from the point of view of a young child or a wise elder.

For emphasis, the guide can repeat key words or phrases uttered by the traveler, or request that he/she reiterate them.

In the processing period following the music, the therapist may incorporate Gestalt techniques that are not usually employed in BMGIM sessions. For instance, the client might be asked to imagine that a key figure from music-evoked imagery is sitting in an empty chair, and to engage in a dialogue with this character. As the conversation develops, the client could be directed to "switch roles" and take a turn sitting in the chair to speak from another point of view. Shuttling back and forth between seats/viewpoints can open up new perspectives and possibilities for clients.

During the processing period, the therapist might detect the client's fear about putting into practice a new mode of behavior or course of action that was visualized during the music session. At this point it would be appropriate to use the Gestalt method of "rehearsing" the behavior or action through role playing. For example, a woman might practice asserting herself, while the therapist enacts her employer criticizing her work performance.

Gestalt techniques appear to fit remarkably smoothly into the BMGIM format. Without the music, Gestalt exercises might simply heighten awareness in the here and now; with the music, the session has the potential to be a profound, transcendent experience that taps both ordinary and non-ordinary states of consciousness. Gestalt and BMGIM methods mutually support one another; the former teach clients to notice attentively their changing corporal and emotional responses, and the latter evoke psychodynamic and transpersonal insights with carefully chosen music.

## *References*

Naranjo, C. (1993). *Gestalt Therapy: The Attitude and Practice of an Atheoretical Experientialism*. Nevada City, CA: Gateways/IDHHB Publishing.

Perls, F. (1973). *The Gestalt Approach and Eye Witness to Therapy*. North Vancouver B.C.: Aquarian Productions, Ltd. (Science and Behavior Books).

Perls, F., Hefferline, R., & Goodman, P. (1951). *Gestalt Therapy: Excitement and Growth in the Human Personality*. Highland, NY: The Gestalt Journal Press.

Polster, E. & Polster, M. (1973). *Gestalt Therapy Integrated*. New York: Vintage Books.

Zinker, J. (1977). *Creative Process in Gestalt Therapy*. New York: Random House, Inc.

*Chapter Fourteen*

# A SPIRITUAL ORIENTATION TO THE BONNY METHOD: TO WALK THE MYSTICAL PATH ON PRACTICAL FEET

## Roseann E. Kasayka

The journey we make along the spiritual path is at once intensely personal and at the same time integrally part of the collective journey of all humankind. As we search for answers to questions that deal with ultimates, as we explore our concerns about and our connections to the Divine, by whatever name we call it, we plumb the depths of spirituality. O'Murchu (2000) describes spirituality as "a search for meaning that embraces a 'beyondness'; a sense of being embraced and held by a larger life-force, at one time very earthly, and yet inclusive of everything that belongs to the life-spectrum of past-present-future" (p. 204). Chittister, a Benedictine sister, in an interview with Joseph Driscoll (1996) calls spirituality "theology walking." The anthropologist Arrien (1987) believes that spirituality involves "walking the mystical path with practical feet" (pp. 41–42). Kinerk (1988) speaks of spirituality as "the expression of a dialectical personal growth from the inauthentic to the authentic" (p. 21).

Each of these descriptions is apt for our contemporary world. Each describes an aspect of how we read the sacred and apply what is holy in our inner life to the outer world. Each implies that spiritual development is dynamic and dialogic. The spiritual revolution currently taking place in our society tends to be creation-centered, sometimes only adjacent to if not separated from organized religion and grounded in a belief system of connectedness that is as old as time itself. The renewed interest in spirituality cannot be contained by dogma nor eliminated by sanction. The explosive interest in rediscovering what it means to be spiritual beings leads us to seek experience of the material world and the nonmaterial world. It takes us to the edge of the realm that mystics and musicians, poets and artists, healers and visionaries know as home. The exploration of spirituality calls us into that same realm and promises to make for us too a home.

## BONNY'S ORIGINAL BELIEFS

Consummate musician and mystic, Helen Bonny located the theory and the practice of her method solidly in an evolving personal spirituality. This spirituality is reflected in the seminal story of her experience of playing the violin before a prayer group and being transported to a place of beauty, grace and pure music that she knew to be real but also was somewhat incomprehensible. Bonny (1994) refers to this experience as one of similar import to that of the apostle Paul on the road to Damascus. As a conversion experience, the knowing gained in it never drifted far from Bonny's awareness. The questions this experience raised about the connection of music and prayer, music and mysticism, music and spirituality became the starting point for much of her exploration. While these questions are not always overtly explored in her early writings about the Bonny Method, they are always quietly present.

Bonny looked to the works of humanistic psychologists such as Abraham Maslow, and mystics of Western Spirituality such as Teresa of Avila and Underhill for language to describe her experience and theory to parse it.

Maslow's description of peak experiences closely approximates Bonny's performance experience as well as the effect this experience had on her thought in regard to what she originally called "Guided Imagery and Music" of GIM. Maslow (1962) speaks of peak experiences as "moments of pure, positive happiness when all doubts, all fears, all inhibitions, all tensions, all weaknesses, were left behind" (p. 9). In this same article, he goes on to note further that, when in the process of peak experience, self-consciousness is lost, separateness and distance from the world disappears, and there is the sense of experience of oneness with all things. In his later writings, Maslow (1970) describes various aspects and results of peak experiences (pp. 59–68). He notes that during peak experiences there is a tremendous concentration of a type that does not generally occur. This concentration permits the individual to move closer to the essence of the thing, person, or situation experienced.

Bonny (1994) detailed the beginnings of GIM and its relation to the aforementioned performance experience. She tells that she, though at first extremely nervous, began to play music of such exquisite beauty that she had the sense that the music was not being produced by her but rather through her. In so concentrating and in so becoming one with the music, she attained a peak state. In this state of unity with the music, even her efforts to sabotage her playing by eliminating the vibrato did nothing to lessen the beauty that not only she but that all listening experienced. Many of the elements Bonny describes in this interview—namely, the sense of unity with the music, the sense of the beauty of the music, the sense of concentration as she played—are similar to the characteristics discussed by Maslow. Bonny's experience of trying to sabotage the music without effect matches another of Maslow's concepts about peak experiences as a receptive rather than active phenomenon. Maslow (1962) says, ". . . most of them (peak experiences) are receptive phenomena. They invade the person and he must be able to let them. He can't force them, grasp them, or command them. Will power is useless; so is striving and straining. What's necessary is to be able to let go, to let things happen" (p.17). Bonny noted that the experience she had during that performance has never been repeated. But she continued to pursue the essence of that experience in her writing and her design of Guided Imagery and Music.

In an early article, "The Use of Music in Psychedelic (LSD) Psychotherapy" Bonny and Pahnke (1972) speak of ways in which music complements therapy and moves forth therapeutic objectives. One way noted is that music contributes toward a peak experience. The authors note (p. 69) that reaching such an experience was a goal of the LSD therapy in which they were engaged. The reason for this goal lay in the hypothesis that these experiences had the potential to produce in the client the greatest life-changing and most enduring results. In this section, six major psychological characteristics of peak experiences previously discussed by Pahnke (1969) are listed. They are: a sense of unity or oneness; transcendence of time and space; deeply felt positive mood (joy, peace, love); sense of awesomeness, reverence and wonder; meaningfulness of psychological and/or philosophical insight; and ineffability (sense of difficulty in communicating the experience by verbal description). These characteristics are reminiscent of Maslow's description of peak experiences. The hypothesis that these experiences produce lasting change in a person's life also parallels Maslow's beliefs. While Bonny is considering peak experiences in psychological language in this article, the description of the peak experience is decidedly spiritual. Since Bonny (1994) had been counseled not to mention spirituality or mysticism when she began her music therapy training and since this is one of her first published articles, one can follow the logic of the change of focus. However, one can also question the loss to the development of the GIM method in the main stream music therapy community that comes as part of that restriction. If from the very beginning Bonny had been free to discuss publicly not only the psychological but also the spiritual ramifications of her newly developing method, how would it have impacted not only GIM but also the field of music therapy as a whole?

In *Music and Your Mind* (1973), written before Bonny began working with dyads (i.e., in individual sessions), she and Louis Savary describe the peak and religious experiences of persons at the First International Conference on Psychobiology and Transpersonal Psychology (pp. 111–127). In speaking of the experiences of the group, Bonny and Savary return to the language of spirituality but continually distinguish between peak and religious experience. In a chapter which provides exercises and music to open the potential for spiritual experience, Bonny and Savary note that each of the suggestions allow the reader to bring to the listening experience their own ideas about humankind, nature, God, religion, and the transcendent. Each of the pieces that will later be programmed as the *Peak Experience Tape* appear in one or another of the suggestions for music for these experiences. This music is evocative of the spiritual and permits and encourages openness to higher realms of the transcendent, to higher vibrations, to gratitude, and to joy.

In summary then, Bonny's performance experience could be classified as a high peak experience that changed her life and set her on a spiritual journey. Music was her constant companion on this journey. Throughout all of her work, Bonny held to the belief that music could open an individual to the spiritual and could effect healing. Guided Imagery and Music is one of the products of Bonny's ongoing exploration and search to understand the Divine, to answer ultimate questions, and to bring healing into the world. In its inception, the process of Guided Imagery and Music had as a focus work in groups. This is evidenced and described in *Music and Your Mind*. As discussed in this book, GIM often began a spiritual exploration and almost always led to spiritual or peak experiences.

As Bonny (1994) began to work at Maryland Psychiatric Institute, and explored the effects of music with clients there, the GIM process developed in a way that more closely resembles the traditional individual form of GIM, which is now called the Bonny Method of GIM (BMGIM). While dyadic work does not preclude the possibility of doing the work of spiritual growth, it is often not the immediate primary focus. Personal growth work is holistic and multileveled. As a process, BMGIM also could be considered holistic and multileveled. It would do violence to the process of BMGIM and the personal process of the individual client if an artificial boundary or distinction allocated work done to a purely psychological or purely spiritual or purely transpersonal level. BMGIM works on each of those levels, often simultaneously. Yet, in tracing the development of Bonny's original thought, it serves well to notice the difference in focus between *Music and Your Mind* and the work done at Maryland Psychiatric Institute. The former was decidedly more toward spiritual growth and transpersonal experience with the work primarily done in groups; the latter more toward personal insight and ego development with the work primarily done in dyads. For the sake of clarity, the former will be called Group GIM, and the latter individual form will be referred to as BMGIM.

Currently, in the development of Group GIM and BMGIM, there is a movement to reclaim all of the potential foci. Thus, in the past few years, there has been a renewed interest in the spiritual growth process. This particular spectrum of GIM work moves the focus from using individual or group forms of GIM as a psychotherapeutic tool to using them as a spiritual guidance process. Several fellows of the Association for Music and Imagery who have developed programs or retreats use Group GIM in this way. Some of these programs will now be presented. Note that they are all group forms of GIM, and should be distinguished from the use of BMGIM for purposes of spiritual development.

## TAKING DIFFERENT PATHS

### Holligan and Marr

Holligan and Marr (1999) evolved a framework for working with groups for spiritual growth. The core reason for offering GIM in this format is the realization that when the power of classical music, the power of God's Word as read in Scripture and the faith life of the participants in the group come together in a safe and supportive atmosphere, powerful movement takes place in the lives of the participants. Holligan and Marr rely strongly on O'Murchu's (1992) definition of spirituality, namely, "the deeper realm of the human psyche—a quality of inner experience shared by all people and unique to each person. Its focal point in human behavior is the search for meaning which each person pursues in the depth of his or her own heart, and which we humans articulate collectively in a vast range of social and ritual behaviors" (p. 57). They also look to James Fowler's (1981) stages of faith and Ken Wilber's (1977) spectrum of consciousness as underpinnings for their work.

The format that Holligan and Marr suggest for this work is basically the traditional group GIM format. That includes: preliminary discussion; prayer (this is an added step); relaxation/induction; transition focus to the music; music listening; processing with mandala, clay, and/or writing; verbal sharing; closure—prayer. The main difference in the implementation of this traditional format is that the instead of the usual induction, the focus is drawn from Scripture, preferably a short selection and a story with natural imagery following a theme (e.g., parable and miracle stories from Gospel readings).

Holligan and Marr (1999) list some primary differences between therapy groups and this type of GIM spiritual growth group. They include:

- People come for spiritual growth, *not* therapy. This fact is spoken and understood from the beginning.
- There is more emphasis on the Spirit leading/guiding the group process.
- There is a different method of processing with the group sharing which allows participants space to hear where the Spirit is leading. Questions which typically facilitate the process might be: "Where do you sense the Spirit (God) in all of this?" or "Is there some passage in Scripture that comes to you as being connected to this experience?"
- When responding to another person's sharing, group members are invited to give a "response from the heart." This avoids any tendency to analysis or judgment.
- A candle is placed in the midst of the group at the time of sharing. This is an invitation for all to gather around the Light in whatever way they understand the light.
- The impact of the group process is often significant and it seems that group members make soul connections and find kindred spirits. Because of the depth of the shared faith experience, people often continue to support each other beyond the time of the group. This is a kind of community building.
- The usual precautions are taken at the end of the group experience. If unresolved issues have surfaced participants are urged to seek counseling or spiritual direction. However, an invitation to trust in God's Spirit, or whatever image of God is comfortable for the individual, is also given.

While this particular type of group work is orientated to those of the Christian tradition, Holligan and Marr suggest that it could be translated into any belief system or philosophy by replacing the reading taken from the Christian Scriptures with readings from other sacred books, from poetry or from appropriate prose.

Holligan (1994) and Marr (2001, article in press) have each written about the use of GIM in retreat work. In her article, Marr presents a full outline for a two-and-a-half-day program including induction, image focus, and music suggestions.

## Borling and Borling

A second process for using Group GIM in spiritual development was created by Borling and Borling (1999). *Music, Imagery and Universal Truths* is a five-week series. Each of the weekly sessions lasts about two hours. Typically the sessions are held in a church or some type of spiritual community. The language of the series is made relevant to the belief system of the particular church or spiritual community. The basic theory underlying the sessions lies in the client-centered work of Carl Rogers, the humanistic work of Abraham Maslow, the psychology of Carl Jung, and the transpersonal focus of Stanislav Grof.

The format for each of the classes is the same. It is:

- Opening prayer and lighting of candle
- Discuss music/imagery/healing (first class only)
- Check in from previous class (classes 2–5 only)
- Group discussion of the "Truth of the Week"
- Write intention for journey in journal
- Induction/music experience
- Mandala drawing
- Group discussion and processing
- Closing prayer and extinguishing of candle

Each of the classes is focused around a theme identified as a universal truth. These include: Pure Potential; Trust of God and Self: Letting Go; Forgiveness of Self and Others; Transformation; Living from the "Christ." In their presentation, Jim and Nannette Borling outlined goals and objectives for each of the classes, discussed emotions that might emerge during them and offered short music programs that would be appropriate.

## Beck

In the format of a retreat and through several conference presentations, Beck has also styled a theory and a framework for working with GIM and spiritual growth, which she calls "Listening with Open Ears." Beck (1996–1997) lays out some of the major tenets of Adrian van Kaam's formation science. Two of the terms often used, namely consonance and dissonance, have distinctly musical applications. Beck notes that the term "consonance is used to express the inner and outer harmony of form and formation . . . ; it refers to the agreeable correspondence of sounds and hence, more generally to any state or form of being consonant" (p. 28). Dissonance marks a life that "opposes the consonance with the mystery we are called to image" (p. 28). Contrary to a transcendent consonant life, the dissonant life is centered only in functional achievement, vital gratification, or social adjustment. In order to move from consonance to dissonance, Beck holds that music must be approached and listened to with an "open ear." She says: "Mindful that dissonance in life may be a call to transcendence we may seek dissonance in order to tend to the soul's deepest longing. Music listening may open the heart to a deeper response in loving compassion for self and others and thus lead us to a more authentic way of being in the world of people, events and things" (p. 31). The language of transcendence and of compassion is key in this approach to spirituality. Open-ear listening experiences are the touchstone of the retreats and presentations given by Beck. During these experiences, ultimate and generally unanswered spiritual questions arise. These questions might be: Who am I? What will become of me? What is the meaning of life? How do things hang together? What is important in my life? Each of these questions is viewed as a call to the More. As they are approached and lived within the music, these questions support, in Beck's words, "a consonant unfolding. This consonance is not a mere abstraction, idea or fantasy. It is the living harmony of all aspects of our being. It is the coming home to the depth of the mystery of who we are" (p. 34).

## Clark and Kasayka

"Music Passages" is a retreat set comprised of four separate sessions held during each of the seasons. Each of the sessions is complete in itself with a particular focus, yet the general purpose of all of the sessions is to bring people through a worshipful retreat based on simple themes using the power of music as a bridge to God. Nonsectarian and nondenominational, the retreat sessions are open to anyone looking for and wanting to experience spirituality with the use of music as a connector to spirit. It is intended to bring people of different lifestyles and backgrounds together in a safe space to explore the question of their lives and to reconnect to a sense of personal spirituality.

The format for this two-and-a-half-day residential retreat is as follows: guidance in using music as a passage to inner spiritual experiences; listening sessions; use of expressive arts as a tool for processing; time for personal meditation and reflection; readings from sacred and inspired texts; and suggestions for regular practice and support.

The program titles for the sessions are:

- Grieving Retreat—From Darkness to Light: Grief in Life (Spring)

- Healing Retreat—Abundance and Praise: Embodying Joy (Summer)
- Atonement Retreat—Forgiveness and Resolution: Self and Others (Fall)
- Gratitude Retreat—Light in the Darkness: Claiming the Altruistic Spirit (Winter)

At the beginning of each of the sessions, time is spent distinguishing and discussing spiritual experience/growth versus a psychotherapeutic experience. Direction of the specific creative arts ideas and the questions or comments made during the processing sessions support this focus.

## THE PRIMACY OF MUSIC

Each of the programs described above puts emphasis on the importance of music in the format of the programs and the catalytic effect that it has in evoking the spiritual. Once again, it would be appropriate to look at Bonny's thought about the primacy of music.

Bonny's performance experience, one of music of pure and exquisite beauty, is, as previously stated, the touchstone for the prime position given to music in the process. Looking first at her life and her writing, one can see that throughout her career Bonny continues to try to understand and explain the power music brings to the GIM experience be it used in psychotherapy, healing, or spiritual growth. She continues to perform and to cultivate her relationship with music so that her learning, her presentations, and her writing is grounded in the intimacy that comes from "repeated closeness" (Bonny, 1993, p. 9). From this closeness and from her respectful curiosity, Bonny continues to explore just how classical music has the power to open individuals to spiritual growth and healing.

In her earliest work—the three monographs—Bonny (1978) dedicates the second to the role of the taped music programs in the GIM process. In this monograph, Bonny presents Hevner's mood wheel. It is important to note that the adjectives listed under category one touch into the spiritual. These adjectives are: spiritual; lofty; awe-inspiring; dignified; sacred; solemn; sober; serious. In the description of how the music programs for GIM are put together, Bonny talks of each selection being an "affective building block." When considering how to choose music for a spiritual growth program, one might look for those that are "spiritual building blocks." Bonny and Savary (1973) have given some indication of this type of music in Appendix C of *Music and Your Mind*.

In *Musical Lifeline*, a talk given to the Eleventh Annual Conference of Canadian Music Therapists, Bonny (1984) states: "I think that we must lay music down and dissect her every dot, trill and rest, according to the most discrete scientific specificity and that we should look at the effects of music on the person from a holistic perspective" (p. 22). While this charge might appear somewhat reductionistic, it expresses the seriousness with which Bonny believes that we must approach music and the power it has in working with individuals. In the same talk she notes that music can be the bridge from the old to the new. It is a lifeline. It can bridge the old spirituality and that which is developing in the world right now. It can connect to the positive energy that is present in both of those realities.

In a later article, Bonny (1997) offers a caution. She says: "The great gift of music requires our best efforts—to hone our responses to her many faces, many of which can be seductive and misleading. Music is a product of man and the complex psychological/biological/spiritual being that man may become" (p. 70). This caution is to be heeded especially when dealing with music in the spiritual realm of healing. As a biophysical and a spiritual phenomenon, healing is affected by music on several planes. The vibrations and the rhythm of music affect the physical body. The large collection of sacred music that has been part of civilization since its beginnings call to the spirit and draw it, with its unlimited potential, into the healing process. While we know this to be true, we do not know exactly how it is so. It is well to heed Bonny's advice to honor the complex phenomenon that both music and each of us is.

While Bonny offers cautions and guidance, she also offers encouragement to those trained in her method to explore different applications, and the use of different music in forming those applications. Each of the programs outlined in this chapter draw heavily on the power of music to support the process of spiritual growth. The music used by Holligan and Marr is classical music. Explaining the reason for the choice of classical music, Marr (2001, in press) states:

> The music used to evoke imagery for this process is from the classical repertoire. It is the most effective music in its ability to evoke the depths of the human psyche. It is great art and as such, contains elements of the composer's emotion, passion and experience. Great art is universal and these connections can be felt through the depth and power of music form and structure (p. 2).

Marr's statement closely reflects Bonny's belief regarding the use of classical music.

Borling and Borling (1999) generally use classical music in their *Music, Imagery and Universal Truths*. However, some more contemporary pieces are also used (e.g. "The Cello's Song" from *A Childhood Remembered* and "Gabriel's Oboe" from *The Mission Soundtrack*). These selections are used during the first class whose goal is to use music to begin exploration of the psyche with the understanding that we have within us the "pure potential" for all things. Since this is the first experience of using music for the group there is a logic to using music that might be more familiar.

In her retreats, programs, and presentations Beck (1996–1997) uses classical music, contemporary and traditional religious music, and contemporary songs. The choice of the type of music is directed to offer an opportunity to resolve the dissonant experience in one that is consonant, thus producing spiritual growth and harmony.

Clark and Kasayka employ a predominance of classical music, generally of a form that matches the theme. For example, in the spring retreat whose theme was grieving, a number of Requiems were used. Other contemporary and world music is part of the format of the program. This music is chosen for the situation and experience with eyes toward selections that have form and a sense of soul.

## A SPIRITUAL FOCUS

As has been previously mentioned, the focus for each of the programs outlined is the use of the individual or group form of GIM as a spiritual growth tool. Thus, the container for each of the experiences is fashioned to support spiritual experience. Clark (1998–1999) notes that GIM is a technique in which "music is carefully chosen as an aesthetic container offering a space for exploration into all parts of the self" (p. 60). Thus, the music chosen for the spiritually-focused experience, the intention stated at the beginning of the experience, and the methods of processing material, are the fabric of this container. Such a container sets intentional boundaries for the experience while not at all denying or ignoring the fact that psychotherapeutic or transpersonal work might also take place within these boundaries. Bonny's original sentence leading into a musical experience, "Let the music take you where you need to go," is still the overtly spoken or implied permission given to the self to enter into and to use the musical experience as necessary. Clark (1998–1999) notes that GIM is a "method which can assist in the movement through develop-mental stages not only of a psychological nature but also of a spiritual nature and further discusses the distinctions involved in spiritual and transpersonal work. She does this by looking at the ways GIM can be used in ego work, faith development and transpersonal work. Clark (1998–1999) holds, as does Wilber (1997) that spirit infuses and informs each of these types of work. Each of these types of work is distinct and in Clark's framework, developmental. But, in the context of GIM, itself a multileveled process, work on each of these levels is not only possible but to be expected.

# CONCLUSION

This chapter attempts to capture some of the spiritual goals, uses, and outcomes of Group GIM that have been part of the process since Helen Bonny's initial thought in formulating the process. The four spiritual growth/retreat programs described are examples of how Bonny's process has been adapted to meet contemporary spiritual goals. While representative of this effort, they are not exhaustive. The process of GIM and spiritual growth has become a point of interest of many in the GIM community. The primary of music in the process and the possible kinds of music used is of equal interest.

Underhill (1911) in her classic work on mysticism outlines four of its characteristics. She says that mysticism is active and practical, not passive and theoretical. It is an entirely spiritual activity whose business and method is love. Mysticism entails a definite psychological experience. It is never self-seeking. Looking back over Bonny's performance experience and the application she made of it while developing her method, it is apparent that Bonny has "walked the mystical path on practical feet." Believing, like Underhill, that mysticism or spirituality is a power latent in the whole human race, Bonny moved her mystical experience from the solely personal and made it an active and practical expression of her love for classical music. Thus the Bonny Method of Guided Imagery and Music and all of its variations came to be.

Bonny challenges each of us to do the same—to claim our latent power to touch what is holy, to walk with the holy, to manifest the holy in our daily lives. Writing about Helen Bonny, Clark (2000) states:

> As an encourager of the pioneering spirit, Helen has brought many people to the Bonny Method of Guided Imagery and Music. They have been touched, many have been transformed by that encouragement. As a lover of the beautiful spirit in great music, Helen has shown people how they, too, can be close to great music. As a mystic and a healer, Helen has taught people that there is a divine transforming spirit available to them as it has been made available to her.

The personal journey that we make along our spiritual path and the collective journey that brings us together in a spiritual community are a return home from exile. Today's interest in spirituality is, at its core, an interest in remembering who we really are and what we are meant to be. Processes like Guided Imagery and Music as well as retreat and spiritual growth programs are guideposts to keep us on the path. Music is the spirit that sings us along the way.

## References

Arrien, A. (1987). *The Tarot Handbook: Practical Applications of Ancient Visual Symbols.* Sonoma, CA: Arcus Publishing Co.

Beck, D. M. (1996–1997). Listening with open ears. *Journal of the Association for Music and Imagery ,* 5, 26–35.

Bonny, H. (1975). Music and consciousness. *The Journal of Music Therapy,* 12 (3), 121–135.

Bonny, H. (1978). *The Role of Taped Music in the GIM Process. (GIM Monograph No. 2).* Salina, KS: The Bonny Foundation; New Edition (1998).

Bonny, H. (1984). *The Musical Lifeline.* Proceedings of the Eleventh Annual Conference of the Canadian Association for Music Therapy. 6, 3–12.

Bonny, H. (1986). Music and healing. *Music Therapy,* 6A (1), 3–12.

Bonny, H. (1993). Body listening: A new way to review the GIM tapes. *Journal of the Association for Music and Imagery,* 2, 3–10.

Bonny, H. (1994). Address at Association for Music and Imagery, Annual (June) Meeting, Wildacres Retreat Center, N.C.

Bonny, H. (1997). The state of the art of music therapy. *The Arts in Psychotherapy,* 24 (1), 65–73.

Bonny, H. & Pahnke, W. (1972). The use of music in psychedelic (LSD) Psychotherapy. *Journal of Music Therapy,* 9 (2), 64–83.

Bonny, H. & Savary, L. (1973). *Music and your mind.* New York: Harper & Row; 2$^{nd}$ Edition (1990). Barrytown, NY: Station Hill Press.

Borling, J. & Borling, N. (1999). *Music, Imagery and Universal Truths.* Presentation, Association for Music and Imagery Annual (June) Meeting, Northeastern University, Chicago, IL.

Clark, M. (1998-1999). The Bonny Method and spiritual development. *Journal of the Association for Music and Imagery,* 6, 55–62

Clark, M. (2000). Personal communication, September 2000.

Driscoll, J. (1996). Defining spirituality. Theology walking. *Vision,* 6 (9) 9.

Fowler, J. (1981). *Stages of Faith.* New York: HarperCollins Publishers.

Holligan, F. (1994). Using guided imagery and music in retreat. *The Journal of the Association for Music and Imagery,* 3, 59–63.

Holligan, F. & Marr, J. (1999). *Taking a different path: The use of GIM in groups seeking spiritual growth.* Presentation, Association for Music and Imagery Annual (June) Meeting, Northeastern University, Chicago, IL.

Kinerk, E. (1988). Toward a method for the study of spirituality. In D. Fleming, (ed.), *The Christian Ministry of Spiritual Direction,* St. Louis: Review for Religious Press.

Marr, J. (2001). The use of Guided Imagery and Music in spiritual growth. *Journal of Pastoral Care* (in press).

Maslow, A. (1962). Lessons from peak experiences. *Journal of Humanistic Psychology,* 2, 9–18.

Maslow, A. (1970). *Religion, values and peak experiences.* New York: Penguin Books.

O' Murchu, D. (1992). *Our World in Transition: Making Sense of a Changing World.* UK: The Book Guild Ltd.

O'Murchu, D. (2000). *Religion in Exile: A Spiritual Homecoming.* New York: The Crossroads Publishing Co.

Pahnke, W. (1969). Psychedelic drugs and mystical experiences. In E.M. Pattison (ed.), *Clinical Psychiatry and Religion.* International Psychiatry Clinics. 5 (4), 149. Boston: Little & Brown.

Underhill, E. (1911). *Mysticism.* New York: E. P. Dutton & Co., Inc.

Wilber, K. (1977). *Spectrum of Consciousness.* Wheaton, IL: Quest Books.

Wilber, K. (1997). *Eye of Spirit.* Boston: Shambala.

# Part Four:

# Developments

*Chapter Fifteen*

# CLIENT ASSESSMENT IN THE BONNY METHOD OF GUIDED IMAGERY AND MUSIC (BMGIM)

## Kenneth E. Bruscia

Assessment is that part of the BMGIM process wherein the therapist elicits and organizes information from various sources, in order to gain greater understanding of the client—his/her life story, problems, goals, needs, potentials, and resources. While such understanding is essential when working with all clients, the depth and breadth of assessment efforts may vary considerably according to the client's goals, and the nature of the work. When the client's goals are related to self-actualization or spiritual growth, or when the work is short-term, assessment efforts may be limited accordingly; however, when the client's goals are psychotherapeutic in nature, and when the work will extend over a significant period, assessment is an integral part of the BMGIM process. This chapter describes the kinds of assessment efforts that can be helpful when BMGIM is used as psychotherapy.

## GOALS

A comprehensive approach to assessment may involve several goals. The four main types relevant to BMGIM are: diagnostic, prescriptive, interpretive, and evaluative.

### Diagnostic Goals

When the goal is *diagnostic*, the therapist gathers data to better understand the specific nature of the client's problem or condition. The first task is to determine if the client has been diagnosed by another health professional as having a particular medical or psychiatric condition. If so, the therapist needs to understand the causes, symptoms, and life problems that may accompany that condition and its treatment. Of particular concern is whether the client's health and safety could be compromised in any way by participation in BMGIM. Important questions are: Does the client have a condition that will not permit full participation in BMGIM? Would the client's condition be worsened in any way by BMGIM? Does the client's condition warrant some kind of modification in BMGIM or in the client's level of participation?

A diagnostic assessment always has as its top priority a fundamental issue—whether BMGIM is indicated or contraindicated. Summer (1989) pointed out that it is *indicated* only when the client:

- Is capable of symbolic thinking;
- Can differentiate between symbolic thinking and reality;
- Can relate his experience to the therapist; and
- Can achieve positive growth as a result of the GIM therapy (p. 41).

Additionally, the present author (Bruscia, 1992) has found that BMGIM is *contraindicated.* whenever a client *lacks:*

- The *medical and physical stamina* needed to experience the music and the images that may arise from the music;
- The *emotional stability and ego strength* needed to undergo the feelings that may arise in response to the music and images evoked;
- The *intellectual abilities* needed to understand his/her own experiences in BMGIM, and not be dangerously overwhelmed or confused by them;
- The *verbal abilities* needed to dialogue with the guide during and after the imagery experiences;
- *Sufficient reality orientation* to distinguish between the imaginary and real worlds; and
- The *ego boundaries* needed to maintain a separate sense of self after deep imagery experiences where boundaries between self and other (or the environment) may merge.

Of course not all clients who seek BMGIM have a medical or psychiatric condition. Many clients come to BMGIM to resolve psychological or life problems that are not classified as disorders. In these cases, diagnostic goals are still problem-oriented. The therapist seeks to gather data that will provide a better understanding of the precise nature of the client's problem—its causes, its effects on the client and significant individuals in the client's life, and its overall implications for the client's life.

## Prescriptive Goals

When the assessment goal is *prescriptive* in nature, the therapist gathers data to understand how to best work with the client. Certainly, all diagnostic information gathered will provide valuable clues about any precautions or modifications that may be necessary in working with the client in BMGIM. In addition, the therapist has to observe the client during each component of the session, and explore ways to engage the client in the experience, as fully, as safely, and as comfortably as possible. This may include discovering: how to listen and respond to the client during verbal discussions, what music is the most appropriate or relevant, how to design and deliver inductions, how to guide during the music imaging experience, and so forth. The earlier the therapist makes these determinations, the more effective BMGIM will be, and the safer the client will be within the process.

## Interpretive Goals

When the goal of assessment is *interpretive*, the therapist works with the client to find meaning, not only in the music and imagery experiences within each session, but also in the client's life experiences outside of therapy. By its very nature, BMGIM reveals the client's life story, and the various narratives and metaphors that are a part of that story, and as these unfold, the client often needs to derive or discover meaning from them. Sometimes the client and therapist work to find such meanings from the client's point of view—that is, as they are presented and interpreted by the client, within the context they are presented, and as applied to the client's life. In contrast, sometimes the meanings can be understood from an outside perspective (e.g., therapist), or within the context of an external theory (e.g., psychodynamic). Interpretive assessment takes place naturally at the end of each session, when the client and therapist discuss the imagery experience. It may also take place in later sessions, or in special sessions specifically devoted to reviewing transcripts of previous sessions.

## Evaluative Goals

Finally, when the goal of assessment is *evaluative*, the therapist seeks to determine whether the client has changed as the result of BMGIM, and if so, in what ways. This may be accomplished by gathering specific data at the beginning of therapy for comparison at the end of therapy. It may also be accomplished by reviewing session transcripts at various intervals throughout the work.

Because the above goals may be pertinent at various stages of therapy, assessment is an ongoing concern in BMGIM therapy. It is not a single task or procedure; rather it is a continuous way of focusing on what the client presents, and accumulating and organizing information needed to understand the client and his/her therapeutic needs in increasingly more holistic ways. Assessment, therefore, begins as soon as the client enters BMGIM, and continues throughout the entire process. What follows is a description of methods commonly used to assess the client at various stages within the process.

# INTAKE

Intake assessment procedures vary according to whether the therapist will be working with the client in private practice or in an institutional setting (e.g., hospital, hospice, day program, residential center), and whether the client has been referred to BMGIM by another health professional. When the therapist is working in an institutional setting, a primary source of data will be the institution's records on the client. When the therapist is working in private practice and the client is referred by another health professional, it is important for the therapist to obtain pertinent information from the professional who has been working previously with the client. Whether the therapist consults the client's records or other therapists, a key concern is whether there are any contraindications for working with the client in BMGIM, and whether any aspect of the process might need to be modified.

In addition to consulting these outside sources of data, the therapist will also seek information directly from the client. In fact, many BMGIM therapists devote the entire first session to an "intake" assessment. The intake session may involve having the client fill out informational questionnaires, interviewing the client in depth, and introducing the client to BMGIM through brief demonstrations and experiences. Most therapists take notes during or after the intake assessment, and then file the results in the client's folder.

## Questionnaires

Tables 1 and 2 provide examples of questionnaires that might be presented to the client in the first or intake session. Table 1 is a form that elicits basic facts about the client that are valuable for the therapist to have. The information also provides a springboard for further elaboration and discussion.

Table 2 is an example of another kind of intake assessment, which each therapist can design to assess the specific problems or symptoms that are characteristic of his or her clientele. The list can be constructed based on the literature dealing with the condition or client population, or on therapist's own work experience. Such assessments are particularly useful when therapists work with clients who are homogenous, or who have the same medical condition (e.g., cancer, arthritis) or psychological problem (e.g., obsessive compulsive disorder, anxiety). Besides identifying what problems the client is experiencing, and predicting what kinds of issues might emerge in the imagery, this type of assessment also provides the basis for evaluating the client's progress. The Likert Scale allows easy statistical comparison between the severity of symptoms before and after therapy.

Yet another approach has been suggested by Bonny (1980), who in a series of early research studies, developed a "Music Experience Questionnaire" to "estimate a subject's musical sophistication" (p. 4) prior to having a music-assisted LSD experience. The questionnaire sought information on: 1) whether the client had experience playing or studying instruments or voice; 2) how much the client listened to music, and in what ways; 3) what types of music were most preferred by the client; 4) what were the client's favorite recordings, compositions, composers, and/or artists; and 5) whether the client's hearing was normal.

In addition to questionnaires, therapists can also administer standardized tests that can be used for evaluation purposes. For example, Wrangsjö and Körlin (1995) had their clients take three tests: the Hopkins Symptom Checklist, the Inventory of Interpersonal Problems, and the Sense of Coherence Scale. Comparisons were made before and after therapy to determine progress.

## Interview

The first or intake interview has two main purposes: to gather assessment data from the client, and to provide the client information about the nature of BMGIM. It is usually best to follow the client's inclinations as to which purpose to pursue first. Often the client will begin by explaining why he or she has come for therapy, and specifically BMGIM. This quite naturally leads into discussions about the problems the client is experiencing, his/her developmental goals, or the kinds of life changes the client would like to make.

Table 1.
Client Intake Sheet

Name_____ Date_____
Address_____ D.O.B._____
City_____ State_____Zip_____
Telephone: Home_____ Work_____
E-mail_____ Occupation_____
Marital Status_____ Spouse's name_____
Person to contact in case of emergency:
Name_____ Relationship_____
Address_____ Home Phone_____
_____ Work Phone_____
Please list any medical conditions you currently have, and indicate treatment or medication.
Condition                          Treatment/Medication
_____    _____
_____    _____
_____    _____
Have you ever been hospitalized for psychiatric reasons? If yes, please explain:


Are you currently taking any medication for depression, anxiety, obsessive-compulsive disorder, or any other psychological condition? _____If so, please identify:

Have you previously had any other form of psychotherapy? _____
Are you currently receiving any form of counseling or psychotherapy?_____
If yes to either, please give name, address, and telephone of therapist.



Are you affiliated with any religion, church, or spiritual practice? _____
If yes, please identify:



What goals would you like to pursue through BMGIM?

Table 2.
Problem Checklist

Name_____Date_____

Indicate how troubled you are by each of the following by putting a check mark along the line. Answer quickly, giving your immediate reaction.

Stress
                |_____|
                Least troubled                Most troubled

Depression
                |_____|
                Least troubled                Most troubled

Anxiety
                |_____|
                Least troubled                Most troubled

Insomnia
                |_____|
                Least troubled                Most troubled

Fatigue
                |_____|
                Least troubled                Most troubled

Fear of Getting Worse
                |_____|
                Least troubled                Most troubled

Fear of Losing Job
                |_____|
                Least troubled                Most troubled

Relationship Problems
                |_____|
                Least troubled                Most troubled

Sometimes, however, the client may be more interested in finding out about BMGIM first, before disclosing very much personal information. In this case, the client will immediately begin to ask questions about BMGIM, and thereby try to determine if it will be the most appropriate form of therapy to pursue.

The kind of assessment data to gather in the initial interview depends upon whether the therapist uses any preliminary questionnaires. Some answers on the questionnaire are self-explanatory and do not need to be discussed; however, some may also require further elaboration. Since this is the very first meeting, the therapist has to be careful not to probe too much too soon. Getting to know the client has to be a gradual, relaxed process; at the same time, the therapist must be sure to gather information needed to engage the client in BMGIM safely. Data on clinical history and current health status are essential. At the same time, judgment and sensitivity are required.

Certainly, the most natural topic of conversation is what the client hopes to gain from BMGIM. During the course of this conversation, the therapist has to gain a clear understanding of what the client's therapeutic goals and needs are, and whether BMGIM therapy is indicated. Meanwhile, the client has to gain a clear understanding of whether BMGIM can help, and if so, how it works. At this juncture, the therapist explains how the BMGIM session is structured, what the client is likely to experience during the music imaging, the role of the music, how the therapeutic process unfolds, how BMGIM effects change, and so forth.

Once these topics have been covered, the conversation can easily go into the client's musical background and preferences—or what may be more broadly described as the client's relationship to music. This may include:

- Whether the client has studied music
- Whether the client plays an instrument or sings
- How much the client listens to music, and under what circumstances
- The kinds of music the client likes to listen to (e.g., style, media, artist)
- The client's attitudes toward classical music
- Whether there are any specific types or pieces of music that have special significance
- Whether the client has any musical dislikes or whether there are any negative associations to music
- What the client understands about the therapeutic potential of music

In addition to the client's relationship to music, the therapist will also be interested in gleaning basic information about the client's previous experiences with altered states of consciousness and imagery. Areas to explore may include:

- Whether the client has had any previous experiences with meditation, self-relaxation, hypnosis, etc., and whether these experiences have been positive
- What factors might affect the client's ability to enter an altered state of consciousness
- Whether the client has any preferences or special needs related to relaxation inductions
- Whether the client has had any previous experiences with imaging, and especially within a therapeutic context, and whether these experiences have been helpful or troubling
- What kinds of images the client is most inclined to create

- What factors might affect the client's ability to image freely

Once such topics have been sufficiently addressed, the therapist may either give the client: short practice exercises on the various components of BMGIM (i.e., relaxation, imaging, music listening), a short GIM experience, or a full GIM session. This naturally leads into another approach to assessment, observing the client's way of responding in BMGIM.

## OBSERVATIONS

Aside from all the information gathered through verbal discussion, the therapist also learns a great deal about the client by observing how s/he responds to or manages each aspect of the BMGIM process. Table 3 shows aspects of client responsiveness that may be readily observed and rated by the therapist. The table is a condensed version of an assessment scale (Bruscia, 2000), developed for the following purposes:

- To identify those components of the BMGIM experience which are easy or difficult for the client, and to gain insight into the client's defenses;
- To identify possible contraindications or areas where modifications in the BMGIM experiences may be needed;
- To suggest ways that the therapist may work more effectively with the client, and especially with regard to guiding;
- To assess the client's potential for engaging fully in the transformational or therapeutic aspects of the BMGIM process;
- To provide a pre- and post-test measure of the client's growth as evidenced in his or her ability to negotiate and fully engage in the BMGIM experience.

The original scale allows the therapist to rate the client on each item using a five-point scale. Though certainly not required, such numerical ratings are particularly useful when the therapist wants to evaluate and measure progress, by comparing client responsiveness at the beginning and end of therapy. The reliability and validity of these ratings have been examined by Meadows (2000).

# VERBAL DATA FROM
# SUBSEQUENT SESSIONS

Every GIM session provides two opportunities for the client to verbally inform the therapist about his/her life: in the preliminary conversation, and in the postlude discussion. The preliminary conversation usually begins with theclient giving the therapist an update on his/her life since the last GIM session.

This may include not only what has happened in that period, but also how the client has been thinking or feeling. These topics quite naturally lead to discussions of the client's past, and how previous events, situations, and experiences provide a foundation for the present. As such, when taken together, the preliminary conversations of each session provide a continuous and cumulative account of the client's life story, with each conversation offering bits and pieces to the whole narrative, while also providing a context for understanding the present in terms of the past.

In the postlude discussion, the kind of life information gained is somewhat different, but equally valuable. Here the conversation begins with the client reviewing the images that he or she has just created while listening to the music. The purpose of this discussion is to help the client better understand the images and the implications they may have for the client's life. In that process, the therapist can learn much about the client's life that was not revealed in the preliminary conversation. The reason is that the preliminary conversation deals essentially with factual information about the client's life that is already in his/her consciousness; in contrast, the postlude discussion deals with images of the client's life emanating from his/her unconscious. Thus, the former gives facts, the latter meaning. This leads to the next source of data assessment, the images themselves.

# ANALYSIS OF IMAGERY

Assessment in BMGIM always involves efforts to understand the client's imagery experiences and what they might mean; however, like dreams, the imagery generated in a BMGIM session can be understood on many different levels and from many different perspectives. Because the client creates the images, it is imperative that the client play a significant role in deciphering their meaning or ascribing meaning to them.

## Table 3.
## Aspects of Client Responsiveness

RELAXATION

- Responsiveness to Induction: how well the client responded to the relaxation induction given in preparation for the music -imaging experience.
- Depth of Relaxation: how deeply the traveler went into an altered state.
- Duration and Continuity of Relaxation: how easily the client sustained an altered state of consciousness during the music-imaging experience.
- Completeness of relaxation: how completely the traveler allows self to enter altered state, as demonstrated by body, face, imaging, pace, and verbal ability.

IMAGERY EXPERIENCES

- Productivity: how freely and easily the client generated images or inner experiences.
- Pacing: extent to which the client stayed with each image for a sufficient amount of time.
- Vividness: how vivid the client's images were to him/her.
- Body involvement: how physically involved the client was in the images.
- Emotional involvement: how emotionally involved the client was in the images.
- Congruence: extent to which the client's physical and emotional reactions were consistent with the imagery.
- Personal Relevance: extent to which the client's images pertained to the client's life.
- Engagement: how actively the client participated as a character in the images, or interacted within the images.
- Sensorial Richness: extent to which client was able to have images in different sensory modalities (visual, kinesthetic, auditory).
- Proneness to Fantasy: extent to which client was open to images that are unusual, fantastic, or out of the ordinary.

- Acceptance: how accepting the client was of his/her own inner experiences and images.

MUSIC EXPERIENCES

- Relationship of Images to Music: extent to which the client's images fit the music and ongoing changes therein.
- Body Involvement: extent to which client reacted physically to the music.
- Emotional Involvement: extent to which client reacted emotionally to the music.
- Use of Music: extent to which client found the music helpful or useful during the imaging experience.

RESPONSES TO GUIDE

- Reporting: extent to which the client reported images in a timely and informative way.
- Responsiveness: how responsive the client was to the interventions provided by the guide.
- Use of guide: extent to which the client found the guiding process helpful.

VERBAL PROCESSING

- Willingness: how willing the client was to talk about and further examine various details of the music imaging experience.
- Ease: how easy it was for client to verbally describe experiences and images during the music.
- Interest: how interested the client was in understanding and finding meaning in the imagery experience.
- Relevance: extent to which client found imagery experience relevant to self and own life.

GENERAL

- Meaningfulness: how meaningful the client found the GIM session.
- Comfort: how comfortable the client was with the GIM process.

On the other hand, therapists can also have insight into what the client's imagery might mean, based not only on their experience and expertise in BMGIM, but also on their knowledge of the client. Thus, whenever the assessment process is aimed at understanding or interpreting the client's imagery, the process is an interactive one, with the client leading and the therapist following, or the therapist leading within the limits and resistances put forth by the client. Either way, the therapist approaches this kind of assessment carefully and respectfully, steeped in the notion that the client ultimately must—and eventually will—find his/her own meanings.

All this said, it is still important to recognize that clients come to psychotherapy, and BMGIM in particular, to gain a better understanding of themselves, and to find greater meaning in their lives. And by inference, they are also coming because they want to learn how to accomplish these aims more effectively and independently than they have in the past. Thus, an integral part of a therapist's responsibility is helping clients to become better meaning-makers. In BMGIM, the therapist does this, not by telling the client "what" images mean, but by helping the client understand "how" images mean. One might even say that the therapist "teaches" the client about the many layers of meaning available within the music-imagery experience. Several approaches can be used, separately or together.

## Focus on Meaning-Laden Imagery Experiences

The first approach is to focus the client on images or aspects of the imagery experience that seem to hold particular significance for the therapeutic process. Table 3 presents those aspects of the imaging process that the therapist can observe during the music experience, and possibly to examine further with the client in the postlude discussion. In addition, there are many other types of imagery experiences that are important to explore for purposes of assessment. They are:

1) Highly charged images, such as: those accompanied by strong physical or emotional reactions (transcendent or painful); those that are exceptionally or uncharacteristically vivid; and those that seem to "stick" in the client's awareness or memory.

2) Reiterative or cyclic images, such as: a single image that recurs with very little change, either within the same session or subsequent sessions; recurring images that are different but actually share the same emotional theme; images within the same

session that contain the same sequence of events or experiences, but in different situations.

3) Rapidly or randomly changing images, such as: sudden changes in scenery or characters (especially when the image is highly charged), extremely fast imagery sequences, and unpredictable changes from one image to another (especially when the previous image is incomplete or unresolved).

4) Puzzling or troubling images, such as: images that cannot be fully apprehended or understood; incomplete images; images that have blind pots; images that vanish without closure; images that present questions, dilemmas, or paradoxes; images that are haunting; and images that are highly uncharacteristic or unusual for the client.

5) Communicative images, such as: images that contain voices or characters that give messages to the client about a particular situation; physical images in which the body sends a message to the client, and so forth.

6) Body images and experiences, and especially those that are out of the ordinary, such as: exaggerated body parts or structures, unusual or distorted bodily processes, significant pain, signs of deterioration or disease, physical transformation, and so forth. These kinds of images can give important information on the physical or medical condition of the client, as well as clues about the healing process that will be needed. Body images and experiences also provide psychological or metaphorical links between the body, mind, emotions, and spirit. For examples, see Short (1991), Hale (1992), and Merritt (1993),

7) Detached or dissociative images, such as those that the client observes from a distance or disengages from, or those identified by Pickett and Sonnen (1993) as dissociative, for example: visual images that are confounded by kinesthetic memories, feeling states of unreality where there is distance between the imager and the image, fragmentation and shifts in identity, and multiple ego states.

Also important to note are images that are very disturbed, or even psychotic in nature. While such images may seem meaning-laden, further elaboration of them with the client is usually not indicated. In fact, when clients offer such imagery, therapists must exercise great care, and seriously consider whether to continue the imagery experience or bring the client back to ordinary awareness immediately. The appearance of severely disturbed or psychotic images usually signals that BMGIM is contraindicated. Examples of images to be evaluated as potentially dangerous are: troublesome loss of self (through dissociation, disintegration, self-annihilation), paranoid images, intense emotional flooding, bizarre or sickening images that are exaggerated in scale, extremely inflationary images, images that lack coherence or ideational organization, and extreme physical reactions. It is important to note that all of these kinds of images may also be quite normal—what distinguishes normal from pathological imagery is not content alone but also their scale or degree of intensity.

## Clarify Images and Sequences

The next way a therapist facilitates the meaning-making process is to help the client elaborate and clarify meaning-laden images and imagery sequences. This is an important step because, during the imagery experience, the client is frequently unable to report everything that he or she is apprehending at the time; in addition, there may be aspects of the image that the client apprehended, but did not attend or register at the time, simply because his/her attention was riveted elsewhere in the image. The role of the BMGIM therapist, then, is to help the client recover important details about the images that may give additional insight or understanding about them. Often, this can be easily accomplished by asking questions that will "fill in" the missing information about the basic elements of most images. The basic elements that may require clarification include:

1) Characters and objects in the image: the qualities and characteristics of each "entity" in the image.
2) Settings: the environment, context, or situation in which the characters and objects are operating.
3) Relationships: how the characters, objects, and settings relate to one another dynamically.
4) Action sequences: what happens when.

In addition to clarifying the image itself, it is also useful to explore precisely how the client changed from one image to another, and how the various images related to one another. This requires going through the session afterward and looking for where each image began and ended, and then exploring where the experience was discontinuous, reiterative, or focused. Specifically:

## DISCONTINUOUS SEQUENCES:

1) Did the image change when the client was involved in a difficult event or experience, and was the change unsupported by the music or the interventions of the guide? If so, the change can point to a problem that the client is struggling to resolve, yet defending against at the same time. Similarly motivated changes will probably be found in subsequent imagery sequences.

2) Did the image change unpredictably when the music changed? While the therapist continually makes efforts to keep the client's experience responsive to the music, clients can also use the end of each piece as an opportunity to escape what is likely to unfold in the ongoing image, by simply starting a new imagery sequence. Sometimes the change is compatible with the change in music, and sometimes it is not. In either case, it is the change that is of interest, for the client may be using the music as a defense against the full development of an image, or the client may be depending on the music to rescue him or her from difficult imagery work.

## RE-ITERATIVE SEQUENCES:

1) Did a particular image (e.g., bird) appear repeatedly in completely different imagery scenarios, and was its appearance somewhat puzzling? If so, depending on the qualities of the image, it may symbolize a conflict or problem that may need to emerge in the client's work, or it may suggest how the problem underlying the images might be resolved. In both cases, the recurring image is like a message from the unconscious trying to enter into the client's awareness.

2) Did different unresolved images in the session have the same theme or sequencing of events or feelings? If so, depending on the images themselves, the client may be trying out different ways of solving a problem, but has not found the most appropriate or satisfying solution. Or, the client may be consistently resisting resolution of the problem. In both cases, the unconscious may be saying that the work has not been completed yet.

3) Did the same image or imagery sequence repeat cyclically throughout the session, each time adding something new? If so, depending on the images themselves, the client may need to work gradually in confronting the full nature of the problem, or take

more time to realize the fullness of a particular achievement or blessing.

PROGRESSIVE SEQUENCES:

1) Did the client begin with a particular focus, and then work on that focus through a continuous and meaningful progression of images? Did this require continual reframing of the music by the client to fit with the unfolding imagery sequence? When this occurs, the entire session builds a coherent narrative around a central theme, and it usually indicates deep, full work.

## Link Images to Real World

Once the most relevant aspects of the imagery experience have been sufficiently elaborated, the next step is to help the client find links between elements in the imagery experience and aspects of his/her real world. The most obvious link occurs when a real person, object, setting or relationship in the client's real world—past or present—actually appears in the client's imagery experience. This link occurs when the imagery is "biographical" in some way.

There are many examples of biographical images in the literature. Pickett (1995) described her work with a young man who created images of a priest who had abused him, and his parents who had abandoned him. These images allowed the man to work through the anger and sadness connected to these early life experiences.

The next common link is when an aspect of the client's real world is represented or manifested in the image through symbols, analogies, and metaphors. For an in-depth discussion of how these are distinct but closely related, see Bonde (2000). In this kind of link, something or someone in the image symbolically represents something or someone else in the real world, or one situation or relationship in the image is analogous to a real-life situation or relationship, or one way of construing or configuring an episode in the image is a metaphorical representation of how the episode is construed or configured in the real world.

The assessment task here is to find the correspondence between the element in the image and the client's real world, and then exploring what insights can be gained about the client's real world from the symbol, analogy, or metaphor in the image. An example would be when a person in the client's life appears in the image as an animal. Here, the nature of the animal and its symbolic meanings shed light on how the client perceives the person in his/her life. Going even further, the way the animal and the client interact in the image is an analogy for how the person and the client interact(ed) in the real world; and the way the client construed and configured the interaction in the image is a metaphor for how he or she is experiencing the interaction in the real world. Eventually, the entire story that unfolds between the animal and the client in the image provides a metaphoric narrative of how their relationship actually unfolded in the real world.

Bonde (2000) identified three levels of metaphor commonly observed in BMGIM:

1) The client's imagery contains a core metaphor that characterizes the client's problem in the real world. For example, in a case by Bush (1995), a giant octopus in the client's imagery served as a metaphor for how she was being overcome by her life circumstances.

2) The client's imagery contains a metaphor that describes how various parts of the client's self are configured in relation to a life problem or therapeutic issue. For example, in a case by Pickett (1991), a client with addictions wrestled with several sub-personalities, each with its own name, and each with its own needs and demands.

3) Several metaphors are put together to form a complete narrative. For example, in a case by Bruscia (1998), the client watches a man being stoned to death by an angry crowd, and through his identification with both the man and the crowd, the client discovers his own self-destructive tendencies, and the feelings of guilt and anger that supported them.

So far in this discussion, the client's images have been linked to biographical aspects of the real world. Another important real-world link is to the therapy experience itself. Images may be metaphors for the client's feelings toward the therapist, the music, or the therapeutic process itself. A particularly important link is between the client's images and the client-therapist relationship. Specifically, characters in the client's images may be representations of the therapist, and interactions among the characters may serve as metaphors for the relationship between the client and therapist, as perceived by the client.

These imaginal representations of the client-therapist relationship give feedback to the therapist about how the client perceives their relationship, consciously or unconsciously, while also suggesting whether the client's perceptions are accurate or distorted. This information in turn reveals whether the client has a "transference" toward the therapist. In a transference relationship, the client perceives and reacts to the therapist as if s/he were a significant person in the client's life, and then tries to relive that relationship with the therapist. In psychodynamic forms of therapy, working through the transference relationship is an essential step in the therapeutic process. For examples in BMGIM, see Bruscia (1995) and Pellitteri (1998).

## Link Imagery to Myths and Archetypes

In addition to having links to the client's real world and its many life narratives, imagery that arises in BMGIM also move beyond the individual psyche to realms and stories that belong to groups, cultures, and even the entire species. As such, these imagery experiences move the client from his/her own individual unconscious to collective levels of consciousness.

Myths are tales and stories that survive the passage of time, being passed on from generation to generation through oral telling, story books, literature, and various secular and religious rituals. Myths and fairy tales are also encountered in deeply altered states of consciousness, music experiences, and BMGIM (Clark, 1995; Short, 1996–97). Seeing the links between one's own life and the great myths and fairy tales has many therapeutic values. "Through the experience of GIM, persons can begin to search out what myth it is they are living. The metaphorical language which music and imagery evokes enables persons to see the workings of mythological patterns in their lives" (Clark, 1995, p. 51). For this reason, an integral part of assessment in BMGIM involves finding links between the client's images and the great myths of our time. Often this process can be facilitated by music programs that are based on myths, such as the "Hero's Journey" (Clark, 1995; McIvor, 1998–99).

Closely related to myths and fairy tales are archetypes. First defined by Carl Jung, and later described in various ways, archetypes are symbolic structures shared by human beings at a collective unconscious level. Examples include: Mother, Father, Wise Man, Goddess, Trickster, King/Queen, Anima/Animus, and so forth. Such archetypes are often encountered in dreams and images, and are particularly vivid in the BMGIM setting. For this reason, BMGIM therapy often involves linking the client's imagery to various archetypal figures and processes. Examples in the literature include: Merritt (1993), Tasney (1993), Ventre (1994), Wesley, 1998–99), and Brooks (2000),

## Link Images to Spiritual and Transpersonal Realms

As the client's imagery moves from descriptions of his/her real life to expressions of myths and archetypes, there may also be a shift toward religious imagery, and/or spiritual, or transpersonal experiences. This shift can be seen as a normal step in the process of healing and spiritual development that arises in

BMGIM (Clark, 1998–99). Sometimes, death-rebirth experiences initiate an opening to these realms, moving the client from self-concern to transpersonal experiences of Self (Borling, 1992; Bunt, 2000). These transpersonal experiences are quite varied; yet seem to share many common features (Lewis, 1998-99). From an assessment point of view, these images and experiences provide a better understanding of the client's spiritual beliefs, goals, obstacles, and resources.

## MANDALAS

From the earliest days of GIM, Bonny used mandalas to better understand her clients, and to facilitate their work (Bonny, 1995). Mandalas are drawings created by adding color and design to an unfilled circle. Bonny first encountered the mandala in 1972, when she met Joan Kellogg, an art therapist who had been doing intensive research on its diagnostic and clinical uses. It was that year that Kellogg had begun consulting with the LSD research team at the Maryland Psychiatric Center where Bonny was working (Kellogg, MacRae, Bonny & Di Leo, 1977). As Bonny became more acquainted and impressed with Kellogg's work, she began to ask her clients to draw mandalas as part of her experimental work in GIM. At the time, Bonny had just begun exploring the use of music to expand states of consciousness without drugs (Bonny, 1995). By 1977, Bonny had reported on a case study in which she asked her client in BMGIM to draw a mandala at the end of most sessions (Kellogg, MacRae, Bonny & Di Leo, 1977). Then, to research the accuracy of information obtained through the mandala, Bonny sent each drawing without any other information except for the date and patient's gender to Kellogg. Without any discussion of the case, Kellogg would then return her diagnostic interpretations. At the end of the study, Bonny concluded:

> It was found that the drawing of the mandala at the close of the session was useful in several ways. Immediately following experiences that were sometimes very intense, concentration on the making of a circular design gave the client a needed opportunity to unwind. In doing so, she gave outward expression to the inward experience of the preceding hour.
>
> Here we will concentrate, however, on demonstrating the richness, depth, and accuracy of the information that can be derived from the mandala. There is evidence that it can provide not only a valuable diagnostic tool but also a way of checking on the therapist's

immediate impressions—even at times, a source of valid predictions that may warn us of pitfalls and guide us in the direction of constructive therapeutic maneuvers (Kellogg, MacRae, Bonny, & Di Leo, 1977, p. 126).

For another case example, see Bonny and Kellogg (1977). Use of the mandalas as an adjunct to BMGIM has continued and developed since these early days. Today, many BMGIM practitioners use the drawings to facilitate or deepen the music-imaging experience, and to help clarify the images evoked by the music.

In addition to the drawings, many practitioners, upon completion of the necessary training, have used Kellogg's "MARI Card Test" (1978) as an important component of assessment and evaluation. In the card test, the client is presented with thirty-nine clear plastic cards, each embossed in black with a basic mandala design. The thirty-nine cards consist of three versions of thirteen basic designs that Kellogg identified as archetypal. After selecting five designs that are most preferred, the client is presented thirty-eight opaque color cards (plus one silver and one gold Florentine card). The client then chooses five preferred color cards, and is asked to match the preferred colors with the preferred designs. The client can experiment by placing the color cards under the design cards. It should be mentioned that some testers also ask for the least preferred design matched with the least preferred color, plus a possible healing color.

The tester then places the selected cards on the "Great Round of the Mandala" created by Kellogg. The Great Round is a circular arrangement of the 13 archetypal designs into developmental stages or structures. The card choices and their placement on the Great Round are then analyzed and interpreted according to guidelines set forth by Kellogg (1978). For an example of how mandala drawings and the MARI Card Test are used in conjunction with BMGIM, see the case study by Bush (1992).

In closing, it should be mentioned that in addition to mandalas, BMGIM therapists may also engage their clients in other projective arts experiences, such as clay, sand play, journaling, song discussion, and music improvisation. Each of these experiences adds even more information to the rich array of assessment data available within the BMGIM session.

## SUMMARY

Client assessment is an ongoing process in BMGIM, beginning with the gathering of referral information and continuing throughout the various stages of therapy. The goals may be diagnostic, prescriptive, interpretive or evaluative in nature. During intake, a key concern is whether BMGIM is indicated or contraindicated. The BMGIM process affords a variety of data sources and methods of data collection, including: intake questionnaires, verbal inquiry during sessions, observation of the client's responsiveness during the music-imaging experience, analysis of the client's imagery, mandalas, and other projective devices.

## *References*

Bonde, L. O. (2000). Metaphor and narrative in Guided Imagery and Music. *Journal of the Association for Music and Imagery, 7*, 59–76.

Bonny, H. (1980). *GIM Therapy: Past, Present and Future Implications. Monograph #3.* Salina, KS: Bonny Foundation.

Bonny, H. (1995). *The Mandala Rediscovered: The Work in Retrospect.* Unpublished speech given at a conference on mandalas held in Baltimore MD, June 1965.

Bonny, H. & Kellogg, J. (1977). Guided Imagery and Music and the mandala: A case study illustrating the integration of music and art therapies. *Creativity and the Art Therapist's Identity: Proceedings of the Seventh Annual Conference of the American Art Therapy Association (October, 1976).* Baltimore, MD: American Art Therapy Association, pp. 71–75.

Borling, J. (1992). Perspectives on growth with a victim of abuse: A Guided Imagery and Music (GIM) case study. *Journal of the Association for Music and Imagery, 1*, 85–98.

Brooks, D. (2000). Anima manifestations of men using Guided Imagery and Music: A case study. *Journal of the Association for Music and Imagery, 7*, 77–87.

Bruscia, K. (1992). *Manual for Level One Training in Guided Imagery and Music.* Unpublished manuscript.

Bruscia, K. (1995). Manifestations of transference in Guided Imagery and Music. *Journal of the Association for Music and Imagery, 4*, 17–38.

Bruscia, K. (1998). Modes of consciousness in Guided Imagery and Music: A therapist's experience of the guiding process. In K. Bruscia (ed.), *The Dynamics of Music Psychotherapy,* pp. 491–526. Gilsum NH: Barcelona Publishers.

Bruscia, K. (2000). A scale for assessing client responsiveness to Guided Imagery and Music. *Journal of the Association for Music and Imagery, 7*, 1–7.

Bunt, L. (2000). Transformational processes in Guided Imagery and Music. *Journal of the Association for Music and Imagery, 7*, 44–58.

Bush, C. (1992). Dreams, mandalas and music imagery: Therapeutic uses in a case study. *Journal of the Association for Music and Imagery,* 1, 33–42.

Bush, C. (1995). Healing Imagery and Music: Pathways to the Inner Self. Portland, OR: Rudra Press.

Clark, M. (1995). The hero's myth in GIM. *Journal of the Association for Music and Imagery,* 4, 49–66.

Clark, M. (1998–99). The Bonny Method of Guided Imagery and Music and spiritual development. *Journal of the Association for Music and Imagery,* 6, 55–62.

Hale, S. (1992). Wounded woman: The use of Guided Imagery and Music in recovering from a mastectomy. *Journal of the Association for Music and Imagery,* 1, 99–106.

Kellogg, J. (1978). *Mandala: Path of Beauty.* Clearwater FL: MARI.

Kellogg, J., MacRae, M., Bonny, H., & Di Leo, F. (1977, July). The use of the mandala in psychological evaluation and treatment. *American Journal of Art Therapy,* 16, 123–134.

Lewis, K. (. (1998-99). The Bonny Method of GIM: Matrix for transpersonal experience. *Journal of the Association for Music and Imagery,* 6, 63–86.

McIvor, M. (1998-99). Heroic journeys: Experiences of a Maori group with the Bonny Method. *Journal of the Association for Music and Imagery,* 6, 105–118).

Meadows, A. (2000). The validity and reliability of the Guided Imagery and Music Responsiveness Scale. *Journal of the Association for Music and Imagery,* 7, 8–33.

McKinney, C. (1993). The case of Therese: Multidimensional growth through Guided Imagery and Music. *Journal of the Association for Music and Imagery,* 2, 99–110.

Merritt, S. (1993). The healing link: Guided Imagery and Music and the body/mind connection. *Journal of the Association for Music and Imagery,* 2, 14–28.

Pellitteri, J. (1998). A self-analysis of transference in Guided Imagery and Music. In K. Bruscia (ed.) (1998), *The Dynamics of Music Psychotherapy,* pp. 481–490.Gilsum NH: Barcelona Publishers.

Pickett, E. (1991). Guided Imagery and Music (GIM) with a dually diagnosed woman having multiple addictions. In K. Bruscia (ed.), *Case Studies in Music Therapy,* pp. 497–512. Gilsum NH: Barcelona Publishers.

Pickett, E. (1995). Guided Imagery and Music: A technique for healing trauma. *Journal of the Association for Music and Imagery,* 4, 93–102.

Pickett, E., & Sonnen, C. (1993). Guided Imagery and Music: A music therapy approach to multiple personality disorder. *Journal of the Association for Music and Imagery,* 2, 49–72.

Short, A. (1991). The role of Guided Imagery and Music in diagnosing physical illness and trauma. *Music Therapy: Journal of the American Association for Music Therapy,* 10 (1), 22–45.

Short, A. (1996–97). Jungian archetypes in GIM therapy: Approaching the client's fairytale. *Journal of the Association for Music and Imagery,* 5, 37–50.

Smith, B. (1996–97). Uncovering and healing hidden wounds: using GIM to resolve complicated and disenfranchised grief. *Journal of the Association for Music and Imagery,* 5, 1–23.

Summer, L. (1989). *Guided Imagery and Music in the Institutional Setting.* St. Louis: MMB Music.

Tasney, K. (1993). Beginning the healing of incest through Guided Imagery and Music. *Journal of the Association for Music and Imagery,* 2, 35–47.

Ventre, M. (1994). Guided Imagery and Music in process: The interweaving of the archetype of the mother, mandala, and music. *Music Therapy: Journal of the American Association for Music Therapy,* 12 (2), 19–38.

Wesley, S. (1998–99). Music, Jung, and meaning making. *Journal of the Association for Music and Imagery,* 6, 3–14.

Wrangsjö, B., & Körlin, D. (1995). Guided Imagery and Music as a psychotherapeutic method in psychiatry. *Journal of the Association for Music and Imagery,* 3, 35–48.

*Chapter Sixteen*

# GROUP MUSIC AND IMAGERY THERAPY: EMERGENT RECEPTIVE TECHNIQUES IN MUSIC THERAPY PRACTICE

## Lisa Summer

Emerging from the fringes of pharmaceutical/psychological experimentation, Helen Bonny crafted a therapeutic approach to the unconscious which would obviate the necessity of Albert Hoffmann's chemical approach: Lysergic acid diethylamide tartrate Delysid, a.k.a. LSD-25. "My ego," the drug's inventor explained, "was suspended somewhere in space" (reported in Parfrey, 1987, p. 58). Bonny's nonpharmaceutical recreation, Guided Imagery and Music, a.k.a. GIM, was developed during the 1970s to duplicate the life-changing peak experiences engendered by the ingestion of LSD, without the chaotic and dangerous psychological aftereffects caused by the drug's invasive entry into the usually well-defended unconscious. Bonny discovered that relaxation was a safer method to penetrate beyond a client's normal ego defenses deep into the unconscious, using music as the (metaphorical) trepanation tool.

Bonny initially experimented with group music and imagery procedures using groups of therapists, friends, and students (Bonny & Savary, 1973). Although she dabbled in developing an application of GIM for groups that she called "group GIM," the training and the practice that Bonny developed were solely devoted to individual work with its goal of stimulating life-changing, reconstructive imagery experiences. This individual form was eventually renamed the "Bonny Method of Guided Imagery and Music" or BMGIM.

Group sessions were used as a stepping stone to interest people in individual BMGIM sessions—either to become a client or to become a trainee. Group GIM was a pedagogical technique, used in lectures, workshops, and trainings; not a classic version of group psychotherapy, but rather a helpful tool. A workshop leader could use group GIM to introduce large audiences to the idea of individual BMGIM, without the time-consuming process of having to give each potential practitioner and/or client an individual two-hour session.

Because group GIM mimicked an individual session as closely as possible, adapting it for the group only when necessary (as in the element of individual guiding), many students of the technique (including myself) confused the pedagogical tool for the technique itself.

As a student at Western Michigan University, I studied French horn with Neill Saunders, a former symphony mate of Dennis Brain (the reference will impress horn players). During one lesson I was playing the second movement of Mozart's fourth horn concerto (K 495), and Mr. Saunders admonished me for my playing. He said I was playing Mozart like it was Beethoven, with a dark, heavy, and serious tone. He wanted my tone, articulation, and phrasing to sound "light and effortless." "Liser," he said sternly, metamorphosizing my name in his heavy British accent, "lift up your right foot and bend it at the knee." Obedient to his instructions, I imitated the appearance of a resting stork. "Play from the beginning of the movement again." After a moment of disbelief at having to accomplish this seemingly absurd and impossible task, I played the first ten measures of the second movement standing on one foot. To my amazement, my sound became light and effortless just as my teacher desired. As clever a tool as it was, standing on one foot was merely a pedagogical technique. Saunders was not suggesting that I should commence performing on one leg outside of the practice room, in the real world of music performance.

In my early practice of group work, it did not take long to discover that the philosophy and technique of group GIM did not work in the real world of group music psychotherapy. When I began to apply group GIM in clinical settings as a therapeutic technique, I discovered that I was, in essence, conducting sequential individual BMGIM sessions with each member of my therapy group, which was antithetical to the desideratum of stimulating therapeutic group process. I was performing group therapy while standing on one leg.

Similarly, many GIM practitioners have confused the concept of group GIM practice with the pedagogy employed in the teaching of individual BMGIM. Like my horn technique, group work needed a lighter adaptation of music and imagery to facilitate group, instead of in-depth, individual process.

Recognizing the need for group GIM to become more directed toward clinical goals, several music therapists altered the technique from its incipient form as a pedagogical technique into a valid tool for group music psychotherapy (with sundry attendant changes in nomenclature.) I discussed adaptations with the elderly in 1981, calling the work "group GIM" (Summer, 1981); and in my 1988 monograph, *GIM in the Institutional Setting,* I discuss individual and group work with hospitalized psychiatric clients (Summer, 1988), and proposed a differentiation between group GIM and GIM-related techniques. Short (1992) described her group work with physically disabled elderly clients, titling it "music and imagery." In 1994 Goldberg described "modified GIM therapy for groups" of hospitalized psychotic patients; Blake and Bishop (1994) described adaptations for hospitalized clients with Post-Traumatic Stress Disorder (PTSD), with the term "group GIM therapy"; and in work with clients with eating disorders, Justice (1994) labeled her group work techniques as "music-reinforced relaxation" and "insight-oriented music and imagery."

Concurrent with the maturation of the group work was the increased acceptance of Bonny's pioneering work in the training and practice of professional music therapy. Many university music therapy programs adopted elements of GIM into the curriculum, and under the aegis of *receptive music therapy* techniques commenced the instruction and application of group music and imagery techniques. Group music and imagery techniques, integrated into the music therapy curriculum along with other receptive and active music therapy techniques, conform with Wheeler's (1983) established schema of levels of practice; viz: supportive, reeducative, and reconstructive (Summer, 1999). Whereas the original group GIM technique has been misapplied, not as a pedagogical tool, but rather as an awkward form of seriatim individual BMGIM (both by music therapists and practitioners of BMGIM alike), the group music and imagery therapy is clearly in the domain of music therapy practice because of its emphasis on stimulating interactive group process through music. The practice of group music psychotherapy, including group music and imagery therapy, should be understood to require the education and training afforded professionally accredited music therapists.

## SUPPORTIVE
## GROUP MUSIC AND IMAGERY THERAPY

Most groups in institutional settings are comprised of clients whose psychological issues, cognitive or speech/language disabilities, or physiological limitations militate against bypassing conscious issues in favor of the unconscious. These client groups, as well as any client group in short-term therapy, require a more structured technique that stimulates conscious rather than unconscious imagery. For these groups the preferred level of treatment, supportive music therapy, fosters the growth of trust and unity among group members. In the beginning phase of group therapy, clients need to develop a feeling of trust for the leader as well as for each other, in order to become fully engaged in the therapeutic process. As interaction increases and trust deepens, participants will perceive each other as not only individuals but also as members of a collective unity.

In an environment lacking trust and unity, group members cannot become fully engaged in a therapeutically beneficial group interaction. Group leaders may erroneously overlook the necessity of first developing group unity and cohesion in favor of a superficially meatier session involving what appears to be insight and self-understanding, but what is, in actuality, a simulacrum of insight and self-understanding. This simulacrum of group therapy plays well on movies and television, such as in the CBS group therapy parody "Big Brother," where confrontation between group members is entertaining to the viewers; but sideshow antics are nugatory from a therapeutic perspective.

Nor do therapeutic benefits arise from group members merely relating personal experiences or internal conflicts to each other. "There is nothing more deadening than a therapy group meeting in which a large group of people sit around unenthusiastically listening to one member discuss in great detail some aspect of his or her past or present life situation" (Yalom, 1983, p. 48). In the case of group GIM, Yalom's comment applies equally to the directionless sharing of complex imagery experiences, which "frequently . . . will have little meaning to the majority of other patients, especially to those who have had little opportunity to develop a close relationship with the narrator. At best, the listeners hope for a 'taking turns' format: that is, they hope that in time their turn will come when they, too, will be allowed to present their life problems" (p. 48) or, analogously, imagery experiences. Yalom remarks, "Time after time I observed well-trained clinicians who were ineffective group leaders because they did not know how to turn the group's attention onto its own process" (p. 21). Successful group therapy must be built on a solid foundation of the group's sense of community. Without this foundation, in-depth interpersonal work cannot be effective.

The imagery stimulated in supportive group music and imagery therapy must provide the clients with a catalyst for immediate and positive interpersonal interaction. "A group in which members continually express their observations of, and feelings toward, one another is a group in which no member of the group is very far from center stage. All members have the sense that they may be centrally involved at any moment in the group . . . A group focusing on the here-and-now, on its own interaction, is almost invariably a vital, cohesive group" (Yalom, 1983, p. 48).

Positive interaction among group members requires imagery experiences that are easily described and understood. There should be no obstacle to the group members relating to and validating each other's imagery. The group leader, or the group itself, should develop a simple induction to frame the music experience. The induction can be a feeling, a concept, a word, or a visual image that provides a topic upon which group members will focus during the music. It should clearly present a positive internal experience rather than a conflictual one. A positive image allows for increased feelings of safety, positive self-esteem, and a strong feeling of being part of the group. When clients have psychological conflicts and anxiety that are close to the surface, it can be difficult for them to focus upon a positive internal experience. At the beginning of therapy it is imperative for the leader to take the responsibility for helping to hold these conflicts in abeyance until the group builds enough unity to address conflicts effectively. Like the role of a parent in protecting a newborn child from unmanageable anxiety, the leader's role is to hold away conflictual material in favor of an initial positive experience. Typical inductions that stimulate a positive experience are words such as "connection," "support," or "strength"; a visual image of a supportive family member, friend, or group member; or suggestions of feeling safe, relaxed, or energized.

The induction must also provide a strong common denominator—a shared platform upon which group members can easily interact. When group members enter a group they are naturally preoccupied with their own sui generis life concerns. These individual concerns are often so threatening as to obstruct the group cohesiveness necessary for trust. The group therapist must create an experience in the here-and-now to help group members set aside their individual concerns so that they can discover a positive common denominator upon which it is possible to construct the prerequisites for true group process. Leading the individual group members to common ground is a necessary first step in group therapy. The induction in supportive work is usually task oriented as opposed to an induction that encourages exploration. For example, directions to create a short poem about a feeling, such as "safety" or "security," or to draw a visual image that is "relaxing" provide a simple and concrete task that holds the clients in a common, positive feeling that will establish a sense of group unity during and after the music is played.

The role of the music in supportive group music and imagery therapy is to provide a common aesthetic experience; a musically bound common denominator which will engender a feeling of group unity. Music contains and focuses the imagery experience. With short-term inpatient psychiatric groups Goldberg (1994) found that "Because of the possibility of eliciting overwhelming affect and conflict laden images, the music must stimulate an emotional response and allow images to emerge while concurrently limiting their dynamic movement" (p. 27). Goldberg recommends the use of "music with a narrow range" (p. 31) to allow a "very brief imagery experience without the dynamic unfolding that is characteristic of standard GIM sessions" (p 28). Either classical or non-classical music, of five to ten minutes duration, with minimal musical development and considerable repetition helps clients to keep focused upon one image. In the classical genre, pieces or movements of pieces from the baroque, classical, and or light romantic eras with little musical development can be utilized. Pieces such as Reger's *Lyric Andante*; Dvorak's *Serenade for Strings*, opus 22, movement 1; Warlock's *Pieds en L'Air*; Bach's *Shepherd's Song from the Christmas Oratorio*, BWV 248; and Mozart's *Horn Concerto #4* (K. 495), 2nd movement are examples from the classical genre. Nonclassical pieces that I have used include "River Run" from Paul Winter's *Canyon*, "Caribbean Sea" from *Earth Tribe Rhythms*, and "Celestial Soda Pop" and "Falling in the Garden" from Ray Lynch's *Deep Breakfast*.

After the heart of the session, the therapist must consider how to reinforce any positive feelings that have emerged from the music and imagery experience and determine a strategy which encourages the continued growth of group unity through an interactive music therapy technique. To "hold" the group in the positive feelings that have been elicited, the therapist employs music-making techniques such as spontaneous song-writing, structured improvisation, or singing. For example, in a group session in which group members have created poetry about feelings of safety as described in the induction above, the therapist could utilize a song writing technique in which each poem is turned into the verse of a song, structured musically by the therapist. Alternatively, the group could work cooperatively to create a group song by writing lyrics that combine key words from their poems. Creating an instrumental or vocal improvisation or simply choosing a precomposed song whose words and music reflect positive feelings of safety and group unity will encourage the group to sustain its cohesiveness until the end of the session.

# REEDUCATIVE
# GROUP MUSIC AND IMAGERY THERAPY

Reeducative group music and imagery therapy fosters change through insight. The reeducative level of treatment is utilized in the second phase of group therapy—the working phase—and only after group trust and unity have been established by prior successful sessions of supportive group music and imagery. In the working phase of the group process, the group can interact more independently from the leader since the group has developed active, supportive relationships among themselves. The reeducative level is the usual type of treatment for long-term group work, or for an institutionalized client group whose members have good basic ego strength.

The goals of reeducative group music and imagery techniques are to help each client to experience himself in relation to other group members and to bring greater self-awareness and self-understanding. The leader facilitates group members to help each other become aware of maladaptive patterns of interpersonal relating that are hindering daily life. "By helping individual patients to see themselves as others see them and to understand their maladaptive ways of relating to others in the group, the therapist will help patients understand what has gone wrong in their individual social worlds at large" (Yalom, 1983, p. 175). In the beginning phase of group work, focusing upon each client's differing psychological conflicts is detrimental to the establishment of group unity. However, once the group is cohesive, self-understanding can occur as group members, no longer threatened by their differences, can learn from them.

In reeducative group music and imagery therapy, the induction continues to serve as an initial frame for the music experience. The induction can now be designed to stimulate significant differences among group members' imagery experiences. Since supportive interpersonal relationships have already been established, the group process can now address the serious individual psychological issues of its members. Rather than holding the group away from conflict, the induction can now serve as a platform upon which group members can interact regarding their own psychological conflict. Inductions that allow for a more internal individualized topic usually include a relaxation procedure such as deep breathing exercises, a simple muscle relaxation, or a centering exercise. Topics for a reeducative induction include the client's current mood, a specific relationship, a current life question (such as "Where is my life going?"), and a conflictual life situation.

The music chosen for the reeducative level of practice serves the same aesthetic and containing functions as in the supportive level. It should be repetitious, with little musical development. However, to stimulate a greater variety of responses in group members, the music should be of greater length and complexity (structural and textural). In the classical genre, some simpler slow movements from classical or romantic symphonies as well as the exposition sections of first movements of romantic symphonies can be used. I have found Webern's *Langsamer Satz,* the opening six minutes of Wagner's *Siegfried Idyll,* and the second movement, in its entirety, of Beethoven's seventh symphony, to be useful.

Reeducative group music and imagery therapy usually proceeds to verbal, rather than musical, processing, though the discussion should not concentrate upon the solution of the conflictual issues brought up by the induction and the music. In the postlude of the session group members can do little to help each other solve conflicts, but group members have a great deal to reveal to each other in regard to their perceptions of each other's imagery and in regard to how they present their imagery to the group. The goal of processing imagery experiences in re-educative group music and imagery is not to simply reinforce the experience generated by the music as it is at the supportive level, nor is it to relate the imagery experience to the client's conflicts outside the group. The interactive processing of the imagery experience serves to help each client investigate how his internal conflicts are represented through the imagery experience, and how these conflicts impact his interpersonal relationships with specific members of the group. The therapist facilitates each group member to respond emotionally to each other's imagery, and utilizes the group's images to stimulate significant supportive and confrontive interaction among group members. The group becomes a therapeutic agent for each group member through their natural emotional responses to each other's imagery.

## RECONSTRUCTIVE
## GROUP MUSIC AND IMAGERY THERAPY

The reconstructive level of group music and imagery therapy fosters reconstructive ego change through personal and transpersonal transformation. It is used infrequently since it is only appropriate for long-term group work and for clients with good ego strength. It is only utilized for groups with consistent and committed group members, and only when the group is in existence long enough to delve into more serious underlying personal, existential, and spiritual questions.

Inductions used in reconstructive group music and imagery sessions are similar to those used in the reeducative level in that they serve to stimulate significant differences among group members' imagery experiences. However, at the reconstructive level they include an extended relaxation procedure to allow for a deeper state of consciousness and focus upon existential or spiritual issues.

Evocative classical selections of approximately ten minutes in duration with a wide range of elements and more complex development sections are used in reconstructive work. Selections from the classical genre such as middle movements from larger romantic works are appropriate for reconstructive group music and imagery sessions. Some pieces I have found especially useful are the third movements from Brahms first and third symphonies, and the fourth movements from Mahler's fifth and seventh symphonies.

As in the reeducative level of group work, the verbal processing in reconstructive group music and imagery still keeps the focus upon an active group process of support and confrontation.

Of course, group process is not as cut-and-dried as the linear three-level description above. The type of group process to be activated is determined by the spontaneous needs of the client group. Many groups will remain in the supportive, or beginning, stage for the entire life of the group. This is quite usual for inpatient groups whose membership consists of clients with serious diagnoses, for short-term groups, and for groups with high client turnover. Other groups will quickly develop a sense of cohesion, and be ready for the working stage within a short time period. In addition, the three levels of practice indicate the intention and goals of the group leader, not the actual result of the group. For example, in leading a supportive music and imagery group, group members will, of course, develop insight even though this is not the focus of the group.

## CONCLUSIONS

Group music and imagery therapy, which was born of the pedagogy of GIM, has grown up, and in order to attain its potential as a therapeutic tool must be recognized as a critically different entity than its parent. BMGIM is a psychotherapeutic tool that pertains to the individual, to the unconscious, and to a broad range of personal and transpersonal issues. Group music and imagery therapy pertains to the collective, to the conscious, and to a narrow range of immediately relevant personal issues. In BMGIM, the imagery is often unpredictable and difficult to verbalize; even, at times, ineffable. It may leap effortlessly from conflict to accord. Contrarily, the process necessary for beneficial therapeutic results in group music and imagery requires controlled and linear positive imagery that can be easily verbalized and described. Discordant imagery is to be avoided until and unless prerequisite group harmony has been achieved in preliminary supportive group sessions. The process of BMGIM is intrapersonal and dwells in the past; group music and imagery therapy is interpersonal, highly interactive, and anchored in the here-and-now. The BMGIM practitioner uses music that is evocative, hence the prevalence of Romantic period pieces with extended development and textural complexity; whereas the group leader in group music and imagery therapy must utilize music that is contained and minimally textured, hence the reliance on pieces focused on exposition with minimal development and orchestral textures of greater simplicity as well as the inclusion of nonclassical music with its modicum of musical depth. Finally, the group music and imagery techniques described in this chapter are not group versions of BMGIM. They are techniques of receptive group music therapy, and reside in the bailiwick of the music therapist, whose education in the immediacy of interaction through the interweaving of receptive and active music techniques is a necessary pre-requisite for true group music therapy to occur.

# References

Blake, R. L., & Bishop, S. R. (1994). The Bonny Method of Guided Imagery and Music in the treatment of post-traumatic stress disorder (PTSD) with adults in the psychiatric setting. *Music Therapy Perspectives,* 12 (2), 125–129.

Bonny, H. L. (1994) Twenty-one years later: A GIM update. *Music Therapy Perspectives,* 12 (2), 70–74.

Bonny, H. L., & Savary, L. M. (1973). *Music and Your Mind.* Barrytown, NY: Station Hill Press.

Goldberg, F. S. (1994). The Bonny Method of Guided Imagery and Music as individual and group treatment in a short-term acute psychiatric hospital. *Journal of the Association for Music and Imagery,* 3, 18–33.

Justice, R. W. Music therapy interventions for people with eating disorders in an inpatient setting. *Music Therapy Perspectives,* 12 (2), 104–110.

Parfrey, A. (ed.) (1987). *Apocalypse Culture.* New York: Amok Press.

Short, A. E. (1992). Music and imagery with physically disabled elderly residents: A GIM adaption. *Music Therapy,* 11 (1), 65–98.

Summer, L. (1981). Guided Imagery and Music with the elderly. *Music Therapy,* 1, 39–42.

Summer, L. (1988). *Guided Imagery and Music (GIM) in the Institutional Setting.* St. Louis: MMB Music.

Summer, L. (1999, November). *Introduction to Guided Imagery and Music.* Paper presented at the World Congress of Music Therapy, Washington, D.C.

Wheeler, B. (1983). A psychotherapeutic classification of music therapy practices: A continuum of procedures. *Music Therapy Perspectives,* 1 (2), 8–12.

Yalom, I. D. (1983). *Inpatient Group Psychotherapy.* New York: Basic Books.

*Chapter Seventeen*

# DEVELOPMENTS IN MUSIC PROGRAMMING FOR THE BONNY METHOD

## Kenneth E. Bruscia

### MUSIC PROGRAM DEFINED

In the Bonny Method of Guided Imagery and Music (BMGIM), a program is a specially selected, recorded sequence of western classical music (mostly from the eighteenth to the twentieth century), designed to help the imager explore inner experiences and various levels of consciousness. Each program consists of two or more pieces, by one or more composers, either in the same or different musical style and mood, altogether lasting anywhere from ten to fifty minutes. These recorded programs may be used alone or in various combinations, with or without some modification, depending upon the client's needs and the length of the session. Each program has a title that broadly suggests possible uses; however, these titles are not regarded as accurate predictors of specific imagery, emotional processes, imager reactions, or therapeutic outcomes. Thus, selecting which program to use requires considerable knowledge, skill, and judgment.

A recurring issue in the history of BMGIM has been whether music outside of the western classical tradition (e.g., new age, movie music, popular jazz, folk or indigenous music) is appropriate for individual and group work. A related question has been whether the use of such music is consistent with the Bonny Method. While Bonny did experiment with non-classical music in group workshops and educational settings (Bonny & Savary, 1973), the programs that she developed specifically for individual work contain only music from the western classical tradition; moreover, in her writings and speeches, she has argued continuously for its advantages over other styles, and she only provides guidelines for the selection and sequencing of classical music (Bonny, 1978).

Thus, in this chapter, and throughout the book, only classical music is considered indigenous to the individual form of the Bonny Method, while the use of classical and/or nonclassical music is considered more characteristic of Bonny's group form and adaptations thereof. Going even further, the use of pre-sequenced recorded programs is considered indigenous to the individual form of the Bonny method, while spontaneous selection of one or more pieces is considered more characteristic of Bonny's group form and adaptations thereof

## A HISTORY OF MUSIC PROGRAMS

Since the inception of BMGIM, an entire library of programs has been created by Bonny and her followers, all for use primarily in individual sessions. As shown in the various Appendices, nearly one hundred programs have been developed by various programmers. What follows is an historical account of how and why these programs have been developed, and the myriad factors affecting their distribution and use.

### The Early Taped Programs

In the early 1970s, the Institute for Consciousness and Music advertised and sold Bonny's original taped programs (as well as a few by other programmers) to individuals who were doing the GIM training, as well as to other interested professionals. As training in GIM became more formalized over the next two decades, distribution of the tapes became more closely linked to the different levels of training, the premise being that appropriate use of the programs depended upon the readiness of both guide and imager for the music contained. The Institute for Music and Imagery distributed seventeen taped programs across the three levels of training already established at the time, thirteen by Bonny and the other four by Keiser Mardis (see asterisks).

Level I programs were those used in the early stages of work by beginning guides. These programs included: *Group Experience* (later called *Explorations*), *Imagery, Quiet Music, Nurturing, Relationships, Creativity I\**.

Level II programs were those considered more intense or working programs, and thus appropriate for more experienced imagers, and guides with more advanced training. These included: *Comforting/Anaclytic, Positive Affect, Transitions, Grieving\*, Emotional Expression I, Mostly Bach, and Peak Experience.*

Level III programs were those considered both advanced and specialized for both imager and guide. These included: *Affect Release, Death-Rebirth, Expanded Awareness\*,* and *Creativity II\*.*

In addition to these seventeen, there were a few other original taped programs advertised in the *ICM Newsletter* that were not as widely used, and not regularly distributed as part of training. These included: *Children's Imagery Tape, Cosmic Astral, and Serenity.*

## The Bonnytapes

In the late 1980s as the master tapes began to wear from repeated copying, Bonny began the task of remastering all of the original programs, and created a series of metal tapes under the name "Bonnytapes © 1989." In the process, she discovered that some of the original performances were no longer commercially available, and that she would have to find other acceptable performances. Bonny also took this opportunity to release three new programs of her own: *Body Tape, Inner Odyssey, and Emotional Expression II.* Also included in the series were: *Creative Listening I* (originally by Lou Savary), *Hero's Journey* (by Lisa Summer), *and Conversations* (by Ruth Skaggs).

## The Copyright Dilemma

It is important to realize that most, if not all, of the music programs created in the first two decades of BMGIM practice were mastered and copied on audiotapes. This practice came to a screeching halt when Congress passed The Home Audio Recording Act of 1992. With this act, new copyright laws were put into effect, and it became illegal in the United States to reproduce recorded music without the appropriate copyright releases from the recording company and score publisher, and without paying the appropriate royalties. Distribution and sales of all BMGIM tapes had to be discontinued immediately to be in compliance with the law. Thereafter, if someone wanted to own or use a program, the person had to buy CDs of every piece contained on the program, and then make a tape or CD using the appropriate sequence of pieces. Aside from the exorbitant cost of doing this, a major problem was finding the best performances and recordings. By this time, the commercial recording business had converted from LPs to CDs, and many of the original performances on LPs were no longer available.

## The Twelve Core Programs

In October 1994, Helen Bonny and Linda Keiser Mardis met for several days to consider the various dilemmas confronting the GIM community with regard to the music programs. As a result, they developed the concept that there were twelve "core" programs.

> Our feeling is that if a student of GIM comes through three levels of training with a through knowledge of these 12 programs, their uses, their musical intricacies, their guiding possibility, etc., and with the experience of many personal sessions to these programs, then s/he will be very able to conduct sessions with a full range of affective and therapeutic potential. We also feel that the purchases of recordings necessary for 12 programs can be handled reasonably by a student during the length of the three levels of training; and that the time spent in the preparation of the actual tapes will prove very meaningful in the student's relationship with the music and also the machinery necessary in the practice of GIM (Bonny & Keiser Mardis, 1994, p. 1).

The twelve programs they selected as "core" included: eight by Bonny (*Explorations [Group Experience], Imagery, Emotional Expression I, Quiet Music, Mostly Bach, Peak Experience, Transitions, Positive Affect);* two by Keiser Mardis *(Creative I, Grieving)*: and two new ones developed by Bonny and Keiser Mardis *(Recollections* and *Caring). Recollections* and *Caring* were developed because of difficulties in finding suitable recordings for some of the pieces on the *Nurturing* and *Comforting* programs.

The twelve programs were presented as a discography (Bonny & Keiser Mardis, 1994) with specific recommendations for performances and CDs, and the following caveat:

> All the CDs on the discography are currently available as of the writing of this memo. We will have to review the discography each year, because certain CDs are taken off the market each year. We will become very fluid in outlook on these programs! . . . Some of the older programs are not included on this list because we are having difficulty finding current CDs. This now must be taken into consideration. It does not mean that the older programs are no longer valid. It means that as we progress into these new concepts of program production, the availability of CDs must be considered and

will provide us with the creative opportunity to revise programs periodically (Bonny & Keiser Mardis, 1994. p. 2).

## Music for the Imagination

In 1996, Barcelona Publishers entered into an agreement with Naxos of America to produce CDs containing several BMGIM programs. The result of this joint venture was *Music for the Imagination*, a set of ten CDs recorded by Naxos and distributed by Barcelona Publishers.

Naxos was selected for the project because it had a very large library of recordings with many fine performances, and because its executives were very supportive of the idea of using music for therapeutic purposes. Nevertheless, two problems were encountered in trying to create CD versions of BMGIM programs from a single recording library. First, while the Naxos library had much of the music contained in the BMGIM programs, it did not have every piece needed to reproduce each program exactly as designed; thus, either the missing piece had to be substituted with another one, or a gap had to be left in the program. Second, at the time, Naxos traditionally recorded only one performance for each piece in their library. While the quality of most of its performances is quite high, some were either unacceptable or unsuitable for specific use in a BMGIM program. Thus either the piece had to be eliminated or substituted on the CD, or it had to be included in the program despite reservations about the performance.

Recognizing the pros and cons of leaving gaps, the present author, in consultation with Helen Bonny, worked to find acceptable solutions to these two problems. As a result, *Music for the Imagination* contains twenty-five GIM programs, some which appear exactly as designed by the programmer, some which have been modified according to the Naxos library by the author and Helen Bonny, and some which have been newly created by the author. Programs included in the set are: *Explorations, Imagery, Creativity I–II, Relationships, Caring, Nurturing, Positive Affect, Emotional Expressions, Grieving, Peak Experiences, Transitions, Death-Rebirth, Affect Release, Inner Odyssey, Body Tape, Solace, Mournful, Consoling, Pastorale,* and *Searching.* See the Appendix for detailed information on these programs and their modification.

While opinions vary on some of the performances included in the CDs, and on the various substitutions made in actual pieces, *Music for the Imagination* has been an important development in music programming for the GIM community. Besides making the GIM programs more easily and economically available to students and practitioners, it has also changed many aspects of music programming. A major change has been that it has encouraged GIM practitioners to use CDs instead of audiotapes.

CDs offer two main advantages over tapes. First, they have much greater fidelity and clarity of sound than tapes. Second, CDs offer considerably more freedom in music programming. CDs make changing from one program to another or one piece to another much easier; moreover, unlike tapes, CDs provide immediate access to any piece in a program and to several programs at once. In essence, CDs give practitioners free, easy, and immediate access to a huge repertoire of BMGIM music. The implications of this are profound—free access to more music encourages practitioners to become more involved in programming the music while guiding.

## NEW LEVELS OF PROGRAMMING

Based on how *Music for the Imagination* has been used since its release, three levels of programming have emerged. They are:

- At a *basic* level, the guide: a) chooses whether to use an original or modified program, and then follows the pre-designed program faithfully, without making any modifications in it; b) selects between two options already provided within a pre-designed program; c) switches from one program to another as dictated by traveler needs; and d) adds tags that have already been suggested for each program.
- At *intermediate* level, the guide: a) extemporaneously selects options within a pre-designed paradigm or program theme; and b) extemporaneously sequences previously designed parts of different programs. The main condition at this level is that musical selections have already been made, options and sequences already exist, and the guide is merely selecting and sequencing the music in new ways. Decisions at this level can be found in *Music for the Imagination*, where some of the CDs provide multiple options for programs and music sequences. Keiser Mardis (1996) has also proposed a similar programming paradigm.
- At an *advanced* level, the guide selects new music, designs new sequences or options within a program, creates new programs, designs special programs for clients prior to a session, and extemporaneously programs music while guiding the client. Two BMGIM practitioners have been developing concepts of extemporaneous programming: Madelaine Ventre and Lisa Summer.

Needless to say, each level of programming requires different knowledge and skills. Given that there is considerable variability in musical expertise among BMGIM practitioners and students, the advancement of programming concepts has important implications for training and ethics. It is important that every training program formulate clear learning objectives with regard to programming at one or more of these levels, and that all practitioners and students take care to program music at the level consistent within their own competence.

## Other Programmers

Meanwhile, as interest in BMGIM has continued grow, many additional programs have been created by Bonny's followers. Music programs have grown in number and variety as the result of many factors. First, new programs have arisen out of the expansion of the method. As the applications of BMGIM have expanded, different music programs have been needed to address the unique characteristics of each new population and the new goals that have evolved from working with them. Second, as BMGIM training opportunities have increased, there are more qualified individuals who are interested in creating programs. And third, new music programs have evolved as the result of changes in the commercial availability of various pieces and preferred performances, and the legality of copying and distributing copies of the recorded programs.

Of all the programs now in existence, Bonny's are certainly the ones most widely used by GIM practitioners and students, attesting to their effectiveness as well as their musical integrity. There are many reasons, however, that the BMGIM library include the work of other programmers. Given the centrality of music in the process, the very potential of BMGIM depends upon the range of music and music programs available. Each program presents certain musical spaces, with certain musical challenges and resolutions, all determined by the musical preferences and psychological range of the programmer. The world of music is vast and constantly growing, and there are many different musical tastes and psychological ranges.. at the same time, listeners are growing in exposure to and appreciation of various genres and styles of music, thus making it necessary to gear BMGIM programs to growing musical needs of clientele. Keiser Mardis (1996) has underlined the importance of seeking input from clients on the kinds of music they need to accomplish their goals. For all these reasons, the continual development of programs is an integral to the continued growth and efficacy of BMGIM.

## REFERENCING PROGRAMS

Given the number of programs now in existence, and the numerous modifications and revisions that have been made over the years, problems have arisen in finding an accurate and consistent way for referring to the programs, and making the appropriate distinctions between the original and modified versions thereof. The present editors propose the following system:

- In citing an original program, give the name of the programmer and the date of the publication that is being cited. Thus "*Positive Affect*" (Bonny, 1973) refers to the original version as listed in the *ICM Newsletter* that year. When the program has two creators, use both names separated by an "&". Thus, "*Caring*" (Bonny & Keiser Mardis, 1994) refers to the original version as presented by both programmers in their paper on Core Programs.

- Care should be taken to cite the original source for each program. Otherwise there can be considerable confusion between the various references that contain the program. For example, because the *Transitions* program has been published in three different places, a writer could cite three different bibliographic sources for it: "Bonny, 1978" (her second GIM Monograph); "Keiser Mardis 1986" (which is her book entitled "Conscious Listening"); or "Bonny & Keiser Mardis 1994" (which is the discography they developed for the Core Programs). Only the first reference (Bonny, 1978) comes close to being accurate, because *Transitions* was created by Bonny prior to 1978. The other two references are really confusing because, without further explanation, they imply either that Keiser Mardis created the program in 1986 or that both Bonny and Keiser Mardis created it in 1994.

- All references to programs should include any modifications or revisions made to the program. A modification or revision is defined as an addition, omission, or substitution of any piece of music included in a program by the originator, or a change in the sequence of those pieces, whether these changes are made by the originator of the program or another person. A modification or revision does not include changes in the performance of any piece of music.

- When referring to a program that has been modified or revised, always give the name of the program, the programmer, and the original reference first; then cite who modified the program and its reference. Thus, to refer to a modified version of the *Positive Affect* program, say: *Positive Affect* (Bonny, 1973), as modified by Bruscia (1996).

## CONCLUSION

One of the most innovative features of the Bonny Method is the use predesigned, recorded programs of classical music for purposes of therapy, healing, and self-development. Through her experimentation and research, Bonny developed criteria for selecting music most appropriate for BMGIM, along with principles of sequencing the music to support various kinds of imaginal journeys through consciousness. (See Chapters Five and Six). Thus, Bonny's legacy consists not only of the programs that she herself developed, but also her method of programming. Meanwhile, the advent of CDs, changes in copyright laws, increases in the applications of BMGIM, and the programming efforts of Bonny's followers have all contributed to the development of new programs for BMGIM (See Appendices), as well as new approaches to programming.

## *References*

Bonny, H. (1978). *The Role of Taped Music Programs in the GIM Process (Monograph #2).* Salina, KS: The Bonny Foundation.

Bonny, H. (1989). *Bonnytapes.* Salina KS: The Bonny Foundation.

Bonny, H., & Keiser Mardis, L. (1994). *Music Resources for GIM Facilitators: Core Programs and Discography of Core Programs.* Olney, MD: Archedigm Publications.

Bruscia, K. (1996a). *Music for the Imagination (Ten CD set).* Gilsum, NH: Barcelona Publishers.

Bruscia, K. (1996b). *Music for the Imagination: Rationale, Implications and Guidelines.* Santa Cruz, CA: Association for Music and Imagery.

Keiser Mardis, L. (1986). *Conscious Listening: An Annotated Guide to the ICM Taped Music Programs.* Olney, MD: Archedigm Publications.

Keiser Mardis, L. (1996). *Program 33: A New Program and a New Programming Concept.* Olney, MD: Archedigm Publications.

*Chapter Eighteen*

# METHODS OF ANALYZING MUSIC PROGRAMS USED IN THE BONNY METHOD

## Brian Abrams

Music programs, or recorded sequences of classical music selections, are one of the cornerstones of the Bonny Method of Guided Imagery and Music (BMGIM). A music program constitutes the backdrop, terrain, and very fabric of a BMGIM experience. Each program embodies the potentials that any given session holds for a traveler. For this reason, practitioners and researchers have had a long-standing interest in analyzing the music programs commonly used to discover the ways in which they work, and how to use them most effectively.

Since the inception of BMGIM, a number of different approaches to program analysis have emerged. Each approach is based upon a distinct set of assumptions concerning both the nature of music programs and what matters most about their potential applications in BMGIM work. Methods of program analysis can be divided into three principal categories: *musical approaches*, *phenomenological approaches*, and *heuristic approaches*. These three categories are related in a *nested* manner. That is, in the order presented here, each successive category includes the basic properties of the previous one(s), yet adds a layer of properties which distinguishes the new category. The purposes of this chapter are to review methods within each category, to compare methods within each category, and to summarize general variations across all methods.

## MUSICAL APPROACHES

Certain approaches to analyzing BMGIM programs are *musical*, in that they focus primarily upon properties of the music itself, and their metaphorical implications for BMGIM work. This includes the analyzer's own qualitative impressions of the music heard in recordings of music selections, as well as the analyzer's identification of elements and structures evident both in recordings and in printed scores of the music.

## Bonny

Bonny (1978) has designed a system of analyzing BMGIM programs, for the purpose of guiding the development of new programs. Bonny's system is based upon the ways in which the original programs were created. The system includes guidelines for examining musical properties both within and across the individual music selections in programs.

For analysis within each selection of a program, the analyzer begins by evaluating the degrees of variability in certain musical elements. The analyzer then considers the metaphorical implications of these elements and their relative variability, revealing the psychological processes the program is likely to promote. According to Bonny, the primary musical elements to consider are pitch, rhythm/tempo, timbre, and melodic line, each of which carries specific metaphorical implications.

Pitch carries a number of implications. High pitch levels can imply uplifted emotions, femaleness, high religious states, or transcendence. Low pitch levels can imply groundedness, subterranean qualities, death, sadness, heaviness, warmth, security, support, or basic worth. Degrees of pitch variability imply degrees of variability in the qualities listed above.

Tempo is associated with the speed of imaginal activity and of internal time as perceived by the traveler. A faster tempo tends to facilitate or reflect transience in imagery, whereas a slower tempo generally encourages contemplation, insight, and development within the traveler's inner world. Steadiness of rhythm and tempo engender safety, security, structure, reassurance, and predictability, whereas greater variability in rhythm and tempo represents instability, and is contraindicated for use in BMGIM.

Timbre, or tone colors and other qualities of sound, can represent particular characters or persons in the traveler's life or imagination, as well as projected aspects of the traveler's own identity. Timbre which involves the use of human voices relates to actual human voices in life, and can provide a sense of closeness, relationship, humanness, and reassurance. Degree of variation in timbre is associated with the traveler's potential range of sensory and emotional experience, as well as the range of support and structure available to the traveler while negotiating internal conflicts and problems.

Finally, melodic line is associated with the directionality of imagery and psychological processes. Thus, degrees of variation in melodic direction relate to degrees of variation in experiential directionality.

Bonny has also suggested identifying the predominant mood(s) of each selection in a program using Hevner's (1937) *mood wheel*, a model in which moods are categorized according to their relative similarity and dissimilarity to one another. Bonny has indicated a preference for music selections with well-integrated, clearly focused moods, as opposed to those with shifting or ambiguous moods.

For analysis across selections of a program, Bonny's method calls for the formulation of an affective-intensity profile, or a contour of the rising and falling mood and energy levels which occur over the course of the program. An affective-intensity profile is diagrammed as a continuous line with peaks, valleys, and plateaus according to the analyzer's perceptions of relative intensity levels across all selections in the program. Individual selection titles are placed sequentially along the bottom of the diagram, for reference.

According to Bonny, affective intensity should be as continuous and smooth as possible between music selections, to minimize the amount of internal adjustment required on the part of the traveler, thereby promoting an uninterrupted, non-ordinary state of consciousness. In addition, performance quality should be as consistent as possible across music selections within a program. Bonny has advised that analyzers (or programmers) utilize the affective-intensity profile in order to gauge the extent to which programs are likely to function in accordance with the programmer's intent.

## Skaggs

Another approach to program analysis has been developed by Skaggs (1994). Like Bonny's affective-intensity profile, the purpose of Skaggs's approach is to evaluate how well music programs function in accordance with the programmer's intent.

First, the analyzer identifies the program's intended psychological theme(s) and process(es). Next, the analyzer considers the role of each selection within the overall program. This involves obtaining relevant background material on each selection (i.e., the history, the score, etc.), listening to the selection, and providing a description of the selection.

The analyzer describes the music primarily as it is heard, in the form of a narrative. The description includes both objective aspects (i.e., factual, formal elements) and subjective aspects (i.e., qualitative impressions and interpretations). In the process of formulating this description, the analyzer considers the imaginal potentials of the music, pertinent to the program's intended purpose. For example, if the program is designed to promote an inner dialogue for the traveler, the analyzer attempts to imagine ways in which the music could embody dialoguing (i.e., through antiphony, solo-tutti forms, a subjective sense of alternation in musical qualities, etc.).

Once all individual selections have been considered, the analyzer summarizes elements common to all selections of the program. Finally, the analyzer considers the program as a whole, and evaluates the extent to which it is likely to function as originally intended.

## Summer

Summer (1995) has proposed an approach to program analysis designed to evaluate how well music selections meet particular therapeutic needs of individual travelers. Specifically, the analyzer assesses the interplay between degrees of *holding* and *stimulation* embodied in the musical form.

*Holding* refers to relatively stable periods in the music, through which the music reflects the traveler's present state of being. This musical holding engenders a symbiotic relationship between the music and the traveler, as well as a sense of safety, nurturance, and "home" for the traveler. *Stimulation* refers to less stable periods in the music, during which the musical form shifts away from its "home base" through passages of creative musical development. This encourages the traveler to imagine and experience possibilities for self-transformation, beyond the present limits of her or his present state of being. For Summer, when the interplay between holding and stimulation in the music is sufficient to provide the traveler with opportunities for psychological development, the music functions in a manner analogous to a mother promoting the development of her child.

To explore manifestations of holding and stimulation in the music, the analyzer first examines each piece of music in the program both through listening and through score analysis, to create a framework of salient, formal divisions in the music (such as theme and variations, exposition and developments, recapitulation, etc.). The analyzer then examines all musical elements (e.g., rhythm, melody, harmony) within each formal division, attending specifically to their metaphorical implications for holding and stimulation. The analyzer then provides a written summary of the musical properties within each formal division.

Summer has emphasized that musical holding and stimulation are broad constructs, not limited to specific meanings, images, feelings, or psychological issues. Essentially, these constructs provide an understanding of the music as a therapeutic "space" within which any number of experiences may unfold. Summer has cautioned that the analyzer need not adhere to any single theory of psychological development in deciding when and how holding and stimulation occur in the music, and that the analyzer must consider a traveler's idiosyncratic, therapeutic needs in order to make decisions about whether or not the particular holding-stimulation profile of a given BMGIM music program is adequate for that traveler.

## Comparison of Musical Methods

The three approaches presented here differ in their central purposes and priorities. The approaches of Bonny and Skaggs are music-centered, in that they prioritize evaluating and understanding the music according to its intended function, independently of any specific application with a traveler. In contrast, Summer's approach is traveler-centered, in that the fundamental question posed concerns the adequacy of the music for a given traveler.

All three approaches to analysis involve a consideration of formal, musical elements, yet each emphasizes something different about these elements. Bonny's approach specifies a particular set of elements for the analyzer to consider. Summer's approach emphasizes elements which pertain to holding and stimulation in the music. In Skaggs's approach, the analyzer identifies whichever elements seem most significant in the context of reviewing the program.

All three approaches incorporate the analyzer's own interpretations and qualitative impressions of the music. Bonny's approach incorporates the analyzer's interpretations of musical elements and sense of mood within selections, as well as the analyzer's impressions of affective intensity across music selections. Skaggs's approach involves the analyzer's imaginative interpretations of the music, as well as the analyzer's impressions of the music in terms of the intended function of the program. Summer's approach includes any of the analyzer's interpretations or qualitative impressions pertaining to holding and stimulation.

Specificity of musical meaning is another distinguishing factor among the three approaches. Bonny's and Skaggs's approaches emphasize the importance of identifying or affirming specific meanings, moods, imagery potentials, and psychological agendas embodied in the music. In contrast, Summer's approach focuses only upon the general interplay of holding and stimulation in the music, without proposing any particular psychological meanings. Of the two methods which do identify specific musical meanings, Bonny's approach includes a set of preconceived, psychological correlates of musical elements, whereas Skaggs's requires that the analyzer discover specific meanings of the music.

Treatment of time is yet another way in which these approaches differ. In Bonny's approach, the way a program unfolds through time is represented through the continuous, affective-intensity diagram. However, within each piece, musical elements are recorded as static, condensed summaries. Similarly,

Summer's approach involves a temporally sequenced account of the overall formal development of the music, with summaries of each formal musical division in static form. In Skaggs's approach, the music is described primarily in narrative, time-ordered form, as heard by the listener.

# PHENOMENOLOGICAL APPROACHES

*Phenomenological* methods of program analysis are based upon how actual travelers have responded to the music experientially, generally in the form of imagery. Traveler experiences are considered as they have actually unfolded through the *lived time* of BMGIM sessions (or under closely related conditions involving listening in non-ordinary states). Phenomenological methods are also *musical*, as each includes a consideration of the music to establish a temporal framework for organizing reported imagery (or other responses) and for evaluating relationships between music and imagery.

## Kasayka

Kasayka (1991) has designed a method of program analysis for exploring the ways musical aspects of a program facilitate particular forms of experience. Kasayka's approach involves two primary phases: exploring the music, and reviewing travels to the music program.

The first phase in Kasayka's approach, exploring the music, is based upon Ferrara's (1984) phenomenological approach to musical analysis. This phase involves five basic steps which are applied to each music selection in the program. Each step culminates in a written summary. In advance of implementing this phase, the analyzer obtains audiotapes and printed scores of each music selection.

The first step in exploring the music is *open listening*, in which the analyzer listens to a recording of a given selection, making note of any impressions of the music and its meaning. Bonny (1993) has suggested commenting out loud during an open listening, to maximize one's intuitive awareness of the music. The second step is *listening for syntax*, in which the analyzer focuses upon formal aspects of the music, both as heard and as printed in score form. In this step, the analyzer divides the music into significant passages, marked off by score measure numbers. In one implementation of Kasayka's approach (Dutcher, 1992), the syntax of an entire program was condensed into a single chart summarizing salient musical features within each music selection.

The third step is *listening for semantics*, in which the analyzer attends to anything the music seems to suggest beyond itself, such as feelings, sensations, metaphors, associations, interpretive meanings, etc. The fourth step is *listening for ontology*, in which the analyzer considers the music within the context of its composer's life and identity. The fifth and final step is a *second open listening*, unstructured as in the first open listening, yet informed by all of the previous steps.

Through all of these steps, the analyzer considers the significance of each selection within the context of the program as a whole. After applying the five-step method across all selections in the program, the analyzer may perform a metacritique, to evaluate the various strengths and weaknesses of the analysis process and its implementation.

The second phase in Kasayka's approach, reviewing travels to the music program, also involves five steps, each culminating in written summaries. This phase is based upon the work of Forinash and Gonzalez (1989). Each step in this phase is applied to entire processes of travelers in past BMGIM sessions that featured the program. In advance of this phase, the analyzer obtains traveler background information, audiotapes of sessions, and written BMGIM session transcripts.

The first step in analyzing a traveler's imagery is providing *historical information*, or the traveler's psychosocial and therapeutic background. The second step is *session summary*, or a description of the traveler's general BMGIM process within the session, excluding imagery details. The third step is reviewing the imagery for *syntax*, or framing the imagery according to when it occurred during the music of the program. This is represented in a chart which positions summaries of musical passages (identified in the first phase) next to corresponding passages of imagery.

In the fourth step of imagery analysis, reviewing the imagery for *semantics*, the analyzer considers possible meanings of the imagery, as well as relationships between the imagery and the music. The fifth step, reviewing the imagery for *ontology*, involves a consideration of the traveler's life situation and state of being at the time of the BMGIM session. Following these five steps, the analyzer may create a general summary of the session imagery and its significance, and perform a metacritique on the impact of the analysis.

Upon conclusion of the analysis, the analyzer considers the summaries generated from both phases together. The analyzer then assesses how particular aspects of the music in the program promote and support particular kinds of experience.

# Lem

A system of analysis by Lem (1998) was developed for the purpose of examining both experiential and physiological responses to individual music selections within BMGIM programs. In this approach, the analyzer first examines the formal and affective components of one music selection from a program. Formal components are considered through a structural analysis procedure similar to *listening for syntax* in Kasayka's approach. Affective components are considered through the application of Bonny's *affective-intensity profile* (in this case, the profile is represented by verbal descriptions, as opposed to a visual line, and is applied within the single selection, as opposed to across all selections in the program). Based upon a combination of both formal and affective components, the analyzer then divides the music into meaningful segments.

Next, the analyzer utilizes digital-audiovisual technology to generate a graphic wave-form representation of the entire music selection, based upon the contour of its sound properties (a composite of amplitude and harmonic properties) across time. The wave-form is then divided according to the segments identified in the formal-affective analysis. Then, based upon meaningful patterns evident in both the formal-effective analysis and wave-form, a number of major divisions in the music are identified (each containing a number of the segments identified earlier). Lem refers to the entire, resulting structure as a *psycho-acoustic profile* of the music.

Responses to the music are evaluated in terms of the imagery of several listeners, each of whom images to the music selection in a relaxed state, without a guide (a condition related to, yet different from, true BMGIM). Listeners summarize their imagery after the music has ended. The analyzer sorts the imagery of all listeners into categories, such as "visual imagery" and "sudden, unexpected imagery." In addition, appropriate technology is utilized to measure EEG responses during music listening, as an assessment of neuropsychological arousal levels. Following EEG measurements, graphic representations both of individual measurements and of a composite (mean) of all measurements are generated.

In the final stages of the analysis, the analyzer can examine various interrelationships among the distribution of imagery across categories, the EEG measurements, and the psycho-acoustic profile of music. Through a consideration of these interrelationships between the music and listener responses, the analyzer can draw conclusions about the experiential potentials in the structural and qualitative nature of the music selection.

# Grocke

Grocke (1999) has developed a method of music program analysis closely related to Kasayka's, both in purpose and in form. In advance of implementing the analysis, the analyzer obtains recordings and printed scores of music program selections, as well as written transcripts of BMGIM sessions featuring the program under examination. Four distinct phases of analysis then follow.

The analyzer begins the first phase in the analysis by listening to the entire music program, and providing a running narrative of salient musical features. The analyzer then listens to the program again, this time while reviewing printed scores of each selection in the program, to ground and enrich the narrative of the first listening. Next, within each piece, the analyzer identifies meaningful units of music, or musical passages distinguished by significant events or changes (e.g., the introduction of themes, shifts in tempo, variations in orchestration, etc.), and assigns a title or heading to each.

In the second phase, the analyzer reviews imagery transcripts from past sessions involving the program, making note of when each new music selection began within the imagery. Next, the analyzer reviews the imagery within the boundaries of each music selection, identifying and assigning titles to meaningful imagery passages, each distinguished by significant aspects of (or shifts in) content, tone, mood, dialogue, or any other relevant features.

In the third phase, the analyzer creates a general description of the music in the program by linking titles of the meaningful music units with key features of each music selection. Similarly, the analyzer also creates a general description of the imagery by linking imagery unit titles and key features of the imagery. These two general descriptions are then placed side by side for comparison (without attempting to identify exact points of correspondence between the music and imagery).

In the fourth and final phase, the analyzer applies Grocke's Structural Model of Musical Analysis (SMMA) to the program for an in-depth comparison among its music selections. In the SMMA, the analyzer notes all relevant musical elements within each of the following categories: style and form, texture, time (e.g., meter), rhythmic features, tempo, tonal features, melody, ornamentation and articulation, harmony, timbre and instrumentation, volume, intensity (e.g., tension-resolution, intensity peaks), mood, symbolic and associational components (e.g., culture-based associations, metaphoric associations), and performance (e.g., quality, techniques, stylistic and artistic interpretation).

## Marr

Marr (2000) has designed a method similar to both Kasayka's and Grocke's, in purpose and form. In this method, the analyzer first obtains audiotapes and printed scores of the program, as well as audiotapes of actual travels to the program. Three main analysis phases then follow.

In the first phase, the analyzer begins by listening to each music selection as a complete work while reviewing a printed score of the selection. While listening, the analyzer marks off significant musical structures and elements directly on to the score, and divides the music into distinct, meaningful segments. The analyzer then listens several more times, marking down further details onto the score during each listening. To identify significant musical features within each segment of music, the analyzer applies Grocke's SMMA.

The analyzer then provides a running, verbal description of each selection in the program, incorporating Kasayka's concepts of both musical *syntax* and musical *semantics*. In addition, the analyzer incorporates the concept of musical *ontology*, to frame the musical narrative in terms of the history, life, times, and compositional style of each selection's composer.

In the second phase, the analyzer transcribes imagery from multiple travelers' sessions directly alongside of each other and the musical narratives, all positioned in the text according to exactly when the imagery occurred during the music. The analyzer then examines the imagery sequences of multiple travelers within music segments to identify relationships between particular moments in the music and particular passages of the travelers' imagery, taking into account content, sensory modalities, physical state, emotions, consciousness, and symbolism, across all travelers. The analyzer describes these relationships in terms of any relevant music features involved, as well as relevant aspects of each traveler's life context.

In the third and final phase, the analyzer summarizes the overall influence of the music program on the participating travelers' imagery. This summary incorporates all aspects of analysis from the previous phases.

## Comparison of Phenomenological Methods

All phenomenological methods of program analysis presented here are related in purpose and form. All were designed to examine how particular aspects of the music support, underpin, or influence particular aspects of imagery, and all attempt to examine programs in terms of the lived BMGIM experiences of multiple travelers. However, their purposes differ in that Kasayka's approach was designed to examine relationships between one program and one form of experience, Lem's was designed to examine relationships between single selections from programs and various experiential and neurological responses, Grocke's was designed to examine relationships between various programs and one form of experience, and Marr's was designed to examine relationships between one program and various experiences.

Another differentiating factor is the approach to structural music analysis. Kasayka's and Lem's approaches employ traditional, formal analyses, whereas Grocke's and Marr's approaches employ a system specifically designed for BMGIM program analysis in which numerous, fixed categories of musical elements are considered (i.e., Grocke's SMMA).

Yet another factor concerns precision of correspondence between music and imagery. Kasayka's and Marr's approaches involve precise, temporal correspondence between musical and imagery, implying that such a moment-to-moment relationship is critical in understanding BMGIM programs. Lem's approach utilizes condensed, static summaries of imagery, generated completely outside of lived experiences of the music. While EEG is measured as the music unfolds within this approach, EEG is an expression of neuropsychological arousal that can only *imply* the occurrence of inner experience, and cannot specify content. (For accuracy, Lem's method should be considered *pseudo-phenomenological*.) Grocke's approach considers correspondence between music and imagery, but only according to meaningful links between music units and imagery processes, as opposed to their precise chronological occurrences.

## HEURISTIC APPROACHES

In certain approaches to program analysis, the analyzer's own experiences of programs serve as primary guiding factors in understanding the program. These approaches are *heuristic* (i.e., involving the researcher's self as a primary instrument of analysis). In these heuristic approaches, the analyzer's experiences of the program are acquired under conditions identical or similar to actual BMGIM sessions. Thus, heuristic forms of analysis consider BMGIM programs within their indigenous contexts, and provide the analyzer with the most direct links to experiential aspects of the music.

Heuristic approaches are *phenomenological*, in that each considers experiences as they manifest in actual, lived time. They are also *musical*, in that they inherently involve some implicit or explicit consideration of structures and elements in the programmed music.

## Bonny

Bonny (1993) proposed a heuristic form of program analysis called *affective-intuitive listening*. It was designed to facilitate analysis from an experiential perspective, and to open the analyzer's awareness more directly to sensory and emotional aspects of the music. As a specific approach to this form of listening, Bonny has suggested *body listening*. This approach involves the following instructions to the analyzer:

1) stretch, relax, and quiet the mind;
2) begin playing the program, and lie on the floor;
3) visualize the body, and become aware of whatever it is experiencing;
4) move freely, expressing whatever the music seems to suggest to the body; and
5) reflect upon the nature of the program in terms of how the music was experienced in the body, and how the body has expressed these experiences.

## Bruscia

Bruscia (1999) has designed a system of program analysis for examining various potentials of a given program. Bruscia's method is composed of several specific phases, each involving experiencing the music from a distinct perspective. These perspectives are eventually integrated into a single, comprehensive, experiential description of the program, including a consideration of the program's possible uses in BMGIM work.

Bruscia's approach begins with a preliminary, preparatory phase. In this phase, the analyzer makes decisions about who will participate in the analysis (analyzer, peers, clients, etc.), how individualized or generalized the analysis will be, what the specific purpose or use of the analysis will be, etc. The analyzer also uses this phase to make a practical plan for implementing the analysis. In addition, the analyzer gathers available, relevant information about the program by considering such sources as case studies, written scores of the music, the composer's biography, and any material provided by the composers of the music, the author of the program, or previous analyzers of the program.

In the first main phase, the analyzer considers experiences of the program's musical properties, both from traveler and guide perspectives. The analyzer first listens to the entire program in a non-ordinary state of consciousness, as traveler, commenting out loud about anything she or he senses or imagines specifically about the sound, instruments, performers, etc. The analyzer deliberately pursues, intensifies, and deepens these music experiences, without using preconceived structures or categories to guide the listening. Whenever material which does not directly concern the music emerges, the analyzer simply allows it to pass, and re-focuses upon the music. Ideally, a guide assists the analyzer in this phase. The analyzer tape-records all comments for written transcription later on.

The analyzer then repeats the music-centered listening in an alert state, in the simulated role of guide, again tape-recording for subsequent transcription. When transcribing, the analyzer places comments from both perspectives on separate halves of the same paper (side by side), roughly aligned according to naturally occurring segments of musical experience and distinct shifts in the analyzer's experience or attention. Separate paper is used for each piece in the program.

The first phase continues with a review of written scores of each piece in the program, to inform, develop, and elaborate upon listening experiences. The analyzer considers any apparently salient aspects of the score, including those of form, tempo, volume, rhythm, tonality, melody, harmony, texture, timbre, style/idiom, etc. In addition, the analyzer looks for relationships between musical form and the division of segments in the listening experience. The analyzer then synthesizes listening experience and score review material into a single, running narrative of the entire program, emphasizing salient musical aspects. To conclude this phase, the analyzer listens yet again to the entire program, making any appropriate revisions or additions to the narrative.

The second main phase involves analyzing the program specifically in terms of its imagery potentials. First, the analyzer travels to the program, in a non-ordinary state, with a guide (i.e., a "standard" BMGIM session). The session is tape-recorded, then later transcribed. The analyzer organizes transcriptions according to the musical segmentation within each piece (as identified in the first phase), again using separate paper for each piece in the program. The analyzer then once again listens to the entire program in an alert state, focusing upon imagery potentials of each musical segment, within each piece. As part of this, the analyzer considers aspects of each piece which may have implications for the traveler (including musical elements and their metaphorical significance), as well as extramusical components such as meaningful associations, programmatic aspects, lyrics, composer's intent, programmer's intent, etc. In addition, the analyzer incorporates Bonny's mood and intensity profiles of the program into the imagery analysis. The analyzer then guides others to the program, recording and transcribing the imagery.

Next, segment by segment, the analyzer identifies principal categories of imagery, which may include visual, tactile-kinesthetic, metaphorical fantasy, emotional, spiritual-religious, transpersonal, etc. Finally, the analyzer formulates a second running narrative, sequenced according to how imagery in the overall program tends to unfold (considering both potential and actual manifestations).

In the third and final main phase of the analysis, the analyzer reviews musical and imagery narratives, and considers the nature of the program as a whole. This includes effective inductions, functions of and interrelationships among individual pieces in the program, the kinds of resolution or extension which may be needed following the end of the program, etc. In addition, the analyzer considers the program's possible uses and functions, when and why it should be used within a larger BMGIM series, its indications and contraindications for particular client populations, and so forth.

## Booth

Booth (1998–1999) has devised an approach to program analysis, primarily for the creation and evaluation of new programs. Like Bruscia's, the approach was designed to evaluate the various potentials of a program, through a number of distinct phases. Booth's approach was also designed to evaluate how well a program works in accordance with its programmer's intent. Prior to beginning, the analyzer identifies the intended function of the program, and gathers all materials required for performing the analysis.

First, the analyzer considers the general architecture and various formal elements of the music, in terms of how these seem to support the function of the program as intended by the programmer. Second, to evaluate the experiential potentials of the program, the analyzer experiences each selection of music in a non-ordinary state of consciousness without a guide, recording any immediate musical impressions or emotional responses. This includes any impressions of performance quality within each selection. (When applying the analysis in the context of designing a new program, this second phase is utilized to make decisions about how to sequence music selections, as it involves a sense of the music prior to much intellectual processing.)

Third, the analyzer reviews the printed score of each music selection in the program, identifying, labeling, and marking major musical events as reference points for future examination. Fourth, for further insight into the potential significance of the music, the analyzer gathers corroborative, biographical information concerning the composers and respective life circumstances surrounding their compositions.

Fifth, the analyzer assesses actual BMGIM dyads involving the program. This phase includes recording relevant information about each participating traveler, summarizing the imagery corresponding to marked passages of the music (as identified earlier), and eventually summarizing each traveler's overall process, including its significance with respect to the program as a whole. Sixth, the analyzer has various participants draw while listening to the entire program, in a light non-ordinary state of consciousness. As participants work, the analyzer notes when various shapes are drawn and when various colors tend to be utilized during the progression of the music. In addition, to evaluate measurable shifts resulting from experiencing the program, the analyzer can administer a quantitative instrument (such as a mood questionnaire) prior to and following each participant's experience of the program.

Seventh, the analyzer evaluates the overall program, based upon information gathered from all previous phases. This is accomplished by addressing the following questions: (a) In which ways does the program function in accordance with the intentions of the programmer, and in which ways does it not? (b) Do archetypes emerge through listening experiences of the program, and does any single archetype seem to predominate? (c) Are there isolated and/or consistent relationships between expressions of how the program is experienced, such as imagery, drawings, and aspects of the music? (d) How generally may the program be used, and what are its potential indications and contraindications with respect to specific populations? (e) What other potentially important information is conveyed through various experiences of the program? (f) What do the various experiences suggest about long-term effects of the program? Based upon this evaluation, the analyzer concludes the analysis by providing a summary of the nature, function, and virtues of the program for use within BMGIM work.

## Comparison of Heuristic Methods

Although related in various ways, the primary purposes of each method reviewed here differ. Bonny's method was developed primarily to deepen the analyzer's intuitive understanding of existing programs. Booth's was designed primarily for evaluating new programs. Bruscia's was designed *both* for deepening the analyzer's understanding of existing programs *and* for evaluating new programs.

Another distinguishing factor concerns examination of the music. Both Bruscia's and Booth's approaches include explicit analyses of musical structures and elements. The result is a time-ordered, musical framework upon which various experiential aspects of the program can be superimposed. In contrast, Bonny's approach does not involve a formal consideration of musical material. Rather, the music is considered implicitly as the experiential underpinning to the listener's direct, intuitive, moment-to-moment responses.

All three heuristic methods of program analysis presented here involve the analyzer's own experiential perspectives of the program. However, the specific nature of these perspectives and the ways in which they are obtained vary across methods. In Bonny's method, the analyzer examines program in terms of body experiences and physical movement to the program while listening, unguided, in a non-ordinary state of consciousness. Booth's approach also incorporates unguided, non-ordinary-state listening, but focuses upon musical and emotional properties, as opposed to body responses.

Bruscia's method incorporates multiple, experiential perspectives on the part of the analyzer, comprising the full set of perspectives indigenous to GIM (i.e., focusing upon both music and imagery, each from perspectives of both traveler and guide). Furthermore, in Bruscia's method, the analyzer is advised to enlist the assistance of a guide during non-ordinary-state listening, to re-create the authentic dynamics of an actual BMGIM process. Moreover, while Bonny's approach involves the analyzer's experiences only, both Bruscia's and Booth's approaches incorporate the experiential perspectives of others, to expand upon and ground the analyzer's own experiences. (It is notable that Booth's approach also incorporates the process of having others draw to the music, as yet another way of examining creative expressions of the program.)

# VARIATIONS ACROSS ALL METHODS

In general, the methods of program analysis considered here vary according to two fundamental factors. The first concerns the purpose(s) for analyzing the music, or what the analyzer hopes to learn about the music through the analysis. This factor carries implications about how the analyzer understands the nature and significance of the music with respect to BMGIM. The second concerns the particular manner in which an analysis is implemented. Because form follows function in each analysis method, the two factors identified here are interrelated.

In certain approaches (e.g., Lem's and Marr's), the analyzer seeks to evaluate cause-effect relationships between music selections and reported imagery (or other variables). This implies an understanding of the music in BMGIM as a stimulus for eliciting particular psychological responses. These approaches utilize empirical data from actual travelers, to identify precise, moment-to-moment correspondence between instances of music and responses within particular sessions. This further implies an understanding of the music as a collection of individual *parts*, each carrying an evocative effect independent of the overall program.

In certain other approaches (e.g., Bruscia's and Summer's), the analyzer seeks to discover the nature of a given program's potentials (as opposed to its specific influences on imagery). This implies an understanding of the music as a dynamic form which can support creativity, imagination, and therapeutic work in any number of ways (as opposed to in a very specific, determined way). Approaches for addressing this purpose may entail drawing inferences about a program's potentials based upon purely musical properties (e.g., Summer's), or discovering potentials of the music by experiencing it directly in various modes of consciousness (e.g., Bruscia's).

From the latter perspective on program analysis, there is no need for precise, moment-to-moment correspondence between music and traveler responses, as potentials of the music unfold perpetually throughout the course of the entire program. The program is understood as an indivisible, irreducible *whole* (as is are any phenomena that emerge when exploring the program's potentials). Any individual musical structures or elements are meaningful only within the context of the program as a whole, and are analyzed solely for the purpose of better informing the analyzer's sense of this whole.

There are a number of additional, distinguishing purposes for analysis among methods considered here. Some of these are (a) development of new programs (e.g., Bonny's [musical] and Booth's); (b) considering developmental processes supported by the music (e.g., Summer's); (c) evaluating a program for its general and/or individual suitability for therapy, including indications and contraindications (e.g., Bonny's [musical], Booth's, Bruscia's, and Summer's); and (d) evaluation of objective, organismic response variables (e.g., Lem's).

There are also a number of additional, distinguishing aspects of implementation. These include (a) use of a particular theme or process as a central principle throughout analysis (e.g., Summer's); (b) use of intuitive means of analysis (e.g., Bonny's [heuristic]) versus rational means (e.g., Lem's); (c) inclusion of participants in the analysis process (e.g., Booth's, Bruscia's, and Kasayka's); (d) use of systematic, exhaustive forms of musical analysis (e.g., Grocke's) versus forms which consider only those elements judged salient by the analyzer (e.g., Bruscia's and Skaggs's), and the advantages of each with respect to revealing *implicit* or *unconscious* aspects of the program experience; and (e) describing music and/or music experiences temporally, in narrative form (e.g., Bruscia's and Skaggs's), versus condensing these into static descriptions (e.g., Lem's).

## CONCLUSION

Clearly, analyzing the music used in BMGIM is important, both when designing new programs and when deepening understandings of existing programs. Program analysis constitutes an in-depth consideration of the music from multiple perspectives, beyond musical and aesthetic properties alone. Minimally, analysis must address implications that the music holds for healing and development through listening, in non-ordinary states of consciousness, with a guide.

The need for continued exploration and refinement of existing approaches to analysis, as well as for development of new approaches, is clear. These pursuits will undoubtedly benefit the BMGIM discipline by enriching understandings of how the music can be used in BMGIM work.

## References

Bonny, H. L. (1978). *The Role of Taped Music Programs in the GIM Process: GIM Monograph #2*. Baltimore, MD: ICM Books.

Bonny, H. L. (1993). Body listening: A new way to review the GIM tapes. *Journal of the Association for Music and Imagery, 2*, 3–10.

Booth, J. M. (1998-1999). The Paradise Program: A new music program for Guided Imagery and Music. *Journal of the Association for Music and Imagery, 6*, 15–35.

Bruscia, K. E. (1999). *Manual for Level II GIM Training*. Philadelphia, PA: Author.

Dutcher, J. (1992). Tape analysis: Creativity I. *Journal of the Association for Music and Imagery, 1*, 107–118.

Ferrara, L. (1984). Phenomenology as a tool for musical analysis. *The Musical Quarterly, 70*(3), 355–373.

Forinash, M., & Gonzalez, D. (1989). A phenomenological perspective of music therapy. *Music Therapy, 8*(1), 35–46.

Grocke, D. E. (1999). *A Phenomenological Study of Pivotal Moments in Guided Imagery and Music (GIM) Therapy*. Bell and Howell, Dissertation Publishing #9982778.

Hevner, K. (1937). An experimental study of the affective value of sounds and poetry. *American Journal of Psychology, 49*, 419–434.

Kasayka, R. E. (1991). *To Meet and Match the Moment of Hope: Transpersonal Elements of the Guided Imagery and Music Experience* (Doctoral dissertation, New York University, 1991). *Dissertation Abstracts International, 52* (6), 2062.

Lem, A. (1998). EEG reveals potential connections between selected categories of imagery and the Psycho-Acoustic Profile of Music. *Australian Journal of Music Therapy, 9*, 3–17.

Marr, J. K. (2000). *The Effects of Music on Imagery Sequence in the Bonny Method of Guided Imagery and Music (GIM)*. Unpublished master's thesis, University of Melbourne, Australia.

Skaggs, R. (1994). Conversations: An analysis of the music program. *Journal of the Association for Music and Imagery,* 3, 69–75.

Summer, L. (1995). Melding musical and psychological processes: The therapeutic musical space. *Journal of the Association for Music and Imagery,* 4, 37–48.

# Part Five:

# Theory and Research

*Chapter Nineteen*

# TRANSPERSONAL DIMENSIONS OF
# THE BONNY METHOD

## Brian Abrams

The term *transpersonal* conventionally refers to aspects of human experience and development that transcend the usual scope of individual identity, personality, or ego (Anderson, 1998; Grof, 1996; Scotton, 1996; Walsh & Vaughan, 1980). The term also denotes an entire orientation which holds that human consciousness has the fundamental potential for development beyond individual, personal proportions (Walsh & Vaughan, 1996; Wilber, 1997).

The earliest documented use of the term *transpersonal* was by the psychologist and mystic researcher William James, in 1905 (Vich, 1988). Since that time, it has been utilized in a variety of contexts, and has been associated with a number of related terms, such as *archetypal, collective, cosmic, mystical, numinous, paranormal, peak, religious, spiritual, transcendent, ultimate,* and *unitive.* Wilber (1997) has offered the following, specific definition of the term:

> The word "transpersonal" itself simply means "personal plus." That is, the transpersonal orientation explicitly and carefully includes all of the facets of personal psychology and psychiatry, but then *adds* those deeper or higher aspects of human experience that transcend the ordinary and the average—experiences that are, in other words, "transpersonal," or "more than the personal," or personal plus (p. 31).

Relationships between transpersonal experiences and psychological well-being have been understood for some time. Clinical, psychotherapeutic applications of transpersonal experience date back to the early part of the twentieth century. Developments in this area, together with advances in transpersonal research and theory, eventually led to the establishment of the *transpersonal psychology* field in 1968 (Chinen, 1996). It was also during the late 1960s when a clinical research project on music and non-ordinary states of consciousness began, out of which emerged the Bonny Method of Guided

Imagery and Music (BMGIM), a form of psychotherapy consistent with many of the basic tenets of the transpersonal orientation. Helen Bonny, creator of BMGIM, has claimed that the method itself is transpersonal (Bonny, 1978a), and that one of its most significant functions is as a medium for transpersonal work (Bonny, 1978b). Specifically, she has stated that BMGIM is ideal for those interested in "seeking fuller experience and insight in the areas of the humanistic and transpersonal" (Bonny, 1980, p. 25).

Two basic components of BMGIM, music and imagery, have each played important roles in transpersonal work. The literature cites numerous links between transpersonal experiences and music (e.g., Keutzer, 1978; McClellan, 1988), some which specifically involve classical music listening (Panzarella, 1980) or performance (Bonny, 1995). There are also a number of sources which describe transpersonal experiences of music in psychotherapy (Assagioli, 1971; Bonny & Pahnke, 1972; Bravo & Grob, 1996; Grof, 1985, 1988; Lee & Speier, 1996). In addition, the literature refers to uses of imagery both in transpersonal forms of healing (Achterberg, 1985) and in transpersonal psychotherapy (Houston, 1997; Progoff, 1963; Sheikh, 1986).

A number of BMGIM music programs have been designed specifically for promoting transpersonal experience (Kasayka, 1991; Lewis, 1998–1999). Among these are *Expanded Awareness* (Keiser Mardis, 1986), *Faith* (Bruscia, 1997a), *Peak Experience* (Bonny, 1978b), *Positive Affect* (Bonny, 1978b), *Sublime I* (Bruscia, 1997b), *Sublime II* (Bruscia, 1997c), and *Transitions* (Bonny, 1978b).

BMGIM training typically includes an orientation to transpersonal experiences and their transformational value (Association for Music and Imagery [AMI], 1996), in certain cases encompassing entire training modules (e.g., Stokes-Stearns, Bush, & Borling, 1998). Various printed materials which accompany training address matters of identifying, understanding, and guiding transpersonal BMGIM experiences (e.g., Bruscia, 1996a, 1998b; Stokes-Stearns, Bush, & Borling, 1998).

A variety of topics have been addressed through research on transpersonal BMGIM (Abrams, 2001; Dahlstrom, 1991; Hintz, 1995; Kasayka, 1991; Lewis, 1998–1999; Maack & Nolan, 1999; Rugenstein, 1996; Shaw, 1995). Furthermore, a number of theories on transpersonal dimensions of BMGIM have been proposed (Bonny, 1975, 1978b; Bruscia, 1998a; Bush, 1995; Summer, 1992).

Because transpersonal phenomena comprise a core element of the BMGIM discipline, they demand careful consideration. The term *transpersonal phenomena* as used here encompasses both transpersonal experience and transpersonal aspects of inner development or self-transformation. The purposes of this chapter are to review theoretical foundations of the transpersonal orientation, to review the literature on transpersonal dimensions of BMGIM, and to consider aspects of BMGIM which call for an indigenous (i.e., BMGIM-specific) theory of transpersonal phenomena.

## THEORETICAL FOUNDATIONS OF THE TRANSPERSONAL ORIENTATION

The ways in which transpersonal work is understood, both generally and specifically with respect to BMGIM, have much of their foundations in the theories of five figures, arguably the most notable contributors to the development of the transpersonal orientation. These figures are Carl Jung, Abraham Maslow, Roberto Assagioli, Stanislav Grof, and Ken Wilber.

### Carl Jung

Carl Jung is generally considered the first transpersonal psychiatrist and depth psychologist (Grof, 1985; Scotton, 1996). Jung's earliest documented use of the term *transpersonal* (in its German form, *überpersonlich*) was in a 1917 paper on analytical psychology (Vich, 1988). Jung's theories have had a considerable influence on concepts of transpersonal phenomena.

Jung valued spiritual and mystical dimensions of consciousness as integral to human growth and development. He further believed that creative, symbolic forms of psychotherapy promote experience and development surpassing individual ego boundaries (Jung, 1956). These views are well incorporated into much of the BMGIM literature.

Jung theorized a great deal on the *collective unconscious*, or that component of the psyche containing shared experiences of humankind. He also wrote extensively on *archetypes*, or universal aspects of being which manifest in myths, dreams, and imagination (Jung, 1969). Both of these constructs are found in much of the clinical and theoretical BMGIM literature concerning transpersonal work.

### Abraham Maslow

Abraham Maslow, in collaboration with several others, officially established the discipline of transpersonal psychology (Chinen, 1996). Throughout the 1960s, he explored the further reaches of human potential, which included such phenomena as peak experiences (Maslow, 1970) and transcendence (Maslow,

1971). Maslow believed that human beings are capable of attaining levels of psychological health beyond "normal" ego functioning, and that transcendent experiences are signs of supernormal health (Maslow, 1970, 1971). Maslow's concepts served as major foundations for the research that led to the creation of BMGIM (Bonny & Pahnke, 1972), and are integrated into much of the literature on transpersonal BMGIM work.

## Roberto Assagioli

Roberto Assagioli was a psychoanalyst who pioneered many clinical applications of transpersonal principles. As early as the 1920s, he began developing a transpersonal system of psychotherapy known as *psychosynthesis* (Assagioli, 1971). Psychosynthesis includes a seven-part model that distinguishes personal (or individual) aspects of the psyche from those beyond the personal. This model has served as a valuable framework for understanding transpersonal BMGIM work (Bonny & Savary, 1990).

Unlike Jung, Assagioli considered the concepts *collective* (i.e., shared) and *transpersonal* distinct from one another. This distinction is reflected in understandings of transpersonal phenomena in BMGIM, as not all BMGIM experiences considered *collective* are considered *transpersonal*, nor vice versa (Abrams, 2001).

## Stanislav Grof

Psychiatrist and psychoanalyst Stanislav Grof has been another major contributor to the development of the transpersonal orientation. Grof's work has had a unique impact on concepts of transpersonal work in BMGIM.

In the 1950s, Grof began extensive research on the psychotherapeutic value of non-ordinary states of consciousness, particularly of those promoted through psychedelic substances. Grof's consciousness research became the basis for his creation of *holotropic therapy* (Grof, 1988), a technique based on non-ordinary states of consciousness facilitated by deep breathing. As chief of psychiatric research at the Maryland Psychiatric Research Center, Grof spent considerable time collaborating with Helen Bonny (Grof, 1985, 1988), which contributed significantly to Bonny's creation of BMGIM.

Grof's (1985, 1988) research revealed that psychological well-being is profoundly shaped by four basic types of primal birth experiences. When relived in non-ordinary states of consciousness, these primal experiences can elicit transpersonal phenomena. The concept of accessing transpersonal phenomena through primal birth experiences is acknowledged in BMGIM training materials (e.g., Stokes-Stearns, Bush, & Borling, 1998).

Grof (1988) has identified numerous categories of transpersonal experience, based primarily upon his own research findings. These categories of transpersonal experience and their relationships to BMGIM work can be found in the BMGIM training literature (e.g., Bruscia, 1996a, 1998b; Stokes-Stearns, Bush, & Borling, 1998).

## Ken Wilber

Ken Wilber's theories have had a profound impact on the transpersonal orientation. Since the 1970s, Wilber's views have contributed substantially to the disciplines of transpersonal psychology and transpersonal psychotherapy, as well as to concepts of transpersonal work specifically in BMGIM.

Through a synthesis of Eastern, Western, ancient, and modern wisdom from a vast range of fields, Wilber (1995, 1996b, 1997) has created a model addressing the nature of existence, including matter, life, mind, culture, society, morality, and spirituality. The model is composed of four "quadrants," each embodying a developmental continuum concerning a particular facet of reality. Each continuum signifies the manner in which any given aspect of being represents a *whole* which encompasses yet also transcends its *parts*, or all of those aspects along the continuum of lesser depth and complexity.

Wilber (1995, 1996b, 1997) has written most extensively on the facet of reality concerning consciousness, or a person's interior, subjective experience. Wilber's (1993) *spectrum of consciousness* model illustrates the kinds of interior experiences possible at various stages of a person's development. Wilber has represented the spectrum in various forms, such as a circle (Wilber, 1996c), a ladder (Wilber, 1996b), and as a sequence of developmental "fulcrums," or branches (Wilber, 1986).

According to Wilber (1986, 1993, 1995, 1996a, 1996c), there are three basic, developmental divisions in the spectrum of consciousness. These consist of (a) the *prepersonal*, wherein it is only possible to experience reality in ways preceding a sense of distinct, individual self; (b) the *personal*, in which it becomes possible to experience reality in terms of an individual ego; and (c) the *transpersonal*, in which it becomes possible to experience reality in ways transcending ego and individual identity. Wilber has emphasized that prepersonal and transpersonal phenomena tend to be confused with one another, due to superficial similarities. To a certain extent, the threat of this confusion is acknowledged within the BMGIM literature, such as in cases where regressive, infantile experiences of grandiose, "cosmic" proportions are carefully distinguished from experiences of authentic ego transcendence (e.g., Clarkson, 1994).

Wilber (1997) has contended that experiences in temporary *states* of consciousness within the transpersonal division eventually result in stable, enduring, *traits* of consciousness within this division. This has represented a valuable construct in conceptualizing the basic process and mechanism underlying transpersonal BMGIM work. Furthermore, Wilber's (1995, 1996a, 1997) identification of specific developmental stages within the transpersonal division has provided a model for tracking client progress in transpersonal BMGIM work (Rugenstein, 1996).

## LITERATURE ON TRANSPERSONAL
## DIMENSIONS OF BMGIM

The literature contains a variety of philosophical perspectives, theoretical models, and typologies concerning transpersonal aspects of BMGIM. Also in the literature are a number of clinical cases and research studies on BMGIM that feature transpersonal phenomena. Each of these will now be considered.

### Philosophical Perspectives

Several authors have articulated philosophical positions on transpersonal dimensions of BMGIM. For example, Bonny (1978a) has asserted that BMGIM is consonant with transpersonal psychology, in that it promotes total development, both within and beyond the boundaries of individual personality. Kovach (1985), likening BMGIM to shamanism, has noted that it involves transcendent experiences as part of healing and self-transformation. Bush (1995) has claimed that BMGIM touches the soul and gives way to spiritual encounters with the higher self, upon which is elaborated in the following:

> A transpersonal experience within GIM can be a profoundly integrative experience . . . It becomes an encounter with consciousness that is often expansive, beyond yet including the personal. It can be spiritual in nature, evoking our depths while opening consciousness to the experience of anything in the known and unknown universe (pp. 92-93).

Clark (1998–1999), considering transpersonal aspects of BMGIM specifically in terms of the music, has claimed that "in the transpersonal states, music is the fluid, unifying and energizing medium through which and in which the personality is transcended and unitive states are attained" (p. 60). Clark has further asserted that such experiences of music in BMGIM provide opportunities for inner development of transpersonal proportions.

## Theoretical Models

The literature contains a number of theoretical models concerning transpersonal BMGIM phenomena. As one example, Bonny (1975, 1978b) has proposed a transpersonal model of human consciousness illustrated by a "cut-log" diagram (refer to Figure 1). The diagram consists of a set of concentric circles, each representing one distinct layer of human consciousness. The innermost circle represents ego consciousness (i.e., awareness at an ordinary, personal level), whereas each successively larger circle represents consciousness at a more expansive, extraordinary, transpersonal level. Each circle is drawn with a dashed line, indicating that any layer(s) of consciousness can be traversed through non-ordinary experiences, such as those attained through the music in BMGIM work. On this matter, Bonny (1975) has written, "The multidimensional qualities of musical sound allow it to touch many levels of consciousness both simultaneously and/or in sequence" (p. 130). Variations on Bonny's "cut-log" diagram include another concentric-circle diagram by Goldberg (1994), as well as a three-dimensional, funnel diagram by Bush (1995).

Summer (1992) has proposed another model of the transpersonal potentials in BMGIM work. According to Summer, the classical music masterworks used in BMGIM introduce and develop various musical ideas and materials in profoundly aesthetic ways, representing beauty on a universal, transpersonal level. A client who experiences these masterworks with sufficient depth accesses their transcendent beauty, and thus gains opportunities for entering realms of consciousness beyond individual identity.

Yet another model pertaining to transpersonal BMGIM phenomena has been proposed by Bruscia (1998a). Through a diagram based upon Wilber's (1995, 1996b, 1997) four-quadrant diagram, Bruscia has illustrated the manner in which music experiences (such as those occurring through BMGIM work) become transpersonal (refer to Figure 2). According to Bruscia, experiences of music begin with one of four primary emphases, represented in the diagram by four quadrants. These emphases include the *subjective* (personal meanings and representations of music experience), the *objective* (stimulus, organismic, and response variables of music experience), *collective* (communal, ritual, or archetypal aspects of music experience), and *universal* (natural laws and organic patterns of music experience). When a music experience becomes sufficiently profound, it surpasses any particular emphasis, retaining only the intrinsic properties and values of the music itself. This is an *aesthetic music experience*, represented in the diagram by a circle overlapping the inner corners of the four quadrants.

Figure 1.
The Cut Log Diagram

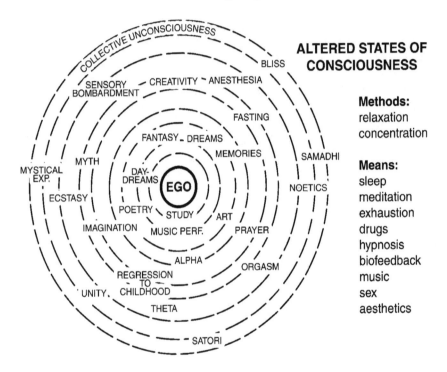

According to Bruscia's (1998a) model, when a music experience becomes so profound that it transcends individual ego boundaries (as can occur for BMGIM clients), it becomes a *transpersonal music experience*. Essentially, this is an aesthetic music experience, deepened to the extent that neither the music nor sense of self are apprehended as separate, finite entities. Thus transpersonal music experience is represented in the model diagram by a circle within the aesthetic music circle. Also according to Bruscia's model, music can function either as a *transpersonal vehicle* or as a *transpersonal space*. Music serves as a transpersonal vehicle when transcendent experiences of the music function as means to transpersonal states of consciousness not integrally linked to the music itself. In contrast, music serves as a transpersonal space when transcendent experiences of the music are ends in themselves.

Figure 2.
Four-Quadrant Diagram of Music Experience

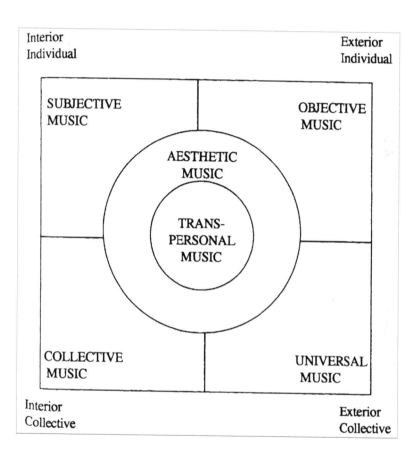

## Typologies

Typologies of BMGIM experiences identify and elaborate upon the various categories of BMGIM experiences, including the transpersonal category. Typologies of this kind are found in a number of BMGIM training manuals.

For one BMGIM training manual, Bruscia (1996a) has compiled a typology consisting of imagery associated with transpersonal BMGIM experiences. Generally, this typology describes forms of imagery which (a) reach beyond the personal; (b) manifest as peak experiences of a religious or spiritual nature; and (c) tend to feel supportive, nurturing, or awesome.

Similarly, typologies in training manuals by Bruscia (1998b) and by Stokes-Stearns, Bush, and Borling (1998) identify a wide variety of transpersonal BMGIM experiences, such as those involving clear light, transforming colors, energy fields, spirit guides, angels, past lives, feelings of incredible beauty and awe, profound silences, a sense of self expanded beyond the body, the surrender of ego to larger forces, unity with God, or unity with the music.

## Clinical Case Studies

A number of clinical BMGIM case studies feature transpersonal dimensions. Some of these cases refer to transpersonal experiences through the term *transpersonal* itself (e.g., Bonny, 1975; Bonny & Savary, 1990; Clark, 1998–1999; Marr, 1998–1999; McKinney, 1993), whereas others imply these experiences through the use of related terms, such as *peak* (e.g., Buell, 1999; Clark, 1991; McIvor, 1998–1999), *spiritual* (e.g., Beck, 1996–1997; Borling, 1992), *transcendent* (e.g., Skaggs, 1997), and *unitive* or *unity* (e.g., Merritt & Schulberg, 1995).

In two cases (Bonny & Savary, 1990; Buell, 1999), clients themselves explicitly conveyed the transpersonal nature of their own experiences (using the term *transpersonal* and/or related descriptive terms). In all other cases, transpersonal experiences were inferred by the BMGIM guide, based upon existing, identifying criteria. A condensed review of BMGIM cases involving transpersonal dimensions will be provided here. (For a detailed summary with references to specific cases, refer to Abrams [2001].)

Transpersonal forms of experience in BMGIM case studies include profound experiences of light; extraordinarily powerful or otherworldly physical sensations; deeply felt positive emotion; identity metamorphoses; collective experiences, or those involving a profound sense of identification with a community, culture, or all humanity; and unitive experiences, or those involving a sense of oneness. Other transpersonal experiences include encounters with sacred spaces, such as religious buildings, heavenly realms, or other transcendent domains; special objects possessing sacred power, wisdom, or healing potential; and supernormal presences or religious guide figures who impart wisdom, blessings, or love. It is worthy of note that not all transpersonal experiences in these cases are positive or pleasant, as some involve pain, fear, hellish visions, or a profound sense of lacking.

Certain BMGIM cases convey struggles of clients and guides in identifying and describing transpersonal experiences, due to their characteristic elusiveness and ineffability. Some of these cases demonstrate the use of logically paradoxical language as an attempt to express the verbally inexpressible.

Although no single music selection or program is featured in BMGIM cases involving transpersonal experiences, the music typically has a sublime, expansive, ethereal, or liturgical character. Across these cases, the programs featured most often are *Peak Experience* (Bonny, 1978b) and *Positive Affect* (Bonny, 1978b), both of which are generally recognized within the BMGIM discipline for their promotion of transpersonal experience (Bruscia, 1996b; Stokes-Stearns, Bush, & Borling, 1998). Other programs which appear often are *Emotional Expression I* (Bonny, 1978b), *Explorations* (originally *Group Experience*) (Bonny, 1978b), *Mostly Bach* (Bonny, 1978b), and *Nurturing* (Bonny, 1978b). Some of these cases contain accounts of transpersonal experiences, explicitly described in terms of the music itself.

Because transpersonal experiences in the BMGIM cases considered here occurred within clinical contexts, each case accounts in some way for the therapeutic benefits of these experiences. Such benefits range from healing and other aspects of change around personal issues, to forms of transformation that transcend matters of the client's individual identity.

## Research

There are three major categories of research concerning transpersonal dimensions of BMGIM. These include investigation of transpersonal BMGIM phenomena based upon (a) researcher self-study, (b) observation, and (c) participant self-report. Descriptions of research within each category now follow.

SELF-STUDY. In a researcher self-study, Hintz (1995) explored the process of empowerment through spiritual experiences in BMGIM. In the study, the researcher used the term *spiritual experience* interchangeably with *transpersonal experience*, and defined it as imagery of a supernatural or religious nature. Hintz noted how these BMGIM experiences led to inner transformation as various forms of self-empowerment.

OBSERVATIONAL STUDIES. Rugenstein (1996) conducted a study in which transpersonal BMGIM experiences and the levels of human development addressed through them were classified using Wilber's (1993) *spectrum of consciousness* framework. Based upon observations of one participant's BMGIM process, the researcher classified several aspects of the participant's experiences as transpersonal, according to Wilber's constructs.

Lewis (1998–1999) utilized an indirect form of observation to explore the transpersonal potential of BMGIM. Through analysis of 148 BMGIM session transcripts, the researcher derived eight categories of transpersonal experience, utilizing the transpersonal psychology literature to guide the categorization. Categories consisted of *archetypal/spiritual* experiences, *body changes*, *deeply positive emotion*, experiences of *light/energy*, *past lives/other psychic* experiences, experiences of *space/time*, *unitive experiences*, and *wisdom*. Because a significant portion of imagery in the 148 transcripts fit into transpersonal categories, the researcher concluded that BMGIM does effectively promote transpersonal experience. In addition, the researcher found that the BMGIM music programs utilized in the most comprehensively transpersonal sessions were (in descending rank order) *Peak Experience* (Bonny, 1978b), *Mostly Bach* (Bonny, 1978b), and *Positive Affect* (Bonny, 1978b).

Kasayka (1991) also explored the transpersonal potential of BMGIM, specifically in terms of the *Peak Experience* (Bonny, 1978b) music program. First, the researcher performed a musical analysis of the program. Next, the researcher examined the extended BMGIM process of several participants, including an in-depth analysis of the session within each participant's process featuring the *Peak Experience* program. In this examination, the researcher made note of where, when, and how segments of the music program occurred with transpersonal experiences based upon conventional definitions of these experiences. Transpersonal experiences identified included those involving phenomena such as clear or golden light, deep emotion, healing or empowering energy, inner transformation, purity, spiritual figures and symbols, unity, etc. The researcher concluded not only that the *Peak Experience* music program effectively promotes transpersonal BMGIM experience, but also that such experience can result in positive inner changes for a client.

SELF-REPORT. Maack and Nolan (1999) investigated the therapeutic value of BMGIM by designing and distributing printed surveys on self-perceived change through BMGIM work, including changes specifically of a transpersonal nature (such as *development of psychic abilities*, *discovery of new parts of the self*, and *spiritual growth*). Survey responses from twenty-five participants (each of whom had some past experience as a BMGIM client) indicated that positive transpersonal changes within the category of *spiritual growth* were fairly common, and that participants considered these changes to be especially important.

Shaw (1995) examined the nature of transpersonal BMGIM experience by interviewing and administering surveys to seventeen BMGIM trainees and one BMGIM trainer. From participant self-reports in the interviews and surveys, the researcher was able to identify a number of experiential themes on transpersonal imagery in the participants' own past BMGIM experiences. These themes included *acquisition of special knowledge and wisdom*, *dialogues with deceased persons*, *encounters with deities and archetypal figures*, *encounters with natural or elemental forces*, *expansion of consciousness*, *inner energy shifts and other unusual physical sensations*, *perceptions of colors and light*, *transformation experiences*, and *unity experiences*. Additional themes included *ineffability*, *lapses in awareness*, and *transcendence of all form and imagery*. Participants reported enduring benefits of these transpersonal experiences, including new outlooks on life, healing, and deepened spirituality.

Dahlstrom (1991) obtained self-reports of sixteen middle-aged women on their experiences of expanded awareness in a group adaptation of BMGIM. The researcher analyzed the self-report contents according to the same eight categories of transpersonal experience identified by Lewis (1998–1999). Findings revealed that thirteen of the sixteen women reported experiences of expanded awareness, some of which fell into transpersonal categories.

Finally, Abrams (2001) examined defining features of transpersonal BMGIM experiences according to self-reports of nine participants with extensive experience as BMGIM clients. Each participant underwent a total of three interviews. In the first interview, participants identified and briefly described several BMGIM experiences which they considered transpersonal, and several which they did not. In the second interview, with the aid of a user-interactive computer program, participants identified various similarities and differences among their own experiences. In the third interview, participants elaborated upon some of the comparisons they made in the second interview. Through a qualitative analysis of all interview data, the researcher derived both an individual definition of transpersonal BMGIM experience for each participant, as well as a model expressing a single composite of all individual definitions.

Abrams (2001) has provided a diagram of the composite model (refer to Figure 3). The diagram consists of two primary dimensions of BMGIM experience, illustrated by a pair of axes. The horizontal axis represents a polarity between the qualities of separateness and unity in both music and imagery components of BMGIM experience, whereas the vertical axis represents a polarity between the qualities of particularity (i.e., specificity and ordinariness) and universality (again, in both music and imagery components of BMGIM experience). As illustrated in the upper right region of the diagram, participants collectively conveyed that the degree to which BMGIM experiences are transpersonal is generally determined by the degree to which both music and imagery components are both unitive and universal.

# TOWARD AN INDIGENOUS THEORY

BMGIM shares elements in common with certain practices involving transpersonal dimensions, such as music-assisted meditation, LSD psychotherapy, biofeedback, and breath work. However, no practice combines elements in quite the way that BMGIM does. This uniqueness of the BMGIM form, along with the diversity of literature on its transpersonal dimensions, calls for an *indigenous* theory of transpersonal BMGIM phenomena, or a coherent set of principles on transpersonal phenomena formulated specifically in accordance with the unique parameters of BMGIM. Such a theory would serve BMGIM practitioners and researchers by providing a relevant, meaningful framework for understanding the transpersonal dimensions of their discipline.

Figure 3.
Diagram of Model Defining Transpersonal BMGIM Experience

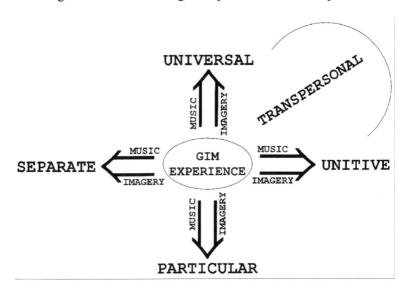

There are several basic requirements for an indigenous theory of transpersonal BMGIM phenomena. First, it must address ways of understanding transpersonal dimensions of BMGIM, specifically in terms of the four primary components comprising the BMGIM form, both individually and in unique combination with one another. These components include classical music listening (more specifically, *music program* listening), imagery, consciousness, and guide. Second, it must include a process model, or a description of the unique manner in which transpersonal BMGIM phenomena occur, and the contexts surrounding their occurrence. Third, it must include a comprehensive definition of transpersonal BMGIM phenomena.

Transpersonal BMGIM phenomena can be understood specifically in terms of the music (Abrams, 2001; Bruscia, 1996b, 1998a; Clark, 1998–1999; Summer, 1992). Many within the BMGIM discipline acknowledge transcendent experiences of the beauty and creativity inherent in music programs (Abrams, 2001). Imagery is another component integral to understanding transpersonal BMGIM phenomena (Abrams, 2001; Kasayka, 1991; Lewis, 1998–1999; Shaw, 1995). This is exemplified by typologies that identify certain forms of imagery as transpersonal (e.g., Bruscia, 1996a, 1998b; Stokes-Stearns, Bush, & Borling, 1998).

It is widely recognized within the BMGIM discipline that transpersonal states of consciousness can be attained through the expansion and deepening of awareness through BMGIM work (i.e., Abrams, 2001; Bonny, 1975, 1978b; Bruscia, 1998a; Bush, 1995; Goldberg, 1994; Summer, 1992). Abrams (2001) has specifically proposed an entire mode of transpersonal consciousness unique to the BMGIM form. The client's relationship to the guide is yet another component inextricable from the BMGIM form. To a certain extent, transpersonal dimensions of this component have been addressed, primarily in the form of instructions for guiding transpersonal BMGIM experiences (e.g., Bruscia, 1998a, 1998b; Stokes-Stearns, Bush, & Borling, 1998). However, the overall matter warrants further consideration.

Although considering transpersonal dimensions of BMGIM in terms of individual BMGIM components helps establish the foundations of an indigenous theory, such a theory must also address an understanding of transpersonal dimensions in terms of *all* components, *in combination with one another*. It must address an understanding that transcends *parts* alone, and that embraces the BMGIM form as a single, indivisible *whole*. Through such an understanding, it becomes possible to conceptualize transpersonal phenomena in terms of the utterly unique, intrinsic nature of BMGIM. Moreover, it becomes possible to formulate part-whole relationships, or the unique roles of each BMGIM component in relation to the overall form, with respect to transpersonal phenomena.

Because BMGIM is a process, an indigenous theory must also incorporate a *process model*, or an elaboration both upon the unique manner in which transpersonal BMGIM phenomena occur, and upon the unique circumstances surrounding their occurrence. A process model carries particularly important clinical implications, as it informs the BMGIM guide about specific ways to proceed when engaging in transpersonal work with a client, and may carry implications regarding the efficacy and clinical value of transpersonal BMGIM work. Several existing models of transpersonal BMGIM phenomena imply aspects of a process (e.g., Bruscia, 1998a; Bush, 1995).

A process model must delineate a developmental progression of transpersonal phenomena, specifically as they manifest within and across BMGIM sessions. Included in this may be a specification of directionality with respect to the process, such as sequential progression in one direction only (unidirectional), in several directions (multidirectional), in a circle (cyclical), or in a manner which does not involve a discrete sequence (nonlinear). The model must also specify the contexts surrounding the emergence of transpersonal BMGIM phenomena. This includes anything within or across BMGIM sessions that elicits, inhibits, is a prerequisite of, or results from transpersonal BMGIM phenomena.

Finally, an indigenous theory requires a comprehensive definition of transpersonal BMGIM phenomena. This definition must take into consideration all relevant components and process elements of BMGIM (such as those considered in the foregoing), and must provide criteria sufficient for distinctly identifying those phenomena which *both* fall within the domain of BMGIM and qualify as transpersonal. (For potentially relevant contributions to a comprehensive definition, refer to Abrams [2001].)

# SUMMARY

Given the value of transpersonal BMGIM work, it is imperative that it be understood in coherent, meaningful ways. These understandings depend upon the discoveries, insights, and perspectives obtained through research, as well as upon the framework of principles and meanings provided by the formulation of an indigenous theory. Thus, there is the need for continuing proliferation of both research and theory development, as both will play an indispensable role in focusing and guiding future work concerning transpersonal dimensions of BMGIM.

## *References*

Abrams, B. (2001). *Defining Transpersonal Experiences of Guided Imagery and Music (GIM)* (Doctoral dissertation, Temple University, 2000). Dissertation Abstracts International-A, 61 (10), 3817.

Achterberg, J. (1985). *Imagery in Healing: Shamanism and Modern Medicine.* Boston, MA: Shambhala.

Anderson, R. (1998). Introduction. In W. Braud and R. Anderson (eds.), *Transpersonal Research Methods for the Social Sciences* (pp. xix–xxxi). Thousand Oaks, CA: Sage.

Assagioli, R. (1971). *Psychosynthesis (Revised Edition)*. New York, NY: Viking Press.

Association for Music and Imagery. (1996). *AMI Training Directory*. Santa Cruz, CA: Author.

Beck, D. M. (1996–1997). Listening with open ears. *Journal of the Association for Music and Imagery, 5*, 25–35.

Bonny, H. L. (1975). Music and consciousness. *Journal of Music Therapy, 12*(3), 121–135.

Bonny, H. L. (1978a). *Facilitating Guided Imagery and Music Sessions. Monograph #1*. Salina, KS: Bonny Foundation.

Bonny, H. L. (1978b). *The Role of Taped Music Programs in the GIM Process. Monograph #2*. Salina, KS: Bonny Foundation.

Bonny, H. L. (1980). *GIM Therapy: Past, Present, and Future Implications. Monograph #3*. Salina, KS: Bonny Foundation.

Bonny, H. L. (Speaker). (1995). *The Story of GIM as Told by Helen Bonny* [Video recording]. Santa Cruz, CA: Association for Music and Imagery.

Bonny, H. L., & Pahnke, W. N. (1972). The use of music in psychedelic (LSD) psychotherapy. *Journal of Music Therapy, 9*(2), 64–87.

Bonny, H. L., & Savary, L. M. (1990). *Music and Your Mind: Listening with a New Consciousness (Revised.Edition)*. Barrytown, NY: Station Hill Press.

Borling, J. E. (1992). Perspectives on growth with a victim of abuse: A Guided Imagery and Music (GIM) case study. *Journal of the Association for Music and Imagery, 1*, 85–97.

Bravo, G., & Grob, C. (1996). Psychedelics and transpersonal psychiatry. In B. W. Scotton, A. B. Chinen, and J. R. Battista (eds.), *Textbook of Transpersonal Psychiatry and Psychology* (pp. 176–185). New York, NY: BasicBooks.

Bruscia, K. E. (1996a). *Guided Imagery and Music: Level One Training Manual*. Phoenixville, PA: Author.

Bruscia, K. E. (1996b). *Guided Imagery and Music: Level Two Training Manual*. Phoenixville, PA: Author.

Bruscia, K. E. (Programmer). (1997a). *Faith* [Music program]. See Appendix E.

Bruscia, K. E. (Programmer). (1997b). *Sublime* [Music program]. See Appendix E.

Bruscia, K. E. (Programmer). (1997c). *Transcendence* [Music program]. See Appendix E.

Bruscia, K. E. (1998a). *Defining Music Therapy (Second Edition)*. Gilsum, NH: Barcelona Publishers.

Bruscia, K. E. (1998b). *Guided Imagery and Music: Level Three B Training Manual.* Phoenixville, PA: Author.

Buell, R. (1999). Emerging through music: A journey toward wholeness with Guided Imagery and Music. In J. Hibben (ed.), *Inside Music Therapy: Client Experiences* (pp. 45–51). Gilsum, NH: Barcelona Publishers.

Bush, C. A. (1995). *Healing Imagery and Music: Pathways to the Inner Self.* Portland, OR: Rudra Press.

Chinen, A. B. (1996). The emergence of transpersonal psychiatry. In B. W. Scotton, A. B. Chinen, and J. R. Battista (eds.), *Textbook of Transpersonal Psychiatry and Psychology* (pp. 9–18). New York, NY: BasicBooks.

Clark, M. (1998-1999). The Bonny Method and spiritual development. *Journal of the Association for Music and Imagery, 6,* 55–62.

Clark, M. F. (1991). Emergence of the adult self in Guided Imagery and Music (GIM) therapy. In K. E. Bruscia (Ed.), *Case Studies in Music Therapy* (pp. 321–331). Gilsum, NH: Barcelona Publishers.

Clarkson, G. (1994). Learning through mistakes: Guided Imagery and Music (BMGIM) with a student in a hypomanic episode. *Journal of the Association for Music and Imagery, 3,* 77–93.

Dahlstrom, S. P. (1991). *The Use of Evoked Experiences of Expanded Awareness in the Adult Woman's Search for Meaning and Purpose in Life* (Doctoral dissertation, The Fielding Institute, 1990). Dissertation Abstracts International-B, 51(8), 4044.

Goldberg, F. S. (1994). Guest editorial: Introduction to the special issue on psychiatric music therapy. *Music Therapy Perspectives,* 12(2), 67–69.

Grof, S. (1985). *Beyond the Brain: Birth, Death, and Transcendence in Psychotherapy.* Albany, NY: State University of New York Press.

Grof, S. (1988). *The Adventure of Self-discovery.* Albany, NY: State University of New York Press.

Grof, S. (1996). Theoretical and empirical foundations of transpersonal psychology. In S. Boorstein (ed.), *Transpersonal Psychotherapy (Second Edition)* pp. 43–64). Albany, NY: State University of New York Press.

Houston, J. (1997). *The search for the Beloved: Journeys in Mythology and Sacred Ppsychology (Second Edition).* New York, NY: Jeremy P. Tarcher/Putnam.

Hintz, M. (1995). *Empowerment through Spiritual Experiences in Guided Imagery and Music: A Self-exploration.* Unpublished master's project, Temple University, Philadelphia, PA.

Jung, C. G. (1956). *Symbols of Transformation.* Princeton, NJ: Princeton University Press.

Jung, C. G. (1969). *The Archetypes and the Collective Unconscious (Second Edition).* Princeton, NJ: Princeton University Press.

Kasayka, R. E. (1991). *To Meet and Match the Moment of Hope: Transpersonal Elements of the Guided Imagery and Music Experience* (Doctoral dissertation, New York University, 1991). Dissertation Abstracts International, 52 (6), 2062.

Keiser Mardis, L. (1986). *Conscious Listening: An Annotated Guide to the ICM Taped Music Programs.* Olney, MD: Archedigm Publications.

Keutzer, C. S. (1978). Whatever turns you on: Triggers to transcendent experiences. *Journal of Humanistic Psychology,* 18 (3), 77–80.

Kovach, A. M. S. (1985). Shamanism and Guided Imagery and Music: A comparison. *Journal of Music Therapy,* 22 (3), 154–165.

Lee, K. J., & Speier, P. L. (1996). Breathwork: Theory and technique. In B. W. Scotton, A. B. Chinen, and J. R. Battista (eds.), *Textbook of Transpersonal Psychiatry and Psychology* (pp. 366–376). New York, NY: Basic Books.

Lewis, K. (1998–1999). The Bonny Method of Guided Imagery and Music: Matrix for transpersonal experience. *Journal of the Association for Music and Imagery,* 6, 63–85.

Maack, C., & Nolan, P. (1999). The effects of Guided Imagery and Music therapy on reported change in normal adults. *Journal of Music Therapy,* 36 (1), 39–55.

Marr, J. (1998–1999). BMGIM at the end of life: Case studies in palliative care. *Journal of the Association for Music and Imagery,* 6, 37–54.

Maslow, A. H. (1970). *Religions, Values, and Peak experiences.* New York, NY: Arkana.

Maslow, A. H. (1971). *The Farther Reaches of Human Nature.* New York, NY: Arkana.

McClellan, R. (1988). *The Healing Forces of Music.* Amity, NY: Amity House.

McIvor, M. (1998–1999). Heroic journeys: Experiences of a Maori group with the Bonny Method. *Journal of the Association for Music and Imagery,* 6, 105–118.

McKinney, C. H. (1993). The case of Therese: Multidimensional growth through Guided Imagery and Music. *Journal of the Association for Music and Imagery,* 2, 99–109.

Merritt, S., & Schulberg, C. (1995). GIM and collective grief: Facing the shadow of the holocaust. *Journal of the Association for Music and Imagery,* 4, 103–120.

Panzarella, R. (1980). The phenomenology of aesthetic peak experiences. *Journal of Humanistic Psychology,* 20(1), 69–85.

Progoff, I. (1963). *The Symbolic and the Real.* New York, NY: Julian Press.

Rugenstein, L. (1996). Wilber's spectrum model of transpersonal psychology and its application to music therapy. *Music Therapy,* 14 (1), 9–28.

Scotton, B. W. (1996). Introduction and definition of transpersonal psychiatry. In B. W. Scotton, A. B. Chinen, and J. R. Battista (Eds.), *Textbook of Transpersonal Psychiatry and Psychology* (pp. 3–8). New York, NY: Basic Books.

Shaw, P. (1995). *Imaging and spirituality in Guided Imagery and Music.* Unpublished master's thesis, University of Auckland, Auckland, New Zealand.

Sheikh, A. A. (Ed.). (1986). *Anthology of Imagery Rechniques.* Milwaukee, WI: American Imagery Institute.

Skaggs, R. (1997). The Bonny Method of Guided Imagery and Music in the treatment of terminal illness: A private practice setting. *Music Therapy Perspectives,* 15(1), 39–44.

Stokes-Stearns, S. J., Bush, C. A., & Borling, J. (1998). *Music and Transpersonal.* Virginia Beach, VA: Mid-Atlantic Training Institute.

Summer, L. (1992). Music: The aesthetic elixir. *Journal of the Association for Music and Imagery, 1,* 43–53.

Vich, M. A. (1988). Some historical sources of the term "transpersonal." *Journal of Transpersonal Psychology,* 20(2), 107–110.

Walsh, R., & Vaughan, F. E. (1996). Comparative models of the person and psychotherapy. In S. Boorstein (Ed.), *Transpersonal Psychotherapy (Second Edition)* pp. 15–30). Albany, NY: State University of New York Press.

Walsh, R. N., & Vaughan, F. (Eds.). (1980). *Beyond Ego.* Los Angeles, CA: J. P. Tarcher.

Wilber, K. (1986). The spectrum of development. In K. Wilber, J. Engler, and D. P. Brown (eds.), *Transformations of Consciousness* (pp. 65–105). Boston, MA: Shambhala.

Wilber, K. (1993). *The Spectrum of Consciousness (Second Edition).* Wheaton, IL: Quest Books.

Wilber, K. (1995). *Sex, Ecology, Spirituality: The Spirit of Evolution.* Boston, MA: Shambhala.

Wilber, K. (1996a). *The Atman Project: A Transpersonal View of Human Development (Second Edition).* Wheaton, IL: Quest Books.

Wilber, K. (1996b). *A Brief History of Everything.* Boston, MA: Shambhala.

Wilber, K. (1996c). *Eye to Eye: The Quest for the New Paradigm (Third Edition).* Boston, MA: Shambhala.

Wilber, K. (1997). *The Eye of Spirit: An Integral Vision for a World gone Slightly Mad.* Boston, MA: Shambhala.

*Chapter Twenty*

# A HOLOGRAPHIC FIELD THEORY MODEL OF THE BONNY METHOD OF GUIDED IMAGERY AND MUSIC (BMGIM)

## Frances Smith Goldberg

*A man's [woman's] conscious wit and will are aiming at something only dimly and inaccurately imagined. Yet all the while the forces of mere organic ripening within him [her] are going on to their own prefigured result, and his [her] conscious strainings are letting loose subconscious allies behind the scenes which in their way work toward rearrangement, the rearrangement toward which all these deeper forces tend is pretty surely definite, and definitely different from what he [she] consciously conceives and determines. It may consequently be interfered with (jammed as it were) by his [her] voluntary efforts toward the true direction. (Hence,) When the new center of energy has been subconsciously incubated so long as to be ready to burst into flower, "hands off" is the only word for us; it must burst forth unaided (William James, cited in Dewey, 1934).*

James wrote this about religious experience, and Dewey saw that James' ideas might well have been written about the antecedents of the creative process. These words equally apply to the BMGIM experience in its exploration of consciousness, a creative process in itself, through the creative genius of classical music. The spiritual, psychological, and creative forces of organic ripening are going on within the psyche, waiting for the proper time to burst forth into flower, carried by the music, the fuel for the BMGIM exploration. "Hands off" is the only word for us; it must burst forth unaided.

In this chapter an expanded, holographic version of the original Field Theory Model of BMGIM (Goldberg, 1992) will be presented. This model is designed to describe the process of bursting into flower through BMGIM. The original model stemmed from many questions about the BMGIM process. How does music evoke imagery? How does music evoke emotion? What accounts for the various expressions of imagery and emotion in response to music or the lack thereof? The original Field Theory Model of BMGIM answered some of these questions, but there were others still unanswered. These further questions had to do with the integrative and transcendent aspects of BMGIM and the relationship to consciousness. Bonny states that consciousness serves as the personal faculty that integrates one's varied perceptions of reality. And she describes BMGIM as an exploration of consciousness (Bonny, 1978). The original Field Theory Model was focused primarily on one part of this exploration. The expanded model attempts to embrace a larger spectrum of the vast potential of BMGIM to actualize one's inner potential in this exploration of consciousness through a creative leap into a new dimension of musical experience and meaning.

The chapter is organized into three sections. First, the original Field Theory Model will be discussed and then new elements will be presented. Finally, implications for clinical practice will be discussed.

## THE ORIGINAL FIELD THEORY MODEL

The original Field Theory Model is based on the literature on music, imagery, and emotion theory; its purpose was to arrive at some understanding of the complex interaction among these elements of the BMGIM experience and the impact of this interaction on the process. Thus, the model puts forth music, imagery, and emotion as the primary elements of the BMGIM experience.

In the model, "music" refers to Western classical music, except where stated otherwise. "Imagery" or "image" refers to experiences of the music during the listening phase of BMGIM, including images in all sensory modalities, kinesthetic images, body sensations, feelings, thoughts and noetic images (an intuitive sense of imaginal events that arise outside of other imagery modes).

Defining emotion requires more discussion. The literature in both emotion theory and psychodynamic psychotherapy are fraught with the use of the same terms in a myriad of ways, making effective communication both within each field and between the two fields difficult. In the psychotherapy literature (Basch, 1988) "affect" is used to describe an overt response that is carried by the autonomic nervous system and comes unbidden from within. This may be experienced before becoming consciously aware of the nature of the stimulus and the reason for the response. "Feeling" is when the basic involuntary affective reaction is related to the self; thus one can say, "I am angry." "Emotion" results from joining feeling states with experience to give personal meaning to complex concepts such as love, hate, etc. Basch considers this to be a model of affective development from infancy to mature adulthood, with the final phase being empathic understanding.

Scherer (2000) has reviewed the literature in emotion theory research over the past few decades. He, and many other emotion theorists, consider emotion to be subsumed under affective states, an umbrella term that also includes mood, interpersonal stance taken toward another person, attitudes, and personality traits (emotionally laden, stable behavior tendencies, e.g., nervous, anxious, hostile, etc.). Most emotion theorists subscribe to a multi-component definition of emotion. The three components, called the "reaction triad" of emotion, are: 1) physiological arousal, 2) motor expression and 3) subjective feeling. These three components of emotion are felt as a unitary experience. (Scherer, 2000).

Since the BMGIM model described here is derived from emotion theory, the working definition of emotion throughout this chapter is: "Emotions are episodes of coordinated changes in several components (including at least neurophysiological activation, motor expression, and subjective feeling but possibly also action tendencies and cognitive processes) in response to external or internal events of major significance to the organism" (Scherer, 2000, p. 138). Subjective feeling is a reflection in the central nervous system of all changes in both the central and peripheral systems during an emotional episode (p. 155). Emotion does not become a subjective feeling until it has been evaluated (Mandler, 1980, 1984; Plutchik, 1984; Scherer, 2000).

In spite of the various definitions of specific terms, the literature in emotion theory and psychotherapy agree that emotional responses begin as physiological arousal (which can occur on the unconscious level), and that an appraisal of the meaning of the arousal is an important part of the process.

## Major Propositions

The original Field Theory Model consisted of five main propositions. These will be presented below.

*Proposition One: In the BMGIM experience image formation is a function of the emotional response to music.*

*Proposition Two: Music may generate conscious or unconscious emotion through direct stimulation of the autonomic nervous system (ANS); emotion, in turn, may evoke the image. Subsequent images may flow from the first as long as emotion connected with that sequence remains. Then the emotional influence of the music may return and a new series of images ensues. This results in a series of music-emotion-imagery cycles.*

Propositions one and two go hand in hand. The emotional element of music is one of the primary factors in the BMGIM process. This is evident in clinical practice where emotionally laden images and overt emotional expression are frequent responses. Music may act directly on the ANS to evoke an emotional response. There is evidence that auditory information may be conveyed by neural circuits within the limbic areas (a part of the brain that is associated with emotion processing) to the hypothalamus (Nauta & Domesick, cited in Thaut, 1990). The hypothalamus is directly connected with the autonomic nervous system. The hypothalamus, in turn, projects to the amygdala (a part of the limbic area that is involved in emotion processing) and the cortex (Aggleton & Mishkin, 1986). This implies a direct connection of music to the autonomic nervous system, the emotion-processing areas of the brain, and to the cortex where it may be processed to conscious awareness.

Emotional responses begin in the autonomic ANS as physiological arousal (Ervin & Martin, 1986; James, 1910; McLean, 1949; Papez, 1937; Schacter & Singer, 1962; Scherer, 2000). Actual ANS arousal supports the intensity and quality of emotional experiences (Mandler, 1984).

Image contents are influenced by emotional states and imagery experiences, in turn, evoke further emotion. Emotion and image are bound and one may lead to the other when the other is out of conscious awareness (Horowitz, 1983, Perry, 1974). The image may hold a central role as translator between the ANS and the brain (Achterberg, 1985). This view is shared by Lusebrink (1990) who states that the image is a bridge between body and mind and between levels of information processing and changes in the body.

If music acts directly upon the ANS and emotion begins in the ANS, and if the image is the mode of communication between the ANS and the brain, it follows that the image would appear to be a representation of emotion during the BMGIM experience. Thus the BMGIM experience may consist of a series of music-emotion-imagery cycles.

*Proposition Three: Imagery arises in the BMGIM experience according to a personal hierarchy.*

The BMGIM process may be likened to that described in Gestalt field theory which refers to a differentiation of a part of the field of awareness into a place of central importance without losing touch with the rest of the field (Latner, 1974; Perls, Hefferline & Goodman, 1951). The music field is always present, but may recede in conscious importance or even seem to disappear as the gestalt, which is the image or emotion, comes into the center of attention.

This gestalt represents whatever is "spontaneously dominant" and is the top of the hierarchy of urgency at that time.

Figure 1.
Field Theory Model of Guided Imagery and Music

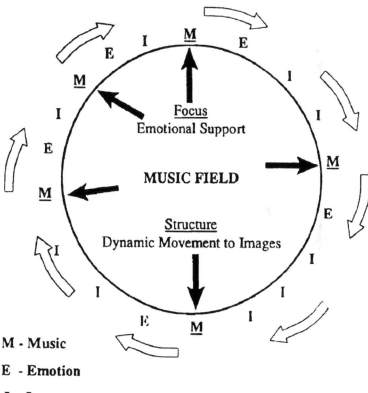

M - Music

E - Emotion

I - Imagery

Figure 1 represents the Field Theory process. The music field stimulates emotion, which evokes the image, and the image in turn may evoke more imagery, generated by the emotional aspect of the image. This creative process continues until the emotion is spent, and then the process begins again, continuing the cycle of music, emotion and imagery. Even though the music may recede from conscious awareness it continues to provide focus and structure for the inner experience, dynamic movement to the images, and emotional support for the listener in the context of an aesthetic experience.

*Proposition Four: Defensive maneuvers develop as a result of the emotional response to music during the BMGIM experience. These are essential to avoid fragmentation or disintegration of the ego.*

The concept of the defensive maneuver is related to the components of an emotional response. Emotions have been called "relevance detectors" because a personal meaning is ascribed to them. The nature of the evaluation determines both the functional response—whether directed toward adaptation to or mastery of the event or situation—and the nature of the person's mental changes that will occur during the emotional episode (Scherer, 2000, p. 138). According to Plutchik (1984), this action/reaction results in a feedback loop in which overt behavior may change the stimulus event in some way and thereby change the inferred cognition, the subjective feeling, the arousal, and the impulses to action. The overall effect is to reduce the threat, stress, or emergency, and re-create a temporary behavioral homeostatic balance.

In BMGIM, the chain of events included in the evaluation leading to action comprises not only the emotional arousal, but also music and imagery. The action may be directed toward the music itself, or toward diverting the emotional response or the image representing the emotion. The emotion may be blocked while the image emerges bereft of feeling, the image itself may be transformed into a less threatening form, or the issue related to the emotion or image may be suppressed. Sometimes the therapist is also included in the emotional evaluation. This may lead to transference and countertransference. Any portion of this process may proceed on either the conscious or unconscious level. The function of the action is to reduce threat or stress posed by the emotional response to music.

In the model, this evaluation/action process in the emotional response has been referred to as a "defensive maneuver." Defensive maneuvers in BMGIM are an adaptive means of coping with deeply emotional and potentially stressful or threatening experiences, and they are essential to avoid fragmentation or disintegration of the ego. Defensive maneuvers have been observed on all levels of BMGIM experience from psychodynamic to transpersonal. This process is not synonymous with the Freudian defense mechanism, however. Defensive maneuvers also include positive experiences, such as the appearance of helpers in the form of animals, people, or archetypal or spiritual figures. Defensive maneuvers are those that help the person not only to cope with stress or threat during the BMGIM experience, but also to achieve mastery and build power to move deeper into the issues at hand.

*Proposition Five: Deep emotional responses to music (including positive emotions, such as joy or bliss, as well as the more negative emotions, such as sadness or anger) will result in conscious or unconscious images and the possibility of defensive maneuvers.*

This proposition has to do with levels of emotional arousal to music along the dimension of intensity (see Thaut, 1990). Obviously, all music experiences do not lead to potentially stressful or threatening emotion. The critical factors seem to be the emotional state of the listener, the degree of focus on the music, the match between the music and the listener, and the music itself. Although these factors interact in a very complex way, it appears that provided there is a good enough match between the person and the music:

(a) To the extent that emotionally charged issues are active in a person's life, the music will stimulate a deep emotional response and conscious or unconscious images; and

(b) The more intense the focus on the music and the inner experience the more likely the deeper emotional response will be experienced, along with conscious or unconscious images.

## Summary of the Original Field Theory Model

These five propositions draw a very complex picture of the interaction of the three major elements of the BMGIM process: music, emotion, and imagery. Imagery in the BMGIM process may be a function of the emotional experience of music. The mechanism for the emotional response to music may be direct action on the ANS, producing imagery that carries sufficient emotional content to generate more images. When the initial emotion is spent the process begins again, resulting in a circular experience of music perception, conscious and unconscious emotional stimulation, and imagery experience. The gestalt of emotion and imagery in the BMGIM experience may arise in a personal hierarchy representing whatever is spontaneously dominant for the listener.

The intensity of emotional experience may result in the formation of defensive maneuvers as a means of coping with stress or threat. These maneuvers may be the outcome of unconscious evaluation of the emotional experience and an action to manage the resulting stress or threat. This maneuver may explain such phenomena in BMGIM sessions as sudden shifts in image content, little or no overt emotion in spite of emotionally laden images, or the appearance of helpers. Defensive maneuvers are an adaptive means of coping with the emotional response to music and are essential to avoid fragmentation or disintegration of the ego. These maneuvers may also explain how the person achieves mastery and builds power to continue to confront difficult issues in the BMGIM experience.

The conditions necessary to sufficient emotional intensity for images to be generated while listening to music are rather complex. However, the focus on the music and inner experience, the extent to which emotionally charged issues are present, and the match between the person and the music seem to be primary factors, along with the qualities of the music itself. Under such conditions images may emerge in many situations, such as in concert halls, at home, while performing, or during improvisational music. In BMGIM every effort is made to provide sufficient inner focus and to make a good enough match between the state of the client and the music selected for the session, resulting in the rich imagery experience characteristic of BMGIM sessions.

## THE HOLOGRAPHIC MODEL

The inspiration for this part of the Holographic Field Theory Model (in addition to the questions raised at the beginning of this chapter) began when reading Wilber's (1979) ideas about the need for various therapies to address various parts of the person. He suggests that the many models and systems of therapy were developed in an effort to meet differing levels of the person's self-identity, which he describes as the spectrum of consciousness. It was clear that BMGIM therapy addresses all of these self-identities or aspects of the Self. BMGIM is an exploration of consciousness, the entire spectrum. Emotion and imagery represent the content of this exploration. This model also owes a debt of gratitude to Kenny (1989) whose Field of Play theory of music therapy so beautifully illustrates the usefulness of fields in describing the essentially nonverbal experience of music in therapy.

The new elements of this model build on Bonny's (1978) Cut Log diagram of consciousness, integrating the original Field Theory Model, and expand the diagram in two ways. First, the rings have been described in keeping with current ideas about consciousness, object relations theories of therapy, Jungian depth psychology, transpersonal psychology, and the interaction of spiritual and psychological growth. Second, the model has been expanded to a holographic field.

The holographic model brings four new propositions which describe: The nature of the model, the various states of consciousness encountered in the BMGIM process, the role and locus of the Self, and the process of growth and its psychospiritual aspects.

*Proposition Six: The BMGIM process can be viewed as a holographic field including music, the music-emotion-imagery cycles, the Self, and states of consciousness.*

Imagine the original Field Theory Model (Figure 1) as a hologram embedded in the field of music. This implies a more fluid movement through the music-emotion-imagery cycles since any part of a hologram carries all parts of the hologram. In this holographic field, however, rather than one circle of music-emotion-imagery sequences, there is an infinite number—vast possibilities in the form of circles. These rings of possibilities represent various states of consciousness.

It is as if the rings of the Cut Log diagram have been separated and each has its own independent axis around a central nucleus. These rings are the music-emotion-image sequences in various states of consciousness. This infinite number of holographic rings embedded in the field of music represents consciousness, the whole Self, the vast world that represents our true Selves. Here "Self" refers to that part of the person that is not the ego; it is larger than the ego. It is the Self in both Jungian and spiritual terms, the totality of the person. At the same time, the Self is at the core of these rings and is the nucleus around which the whole is organized. (See Figure 2.)

Some of the states of consciousness are named. Closest to the center of the hologram are rings representing the ego, and the persona (the face that we present to the world, the roles that we play in everyday life). Other rings near the center represent those states of consciousness where we encounter conscious and unconscious issues through images. This is the world of biographical material that needs to be worked through in order to address internal conflicts and strengthen the ego; it is the psychodynamic domain. Also among these rings are body states of consciousness where both psychodynamic and physical issues are encountered. Other body states of consciousness communicate through body sensations that great change or transformation is taking place within, even though the change cannot yet be named. Further out (or deeper in consciousness) is that state where mind and body come together, an experience of true integration and congruence of the body-mind.

Figure 2
Holographic Model of GIM

Other rings include various states of consciousness that serve both psychodynamic and spiritual growth. These are where the perinatal matrices (Grof, 1985), fairy tales and myths, the shadow, the collective unconscious, and the archetypes are encountered. Also included here are creative states of consciousness and aesthetic states. The aesthetic states of consciousness are of particular interest in this model, because, among other experiences, they represent an encounter with the music. BMGIM fosters a relationship with the music beyond listening. It is in these states that there is potential to actually become the music, of music to bring healing of the body-mind, of music to become the caring, omnipotent "other," offering an experience of unconditional love that is far beyond the capacity of the very best therapist. It is in this relationship with music that many experience the spiritual, an encounter with the Divine.

Then there are the rings where transcendental experiences such as death and unity consciousness are encountered. These are rings of transpersonal and spiritual states of consciousness. It is in these states that the journey beyond the ego proceeds.

*Proposition Seven: The Self is both a centering, organizing principle and a part of all states of consciousness that knows what it needs, and seeks and finds it through its own personal hierarchy.*

Consciousness represents all that is, the complete whole. Therefore the Self is already the whole. It is a part of each state of consciousness and also the nucleus of the holographic field. It is the center, the place where integration takes place. The Self is also a spiral, weaving through the states of consciousness in the service of integrating them in the center. The state accessed at any given moment is determined by whatever is spontaneously dominant on a personal hierarchy. This hierarchy not only includes content or issue (as stated above), but also the state of consciousness through which to approach the content.

The Self is also an observer of the process, leading to reflective distance on the psychodynamic level. On the transpersonal level this observation may lead to disidentification from egoic self-concepts. The Self also strives to reveal its true nature as it seeks spiritual growth and ultimately unity consciousness and the experience of the Divine.

*Proposition Eight: The BMGIM process is one of expansion of the Self, fueled by the music, to ever increasing access to the various parts of the Self that have been here-to-fore unencountered, undeveloped or out of conscious awareness, bringing them back to the center for integration.*

The Self is a spiral that seeks what it needs to grow and expand by spiraling through the field of consciousness, exploring the space, and attaching wherever it needs to be to do its work. Imagine this spiraling and attachment like that of the tendril of a vine. The tendril reaches out and waves around until it finds where it needs to be and then grabs hold, eventually moving on to another place as it grows. So, too, does the Self in its exploration carried by the music. Like the spiral in nature the spiraling Self attaches in whatever state of consciousness it needs in the moment. This may be one state for an entire session or over several sessions; or it may be different states during one session or over several sessions.

As the Self explores, it encounters the shadow, confirms its own beauty, and touches the numinous. The music vivifies the process and brings the Self face to face with its demons, its fears, its polarities, its very soul, and brings it back to the center for integration. It is a process of multidimensional expansion of the Self, fueled by the music. BMGIM enables the person to grow and expand from building the ego to ego transcendence.

*Proposition Nine: The BMGIM process facilitates psychological and spiritual growth in an integrated manner.*

The integration of spiritual and psychological growth seems to be inherent in the BMGIM experience for those who have reached sufficient growth in one area to proceed in the other. Many people move in and out of spiritual states of consciousness throughout their BMGIM therapy. Ego development and spiritual development need to proceed hand in hand (Almaas, 1988; Engler, 1993; Vaughan, 1995), and BMGIM seems to be particularly suited for this purpose.

## Summary of the Holographic Model

In the Holographic Field Theory Model of BMGIM the field represents consciousness, the whole Self, the larger Self in Jungian and spiritual terms, embedded in the field of music. The field consists of the Self, music-emotion-imagery cycles, various states of consciousness, and the music. Each of the holographic rings representing various states of consciousness has its own axis around a central nucleus, the Self, and consists of music-emotion-imagery cycles. Some of the rings have been named, but their number is infinite, and the boundaries among them are blurred. There is a great deal of overlap among them at the same time that they are discrete states and part of the larger holographic whole. There is also no hierarchy in this field. One state is not better, worse, higher, or lower than another. The only hierarchy is the personal one of each person, each psyche. The music fuels the movement of the Self through this field.

The Self is located in all parts of the hologram and serves an integrative function by spiraling through states of consciousness to bring various aspects of the Self to the center for integration. The Self proceeds on a personal hierarchy that includes content and issue through emotion and imagery that arise in a gestalt out of the field of music. This hierarchy also includes the state of consciousness through which to do its work. The Self also has an observing role that may lead to reflective distance and to disidentification with egoic self-concepts.

The Self also appears to move inherently toward revealing its true nature, that of a spiritual being. Spiritual states of consciousness are regularly accessed in the psychotherapy of many people, which seems to indicate that BMGIM is especially suited to the integration of psychological and spiritual growth. The entire process is one of expansion as the Self gathers more and more in the various states of consciousness and brings them to the center for integration.

Defensive maneuvers arise during the BMGIM experience as a means of coping with emotional stress or threat during the exploration of consciousness.

These maneuvers are a necessary process in order to protect the ego from fragmentation or disintegration. Some people are not able to generate sufficient defensive maneuvers and will need some type of modification of the BMGIM procedure. Everyone who embarks on this journey is not yet ready for its intensity.

## IMPLICATIONS FOR CLINICAL PRACTICE

### Guiding

The first implication for clinical practice is confirmation of nondirective guiding. As guides, we need to keep hands off and allow the personal hierarchy to unfold, as long as the person is not in danger of emotional flooding. One of the most important aspects of BMGIM therapy is to come to trust that inherent movement toward growth and healing that is in each person. If we impose ourselves too much in the BMGIM process, the client is robbed of the chance to truly experience this. We have to allow the music to energize this inherent movement toward wholeness at its own pace.

### Process

As guides, we must also respect the process and understand the role of defensive maneuvers. Throughout the BMGIM process defensive maneuvers may be more or less evident, depending on the individual's perception of threat or stress, the person's psychological structure, and the degree to which the person is already stressed and therefore compromised in coping capacity. The presence of defensive maneuvers is a sign of healthy ego strength. The therapist can observe defensive maneuvers as a guide for managing each BMGIM session as well as the BMGIM series and course of the therapy or growth work. Defensive maneuvers give important clues to ego strength or lack of it and also provide flags for emotionally laden issues.

The healthier person generates defensive maneuvers when necessary and also uses the music as a transitional object to keep tension and anxiety at a manageable level (Goldberg, 1995). These healthier persons are likely to move through defensive maneuvers fairly quickly during a session or series. Defensive maneuvers may be what enable clients to build power and move deeper and deeper into their conflicts, achieving mastery and healing.

It was undoubtedly observation of defensive maneuvers that led to early impressions that BMGIM is a self-limiting process and that people will not go where they are not ready to go. Clinical practice over the years has shown that this early impression does not apply to everyone, especially many people who come into therapy. Special care is required in BMGIM sessions with these clients (E. Bonny, 1988; H. Bonny, 1980, 1994; Goldberg, 1994, 1995; 2000, Summer, 1988).

## Managing Clinical Populations

Those clinical populations, who by their nature have compromised ego strength, are less able to form defensive maneuvers and are more vulnerable to overwhelming emotion and unmanageable anxiety. Here clinical populations include those who have well-developed ego structure, but are dealing with major life situations that bring narcissistic wounding. This may include people suffering from PTSD, sexual abuse, auto accidents, or major illnesses, such as cancer or AIDS. Any number of life issues can propel people into a vulnerable state that compromises their ability to cope. Often their only recourse in BMGIM sessions is to precipitously stop the session or refuse further treatment. Some people are not even able to do that, and they are susceptible to emotional flooding or re-traumatization during the BMGIM process.

There are other people who appear quite healthy on the surface, but need to cut themselves completely off from their emotions to such an extent that they are not able to have a BMGIM experience. This may be termed the ultimate defensive maneuver. Some of these people are able to eventually use BMGIM if they are first involved in some of the modifications discussed below. Observation of defensive maneuvers, or the absence of them, provides important information for managing sessions with more vulnerable people. The maneuvers can be a guide to the frequency of BMGIM sessions, the degree of structure the client requires, the type of music, the length of the session, and how much and what type of support the client needs during the session.

## Modifications

FREQUENCY OF SESSIONS. It may then be necessary to modify the BMGIM approach. This includes how frequently BMGIM sessions are given as opposed to talk sessions. The use of other arts, such as drawing and writing, with or without music, are excellent alternatives under these circumstances. These activities allow people to externalize threatening emotion, which helps to build ego strength.

MUSIC. Another modification is to give shorter music sessions by not using a whole music program (see Ritchey-Vaux, 1993). Spontaneous programming—cutting and pasting cuts from different music programs—can also be effective, choosing each selection to provide whatever support the client requires in the moment. For example, spontaneous programming can be used to provide more musical structure throughout the music session. More structure can be provided, for example, by choosing Bach or Pachelbel instead of Vaughn-Williams or Ravel. Spontaneous programming can also be used to develop a less emotionally intense program. It may be necessary to use non-classical music, such as the more grounded new age music, to sufficiently reduce emotional intensity. My experience is that vulnerable clients can do excellent work with music that has no big shifts, such as increase or decrease in volume or sudden shift in orchestration. Simpler music seems to be more effective because it keeps tension at a manageable level, thereby increasing the client's ability to form defensive maneuvers when needed.

GUIDING. Sometimes modifying guiding technique is necessary. Often when people have little coping capacity, they need help in developing defensive maneuvers. This might mean being more directive by asking leading questions, such as, "Is there anyone there who can help you?" or "Is there someplace else you'd like to be?" It may be necessary to become very directive and suggest the client find a safe place or guide the client to a safe place when the experience is too overwhelming.

## PSYCHOSPIRITUAL GROWTH
## AND DEVELOPMENT

Another implication of this model has to do with the interaction between psychological growth and spiritual growth. The movement through various states of consciousness often involves moving in and out of spiritual states even though the client is in the midst of major psychodynamic work. Almaas (1988) and Vaughan (1995) have both addressed the issue of the need for psychological and spiritual growth to proceed hand in hand. This is quite evident in BMGIM and should be addressed directly by the therapist when it shows up in the client's sessions. BMGIM guides need to be familiar with this interaction and prepared to deal with it with their clients. Difficulties in spiritual development impede psychological growth and development, and if that is a factor in a stuck therapy process the therapist needs to recognize it. By the same token psychological problems can impede spiritual growth.

The BMGIM therapist also needs to recognize and understand spiritual emergency and be able to make a referral or get a consultation for additional help. Wilbur (1986) outlines some of the dangers on the spiritual path. These can be helpful in evaluating possible spiritual emergency and determining appropriate referral or consultation. (See also Bragdon, 1988; Grof & Grof, 1990; Lukoff, Lu & Turner, 1990; Walsh & Vaughan, 1993.)

Some people seek out BMGIM therapy as a means to spiritual transcendence, but are not willing to do the basic work. The ego must develop before it can be transcended. As Engler (1993) points out, one must be somebody before one can be nobody. When the BMGIM therapist finds this tendency in a client, this must be addressed.

One more implication of this aspect of the theory is that the BMGIM therapist must do her/his own work toward spiritual development. It is only when the therapist has some sense of the journey that he/she is able to identify and respond to spiritual issues as they arise in BMGIM therapy.

## SUMMARY

In this chapter the original Field Theory Model of BMGIM has been reviewed and updated to The Holographic Field Theory Model of BMGIM. Implications for clinical practice have been discussed. An important aspect of this model is the concept of the defensive maneuver, which when heeded by the therapist allows BMGIM therapy to proceed in safety. This model is a description of the holistic, person-centered process of BMGIM that is grounded in humanistic and transpersonal psychology values. It is a hologram that acknowledges the inner wisdom of the client to use the energy of the music to carry her or him on an exploration of consciousness in the client's own personal hierarchy. Through this exploration the Self spirals through various states of consciousness in the form of music-emotion-imagery cycles and brings back to the center parts of the Self that have been previously unrecognized. BMGIM appears to be especially effective for the integration of spiritual and psychological growth as is evidenced by the frequency of spiritual states of consciousness occurring during psychodynamic therapy. The Bonny Method of Guided Imagery and Music is a multidimensional process of expansion toward integration, healing and transformation.

## *References*

Achterberg, J. (1985). Imagery in Healing: Shamanism in Modern Medicine. Boston: New Series Library.

Aggleton, J., & Mishkin, M. (1986). The amygdala: Gateway to the emotions. In R. Plutchik & H. Kellerman [eds.] *Emotion: Theory, research, and experience: Volume Three – Biological Foundations of Emotions* (pp. 281–299). New York: Academic Press.

Almaas, A. H. (1988). *The Pearl Beyond Price.* Berkeley, CA: Diamond Books.

Basch, M. F. (1988). *Understanding Psychotherapy.* New York: Basic Books.

Bonny, E. (1988). *Clinical Treatment of Adult Children of Alcoholics with Guided Imagery and Music.* Unpublished manuscript.

Bonny, H. (1978). *The Role of Taped Music Programs in the GIM Process.* Monograph # 2. Salina, KS: Bonny Foundation.

Bonny, H. (1980). *G.I.M. Therapy: Past, Present and Future Implications.* Monograph #3. Salina, KS: Bonny Foundation.

Bonny, H. (1994). Twenty-one years later: A GIM update. *Music Therapy Perspectives,* 12 (2), 70–74.

Bragdon, E. (1988). *A Sourcebook for Helping People in Spiritual Emergency.* Los Altos, CA: Lightening Up Press.

Dewey, J. (1934). *Art as Experience.* Harvard lectures on aesthetics.

Engler, J. H. (1993). Becoming somebody and nobody: Psychoanalysis and Buddhism. In R. Walsh, and F. Vaughn. [eds]. *Paths Beyond Ego.* Los Angeles: Tarcher.

Ervin, R. & Martin, J. (1986). Neurophysiological bases of the primary emotions. In R. Plutchik & H. Kellerman [eds.] *Emotion: Theory, research, and experience: Volume Three – Biological Foundations of Emotions* (pp. 145–170). New York: Academic Press.

Goldberg, F. (1992). Images of emotion: The role of emotion in Guided Imagery and Music. *Journal of the Association for Music and Imagery,* 1, 5–17.

Goldberg, F. (1994). The Bonny Method of Guided Imagery and Music as individual and group treatment in a short-term acute psychiatric hospital. *Journal of the Association for Music and Imagery,* 3, 19–33.

Goldberg, F. (1995) The Bonny Method of Guided Imagery and Music. In T. Wigram, B. Saperston & R. West. (eds), *The Art and Science of Music Therapy: A Handbook.* Switzerland: Hardwood Academic Publishers.

Goldberg, F. (2000). I am the creator and the created: A woman's journey from loss to wholeness. *Beiträge zur Musiktherapie*, 10, 47–58.

Grof, C. & Grof, S. (1990). *The Stormy Search for the Self*. Los Angeles, CA: Tarcher.

Grof, S. (1985). *Beyond the Brain*. Albany, NY: SUNY Press.

Horowitz, M. (1983) *Image Formation and Psychotherapy* [rev.ed.] New York: Aronson.

Kenny, C. (1989). *The Field of Play: A Guide for the Theory and Practice of Music Therapy*. Atascadero CA: Ridgeview Publishing Company.

James, W. (1910). *Psychology*. New York, NY: Holt.

Latner, J. (1974). *The Gestalt Therapy Book*. New York, NY: Bantam Books.

Lukoff, D., Lu, F., & Turner, R. (1992). Toward a more culturally sensitive DSM IV, Psychoreligious and psychospiritual problems. *Journal of Nervous and Mental Disease*. 180 (10), 673–682.

Lusebrink, V. (1990).. *Imagery and Visual Expression in Therapy*. New York: Plenum Press.

Mandler, G. (1980). The generation of emotion: A psychological theory. In R. Plutchik & H. Kellerman (eds.) *Emotion: Theory, research, and experience: Volume One – Theories of Emotions*. New York, NY: Academic Press.

Mandler, G. (1984). Consciousness, imagery and emotion—With special reference to autonomic imagery. *Journal of Mental Imagery*, 8, 87–94.

McLean, P. (1949). Psychosomatic disease and the "visceral brain." *Psychosomatic Medicine*. 11, 338–353.

Papez, J. (1937). A proposed mechanism of emotion. *Archives of Neurology and Psychiatry,* 38, 725–743.

Perls, F. Hefferline, R. & Goodman, P. (1951). *Gestalt Therapy*. New York: Dell.

Perry, J. (1974). *The Far Side of Madness*. Englewood Cliffs, NJ: Prentice Hall.

Plutchik, R. (1984). Emotions and imagery. *Journal of Mental Imagery*, 8, 195–112.

Ritchey Vaux, D. (1993). BMGIM applied to the 50-minute hour. *Journal of the Association for Music and Imagery*. 2, 29–34.

Schacter, S. & Singer, J. (1962). Cognitive, social and physiological determinants of emotional state. *Psychological Review*, 69, 379–399.

Scherer, K. R. (2000). Psychological Models of Emotion. In J. Borod [ed]. *The Neuropsychology of Emotion*. Oxford, UK: Oxford University Press.

Summer, L. (1988). *Guided Imagery and Music in the Institutional Setting*. St. Louis, MO: MMB Music.

Thaut, M. (1990). Neuropsychological processes in music therapy. In R. Unkefer (ed.) *Music therapy in the Treatment of Adults with Mental Disorders*. New York: Schirmer Books.

Vaughan, F. (1995). *The Inward Arc (Second Edition)*. Nevada City, CA: Blue Dolphin.

Walsh, R. & Vaughan, F. (1993). *Paths beyond Ego*. Los Angeles, CA: Tarcher.

Wilbur, K. (1979). *No Boundary*. Boston: New Science Library.

Wilbur, K. Engler, J. & Brown, D. (1986). *Transformations of Consciousness*. Boston: Shambhala.

*Chapter Twenty-One*

# A NEUROPSYCHOLOGICAL THEORY OF TRAUMATIC IMAGERY IN THE BONNY METHOD OF GUIDED IMAGERY AND MUSIC (BMGIM)

# Dag Körlin

The Bonny Method of Guided Imagery and Music (BMGIM) is a holistic process, where the music interacts with the mind to evoke memories, affects/emotions, imagery for all senses, and cognitions (Bonny, 1978a, 1978b, 1980). The images present as symbols, but also as unprocessed sensory, bodily, and affective experiences. Symbolic images may encompass any combination of aesthetic, psychodynamic, archetypal, and transpersonal realms. This world of imagery is evoked by listening to selected classical music while in an altered state of consciousness, facilitated and safeguarded by a guide.

The symbolic imagery evoked in BMGIM can be seen as representations of the traveler's resources and difficulties as they are shaped by important relationships and events. However, overwhelming physical and psychological abuse, sudden illness, accidents, or loss of important persons are often not manifested in symbolic imagery. Instead, memories of the trauma tend to recur as direct sensory and affective reexperiences. Bodily pain and other perceptions may be disconnected from each other and the recall of, for example, abuse by a parent, spouse, or peers. Affects of fear, despair, rage. and loss may also be disconnected, chaotic, or numbed, and difficult to communicate during the music experience. In talking about the experience afterward, the event itself may be remembered correctly or with distortion of the where, what, when. and why of the trauma. In some cases, memory of the traumatic episode is totally disconnected from the reexperience in the music. The self is perceived to be vulnerable, incompetent, worthless, or even nonfunctional.

This chapter explores, in neuropsychological terms, this spectrum of reactions to trauma, and the potential of BMGIM to access and reintegrate traumatic memories. The usefulness of BMGIM in the treatment of traumatic conditions has been prominently described in the literature (e.g. Bonny, 1989; Borling, 1992; Bishop, 1994; Goldberg, 1992, 1994; Picket and Sonnen, 1993). Integration of neuropsychology and psychotherapy is a fruitful new field of investigation (e.g. Siegel, 1995; Shevring, 1996). For readers unfamiliar in this field, the neuropsychological concepts of this chapter may require an extra effort.

From a neuropsychological point of view, traumatic imagery represents a failure of the brain's information processing systems to integrate traumatic perceptions and affects into a cognitively and emotionally coherent narrative. The brain has a multitude of "mind languages," such as perceptions from the senses, autonomic and affective reactions, memories, images, and thoughts—all forming neuropsychological units, and all within the range of imagery that may occur in BMGIM. Each of these information systems uses a distinct code that cannot be directly understood by another system. The translation is done by associational linking of the different sensory codes into a larger so-called neuronal network, speaking yet another language. Normally, the experience of an event from each of the sensory languages, together with sensory memories, are translated into a meaningful whole perception. This information is associated with the languages of bodily and emotional memory and social cognition and translated into images and words. In the process, larger and larger associational networks are formed (see Siegel, 1999). The constant integration of different qualities of information into a coherent whole creates autobiographical memory—a sense of continuity of self across time, linking past experiences with present perceptions and anticipations of the future. The integrative process strives toward narrative coherence, reflected in both the way a life story is told, and the nonverbal manner in which life activities are lived (Siegel, 1999; Tulving et al, 1994).

The integrative process of associational linking is thought to be disrupted through the excessive and prolonged release of stress hormones caused by overwhelming traumatic events. Protective "divided attention" during an overwhelming experience also impairs the associational process. Experiences tend to remain as unintegrated perceptual and affective memories that, when triggered by external or internal associations, intrude into awareness without conscious control. This impairs, or destroys, the sense of functioning self.

Several concepts, important for a neuropsychological understanding of trauma, will be briefly outlined as a prelude to the statement of the theory. They are discursive and analogic symbolization, explicit and implicit memory, vitality affect, categorical affect, emotion, and dissociation.

Discursive and analogic symbolization are two major forms of information processing, using different codes or languages. Simply put, discursive symbolization processes information through the word and analogic symbolization through the image. These major forms of symbolization utilize explicit (verbal and conceptual) memories and implicit (nonverbal, perceptual, bodily, and emotional) memories (Siegel, 1999, chapters 2 and 5).

Traumatic images are essentially implicit (nonverbal) memories dissociated from autobiographical memory. They are not repressed in the sense of a stable defense mechanism. Repressed memories and affects have lost contact with consciousness in a stable way (Basch, 1988). Traumatic memories are essentially dissociated, which means that they have an on-off quality, being either unconscious or intruding into consciousness (van der Kolk, 1996).

Dissociation is a term with many meanings (Spiegel, 1996; Waller et al, 1996; Putnam, 1997). For the purpose of this chapter, it is used in the sense of disconnection between psychological functions that are normally integrated (American Psychiatric Association, 1994). The focus will be on dissociation of discursive and analogic symbols, explicit and implicit memories, and affect.

Vitality affects are bodily profiles of arousal such as surges of energy and strength (Stern, 1985). Categorical affects, for example, interest, enjoyment, fear, and distress (Tomkins, 1962–1963) differentiate into emotions by being related to the self, relationships, and to discursive concepts (Basch, 1988), enabling one to say "You make me glad." Dissociated affect may manifest as alternating states of chaotic affect and numbness, both being disconnected from the self and the discursive word.

The establishment of a coherent perceptual memory and cognitive understanding of trauma are partial goals. Cognitive understanding has to be integrated with emotion, social context, and imagery to reestablish a sense of functioning self and autobiographical memory.

Based on these concepts, and the author's experience working with over 200 traumatized patients in group and individual BMGIM, a theory will be forwarded that attempts to explain the evocation and integration of traumatic memories.

Music will be proposed to evoke traumatic imagery, or cause degradation of symbolic imagery, in two ways. One pathway carries psychophysical alarm qualities of strong dynamics, transience, or rhythmicity. The other mediates threatening symbolic musical gestalt.

Through cyclical resource imagery (Bishop, 1994), traumatic imagery and affects can be "owned" and made available for symbolization. Inner resources are proposed to include functional, implicit memories and vitality affects of protection and nurturing.

Processing of traumatic imagery is mediated by the interplay between discursive symbolization (through the word), and analogic symbolization (through imagery and creative expression). This interplay is illustrated by the metaphor of the "Symbolization Triangle." Reassociation of traumatic affects with images and words creates autobiographical memory.

Informed by this perspective, implications for management and music choice will be outlined.

To provide a basis for the following theory, which uses unfamiliar concepts for those not schooled in neuropsychology, some basics are described, including their relevance for BMGIM and trauma. These basics include neuroanatomy (Figure 1a, b, and c), memory, symbolic representation, affect/emotion, perception and imagery. This prepares the ground for the treatment of the theory, beginning with the paragraph "Symbolic and Traumatic Imagery in BMGIM." From this point, structure will basically follow the theoretical propositions above.

For further study, the reader is referred to *The Developing Mind: Toward a Neurobiology of Interpersonal Experience* by Siegel (1999).

## BASIC NEUROANATOMY

The brain is considered to consist of three interconnected parts—the subcortical or "lower" areas, the "higher" neocortex, and the intermediately located limbic system.

The subcortical areas, including the brain stem, mediate states of arousal and the physiological states of the body, like temperature, respiration, and heart rate. The thalamus, at the top of the brain stem, serves as a gateway and relay station of incoming sensory information. It has extensive connections with other parts of the brain, including the limbic system and the areas of sensory perception in the neocortex.

The neocortex hosts areas for perceptions of the different sensory modalities like sight, sound, smell etc. It mediates more complex information processing such as perception, coordination of movement, encoding of permanent memory, and symbolization. The orbitofrontal cortex (frontal cortex behind the eyes), is by some regarded as an extension of the limbic system. The orbitofrontal cortex in the right hemisphere (right half of the brain) especially may play a major role in integrating memory (Wheeler et al., 1997), attachment (Shore, 1997), emotion (Tucker, 1992), bodily representation and regulation (Damasio, 1994), and social cognition (Baron-Cohen, 1995).

Figure 1.

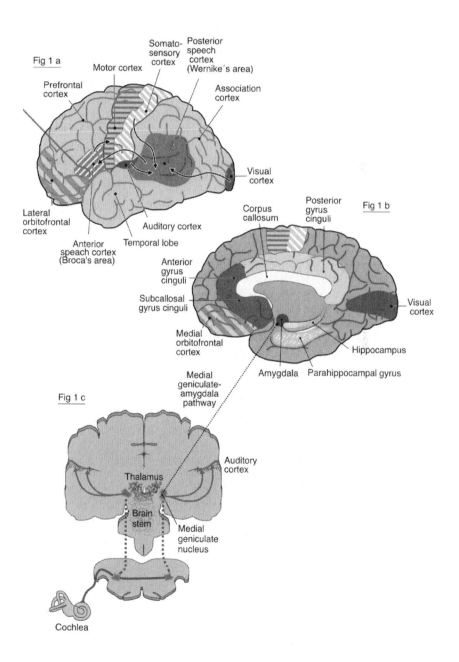

The centrally located limbic system plays a role in coordinating the activity of higher and lower brain structures and consists of two parts, functioning through respectively explicit (verbal) and implicit (nonverbal) memory (Mega et al, 1997). The explicit system includes the lateral (toward the side) orbitofrontal cortex, the hippocampus, and the posterior (toward the back) part of the gyrus cinguli. It plays a central role in consciously accessible verbal memory, and attention to external reality. The implicit system includes the medial (toward the middle) orbitofrontal cortex, anterior (toward the front) gyrus cinguli, and the amygdala. These are thought to mediate unconscious appraisal of meaning, emotion, and social cognition. The amygdala which, simply put, determines like-or-dislike of incoming sensations, including music, serves as an "alarm bell," warning the brain of danger. This system, and the lower parts of the brain, also house the hypothalamus and the pituitary which are responsible for bodily equilibrium.

There is an estimated one hundred billion neurons, each with an estimated ten thousand connections, or synapses, with other neurons. In the synapse, the signal may branch to other connected neurons, which in turn may branch to yet another set of neurons, making an estimated sum of one million billion connections (Green et al, 1998; Kandel and Schwartz, 1992). This branching forms complex "neural networks," capable of firing in a myriad of patterns called "neural net profiles." A firing pattern is considered to constitute specific information (Tucker, 1992; Rolls & Treves, 1994). Perceptions, memories, emotions, words, and symbols all are constituted by specific net profiles. Neurons that fire together will wire together, through strengthening of synaptic connections. Short-term biochemical strengthening is thought to constitute short term memory. Long-term creation of new synapses, through interaction with the DNA, is proposed to create long-term memory (Siegel, 1999, p. 26).

## EXPLICIT AND IMPLICIT MEMORY

Memory is the way past events affect future function. This definition is much wider than the everyday notion of memory as a conscious recollection of facts, concepts, and events, which is here termed explicit or declarative memory. Explicit memory is thought to consist of semantic and episodic memory. Semantic memory is about facts (rose) and abstractions (flower), that can be declared with words and assessed as "true" or "false" (Siegel, 1999).

Whether episodic, or autobiographical, memory is the ability to put events into the context of self, place, and time—a sense of recollection of the self at a given time in the past, awareness of the self in the living present, and projection of the self into the imagined future (Wheeler, Stuss & Tulving, 1997).

The hippocampus is central to the encoding of explicit memory. It is activated by focal conscious attention on the event to be remembered. From the huge amount of perceptual, bodily and emotional representations of the event, selected items are placed in short-term (working) memory, a process where the lateral prefrontal cortex is thought to be essential (Andreasen et al., 1995). Working memory has been compared to a "chalkboard" of the mind, where items perceived in the present may be linked together with perceptual, bodily, and emotional items recalled from the past. The hippocampus is active in "cognitive mapping" which involves sequencing of the order of events and the establishment of a spatial representational map of the location of things in the world (Squire et al., 1993). The hippocampus then transfers some of the associated items into long-term, explicit memory in the associational neocortex. All these functions are vulnerable to traumatic stress.

Long-term memory may then become permanent, explicit memory through a process called "cortical consolidation," taking weeks, months, or even years to form. Permanent memory is finally independent of the hippocampus. Some suggest that this requires a nonconscious rehearsal involving the incorporation of previously unintegrated information into existing memory networks (Milner et al., 1998). Dreams are proposed to be essential for this process and may be a fundamental way in which the mind consolidates the myriad of new explicit recollections into a coherent set of representations (Winson, 1993). The BMGIM process is proposed to have a similar function.

In contrast to explicit memory, implicit or nondeclarative memory (Siegel, 1999) is activated outside of conscious control and without a subjective experience of recall, self, or time. Implicit memory includes everyday behaviors, affects/emotions, and perceptual images. Behavioral memory, such as the ability to walk, is thought to be mediated by the motor cortex and basal ganglia. The latter are subcortical coordinating centers of movement (not shown in Figure 1). Perceptual memories are thought to involve the perceptual and association cortices. Emotional memories may be mediated by the amygdala, anterior gyrus cinguli, and the medial orbitofrontal cortex. Though research has not explored somatosensory (bodily) memory, this form of nonverbal recall might also be implicit. Bodily memories may be mediated by the somatosensory cortex in addition to the structures mentioned for the memory of affect/emotion (Siegel, 1999).

Implicit memories involve parts of the brain that do not require conscious encoding and retrieval (Squire et al., 1993), start forming at birth and continue to develop throughout life. Infants demonstrate recall for behaviors, perceptions, and emotions. If frightened by a noise associated with a particular toy, they will get upset when shown that toy in the future, without the internal sense that something is being recalled. If allowed to feel the shape of a nipple in a dark room, they later will be able to pick out the familiar nipple from a visual display. Their minds have created a mental image from touch, so called amodal perception (Stern, 1985). Implicit memories of faces, voices, touch, behavioral interactions, and pleasant or unpleasant internal states begin to synthesize into so-called mental models of being with caregivers. By eighteen months, it is postulated that children can bring a comforting image of an attachment figure forward in their minds (Freyd, 1987).

In the presence of good-enough mothering, these implicit memories are functional, and proposed to manifest as the psychodynamic dimension of resource imagery in BMGIM. Traumatic images are dysfunctional implicit memories that are dissociated (disconnected) from autobiographical memory following traumatic events (Siegel, 1995).

## REPRESENTATIONS AND SYMBOLS

To adapt to repeated experiences, the mind organizes information in increasingly generalized representations, which carry information about similarities, differences, associations, and generalizations of experiences. With increasing complexity, they have increasing symbolic value in the original sense of the Greek word "symbolon:" to throw or put together. Symbols are experienced as words, concepts, and images that carry meaning beyond themselves, and themselves initiate further processing in the mind (Siegel, 1999, pp. 162-164).

Two major forms of symbolic representation, discursive and analogic, are important for the theory proposed in this chapter. Discursive (Langer, 1957), lexical (Horowitz, 1983), or digital (Siegel, 1999) processes are slow, sequential, and linear, utilizing monosemantic, strictly defined "packets" of information. Examples of this are reading the words of this sentence, or determining the sequence of items in this chapter. The information packets can be manipulated with analytical, logical thought and communicated through words. Discursive symbolization, termed the "interpreter" (Gazzaniga et al., 1996), attempts to use reason to categorize and explain cause-effect relationships from whatever information that is available. The word is the basic form of conscious discursive representation both in thinking, writing, and speaking.

Analogic processes are fast-acting, parallel, and holistic. They contain nonverbal representations of sensations, images, and the polysemantic meaning of words. They allow us to understand metaphor, paradox, humor, and prosody. They are involved in intentions, attitudes, perceptions, emotions, and in perceiving the mental state of self and others, or social context (Baron-Cohen, 1995). Analogic symbolization gives a direct and immediate image of the world as it is, with complex relationships intact and little attempt at reduction and analysis.

The difference between discursive and analogic processing has been summarized as the difference between rational and intuitive, text and context, external and internal attention and action (Ornstein, 1997; Rotenberg, 1994). In addition to the the hippocampus, left prefrontal and orbitofrontal cortex, the posterior and anterior speech centers of the left hemisphere (Wernicke's and Broca's areas) also mediate explicit memory. The arrows of Figure 1a indicate some aspects of the understanding and generation of language. The left hemisphere is thought to be more capable for detailed assessment of a single mode of perception. Analogic processing is thought to be mediated mainly by the right hemisphere, which seems more capable of dealing with context, complexity and for integrating various modes of perception such as sight and sound (e.g., Goldberg & Costa, 1981; Zaidel et al., 1990), and different sensations of the body (Damasio, 1994). It seems more capable than the left to regulate states of bodily arousal (Stern, 1985).

These functions, (discursive, explicit, analogic, implicit) interact extensively, which makes for example the left-right dichotomy oversimplified. Reading this text primarily engages the left hemisphere, while lyrics and emotional narrative activate both left and right hemispheres.

The rational "interpreter" (Gazzaniga et al., 1996), uses pure rational cognition to understand the where what, when, and why of an event, and tries to create an explanation even without information of social context or emotion. In this chapter, the memory of the interpreter is referred to as cognitive. Autobiographical memory results from the integration of the interpreter's cognitive processing with analogic, emotional, context-dependent information, that subconsciously provides the themes of narrative (Siegel, 1999). The difference between cognitive and autobiographic memory is an important distinction of this chapter.

The BMGIM process provides several tools for stimulating discursive symbolization: first through the dialogue with the guide during the music experience, second through cognitive imagery, third in the post-session verbalization of artwork, and fourth by written processing between sessions. However, autobiographical stories, fairy tales, metaphors, and poems have increasingly strong contributions of analogic processing, and represent an integration of discursive and analogic processing. This side of BMGIM has been investigated by Bonde (2000). In this chapter, additional aspects of integration between discursive word, internal analogic image, and external analogic art work in BMGIM are explored.

Analogic processes are involved in the preverbal communication between the baby and the mother, linked to specific states of consciousness of the child (e.g., Trevarthen, 1996). The musical qualities of this "protoconversation" have been investigated by Stern (1996; Trevarthen & Malloch 2000). The concept of the music's evocation of analogic symbols has been seen as most compatible with the complexity of the BMGIM process (e.g., Goldberg, 1992; Summer 1985). In this tradition Kurth (1931), Meyer (1956), and Nielsen (1971) have argued that formal elements are musical reflections of psychic phenomena. According to Langer (1957), these forms include flow, energy, modulations, and ambiguity. She saw music as a presentational symbol, similar to art and images in its capacity to represent several meanings simultaneously and where the elements have no definite dictionary of meaning.

## AFFECT AND EMOTION

Pratt (1931), applying the perspective of analogic symbol to emotions, made the poetic statement that "[musical] characters are not emotions at all, they merely sound the way mood feels," Langer (1957) argued that "music is not a specific cause or cure of feelings," that it does not classify feelings in the terms of cognitive or discursive symbols, and that instead "music articulates feelings in forms that language can not set forth." Music's analogic evocation of emotion has been central in most theories of imagery in BMGIM (e.g. Goldberg, 1992). In this chapter, it is proposed that music evokes affect and emotion not only through its highly processed analogic form, but also through alarm qualities of sound, acting directly on the amygdala before higher processing takes place. These alarm qualities of sudden and strong sounds set off a reaction of startle, fear, and chaotic affective states.

Affect and emotion are controversial subjects in neuropsychology (Brothers, 1997). The following synthesis is compatible with the affect differentiation theory of Tomkins (1962–1963) and Basch (1988). Sensory representations from a situation is evaluated by the amygdala as "good" or "bad," The initial evaluation of the amygdala is sent to the anterior cingulate and orbitofrontal cortex for further evaluation of, for example, facial expression, direction of gaze, and other aspects of nonverbal behavior revealing the state of mind of the other (Allman & Brothers, 1994). These areas also register the state of the body, and directly affect its state of activation (Porges et al., 1994). Information from these areas are also passed to the hippocampus for cognitive mapping and in some cases transfer into explicit memory. The orbitofrontal cortex also plays a major role in coordinating these appraisal processes with more complex neocortical representations of social context and symbols (Price et al., 1994; Shore, 1994). During this process, it is conceivable that the originally undifferentiated affective states in the limbic system, through the intermediary stage of feeling, become nuanced emotions, as described by Basch. Emotions are possible to describe, reflect, and act upon.

Excessive release of stress hormones impair the structures that differentiate the amygdala's inital fear response, resulting in "affect dysregulation" (van der Kolk et al., 1996). In the resulting state, affects are chaotic, intermixed, unmanageable, and hard to describe in words. Alternately they are dissociated and replaced with a sense of numbness. This leads to avoidance of relationships and withdrawal from social life.

## PERCEPTION, ENGRAMS, AND IMAGERY

Sensory perceptions are experienced in the visual, auditory, somatosensory, and gustatory/olfactory areas of the cerebral cortex. The light waves of a tree are reflected onto the retinal cells of the eye, where a conversion into electrical nerve impulses take place. These travel along the optic nerve, crossing to the opposite side of the brain to arrive at the primary visual cortex. A stepwise interpretation of light, shape, and color takes place in the secondary visual areas. Incoming information is analyzed and compared with memories of previous experiences, in order to categorize the sensation as the sight of a tree. The neural activation profile representing the tree is called a perceptual representation (Siegel, 1999).

Similarly, the sound of the wind rustling the leaves is registered and interpreted by the auditory cortex. The somatosensory cortex receives information from a number of sense organs registering touch, vibration, pressure, pain, temperature, muscular tension, balance, and movement when climbing the tree to rest in its branches. Taste of its fruit and smell of its flowers are projected to the gustatory and olfactory cortex. The emotions of the adventure may be mediated, among other areas, in the amygdala, anterior gyrus cinguli, and orbitofrontal cortex (Halgren & Marinkovic, 1995). Different sensory experiences of the tree are stored in modality-specific code. The initial sensory impact on the mind has been called an engram (Schachter, 1996).

The different sensory codes of the tree are linked together by the association cortices into larger networks, creating a coherent perceptual representation. If the amygdala is activated, the engram is thought to be marked as significant, a "value-laden" memory (Edelman, 1992). To put the tree-engram into a coherent explicit and implicit context, it is associated in even larger networks, thought to be encoded and retrieved by the orbitofrontal cortex (Buckner, 1996; Kapur et al., 1995; Wheeler et al., 1997). Remembering the tree is not merely the reactivation of the original engram; it is the construction of a new neural net profile, with features of the old engram, elements of memory from other experiences, as well as influences from the present state of mind (Siegel, 1999).

Recent PET-scan studies in normal subjects (e.g., Kosslyn et al. 1999) suggest that the same areas of the visual cortex (visual areas 17 and 18) are active both in visual perception of, for example, the tree and in visualization of the tree, originating within the brain (imagery). Similarly, imagery for music may be mediated primarily by the right auditory association cortex (Halpern & Zatorre, 1999). From this, it can be assumed that imagery for other sensory modalities are evoked by activating their respective associational sensory areas. The internal activation of imagery is considered to start with the evocation of memories (Roland & Gulyas, 1994). Thus it can be proposed that imagery of the tree reflects the activation of memories, emotions, and higher representations that include the tree-engram.

## SYMBOLIC AND TRAUMATIC
## IMAGERY IN BMGIM

Imagery of a tree may be very different, depending on the size and level of integration of the associated net profile. In a transpersonal experience, the traveler may be one with the tree, the wind, the movement, and the light of the sun reflected from the leaves. In an archetypal dimension, the tree may symbolize inborn capacity of nurturing, growth, continuity, and safety independent of personal history. In a psychodynamic perspective it may represent nurturing, protective relationships, and self-image.

The following case (Case 1) will provide an example of initial resource experience followed by gradual degradation of imagery ending in traumatic re-experience. This patient had been confined in a smaller community and systematically beaten and raped for several months in an abusive relationship. Her only place of refuge was a large old tree where she could seek a moment of respite and strength.

Figure 2.

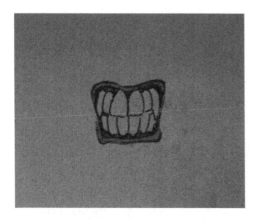

In an early session the patient experienced the tree with a growing sense of relief and protection. She felt as one with the tree, which became surrounded by a light that filled her with strength and security beyond words. This quality indicates a transpersonal experience. In a subsequent session, another tree was threatened with active destruction by her abuser who was equipped with a chain saw. This image is representative of her massive intrusive traumatization and the near destruction of the self. In the next session, the patient had a partial visual reexperience of the perpetrator's teeth (Figure 2), accompanied by nausea and chaotic affect. The reader may question if such imagery is therapeutically helpful. The patient's answer is typical of many others: "I much prefer experiencing this in the music, with someone I trust, than alone." It may be added: provided there is a safe clinical framework. The place where she was abused also had a prominent windmill, which will feature in the resymbolization described later.

This case is characterized by a cognitive connection with the traumatic events, insufficient analogic symbolization, and no integration of affect. There is little sense of functioning self.

Figure 3.

Fragmented memories may appear without connection to the actual traumatic event. The depressed woman of Case 2 had episodes of stomach pains and nausea, constituting a reexperience of her bodily condition during a traumatic stillbirth. During a BMGIM session she reexperienced the pain and nausea, without making a cognitive connection with the traumatic event, and afterwards depicted her bodily sensations with the visceral forms in Figure 3.

Another client (Case 3), could not relax and experienced what she described as a panic attack during the music. When encouraged to depict the experience she drew an hourglass-shaped figure representing a constriction of her throat, with pain and muddled affect below the constriction and a dizzy, empty feeling above (Figure 4). In this case, there was an explicit memory of being beaten and hung up by a rope at the age of ten, but no cognitive connections with her panic attacks that may be interpreted as affective and bodily flashbacks.

Figure 4.

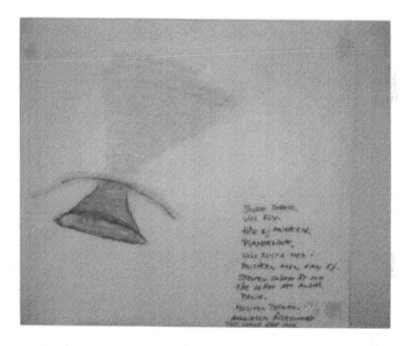

The cases illustrate visual, bodily, and affective reexperiences, one with and two without cognitive connection to the traumatic events. It should be noted that reexperiences seldom are completely unsymbolized. These pictures all manifest a measure of low-grade analogic symbolization: the affects of both perpetrator and victim contained in the teeth (Figure 2), the visceral forms of the body imagery (Figure 3), and the constriction of the panic spiral (Figure 4). This "protosymbolization" may be there already in the inner experience or may be introduced in the external act of painting. As will be described in the paragraph on symbolization, further processing will develop from these origins.

# PATHWAY OF PRESYMBOLIC
# MUSIC INFORMATION
# TO THE AMYGDALA

The traumatic imagery of these patients were all evoked by the same transient and dynamic music passage: the strong staccato piano chords in the second movement of Beethoven's *Fifth Piano Concerto.* They are representative cases from the authors experience with over 200 traumatized patients, where intrusive imagery, or degradation of symbolic imagery, is frequently evoked by unexpected, sudden, or strong musical elements. Examples of such elements are crescendos and instruments characterized by fast transients such as drums. Haydn, according to legend, included an unexpected tympani crescendo in the slow movement of his *Symphony in G major,* to wake up a dozing audience. He seems to have known that musical suddenness and dynamics alone may evoke the alarm reaction. Recent research suggests that this effect may be relayed via subcortical input to the amygdala. This input contains alarm information, processed at the level of the brain stem and thalamus. This occurs before the sound information reaches the neocortex, where it is transformed into music information through higher processing.

Sound information is relayed and interpreted through several nuclei, or relay stations in the brain stem, before reaching the thalamus, the gateway for incoming sensory information. Sound is analyzed in terms of frequency and temporal aspects in the medial geniculate nucleus. This psychophysical information is relayed not only to the auditory cortex for higher processing, but also in subcortical pathways to the amygdala for affective evaluation, and probably also to other parts of the limbic system. Sudden sounds have been shown to evoke fear and bodily alarm reactions through activation of the amygdala directly from the medial geniculate nucleus (LeDoux, 1990). This pathway (Figure 1c-b) may mediate the frequently observed evocation of traumatic reexperiences by psychophysical musical alarm properties of dynamics, transience (suddenness), and sheer volume.

# ACTIVATION OF TRAUMATIC IMAGERY
# THROUGH SYMBOLIC MUSICAL GESTALT

Analogic symbolic imagery reflects not only existing but also new combinations of memories and representations, suggesting a creative process in the altered state. Continuing the example of the tree, it may grow eggs instead of fruit, or transform into a living creature. It is conceivable that the evoked neural networks even may spark a general activation of the limbic system, thought to be the neuropsychological event behind a transpersonal experience (Saver & Rabin, 1997). High functioning travelers generally manage these experiences, which often reflect creativity, mythology, and internal difficulties. In the author's experience, traumatized patients have difficulties in managing complex imagery, especially with longer sequences of evocative music. Symbolic images like snakes or arrows may quickly become intrusive and degrade into traumatic reexperiences, also in the absence of alarm qualities in the music. Transpersonal experiences are more prone to assume destructive qualities than in the high-functioning traveler.

Complex, creative imagery presupposes higher processing and perception of music in the neocortex. Cortical processing of music is mediated through the pathway from the medial geniculate nucleus via the primary, secondary, and association auditory cortices. Perception of melody, timbre, and intensity is thought to be mediated by the right hemisphere, pitch and rhythm by the left (Halpern & Zatorre, 1999; Platel et al., 1997). In BMGIM, it is proposed that music, in the altered state, subsequently may activate brain areas that integrate memory, visceral functions, affect/emotion, perception, and discursive and analogic representations.

## PET-SCAN VISUALIZATION
## OF TRAUMATIC IMAGERY

The clients above exemplify perceptual, bodily, and affective reexperiences, all with a component of fear, and in two cases without cognitive links to traumatic events. Similar experiences have been visualized with the help of neuroimaging techniques in patients with Post Traumatic Stress Syndrome (PTSD).

In one of these studies, traumatic re-experiences were elicited by listening to verbal accounts of traumatic events (Rauch et al., 1996). The patients all had flashbacks from diverse traumata such as childhood sexual and physical abuse, rape, domestic violence, combat exposure, car accident with death of child and witnessing of burn victims. Activity of the brain regions were compared under two conditions: first while imagining the trauma listening to a narrative of the event from audiotape (Figure 5A–C), and second while imagining a personally neutral narrative (Figure 5D).

In the traumatic condition, patients showed activation of brain structures of the limbic system, among them the right amygdala, orbitofrontal, and anterior gyrus cinguli. Activation of the right amygdala has consistently been linked to the experience of fear (Davis et al., 1995). The orbitofrontal cortex, as mentioned previously, is involved in bodily and emotional experience and the integration of memories, and the anterior gyrus cinguli to a role in mental (distinct from sensory) imagery. The anterior gyrus cinguli also is involved in emotion, bodily representation and regulation (Shin et al., 1997). There was also activation of brain structures not mentioned so far: the anterior insula (not shown in Figure 1), which may register bodily consequences of negative emotions (Cheketto & Saper, 1990), and the anterior and medial temporal cortex, both implicated in anxiety and other negative affect (Drevets et al., 1992). Simultaneously, increased heart rate was measured and subjects experienced fear and other affects. The evoked activity then spread into the secondary visual cortex (Figure 5 A and B) consistent with reported visual imagery.

Figures 5A-D.

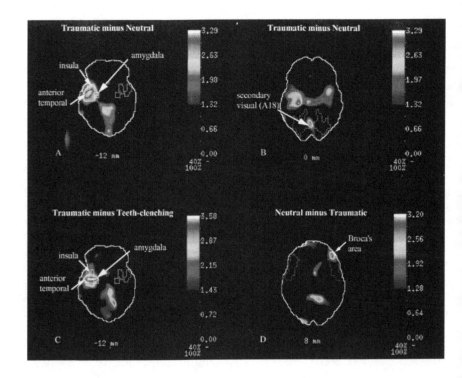

Activation of the amygdala, anterior gyrus cinguli, and orbitofrontal cortex with a preponderance for the right side have been the most consistent findings in similar studies of PTSD subjects, and to a lesser degree also in traumatized subjects without PTSD (Rauch et al., 1996; Shiffer et al., 1995). The activation of the visual areas is consistent with the view that visual imagery involves the same area as visual perception and has been found also in imagery elicited by viewing aversive pictures (Kosslyn et al., 1999). The PET scan conceivably reflects also what happens during traumatic imagery in BMGIM.

## TRAUMATIC STRESS AND SYMBOLIZATION

Following traumatic stress, there is impairment of discursive processing through words and abstract concepts.

As mentioned, the flashback is hard, sometimes even impossible to verbalize. In the PET-scan the anterior speech center, or Broca's area, is silent during traumatic imagery (Figure 5 A-C), but active when listening to a neutral narrative (Figure 5 D). Broca's area is thought to be involved in speech production and inner speech (Kertesz et al., 1997; McGuire et al., 1996; Pauleso et al., 1993; Petersen et al., 1989). Decreased activity of Broca's area has been found also in other PET studies of PTSD (Fisher et al, 1996; Shin et al, 1997, 1999). In all these studies, the silence of Broca's area is interpreted as manifesting impairment of discursive processing during the reexperience of traumatic events.

Excessive or long-standing release of stress hormones impairs other structures involved in explicit memory in a number of ways, leading to parts of the experience being encoded implicitly but not explicitly. Impairment of the hippocampus may disrupt its associational networks, fragmenting different parts of a traumatic experience (Pitman & Scott, 1995). This may also result from "divided attention" during overwhelming trauma, where the individual may focus her attention on nontraumatic aspects of the environment or on imagery, as a means of escape (Siegel, 1995). Impairment of the hippocampus and orbitofrontal cortex may prevent encoding of both cognitive and autobiographical memory (Bower & Sivers, 1999). Excessive release of stress hormones may influence the amygdala to "overinclusion," associating the fear reaction with harmless external and internal perceptions (Davis et al., 1995).

A situation that is perceived as dangerous, for example a face reminding of a perpetrator or a sudden sound in the night, activates the oversensitive amygdala to set off an alarm reaction and physiological stress response, accompanied by the affect of fear. If overwhelmed by conflicting emotion and affect, the mind may regress back to a more undifferentiated affective state, where the affective components are disconnected and no longer recognizable. This chaotic state may be alternately dissociated, resulting in numbing, or intrude into consciousness as overwhelming affect (van der Kolk et al., 1996).

## CYCLICAL RESOURCE IMAGERY, AFFECT DIFFERENTIATION, AND AUTOBIOGRAPHICAL MEMORY

Traumatization often leads to low self-esteem and dysfunctional self-assumptions of vulnerability, incompetence, and worthlessness (van der Kolk, 1996). This wounded person is faced with the task of confronting overwhelming reexperiences. In the BMGIM session, inner resources that are silent during ordinary consciousness may become conscious during the experience of music in an altered state (Bonny, 1989; Borling, 1992; Bishop, 1994; Goldberg, 1992, 1994; Picket & Sonnen, 1993; Tasney, 1993).

These inner resources have a wide range of manifestations, from bodily experiences to archetypes representing empowerment (Jung, 1959). There may be experiences of protection from, or management of, inner threats that may alleviate the sense of vulnerability and incompetence. Here, the focus is on bodily manifestations with qualities of warmth, energy, strength, movement, nourishing, and healing, all belonging to the implicit realm of positive vitality affects and mental models. For example, gently swinging in the branches of a tree, feeling safe, and hearing mother's voice in the music, may reflect good moments of being with mother. Meeting a bear, feeling its strength in the body, may manifest the traveler's mental and physical resilience. Experiences of nurturing are important, since they may alleviate the sense of worthlessness, and encourage emotional relating.

Bishop (1994) has described a cyclical process of mobilization of resources followed by confrontation with traumatic material, ending in resolution and new resource mobilization. During this process, improvement of defenses can be observed. One frequent example in the author's experience is the protective place, that often implies a dilemma. The more protection, the more isolation. The higher and thicker the protective hedge, the more it prevents relationships. This situation reflects the traumatized persons distrust of relationships and avoidance of emotional interaction (Levin et al., 1999). A more flexible safe place was experienced by the woman of Case 3. She experienced a panic attack provoked by the staccato chords of Beethoven's *Fifth Piano Concerto,* depicted in Figure 4. In a subsequent session she was given the less transient and evocative Albinoni´s *Sinfonia in G minor*. This music allowed her to find a safe place on a beach and a sense of mastery, which allowed her to manage the arrival of a potentially dangerous eagle. Her fear and rage could be more comfortably explored in this symbolic form.

As mentioned before, autobiographic memory implies a functioning self, with social cognition and emotionality. By contrast, cognitive memory, in the sense of the interpreter, uses pure cognition to understand the where, what, when, and why of an event. This discursive interpreter does not feel the need to incorporate emotionality and relationship in its narrative. This distinction explains why some traumatized persons, with apparent explicit recollection and cognitive understanding of a traumatic event, still suffer from traumatic re-experiences and lack a sense of functioning self. The shutting off of emotion and relationship is a central issue in integrating traumatic into autobiographical memories.

In sum, mobilization of resources and transformation of cognitive into autobiographical memory are central in the symbolic processing of traumatic memories to be described below. With resource mobilization, and increased self-esteem, traumatic imagery can be owned and made available for symbolization. Replacing alternating intrusive affect and numbing with owning of affect is essential for its differentiation into emotion. Without this process, the author holds, the central issue of emotional isolation cannot be resolved, and withdrawal from life continues.

## SYMBOLIZATION IN THE BMGIM PROCESS

An important feature of discursive and analogic symbolization is that they almost always interact in the BMGIM session. This interaction can be depicted as a "symbolization triangle" with image, artwork, and word at each of the three corners (Figure 6, adapted from Franzke, 1994). The word is the basic unit of discursive symbolization. The image may be a traumatic image or analogic symbol. The separate corners for image and artwork introduces a clinically important distinction between internal and external analogic symbolization.

The line between the image and the word depicts discursive symbolization during the music, when the guide and traveler dialogue about the imagery. The process not only goes from image to word; the word also stimulates change of the images. The image-word line also depicts talking about the imagery in the verbal post-session. The writing of enchantment and poetry between sessions is another means of integrating the image and the word, employing both discursive and analogic symbolization.

Discursive symbolization of the traumatic image is, simply put, first about recognizing that the traumatic image belongs to a certain event, second the ability to describe in words when, where, and how it happened (cognitive episodic memory). In attempting to explain why, semantic concepts and logic are used. Overwhelming traumatic reexperience during the music will, in the extreme case, result in silence. The inactivity of Broca's area of Figure 5 (A-C) is a visualization of one of many possible neuropsychological impairments of discursive narrative.

Figure 6.

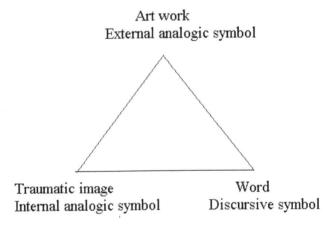

Art work
External analogic symbol

Traumatic image                          Word
Internal analogic symbol          Discursive symbol

Analogic symbolization is about transforming the intruding traumatic perception into symbolic image, which carries additional, parallel information. Whereas the traumatic image intrudes spontaneously into the everyday waking state, the highly processed symbolic image is normally possible to access only in an altered state of consciousness. The symbolic image may bind the traumatic affect (Perry, 1974). In addition to representing the trauma, it may also show realities of the event and suggest ways of understanding and managing a similar situation in the future. It may demonstrate effects of the trauma on self-assumptions and relationships. In addition, the analogic image regularly manifests resources.

Failure of analogic symbolization manifests in the repetition of the traumatic image. Often, there is impairment of both discursive and analogic processing during the music experience. It is in this situation that external analogic symbolization is essential. In painting the traumatic image, symbolic qualities regularly emerge in the picture giving clues for episodic memory. The picture can contain and externalize the experience, be put away, and brought back to the next session. In this external form, it can be talked about more easily than it is possible to do about the internal traumatic image. The picture may then be allowed to serve as a focus for the next experience.

The described interaction of processing through image, artwork and word will be illustrated by vignettes of two of the previously presented cases.

Figure 7.

Internal analogic symbolization is illustrated by Figure 7 (Case 1). Figure 2 illustrated a partial flashback of the perpetrator's teeth, accompanied by chaotic affect. In this case there was a cognitive awareness of the memory of being systematically beaten and raped in an isolated community (cognitive memory). However, affect was dissociated and there was no functioning sense of self. Figure 7 illustrates a symbolic transformation of this perpetrator during a music experience, represented as a wildly swinging windmill with sharp teeth. There was a greater sense of internal management of the windmill, than of the teeth of Figure 2. The windmill was stuck in its place, but the traveler was able to move away in the music. She realized, when talking about the picture, that she was now in safety. When further symbolized, the windmill might develop into a beast, capable of representing a wider range of emotions and relationships and also carrying a mythological potential. This sequence is an example of inner analogic symbolization during the music experience.

Discursive symbolization is illustrated by Case 2. During a BMGIM session she reexperienced stomach pain and nausea, disconnected from memories of a traumatic stillbirth, and after the session depicted this as a series of visceral forms (Figure 3). She went into the next session with these forms as a focus. Evoked by the tympani crescendo of Elgar's *Ninth Enigma Variation* (selected because of her good ego strength), a sensation of stomach kicks emerged, first accompanied by fear. The kicks were the link with the where and when—the kicks of the baby before birth. This explicit memory made it possible for her to make a cognitive connection between the stomach pains and the traumatic stillbirth. The intensity and transience of the tympani were needed to provoke the body memories of the kicks. Since they were accompanied by fear, it is conceivable that this involved the geniculate-amygdala pathway.

The focus of the first case was of analogic symbolization and the second of discursive symbolization in the music. However, both processes would probably not be possible without the external artwork, and discursive reflection. Another necessary feature of resolution is the affective processing of these patients.

In Case 1, the realization of safety made it possible to confront the so far dissociated affective chaos and in further sessions investigate the component experiences of fear, bodily disgust, rage, and loss. This alleviated the sense of chaos, and made it possible to "own" the affects, and link them with the cognitive memories of beating and rape.

In Case 2, the emergence of the cognitive memory in the Elgar tympani crescendo was followed by Puccini's "Humming Chorus" from *Madama Butterfly* which provided a musical gestalt symbolic of caring, evoking memories of sewing baby clothes, strong experiences of loss, and anger at obstetric mistakes. This very rapid restructuring of affect was further worked through in painting and verbal processing.

In integrating these affects with the cognitive memories, it is conceivable that autobiographical memory was beginning to form in both these cases.

## IMPLICATIONS FOR MANAGEMENT OF SESSIONS AND MUSIC CHOICE

High functioning traumatized clients may work in BMGIM with only minor modifications of the method. At the other end of the spectrum, clients with complex PTSD or early traumatization need modifications of guiding, music choice, and additional framework. In cases of severe dissociative symptoms and distrust, a co-therapist (preferably making up a male/female combination), resources for hospitalization, and long treatment times are all needed.

A common feature of all traumatized is the strong need for security and protection to enable the confrontation with reexperience imagery. Gradually, this need may diminish as inner resources are mobilized, reestablishing a sense of functioning self. Facilitating this process is the first priority in verbal work, guiding, and music choice.

To strengthen the mobilization of resources, it is helpful to find out about good and protective relationships in the past. Often there will be a grandmother, or other figure who provided food and security. Making grandmother the focus of the next session often reveals further protective figures and coping.

The finding of a musical home is essential. The question in the mind of the guide may be: with what musical elements is the traveler comfortable? It should be realized that persons with complex PTSD or early traumatization often are distrustful of the conventionally nurturing, or invaded by the conventionally protective, for example the insistent Pachelbel's *Canon*. Instead, they may find their first musical home in dissonant, fluent, or otherwise conventionally insecure music. Once the home is found the traveler may spend long periods working with the same piece. One traveler used the beginning and end of the second movement of Mozart's *Clarinet Concerto* as a home for fifteen straight sessions. She closed her ears during the middle, more evocative part, but still insisted on its presence. Gradually she could begin to work also with this more ego-alien sequence of the music.

Some clients periodically need to revert to the protection and reassurance of the therapist. These are the situations where favorite music is used more as a presence in the room during sessions, and when guiding approaches the dialogue of a verbal session.

Of course, transference also influences both imagery and music experience. One common phenomenon is for both guide and traveler to switch between perpetrator and victim positions. There is substantial danger for the guide to be traumatized by the traveler's imagery.

Sooner or later, the client needs to enter the "negative" phase of the BMGIM cycle to confront traumatic imagery and affect. The challenge for the guide is to combine the resource-building strategy with a readiness to be with the traveler's reeexperiences. Here, the countertransference issues of the guide become important. The client's need is to be in the imagery with music and someone they trust, since they have had enough of being there alone. In the author's experience, active exploratory guiding with the intent of stimulating the traveler's verbalization is helpful when traumatic imagery appears. With the same intent, there is need of a dialogue with features of guiding during the post-session artwork, when the traveler moves from internal image to external analogic symbol.

As proposed, traumatized persons are sensitive to psychophysical alarm qualities of music like transience, dynamic changes, and rhythm. They are also sensitive to highly processed elements like dissonance, harmonic changes and general evocative potential. Consequently, when the guide notices the need to minimize the evocation of traumatic imagery, these musical elements should be avoided, and the music-listening phase of the session should be short.

Music that varies primarily in the dynamic dimension is useful for monitoring the balance between traumatic and symbolic imagery. The BMGIM program *Peak Experience* (Bonny, 1978b) is an excellent step-by-step evaluative tool of this balance in a more high functioning traumatized person. The pieces are wide-purpose, fairly holding and with little dissonance. Significantly, the program contains a sequence of increasingly dynamic passages: one of the piano sequences in the slow movement of Beethoven's *Fifth Piano Concerto,* the crescendo toward the end of Bach's *(Toccata, Adagio & Fugue in C)*, and in the middle of Wagner's *Lohengrin* (Prelude to Act 1). In the authors opinion, the Wagner crescendo is not only the strongest, but also the least contained one in the program. During evaluative sessions, guiding should be present and explorative in these passages. If the intense parts evoke unprocessed traumatic memories, provoke symbolic imagery to degrade, or assume threatening qualities, the guide should consider lowering the volume or avoiding the next crescendo altogether. This decision is influenced by the presence and quality of resources and defenses earlier in the session. *Peak Experience* provides several qualities of supportive, nonchallenging music by Vivaldi (*Gloria, Et in Terra Pax*), Faure (*Requiem* [In Paradisum]) and most of the Beethoven. One may be chosen, depending on the traveler's previous response, to shorten the session. Other options within the BMGIM repertoire are

Bach's *Air,* Vaughan-Williams' *Rhosymedre Prelude,* Warlock's "Pied en l'air" from the *Capriol Suite* and, possibly, Pachelbel's *Canon.* In addition, the BMGIM guide should have an ample supply of low-intensity, nonevocative, nurturing music outside of the formal BMGIM repertoire.

Marked rhythm may activate traumatic memories of, for example, beating, but also positive implicit experiences of mobility. One client, who had been beaten by her father, had very specific musical requirements and wanted to travel to steady andante beats. She had anxiety attacks with a sense of being stuck and somatic symptoms that partly were body memories of beating. The Andante of Mendelssohn's *Italian Symphony* first allowed her to move with the walking beat, breaking the sense of stuckness. The next session, the steady beat evoked imagery of fences that in the post-session reminded her of the father's strict enforcing of rules. Then, the rhythms become actual beatings, evoking the same pain that she experienced in her panic attacks. These were defensively transformed into a scene from an historical painting depicting a whipping. The next session she was again walking with the beat, this time freely in an open landscape. This illustrates how positive and negative potentials of a specific musical element can be experienced by the traveler in a cyclical fashion.

The traumatized traveler's avoidance of affect and relationship is an important aspect of music choice. The issue for the guide is to listen for the affective potential of musical parameters in the mutual musical field of play. Usually, affective content should be kept low in the beginning. An interesting development is short neoclassical music with little emotion, emphasis on form, and low evocative potential. The BMGIM program *Soliloquy* (Bruscia, 2000) contain useful examples. At the other extreme is music with strong harmonic content and change, exemplified by composers like Tschaikovsky and Dvorak, and prominent interplay between instruments as in Debussy's *String Quartet.* That last piece also features dissonance, which regularly elicits strong ambivalent response. In the authors experience, vocal music with holding qualities like Puccini's "Humming Chorus" from *Madama Butterfly* and Mozart's "Laudate Dominum" from the *Vesperae Solemnes* are useful stepping-stones into holding and differentiation of affect.

## SUMMARY

Traumatic reexperiences represent information that is disconnected from, and no longer "understood" by, the integrating functions of the mind. The BMGIM process provides the means necessary for evocation and reintegration of traumatic information. The music evokes the disconnected sensory and affective memories and mobilizes inner resources. These enable the traveler to own the reexperiences and make them available for symbolization. Reintegration consists of a number of interweaving processes. These are: transformation of traumatic imagery into symbolic imagery, establishment of cognitive memory and understanding, and integrating the resulting discursive symbols with analogic symbol and affect. The resulting weave forms the coherent narrative of autobiographic memory.

## References

Aguirre, G. K., Detre, J. A., Alsop, D. C., & D´Esposito, M. (1996). The parahippocampus subserves topographical learning in man. *Cerebral Cortex,* 6, 823–829.

Alarcon, R. D., Glover, S. G., & Deering, C. G. (1999). The cascade model: An alternative to comorbidity in the pathogenesis of posttraumatic stress disorder. *Psychiatry.* Summer, 62(2), 114–124.

Allman, J., & Brothers, L. (1994). Neuropsychology. Faces, fear and the amygdala. *Nature.* Dec. 15; 372 (6507*),* 613–614.

American Psychiatric Association. (1994). *Diagnostic and Statistical Manual of Mental Disorders.* (4th ed.). Washington, DC.

Andreasen, N. C., O'Leary, D. S., Arndt, S., Cizaldo, T., Hurtig, R., Rezai, K., Watkins, G. L., Ponto, L. L. B., & Hichwa, R. D. (1995). Short-term and long-term verbal memory: A positron emission tomography study. *Proceedings of the National Academy of Sciences USA,* 92, 5111–5115.

Baron-Cohen, S. (1995). *Mindblindness: An Essay on Autism and Theory of Mind.* Cambridge, MA: MIT Press.

Basch, M. F. (1988). *Understanding Psychotherapy.* New York: Basic Books.

Bechara, A., Tranel, D., Damasio, H., & Damasio, A. R. (1996). Failure to respond autonomically to anticipated future outcomes following damage to prefrontal cortex. *Cerebral Cortex,* 6, 221–225.

Bishop, S. (1994). *The Use of Guided Imagery and Music with Adult Female Survivors of Abuse in an Inpatient Psychiatric Setting.* Salinas, KS: Bonny Foundation.

Blake, R. (1994). Vietnam veterans with posttraumatic stress disorders: Findings from a music and imagery project. *Journal of the Association for Music and Imagery,* 3, 5–18.

Blood, A. J., Zatorre, R. J., Bermudez, P., & Evans, A. C. (1999). Emotional responses to pleasant and unpleasant music correlate with activity in paralimbic brain regions. *Nature Neuroscience,* 2 (4), 382–387.

Bonde, L. O. (2000). Metaphor and narrative in Guided Imagery and Music. *Journal of the Association for Music and Imagery, 7,* 59–76.

Bonny, H. (1978a). *Facilitating GIM sessions. Monograph #1:* Salina, KS: Bonny Foundation.

Bonny, H. (1978b). *The role of taped music programs in the GIM process. Monograph #2:* Salina, KS: Bonny Foundation.

Bonny, H. (1989). Sound as symbol: Guided Imagery and Music in clinical practice. *Music Therapy Perspectives, 6,* 7–10.

Borling, J. (1992). Perspectives of growth with a victim of abuse: A Guided Imagery and Music (BMGIM) case study. *Journal of the Association for Music and Imagery, 1,* 85–98.

Bower, G. H., & Sivers, H. (1998). Cognitive impact of traumatic events. *Developmental Psychopathology Fall,* 10(4), 625–653. Review.

Braver, T. S., Cohen, J. D., Nystrom, L. E., Jonides, J., Smith, E. E., & Noll, D. C. (1997). A parametric study of prefrontal cortex involvement in human working memory. *NeuroImage 5,* 49–62.

Brothers, L. (1997). *Friday's Footprints: How Society Shapes the Human Mind.* New York, NY: Oxford University Press.

Buckner, R., Raichle, M., & Petersen, S. (1995). Dissociation of human prefrontal cortical areas across different speech production tasks and gender groups. *Journal of Neurophysiology, 74,* 2163–2173.

Buckner, R. L. (1996). Beyond HERA: Contributions of specific prefrontal brain areas to long-term memory retrieval. *Pscychonomic Bulletin, 3,* 149–158.

Bunsey, M., & Eichenbaum, H. (1993). Critical role of the parahippocampal region for paired-associate learning in rats. *Behavioral Neuroscience, 107,* 740–747.

Cheketto, D. F., & Saper, C. B. (1990). Role of the cerebral cortex in autonomic function. In D. A. Loewy, & K. M. Speyer (eds.). *Central Regulation of Autonomic Function.* New York: Oxford University Press.

Damasio, A. R. (1994). *Descartes' Error: Emotion, Reason, and the Human Brain.* New York: Grosset/Putnam.

Davidson, R., Ekman, P., Saron, C.D., Senulis, J. A., & Friesen, W. V., (1990). Approach-withdrawal and cerebral asymmetry: Emotional expression and brain physiology. I. *Journal of Personality and Social Psychology.* Feb, 58(2), 330–341.

Davis, M., Campeau, S., Kim, M., & Falls, W. A. (1995). Neural systems of emotion: The Amygdalas role in fear and emotion. In J. L. McCaugh, N. M. Weinberger, & G. Lynch, (Eds.). *Brain and Memory. Modulation and Mediation of Neuroplasticity.* New York: University Press.

Drevets, W. C. (1997). Subgenual prefrontal cortex abnormalities in mood disorders. *Nature, 386,* 824–827.

Drevets, W. C., Videen, T. O., MacLoud, A. K., Haller, J. W., & Raichle, M. (1992). PET images of blood flow changes during anxiety: correction. *Science*, 256, 1696.

Edelman, G. (1992). *Bright Air, Brilliant Fire*. New York: Basic Books.

Farah, M. J. (1988). Is visual imagery really visual? Overlooked evidence from neuropsychology. *Psychology Review*, 95, 307–317.

Farah, M. J. (1989). Mechanisms of imagery-perception interaction. *Journal of Experimental Psychology. Human Perception and Performance*, 15, 203–211

Farah, M. J. (1995). The neural bases of mental imagery. In M. S. Gazzaniga (ed.). *The Cognitive Neurosciences*, 963–975. Cambridge, MA: MIT Press.

Farah, M. J., & Smith, A. F. (1983). Perceptional interference and facilitation with auditory imagery. *Perception and Psychophysics*, 33, 475–478.

Farah, M. J., Weisberg, L. L., Monheit, M., & Peronnet, F. (1989). Brain activity underlying mental imagery: Event-related potentials during mental image generation. *Journal of Cognitive Neuroscience* 1, 302–316.

Fisher, H., Wik, G., & Fredriksson, M. (1996). Functional neuroanatomy of robbery re-experience: affective memories studied with PET. *Neuroreport, 1996–1997*, 2081–2066

Franzke, E. (1994). Växelspel mellan ord och bild inom psykoterapin (Interplay between word and image in psychotherapy). *Proceedings of the 52nd Continued Psychiatric Education Seminar*. Växjö Psychiatric Clinic.

Freyd, J. J. (1987). Dynamic mental representations. *Psychological Review*, 94, 427–438.

Gabrieli, J. D. E., Desmond, J. E., Demb, J. B., Wagner, A. D., Stone, M. V., Vaidya C. J., & Glover, G. H. (1996). Functional magnetic resonance imaging of semantic memory processes in the frontal lobes. *Psychology Science* 7, 278–283.

Galaburda, A.M., & Sanides, F. (1980). Cytoarchitectonic organization of the human auditory cortex. *The Journal of Comparative Neurology*, 597–610.

Gazzaniga, M. S., Eliassen, C., Nisenson, L., Wessinger, C. M., & Baynes, K. B. (1996). Collaboration between the hemispheres of a callosotomy patient: Emerging right hemisphere speech and the left brain interpreter. *Brain*, 119, 1255–1262.

Goldberg, E., & Costa, L. D. (1981). Hemispheric differences in the acquisition and use of descriptive systems. *Brain and Language*, 14, 144–173.

Goldberg, F. S. (1992). Images of Emotion. *Journal of the Association for Music and Imagery*, 1, 5–18.

Goldberg, F. S. (1994). The Bonny Method of Guided Imagery and Music (BMGIM) as individual and group treatment in a short-term acute psychiatric hospital. *Journal of the Association for Music and Imagery.* 3, 5–18.

Goldenberg, G., Podreka, I., Steiner, M., Willmes, K., Suess, E., & Deecke, L. (1989). Regional cerebral blood flow patterns in visual imagery. *Neuropsychologia*, 27, 641–664.

Green, T., Neinmann, S. F., & Gusella, J. F. (1998). Molecular neurobiology and genetics: Investigation of neural function and dysfunction. *Neuron*, 20, 427–444.

Halgren, E., & Marinkovic, K. (1995). Neurophysiological networks integrating human emotions. In M. S. Gazzaniga (ed.). *The Cognitive Neurosciences*, 1137–1151. Cambridge MA: The MIT Press.

Halpern, A. R., & Zatorre, R. J. (1999). When that tune runs through your head: a PET investigation of auditory imagery for familiar melodies. *Cerebral Cortex*. 9(7), 697–704.

Horowitz, M. J. (1983). *Image Formation and Psychotherapy*. New York and London: Jason Aronson, Inc.

Hubbard, T. L., & Stoeckig, K. (1988). Musical imagery: generation of tones and chords. *Journal of Experimental Psychology: Learning, Memory and Cognition*, 14, 656–667.

Jung, C. G. (1959). *Basic Writings of Jung*. Garden City, New York: Doubleday.

Kandel, E. R., & Schwartz, H. (eds.). (1992). *Principles of Neural Science* (2nd ed.). New York: Elsevier.

Kapur, S., Craik, F. I. M., Jones, C., Brown, G. M., Houle, S., & Tulving, E. (1995). Functional role of the prefrontal cortex in retrieval of memories: A PET study. *Neuroreport*, 6, 1880–1884.

Kertesz, A., Lesk, D., & McCabe, P. (1977). Isotope localization of infarcts in aphasia. *Archives of Neurology*, Oct. 34, (10), 590–601.

Klein, D., Milner, B., Zatorre, R. J., Evans, A. C., & Meyer, E. (1995). The neural substrates underlying word generation: a bilingual functional imaging study. *Proceedings of the National Academy of Science, USA* 92: 2899–2903.

Kosslyn, S. M., Alpert, N. M., Thompson, W. L., Maljkovic, V., Weise, S. B., Chabris, C. F., Hamilton, S. E., Rauch, S. L., & Bounanno, F. S. (1993). Visual mental imagery activates topographically organized visual cortex: PET investigations. *Journal of Cognitive Neuroscience* 5, 263–287.

Kosslyn, S. M., Shin, L. M., Thompson, W. L., McNally, R. J., Rauch, S. L., Pitman, R. K., Alpert, N. M. (1996). Neural effects of visualizing and perceiving aversive stimuli: A PET investigation. *Neuroreport*, 7, 1569–1576.

Kosslyn, S. M., Pascal-Leone, A., Felician, O., Camposano, S., Keenan, J. P. & Thompson, V. (1999). The role of area 17 in visual imagery: convergent evidence from PET and rTMS. *Science,* Apr 2, 284 (5411), 167–70

Kurth, E. (1931). *Musikpsychologie.* Berlin, Germany: Max Hesses Verlag.

Langer, S. K. (1957). *Philosophy in a New Key.* Cambridge, Massachusetts: Harvard University Press.

LeDoux, J. E. (1990). Information flow from sensation to emotion: plasticity of the neuronal computation of stimulus value. In M. Gabriel & J. Moore (eds.). *Learning and Computational Neuroscience: Foundations of Adaptive Networks,* 3–51. Cambridge MA: MIT Press.

Levin, P., Lazrove, S, & van der Kolk, B. (1999). What psychological testing and neuroimaging tell us about the treatment of Posttraumatic Stress Disorder by Eye Movement Desensitization and Reprocessing. *Journal of Anxiety Disorder,* 13 (1–2): 59–72

McGuire, P. K., Silbersweig, D. A., Murray, R. M., David, A. S., Frackowiak, R. S., & Frith, C. D. (1996). Functional anatomy of inner speech and auditory verbal imagery. *Psychol Med..* Jan, 26(1), 29–38.

Mega, M. S., Cummings J. L., Salloway, S., & Malloy, P. (1997). The limbic system: An anatomic, phylogenetic and clinical Perspective. In S. Salloway, P. Malloy, & J. L. Cummings (eds.). *The Neuropsychiatry of Limbic and Subcortical Disorders.* Washington: American Psychiatric Press.

Meyer, L. B. (1956). *Emotion and Meaning in Music.* Chicago: University of Chicago Press.

Milner, B., Squire, L. R., & Kandel, E. R. (1998). Cognitive neuroscience and the study of memory. *Neuron,* 20, 445–468.

Nakamura, S., Sadato, N., Oohashi, T., Nishina, E., Fuwamoto, Y., & Yonekura, Y. (1999). Analysis of music-brain interaction with simultaneous measurement of regional cerebral blood flow and electroencephalogram beta rhythm in human subjects. *Neuroscience Letters* 275, 222–226.

Nielsen, P. (1971). *Musical Form Analysis. From A. B. Marx "Kompositionslehre" to Contemporary Structural Analysis.* Copenhagen: Borgen.

Nyberg, L., Cabeza, R., & Tulving, E. (1996). PET studies of encoding and retrieval. *Psychonomic Bulletin & Review.* 3, 135–148.

Ogawa, J. R., Sroufe, L. A., Weinfeld, N. S., Carlsson, E. A., & Egeland, B. (1997). Development and the fragmented self: Longitudinal study of dissociative psychopathology in a non-clinical sample. *Development and Psychopathology,* 9, 855–880.

Ornstein, R. (1997). *The Right Mind: Making Sense of the Hemispheres.* New York: Harcourt Brace.

Paulesu, E., Frith, C. D., & Frackowiak, R. S. (1993). The neural correlates of the verbal component of working memory. *Nature.*. Mar 25, 362(6418), 342–5.

Perry, B. D. (1997). Incubated in terror: Neurodevelopmental factors in the "cycle of violence". In J. Osofsky (ed.). *Children in a Violent Society*, 124–149. New York: Guilford Press.

Perry, D. W., Zatorre, R. J., Petrides, M., Alivisatos, B., Meyer, E., & Evans, A. C. (1999). Localization of cerebral activity during simple singing. *Neuroreport* 10, 3979–3984.

Perry, J. (1974). *The Far Side of Madness*. Englewood Cliffs, NJ: Prentice Hall.

Petrides, M., Alivisatos, B., Meyer, E., & Evans, A. C. (1993). Functional activation of the human frontal cortex during the performance of verbal working memory tasks. *Proceedings of the National Academy of Science, USA*, 90, 878–882.

Petersen, S., Fox, P., Posner, M., Mintun, M., & Raichle, M. (1988). Positron emission tomographic studies of the cortical anatomy of single-word processing. *Nature,* 331, 585–589.

Petersen, S. E., Robinson, D. L., & Currie, J. N. (1989). Influences of lesions of parietal cortex on visual spatial attention in humans. *Experimental Brain Research*, 76(2), 267–280.

Petrides M, & Pandya D. N. (1988). Association fiber pathways to the frontal cortex from the superior temporal region in the rhesus monkey. *Journal of Comparative Neurology.* Jul 1, 273(1), 52–66.

Picket, E., and Sonnen, C. (1993). Guided Imagery and Music: A music therapy approach to multiple personality disorder. In E. S. Kluft (ed). *Experiential and Functional Therapies in the Treatment of Multiple Personality Disorder*. Chapter 4. Springfield, IL: Charles C. Thomas.

Pitman, R. K., & Scott, P.O., (1995). Psychophysiology of emotional memory networks in Posttraumatic Stress disorder. In J. L. McCaugh, N. M. Weinberger, & G. Lynch (eds.). *Brain and Memory. Modulation and Mediation of Neuroplasticity.* New York: Oxford University Press.

Platel, H., Price, C., Baron, J. C., Wise, R., Lambert, J., Frackowiak., R. S., Lechevalier, B., & Eustache, F. (1997). The structural components of music perception. A functional anatomical study. *Brain*, 120, 229–243.

Porges, S. W., Doussard-Roosevelt, J. A., & Maiti, A. K. (1994). Vagal tone and the physiological regulation of emotion. *Monographs of the Society for Research in Child Development,* 59(2–3), 167–186

Pratt, C. C. (1931). *The Meaning of Music.* New York and London: McGraw Hill Book Co.

Price, J. L., Carmichael, S. T., & Drevets, W. C. (1994). Networks related to the orbital and medial prefrontal cortex: A substrate for emotional behavior? *Progress in Brain Research*, 107, 523–536.

Putnam, F. W. (1997). *Dissociation in Children and Adolescents: A Developmental Perspective.* New York: Guilford Press.

Rao, S. M., Harrington, D. L., Haaland, K. Y., Bobholz, J. A., Cox, R. W., & Binder, J. R. (1997). Disturbed neural systems underlying the timing of movements. *Journal of Neuroscience,* 17,5528–5535.

Rauch, S. L., van der Kolk, B. A., Fisler, R. E., Alpert, N. M., Orr, S. P., Savage, C. R., Fischman, A. J., Jenike, M. A., & Pitman, R. K. (1996). A symptom provocation study of posttraumatic stress disorder using positron emission tomography and script-driven imagery. *Archives of General Psychiatry,* 53, 380–387.

Roland, P. E., & Gulyas, B. (1994). Visual imagery and visual representation. *Trends in Neurosciences,* Jul, 17(7), 281–287; discussion 294–297. Review.

Rolls, E. T., & Treves, A. (1994). Neural networks in the brain involved in memory and recall. *Progress in Brain Research,* 102, 335–341.

Romanski, L. M., Bates, J. F., & Goldman-Rakic, P. S. (1999a). Auditory belt and parabelt projections to the prefrontal cortex in the rhesus monkey. *Journal of Comparative Neurology*, Jan 11, 403(2), 141–157.

Romanski, L. M., Tian, B., Fritz J., Mishkin, M., Goldman-Rakic, P. S., & Rauschecker, J. P. (1999b). Dual streams of auditory afferents target multiple domains in the primate prefrontal cortex. *Nat Neuroscience* Dec, 2(12), 1131–1136.

Rotenberg, V. S. (1994). An integrative psychophysiological approach to brain hemisphere functions in schizophrenia. *Neuroscience and Biobehavioral Reviews,* 18, 487–495.

Saver, J. L. & Rabin, J. (1997). The neural substrate of religious experience. In S. Salloway, P. Malloy, & J. L. Cummings, (eds.). *The Neuropsychiatry of Limbic and Subcortical Disorders.* Washington, D.C: American Psychiatric Press.

Schachter, D. L. (1996). *Searching for Memory: The Brain, the Mind, and the Past.* New York: Basic Books.

Shalev, A. Y., Freedman, S., Peri, T., Brandes, D., Sahar, T., Orr, S. P., & Pitman, R. K. (1998). Prospective study of posttraumatic stress disorder and depression following trauma. *American Journal of Psychiatry.* May, 155(5), 630–637.

Shevring, H. (1996). *Conscious and Unconsious Processes—Psychodynamic, Cognitive and Neurophysiological Convegence.* New York: Guilford Press.

Shiffer, F., Teicher, M. H., & Papanicolaou, A. C. (1995). Evoked potential evidence for right brain activity during recall of traumatic memories. *Journal of Neuropsychiatry, 7*, 187–250.

Shin, L. M., Kosslyn, S. M., McNally, R. J., Alpert, N. M., Thompson, W. L., Rauch, S. L., Macklin, M. L., & Pitman, R. K. (1997). Visual imagery and perception in Posttraumatic Stress Disorder: A positron emission tomographic investigation. *Archives of General Psychiatry, 54*, 233–241.

Shin, L. M., McNally, R. J., Kosslyn, S. M., Thompson, W. L., Rauch, S. L., Alpert, N. M., Metzger, L. J., Lask, N. B., Orr, S. P., & Pitman, R. K. (1999). Regional cerebral blood flow during script-driven imagery in childhood sexual abuse-related PTSD: A PET investigation. *American Journal of Psychiatry*. Apr, 156(4), 575–584.

Shore, A. N. (1994). *Affect Regulation and the Origin of the Self: The Neurobiology of Emotional Development*. Hillsdale, NJ: Erlbaum.

Shore, A. N., (1997). Earlier organization of the nonlinear right brain and the development of a predisposition to psychiatric disorders. *Development and Psychopathology 9*, 595–631.

Siegel, D. J. (1995). Memory, trauma, and psychotherapy: A cognitive science view. *Journal of Psychotherapy Practice and Research, 4*, 93–112.

Siegel, D. J. (1999). *The Developing Mind—Toward a Neurobiology of Interpersonal Experience*. New York: The Guilford Press.

Smith, E. E., & Jonides, J. (1997). Working memory: A view from neuroimaging. *Cognitive Psychology, 33*, 5–42.

Spiegel, D. (1996). Dissociative disorders. In R. E. Hales & C. S. Yudovsky (eds.). *American Psychiatric Press Synopsis of Psychiatry*, 583–604. Washington, D.C.: American Psychiatric Press.

Springer, S. P., & Deutsch, G. (1993). *Left Brain, Right Brain*, 4th ed. New York: Freeman.

Squire, L. R., Knowlton, B., & Musen, G. (1993). The structure and organization of memory. *Annual review of Psychology, 44*, 453–495.

Stefanacci, L., Suzuki, W. A., & Amaral, D. G. (1996). Organization of connections between the amygdaloid complex and the perirhinal and parahippocampal cortices in macaque monkeys. *Journal of Comparative Neurology. 375,* 552–582.

Stern, D. N. (1985). *The Interpersonal World of the Infant*. New York: Basic Books.

Stern, D. N. (1996). *Temporal Aspects of an Infants Daily Experience: Some Reflections Concerning Music*. Presentation at the International Congress of the World Federation of Music Therapy. Hamburg, Germany, July 1996.

Stroebe, M., vanSon, M., Stroebe, W., Kleber, R., Schut, H., & van den Bout, J. (2000). On the classification and diagnosis of pathological grief. Review.*Clinical Psychology Review*, Jan, 20(1), 57–75.

Summer, L. (1985). Imagery and music. *Journal of Mental Imagery*, 9(4), 83–90.

Tomkins, S. S. (1962–1963). *Affect, Imagery, Consciousness.* Vols. I and II. New York: Springer Publishing.

Trevarthen, C. (1996). Lateral asymmetries in infancy: Implications for the development of the hemispheres. *Neuroscience and Biobehavioral Reviews,* 20, 571–586.

Trevarthen, C., & Malloch, S. (2000). The dance of well-being: Defining the musical therapeutic effect. *The Nordic Journal of Music Therapy,* 9 (2), 3–17.

Tucker, D. M. (1992). Developing emotions and cortical networks. In M. R. Gunnar & C. Nelson (eds.). *Minnesota Symposia on Child Psychology: Vol 24. Developmental Behavioral Neuroscience*, 75–128. Hillsdale, NJ: Erlbaum.

Tulving, E., Kapur, S., Craik, F. I. M., Moscovitch, M., & Houle, S. (1994). Hemispheric encoding/retrieval asymmetry in episodic memory: Positron emission tomography findings. *Proceedings of the National Academy of Sciences USA*, 91, 2016–2020.

Van der Kolk, B. A., McFarlane, A. C., & Weisaeth, L. (eds.). (1996). *Traumatic Stress: The Effects of Overwhelming Experience on Mind, Body and Society.* New York: Guilford Press.

van der Kolk, B. A., Pelcovitz, D., Roth, S., Mandel F. S., McFarlane, A., & Herman J. L. (1997). Dissociation, somatisation & affect dysregulation: The complexity of adaption to trauma. *American Journal of Psychiatry,* supplement 153:7.

Waller, N., Putnam, F. W., & Carlsoon, E. B. (1996). Types of dissociation and dissociative types. A taxometric analysis of dissociative experiences. *Psychological Methods,* 1, 300–321.

Wheeler, M. A., Stuss, D. T., & Tulving, E. (1997). Toward a theory of episodic memory: The frontal lobes and autonoetic consciousness. *Psychological Bulletin,* 121, 331–354.

Winson, J. (1993). The biology and function of rapid eye movement sleep. *Current Opinion in Neurobiology,* 3, 243–248.

Zaidel, E., Clarke, J. M., & Suyenobu, B. (1990). Hemispheric independence: A paradigm case for cognitive neuroscience. In A. B. Scheibel & A. F. Wechsler (eds.). *Neurobiology of Higher Cognitive Function*, 297–355. New York: Guilford Press.

Zatorre, R. J. (1988). Pitch perception of complex tones and human temporal-lobe function, *Journal of the Acoustical Society,* 84, 566–572.

Zatorre, R. J., Evans, A. C., Meyer, E., & Gjedde, A. (1992). Lateralization of phonetic and pitch processing in speech perception, *Science* 256, 846–849.

Zatorre, R. J., Halpern, A. R., Perry, D. W., Meyer, E., & Evans, A. C. (1996). Hearing in the mind's ear: A PET investigation of musical imagery and perception. *Journal of Cognitive Neuroscience* 8, 29–46.

Zatorre, R. J., & Halpern, A. R. (1993). Effect of unilateral temporal-lobe excision on perception and imagery of songs. *Neuropsychologia,* 31, 221–232.

Zatorre, R. J., & Samson, S. (1991). Role of the right temporal neocortex in retention of pitch in auditory short-term memory. *Brain,* 114, 2403–2417.

Zola-Morgan, S., Squire, L. R., Amaral, D. G., & Suzuki, W. A. (1989). Lesions of perirhinal and parahippocampal cortex that spare the amygdala and hippocampal formation produce severe memory impairment. *Journal of Neuroscience,* 9, 4355–4370.

*Chapter Twenty-Two*

# THE ROLE OF METAPHOR
# IN THE BONNY METHOD OF
# GUIDED IMAGERY AND MUSIC (BMGIM)

## Gabriella Giordanella Perilli

This chapter is an examination of the specific role played by metaphor in the process of therapeutic and growth-oriented change that takes place in the Bonny Method of Guided Imagery and Music (BMGIM). Research has demonstrated that music can evoke imaginative schemas that are embodied at the neuropsychological level, because music presents varied sensory, emotional and motor components that specifically relate to those of the imaginative schemas evoked. These schemas in turn furnish a reference point and foundation for all metaphorical processes, including the creation of new metaphors and the expansion of one's personal inventory of imagery (visual images, fantasies, memories, etc.).

## THE METAPHORIC PROCESS

In second-generation cognitive sciences, the human being is viewed as a complex open system for acquiring new information. This system is characterized by an ongoing process of change aimed at maintaining a dynamic equilibrium and avoiding an increase in internal disorganization. According to this perspective, new information is acquired through concrete body experiences that the person structures according to *imaginative schemas.* These schemas have both motor and perceptual components that provide recurrent structures which help us to organize our experiences (Johnson, 1987). By organizing our experiences in a coherent manner, these schemas serve as models for developing mental representations of them, therein linking sensory perception to cognition

(Johnson, 1987). The schemas may pertain to movement, balance, and rhythm, for example, or more general processes, such as schemas for change.

Once the schemas organize the experience, and the experience is mentally represented, the next step in acquiring new knowledge or making meaning is *metaphorical elaboration* of these schemas. Metaphorical elaboration is a cognitive function which involves moving an imaginative schema from one realm of experience to another. Thus, for example, through metaphorical elaboration, a person transfers information in a nonverbal imaginative schema into other unknown or unactivated realms of experience. This process involves projection and using metaphor to create new patterns of meaning.

For the extension or projection of meaning between the two areas, the person must perceive a commonality between them, which then serves as the basis for projection. For example, a sad person having rather slow motor function may perceive a slow passage of music "as if it were sad." The person perceives his/her motor function and the music as having something in common, and this allows the person to project sadness onto the music. The person thus relates to the music "as if it were sad." Indeed, metaphor is by its very definition an "as if" proposition about the information it represents, which can encourage further elaboration. Thus: the music perceived as "sad" can eventually become a metaphoric representation of various "sad" situations and feelings, which in turn solicit other imaginative schemas with similar rhythmical and motor characteristics. This is why in BMGIM, "sad" music can evoke existing situations that are sad, as well as metaphorically create "sad" situations in the imagery of the listener. It follows then that imaginative schemas and metaphors have differentiated identities, which include not only the concrete initial information but also abstract elements as well. As such, they are functions of operative symbolic thought which move from nonverbal modes (sensory, emotional) to explicit verbal consciousness.

Thus, metaphor is an imaginative structure which originates from the functioning of the body in interaction with its environment, and evolves through a cognitive process that is pervasive, creative, and fundamental for the comprehension and organization of new areas of experience. Johnson (1987) considers the metaphorical process as "one of the central projective operations by which we establish semantic connections" (p. 192). He also notes that "some kinds of metaphor must be regarded as irreducible, primary cognitive functions by which we create and extend structure in our experience and understanding" (Johnson, 1987, p. 192).

Metaphorical projections allow us to construct transversal maps from one domain or knowledge or experience to another, not in an arbitrary manner but according to the very nature of the basic body experiences. This seems to be the process for metaphorically projecting experiential structures (schemas or components) of different categories (sensory, conceptual, emotional), thereby forming new connections and organizations of meaning, and at the same time extending and developing the imaginative schemas of the prelogic stage with nonpropositional (figurative) meanings.

## THE DEVELOPMENT OF METAPHOR

*Metaphors begin to develop in the prelogic stage, with the formation of nonverbal imaginative schemas and the projection of experience from one area to another at a preconceptual level.*

Speaking to the relation between musical and verbal experiences, Gardner (1983) proposed that there is an autonomous musical intelligence which acts in concert with an autonomous verbal intelligence. This notion is supported by other studies showing a significant difference between the processing of musical and verbal stimuli even among newborns (Faienza, 1998), and is useful for clarifying the specificity of the two domains. Gardner also sustains that there are common elements shared by the two types of intelligence, such as intensity, the temporal dimension, etc. If we accept these premises, we can reasonably suppose that the projection of metaphor between the musical and verbal domains is already possible in the prelogic stage.

Nonverbal imaginative schemas are based on experiences embodied kinesthetically. Early experiences, connected to basic somatic sensations and functions (tension/relaxation, balance/imbalance, etc.), are organized and stored in the memory according to schemas with temporal, motor, emotional, and cognitive elements. In addition to the schematic organization of internal body experiences, there is also the more complex organization of experiences connected to motivational systems (reproduction, protection, cohesion) genetically predisposed for the survival of the individual and species (Liotti, 1994). The different imaginative schemas contain a set of innate values that the baby will associate in its memory from the earliest period of life with categories of experiential interaction with its body and environment (Edelman, 1989). With continual repetition in this interaction of kinesthetically perceived experiences with specific characteristics, the baby creates nonverbal schemas which function as internal models that help to define interpersonal relationships and impart subjective meaning with a strong affective value.

*Sounds and music are integral components of early life, in that they carry emotions and provide a means for connecting to the environment and attuning with significant others. In doing so, sounds and music contribute to the formation of nonverbal imaginative schemas.*

Studies carried out with echography have demonstrated that the fetus initially reacts with alarm and crying to sudden intense sounds coming from the external environment. However, with the repetition of the same sounds, the fetus presents more normal motor responses with signs of adaptation and inurement, having experienced the lack of danger of the stimulus. During the period of intrauterine life, the rhythmical and acoustical stimuli coming from both the mother's body and from the external environment stimulate the central nervous system of the fetus, contributing to the formation of engrams which constitute the baggage of basic sensory and affective memory. A fundamental premise here is that human beings organize their internal and external experiences according to categories or temporal schemas, in order to interact with their physical, psychological, and social environment (Giordanella Perilli, 1995).

These neurophysiological schema for organizing internal events and perceiving external ones develop on the psychological level with early psycho-physical experiences of which sound and music are integral parts. Observations of newborns have established that there is an *in utero* apprenticeship. Indeed, sounds perceived repeatedly during the ultimate two months of the fetal cycle are remembered by newborns and preferred to other, unknown sounds (Oliverio, 1986). Newborns calm down upon hearing a musical passage heard previously in the mother's womb, and of which they appear to have a memory associated with sensations of well-being. Likewise, they will also nurse a bottle with a specific cadence activating a recording that reproduces the voice of the mother or a brief musical passage heard several times in the womb (Oliverio, 1986, p. 17). The same tranquilizing effect can be attained by having them listen to a regular heartbeat.

The association of a sound with a positive (or negative) bodily situation can be successively generalized and organized in imaginative schemas. The perception of sounds or analogous rhythms will evoke emotional responses similar to those experienced and stored in the memory, without, however, a corresponding concrete need for satisfaction, and in a completely different situation. Research seems to show that human beings self-referentially develop imaginative schemas in order to attune to their internal and external environments. As with other imaginative schemas, temporal schemas are embodied, and seem to present individual variations as to duration, frequency of occurrence, and intensity in characterizing emotions and other cognitive events (Giordanella Perilli, 1995).

Thus, it can be said that the developing human being already interacts with the mother and the external environment by way of sounds and rhythms during its prenatal life. After birth, a clear example of this interaction of sound and motor schemas is furnished by the act of crying, which is structured in rhythmic sequences with variations in duration, pitch, and loudness. The newborn carries in its behavioral baggage different genetically predisposed configurations of crying to express and communicate affective states or organic needs (hunger, fatigue, anger, pain), so that the person taking care of it can react in an appropriate manner; for example, the crying pattern associated with pain consists of a protracted expiration with constant emissions of sound, followed by a long pause, while the pattern of anger is a single series of sound eruptions in close succession. Crying, an adaptive behavior, is not differentiated in any pathologies, as for example Down's Syndrome.

Organized as it is on the basis of imaginative schemas combining rhythms, sounds, motor functions, sensations, and affects, crying could provide a basis of comparison with the primitive perception of musical stimuli. Musical responses for satisfying the needs of the infant, for example repetitive intoned baby talk when it is sleepy, have the same calming effect in quite different cultures, following as they do the slow respiratory rhythm of the baby on the verge of sleep. These vocalizations, with their simplicity and repetitive melodies, represent a stimulus at once familiar on the cognitive level and reassuring on the emotional level. Lullabies and nursery rhymes, on the other hand, associated with slow or fast rhythms, allow the elaboration of imaginative schemas connected with various internal states, (e.g. joy, arousal) and always take place in a context of affective reciprocity.

Several studies might support the notion that sounds and music contribute to the formation of embodied imaginative schemas. One such study, on cerebral activation in response to sound and musical stimuli, demonstrates that listening to complex musical passages stimulates activity in the cortical and subcortical areas (thalamus, limbic system) (Breitling et al., 1987). A pilot study looking at psychophysical parameters during the listening of two different musical compositions shows varying emotional reactions (relaxation, arousal) on the part of adult listeners, in part conditioned by the structure of the music, either classical (Chopin's *Nocturnes*) or ethno-African (fast rhythms on percussion instruments), and in part dependent on the perceptive "reconstruction" of each single listener. In this study, both musical passages resulted in a decrease in the heart rate of the majority of the listeners (Scrimali et al., 1998). Other studies investigating emotional responses to musical compositions support the hypothesis that slow and moderate music evokes emotions of tranquility/peace or sadness, while quick tempos tend to bring up emotions of joy or anxiety (Imberty 1986; Giordanella Perilli, 1998) associated with the subject's individual psychological situation and self-concept (Giordanella Perilli, 1998).

In any case, a body of evidence demonstrates that music can modify mood, and contribute in this manner to cognitive reorganization (Sutherland et al., 1982). In the context of rehabilitation, research has shown that rhythm and music facilitate recovery of motor functions in stroke victims or persons suffering from Parkinson's Disease, implying an interaction of the auditory and motor systems in physiological responses and the learning of motor skills (Thaut, 2000, p. 19).

To complete this picture of the contribution of sounds to the formation of nonverbal imaginative schemas, it is useful to remember that in its interactions, the newborn initially reacts not to the sense of the spoken word but to the sound of the voice—that is to say, to whether it sounds gentle or angry, according to the intensity and loudness of the intonation. Babies produce identical sounds in all linguistic and cultural contexts (p, b, m, t, a, long a), most likely as a function of their neurological and muscular development. The newborn's production of these sounds, organized in binary rhythms, yields the first words so similar in all languages—"mama" and "papa"—which designate the parents, and carry a strong affective meaning both for the newborn as well as for the parents, who are in this way involved emotionally and encouraged to care for the child.

Thus, repeated early experiences with sounds and music contribute to the organization of schemas with rhythmic, kinesthetic, and affective information conserved in the network of associative memory. Then, as the baby develops further, these nonverbal imaginative schemas are imbued with other meanings.

In the process of attunement to his or her environment, the baby develops a model of the environment structured around several recurring and temporally invariable properties, fundamentally on the basis of subjective schemas which select and furnish personal meaning to events. In this process, the repeated vocalizations in the mother/child interactions are imbued with specific meanings with communicative aims. Stern (1985) writes that metaphors function in mother/child attunement because human beings have the ability, known as synesthesia, to transfer characteristics common to one sensory domain into another in such a way that a sound can evoke a color, a form, or its opposite; this process has been noted by philosophers, poets, and other artists for many centuries. It is still necessary for the adult to establish a synchronized parental interdependence with the baby's emotional states, consisting of parental rhythms and behavioral patterns of which the baby can initially perceive abstract global qualities, such as intensity and temporal schemas (Stern, 1985). At the same time, during the process of development, sensory representations become perceptual representations involving affects, and, successively, symbols and concepts, with the addition of a verbal sign. This process enables different types of psychic identification, including both projective and introjective identification, which, as defense mechanisms, might have a repercussion on the metaphorical process and on metaphor construction.

Obviously, these nonverbal imaginative schemas carry emotions. The mother-child relationship is attuned by the fundamental affects composing the background against which the continuity of relational and emotional experiences develops, with the specific characteristics of each style of attachment. The styles of attachment and care (secure, insecure, etc.) constitute a pattern of recurring behavior which form nonverbal imaginative schemas for *mental representational states* of the various types of relationships and furnish the interpersonal counterpart of self-consciousness. The prototypical emotional qualities which characterize nonverbal imaginative schemas are conducive to the installation of intersubjective relationships to attune the needs of the baby with the adult's care. In this interaction, the basic affects evolve and take on the specifics of emotional categories in the context of experiences associated with the Interpersonal Operative Systems (attachment/care; competition; domination/submission; cooperation, etc.) in function at the moment (Bowlby, 1969; Liotti, 1994). In this light, each emotion can be seen as a process of control relative to the psychological status of the individual (Pribram, 1971) and as an integral part of the nonverbal imaginative schemas conserved in the analogic memory with their sensory, perceptual, and motor components.

*Nonverbal imaginative schemas are stored in long-term memory following a process which begins with the preconscious synthesis of affective, sensory, and motor stimuli and the response of the organism in its interaction with the environment.*

Among the many situations, only those associated with affective states will be classified as significant for the individual (Estes, 1985; Michon and Jackson, 1984, p. 305). The various affective states will be stored in long-term memory by means of schemas which bring into relation basic sensations, perceptions, and motor behaviors. All of the levels involved in the transmission and elaboration of information (experiences)—neural, cognitive, psychological—utilize temporal and spatial codes which become essential attributes of both tacit and explicit understanding and therefore characteristics which help to memorize the structures of nonverbal imaginative schemas. Imaginative schemas for spatial and temporal orientation structure and pervade every experience (Johnson, 1987) and can influence the unconscious and conscious meaning attached to them by the individual.

*Imaginative schemas become nonverbal conceptual metaphors through the metaphorical process.*

Imaginative schematic structures give coherence and meaning to the body's experiences and activities, structuring and attuning perception and cognition (Johnson, 1987, p. 75) in such a way that it is possible to maintain self-consciousness through changing roles and relationships, that is to say, to organize that biographical identity by which the individual is capable of producing metaphors and consequential narrative for his or her own life (Dalle Luche, 2000). The imaginative schemas are extended through metaphorical projections from physical domains into other abstract or symbolic domains. For example, the early experience of being small can be elaborated into the nonverbal metaphor which as an adult leads to feeling "like a small baby," with a sense of inadequacy in the face of difficult or socially demanding situations. Another example is given by the horizontal reclining position of the newborn (imaginative schema), which can generate the nonverbal metaphor "being down" and, by extension on the psychological level, "feeling down." This cognitive modality constitutes the metaphorical process which enables the development of nonverbal conceptual metaphors. As a result of this process, metaphors pervade the network of signs which become interrelated, enabling the individual to understand experience and to self-referentially form new semantic connections (Johnson, 1987).

While imaginative schemas are primary structures for ordering the growth of consciousness, both concrete and abstract, nonverbal metaphors, which develop in the context of other signs, refer to the contents of experience and can be carried to a conscious level as configurations of roles and interpersonal relationships. This evolution from imaginative schemas to nonverbal metaphors takes place in order to give the individual a greater efficiency in acquiring knowledge. Indeed, the mind seems to prefer structure rather than randomness (Hofstadter, 1979). One of the principal structural dimensions of music (other than harmony and melody) is rhythm, which can evoke metaphorical configurations with similar temporal/rhythmic structures and thereby solicit motor and affective experiences of a nonpropositional or prelogic nature.

## METAPHOR DEVELOPMENT
## AT THE LOGICAL LEVEL

A fundamental human strategy for survival and evolution is to enlarge knowledge of self and the environment. This objective can be attained to the extent that we understand things on the basis of the meaning which we attribute to them (Johnson, 1987, p. 176). The development of language, with its capacity for symbolization and abstract reasoning, represents an enormous step forward. With the acquisition of verbal thought, nonverbal metaphors become verbal through the various uses of language, although the verbal, linguistic significance is only a part of the total meaning, which also includes the previous nonverbal meanings (Johnson, 1987, p. 176).

But in contrast to nonverbal metaphor, verbal metaphor carries a specific linguistic connotation, frequently bearing a correlation with bodily functions and sensations, as the human tends to function in a holistic and intentional manner. Verbal metaphor is determined not only by subjective experiences and the overall functioning of the individual, but also by each individual's socio-cultural context.

*Verbal metaphors are formed through a variety of cognitive mechanisms, and are used for a variety of cognitive purposes.*

Metaphors may become verbal by merely attaching word associations to a nonverbal imaginative schema. For example:

> I have a heavy heart
> I have wings on my feet
> I have a tight stomach
> I feel tiny
> I feel reborn
> That makes me sick
> He's a balanced person
> An outburst of joy

As such, metaphors become verbal involve the projective use of language to express or describe nonverbal conceptual metaphors.

Verbal metaphors can also develop from nonverbal conceptual metaphors by extending and transforming imaginative structures from one domain of experience to another. For example:

> Taking on this new job is like climbing a steep mountain
> He fell into black despair
> He's got blinders on
> Toeing the line
> We're up a blind alley
> He's completely rigid

Verbal metaphors provide semantic structures which help to develop categories for our experiences and to place events and ideas in a part-whole relationship. For example:

> Eat like a pig
> Lose one's bearings

Verbal metaphors can be formulated by associating the multiple meanings of words, as well as the meanings which emerge from relationships between the words in one context and their use in another. For example:

> My star, my sun, my flower, my little kitten (referring to persons)
> He's a tiger
> I no longer have the resources to continue
> She's as big as a boat
> She's a real peach

Verbal metaphor connects the word, a conceptual, schematic image and phonic form of things, to an expressive image carrying meaning from subjective experience (e.g., my honey). It uses meaning transfer as a vital and creative resource in confronting new situations (Guiraud, 1955). Such a verbal metaphor may be:

- based on similarity of form, function, or situation (My thoughts are in a tangle, I feel light as a feather; I feel knocked to the ground).
- synesthetic, when a sound becomes associated with a color, an image or a sensation, etc. (it's a bright melody; a disgusting view);
- affective, by assimilating an emotion with an object (sad music).

The kinesthetic sense of the human being is fundamental to this projective use of language, which includes sensations, emotions, images, and motor schemas, all crucial components to the development of self-awareness. Affects, tied to the concept of self, fulfill a primary function in the meaning shifts and other developments of verbal metaphor, produced tacitly or explicitly: "I feel low" as opposed to "I'm in seventh heaven."

*Metaphors become verbal through verbal communication with others.*

Metaphors are expressed through verbal language used in interaction with meaningful attachment/care figures. Verbal communication can influence nonverbal metaphor and imaginative schemas and modify the meaning of the experience (e.g. "cry like a girl"). The consequence can be direct expression of pain and discomfort by the body, as is known to occur with metaphor in psychosomatic disorders. The incompatibility between verbal and nonverbal metaphors can also impede mind-body integration. A study of persons who were physically or sexually abused during their infancy seems to support the idea that traumatic events profoundly distort the representational schemas connected with early relational experiences, leading to a global breakdown in the internal operative models, including the metaphorical process and narrative. In the case of the early loss of a significant parental figure, however, the distortion of the representational models is limited to the possibility of integrating the traumatic event into a coherent narrative (Guerrini Degl'Innocenti et al., 2000), as if a metaphorical projection to and from this tacit experience were not possible, because not achieved through verbal communication with the lost figure.

*Sounds and music are integral components in the formation of verbal metaphors.*

We have seen how sound and music are integral components in the formation of imaginative schemas, bodily and sensory schemas and nonverbal metaphors. With the development of symbolical/linguistic thought, these can transform into verbal metaphors, as for example:

> I'm vibrating with emotion
> We're not in harmony
> They're in tune with each other
> We'll go through the program at a snappy rhythm
> The heart jumped a beat

For Gardner (1983, 1999), music and verbal language are two autonomous types of intelligence which share the auditory system and its organizational characteristics of rhythm, pitch, frequency, loudness, etc. Metaphorical projections seem quite possible between these two areas of knowledge. In therapy, verbal metaphors, represented by stories or memories, are frequently expressed with musical or auditory metaphors. Musical composition itself can be seen as an artistic projection of the metaphorical process, and as a metaphor for bodily functions (heartbeat), kinesthetic sensibility (tension/relaxation), or emotional states (joy, sadness). Even verbal meaning or the sonoric qualities of a word or phrase can be associated with rhythmic or musical metaphors (e.g., in lyric opera and rap music).

In clinical practice, improvising with sounds upon verbally expressed self-identifying characteristics can add a different meaning to the spoken word, as in the case of M., who describes herself as a young girl but who, in musical improvisation, produces slow, descending musical progressions. Musical metaphor here integrates her sadness and elements of her suffering from psychic disorder, with the characteristic description she furnishes at a conscious level. E. describes himself as embalmed and the musical metaphor consists in one long note repeated plaintively without any rhythmic or melodic structure. G., on the other hand, presents himself as courageous, and improvisation on the bongas yields a sound metaphor characterized by a well-articulated, lively rhythm. These sound metaphors evoke a specific kinesthetic effect, a common element which allows the metaphorical projection from the area of nonverbal sound to the experiential, symbolic, linguistic level of imagination.

Musical metaphors can also be imaginative projections, as Wagner relates. The composer conceived the Overture for his opera *Das Rheingold* in a state of somnolence in which he felt immersed in flutes. The sound of the nearby water current became transformed into a musical sound: the E-Major accords pouring out in discrete units with an accelerating rhythm.

Verbal metaphor derived from experience with sounds and music can re-create early imaginative schemas of a bodily/sensory/emotional nature, acting as a shortcut to older levels of memory (including sounds, emotions, bodily states, and verbal definitions).

*Verbal metaphors are modes of constructing or conceptualizing emotions.*

Examples of this are:

> As cold as ice
> A penetrating [cutting, abrasive] glance
> Like a lion in a cage
> Feel like a wreck
> Have a heavy hear

With the development of secondary verbal consciousness (Edelman, 1989), the biological meaning of emotions, associated with motivational systems genetically predisposed for the survival of the individual and species, receives a metaphorical verbal significance connected to the semantic memory developed in interpersonal experiences. This meaning may or may not be coherent with the emotion connected with the memory of the episode and to conceptual metaphors: for example, a child takes fright faced with a barking dog (emotional, biological reaction), the mother calls him a coward (disempowering self-image), and as a result, the child feels misunderstood and sad (metaphorical meaning of the emotion in the incoherent interaction with experience).

*Verbal metaphors are stored in the memory.*

Verbal metaphors are shared within a culture and deeply rooted in our collective unconscious, and serve to elaborate a given theme and enrich it with concepts derived from other areas of collective experience. These are often expressed in idiomatic phrases such as:

> Love is a journey (Lakoff and Johnson, 1999, p. 65)
> This relationship is at a dead end
> We've come to a standstill
> Have the wind in one's sails
> You're just a volcano of ideas
> He's a sphinx
> A Pyrrhic victory
> Have the patience of Job

## THE NATURE OF METAPHOR

*Metaphors are constructed individually, following development in motor/sensory, perceptual, emotional, and cognitive capabilities and in reference to interpersonal experiences.*

To maintain a unified self-consciousness over time, the individual composes a narrative of the episodes in his life, highlighting those situations which metaphorically present elements in common with the current situation. The memories of events which occurred in infancy, therefore, assume a metaphorical value in illustrating the current lifestyle of an individual (Adler, 1927).

Two factors contribute to the elaboration of the subjective repertory of metaphors:

- Self-representation of the body, constantly modified in the light of social and perceptual experience (kinesthetic sense). In one example, a client with anorexia and relational problems perceives herself initially as "behind a wall of glass; even part of my insides is glass, I'm afraid that it will break and become glass shards that would then open my veins and provoke a hemorrhage. Others can see me only with their enormous eyes." Following an effective therapeutic treatment, though, she described feeling "as if my feet were seeds planting themselves in the earth and nourishing me, growing roots which can connect me with other people".

- Language, which develops functionally from affective, motivational use to a more conscious purpose, through two functions—individual (self-satisfaction, self-stimulation, play, etc.) and social (communication, interpersonal relations)—which intersect and blend. Initially language is used principally for its functional expressive value to satisfy immediate physiological needs, before becoming a means by which the baby explores its relationship to the world of things and persons.

Metaphors are socially constructed, in that the different symbolic modalities of language and music transmit a cultural heritage through idiomatic phrases, hymns, and other structures pertaining to history, geography, and the habit and customs of a specific ethnic group.

Data from studies in neuropathology and neurophysiology indicate that subcortical regions of the brain (the regulatory centers of the SNC in the reticular system of the brain stem) carry out an important role in the motivation for social contact and in assimilation of cultural meanings through interpersonal relations and communication. Because of this genetic predisposition, newborns are capable of communicating with the significant attachment/care figures through emotional or motivational expressions (Trevarthen et al., 1997, p. 96). This proto-conversation is based on variations in the pitch, duration and length of interval between vocal emissions (utterances), variations which seem to be associated with emotions expressed by the adult in confrontation with things (emotional referencing), to which the baby pays particular attention toward the age of six months. Even the utterances of very small babies can imitate musical forms such as songs for babies and lullabies, which introduce the individual to the cultural heritage and facilitate the development of socially-constructed metaphors between affects, words, and music.

*Metaphors can either help or hinder development.*

Because they are useful to growth and complete self-realization, it seems to us that metaphors must carry out two functions pertaining to self-representation and personal growth, both of which are essential to the acquisition of knowledge, as described below. Generally, "healthy" metaphors should present an integration of concrete and abstract elements related to each other in a self-referential narrative coherent in its various aspects, as the function of a unified self. Indeed, for effective progress in the area of mental health, the individual needs to construct an inter-subjective self-image, with self-awareness as a being who thinks, acts, and feels emotions in an coherent and articulated mode in relation to others and to the world.

For metaphor elaboration, the individual must be capable of understanding the associative links between events. Indeed, metaphor implies the capacity of confronting and comparing two events, thus constituting a fundamental instrument for the cognitive development conducive to understanding and interpreting the world.

Without this capability of extension, rigidity and limitation can restrict the network of meanings, leading to a reductive, symbolical interpretation of events. Symbols carry an automatic, rigid, preconstituted reading of experience if not mediated by self-referential imaginative schemas such as metaphor (e.g., symbols and symbolic rituals in obsessive-compulsive disorders). In cases of psychological disorders such as delirium it is possible to pass from a metaphorical representation of self characteristics (I'm a magician at the computer) to a delusional global identification where the cognitive "as if" function is lost and metaphor becomes an automatic reading of reality (I have become/I am/I feel like a magician, I have magical powers). It is also possible for an individual to string together a set of metaphors, each with its own possible meaning, without identifying with any, due to a lack of basic emotional-behavioral schemas of reference, a lax cognitive structure or self-referential incapacity (lack of self-monitoring capabilities, dissociative disturbances), as in the following example: "I would like to do love exercises like the water that flows between the fingers in a bottle lit up by the sun, free exercises, without guilt, as it was before eating the apple of knowledge, and as it will be after, like trapeze artists exercise." During the therapeutic interaction, the client redefines him/herself with metaphors such as "I would like to feel myself free and satisfy myself, see myself as a great eagle rather than an old tank."

Other characteristics of "unhealthy" metaphors are linked to:

- Intersubjective disturbances of the self image
- Loss of connection with one's own psychological processes (depersonalization), fragmentation of internal experience, distancing of parts of oneself in internal space
- Dissociation between the observer and the observed self, or between goals and potential, in depressive states

- The loss of self-control and self-critical capacity in maniacal states
- Disorganization in the narration of metaphors and failure to maintain an internal coherence in reasoning and discourse
- Loss of metaphorical thought capacity with a reduction in the acquisition of new information
- Loss of the interpretive function of metaphor, which becomes used as a concrete manifestation of reality rather than as a subjective construction

*An individual can change his/her metaphors by using imagery as a creative process for treating individual knowledge, getting in touch with conflicts, and considering new options and meaningful understanding.*

The function of imagery is to metaphorically represent that which cannot be seen or experienced directly on the basis of memory networks (Achterberg, 1994). It is a cognitive process, a mode of representing knowledge which uses the imaginative code working in parallel to the verbal mode (internal dialogue). Both modalities are connected to the perceptual process and to belief systems through emotive processes (Sacco, 1994). Mental images, as thought structures with symbolical and metaphorical characteristics, can involve one or more of the senses (sight, hearing, internal bodily sensations, kinesthesia, etc.) and can make metaphorical projection possible by means of synesthesia, a function relying on the associative sensory memory networks.

Imagery and the imagination run in parallel to verbal/propositional knowledge. For this reason, internal representational systems used in imagery (visual, verbal, emotional, somatic) are taken into consideration in psychotherapeutic methods. They are also useful for therapeutic purposes in that, as they are more or less associated with the emotions, they can either be evoked spontaneously or triggered. Furthermore, as these systems span conscious and unconscious states, they are linked to the deep structure of the personality, which is the foundation of metaphor construction (Sacco, 1994). Often the operative internal models, constructed in the context of interpersonal relationships, are represented metaphorically in the imagery. However the models may be linked to problematic behavioral patterns, the metaphors developed with the support of the guide in BMGIM can modify incoherent or unadaptive affective structures. It should be understood that the metaphorical process and the development of metaphors spans the entire life cycle. For this reason, incongruities and incoherencies can occur in metaphors at any stage in life. Metaphors emerging in the mature stage of life may refer to goals of self-realization, spirituality, or existential needs, which modify the values and principles behind the choices and goals in life.

As noted above, the role of metaphor in psychotherapy can serve two functions. The first is to find ways for the client to describe, represent, and communicate the self and its own unique psychic structure (a self-representative metaphor); the second is to acquire new knowledge about oneself and the world through some type of growth or creative effort (a knowledge development metaphor).

In discussing the function of the self-representative metaphor, Bonde (2000) proposes "three levels of metaphoric thinking in *GIM*: the narrative episode, configured around a core metaphor; the narrative configuration of self, and the full narrative" (p, 64), or the ensemble of metaphors for narrating the life story within a narrative configuration. Within an effective therapeutic process, metaphors can be grouped along recurrent configurations or themes which can be reconfigured in an integrated and coherent narrative for the individual's well-being.

The other function of the metaphorical process, which is the growth of the domain of knowledge, can be linked to the chaotic cerebral activity seen when, because of an ambiguous and complex perceptual stimulus (e.g., music), a portion of the brain fails to return to its rest state or find an oscillatory frequency in common accord with other areas. This disturbance produces a temporary instability of the system with the advantage of producing new types of cerebral activity, situation which can result in a development of intuitive capacity and in the elaboration of alternative solutions (Freeman, 1998) through the creation of new metaphors conducive to knowledge expansion.

## METAPHOR IN BMGIM

The manner in which metaphors are brought into play in BMGIM is connected to the neuropsychological, esthetic, and spiritual functions of the human being as these unfold in each element of BMGIM: the client-therapist relationship, the altered state of consciousness, the music, and the dialogue with the guide.

### Metaphor and the Client-Therapist Relationship

As discussed above, metaphor construction occurs in a context of intersubjectivity. It unfolds within an interpersonal attunement process. The role of the BMGIM therapist in this process varies according to each part of the session.

In the preliminary conversation, the therapist works to decodify what needs or issues the client is presenting, and based on this decoding finds a relevant theme on which to focus the session work, chooses an appropriate music program, and develops an induction involving the appropriate metaphors (myths, stories, etc.). In a way, the client-therapist discussion before the music-listening experience is a period of examining nonverbal imaginative schemas, and finding verbal metaphors that can guide and focus the work that takes place in the music-imaging period of the session.

During the music-imaging experience, the therapist gives verbal or nonverbal support and assistance needed by the client to explore his or her interior universe and evoke the metaphors which accurately represent the self or which are conducive to personal growth. To do this, the therapist must understand and work within the unique and shared metaphors offered by the client.

In the postlude integration phase, the therapist helps the client to process and elaborate upon the metaphors that have arisen in the imagery, so that their meaning can more fully understood and expressed. In this way, the metaphors can be more easily connected to the client and his/her real world.

During the entire process, it is the duty of the therapist to engage, maintain, and deepen the client's attention so that he/she can enter into an altered state of consciousness facilitating metaphorical projection between the different levels of consciousness.

## Metaphors and Altered States of Consciousness

The various types of attention—vigilant, selective, fluctuating, focused, etc.—favor operations of codification and categorization which enable the individual to receive, elaborate, and integrate internal, body stimuli with those coming from the outside world. With the repetition of experiences and the learning of new information, new neuronal circuits form which serve as bases for perceptual patterns and metaphorical projections. At the same time, these modes of attention can constitute a means of modifying states of consciousness, as for example in yoga, meditation, autogenetic training, and hypnosis. In these non-ordinary states of consciousness, the perceptual process itself can become an object of attention with the inclusion of kinesthetic information relative to embodied experiences. As previously mentioned, it is these repeated embodied experiences that become memorized and rendered automatic in imaginative schemas which provide the platform for the metaphorical process and subjective metaphors, such as self-representation, and therefore the basis for the development of new transpersonal or spiritual understanding.

In these altered states of consciousness (ASC), one can focus the attention on a multidimensional space, enabling metaphors to assume the characteristics of a representative "hologram" of the situation and of the client's growth potential. This "as if" can then represent:

- Situations experienced and maintained in the memory network in various modalities (verbal, nonverbal) and pertaining to different phases of growth (prelogic, verbal, etc.), accessible from various levels of consciousness (preconscious, conscious, etc.); and
- Potential resources for amplifying knowledge and understanding, and thereby facilitating growth or change.

Metaphors arising in altered states of consciousness can appear to be unconnected, to lack an associative network, or to have an idiosyncratic logic as to the content. They can house extraneous elements in a paradoxical manner capable of inspiring laughter (for example, "I fly and ricochet around, I jump all around; it's incredible, I'm having so much fun!") or fear (for example, "I see myself here, and, at the same time, over there on the edge of the precipice, I'm terrorized") out of the same referent and violating physical laws (for example, the law of gravity, space/time dimensions). As the client passes back and forth from ordinary states of consciousness to altered states during the therapeutic experience, with music, relaxation, and dialogue with the guide, metaphorical projections can evolve transversally, linking elements from different states of consciousness and levels of understanding and producing complex metaphors by uniting concrete and abstract elements, remembered experiences and current situations, etc. The hermeneutics of these metaphors can become clearer during the therapeutic process, by elaborating the theme through ever more precisely defined and understandable metaphorical images.

Several examples will help to illustrate the expressed ideas. R. is a thirty-year-old career woman and only child. She enrolled in therapy as a result of a depression following surgery to remove a melanoma. While listening to Beethoven's *Ninth Symphony* (Adagio Molto) in an altered state of consciousness, R. finds herself in the countryside with children playing. She sees a four-year-old boy, who is ashamedly separate from the others, and who obviously wants to join the other children, but doesn't know R. and doesn't dare to approach anyone else either. R. recalls another boy eight years old, new in her class at school, who stayed apart until she, who was of the same age, sat down next to him and proposed that they do their homework together. R. remembers that the boy's mother told her mother how happy he was. Continuing the imaginative experience, R. reverts to an altered state of consciousness and again sees the ashamed boy, whom she invites to play with the others. He gives her a kiss. R. is deeply moved at having succeeded in installing trust in him, having him participate and making him happy. At the end of the musical experience, once more in an ordinary state of consciousness. R. associates the boys with herself and in the dialogue with the guide recalls two episodes of her life in which she felt profoundly excluded and experienced deep sadness: once, at the age of eight, when her "playmate" grandfather died without her having been able to say good-bye, because her parents hid the situation from her; and at the ages of three and five, when her mother, following two spontaneous abortions, went into periods of depression, and R. as a result felt disoriented and abandoned. Both of these dramatic episodes had been completely repressed from R.'s conscious memory.

V., a forty-year-old social worker, divorced with two daughters, has tried various therapeutic approaches both for classically "therapeutic" reasons as well as for reasons of conscious personal growth. She has difficulty in her interpersonal relationships and in integrating masculine and feminine characteristics in her self-image.

While listening to Chopin's *First Piano Concerto* (Romance) V. feels strongly emotional. She sees herself as a male observer watching a ballerina dancing classical ballet in a theater. The walls dissolve and the ballerina continues to dance on a stage in a sunny meadow, while a small girl, eight to ten years old, also watches her from a hypnotized crouch at the edge of the stage. V. recognizes herself in the girl but, she says, this cannot be possible because she sees herself as the man, a removed and unobserved observer. *Metaphorical images link various states of consciousness and levels of knowledge.* The girl and the ballerina dance together, and this evokes for V. her two daughters (modification in the altered state). She wants to continue watching even though she does not feel excluded: "a part of me is on stage," she says, moved. Listening to Respighi's *Fountains of Rome—Villa Giulia,* V., still as the gray man, goes to dance with the ballerina, but feels smothered, and imprisoned in the wet-suit he is wearing (altered state). V. stops dancing with the ballerina and rips the wet-suit open, stepping out into a colored light, still a man but free, lighthearted and joyous inside to the point of feeling as if he/she will burst out of the constraining wet-suit. While listening to Respighi's *Fountains of Rome—Villa Medici*, V. finds herself suspended in air, moving in a zero-gravity atmosphere. She emerges from a blue conic layer, swimming/ flying toward a luminous and dense intermediate layer above which is another layer of more limpid light. She feels supported and protected by these layers which she notices are permeable (*transpersonal metaphor of internal growth*). In the concluding dialogue with the guide, V. says that she sees these experiences as parts of her life story, and that this had never before been so clear to her. In particular, around the age of eight, she was sexually abused by a male friend of the family, a traumatic experience that she had repressed, fearing other eventual attempts at sexual aggression. The male figure imagined should be seen as a metaphor carrying multiple meanings in that it involves both the episodic memory connected to the abuse and her two failed marriages as well as characteristics of herself that await free expression and acceptance.

## Metaphors and Listening to Music

Art, and therefore music, can, by virtue of the symbolical capacities of human beings, be considered as an expression of the metaphorical process proceeding from embodied functions and imaginative schemas. As with other functions necessary for the development of the organism, the metaphorical process seems to present a circular path with a retroactive mechanism: from inside the individual to the external environment with the creation of poetical, figurative, or musical productions and vice-versa, from the external environment to the individual, in a continuous cyclical exchange of information essential for avoiding the encroachment of entropy and the collapse of the system, be it individual or social.

Due to the ambiguity and complexity of the stimuli, musical compositions convey an enormous quantity of data which evoke responses from virtually the entire Central Nervous System, and therefore evoke and solicit metaphors. Studies of the auditory integration system show that sounds produce variations in the rear-brain opioids (Scifo, 1998) and that the opioid system plays a fundamental role in the modification of behavior in mammals, given that endorphins carry out their activity in areas of the brain responsible for integrating sensations, emotions, and affects, such as the limbic system (Panksepp, 1996; Panksepp et al., 1996). Intense emotional experiences can modify the internal operative models, since the affective involvement makes for more efficient cognitive-cortical activity.

Finally, keeping in mind that memory is stored in neural, cortical, and subcortical networks, with superimpositions and intersections (Fuster, 1998), music in its various components (rhythm, tempo, melody, pitch, loudness, etc.) can be easily connected to metaphor production, especially when listened to in an altered state of consciousness. In particular, the increase of endorphins can stimulate unusual sensations—ecstatic emotions and powerful feelings of being part of a whole, as also happens in meditative and mystical experiences. Such experiences are only possible when the "traveler" is willing, and when the "conditions are conducive to transpersonal work" (Bruscia, 1998, p. 150). It is worth adding that the setting for BMGIM, with the music as mediator, can induce a variation in endorphins in the guide as well, as an effect of resonance and empathy with the client's experience and as self-compensation for the assistance given to the client toward the creative productivity of the metaphorical/therapeutic process. The client/therapist relationship, especially in BMGIM, shows some similarities with that of the mother-child relationship. Research in this area underlines the role of the endorphins as a reward which reinforces the mother and improves her ability to respond to the child's needs (Panksepp, 1996; Panksepp et al., 1996).

The state of relaxation and the guidance of the facilitator are conducive to selective attention on the part of the listener to both the musical stimulus and to his or her own current psycho-physical state. In this way imaginative schemas are activated, taking the form of metaphors with affective and cognitive characteristics similar to the internal event of which they provide a representation.

The very perception of music, as a dynamic and an esthetic event, gives birth to new metaphors through the personal responses evoked, in an ongoing process of knowledge. The brain in fact modifies information on the internal and external environment in response to perceptions, thus acquiring new knowledge useful for change and growth.

In the experience of listening, the music itself sometimes remains in the background, and sometimes takes a prominent role in what occurs in the client's imagination or in the relationship with the guide. Even if it remains in the background, however, the musical stimulus, with its structural, psycho-physical, evocative and associative properties, provides the subtext catalyzing the development of the experience, a secure base of support, and the source of information for constructing new metaphors.

The analysis of experiences provoked in various music programs of BMGIM suggest a division of the programs into three categories: those for the initial phase of therapy, those for the intermediate working phase, and those for an advanced phase.

Extensive clinical observations furnish information concerning the categories of transpersonal phenomena associated with different music programs. Lewis (1999) reports changes in the space-time dimension; changes in the perception of the body felt as light and without limits, experiences of light or energy, spiritual images, profound emotions of joy and universal love, feeling of union with the cosmos. Erdonmez Grocke reports the possibility of music stimulating "pivotal moments" (Erdonmez Grocke, 1999); and Wrangsjö and Körlin (1995) report on the benefits obtainable with psychiatric patients.

Of course, from time to time, idiosyncrasies of a psychological, cultural, diagnostic, or therapeutic nature can determine the choice of a program and its eventual adaptation by the specialized guide.

In the author's opinion, music programs used in BMGIM are conducive to provoking at least three imaginative schemas fundamental to the development of the metaphorical process.

The first is the *schema of balance*. Balance is one of the most pervasive aspects of human self-experience, whose nature and meaning emerge from the structure of bodily and perceptual events.

The second is the *schema of movement*, connected with the *schema of balance* insofar as both are functions of the neuromotor system, but characterized by a directional process toward an end. In particular, the schema of movement solicited by music is the *schema of ballistic movement*, which includes functions at the reptilian, subcortical, and cortical levels of the brain, associated with bodily sensations and primary emotions. Scientists suppose that ballistic movements, programmed in anticipation toward an end, might be a basic function of the human brain explaining the higher cognitive abilities, such as linguistic syntax, logical organization, and music (Calvin, 1999). This spatio-temporal schema is based on temporal perception, requiring very short periods of time to program and find cognitive solutions and behaviors conducive to realization of the goal. From both a philogenetic and ontogenetic viewpoint, human intelligence first resolves the problems of movement before moving on to abstract problems. This embodied schema develops in the context of the interaction with the caregiver, especially when the subcortical systems of the brain (i.e., the cerebellum and limbic system) are engaged in order to process and understand the rapid micro-movements in the facial muscles (mouth, eyes), which express the emotional state and level of involvement of the caregiver.

The third basic imaginative schema for the development of the metaphorical process is the *schema of rhythm*, associated with the first two as a function of the neuromotor system, but different in that it furnishes a temporal organization to neurophysiological and psychological events.

The *schema of balance* can be evoked by the structure of the musical compositions and by the organization of each program relative to the sequence of the pieces, while the *schema of movement* is brought into play by the musical components such as melody, intensity, pitch, and speed. The *schema of rhythm* emerges from the rhythmical/temporal dimension of the music which can induce entrainment with the rhythmical-temporal structure of the subject, and thereby reinforce the emotional and cognitive state present at the moment of the experience.

In the case where the client perceives a critical discrepancy between or among different schemas, this discrepancy could provoke a different state of consciousness and bring up memories of a repressed event or engender new metaphors. This can be illustrated by the following example.

C. is a young, hardworking, and successful professional about to make a very important decision regarding his career, but he feels confused and insecure. Listening to Ravel's *Introduction and Allegro*, the decisive rhythm and intense sounds bother him quite a bit, and produce the somatic reaction of a headache. In the concluding verbal reflection, C. states that he felt the music as being in contrast with himself, as happens when arguing with others (his wife, other colleagues) who scream rather than reason, a behavior he finds intolerable. While listening to Mendelssohn's *Fifth Symphony* (Andante), however, C. feels in tune with the music; he finds himself on the open sea and is moved, seeing himself as a boy admiring the stupendous spectacle, experiencing a fabulous sensation. He feels his heart opening up and regenerating. During the verbal discussion afterward, C. associates the sea with peace and serenity, and sees it as a source of vital energy for recharging his inner being at this moment in his life.

In the case where the discrepancy in the rhythmical/temporal organization of the music is too great, and therefore unadapted to the rhythmical/temporal schema of the individual, it will not be processed, and cannot be a useful element for growth in the metaphorical process.

The three imaginative schemas described above organize self-perception in space, time and relationships with others and with the environment. They form at a prelogic stage as nonpropositional structures with preconceptual meanings. For this reason they participate in the sensory and emotional dimension of knowledge as well as in the unconscious realm. From the schemas, linked to bodily experiences, metaphors develop which are at first concrete and then abstract, with the same nature (balance, movement, rhythm) in various areas of experience (emotional, psychological, spiritual, etc.). The three schemas—balance, movement, rhythm—can be seen as parts of a common overriding schema, the *schema of change*, which is the foundation of every biological and therapeutic process as well as of the relative metaphors.

## Metaphors and Imagery Creation

In this chapter, metaphorical processes are viewed as fundamental to the development of knowledge in human beings. Metaphor represents a pervasive modality of knowledge linking sensory, emotional and cognitive functions at different levels of consciousness. At the same time, the metaphors expressed in BMGIM can represent *mental states,* that is to say, recurring patterns of experience and behavior (Horowitz, 1987, 1991) with specific themes, emotions, images, and sensations creating the various types of *imagery* (images, memories, fantasies, emotions, bodily sensations, etc.).

The music programs, with various pieces from the classical literature, have been studied with various aims in mind, including:

- Exploring the quality and modalities (caring, help/support) of relationships
- Identifying resources and elaborating alternate or creative solutions/choices
- Evoking sensations/emotions and bringing up repressed traumatic situations
- Removing blockages in bodily energies
- Furnishing support in the face of difficult or painful situations (chronic or terminal illnesses; struggles, etc.)
- Facilitating "peak" and transpersonal experiences

Metaphors involved in the various types of *imagery* can be associated with both the musical stimulus as mediator, and with the subjective *mental state* and its functional correlations in play at the various moments of the imaginative experience (emotions, memories, fantasies, internal dialogue, perception, bodily sensations, transpersonal experiences, etc.). The client's relative stage in the therapeutic journey will also furnish metaphorical themes represented by the various components of the imagery. An example can illustrate more clearly.

Listening to Ravel's *Daphnis and Chloë, Second Suite*, C. sees the image of a central black point, a whirlpool, and goes toward it, anxious that she might be sucked in, afraid and blocked in her body. This state brings up the memory of the death of her mother when she was three years old. Then, listening to the same piece, the music transforms C. into a bird darting about, freeing the blocked energy and allowing her to overcome her fear of the black void. While listening to Debussy's *Nocturne—Sirènes*), she once again experiences being in a swirling eddy, but here C. feels pleasure and does not feel in danger of being dragged in and drowned, even with the same dark colors and a similar situation to the one imagined during the piece by Ravel. With the two pieces of Duruflé (*In Paradisum, Nôtre Père*), the metaphor is a nocturnal image of the universe as a wave of energy vibrating everywhere. C. feels herself vibrating, at one with infinite space, united with the music in a pure, intense and joyous commotion.

This example specifically illustrates how metaphors use various modalities of imagery (emotions, sensations, memories, fantasies) to represent *mental states* and their correlates (emotions, themes, sensations, etc.). It is possible to follow the passage effected by the client from one mental state to another in the imagery and metaphors, by noting such themes as:

- The loss of a significant attachment/caring figure, with a defensive reaction blocking sensations and emotions to protect against an external situation perceived as annihilating (the image of the whirlpool and anxiety of being sucked in and drowned. As a result of the distortion of the other meanings elaborated in her representational models, C. had not integrated the traumatic experience at a conscious, verbal level, resulting in grave consequences in her emotional, sexual, and relational life);

- Unblocking and awareness of one's proper resources and vital functions—sensations, emotions—(imagery such as the fantasy of being a bird and going up and down at one's pleasure);
- The capacity for mastery faced with difficult situations (imagining oneself in swirling water with dark colors in the center, but feeling relaxation and pleasure);
- Joy, energy, and the feeling of oneness with the environment (imagery representative of a transpersonal experience involving profound and positive emotions and a sense of cosmic unity).

## Metaphors and Verbal Dialogue While Imaging

The ongoing dialogue with the guide is intended to facilitate the exploration of the client's internal world, directing, maintaining, and concentrating the attention on various aspects of the imaginative experience. This focusing of attention is conducive to the creation of new metaphors which enable the client to see him/herself from different perspectives and to modify or amplify the context of his or her experience. In addition, the verbal support (repetition of emotions, key words spoken by the client, solicitation of a description) can help to define vague images and sensations and enable the client to operate intentionally in confronting a difficult situation and elaborating a useful metaphor for change. Following are several illustrative transcripts of the client-therapist dialogue.

FIRST EXAMPLE

C. I'm in the place where I should be [on top of clouds].
T. You're in your place.
C. I feel as if I belong here. I feel that it's my place . . . it's white, bright and cool . . . I see the sun in the distance . . . I see its light all around me . . . I feel its heat all over my body, I face the sun and I 'm completely immersed, without being burned.
T. Does it have a form?
C. At first like a ball, but now it's all around me: it's heat and light.
T. And how are you?

C.  I'm looking at my hands and feet and I know I'm real, I'm walking.

T.  How do your feet feel?

C.  Strong, on solid ground. In the distance I see a large house, I'm going toward it . . .

T.  Do you want to describe it?

C.  Large, quite beautiful, with a stupendous gate opening up. I go inside . . . I know that I am invited.

T.  You feel invited.

C.  Yes, by a person who knows me. I don't know who. I have a feeling of security, tranquility . . . I feel great peace and love in this place.

The words of the guide also tend to assist the client in metaphorically elaborating creative solutions in difficult situations, and paying closer attention to his/her own resources.

SECOND EXAMPLE

The client sees himself as perfect in every way; for this reason he has difficulty reconciling his ideal and real selves. He is listening to Holst's *The Planet—Mars*:

C.  I'm opening a door, and . . . I see a precipice.

T.  Describe it.

C.  There's a void. There are cities at the bottom. I don't know what to do . . .

T.  You can look more closely.

C.  I'm turning around, there's a large umbrella, like a parachute.

T.  What else?

C.  Um, a very steep staircase which I hadn't seen, going down. . . I'm afraid of heights! I'm carrying the umbrella behind me. I could use it as a parachute, but I'm afraid it won't hold. I have my feet on the step, but it's better to keep my back to the void.

T.  What are you feeling?

C.  I'm afraid. I don't know what to do.

T.  How does your body feel?

C.  In shape. The staircase it scares me, it's almost vertical. I'm afraid of the void . . . I feel very agitated.

T.  You feel agitated and in shape. And your legs?

C. Strong . . . there's a handrail, I hadn't noticed. If I don't look down, I'm able to go down slowly, it doesn't matter if I take a long time. I'm calming down.

THIRD EXAMPLE

This client, with a very active lifestyle, tends to impose ever-more demanding and stressful objectives on himself; he has been suffering severe depression. The following exchange took place while listening to Orff's *Carmina Burana*:

C. I'm standing still on a trampoline.
T. What do you want to do?
C. Go down on the ground, pirouette on my toes. . .
T. How do you feel?
C. I have the feeling of being on the ground, but at the same time moving very fast, as if unable to walk.
T. Let the music help you.
C. I'm about to walk, but I'm still up in the air.
T. What can you do?
C. I grab on to a pole with all my strength . . . there's an incredible wind . . .
T. What are you feeling?
C. I've had enough of this situation! I feel as if my arms are very strong, and I can anchor myself to the pole and to the ground.
T. Finally you've succeeded in using your strength to stop yourself!

## Metaphors and Verbal Processing

In the concluding dialogue, the client and guide reflect on the metaphors which came up in the musical and imaginative experience. Their representation and their eventual transformation during the course of the session bring up associations with life situations, indicative of the client's lifestyle, or with possible manifestations of disorders. The verbal meaning given by the client at this point in the encounter is mediated by the experience of the metaphor autonomously constructed in the imagery and is therefore full of those subjective data necessary for effective therapeutic change and/or an enrichment of personal knowledge. It is the responsibility of the therapist to teach, when necessary, how to recognize associative networks for metaphor development as well as how to elaborate metaphors on the basis of symbols by attributing self-referential meaning (for example, the dragon is a symbol of strength; I imagine a dragon transmitting his strength to me, now that I'm aware of my own resources I feel strong like a dragon).

An example taken from the eighth session of Z. helps to illustrate this. Z. imagines that she is hiking along a path on a volcano, in a bleak, barren landscape with a few scattered trees. A dog and a horse join her on her hike up. Then Z. sees a snake, an animal unfamiliar to her, climbing slowly with elegant movements. Z. becomes curious and fascinated with the snake's calmness, as if it wanted to show her how to climb calmly. The snake pulls up next to her and winds itself around her foot, then up her entire body. She feels a sensation of pleasure, as if the snake is smooth as silk. Once it arrives at the height of Z.'s face, the snake opens its mouth and swallows her. Inside, she feels herself becoming a snake which then molts. Z. emerges from her shed skin transformed and feeling light, dressed in a white, luminous dress. In the concluding dialogue to this experience, Z. associates the dog with "loyalty" and the horse with "energy," characteristics which she is aware of having, while she associates the snake with calmness and wisdom in facing difficult situations in life, a characteristic she wants to integrate into her experience. Z. is fully aware during the experience with BMGIM that by participating she truly feels "reborn."

Every six to eight sessions, the therapist and client together often carry out a verbal review, synthesing the data to: 1) note the evolution of the client's suffering through the various metaphors presented; 2) link, in a coherent narrative, those metaphors which present meaningful connections (theme mapping, mental states); and 3) enable the client to extend the information in the metaphor among the different levels of consciousness (logic, prelogic) and various states of consciousness, with the integration necessary for the growth of self-knowledge.

# CONCLUSION

This analysis of the role of metaphor in BMGIM allows us to conclude by saying that, given the basic importance of metaphor to the development of knowledge, BMGIM is a quintessential example of the metaphorical process, and as such is naturally conducive to effecting change in an individual. This can be illustrated by comparing the path made possible in BMGIM with the imaginative voyage of Dante in his epic poem *The Divine Comedy*, a fertile metaphor of man going through the horrors of the Inferno and the eschatological sufferings of Purgatory, to reach, finally, the sublime joy of Divine Love in Paradise. In the great medieval poet's masterpiece, as in each individual case study of GIM, metaphor imposes itself as a primary, irreducible function of knowledge.

## References

Achterberg, J., Dossy, B., & Kolkmeier, L. (1994). *Rituals of Healing. Using Imagery for Health and Wellness.* New York: Bantam Books.

Adler, A. (1927). *Understanding Human Nature.* New York: Greenberg.

Bonde, L. O. (2000). Metaphor and narrative in Guided Imagery and Music. *Journal of the Association for Music and Imagery,* 7, 59–76.

Bowlby, J. (1969). *Attachment and Loss 1: Attachment.* New York: Basic Books.

Bruscia, K. E. (1998). *Defining Music Therapy.* Second Edition. Gilsum, NH: Barcelona Publishers.

Breitling, D., Guenther, W., & Rondot, P. (1987). Auditory perception of music measured by brain electrical activity mapping. *Neuropsychologia,* 25 (5), 765–774.

Calvin, W.H. (1996). *The Cerebral Code: Thinking a Thought in the Mosaic of the Mind.* MIT Press.

Calvin, W.H. (1999). La comparsa dell'intelligenza. *Le Scienze Dossier.* 7, 52–59.

Dalle Luche, R. (2000). Subject and identity: indications from psychiatric practice. *Giornale Italiano Psicopatologia,* 6 (2), 313–318.

Dimaggio, G., Nicolò, G., Semerari, A., Carcione, A., Falcone, M., Pontalti, I., & Procacci, M. (2000). Stati mentali e narrazioni. Come variano nel corso del processo psicoterapeutico? *Quaderni di Psicoterapia Cognitiva* 7 (3, 2), 30–54.

Edelman, G. M. (1989). *The Remembered Present. A biological Theory of Consciousness.* New York: Basic Books.

Erdonnez Grocke, D. (1999). The music which underpins pivotal moments in Guided Imagery and Music. In T. Wigram and J. De Backer (eds.), *Clinical Applications of Music Therapy in Psychiatry.* London: Jessica Kingsley.

Estes, W. K. (1985). Memory for temporal information. In J. A. Michon & J. L. Jackson (eds.) *Time, Mind, and Behaviour.* Berlin: Springer Verlag.

Faienza, C. (1998). Stimolo verbale e musicale e dominanza emisferica nel neonato. In G. G. Perilli & F. Russo (eds.) *La Medicina dei Suoni.* Roma: Borla.

Freeman, W. J. (1998). La fisiologia della percezione. *Le Scienze Quadern,* 101, 32–39.

Fuster, J. M. (1998). Reti di memoria. *Le Scienze Quadern,* 101, 67–75.

Gardner, H. (1982). *Art, Mind & Brain: A Cognitive Approach to Creativity.* New York: Basic Books.

Gardner, H. (1983). *Frames of Mind: The Theory of Multiple Intelligences.* New York: Basic Books.

Gardner, H. (1999). Una molteplicità di intelligenze. *Le Scienze Dossier,* 1, 18–23.

Giordanella Perilli, G. (1995). Subjective tempo in adults with and without psychiatric disorders. *Music Therapy Perspectives,* 13, 2, 104–109.

Giordanella Perilli, G. (1998). Differenti modi di percepire, sperimentare e comprendere gli stessi brani musicali durante il processo riabilitativo e terapeutico. In G. G. Perilli & F. Russo (eds.). *La Medicina dei Suoni.* Roma: Borla.

Guerrini Degl'Innocenti, B., Selvi, A, Valtancoli, A., & Pazzagli, A. (2000). Trauma and internal working models: psychopathological implications of attachment theory. *Giornale Italiano Psicopatologia,* 6 (2), 201–208.

Guiraud, P. (1955). *La Semantique.* Paris: P.U.F.

Hofstadter, D. R. (1979). *Godel, Escher, Bach: An Eternale Golden Braid.* New York: Basic Books.

Horowitz, M. J. (1987). *States of Mind. Configurational Analysis of Individual Psychology.* Second Edition. New York: Plenum Press.

Horowitz, M.J. (1991). States, schemas and control: General Theories of psychotherapy integration. *Journal of Psychotherapy Integration,* 1 (2), 85–102.

Imberty, M. (1986). *Suoni, Emozioni, Significati.* Bologna: Clueb.

Johnson, M. (1987). *The Body in the Mind. The Bodily Basis of Meaning, Imagination, and Reason.* Chicago: The University of Chicago Press.

Lakoff, G. & Johnson, M. (1999). *Philosophy in the Flesh. The Embodied Mind and Its Challenge to Western Thought.* New York: Basic Books.

Lewis, K. (1999). The Bonny Method of Guided Imagery and Music: Matrix for transpersonal experience. *Journal of the Association for Music & Imagery,* 6, 63–85.

Liotti, G. (1994). *La dimensione interpersonale della coscienza.* Roma: NIS.

Liotti, G. (2000). Disorganised attachment, models of borderlines states, and evolutionary psychotherapy. In P. Gilbert & K. Bailey (eds.). *Genes on the Couch: Explorations in Evolutionary Psychotherapy.* Hove Psychology Press.

Michon, J. A. & Jackson, J. L. (1984). Attentional effort and cognitive strategies in the processing of temporal information. *Annals of the New York Academy of Sciences,* 423 (11), 298–321.

Oliverio, A. (1986). Il Senno di prima. In A. Oliverio (Ed.). *L'Evoluzione del Cervello, Scienza & Dossier,* 8, 14–17. Firenze: Giunti Barbera.

Panksepp, J. (1996). *Affective Neuroscience. The Foundations of Human and Animal Emotions.* New York: Oxford University Press.

Panksepp, J., Nerson, E., Bekkedal, M. Y. (1996). Brain systems for the mediation of social separation—distress and social reward. Evolutionary antecedents and neuropeptide intermediaries. In *Proceedings from the New York Academy of Science Conference.*

Pribram, K. H. (1971). *Languages of the Brain. Experimental Paradoxes and Principles in Neuropsychology.* Englewood Cliffs, N.J.: Prentice-Hall.

Sacco, G. (1994). *I Giochi della Mente. Teorie, Ricerche e Applicazioni delle Immagini Mentali.* Roma: Melusina.

Scifo, R. (1998). L'autolesionismo nell'autismo infantile: la teoria degli oppioidi a supporto di trattamenti integrati farmacologici e musicoterapici. In G.G. Perilli & F. Russo (Eds.). *La Medicina dei Suoni.* Roma: Borla.

Scrimali, T., Cultrera, G., Auditore, R. (1998). La dimensione psicofisiologica del suono. In G. G. Perilli & F. Russo (eds.). *La Medicina dei Suoni.* Roma: Borla.

Stern, D. (1985). *The Interpersonal World of the Infant.* New York: Basic Books.

Sutherland, G., Newman, B., & Rachman, S. (1982). Experimental investigations of the relations between mood and intrusive unwanted cognitions. *British Journal of Medical Psychology* 55, 127–38.

Thaut, M. (2000). *A Scientific Model of Music in Therapy and Medicine.* San Antonio: IMR Press.

Trevarthen, C., Aitken, K., Papoudi, D., & Robarts, J. (1997). *Children with Autism. Diagnosis and Interventions to Meet Their Needs.* London: Jessica Kingsley.

*Chapter Twenty-Three*

# QUANTITATIVE RESEARCH IN GUIDED IMAGERY AND MUSIC (GIM): A REVIEW

## Cathy McKinney

Quantitative research has a distinguished history in GIM. In the early days, Helen Bonny recognized the importance of documenting treatment outcomes using methodologies acceptable to the medical and psychotherapeutic communities (Bonny, 1976). Since that time, GIM-trained researchers have begun to develop a substantial body of quantitative literature demonstrating efficacy of the method and also beginning to explore questions about various components of the process.

This chapter will summarize the quantitative literature, focusing first on studies that examine some of the measurable effects of a series of *individual* sessions, herein referred to as the Bonny Method of Guided Imagery and Music (BMGIM). The next section will review studies that have examined various dimensions of spontaneous imaging with music (herein referred to as group GIM), and one study that examined the validity and reliability of an inventory to assess responses to BMGIM. The chapter will conclude with implications for clinical practice and for future research in BMGIM and group GIM.

## OUTCOME STUDIES

The GIM literature has a rapidly expanding body of experimental studies that document therapeutic outcomes resulting from a series of six or more individual BMGIM sessions. These sessions were each one and a half to two hours in length and followed the typical form that includes a preliminary conversation, induction and mental focus, spontaneous imaging with a series of classical music selections, and post-music return and integration (Bonny, 1978a).

Participants in these studies have included healthy adults, individuals with mental disorders, and people with chronic medical conditions. While the sample size of each of these studies is modest, together they offer mounting evidence of the efficacy of the method.

In the first experimental study of BMGIM, Bonny (1976) recruited twenty-four adult volunteers with "mild to moderate neurotic symptomatology" (p. 47). Participants were randomly assigned to BMGIM or "brief intensive psychotherapy without music and imagery" (p. 48) conditions. The length of the series of individual sessions was determined for each participant by the "course of therapy" (p. 48), with a limit of sixty hours of treatment. Although no statistical analysis was reported, Bonny indicated that results included the following:

- Participants in BMGIM required less time in terms of hours spent in therapy, number of sessions, and duration of treatment.
- Not only were the treatment goals of BMGIM participants often met, but other areas not directly addressed were also affected.
- Within six months, nearly half of those in the control group had reentered some type of therapy while none of those in the experimental group had done so.
- This first experimental study began the documentation of BMGIM as an efficacious, cost-effective form of therapy for persons with mild to moderate nonpsychotic mental disorders.

Wrangsjö and Körlin (1995) examined effects of a series of individual BMGIM sesions on psychological distress (Hopkins Symptom Checklist-90), interpersonal relationships (Inventory of Interpersonal Problems), and inner resources (Sense of Coherence Scale) in fourteen adults, ages nineteen to sixty-three. These two men and twelve women, who presented with mild to moderate disturbance, completed the assessment during the first session and at the end of treatment. As in Bonny (1976), the number of sessions varied according to individual need. Wrangsjö and Körlin found that following BMGIM, participants showed a significant decrease in almost every measure of psychological distress, including depression, anxiety, obsession-compulsion, hostility, paranoid ideation, psychoticism, and interpersonal sensitivity. Participants also demonstrated significant improvement in their interpersonal relationships as well as an increased sense of meaningfulness and manageability in their lives.

In a follow-up study, Körlin and Wrangsjö (2000) extended their 1995 work by reporting the results for an accumulated 30 adults. Using a dividing point of two standard deviations above the mean T-score for the pretest global symptom index of the Hopkins Symptom Checklist-90, Körlin and Wrangsjö split the participants into functional ($n = 20$) and dysfunctional ($n = 10$) groups. They found that all of the 10 participants initially scoring in the dysfunctional range at the outset of BMGIM treatment decreased their levels of distress and 6 moved into the functional range after treatment. For this group, effect sizes were large on somatization, depression, psychoticism, and the three composite scores that indicate severity and breadth of symptoms. As might be expected given the lower pretest scores, effect sizes are more modest for the functional group, mostly in the low to moderate range. However, participants in this group demonstrated improvement in several subscales that are considered to measure dimensions that are hard to change in psychotherapy, including the Hostility subscale of the Hopkins Symptom Checklist-90 and the Autocratic, Vindictive, and Cold subscales of the Inventory of Interpersonal Problems. The authors postulate that these changes may be a function of the nature of BMGIM in which most of the processing is done through inner imagery rather than outwardly with a therapist. For the total sample, significant improvement was found in every area with the exception of paranoid ideation. Similar to the findings of their earlier study (Wrangsjö & Körlin, 1995), Körlin and Wrangsjö (2000) report significant improvement in interpersonal relationships (medium effect size) and in meaningfulness and manageability (low and moderate effect sizes, respectively).

While several case studies have described physical benefits of GIM (McDonald, 1986; Merritt, 1993; Pickett, 1987), McDonald (1990) was the first researcher to use quantitative methods in a controlled study to investigate the potential of BMGIM to improve physiological function. He recruited thirty adults, ages twenty-one to seventy-five, who had essential hypertension. He randomly assigned each participant to one of three conditions: BMGIM, verbal psychotherapy, or control. Those in the BMGIM group received six weekly individual BMGIM sessions, those in the verbal psychotherapy group received six weekly verbal therapy sessions, and those in the control group received no treatment. Blood pressure was measured three times at four time points: prior to the sessions, weekly during the treatment period, following the series of sessions, and six weeks after the final session. The mean systolic and diastolic pressures were used as data. McDonald found that those in the group receiving BMGIM demonstrated a significant decline in both mean systolic and mean diastolic blood pressure while the mean blood pressure of those in both the verbal psychotherapy and control groups was unchanged. While diastolic blood pressure in the group receiving BMGIM dropped significantly during the series of sessions and stayed at that level through the follow-up period, systolic blood pressure declined more gradually and demonstrated the sharpest decline during the six weeks after the sessions had ended. This was the first study to demonstrate experimentally not only positive physiological change as a result of individual BMGIM sessions, but also that the change continues beyond the time of the sessions themselves.

In a pilot study of effects of BMGIM in healthy adults, McKinney and colleagues (McKinney, Antoni, Kumar, & Kumar, 1995) worked with eight healthy adults randomly assigned to GIM and wait-list control groups. Participants in the BMGIM group had six weekly individual BMGIM sessions while those in the control were offered a series of six sessions after all measurements were collected. Prior to and one week following the intervention period, participants completed mood assessments (Profile of Mood States). McKinney et al. found that BMGIM significantly attenuated depressed mood. Further, they found that BMGIM accounted for 43 percent of the variance in posttest level of depression. Such a strong association suggests that BMGIM exerts a powerful influence on depressed mood in healthy adults.

In a follow-up study, McKinney, Antoni, Kumar, Tims, and McCabe (1997) examined the effects of a series of individual BMGIM sessions on mood and cortisol, a hormone associated with stress. They recruited twenty-eight healthy adults, ages twenty-three to forty-five, who had been screened for both psychological and physical health and certain health behaviors (e.g., smoking, recreational drug use, alcohol intake) and randomly assigned them to either a BMGIM or a wait-list control condition. Participants in the BMGIM group engaged in six individual biweekly BMGIM sessions while those in the control group had no sessions until all data were collected. Mood was assessed (using the Profile of Mood States) and a sample of blood was collected at three timepoints—entry into the study, one week after the final session, and seven weeks after the final session. Prior to each BMGIM session, participants in the BMGIM group also completed a standardized assessment of mood during the previous week.

McKinney, Antoni, et al. (1997) found that BMGIM significantly reduced depressed mood, fatigue, and total mood disturbance, all of which remained significantly lower through the follow-up period. In addition, BMGIM lowered resting levels of cortisol so that levels were significantly decreased seven weeks following the final session. They note that the observed pattern of change in cortisol lagging behind that of mood indicates that BMGIM may have induced a "shift . . . in the cortisol regulatory system" (p. 398), resulting in decreased stress-related physiological activation.

Through an analysis of the biweekly mood assessments in the BMGIM participants, McKinney, Antoni, et al. (1997) also found depressed mood, fatigue, and total mood disturbance reached a level significantly lower than at entry between the fifth and sixth sessions. They concluded, "for healthy adults unfamiliar with BMGIM, a series of six individual sessions would be a minimum number to demonstrate significant reductions in mood state immediately following the intervention" (p. 398).

Jacobi (1995) explored effects of a series of ten weekly individual BMGIM sessions on pain (McGill Pain Questionnaire); functional measures of disease status, including walking speed, morning stiffness, and number of affected joints; depression (Center for Epidemiological Studies—Depression Scale), and psychological distress (Symptom Checklist-90—Revised) in twenty-seven participants with rheumatoid arthritis. Assessments were made at entry, midpoint, two weeks after the last session, and eight weeks after the last session. She found significant decreases in psychological distress, including depression, anxiety, hostility, phobic anxiety, somatization, and psychoticism; pain; and number of affected joints. Walking speed was significantly increased. Caution is warranted in the interpretation and generalization of these results due to the absence of a control group to rule out change over time due to experimental participation (i.e., Hawthorne effect). Nevertheless, these findings suggest that BMGIM may be efficacious in improving both physical and psychological status of person with rheumatoid arthritis.

In the first experimental study of the effects of BMGIM in persons with cancer, Burns (1999) examined quality of life (Quality of Life—Cancer) and mood (Profile of Mood States) in eight women with a history of either breast or ovarian cancer. Participants were randomly assigned to a BMGIM or wait-list control group. Those in the BMGIM group participated in ten weekly individual BMGIM sessions. Assessments were made at entry, following the series of sessions, and at six-week follow-up. Those in the BMGIM group reported decreased mood disturbance at posttest while mood disturbance for controls remained stable across the same period. This lowered level of mood disturbance in BMGIM participants remained at follow-up. Quality of life for those in the group receiving individual BMGIM increased across time points while levels for the control group were unchanged. Although the small sample size requires that these findings be interpreted cautiously, this study suggests that additional experiments are warranted in the potential of BMGIM for mitigating distress and improving quality of life in persons with cancer.

Little (1999) has explored the effects of a series of six biweekly, individual BMGIM sessions on grief (Grief Experience Inventory) in hospice staff and volunteers. Participants were randomly assigned to experimental ($n = 22$) or wait-list control ($n = 16$) conditions. While there were no significant changes for the control group in any of the dimensions of grief assessed, those who experienced BMGIM experienced a significant reduction in despair.

Taking a different methodological approach to studying effects of BMGIM, Maack and Nolan (1999) used quantitative descriptive methods to survey former BMGIM clients, each of whom had experienced at least six individual BMGIM sessions. Questionnaires sent through BMGIM therapists were returned by twenty-five clients, ages sixteen to eighty-three, who had experienced at least six individual BMGIM sessions. Drawing from published case studies, theoretical literature, and oral reports of BMGIM therapists, Maack and Nolan devised a list of possible areas that might be changed as a result of BMGIM sessions. More than half of the surveyed participants reported gains as a result of BMGIM in the following areas: getting more in touch with emotions, gaining insight into problems, spiritual growth, discovering new parts of self, and increased relaxation. When asked to identify the most three most important outcomes of their work, the participants identified the same five areas plus change in mood and change in self-esteem. Interestingly in light of the experimental findings that change continues beyond the time of the sessions, 67 percent reported that they had continued to improve mentally, 46 percent had continued to improve in physical areas, and 88 percent had continued to improve in transpersonal areas since completion of the sessions.

Once outcome efficacy has been demonstrated in clinically relevant variables for BMGIM, one of the next questions concerns mediating variables. What are the pathways through which BMGIM works to effect psychological and physiological change? While many of these may be beyond the scope of empirical research methodology, McKinney and Antoni (2000) have examined emotional expression as one possible mediating variable. Some GIM writers have proposed a primary role for emotion in the GIM process (Goldberg, 1992; Jacobi, 1995), but no previous experimental study has considered this question.

Prior to and one week following a thirteen week intervention period, McKinney and Antoni (2000) asked twenty-eight adults to write for thirty minutes an essay about the most stressful event of the previous two months. Participants were randomly assigned to GIM or wait-list control conditions. Those in the BMGIM condition experienced a series of six individual biweekly BMGIM sessions; those in the wait-list control group were offered sessions after the data were collected. McKinney and Antoni operationally defined emotional expression as the number of words describing a specific emotion that were used in the essay. Two independent raters tallied the number of emotion words by valence (positive and negative) with satisfactory inter-rater reliability (.92 at pretest, .79 at posttest). The mean length of the essays was the same in the two groups and did not significantly change between pre- and posttest.

McKinney and Antoni (2000) found that the BMGIM participants wrote significantly fewer positive emotion words in their posttest essays while those in the control group showed no pre–post change. There was no significant change in the number of negative emotion words in either group. Thus, BMGIM process may encourage one to describe stressful events with congruent emotion rather than use incongruent emotion words. Further, McKinney and Antoni found that both fewer positive emotion words and more negative emotion words significantly correlated with lower posttest levels of both mood disturbance and serum levels of cortisol, a stress hormone. The correlation with cortisol level indicates that this decreased dissonance is reflected in the body by a decrease in stress-related physiological activation. Whether this increased congruence in emotional expression is a mediating variable or simply a parallel treatment outcome remains to be determined.

## ADDITIONAL STUDIES

In addition to outcome studies that examine therapeutic effects of a series of individual BMGIM sessions, the quantitative literature includes studies that addressed questions concerning various dimensions of the process of spontaneous imaging with music, which is the heart of GIM. These studies have examined the frequency of transpersonal experiences, effects of selected pieces of music on both imagery and physiology, and effects of structured versus unstructured inductions on the imagery. The experimental studies have utilized a single group GIM session. This choice has both positive and negative implications. On the one hand, the shorter time frame allows for permutations of the intervention without interfering with participants' treatment needs. On the other hand, the use of a single session GIM removes from the context of an ongoing therapeutic relationship, reduces the length of music by 70–90 percent, and generally compels the researcher to examine questions related to those music selections most often used as first pieces in a program or series rather than more evocative selections. Despite these limitations, these studies shed much light on a number of questions.

In an effort to study the occurrences of a single type of imagery in individual BMGIM sessions, Lewis (1998–99) analyzed 128 session transcripts, coding the imagery for presence or absence of one of eight categories of transpersonal experience based on Wilber's Spectrum of Consciousness. She found that at least one type of transpersonal experience as defined by Wilbur occurred in 82 percent of sessions. Further, she found that the likelihood of a transpersonal experience was higher for those who either meditated or were associated with spiritual communities (93 percent, $n = 72$) than those who were not (68%, $n = 56$). When the sessions were categorized according to the music program employed, Lewis found that transpersonal experiences were most likely to occur during *Peak Experience, Mostly Bach, Quiet Music, Grieving,* and *Positive Affect* and least likely during *Death/Rebirth*. Lewis asserts that these results "seem to indicate that the music programs have differing potentials for stimulating transpersonal experiences" (p. 76). As Lewis notes, the lack of establishment of the reliability of the rating system, the use of transcripts from a single therapist (who also served as rater and author), among other methodological concerns obligate the reader to exercise caution in the interpretation of these findings. Nevertheless, these data support Lewis' contention that "Bonny Method sessions readily elicit experiences of a transpersonal nature" (p. 77).

Several authors have theorized possible effects of music in the GIM process (Bonny, 1978b; Skaggs, 1992; Summer, 1992; 1995). In an effort to examine effects of a selection of classical music on spontaneous imagery, McKinney (1990) used a quasi-experimental design with two classes of undergraduate music appreciation students, randomly designated as experimental (*n* = 39) and control groups (*n* = 42). After participants completed a demographic questionnaire and a test of imaging ability (Creative Imagination Scale), an induction including physical relaxation, image focus, and bridge was given to both groups. Those in the experimental group then heard a recording of Vaughan Williams' *Rhosymedre* while those in the control group heard silence for the same period. (All participants received the treatment in a group format.) In both the music and silence conditions, participants reported vivid images engaging multiple senses. In fact, this brief selection of music had no effect on the types of imagery experienced, the vividness or activity of the imagery, or the percentage of time imaging or distracted. However, both the music and imaging ability were found to be significant predictors of the intensity of emotions experienced. An analysis of covariance using imaging ability score as a covariate revealed that the music employed in this study significantly increased the intensity of emotions experienced by the participants during the imagery experiences.

When McKinney and Tims (1995) employed a similar procedure, yet further differentiated participants as "high" or "low" imagers on the basis of imaging ability (Creative Imagination Scale) scores, they found that the musical selection itself determined whether or not the intensity of emotions was affected during music imaging. In the first of two experiments reported in this paper, they reanalyzed the data from McKinney (1990); in the second, they replicated and extended that study. In the two studies, sixty-nine and forty-four undergraduates respectively, participated in either music imaging or silent imaging. Each study included a physical relaxation, image focus, and bridge. Whereas the first study used an orchestral transcription of *Rhosymedre* by Vaughan Williams, the second used *Introduction and Allegro* by Ravel. No verbal suggestions were given during the music in either study. The two experimental conditions (music versus no music) and the two imaging ability categories (high imagers versus low) resulted in four cells: high imagers with music, high imagers in silence, low imagers with music, low imagers in silence.

In both experiments, McKinney and Tims (1995) found that high imagers reported significantly more vivid imagery with music than low imagers, although the two types of imagers reported no difference in silence. In addition, the activity of the imagery was increased significantly by the music for high imagers only. While the effect of the two qualitatively different music selections on the vividness and activity of the imagery was a function of imaging ability, participants, regardless of imaging ability, reported greater intensity of emotions in response to the *Rhosymedre* than in silence. However, the *Introduction and Allegro* had no effect on the intensity of emotions, but instead significantly increased the likelihood that the participant, regardless of imaging ability, would experience kinesthetic imagery. The authors concluded that

> music has both broad effects on the [spontaneous] imagery of all persons regardless of imaging ability and also differential effects according to the person's imaging ability. The nature of the broad effects appears to vary with the piece of music used, while some differential effects, particularly on the vividness and activity of imagery, may demonstrate a more consistent pattern from one selection to the next (p. 42).

Band (1996) examined differential effects of two selections of classical music (Bach's *Little Fugue in G Minor"* and Debussy's *En Bateau*) and two types of inductions (structured and unstructured) on vividness of the imagery, absorption in the experience, and mood during the imagery within a group setting. Band recruited 317 undergraduates from six sections of introduction to music. The researcher presented instructions for brief progressive relaxation, an imagery induction, and either music or silence via audiotape. In both inductions, a scene was described and suggestions were given for engaging multiple senses with the scene. The structured induction suggested a specific task for the participant (finding a special object) while the unstructured induction gave no further specific suggestions. Following the imagery experience, participants reported vividness, absorption, and mood during the imagery on visual analogue scales.

The results of the Band (1996) study revealed that there was little difference in the imagery between the two musical selections; however, there were a number of significant effects of music on the imagery. Using composite imaging ability scores as a covariate, music was found to increase the imagery vividness, especially visual detail and bright color; the experience of movement, emotion, and time past; and the participant's level of absorption in the experience. The *Little Fugue in G Minor* significantly increased the vigor/activity experienced during the imagery. The additional structure of a specific task given in the induction was found to increase the appearance of man-made objects in the imagery (perhaps related to the task of "finding an object") and to increase the likelihood that the imager saw him/herself as a participant in the imagery. Otherwise the additional structure of a task exerted little effect on the imagery.

Burns (2000) replicated and extended selected findings of Band (1996) by examining the effect of music and imagery on absorption in and control of visual imagery. Using the research protocol employed by McKinney et al. (1997), she assigned four groups totaling fifty-eight participants to four conditions: music imaging, silent imaging, music listening, and control. Those in the music imaging and music listening conditions heard Ravel's *Introduction and Allegro*. Prior to and following the experimental procedure, each group completed the Tellegen Absorption Scale and the Gordon Test for Imagery Control. Burns found no differences among groups in control of visual imagery and no differences among the three experimental conditions in absorption, although participation in any of the experimental conditions resulted in higher absorption scores than participation in the control condition.

A recurrent question from those who have not experienced GIM concerns the contribution of a relaxation induction to the outcomes documented in GIM studies. In an effort to address this and other questions, McKinney, Tims, Kumar, and Kumar (1997) explored differential effects of music imaging (with induction), silent imaging (with induction), and music listening (without induction) on plasma levels of β-endorphin, a neurohormone the levels of which increase in response to stressful events. Participants ($N = 78$) screened to meet stringent criteria related to health and health behaviors volunteered for one of four groups which were randomly assigned to four conditions: music imaging, silent imaging, music listening, and control, all in a group setting. Using a protocol similar to that employed by McKinney and Tims (1995) for the music imaging and silent imaging groups, they added music listening and control groups. The music used was Ravel's *Introduction and Allegro*. Blood samples were drawn at the beginning and end of the two-hour experimental period. McKinney, Tims, et al. (1997) found that β-endorphin level significantly decreased for those in the music imaging group but was not changed in the other groups. The authors suggest that "the synergistic combination" of music and imagery following an induction may exert a more powerful effect on physiology than music or imagery alone. The findings also indicate that the relaxation suggestions are not sufficient to account for the observed effects since those in the silent imaging group had relaxation suggestions and an image induction identical to that experienced by the music imaging group, yet they experienced no change in β-endorphin.

In a different application of quantitative methodology, Meadows (2000) examined the construct validity and interrater reliability of Bruscia's GIM Responsiveness Scale (GIMR), an instrument designed to "measure the client's responses to various aspects of the GIM experience" (p. 8). Scoring of the GIMR results in subscores for Relaxation, Imagery, Music, Guide, and Verbal, and a total score. In the examination of construct validity, Meadows based his selection of instruments for comparison on Bruscia's assertion that, in addition to providing information concerning imaging ability, the GIMR is intended to "assess the imager's potentials for engaging in the transformative or therapeutic aspects of the GIM experience" (p. 8) which are a function of psychological health and are inversely related to defensiveness. Therefore, Meadows selected Antonovsky's Sense of Coherence Scale (SOC), a measure of psychological health, and Gleser and Ihilevich's Defense Mechanisms Inventory (DMI) for comparison.

Meadows (2000) recruited thirty volunteers who had not previously experienced a BMGIM session. Each participant completed the SOC and DMI prior to having a single, individual BMGIM session, after which the researcher completed the GIMR. Using Pearson correlation coefficients, Meadows found that subscale scores on the GIMR were significantly correlated with each other, suggesting that the subscales are interdependent aspects of the same construct rather than independent measures. The total score did not significantly correlate with any subscale of either the SOC or DMI, suggesting that responsiveness to GIM as measured by the GIMR has no linear relationship with either psychological health as measured by the SOC or defensiveness as measured by the DMI.

Scores from nineteen GIMRs completed by nine raters who either guided or observed a total of seven participant sessions were analyzed by Meadows (2000) to make preliminary calculations of interrater reliability. He found a high level of agreement on individual items (92.3 percent of items were identical or only one point apart on the five-point likert scale) and moderate correlations among raters of the same session. Additional studies including factor analysis of items, reliability of subscales, and evaluation of the reliability of the entire scale with a larger sample will help to determine the validity and reliability of the GIMR.

## IMPLICATIONS FOR CLINICAL PRACTICE

While there are many areas of clinical outcome in GIM that have yet to be explored through quantitative methodology, the extant literature offers indications of clinical efficacy in several areas. The most consistent finding is that BMGIM ameliorates distressed mood. This includes elevating depressed mood in healthy adults (McKinney, Antoni, et al., 1997; McKinney et al., 1995) and individuals with cancer (Burns, 1999), and mitigating depression both in persons with rheumatoid arthritis (Jacobi, 1995) and in individuals with mild to moderate psychiatric disturbance (Wrangsjö & Körlin, 1995; Körlin & Wrangsjö, 2000). Other reported mood effects include reduced fatigue and confusion (McKinney, Antoni, et al., 1997) and reduced anxiety (Jacobi, 1995; Wrangsjö & Körlin, 1995; Körlin & Wrangsjö, 2000). In related findings, Little (1999) found that BMGIM reduced despair in hospice staff and volunteers. Participants in the survey by Maack and Nolan (1999) also indicated that change in mood was one of the most important outcomes of their BMGIM sessions. Therefore, individuals who meet other exclusionary criteria for GIM and who have distressed mood, particularly depressed mood, are likely to benefit from BMGIM sessions.

Another pattern emerging from the quantitative literature is that BMGIM exerts positive effects on human physiology. Documented effects include normalizing blood pressure in adults with essential hypertension (McDonald, 1990), and lowering levels of hormones associated with stress and disease exacerbation (McKinney, Antoni, et al., 1997; McKinney, Tims, et al., 1997). Functional assessments have also demonstrated improvements for those with medical conditions, including decreased pain and improved joint function in persons with rheumatoid arthritis (Jacobi, 1995) and enhanced quality of life for individuals with cancer (Burns, 1999). It is important to note that no studies have reported deleterious effects of BMGIM in persons with chronic medical conditions. Therefore, while it is still premature to suggest to clients that BMGIM will improve their physical status or alter disease progression, there is evidence that BMGIM may improve at least the quality of life and possibly the physical health of persons with chronic physical illness.

Some of the findings of the quantitative literature confirm what is intuitively known or clinically observed by GIM practitioners. For example, the observed fact that transpersonal experiences are common in the BMGIM therapeutic process, confirmed quantitatively by Lewis (1998–99) has led to directed study of and specialized instruction in guiding these types of experiences for GIM trainees (Association for Music and Imagery, 1998). However, other results offer new ways of thinking about the effects of music in the BMGIM process. These results suggest that the music does not evoke imagery, since imagery experienced in silence may be as rich and varied as that experienced in music. Rather, the different musical selections may alter different qualities or dimensions of the imagery, such as intensity of emotions (Vaughan Williams' *Rhosymedre*, in McKinney, 1990; McKinney & Tims, 1995), kinesthetic experiences (Ravel's *Introduction and Allegro*, McKinney & Tims, 1995) or the experience of vigor/activity (Bach's *Little Fugue in G Minor*, Band, 1996). Other possible effects, such as encouraging engagement or forward movement, have yet to be measured experimentally.

GIM research suggests that while the induction is important to the process (McKinney & Tims, et al., 1997), offering structure beyond the suggestion of a scene and suggestions for engaging multiple senses with that scene may not be needed (Band, 1996). Band's study of image inductions with differing degrees of structure indicates that suggesting a task for the participant will have little effect on the imagery.

## IMPLICATIONS FOR RESEARCH

The body of quantitative literature on BMGIM and group forms of GIM raises more questions than it provides answers at this time. There are numerous implications for research suggested by the studies reviewed above. Some of these implications provide guidance to the researcher based on lessons learned. In addition, there are strong indicators of additional areas of potentially fertile investigation.

An important question related to efficiency and cost containment in intervention studies concerns the minimum number of sessions needed to demonstrate significant change and the preferred interval of those sessions. Some BMGIM studies have taken a pragmatic clinical approach, determining the number of sessions and pacing according to individual therapeutic indicators (Bonny, 1976; Wrangsjö & Körlin, 1995; Körlin & Wrangsjö, 2000). Others that have employed a design that calls for a predetermined number of sessions for each participant have found that a series of six sessions is sufficient to document significant change even with modest sample sizes (Little, 1999; McDonald, 1990; McKinney et al., 1995; McKinney, Antoni et al., 1997). McKinney et al. (1995) reported that weekly sessions for a few participants imposed a perceived overload of material with insufficient time for integration prior to the next session. They therefore recommended biweekly sessions if the interval is to be predetermined. However, McDonald (1990) documented significant change following six weekly sessions and both Jacobi (1995) and Burns (1999) used protocols that employed ten weekly sessions. It is important to note, however, than McKinney, Antoni, et al. (1997) have found that six would be the minimum number of sessions needed to document lasting change in distressed mood in individuals unfamiliar with the GIM process.

An important finding for researchers to note, particularly related to physiological change, is that the improvements continue to occur for at least seven weeks beyond the final BMGIM session (Burns, 1999; Jacobi, 1995; McDonald, 1990; McKinney, Antoni, et al., 1997). Studies up to this point have not been designed to measure effects beyond seven weeks. McKinney, Antoni, et al. have documented a lag between psychological change and correlating physiological change resulting from BMGIM. They suggest that the observed lag in physiological change (cortisol level) may have been due to a shift in physiological regulatory mechanisms. Given this, it is imperative that GIM researchers examining physiological variables allow for such a lag. Failure to include at least a six-week follow-up in the design of the study could mean that important changes are missed. In addition, longitudinal studies that include additional follow-up time points are needed in order to learn how long measurable effects last beyond the end of sessions.

The existing GIM outcome literature suggests that research with certain populations would be likely to yield results important to documenting clinical efficacy. Given the consistent pattern of documented mood change, the most obvious population that has yet to be examined is adults with nonpsychotic major depressive disorder. A carefully controlled clinical outcome study comparing GIM with other interventions known to ameliorate depression (e.g., antidepressant medications, cognitive therapy) would be a significant contribution to the quantitative literature in GIM.

Other populations that might offer fertile ground for GIM research include those with chronic medical disorders. McDonald's (1990) report that BMGIM lowers blood pressure in people with essential hypertension and the findings of McKinney, Antoni, et al. (1997) that BMGIM lowers levels of cortisol (elevated levels of which are known to be associated with atherosclerosis) suggest further work with individuals who have or are at risk for cardiovascular disease. Combining the knowledge that elevated levels of cortisol are associated with both suppression of the immune system and enhanced tumor growth with Burns' (1999) findings that BMGIM enhances mood and quality of life in persons with cancer makes a case for further study of psychological and physiological effects of BMGIM in individuals with cancer and other immune-related disorders. The major role of cortisol in the regulation of blood sugar suggests that persons with diabetes may also prove to be a fruitful population for GIM researchers interested in both physiological and psychological outcomes.

Because the study by McKinney, Tims, et al. (1997) concerned a single session of group GIM rather than a series of BMGIM sessions, generalization to BMGIM clinical intervention effects is quite limited. Nevertheless, these results indicate that controlled intervention studies that compare a series of BMGIM sessions with equivalent sessions that employ relaxation strategies, such as cognitive behavioral stress management, are needed. They also provide encouragement that the shorter duration of music generally employed in group settings may yield measurable results.

Researchers employing single-session group designs to study various dimensions of the GIM process, especially those concerning the relationship of music and imagery, would be well-advised to include a measure of imaging ability. McKinney and Tims (1995) found that music affected vividness and activity of the imagery only for high imagers as determined by scores on the Creative Imagination Scale. Similarly, Band (1996) found significant correlations between scores on the Questionnaire Upon Visual Imagery, the Test of Visual Imagery, and the Tellegen Absorption Scale and several dependent measures of imagery. Failure to employ an appropriate measure of imaging ability may obscure findings regarding effects of music on imagery.

Because of the time required for each individual BMGIM session and the number of participants needed for acceptable statistical power, the most challenging aspect of executing intervention studies related to clinical outcome of BMGIM is involving a sufficiently large number of participants to provide for not only a BMGIM condition, but also a control condition and possibly other intervention conditions for comparison purposes. Large-scale studies may necessitate the employment of multiple sites with several experienced GIM therapists. Careful attention to relevant exclusionary criteria, control variables, and reliable and valid outcome measures of clinically relevant change will also enhance the credibility of GIM outcome research and ultimately contribute to increased accessibility of GIM.

Despite the small number of quantitative studies in GIM, especially relative to the number for more established forms of therapy, the results of the existing studies are promising. Additional studies, including replication and extension of existing research, are needed. Nevertheless, substantial groundwork has been laid toward the documentation of BMGIM as the efficacious, life-changing method that facilitators and clients alike know it to be.

## References

Association for Music and Imagery. (1998). *Standards and Procedures for Endorsement of GIM Training Programs.* Blaine, WA: Author.

Band, J. P. (1996). *The Influence of Selected Music and Structured vs. Unstructured Inductions on Mental Imagery* (Doctoral dissertation, University of South Carolina, 1996). Dissertation Abstracts International, 57, 1028.

Bonny, H. L. (1976). *Music and Psychotherapy: A Handbook and Guide Accompanied by Eight Music Tapes to be used by Practitioners of Guided Imagery and Music.* Unpublished doctoral dissertation, Union Graduate School of the Union of Experimenting Colleges and Universities, Baltimore, MD.

Bonny, H. (1978a). *GIM monograph No. 1: Facilitating GIM sessions.* Salina, KS: Bonny Foundation.

Bonny, H. (1978b). *GIM monograph No. 2: The Role of Taped Music Programs in the GIM Process.* Salina, KS: Bonny Foundation.

Bonny, H. (1980). *GIM monograph No 3: GIM therapy: Past, present and future implications.* Salina, KS: Bonny Foundation.

Burns, D. S. (1999). *The Effectiveness of the Bonny Method of Guided Imagery and Music on the Quality of Life and Cortisol Levels of Cancer Patients.* Unpublished doctoral dissertation. The University of Kansas, Lawrence, KS.

Burns, D. S. (2000). The effect of classical music on absorption and control of mental imagery. *Journal of the Association for Music and Imagery, 7,* 34–43.

Goldberg, F. S. (1992). Images of emotion: The role of emotion in guided imagery and music. *Journal of Music and Imagery, 1,* 5–17.

Jacobi, E. M. (1995). *The Efficacy of the Bonny Method of Guided Imagery and Music as Experiential Therapy in the Primary Care of persons with Rheumatoid Arthritis* (Doctoral dissertation, Union Institute, 1995). Dissertation Abstracts International, 56, 1110.

Körlin, D., & Wrangsjö, B. (2000). *Treatment effects of GIM Therapy.* Manuscript submitted for publication.

Lewis, K. (1998–99). The Bonny method of guided imagery and music: Matrix for transpersonal experience. *Journal of the Association for Music and Imagery, 6,* 63–85.

Little, L. H. (1999, June). *The Effect of the Bonny Method of GIM on Grief Among Hospice Staff and Volunteers.* Poster presented at the conference of the Association for Music and Imagery, Chicago, IL.

Maack, C., & Nolan, P. (1999). The effects of GIM therapy on reported change in normal adults. *Journal of Music Therapy, 36,* 39–55.

McDonald, R. G. (1986). *Healing Parasitic Infection Through the Partnership of GIM and Applied Kinesioloy.* Unpublished fellow's paper. Institute for Music and Imagery, Baltimore, MD.

McDonald, R. G. (1990). *The Efficacy of Guided Imagery and Music as a Strategy of Self-concept and Blood Pressure Change Among Adults with Essential Hypertension.* Unpublished doctoral dissertation, Walden University, Minneapolis, MN.

McKinney, C. H. (1990). The effect of music on imagery. *Journal of Music Therapy, 27,* 34–46.

McKinney, C. H. (1995). *The Effect of the Bonny Method of Guided Imagery and Music on Mood, Emotional Expression, Cortisol, and Immunologic Control of Latent Epstein-Barr Virus in Healthy Adults* (Doctoral dissertation, University of Miami, Miami, FL, 1994). Dissertation Abstracts International, 55, 3057.

McKinney, C. H., & Antoni, M. H. (2000). *Emotional Expression, Guided Imagery and Music (GIM) Therapy, and Therapeutic Outcome.* Manuscript in preparation. Appalachian State University, Boone, NC, and University of Miami, FL.

McKinney, C., Antoni, M., Kumar, A., and Kumar, M. (1995). The effects of guided imagery and music on depression and beta-endorphin levels in healthy adults: A pilot study. *Journal of the Association for Music and Imagery, 4,* 67–78.

McKinney, C. H., Antoni, M. H., Kumar, M., Tims, F. C., and McCabe, P. M. (1997). Effects of Guided Imagery and Music (GIM) Therapy on Mood and Cortisol in Healthy Adults. *Health Psychology, 16,* 1–12.

McKinney, C. H., and Tims, F. C. (1995). Differential Effects of Selected Classical Music on the Imagery of High versus Low Imagers: Two studies. *Journal of Music Therapy, 32,* 22–45.

McKinney, C. H., Tims, F. C., Kumar, A., & Kumar, M. (1997). The effect of selected classical music and spontaneous imagery on plasma beta-endorphin. *Journal of Behavioral Medicine, 20,* 85–99.

Meadows, A. (2000). The validity and reliability of the guided imagery and music responsiveness scale. *Journal of the Association for Music and Imagery, 7,* 8–33.

Merritt, S. (1990). Mind, Music and Imagery: Unlocking Your Creative Potential. New York: Plume.

Merritt, S. (1993). The healing link: Guided imagery and music and the body/mind connection. *Journal of the Association for Music and Imagery, 2,* 11–28.

Pickett, E. (1987). Fibroid tumors and response to guided imagery and music: Two case studies. *Imagination, Cognition, and Personality, 7,* 165–176.

Skaggs, R. (1992). Music as co-therapist: Creative resource for change. *Journal of the Association for Music and Imagery, 1,* 77–83.

Summer, L. (1992). Music: The aesthetic elixer. *Journal of the Association for Music and Imagery, 1,* 43–53.

Summer, L. (1995). Melding musical and psychological processes: The therapeutic musical space. *Journal of the Association for Music and Imagery, 4,* 37–47.

Wrangsjö, B., & Körlin, D. (1995). Guided imagery and music (GIM) as a psychotherapeutic method in psychiatry. *Journal of the Association for Music & Imagery, 4,* 79–92.

*Chapter Twenty-Four*


# QUALITATIVE RESEARCH IN GUIDED IMAGERY AND MUSIC (GIM)


## Denise E. Grocke


Qualitative methods are used in BMGIM research to capture the essence of the method and to describe the quality of the experience. BMGIM research requires that methods resonate with the symbolic search for meaning found in the BMGIM experience; for example, the interactive process between the client, music stimulus, and therapist, and the emotional, sensory nature of the imagery experience. The most appropriate research methods that explore these qualitative experiences are case studies of various types and phenomenological studies. In this chapter examples will be given from the GIM literature to illustrate the different types of qualitative research methods.


## CASE STUDIES


Much of the early research in BMGIM is in the form of individual case studies. This may have occurred because training requirements stipulated that advanced-level trainees write a case study of a minimum ten BMGIM sessions. Many of these case studies are published in the *Journal of the Association for Music and Imagery*. Case studies generally do not have a research question, but instead have a clinical focus and a structure that demonstrates the intention of the BMGIM therapy. The typical structure of a case study is:

- background on the client's history and presenting issues;
- goals for the BMGIM series;
- synopsis of key sessions with descriptions and/or interpretation of the imagery, and
- outcomes of the therapy in relation to the client's issues or goals.

The purpose of writing a case study varies, and the different forms can be summarized as:

- Process Case Study: traces the client's working through of significant images or issues (usually written from the therapist's perspective). The purpose is to describe how BMGIM works by tracing significant and recurring images and their transformation, and/or a chronological summary of session content
- Outcome Case Study: traces progress made by clients according to goals set by the therapist, often in collaboration with the client. The purpose is to provide a testimonial of the effectiveness of BMGIM through either an individual case study or a collective case study, documenting the application of BMGIM to a particular population.
- Negative Case Study: traces the client's process in BMGIM sessions, but indicates why the method is not suited to the client, or to the client's presenting issues.
- Hermeneutic Case study: analyzes the images according to one or more theoretical systems. The purpose is to show how BMGIM can be used within a particular orientation to therapy.
- Phenomenological Case Study: the therapist interviews one or more clients to examine their experiences in any aspect of BMGIM.
- Heuristic Case Study: a self-inquiry into the nature of BMGIM, or the nature of one's experience of BMGIM.

Examples of these different types of case studies will be outlined in this chapter. However, this is not a comprehensive review of all case studies in BMGIM. A more complete summary of both individual and collective case studies can be found in Meadows' chapter in the book on psychotherapeutic applications of the Bonny Method.

## Process Case Studies

An example of a process case study tracing key images is Pickett's (1992) account of BMGIM with a woman who had multiple addictions (an eating disorder and addiction to prescribed medication). Pickett traces key images (the wall, the addict, the talking loaf of bread, and the dead tree) and relates them to the client's therapeutic process. She identifies and names the various parts of the client's personality that emerged during the therapy, and concludes that the client was better able to "directly confront her feelings" (Pickett, 1992, p. 66). This impacted positively on the client's ability to develop meaningful social relationships, which had been one of the goals of therapy.

Similarly, Clark (1991) traced key images appearing in a series of twenty sessions of BMGIM with a female client. Clark provides a chronological summary of all sessions and identifies the sequence of key images, whereas Bruscia (1991) shows how key images transformed throughout a series of BMGIM sessions with a man who had AIDS. Images of the black bird, rain, a house, an island cave, and an abandoned child helped the client to ultimately face images of death, and the challenge of living or dying.

A modified form of BMGIM was required in Marr's (1998–1999) case study of a woman in palliative care in the final stages of life. A summary of fifteen sessions is outlined to show how the sessions helped the client in the resolution of key issues in her life.

## Outcome Case Studies (Individual)

The outcome of BMGIM for a man suffering Ankylosis Spondylitis is described by Merritt (1993). At the commencement of therapy the man was in chronic physical pain, his body was stiff and inflexible, and he was unable to feel his spine. After the first series of BMGIM sessions his pain had reduced "from six to a three" (Merritt, 1993, p. 13). Merritt describes his progression through BMGIM sessions by identifying the key images and archetypes that were metaphors for the disease, and which helped the client to confront and resolve painful memories from childhood. After the second series of BMGIM sessions the client was "virtually pain-free" (Merritt, 1992, p. 25).

Both Lewis (1993) and McKinney (1993) document case studies in which the primary goal was personal growth for the client. Lewis identifies goals for the series, then documents various aspects of growth evident in how the client engaged the imagery and music. Lewis concludes with a section detailing "Progress towards stated goals" where the original goals are restated and measured against evidence of the client's life events. McKinney (1993) also identifies specific issues that the female client brought to BMGIM, and describes the client's progress within different relationship paradigms: with friends, family, men, self-image and spirituality. Images from BMGIM sessions enabled this client to reach multidimensional growth in many areas of her life.

## Outcome Case Studies (Collective)

An example of a collective case study is Pickett and Sonnen's (1993) article on BMGIM in the treatment and diagnosis of multiple personality disorder (MPD). The authors draw on a range of clinical vignettes to illustrate the main issues in working with clients who have MPD. Although each client had unique experiences, an overview of common aspects of the client's experiences enables BMGIM therapists to be more informed about specific issues in working with clients who have MPD.

In a study based on 250 sessions with twenty men diagnosed with the AIDS virus, Bruscia (1992) found that for each man the healing process began with visits from the other side—that is, a visitation within the imagery of a significant person who was deceased. Bruscia also categorized the experiences commonly found in BMGIM sessions of gay men carrying the AIDS virus, which included "getting out of limbo," "healing relationships," "finding forgiveness," "putting anger aside," and "embracing life and death."

## Negative Case Study

It is unusual for authors to write a case study to illustrate the limitations of a therapeutic method. Clarkson (1994), however, described difficulties she encountered when using BMGIM with a client in a hypomanic episode, where BMGIM tended to aggravate the client's confusion. In qualitative research this type of study is referred to as a negative case analysis (Creswell, 1999), and these contribute to our knowledge of contraindications of BMGIM practice.

In contrast to Bruscia's (1992) study of men with AIDS, Martin's (1993) exploration of BMGIM with people who are "at the very end of their life" led her to believe that BMGIM was not an appropriate intervention for most patients in advanced-stage cancer. Martin found that most did not want to explore issues in depth (although there were exceptions), particularly when such exploration required a certain amount of energy.

## Hermeneutic Case Study

Hermeneutic studies place case material within a related theoretical system in order to enhance an understanding of the significance of the therapeutic process.

For example, in Borling's (1992) study of a woman survivor of childhood abuse, he documents specific goals that were to be gained through BMGIM as "to assist her in reexperiencing painful issues from the past with the intent of releasing her sense of being stuck" (Borling, 1992, p. 86). He provides a summary of the seventeen sessions given to the client, identifying physical, and embodied responses as the most common experiences of the client. Borling then discusses the outcomes of the therapy from three different frameworks: Bradshaw's *Inner Child*, Grof's *Basic Perinatal Matrices,* and Kellogg's *Mari Card Test*. He concludes that some of his therapist's intuitions were confirmed by the *Mari Card Test*, and that by placing the client's progress in BMGIM alongside the three frameworks it was evident that she was at the same point on each of the three paradigms. He noted that "some work in the area of abuse was accomplished but still remained far from complete" (Borling, 1992, p. 92).

Jungian archetypes have been used by many authors to explain the significance of certain images appearing in BMGIM sessions. Tasney (1993) used a Jungian framework to trace images of healing in a female client who had been subject to incest. Both Jungian interpretation and the Bradshaw dysfunctional family model provided the theoretical framework for Wick's (1990) study of BMGIM with four woman who had eating disorders.

Jungian archetypes also appeared in Erdonmez (1995) case study of five BMGIM sessions with a woman in terminal stages of amyotrophic lateral sclerosis (also known as motor neurone disease). The archetypes included figures (the wise old man, and the old hag) and other significant images of transition (the snake and the tortoise). Similarly, Clark (1991) describes archetypal images and metaphorical fantasy in her case study of twenty sessions with a young woman. The outcome of the BMGIM therapy was an integration of child, mother, and father aspects of the adult self. This growth was mirrored in the imagery sequence evolving from a homeless waif to "the recipient of God's blessing" (Clark, 1991, p. 330).

The three-stage model of Herman (1992) was used by Ventre (1994) to explain the progress of a female client facing memories of abuse. Herman's model identifies three stages of recovery as 1) safety, 2) remembrance and mourning, and 3) reconnection. Ventre illustrates how BMGIM enabled the client to build strength and trust, confront memories and feelings, and make reconnection with ordinary life, within Herman's model of recovery.

Similarly Clark (1995) studied Joseph Campbell's *Hero's Journey* by comparing the imagery of four clients. In delineating the clients' similar processes, Clark proposed a model of *The Hero's Journey* in BMGIM. *The Heroine's Journey* is also explored in McIvor's (1998–1999) study of Maori women in New Zealand, providing an added cultural dimension to Campbell's concept.

Brooks' (2000) study of anima imagery in male clients is an example of hermeneutic research, where a theory or construct is used as a basis for analyzing a text, which in this research comprised the written transcripts of the BMGIM sessions. Brooks conducted six to ten BMGIM sessions with four male clients. Verbatim transcripts were taken of each session. Each transcript was then divided into topical units, so that any response or expression of the client that involved feelings or emotions that related to women, feminine symbols, or archetypes were tagged as anima units. The anima units found in the discussion segment of the session were used to clarify anima themes found in the imagery. In the process of analysis Brooks consulted dictionaries of symbols to verify those symbols interpreted as being feminine. Her findings led to a refinement of the definition of the anima paraphrased as: any quality that a man attributes to or projects onto real women (individually or collectively), female characters (literary or imaginary), symbols or objects which form a pattern or theme in the man's response within BMGIM, and leads to the expression and ownership of emotions, and ultimately individuation (Brooks, 2000, p. 86). Brooks also noted that care should be taken to acknowledge the animus projections of the researcher/therapist in interpreting data.

Other examples of hermeneutic case studies include Bunt's (2000) study of transformations of imagery parallel with changes in the music, inspired by Ovid's *Metamorphoses*, and Bonde's (2000) use of case vignettes to describe metaphor in BMGIM, drawing on the theories of Ricoeur.

## Phenomenological Case Studies

An example of phenomenological case study research is Skaggs' (1984) study of three female clients in BMGIM who had memories of abuse that appeared during the progress of BMGIM. Skaggs interviewed the clients using a phenomenological approach, and identified key statements and meaning units from the clients' experience. She then developed a distilled account of the women's experience.

In a study of pivotal moments (turning points) in BMGIM, Grocke (1999) used a phenomenological research paradigm to interview seven clients (and their BMGIM therapists) about BMGIM sessions that were pivotal, i.e., those moments which stood out as being "turning points" in therapy. There were specific steps in the phenomenological analysis:

- Each interview was transcribed, word by word.
- The transcript was read carefully and key statements that described the pivotal moment were underlined.
- The key statements were grouped into meaning units..
- The meaning units were transformed into a distilled essence of each participant's (or therapist's) experience.
- The interview transcript (with key statements underlined), the meaning units, and the distilled essence were then sent to the participants (or therapists) for verification with the question "Does

the final distilled description capture the essence of your experience? Is there any aspect of your experience that has been left out?"

- When the participants returned the material, any changes or omissions were rectified.
- A horizontal distilling process followed, whereby the common meaning units across all seven interviews (for the clients) and two interviews (for the therapists) were laid side by side, and composite themes were developed.
- Composite themes were distilled into a final global description of the experience of pivotal moments in GIM.

From the seven client interviews, twenty themes emerged. These were (in part):

- Pivotal moments were remembered and described in vivid detail.
- Pivotal moments were emotional and embodied experiences.
- Pivotal moments impacted on the person's life.
- Clients had insight into the meaning of the pivotal moment and the effect was lasting.
- The therapist's presence, or interventions, or silences were important to the pivotal experience.
- The pivotal experience often emerged from unpleasant feelings or images which were uncomfortable, unpleasant, or horrible.

In the second part of the study, the BMGIM therapists were interviewed about their perceptions of the moments identified by the clients as pivotal. From the therapists' interviews, fourteen themes emerged, and these (in part) were:

- The therapists remembered the session identified by their clients as pivotal and also identified other sessions that they thought were pivotal.
- The client's pivotal experience was an emotional experience for the therapist and they anticipated pivotal moments occurring.
- The therapists noted observable changes in the client's body language during a pivotal experience and intentionally intervened to facilitate the pivotal moment, but they were often silent during the precise moment.

## Heuristic Case Study

One of the earliest heuristic studies in BMGIM was Bruscia's (1995) study of his experience as a guide during an exceptional BMGIM session. First he delineated different worlds of consciousness that he entered into (as therapist) during a BMGIM session: the client's world; the therapist's personal world, and the therapist's therapist world. He identified four levels of experiencing (as a therapist): 1) sensorial: the therapist "senses" what is happening for the client through his own body; 2) affective: the therapist identifies feelings and emotions which are aroused by what is taking place for the client; 3) reflective: the therapist tries to integrate meaning out of the sensory and affective experiences; and 4) intuitive, a level of spontaneous response to what is occurring for the client (1995, pp. 170–171).

Bruscia comments that his ability to move his level of consciousness was crucial within the session and that timing was a key factor. The sense of timing was informed from observation of the client's breathing pattern and the speed at which images were reported. When the client spoke haltingly, for example, Bruscia observed that his interventions slowed in response to the client's state (1995, p. 193). He provides a vivid example of these levels of consciousness, by exploring the transcript of one extraordinary session—a session where a client dug up old bones, and sensed that someone had been stoned to death. As the session proceeded the client had a vivid experience of the man being stoned, and the very drawn-out letting go in death. The emotional impact in reading this study is very strong and Bruscia's own reflection is captured in these words:

> It is very difficult to describe what Tom (the client) and I were experiencing in those last few moments of the man's death. Both of our voices were cracking: our words fell into the same rhythm and tonality; and our bodies seemed filled with the same tension and expectation (1995, p. 178).

This study describes a deeper understanding of the interaction between client and therapist during a BMGIM session, and the crucial part that timing plays in the therapist's interventions, the subtleties of voice tone, and body tension in communicating with one's client. The role of the music is also addressed in Bruscia's study:

> The most intimate and powerful aspect of this experience, however, was the music. It seemed to carry us along and into indescribable feelings, almost as if it was composed to support what was happening in Tom's images. And during the long periods of waiting for the man

to let go, the music "held" us in suspense, while also presenting the deep sorrow and regret that both of us were feeling but neither could express (1995, p. 178).

Through the process of heuristic self-inquiry, Bruscia defined and described different states of consciousness through which the therapist might change and shift during a BMGIM session. In so doing, he has created a new theoretical model, which may be used as a framework upon which BMGIM practitioners can better understand and write about their work.

A group of heuristic studies in BMGIM have appeared in Hibben's (1999) edited work *Inside Music Therapy: Client Experiences*. This book differs from all other texts on BMGIM in that the chapters are written by clients, rather than from the perspective of the therapist. In Newel's (1999) account of six BMGIM sessions following surgery, she relates the sequences of images to her stages of recovery. She describes the many insights she gained about the power of the music and the images that were associated with her catastrophic illness.

The journey of BMGIM sessions over one year is captured in Ts heuristic narrative based on his journal entries made after each BMGIM session (T & Caughman, 1999). The narrative description of the BMGIM session is interspersed with his reflections between sessions relative to significant images, memories, and strong emotions. Insight into the significance of images is also captured in Buell's (1999) narrative description of fourteen sessions in BMGIM. Buell comments that changes in her life were foreshadowed by changes in the images within the BMGIM sessions, and that the imagery "was a channel through which my inner knowledge became accessible" (Buell, 1999, p. 51), and spiritual experiences were unexpected. Isenberg-Grzeda (1999) immerses herself in a rich description of the profound effect of the music on her physical and spiritual experiences of BMGIM, and the capacity of the music to hold her during the experience.

## PHENOMENOLOGICAL STUDIES OF THE MUSIC PROGRAMS

In order to study music structures and their relationship with imagery sequences, some studies have adopted the Ferrara (1984) phenomenological model of music analysis. Ferrara's model consists of listening to a piece of music in five different ways:

1) an open listening: the researcher makes an open description of what is heard
2) listening for semantic meaning: the researcher listens for the elements of the music—for example, melody, rhythm, harmony—and describes what is heard
3) listening for mood or feeling of what is being conveyed
4) an ontological listening: hearing the music from the perspective of the composer's life world
5) a final listening: gathering up the insights from the first four listenings.

In one of the earliest studies of the BMGIM music, Kasayka (1991) used the Ferrara model to analyze each of the five pieces on the *Peak Experience* program. She analyzed the music according to its structure by making phenomenological descriptions of each section. She then matched the imagery sequences of the client alongside the descriptive accounts of the music, providing a grid of music description, imagery experiences, and comments about the interrelationship of the two. She noted the timing of specific imagery sequences with certain features of the music.

A further phenomenological approach was undertaken by Hanks (1992) in which she explored transcultural experiences in GIM for American and Taiwanese participants. She used several pieces of music from the Bonny music programs, and several traditional Taiwanese music pieces. She then compared the imagery of both groups of people. One of the most interesting findings was that imagery associated with Brahms' *First Symphony* (3rd movement) was similar for both groups of subjects, that is, both groups had imagery of tall mountains. The ontological connection was that Brahms composed the symphony following a holiday in the Alps where he was inspired by the grandeur of the mountains. Not only was the "imagery" evoked in the American subjects (where Western classical music is a part of the culture), but it was also evoked in the Taiwanese subjects (where the Western classical tradition is not so familiar).

In studying the features of the music that underpinned pivotal moments in GIM, Grocke (1999) made a phenomenological description of the music piece by piece, dividing the music selection into units of musical meaning (e.g., themes, sections of dynamic consistency, and so on). The imagery of the client was placed parallel to the descriptions, and aspects of the music that evoked changes in the imagery were identified. Grocke noted that there were clear instances where the dynamics of the music influenced the imagery of the clients, but there was also evidence where the imagery had "a life of its own" and was not influenced by features/elements in the music.

A phenomenological study of the *Grieving* music program with four clients' imagery was undertaken by Marr (2000). The BMGIM session was audiotaped and the imagery transcribed onto the music score. The four participants' imagery sequences were tabled alongside each other and the music. The music description and the four imagery sequences were examined and compared using "Event Structure Analysis" to discover how the temporal music sequence, and specific musical elements, influenced imagery processes and development.

Marr found that in passages with rapid changes in tonality, dynamic range, rhythmic pulse, and melodic fragmentation, imagery tended to be sparse with long, silent pauses in the reporting of imagery. Tension and resolution that occurred in the music was matched in the imagery sequences. Images expanded with high pitches and light timbres and texture, while it became embodied with low pitches and descending melodic lines. The use of solo instruments often matched somatic and kinaesthetic imagery in specific parts of the body and, when used in dialogue, allowed several aspects of an image to be examined.

## CONCLUSION

In this chapter, various qualitative research methods have been explored to elucidate the relative value of each form. Good qualitative research is based on established procedures which highlight: 1) the need for intentionality and authenticity in what is being studied; 2) rigor in carrying out the analyses; 3) consistent verification by peers, or by the participants themselves; and 4) a commitment to integrity in reporting results.

Qualitative research provides the rich fabric on which an understanding of BMGIM is based. As more research emerges, new methods will be incorporated to best fit the topic being explored.

## *References*

Bonde, L. O. (2000). Metaphor and narrative in Guided Imagery and Music. *Journal of the Association for Music and Imagery, 7,* 59–76.

Borling, J. E. (1992). Perspectives on growth with a victim of abuse: A Guided Imagery and Music (GIM) case study. *Journal of the Association for Music and Imagery, 1,* 85–97.

Brooks, D. N. (2000). Anima manifestations of men using Guided Imagery and Music: A case study. *Journal of the Association for Music and Imagery,* 7, 77–87.

Bruscia, K. (1991). Embracing life with AIDS: Psychotherapy through Guided Imagery and Music (GIM). In K. Bruscia (ed.), *Case Studies in Music Therapy*. Gilsum, NH: Barcelona Publishers.

Bruscia, K. E. (1992). Visits from the other side: Healing persons with AIDS through Guided Imagery and Music (GIM). In D. Campbell (ed*.). Music and Miracles,* pp. 195–207. Wheaton, IL: Quest Books.

Bruscia, K. E. (1995). Modes of consciousness in Guided Imagery and Music (GIM): A therapist's experience of the guiding process. In C. Kenny (ed.). *Listening, Playing, Creating: Essays on the Power of Sound.* Albany, NY: State University of New York Press.

Buell, R. (1999). Emerging through music: A journey towards wholeness with Guided Imagery and Music. In J. Hibben (ed.) *Inside Music Therapy: Client Experiences.* Gilsum, NH: Barcelona Publishers.

Bunt, L. G. K. (2000). Transformational processes in Guided Imagery and Music. *Journal of the Association for Music and Imagery,* 7, 44–58.

Campbell, J. (1968). *The Hero with a Thousand Faces*. Princeton, NJ: Princeton University Press.

Caughman, J. M & T. (1999). Tools of rediscovery: A year of Guided Imagery and Music. In J. Hibben (ed.), *Inside Music Therapy: Client Experiences.* Gilsum: Barcelona Publishers.

Clark, M. F. (1991). Emergence of the adult self in Guided Imagery and Music (GIM) therapy. In K. Bruscia (ed.), *Case Studies in Music Therapy.* Gilsum, NH: Barcelona Publishers.

Clark, M. F. (1995). The hero's myth in GIM therapy. *Journal of the Association for Music and Imagery,* 4, 49–66.

Clarkson, G. (1994). Learning through mistakes: Guided Imagery and Music with a student in a hypomanic episode. *Journal of the Association for Music and Imagery,* 3, 77–93

Creswell, J. (1999). *Qualitative Inquiry and Research Design: Choosing Among Five Traditions*. Thousand Oaks, CA: Sage Publications.

Erdonmez, D. E. (1995). A journey of transition with Guided Imagery and Music. In C. Lee (ed.) *Lonely Waters*. Proceedings of the International Conference: Music Therapy in Palliative Care. Oxford, UK: Sobell Publications.

Ferrara, L. (1984). Phenomenology as a tool for musical analysis. *The Musical Quarterly,* 70, 355–373.

Grocke, D. Erdonmez (1999). *A Phenomenological Study of Pivotal Moments in Guided Imagery and Music (GIM) Therapy*. Doctoral dissertation at the

University of Melbourne. Available on *CD-ROM III* from the University of Witten-Herdecke.

Hanks, K. J. (1992). Music, affect and imagery: A cross-cultural exploration. *Journal of the Association for Music and Imagery*, 1, 19–31.

Herman, J. (1992) *Trauma and Recovery*. New York, NY: Basic books.

Hibben, J. (ed.) (1999). *Inside Music Therapy: Client Experiences*. Gilsum, NH: Barcelona Publishers.

Isenberg-Grzeda, C. (1999). Experiencing the music in Guided Imagery and Music. In J. Hibben (ed.), *Inside Music Therapy: Client Experiences*. Gilsum, NH: Barcelona Publishers.

Kasayka, R. E. (1991). *To Meet and Match the Moment of Hope: Transpersonal Elements of the Guided Imagery and Music Experience*. New York University. UMI Dissertation Services, #9134754.

Lewis, K. (1993). Using Guided Imagery and Music to clarify and support relationship changes: A case study. *Journal of the Association for Music and Imagery*, 2, 87–97.

Marr, J. (1998–1999). GIM at the end of life: Case studies in palliative care. *Journal of the Association for Music and Imagery*, 6, 37–54.

Marr, J. (2000). *The Effects of Music on Imagery Sequence in the Bonny Method of Guided Imagery and Music*. Unpublished master's degree thesis, University of Melbourne, Australia.

Martin, J. (1993). *An Exploration of the Contraindications in the Bonny Method of Guided Imagery and Music with the Terminally Ill*. New York: Creative Therapies Institute.

McIvor, M. (1998–1999). Heroic journeys: Experiences of a Maori group with the Bonny Method. *Journal of the Association for Music and Imagery*, 6, 105-118.

McKinney, C. (1993). The case of Therese: Multidimensional growth through Guided Imagery and Music. *Journal of the Association for Music and Imagery*, 2, 99–109.

Merritt, S. (1993). The healing link: Guided Imagery and Music and the body/mind connection. *Journal of the Association for Music and Imagery*, 2, 11–28.

Newell, A. (1999). Dealing with physical illness: Guided Imagery and Music and the search for self. In J. Hibben (ed.), *Inside Music Therapy: Client Experiences*. Gilsum, NH: Barcelona Publishers.

Pickett, E. (1992). Using Guided Imagery and Music (GIM) with a dually diagnosed woman having multiple addictions. *Journal of the Association for Music and Imagery*, 1, 56–67.

Pickett, E. and Sonnen, C. (1993). Guided Imagery and Music: A music therapy approach to multiple personality disorder. *Journal of the Association for Music and Imagery, 2,* 49–72.

Schulberg, C. H. (1999). Out of the ashes: Transforming despair into hope with music and imagery. In J. Hibben (ed.), *Inside Music Therapy: Client Experiences.* Gilsum, NH: Barcelona Publishers

Skaggs, R. (1984). *The Experience of Incest. Childhood Victims in Later Life.* Unpublished masters thesis, West Georgia College.

Tasney, K. (1993). Beginning the healing of incest through Guided Imagery and Music: A Jungian perspective. *Journal of the Association for Music and Imagery, 2,* 35–47.

Ventre, M. (1994). Healing the wounds of childhood abuse: A GIM case study. *Music Therapy Perspectives*, 12(2), 98–103.

Wick, P. A (1990). *Guided Imagery and Music: Its Use with the Eating Disordered Client.* Unpublished master's degree thesis, New York University.

# Part Six:

# Professional Issues

*Chapter Twenty-Five*

# ETHICAL CONSIDERATIONS IN GUIDED IMAGERY AND MUSIC (GIM)

# Nicki S. Cohen

Ethics is defined as the "beliefs and standards we ascribe to regarding what is right and wrong behavior in personal or professional contexts" (Dileo, 2000, p. 3). As such, ethical conduct always involves relationships (Taylor, 1995). Within a professional context, principles of ethics are upheld through codes that associations develop to direct the practices and scholarly efforts of their members. Ethical codes of professional associations serve as self-regulatory guidelines for their members, in that they "state goals, guide affiliates, and serve as a reference point to discipline those who deviate from the norm" (Darr, 1997, p. 61). Taylor (1995) takes a softer stance when discussing the ethical codes of therapists; she suggests that their purpose is to encourage effective therapeutic behavior and to discourage ineffective therapeutic behavior. Attributing the power of these codes to the fact that they are written down, she explains, "When something is written down in this culture, it gains credibility and begins to shape the way people think and act" (p. 223).

Despite the fluidity of moral standards, certain principles seem to shape the development of moral thinking and therefore direct most ethical codes. Four such principles are beneficence, nonmaleficence, justice, and autonomy (Corey, Corey, & Callahan, 1993; Darr, 1997; Dileo, 2000). Beneficence means doing good, or acting in a positive manner with kindness and charity towards others. Nonmaleficence demands refraining from behaviors which might aggravate a problem or cause a negative response. Such restraint implies the obligation of primum non nocere, or "do no harm" (Darr, 1997; Taylor, 1995). Justice can be described as fairness, that all people should receive what is due to them. The principle of justice is meant to address the problems of social inequity caused by culturally and economically diverse populations. Finally, autonomy encourages us to allow individuals to be as independent as possible, to permit them to make their own choices, and to govern themselves.

# AMI CODE OF ETHICS

No code of ethics existed for the GIM community until the formation of the Association for Music and Imagery (AMI). Upon its inception in 1986, the AMI regarded one of its primary functions to develop an ethics document for the GIM community. The first AMI Code of Ethics was written in 1988 (Marilyn Clark, personal communication, September 11, 2000). The purpose of this chapter is to review the latest revision of the AMI code (See Appendix A), and to explore unique ethical dilemmas inherent to the GIM process.

The most current AMI Code of Ethics (1997) is divided into the Preamble and four sections. The first section, "Personal Integrity," sets forth expectations for AMI members who interact with others in a therapeutic, educational, or research setting. Included are guidelines for continued education, personal growth, and working within the limits of one's competency and training. The second section, "Clients/Students/Research Subjects," pertains to the delivery of services to clients, students, or research participants. These guidelines focus on issues such as discrimination, confidentiality, research behavior, misrepresentation, and dual relationships. The third section, "Peer Relationships," includes suggestions for relating to professional colleagues in an ethical manner, such as working cooperatively with other professionals, not damaging the professional reputation or practice of others, and acknowledging publication credit. The final section, "Public," addresses issues of representation, such as the accuracy and completeness of professional qualifications and materials that are disseminated to the public.

The AMI code addresses all four of the ethical principles of beneficence, nonmaleficence, justice, and autonomy. The code emphasizes nonmaleficence as it cautions GIM practitioners from engaging in behaviors that might cause harm to others. Beneficence, or acting in a kind manner toward others, is an indirect outcome whenever members practice nonmaleficence. Justice, or practicing fairness, is clearly implied in the statement that members will "not discriminate in professional relationships because of race, creed, color, sex, national origin, age or sexual orientation" (p. 2). And autonomy, or allowing individuals to be as independent as possible, is recognized, as each member is encouraged to "respect the dignity and worth of each individual" (p. 2).

## ETHICAL ISSUES UNIQUE TO
## THE GIM SETTING

This section will examine the unique ethical dilemmas that are inherent to the GIM setting. Topics include confidentiality, informed consent, advertising and misrepresentation, professional competence, dual relationships, altered states of consciousness, touch, contraindicated populations and GIM modification, and musical considerations.

### Confidentiality

Confidentiality, which is mentioned in the "Clients/Students/Research Subjects" section, directly relates to the ethical principles of autonomy, beneficence, and nonmaleficence. Confidentiality refers both to the legal and ethical obligation to safeguard clients from unauthorized disclosures of information shared within a therapeutic context (Corey, Corey, & Callahan, 1993). However, client confidentiality rights are not always guaranteed. For example, professionals are legally obligated to reveal personal information if there is a risk of "imminent danger" (p. 2), which occurs when clients threaten immediate danger to themselves or to others (Keith-Spiegal & Koocher, 1985). Therefore, GIM facilitators have the responsibility to share possible exceptions to the confidentiality rule with their clients, and preferably in writing, at the onset of the professional relationship (Corey, Corey, & Callahan, 1993; Taylor, 1995).

### Informed Consent

Informed consent, which is implied in the second section of the code (p. 2), refers to the decision that a person makes—knowingly, freely, and independently—to participate in an event or experience (Dileo, 2000), such as a GIM session, a training workshop, a supervision session, or a research study. As such, informed consent relates to the ethical principle of autonomy.

Before anyone can grant informed consent, they must have the necessary information to make the decision, the capacity to understand what they are being asked to do, and they must voluntarily agree to participate. Thus, for example, when GIM trainees conduct practice sessions, or when they bring one of their clients for a live supervision or consultation, they must obtain written informed consent from each client before doing so. The client must understand that the trainee is not a full-fledged practitioner yet, and that certain information, including audiotaped or videotaped materials, may be shared with the trainee's mentor or GIM supervisor.

Informed consent is also mandatory for GIM trainees or practitioners who are conducting research with human participants. In this case, the researcher is ethically obligated to seek approval from an appropriate Internal Review Board (IRB) before beginning any research project. Most health care facilities can grant in-house IRB approval. Independent IRB agencies are also available for those trainees or practitioners who are not professionally associated with an institution or facility.

For more information on how to design consent forms for various uses, see Dileo (2000).

## Advertising and Misrepresentation

Many GIM practitioners are self-employed, and have to set up their own private practices. When advertising for clients, these practitioners have to be careful to represent GIM accurately in all aspects of their advertising. Advertising must be truthful, fair, complete, and it cannot raise unrealistic expectations for the client (Darr, 1997). Moreover, the AMI Code of Ethics (1997) encourages GIM facilitators to avoid misrepresentation of any kind when presenting themselves to the public.

GIM practitioners are often in a quandary about how to describe their practice when advertising. Should GIM be represented as a form of counseling or psychotherapy, as an alternative health modality, as a spiritual practice, as an advanced music therapy technique, or in some other manner? What complicates this issue even further is the current political climate in some geographical regions. Part of the decision of how to represent oneself is dictated by where the practitioner resides. In some parts of the United States, there are laws or regulations that restrict the practice of various forms of therapy or counseling to those who hold a specialized credential, such as state licensure or national board certification. These laws and regulations are attempts to uphold the ethical principle of nonmaleficence; they are designed to protect the public from any harm that may result from receiving clinical services from individuals who are not qualified to provide those services. Thus, individuals who offer any clinical service without the stipulated qualifications and credentials are not upholding the principle of nonmaleficence.

An ethical dilemma that arises among GIM practitioners is that in some cases a practitioner may have satisfactorily completed all training required by AMI, and are therefore "qualified" to practice GIM, but for a variety of reasons lack the credentials required by the appropriate governing agency to offer their services to the public. Some GIM practitioners attempt to solve this dilemma by modifying their practice to fit within the law, such as specializing only in the supportive techniques, as opposed to more in-depth forms of therapy at the reeducative or reconstructive levels (Wohlberg, 1977). Others lobby for legal exemption status. Still others insist that GIM does not violate any laws, that the practice of GIM therapy is beneficent, and that AMI-endorsed training programs sufficiently prepare individuals to use GIM for various therapeutic purposes.

## Professional Competence

Ethical questions around professional competence arise in three different groups: professionals untrained in GIM, GIM professionals, and GIM trainees.

UNTRAINED PROFESSIONALS. The AMI membership is comprised of GIM practitioners and trainees, all of whom agree to uphold the association's ethical code. However, there are many individuals who are not members of AMI, who use GIM or variations therein, or who use similar techniques within their work as music therapists, counselors, psychotherapists, psychiatrists, educators, musicians, healers, spiritual directors, etc. Notice that some of these professions are clinical or health related, and others are not. These professionals have the same ethical responsibilities as the GIM community: they too are ethically bound to use only those techniques or methods which they are qualified by education and training to use, and which they are legally authorized to offer to the public. It is important for these professionals to realize that training in their own discipline does not prepare them to practice GIM, and that their credential does not automatically qualify them to use GIM with their clients. When professionals untrained in GIM begin to use GIM or related techniques, after completing a workshop or two, or after completing only the initial levels of GIM training, they are violating the ethical concept of nonmaleficence. Often, these professionals, as highly qualified as they may be in their own fields, have no idea of the immense power of music and imagery when experienced in an altered state of consciousness; thus, they may be completely unaware of contraindications, and they may be very ill-equipped to handle the myriad responses that individuals have when experiencing such an-depth techniques. This obviously puts the experiencer in danger of harm, which in turn calls into question the ethical propriety of the professional.

GIM PRACTITIONERS. The AMI Code of Ethics (1997) recommends that all qualified GIM practitioners seek supervision or consultation on an ongoing basis, and it also encourages them to "demonstrate a continuing commitment to professional growth by engaging in continuing education" (p. 1). Unfortunately, however, the number of opportunities for GIM supervision, consultation, and continuing education is limited. GIM practitioners can opt to consult with colleagues from related fields, but these professionals may not be informed about, or may be unsympathetic to, the unique issues which surface in GIM work.

Many ethical issues in therapy concern the interplay between professionals doing what is in their own best interests and doing what is best for their clients (Taylor, 1995), or between therapists meeting their own needs rather than meeting the therapeutic needs of their clients. Most therapists have blind spots and unfinished business that interfere with their effectiveness (Corey, Corey, & Callahan, 1993) in addressing the client's therapeutic needs. The AMI code mandates that practitioners engage in "therapy as needed for personal or professional reasons" (p. 3). The rationale is that only through personal therapy can GIM professionals experience firsthand what their clients experience, and only through personal therapy can GIM professionals keep their own needs separate from their work with clients. It is true that personal GIM therapy is an essential requirement in all AMI training programs. However, as with supervision and consultation, there are a limited number of GIM fellows available for personal therapy. In addition, most GIM practitioners are acquainted with one another through their training experiences or AMI membership, a situation that invites the development of dual relationships.

GIM TRAINEES. An integral part of GIM training is the requirement to do several practice sessions with clients under close supervision by a GIM practitioner. Trainees can encounter a variety of ethical issues when meeting this practice requirement. For example: care must be taken to avoid working with clients who present problems which the trainee is not qualified to address; care must be taken with the number of practice sessions that the trainee does with a particular client without having a supervision or consultation; care must be taken that the trainee works at the level of depth that is commensurate with his/her training; care must be taken that the trainee uses music programs that s/he knows sufficiently well, and that are appropriate to the depth-level of the work.

## Dual Relationships

A dual relationship occurs when a practitioner blends a professional relationship with a client, student, or colleague with another kind of relationship (Cory, Corey, & Callahan, 1993). This incompatibility of roles may occur either at the same time the GIM facilitator is treating the client or after the sessions have been terminated. Although usually defined by sexual intimacy, other types of dual relationships can form. These include nonsexual relationships, such as when professionals provide therapy services for employees, colleagues, students, close friends, family members, or "significant others" (Keith-Spiegal and Koocher, 1985). Dual relationships can also occur when professionals accept gifts from or self-disclose to others (Dileo, 2000). The AMI Code of Ethics cautions GIM practitioners to "avoid dual relationships whenever possible," and stipulates what necessary precautions should be taken—in the form of supervision or consultation—"to insure that professional judgment is not impaired and that no exploitation occurs" (p. 3). Taylor (1995) reinforces that the emphasis should be placed on avoiding exploitation of others, rather than preventing all relationships with multiple facets. That is because multiple relationships are pervasive and difficult to recognize and avoid (Dileo, 2000), especially when working with persons in non-ordinary states of consciousness.

Of special concern to the GIM community is the potential for dual relationships to develop between trainers and trainees. During their training, GIM students receive a required number of personal sessions and supervision/consultations. Because of the small number of members in the AMI community, trainees may be tempted to ask a GIM professional to function both as a supervisor and as a personal therapist. This situation is fraught with dual-relationship possibilities and should be avoided at all costs. In addition, due to the process-oriented nature of GIM training, GIM trainees often share personal information, such as transcripts and mandalas, with student-peers and trainers during the workshops. It may be tempting for trainers or peers to take on a dual role with the trainee. GIM trainers should remain cognizant of such a possibility and should strive to keep professional boundaries intact.

## Altered States of Consciousness

Clients experience more autonomy in ordinary states of consciousness than in altered states. In ordinary states, the personal boundaries between the client and practitioner are usually strong, the client is more consciously aware of what is occurring in the here-and-now, and therefore can more easily exercise control over the situation and his/her interactions with the practitioner. In an altered state of consciousness (ASC), the quality of awareness and perception is different from in an ordinary state (Taylor, 1995). In GIM, the client enters an altered state and remains there for an extended period of time during the music imaging portion of the session. During this time, there is a greater permeability of personal boundaries between client and practitioner, and because the client can become so intensely involved in the music and imagery, it is easy to lose awareness of the here-and-now situation and interactions with the practitioner (Bruscia, 1998). As the experience deepens, the client can lose more and more personal autonomy, and therefore have to depend more upon the practitioner to ensure his/her safety and to protect the integrity of his/her boundaries. Needless to say, when this happens, there is a far greater potential for ethical problems to develop than in ordinary states of consciousness. The practitioner has to be particularly careful during these times to continually help the client to maintain as much autonomy as possible, while also protecting the client from harm and respecting the client's boundaries in all ways. This requires the practitioner to maintain the nondirective approach to guiding that is so indigenous to GIM, while also being ready at any moment to step in with clear directions when the client's safety is at risk.

Meanwhile, it is important to note that the practitioner is also experiencing challenges similar to the client. When guiding a client in an altered state, it is natural for the GIM practitioner to also enter an altered state of consciousness. Both practitioner and client are focused on the same image, while listening to the same music. And as both parties become more involved in the experience, travel into deeper states, the practitioner (like the client) may let down the barriers that normally keep his/her experiences separate from the client's. This allows the practitioners to feel and intuit more of their clients' experiences (Taylor, 1995). While this relaxing of boundaries increases the potential for empathy with the client, it also can pose real challenges to the autonomy of both the client and practitioner. Thus, the practitioner has to be particularly skilled at moving through the various layers of consciousness, and being prepared at a moment's notice to reconstitute the boundaries between client and self and reenter awareness of the here-and-now (Bruscia, 1998).

Each time the practitioner enters into the client's imaginal world, and relaxes the boundaries between them, the practitioner becomes more subject to the client's transference as well as a variety of countertransference issues (Bruscia, 1998). Altered-state forms of therapy often facilitate a mutual confusion of the client's introjects and significant others with the introjects and significant others in the practitioner's life. When this happens, the practitioner becomes very easily influenced by the client through various psychodynamic mechanisms such as resistance, projection, transference, or introjective identification (Bruscia, 1998). Sometimes, the practitioner can even become envious of the client's imagery or therapeutic progress. All of these boundary issues can threaten the practitioner's professional autonomy, and ultimately lessen his or her therapeutic effectiveness. As stated earlier, there is a continuing need for supervision and therapy to protect both the practitioner and client, especially in altered state work.

In short, in order to uphold the ethical principles of autonomy and nonmaleficence, GIM practitioners must do what is necessary to avoid the problems that can arise from the relaxation of boundaries inherent in altered state work. In fact, the AMI code instructs GIM practitioners to "be aware of and not exploit the vulnerability of persons in an altered state of consciousness" (p. 2).

## Touch

Another ethical dilemma in GIM concerns the therapeutic role of touch. Touch is one of our most powerful sensory modalities, and for this reason, even in an ordinary state of consciousness, individuals have strong tactile defenses. The subject of touch in psychotherapy is extremely controversial. On one hand, touch can communicate far more empathy and support than words alone (Corey, Corey, & Callahan, 1993). And in GIM, at the appropriate moment, a skillful placement of hand by the practitioner can help a deeply-altered GIM client feel more grounded or allow the client to move through emotionally-blocked material. On the other hand, touch can certainly be contraindicated, as it has the power to enhance client-practitioner dependency or to be misinterpreted as a sexual overture (Dileo, 2000). Certainly, the permeability of boundaries in the professional relationship in GIM provides a ripe situation for dual relationships and client exploitation to unfold.

In GIM, touch is only appropriate if the practitioner has informed the client, prior to the session, about potential situations where it might be used, and the client has given clear permission to be touched (Corey, Corey, & Callahan, 1993; Dileo, 2000). Touch can also be inappropriate or alarming if the client is in an altered state of consciousness, and the practitioner does not give the client sufficient warning or explanation before touch is used. Practitioners should also not touch clients if it is not congruent with how they feel, as clients can sense non-genuine touch (Corey, Corey, & Callahan, 1993), and it can result in contraindication.

## Contraindicated Populations and GIM Modification

While in non-ordinary states of conscious, clients can often move very directly into the most relevant and emotionally-charged material in the unconscious. Grof refers to this highlighting process as "inner radar" (1990, p. 23). For individuals with well-established boundaries and sufficient ego strength, inner radar can facilitate a most effective passage to self-knowledge and personal transformation. For individuals who lack sufficient ego strength and boundaries, however, GIM can be a frightening and potentially harmful venture into the darker recesses of the self. These persons lack the necessary maneuvers to defend themselves from material too powerful for the conscious mind to fathom. They can become overwhelmed either by the music or by the imagery. For these individuals GIM is contraindicated.

Other contraindicated populations for GIM include individuals who are acutely psychotic, those with dementia, persons in acute phases of substance withdrawal, or those without the necessary cognitive skills to interpret the abstract material from their unconscious.

In this matter, GIM practitioners are bound by the ethical obligation to do no harm. The AMI code tells practitioners to provide their clients with "safety and protection" (p. 2). Therefore, practitioners are taught to screen all potential clientele, to eliminate those for whom GIM may be deleterious, and to refer those clients to counselors who practice more traditional, verbal methods. It goes without saying that the GIM professional's financial needs can never supercede the welfare of potential clients.

In certain cases, GIM can be modified for clientele who are not able to experience safely the traditional GIM method. Goldberg (1994) employed a modification of the classical GIM method in her work with hospitalized acute psychiatric patients. She described these patients as having impaired ego strength and less ability to form defensive maneuvers than healthier individuals. Her method was characterized by the use of structured music to provide an emotionally supportive base, a short music phase, and directive guiding. When working with groups of psychiatric patients, Goldberg started the music before the relaxation, used an extremely brief relaxation, and made the focus the primary emphasis of the session. Goldberg asked her patients to write about their imagery while the music was playing.

Summer (1988) recommends other similar modifications for contra-indicated populations. She used techniques employing music and imagery so that they stayed on a "supportive" level of psychotherapy (Wohlberg, 1977). Before the music, the practitioner's verbal instructions are directive and task-driven. The clients remain seated with their eyes open and engage in a cognitive task, such as drawing or writing, while the music plays. The music itself is brief, tightly-structured, and very repetitive.

## Musical Considerations

In both the modified and traditional methods, music is essential to the GIM process. Three ethical dilemmas pertaining to the music include the selection of the music, copyright law, and commercial compilations of musical recordings.

SELECTION OF MUSIC. Traditionally, practitioners select music that compliments their clients' therapeutic needs. Most GIM practitioners, who tend to know the music intimately, claim that during the prelude, they intuitively hear music that matches the clients, and make their choices accordingly. However, because these same professionals tend to be advanced GIM travelers, they may inadvertently choose music that is appropriate to their level of experience as a traveler, but is actually too strong, evocative, or emotionally challenging for their clients. When a practitioner selects music according to his or her own readiness rather than the client's, the client may have to spend considerable energy warding off perceived threats from the music. This scenario raises the ethical issue of nonmaleficence.

In a somewhat different scenario, when GIM practitioners are too absorbed in their own personal issues during a session, they may choose music to meet their own emotional state rather than the client's. For example, if a therapist is feeling depressed and vulnerable, he or she may not be inclined to select music that is strong, evocative or emotionally intense enough for the client's needs. Or if the therapist is feeling strong and resilient, he or she may not be inclined to select music that is introspective and tender enough for the client's needs.

In both scenarios, whether the issue is client readiness or emotional state, since the practitioner makes the musical decision rather than the client, the principle of autonomy is also called into question. Therefore, GIM practitioners need to have dealt successfully with their own personal issues around musical selection so that these ethical infractions do not occur.

COPYRIGHT LAW. A second ethical problem concerns the use of copyrighted recordings in GIM sessions. Because the original taped music programs created by Helen Bonny are no longer available, due to copyright law, GIM students and practitioners must now purchase all of their musical recordings. In addition, GIM practitioners continue to create new and effective GIM music programs. For these practitioners and trainees to create a comprehensive and ongoing recording library, they must spend a significant amount of money.

An ethical dilemma arises when GIM professionals create illegal audio-recordings in an attempt to save money. In doing so, they break federal copyright law. The AMI Code of Ethics very specifically mandates that members must adhere to "local, state, or federal laws" (p. 2). Therefore, members should refrain from making and using these illegal recordings. Music products that are permitted by law are either the original recording or commercial compilations of recordings that are now available to GIM practitioners.

UNSKILLED USE. A third ethical dilemma involves the unskilled use of commercially available music programs. Certain recording labels, some under the guidance of GIM practitioners, have created excellent compilations of classical musical recordings, which though available to the general public, are quite suitable for use in GIM and related practices. In addition, some compilations have been made specifically for use in GIM by qualified professionals and trainees. An ethical problem occurs when persons who are not sufficiently trained attempt to use these recordings when leading others into experiences involving imagery and altered states of consciousness. While there is no way of controlling how commercially available music recordings are used, it is a violation of the ethical principle of nonmaleficence, when anyone who does not have the required competence uses music in any way that puts the experiencer in harm's way.

## CONCLUSION

This chapter has given an overview of the ethical issues addressed in the AMI code of ethics, as well as those that often arise in GIM because of its unique nature. These include concerns related to: confidentiality, informed consent, advertising and misrepresentation, professional competence, dual relationships, altered states of consciousness, touch, contraindications and modifications of GIM, and the use of music. To be certain, these are not the only ethical concerns essential to GIM practitioners and trainees. It is important for every individual involved in helping others professionally to be aware of the human rights of all those they serve, and to honor all the ethical principles formulated to protect those rights. Four principles which provide a valuable foundation for ethical thinking and practice are beneficence, nomaleficence, justice, and autonomy.

## *References*

Association for Music and Imagery. (1997). *Code of Ethics (Revised)*. Blaine, WA: Author.

Bruscia, K. (1998). Manifestations of transference in Guided Imagery and Music (GIM). In K. Bruscia (ed.). *The Dynamics of Music Psychotherapy* (pp. 407–430). Gilsum, NH: Barcelona Publishers.

Corey, G., Corey, M. A., & Callahan, P. (1993). *Issues and Ethics in the Helping Professions (4th ed.)*. Pacific Grove, CA: Brooks/Cole Publishing Company.

Darr, K. (1997). *Ethics in Health Management*. Baltimore: Health Professions Press.

Dileo, C. (2000). *Ethical Thinking in Music Therapy*. Cherry Hill, NJ: Jeffrey Books.

Goldberg, F. (1994).The Bonny method of guided imagery and music as individual and group treatment in a short-term acute psychiatric hospital. *Journal of Association for Music and Imagery, 3,* 18–34.

Grof, S. (1990). *The Holotropic Mind*. San Francisco: Harper.

Keith-Spiegel, P., & Koocher, G. P. (1985). *Ethics in Psychology*. New York: Random House.

Maranto, C. D. (1981). *Ethics in Music Therapy: A Programmed Text*. Unpublished doctoral dissertation. Louisiana State University, New Orleans.

Summer, L. (1988). *Guided Imagery and Music in the Institutional Setting*. St. Louis: MMB Horizon Series.

Taylor, K. (1995). *The Ethics of Caring. Honoring the Web of Life in our Professional Healing Relationships*. Santa Cruz, CA: Handford Mead Publishers.

Wohlberg, L. R. (1977). *The Technique of Psychotherapy (3rd ed.)*. New York: Grune & Stratton.

*Chapter Twenty Six*


# THE DEVELOPMENT OF TRAINING IN THE BONNY METHOD OF GUIDED IMAGERY AND MUSIC (BMGIM) FROM 1975 TO 2000


# Kirstie Lewis


Training for facilitators of the Bonny Method of Guided Imagery and Music (BMGIM) began in the early 1970s, went through many changes in the 1980s and 1990s, and continues to be offered as a viable professional option today. There were several historical developments in the 1980s that had a large impact on how the method is currently taught. This included the creation of the Association for Music and Imagery (AMI), which, in turn, delineated a process by which training programs and trainers could be endorsed. Minimum standards were set that had to be met by a training program in order for their graduates to be recognized as "Fellows or Facilitators of AMI," i.e., professionals who are fully trained in the Bonny Method. These developments will be traced in the following pages with attention to the initial training model created by Helen Bonny; the subsequent training model refined and modified by Marilyn Clark and Linda Keiser Mardis; and the current AMI model which grew out of the first two.


## THE EARLY YEARS: 1970–1979


The development of BMGIM has been complex and there have been a variety of twists and turns along the way. Helen Bonny has written at least two articles detailing the history of the method that carries her name. "Twenty-one Years Later: A GIM Update," was published in *Music Therapy Perspectives* (1994) and "Celebrating the Tenth Anniversary of the Association for Music and Imagery: Highlights and Perspectives," was published in the Fall 1996 *AMI Newsletter*. Debra Burns, AMI Fellow, also wrote two historical articles ("A

Brief History of the Bonny Method of GIM," and, "Who's Who in AMI: Helen Bonny" which appeared in the Spring 1998 issue of the *AMI Newsletter*. Information in this chapter has been drawn from these articles, from AMI documents, and from several other resources, including copies of early newsletters obtained from Helen Bonny.

The initial creative energy for what has come to be called BMGIM came through the insights of Helen Bonny, a gifted musician and therapist, as well as a spiritual seeker. She was influenced by the writings and approaches to psychology and mysticism of a number of people including Evelyn Underhill, Ken Godfrey, Carl Jung, Abraham Maslow, Carl Rogers, and Hanscarl Leuner, but it was out of her own experiences with music, with the events of her life that might be called spiritual, and with the clinical work she was invited to do at the Maryland Psychiatric Research Center (MPRC) in Baltimore that this unique therapeutic process began to take shape. When Bonny was invited to the Research Center in the early 1970s there was high interest in some psychological and therapeutic circles concerning the question of how different states of consciousness might promote healing. Bonny's particular interest in the potential of music to evoke an altered state of consciousness was creatively applied to clinical populations and eventually her techniques began to coalesce into a method of healing that could stand on its own. Initially Bonny was asked to provide music to accompany therapeutic sessions where LSD was given to the client. Gradually Bonny developed specific music "programs" of carefully sequenced classical music which were used in these sessions, but she also soon realized that the music programs alone had healing potential. After funding for LSD research was withdrawn, she continued to explore the ways in which classical music on its own could be therapeutically applied.

As Bonny's research and experiences at MPRC led to a clearer, more distinct therapeutic method, it became easier to teach it to others. In 1973, Bonny and her friend, Louis Savary, published *Music and Your Mind*, a classic book about the healing potential of music. This book resulted in many requests for music experiences and for copies of the music programs developed by Bonny while working at MPRC. Many individuals wanted to know how they could use GIM in their own mental health work settings. This increasing interest soon led Bonny, Savary, and another colleague, Sister Trinitas Bocchini, to establish the Institute for Consciousness and Music (ICM) in 1973. This nonprofit, educational corporation was designed to be a teaching, publishing, and training vehicle for GIM, and it was also hoped that ICM could contract for the reproduction of the music programs developed by Bonny (Bonny, 1980, p. 39). Sister Bocchini, an educator, became instrumental in setting up the organization of ICM and managing the early workshops it sponsored. The first *ICM Newsletter* was published in the fall of 1973 with listings of materials for sale and scheduled workshops aimed at different professional groups such as music therapists, pastoral counselors, and psychologists. In the *Music Therapy Perspectives* article referred to earlier, Bonny (1994) states that she soon began to feel that "a workshop or series of seminars was not adequate training for people to learn how to use this new and sensitive process" (p. 72). She wrote "GIM therapists would need to be taught a new attitude toward psychotherapy; the expertise to use the method; and a deep understanding of music which would go beyond the traditional playing and training modes. Further training in depth processes of psychology, not a part of the usual training for psychotherapists, would be required of the GIM therapist" and they would need to have "ease in guiding within altered states, personal experience in gaining access to these states and understanding of the need for permissive interaction during such states" (Bonny, 1994, p. 72).

With this perspective in mind, in 1975 ICM began to offer the first training for professionals who wanted to use the Bonny method in their already existing therapeutic and counseling practices. This earliest professional training of BMGIM facilitators was offered in July 1975 and included a five-day seminar/workshop held at a retreat center which was followed immediately by a further five weeks of training. This initial training is described in the ICM Newsletter from that summer and Table 1 is a summary of that information.

This format for training was offered again in July of 1976. By then, Bonny recognized that at least two years of specialized training were needed regardless of previous professional or academic experience (Bonny, 1996). Therefore, an additional requirement of training, the internship, was added. The ICM training flyer from the summer of 1976 states: "The six-week program provides the first stage of training to become a GIM facilitator. Although the participants will gain in the knowledge of the process and the body of material which is available and will acquire some skill in facilitating, it is not designed to produce practitioners who are fully qualified to use this process in every situation. Those who expect to receive full endorsement of ICM should understand that this intensive training is followed by an internship program of approximately one year." The characteristics of the internship program evolved over the next few years and are further elaborated later in this chapter in the section on the middle years of training. It should be noted that those who completed the ICM training were given the title "ICM Fellow."

Table 1.
Bonny's Original Training Model (1975).

| 5-DAY INTENSIVE WORKSHOP | INTENSIVE TRAINING FOR MH PROFESSIONALS |
|---|---|
| *Instruction* | |
| 5-day retreat. | 5-week program of at least 3.5 days per week, plus weekly staff consultations, group seminars, evening sessions, and 5 optional weekend seminars. |
| *Rationale* | |
| "To initiate, deepen, and extend the music and imager experience in participants and to deal with effective methods of GIM use with individuals and groups." | To prepare mental health workers to incorporate GIM procedures into their own therapy and counseling work. |
| *Didactic Content* | |
| 1) Effective methods of using GIM with individuals and groups; 2) New music programs and appropriate choices of music; 3) Techniques of psychodrama, gestalt, and bioenergetics; 4) Using GIM with different populations; 5) Interpreting evoked symbols; and 6) Mapping the psychological sequence of GIM experiences. | While content was not described in the *ICM Newsletter*, the following are titles for the weekend seminars: 1) Sound and movement; 2) Mandala; 3) New techniques expressing Jungian framework; 4) Psychodrama; and 5) Understanding symbols in dreams. |
| *Experiential Requirements* | |
| The objective to "initiate, deepen and extend the music imagery experience" will be approached experientially, and other artistic media (Dance and Art) will be offered. | None specified. |
| *Practica* | |
| None. | Training featured 5 individual staff-facilitated GIM sessions. Participants must give GIM sessions during training (number unspecified). |
| *Outcome* | |
| | "A certificate will be awarded to all who complete the training." |

During these early years, in addition to planning and carrying out training, Bonny was also continuing her own Ph.D. research. Her unpublished doctoral dissertation, "Music and Psychotherapy" (Union Graduate School: Union for Experimenting Colleges and Universities, 1976), was the basis for three published monographs which became important resources for students. The monographs are: *Facilitating GIM Sessions* (1978); *The Role of Taped Music Programs in the GIM Process* (1978), and *GIM Therapy: Past, Present and*

*Future Implications* (1980). In the first monograph, Bonny presented guidelines for facilitators to follow during sessions. In the second, she explored the psychological nature of music experiences and the characteristics of her music programs. In the third monograph Bonny described the genesis of the GIM idea, how GIM can be seen as a radical innovation in the history of psychotherapy, and the results of her investigations into the therapeutic uses of GIM. It is obvious that the content of these monographs was certainly of relevance to the training. It is not clear whether the early training gave Helen ideas for the monographs, or whether the monographs served to help define the training (or both), but certainly Bonny's research and writings, including the monographs and *Music and Your Mind* (1973), contributed to the content and development of the early training which continued to evolve and mature.

## THE MIDDLE YEARS: 1980–1988

In 1974 Bonny began to have health problems. Although she was able to complete her research and her degree, initiate and develop ICM and the training, and continue her writing, eventually, by 1979, heart surgery forced Bonny into semiretirement and she moved from Baltimore to the Pacific Northwest to be with family members. Not wishing the training programs to cease at a time when there was considerable professional interest in this new therapeutic method, Bonny agreed that Marilyn Clark, one of the first two "ICM Fellows" to graduate from ICM (July 1978), and Linda Keiser (who became a fellow in 1979), would assume responsibility to continue the training. Clark and Keiser made some additions and modifications to the training format that had been established by Bonny as they began to offer the ICM training seminars throughout the country as well as in the Baltimore area. There had already been some rather large changes in the internship program that had been added to the training in 1976 as stated previously. By 1980 Bonny described the internship as follows:

> The intern contracts with the ICM Training Seminars to facilitate 100 hours of music sessions, to have sit-in supervision and consultations with the staff, to present a case study, and to design and execute a project using GIM in a creative and innovative way. Intern Retreats are held four times a year during which time projects, case studies, group consultations and specialized workshops are held. Interns are expected to lead and assist in short workshops and help with one Five-Day Intensive Training Session. At the successful termination of

their work, interns are given the title of ICM Fellow and are certified and recommended by the Institute as fully trained in the GIM therapeutic process (Bonny, 1980, pp. 42–43).

Further changes continued from about 1979 through 1982 at which time the training had become a three-phase program with significant prerequisites and practicum requirements. Table 2 is a summary of the training as it had evolved by 1982.

By 1986 the *ICM Newsletter* (1986) held the following description of the three levels of training offered by Clark and Keiser under the auspices of ICM:

The training program in GIM is comprised of three phases each having its own special characteristics, and united by our unique style of combining didactic and experiential learning with the individual needs and interests of those who come to train with us.

In Phase I we present and demonstrate basic techniques of guiding to the music; basic concepts of imagery and music as therapeutic media; and basic processing tools which are compatible with GIM.

Phase II is a six-day residential intensive with a work-study contract to be completed prior to the beginning of the seminar. This includes giving GIM sessions to friends or close associates using some of the basic ICM music programs; receiving personal GIM sessions; reading books about the nature of consciousness, imagery, music, and healing; expanding one's skills in assessing types of music which evoke imagery. Close supervision and sensitive critiquing allow participants to make marked progress in their ability to guide persons through GIM sessions.

Phase III is a two-year period of committed study and use of GIM. The program is self-directed following a carefully prepared outline developed by the Institute. It includes giving and documenting GIM sessions; experiencing a series of personal GIM sessions; receiving supervision during GIM sessions; reading pertinent texts; assisting in GIM workshop leadership; attending adjunct skills workshops; participating in a seven-day Phase III Intensive; conceiving and documenting a project about GIM. This phase of training is for those who intend to use GIM as a prime modality in their life work (p. 3).

Table 2.
Clark and Keiser Training Model (1980–1982)

| PHASE ONE | PHASE TWO | PHASE THREE |
|---|---|---|
| *Instructional Days Required* | | |
| 5-day residential intensive. | 6-day residential intensive. | 7-day residential intensive. |
| *Training Rationale* | | |
| First phase of professional training in GIM. | Refinement of the art of guiding a dyadic music session. | Committed, self-directed study, work, growth and support for those intending to use GIM as major part of professional work. |
| *Prerequisites* | | |
| Previous experience with GIM in a workshop or private session. | Phase One intensive, interview, written application with 3 mandalas, 20 hours of practice sessions; listen to 4 ICM music programs; find short piece of music for GIM; 2 personal GIM sessions, 1 personal growth workshop, 3 books, 3 monographs. | Phase Two intensive and all requirements, interview, written application with 3 mandalas, 40 additional guiding hours, a supervised session, a consultation, 2 personal sessions, 2 personal growth weekends, 4 additional books from list. |
| *Didactic Content* | | |
| GIM and principles of guiding: altered states of consciousness, therapeutic aspects of music. | The art of guiding dyad sessions; essential elements of GIM (guiding, music, imagery). | Review essential elements of GIM, specialized guiding techniques, group work; case studies, workshop procedures, and music evaluations. |
| *Experiential Activities and Requirements* | | |
| Demonstrations of guiding, journaling, clay work, mandalas, movement to music, individual and group music experiences. | Dyads with staff supervision, group consultations, demonstrations of advanced guiding, personal growth through music, journaling, clay, mandalas. | Supervised dyads, demonstrations of specialized guiding, critiques, personal process sessions, group activities and consultations. |
| *Practica Requirements* | | |
| None specified. | See Prerequisites. | 12 personal sessions, 10 days of personal growth workshops, 100 guiding hours, 10 supervisions, written summary of personal growth, assist at Phase One seminar, musical awareness project, case study, written project. |
| *Reading Requirements* | | |
| None specified. | See Prerequisites. | 10 books from list. |
| *Outcome* | | |
| None. | None. | Certified by ICM as Fellow. |

The training continued in this three-level format, and has only varied from this in the last few years when some programs combined the second and third phases into a single level of advanced training.

During the early 1980s, ICM scheduled periodic meetings for their graduates (ICM Fellows) to share information and provide support for one another. By 1986 there were approximately twenty-five graduates, many of whom attended a meeting of ICM Fellows in Chicago in April of that year. For the first time, students of GIM were also invited to this Fellows' gathering. GIM Fellows and students decided that they wanted a formal, nonprofit, professional association to replace the existing informal Fellows group. As a result the Association for Music and Imagery (AMI) was created with the following purpose: "to maintain and uphold the integrity of Guided Imagery and Music and to nurture and support all those who have trained in this method" (*AMI Newsletter,* Winter 1988). Training would still be offered through the auspices of ICM, but once the individual completed the training, then he or she would join AMI, the professional association for all those trained (or are in training) in BMGIM.

By 1988, it had become increasingly difficult for ICM, which had changed its name to the Institute for Music and Imagery (IMI) in 1986, to continue operating on both East and West coasts. Decisions had been made about the production and /selling of the music programs used for GIM which affected the financial health of ICM. It was announced at the 1988 annual meeting of AMI and in *Crescendo*, IMI's newsletter, that the Institute would close in September 1988 because "the needs of the Institute were beyond the scope of what the staff, the board, and the constituency could provide." At the time, several hundred individuals had participated in the training since 1975, a small percentage of whom had completed the entire three-phase training and joined AMI as Fellows.

## THE LATER YEARS: 1988–PRESENT

The closing of the IMI in 1988 resulted in concern as to how training in the BMGIM would continue. Although Bonny's health had improved, she was not in a position to return to a commitment to direct the training, but at the 1988 AMI Conference in Colorado (AMI Minutes, 1988) she announced that she was establishing the Bonny Foundation near Wichita, Kansas, where she would soon begin offering BMGIM training. Madelaine Ventre, an ICM Fellow who had introduced the Bonny method to New York University's music therapy program, stated that the two-year music therapy program at NYU would begin to offer the equivalent of the three phases of BMGIM training, starting in the fall of 1988. Several other Fellows spoke of their plans to initiate training programs. At this 1988 AMI Annual Meeting a Credentialing Committee was created in order to begin developing guidelines for these future training programs. A letter written by AMI's Co-Focalizers (Co-Presidents) and sent to all AMI members after the conference gave the rationale for this committee as follows:

> As a result of the decision to close IMI, AMI's responsibility and role as the professional body for GIM facilitators have both grown broader and more complex. Initially there will be several administrative functions that AMI will take on such as the mailing list, dealing with public inquiries, general public relations, keeping track of all those who completed any phase of GIM training, and so on; the actual training functions, however, will probably spread to diverse programs. Training programs will, in future, be accredited by AMI, and students who complete their GIM training will become Fellows of AMI rather than IMI.

With these concerns in mind, AMI agreed to produce guidelines for training programs and a Code of Ethics for BMGIM facilitators by establishing two committees, the Credentialing Committee and the Ethics Committee.

Several of the most experienced BMGIM facilitators were members of this first Credentialing Committee. Carol Bush, ICM Fellow and chairperson of the committee, reported in the Fall 1988 *AMI Newsletter* that

> the task for this committee this year is to set up credentialing standards for individual GIM facilitators and for GIM training programs. Plans are to create a competency-based credentialing process. Plans also include a grand-mothering clause for individuals who have completed training with ICM or IMI. January 1, 1989, is set as a deadline for establishing standards for training programs. Fellows who wish to establish training programs should go ahead and be creative in that process. However, be sure to inform the committee about your program because this will be the first step in AMI's program credentialing process. Send your proposals to Carol Bush and she will take them to the committee and to the (leadership) circle for approval. AMI will not be able to endorse or certify any programs set up without their knowledge. A more formal credentialing process will be developed between now and our June 1989 meeting.

In the Spring 1989 *AMI Newsletter* the following notice appeared:

> The credentialing committee has formed two sub-groups. Ruth Skaggs and Carol Bush developed the initial draft for Basic and Advanced training requirements. Barbara Collins, Linda Keiser and Carol Bush met for the second draft and have generated requirements for Basic, Intermediate and Advanced level trainings. Requirements for trainers will be included in the proposed guidelines. Fellows who have submitted proposals to begin training programs have been given provisional acceptance until June's meeting.

In the meantime, while AMI committee members were considering how to implement their new responsibility to set guidelines and standards for professional GIM training, Marilyn Clark and Linda Keiser published their book, *Teaching Guided Imagery and Music: An Experiential-Didactic Approach* (1989). In their preface they state:

> We invite persons who are developing new GIM teaching programs to read this manual thoroughly so as to benefit from the years of experience which it represents. Teaching paradigms will change according to the needs of new constituencies and the skills of new leadership; yet the core elements of Guided Imagery and Music remain constant. As GIM training programs begin to proliferate, it is our hope that the training process will remain resonant with GIM and that each trainer will work with personal and professional integrity towards the goal of producing well trained GIM facilitators (p. 4).

These guidelines as well as the experience of Clark and Keiser as trainers in BMGIM clearly influenced the initial AMI document titled "Requirements for AMI-Endorsed GIM Training Programs," which was presented at the third annual AMI conference in July 1989. The introductory statement to this document was as follows:

> GIM training programs may be implemented within a variety of structures, i.e. institutional, independent and mentor programs. For any program to be endorsed by AMI, the program must be taught by AMI-endorsed primary trainers who meet the endorsement requirements herein outlined. Training program requirements reflect minimum components that must be covered at each level. The respective format, content, and resource materials are left to the discretion of the primary trainer (July 1, 1989).

There have been many revisions of these endorsement standards over the years, but they remain similar to the training as it was originally conceived by Helen Bonny, then carried out and modified by Clark and Keiser Mardis. In essence, since 1976, BMGIM training has occurred at three levels, which have been given a variety of names but are currently called: Introductory, Intermediate, and Advanced Training. The training combines both didactic and experiential elements; it requires trainees to give many BMGIM sessions and to receive supervision of their guiding skills; it also requires trainees to receive many personal BMGIM sessions. Other details about training requirements can be found in the documents of AMI. Additional requirements have been added over the years such as continuing education guidelines for Fellows and Primary Trainers, a process for renewal of endorsement, and details of various procedures.

By the Fall of 1989 there were seven AMI-endorsed Primary Trainers who had developed programs and announced training dates in the Fall 1989 *AMI Newsletter*. These initial Primary Trainers and programs were as follows: Helen Bonny (Bonny Foundation); Marilyn Clark (Temple University); Linda Keiser (Archedigm, Inc.); Madeline Ventre (NYU and Creative Therapies Institute); Carol Bush and Sara Jane Stokes (Mid-Atlantic Institute for Music and Imagery); and Ruth Skaggs (Southeastern Institute for Music-Centered Psychotherapy). Numbers of trainers and programs have gradually increased and currently there are more than twenty Primary Trainers and approximately a dozen AMI-endorsed BMGIM training programs worldwide, including several associated with universities. Individual training programs follow the AMI guidelines, but have added elements which serve to make programs unique.

Table 3 is a summarized version of the current AMI "Standards and Procedures for Endorsement of GIM Training Programs" (revised June 1999). These requirements are the minimum necessary for endorsement. Some programs require even more of their students. A study of these requirements will give a good idea of the stages of skill acquisition that a student must move through during this training, from introductory concepts and initial observations of the trainer demonstrating GIM skills, to multiple experiences of conducting sessions both with and without supervision. These requirements have changed over the years and perhaps this is not unexpected since they deal with a method that, at its heart, is about the "exploration of consciousness."

Table 3.
Requirements for AMI-Endorsed Programs (1999).

| INTRODUCTORY | INTERMEDIATE | ADVANCED |
|---|---|---|
| ***Instructional Days Required*** | | |
| 35 hours. | 50 hours, not including practica. | 100 hours, not including practica or other courses. |
| ***Training Rationale*** | | |
| Essential understanding of GIM. | Fundamental skills necessary for practice of GIM. | Expansion of all competencies presented previously, expertise |
| ***Prerequisites*** | | |
| B.A. or equivalent; meets all requirements for therapy practice in own country. | Same as Introductory, plus 2 years mental health experience. | Same as Introductory, plus three years of mental health experience. |
| ***Didactic Content*** | | |
| Introduction to: definition, history, philosophy, current theory, applications, contra-indications, guiding, imagery, music and programs, altered states, session structure, inductions, processing skills, dyadic and group experiences, therapeutic process, practice standards and ethics. | Intermediate concepts of GIM as: medium of personal growth, change, holistic healing, insight, integration, support, and trans-personal process and means of support. Intermediate under-standing of session elements, ethics, standards, contraindications, structure, and dynamics. | Advanced concepts in all areas. |
| ***Experiential Activities and Requirements*** | | |
| Demonstrations by trainer. | Demonstration of dyad session by trainer; 2 dyad experiences (guiding and traveling), group experiences of music-imagery; question and discussion periods; experiences with mandalas, movement, writing. | Demonstrations of physical interventions and several inductions; 3 dyad experiences (guiding and traveling); group experiences with processing of images; feedback on guiding, discussions, other modalities. |
| ***Practica Requirements*** | | |
| None specified. | As stipulated: 4 personal sessions with AMI fellow or advanced trainee, 10 guiding sessions under auspices of trainer. | As stipulated: 15 personal sessions with fellow, 75 practice sessions, 15 supervisions, ongoing case consults, case study, music analysis, papers. |
| ***Reading Requirements*** | | |
| As specified by trainer. | At least 5 books. | At least 15 books. |
| ***Evaluation*** | | |
| Students evaluate training; trainer evaluates students. | Same. | Same. |
| ***Outcome*** | | |
| Eligible to apply for next level. | Eligible to apply for Advanced Training. | With master's degree, eligible to apply for AMI Fellow. |

## ELEMENTS OF BMGIM TRAINING

Several elements of training in BMGIM have been mentioned in the three summary tables without being fully explained. As these aspects of the training are important the following section will discuss them in more detail.

### Supervision

Bonny recognized the importance of direct observation and supervision of trainees. Such supervision is standard procedure in most mental health fields where the subtleties of excellent practice are difficult to teach through "book learning," and must, therefore, be taught by modeling and by timely and specific feedback on the efforts of the neophyte. Therefore, individually supervised sessions have always been an important part of the learning process for trainees in BMGIM. Prior to 1989, each advanced trainee was required to have at least ten supervised sessions; currently, the minimum is fifteen. Observing a student who is engaged in conducting a session is the best and perhaps the only method of determining whether a student has actually gained enough skills and practical expertise in BMGIM to become an independent practitioner. Giving the trainee detailed and thorough feedback is the primary method of ensuring that the trainee has the awareness and understanding to improve her/his skills.

Although supervisions were originally carried out only on-site during a session, as more trainees found themselves in geographic locations with no Fellows near by, the possibility of submitting video-recorded sessions was raised. Since the number of Fellows who can carry out supervisions is limited, this has, in fact, turned out to be an acceptable way to do some of the required supervisions. An audio-recorded session is even less accessible for evaluation as nonverbal interactions are not apparent and much more information is lost to the supervisor. Group supervision sessions can also be helpful to students, but they do not take the place of the individually supervised, one-on-one session.

Linda Keiser Mardis, in her recent paper "Supervising Trainees in the Archedigm Training Program in The Bonny Method of GIM" (Mardis, 2000), has detailed her philosophy about supervision and has given numerous suggestions for applying and improving supervision skills. She states, "The Archedigm concept of supervisions is that they be positive and enriching experiences, carried out with the same spirit of trust and support that is evident in and important to the method itself, thereby providing students a reliable environment in which to own their strengths, confront their weaknesses, and receive additional motivation to strive for excellence." The issue of requirements and training of supervisors is one that is still of interest to AMI Primary Trainers as they seek to improve their training and the excellence of their students.

## Personal Sessions in GIM

Another very important element of this training is the requirement for trainees to participate in a series of personal BMGIM sessions as imager. The minimum number of sessions is specified in the AMI Standards for each level of training, but many programs require more than these minimums. In order to understand the power and potential of BMGIM, a trainee must experience the method personally by having a number of sessions with a Fellow who is not their Primary Trainer. This allows extremely personal and practical learning about music, altered states of consciousness, inductions, guiding interventions, and psychological and spiritual processes to be gained. Such knowledge cannot be gained in any other way. Requiring personal sessions may also help to identify students whose motivation for doing the training is more personal than professional and who then can be redirected to another field of study, if necessary.

Personal sessions also allow the trainee to learn about transference and countertransference from their own experience of these processes. Since these psychotherapeutic processes are essential to understand and almost always occur in BMGIM sessions and series of sessions, having personal sessions is a powerful way to grasp their importance. Bruscia has written two articles about transference for the *Journal of AMI* 1995, Volume 4. His second article, "Manifestations of Transference in Guided Imagery and Music (GIM)," is particularly instructive, and all trainees, trainers, and practitioners of the Bonny Method should be aware of the concepts and experiences he outlines.

## Dyadic Experiences

Another element of the training involves trainees working in pairs or dyads during the days of the intensive workshops for both Introductory and Intermediate training in order to practice the skills of guiding a session. The trainers gradually guide the pairs of trainees through the various steps of an individual session, adding more and more parts of the session as the trainees gain confidence and skill. These practice sessions are followed by feedback periods for both the trainees who were guiding and those who were guided. These dyad practice sessions are done in the group context, and trainers can get a good idea of which trainees are developing their guiding skills adequately and which ones are having difficulty. They also have the opportunity to observe those trainees who may have emotional and personal issues to cope with and they can offer support and suggestions about how these can be handled within the context of the practice session. At the Intermediate level of training, each trainee will usually experience being a guide on three occasions and being guided on three occasions during the intensive workshop, thus allowing a trainee to apply the feedback he receives during subsequent practice sessions. Skills can improve very quickly during these days of intense training.

## Group Imaging Experiences

As a part of the intensive workshops at all levels of training, the trainer usually schedules several group-imaging experiences. These can vary but usually involve trainees listening together to a carefully selected piece of music that is played after a short induction by the trainer. After the music, the group shares their individual experiences and images and draws information from this process. It is an important method of teaching students about the different types of music which are good choices for GIM; about the large variety of imagery which can arise; and about the rather wide range of possible responses that a particular piece of music can evoke.

## Demonstrations

It is difficult to describe in words the nature of the experiences that are possible during a BMGIM session. Therefore, early in training, trainers give both short and longer demonstration sessions in front of the group of trainees so that the potential of this method can be observed directly. Trainers are essentially guiding a real session with a volunteer (not a student) as the imager. Following the session, students are invited to ask questions and make observations about what they have just witnessed. Often what is learned from these sessions is very powerful and is referred to over and over again as the students develop their own skills. It is a powerful opportunity for the trainer to model the skills and expertise for which the trainee will be striving over the course of several years and this experience allows the students to understand more fully the deep impact this method can have on an imager.

There are also other skills, such as many types of inductions, which can be demonstrated by trainers and then practiced by trainees in special laboratory sessions where they receive guidance and feedback.

## Complementary Techniques

Lastly, teachers and facilitators of the Bonny Method have found that there are many possible ways of stimulating the imagination of clients and students. There are also imaginative methods of assisting clients in understanding and integrating their BMGIM experiences into their lives which students must learn. Therefore, during the intensive workshops, many of these techniques are offered to the trainees to use in their own process and to develop as tools for using with clients. These can include things such as working with clay, using journals, drawing mandalas, and moving to music. It is important for students to learn that by developing their own capacity to use their imagination, they will be developing their ability to assist their clients in being at home in the imaginative realm that is this method's strength.

## VARIATIONS OF THE
## BASIC TRAINING MODELS

It is beyond the scope of this chapter to detail each of the AMI-endorsed training programs and their particular format or philosophy of training. All trainings must offer the elements included in Table 3, but they can and do stress different facets of the work and often provide additional or expanded training in some aspects. In the 1998 *AMI Training Directory* twelve programs are listed with brief descriptions of each. Since 1998, the *AMI Training* Directory has not listed program descriptions. Names of trainers, addresses, training dates, and fees are included without further elaboration. Readers will have to seek updated information through the AMI office and from individual trainers. A few of the variations of training described in this directory are summarized below:

- In the Australian program, the Advanced Training is offered through the two-year Graduate Diploma in GIM at the Faculty of Music, University of Melbourne. It consists of eight three-day seminars over the course of two years. This training "is developing within the Australian culture in which archetypal imagery and experiences are reflected from the Australian landscape and historical folklore."
- Madelaine Ventre's training (Creative Therapies Institute) is tailored to fit together with the New York University Music Therapy Department's programs. In general, CTI's requirements for instructional hours and practice are greater than those of AMI.
- The Mid-Atlantic Training Institute offers training with a "strong clinical emphasis and is geared toward the professional who works with client populations."

- The Southeastern Institute for Music-Centered Psychotherapy stresses a high level of musical expertise in its students and offers a two-day course in Music Fundamentals prior to Level II training for students with minimal music backgrounds.
- The Therapeutic Arts Psychotherapy and Training Institute was designed to bring GIM training to European music therapists, psychologists, and psychiatrists and is "geared to help therapists bring their unique individual, cultural and social backgrounds into their training for in-depth GIM therapy in their native lands, in their native languages."

It can be said that the training of professionals in BMGIM evolved steadily since its beginnings in 1975. Since the Bonny Method has expanded into the world with several international programs currently being offered and others being planned, AMI's guidelines and standards have not always been found to fit well within specific cultures. Further variations, therefore, are needed and it is not possible to foresee where these will lead. However, the AMI guidelines will probably continue to serve as a strong framework for some years to come, defining the parameters that experienced trainers have determined are necessary for "good" training.

## PRIMARY TRAINER ENDORSEMENT

In 1988, when AMI members agreed to take responsibility for developing standards for GIM training programs, they also agreed to develop guidelines to use in determining who would do the training of new GIM facilitators. As described in earlier sections of this chapter, Helen Bonny was originally responsible for all training. When she became ill, two experienced GIM fellows, Clark and Keiser Mardis, agreed to continue the training process through ICM. When ICM/IMI dissolved, there were many Fellows prepared to establish their own training programs. Members of AMI decided at that time that certain requirements would have to be met before a candidate could be endorsed as a fully qualified Primary Trainer. These requirements were written and approved by the membership as part of the AMI document "Standards and Procedures for Endorsement of AMI Training Programs"(AMI, 1999). The following description is taken from the 1999 revision of that document:

EDUCATIONAL BACKGROUND

- Fellow of AMI.
- Master's degree or equivalent in a clinical mental health field.
- Evidence of supplementary training through academic coursework, seminars, workshops, examinations, publications, readings, work experience, in-service training, independent study, mentorship, life experience, or other avenues. Supplementary training must cover all of the following areas that were not covered by the graduate or undergraduate curriculum: music competencies, imagery, psychological theory, psychopathology, transpersonal studies, counseling and communication skills, and group dynamics.

EXPERIENCE

- Minimum of three years and 400 client sessions as an AMI Fellow.
- At least one experience as an assistant trainer at an Introductory, Intermediate or Advanced GIM Training.
- Supervision of at least twenty GIM sessions.
- Documented teaching experience.
- Membership in good standing with AMI and completion of continuing education requirements for Primary Trainers as described in the Standards document (p. 12).

# CONCLUSION

In summary, over a space of more than twenty-five years, beginning with the music and imagery technique described in *Music and Your Mind* (Bonny, 1973), changes in name, method, theoretical design, and practice have come about in response to a deeper understanding of the method and the needs of facilitators to provide sophisticated and beneficial therapy to their clients. These have included a number of basic publications, the forming of an endorsing body (AMI) to regulate training at several qualified learning centers, and a professional journal.

The process by which one becomes a skillful practitioner of BMGIM has developed more fully as the power and potential of the method have become apparent. The mental health professional who is seriously intent on using this method is encouraged to seek training through one of the AMI-endorsed programs. In consideration of the intensity of the BMGIM process and the need for the psychological safety of both client and therapist, a supervised training environment is strongly recommended. Both didactic and experiential learning in the depth processes of music and of psychotherapy are a part of the required training to become a competent facilitator of BMGIM.

This chapter has focused primarily on the path that the Bonny Method has followed in becoming an accepted therapeutic approach in the professional world. It has described the mostly formal processes that were developed by the professional organization to ensure that appropriate and regulated training programs would be created so that the integrity of BMGIM could be passed on to new generations. In the description of the earliest training in 1975, through the changes in the 1980s and on into the current standards for training set forth by AMI, one can follow the evolution of a more sophisticated version of training as the years pass by. It is probable that the training will continue to evolve in ways we cannot yet anticipate, especially as this is a creative group of individuals called to practice BMGIM. There will always be some dynamic tension between those who want to preserve the essential elements of the Bonny Method as it has been from the beginning and pass these on to new students, and those whose deepest calling is to elaborate and innovate and thus extend the method into new arenas and challenging clinical circumstances.

However, perhaps what has been lost in these descriptions of the training process is an awareness of the excitement and mystery that remains at the heart of this method. This therapy is unlike most other therapies. It welcomes and evokes experiences that are transpersonal, transformational, and unable to be reduced to pat verbal explanations. This extraordinary method is capable of bringing about spiritual, emotional, and physical healing on deep levels. It is an open-ended, open-minded, and open-hearted therapy that allows for the unexpected to emerge and for those mystical moments which all humans are capable of celebrating. It is not possible to capture the essence of this formidable potential in a simple listing of requirements for training programs and trainers. Nevertheless, because numerous personal sessions in this method must take place for all who become Fellows, and therefore all who become Trainers, we know that the ineffable will probably have been touched by everyone working in this method. We expect there will be breakthroughs and new discoveries in the future. Helen Bonny's desire from the beginning was to create a way in which others could have the kind of peak experiences that she herself had when playing the violin. We know now that this is possible for virtually everyone willing to enter the session space in a receptive state. What we do not know is what the limits of such experiences might be.

## References

Association for Music and Imagery (AMI) (1988). A new professional organization. *AMI Newsletter,* Winter.

Association for Music and Imagery (AMI) (1988). AMI Annual Conference: June 9–11, Lyons, Colorado. *AMI Newsletter,* Fall.

Association for Music and Imagery (AMI) (1989). *Requirements for AMI-Endorsed GIM Training Programs.* Blaine, WA: Author.

Association for Music and Imagery (AMI) (1990). *Minutes of the Fourth Annual AMI Meeting, June 15-19, 1990.* Blaine, WA: Author.

Association for Music and Imagery (AMI) (1994). *Code of Ethics and Standards of Practice.* Blaine, WA: Author.

Association for Music and Imagery (AMI) (1998). *AMI Training Directory.* Blaine, WA: Author.

Association for Music and Imagery (AMI) (1999). *Standards and Procedures for Endorsement of GIM Training Programs.* Blaine, WA: Author.

Bonny, H. L. (1978). *Facilitating GIM Sessions: GIM Monograph #1.* (Revised 1999).Salina, KS: ICM Publications.

Bonny, H. L. (1978). *The Role of Taped Music Programs in the GIM Process: GIM Monograph #2.* (Revised 1998) Salina, KS: ICM Publications.

Bonny, H. L. (1980). *GIM Therapy: Past, Present and Future Implications: GIM Monograph # 3.* Baltimore, MD: ICM Publications.

Bonny, H. L. (1994). Twenty-one years later: A GIM update. *Music Therapy Perspectives,* 12, 70–74.

Bonny, H. L. (1996). Celebrating the tenth anniversary of the Association for Music and Imagery: Highlights and perspectives. *AMI Newsletter.* Fall, Vol. 10, No. 2, 6–7.

Bonny, Helen L. and Savary. L. M. (1990). *Music and Your Mind: Listening with a New Consciousness.* New York: Harper and Row; 2nd Edition. Barrytown, New York: Station Hill Press.

Bruscia, K. (1995). The many dimensions of transference. *Journal of the Association for Music and Imagery,* 3, 3–16.

Bruscia, K. (1995). Manifestations of transference in Guided Imagery and Music. *Journal of the Association for Music and Imagery,* 4, 17–35.

Burns, D. (1998). A brief history of the Bonny Method of GIM. *AMI Newsletter,* Spring, 11 (2), 7.

Clark, M. & Keiser, L. (1989). *Teaching Guided Imagery and Music: An Experiential-Didactic Approach*. Olney, MD: Archedigm Publications.

Institute for Consciousness and Music (ICM) (1976). On the religious imagination. *ICM Newsletter*, 3(3) Spring.

Institute for Consciousness and Music (ICM) (1980). *ICM Newsletter*, 6(2) Spring.

Institute for Consciousness and Music (ICM) Fliers and Announcements:

"Workshop in Guided Imagery and Music: July 14–19, 1975"

"Intensive Training for Mental Health Professionals in Guided Imagery and Music, July/Aug., 1975"

"ICM Training Seminars Presents an Array of Summer Specials, June 1976"

"GIM Summer Training Seminar Is Scheduled to Begin July 5, 1976"

"ICM Presents a Six-Week Training Seminar, June 1977"

"Fall Training in Guided Imagery and Music, Oct. 1978"

"ICM Focuses on Personal Development, Winter 1978"

"Guided Imagery and Music: An Advanced Workshop for Professionals, December 1978"

"Helen Bonny Western Workshops, June 1979"

"GIM Workshop and GIM Training, March 1981"

"Guided Imagery and Music Training, June 1981"

Mardis, L. K. [2000]. Supervision in GIM Training Programs. Unpublished paper.

*Chapter Twenty-Seven*

# SUPERVISION STRATEGIES FOR THE BONNY METHOD OF GUIDED IMAGERY AND MUSIC (BMGIM)

## Darlene Brooks

Supervision is generally regarded as a central component of BMGIM training, yet very little can be found on the subject in the BMGIM literature. In fact, to write this chapter, it was necessary to conduct a survey aimed at gaining insight into the nature of supervisory practices in BMGIM. Toward this end, the author interviewed trainers endorsed by the Association for Music and Imagery (AMI) about their supervisory concepts and practices.

Trainers were selected for these interviews because they are the most knowledgeable about supervision requirements in the training process itself, and because they are also supervisors themselves. Twenty-four trainers were contacted about participating, however, only twelve were available at the time the interviews were scheduled. They were: Jim Borling, Kenneth Bruscia, Marilyn Clark, Frances Goldberg, Denise Grocke, Roseann Kasayka, Kirstie Lewis, Linda Keiser Mardis, Cecilia Schulberg, Ruth Skaggs, Lisa Summer, and Lisabeth Toomey. In addition, written materials were obtained from Madelaine Ventre.

Interviews were conducted on the telephone, and, with the permission of each trainer, the interviews were simultaneously transcribed during the conversation. The interview proceeded informally, relying primarily on open-ended questions, and allowing a natural sequencing of topics. The principal questions were:

- What is your focus during supervision?
- What do you do during supervision?
- Are there specific techniques you use?
- Do you conduct supervisions from audio or video recordings?

- Do you conduct supervision in groups?
- Do you do "consultation" as well as supervisions? How do you distinguish the two?
- Do you approach supervision differently for beginners, advanced trainees, and professionals?
- What problems do you encounter in supervisions
- What makes a good supervisor?
- What makes a good supervisee?
- What makes a good supervision?

On completion of the interview, the transcripts were reviewed and divided into segments according to the questions cited above. Once the interview data were categorized in this way, individual comments made by each trainer were then compared.

In many instances, the data showed that there was general agreement among the trainers. At the same time, on certain topics, each trainer had his or her own unique ideas and emphases. It should also be noted that given the informal and open nature of the interviews, every topic was not discussed by every trainer. Thus, a topic brought about by a trainer in a later interview may not have been specifically pursued by the author in previous interviews.

In the discussion below, all statements about supervision are drawn from the interview data. When no citation is given regarding which trainer(s) made the statement, it can be assumed that there was general agreement or consensus among most, if not all of the trainers on the issue under discussion; when a specific citation is made, it means that only the trainer(s) cited addressed the issue under discussion, either because it was unique to their approach, or because, for any variety of reasons, the topic arose in their interview.

What follows then is a synthesis of the interview data under each of the main topics addressed by trainers in their discussions with the author.

## LEVELS OF SUPERVISION

Three levels of supervision are used in BMGIM: beginning, intermediate, and advanced. At each level, the supervisor has different expectations of the supervisee, and focuses the supervision on different aspects of the guiding process.

## Beginning Level

At the beginning level, the supervisor's primary expectation of the supervisee is he or she has the basic knowledge and experience commensurate with his or her level of training (Keiser Mardis). In addition, the supervisor expects the supervisee to have the maturity and professionalism needed to connect the supervisor's feedback to his/her training, while also remaining open to new and sometimes different ideas (Clark, Skaggs). The focus during the beginning level of supervision is on the basic mechanics of guiding—the ability of the supervisee to implement each segment of the session with basic competence.

## Intermediate Level

At the intermediate level, the supervisee is expected to have had more experience in guiding, and thus be prepared for leading the traveler through more in-depth work. The supervisor expects the supervisee to be able to help the traveler define the "intention" of the session, as developed during the preliminary conversation (Borling). Supervisors then look for the supervisee's ability to relate to, and react appropriately to, the psychological content that evolves as a result of the "intention." Related to this is how the supervisee chooses the music program, and his/her knowledge of the program in relation to the traveler's needs.

At this level, the supervisor is additionally concerned with the supervisee's ability to work with the traveler's resistance effectively so that the traveler has the best or most worthwhile experience possible. Of equal importance is that the supervisee can demonstrate some skill in using a variety of interventions effectively (Clark).

## Advanced Level

At the advanced level, the supervisee is expected to have considerable experience in guiding; an understanding of the relationship between the pre-session dialogue and the music imaging; considerable knowledge of several music programs; and facility in using a variety of interventions (Kasayka).

The focus for advanced supervision is on the supervisee's understanding of the traveler's process, and how he/she is addressing that process within the session. Specifically supervisors are interested in the supervisee's ability to take his/her understanding of the process and weave it into the induction, music choice, and guiding approach, and then pull the main issues together in the post session integration (Clark, Goldberg,Grocke).

An additional focus at this level is the supervisee's understanding of the traveler's images and his/her ability to relate that imagery to the traveler's process (Clark, Goldberg). This is also the level of supervision where supervisors assist supervisees in understanding more about countertransference issues and how they affect the supervisee's responses to the traveler.

## TYPES OF SUPERVISION

In addition to the above levels, there are several types of supervision in BMGIM, including: on-site live observation, video-observation supervision, consultation, transcript supervision, and group supervision.

### On-Site Live Observation

The trainers defined a live observation as a type of supervision where the supervisor sits in the same room and watches the supervisee guide an entire BMGIM session. The purpose of the observation is to actually see how the supervisee implements each segment of a session, and interacts with the traveler in the process.

The on-site observation usually involve three steps: a preparatory meeting in which the supervisor helps the supervisee plan the session with the traveler, the observation of the entire session itself, and a supervisor conference wherein the supervisor can provide support and feedback to the supervisee about the session.

PREPARATION FOR SUPERVISION. The supervisor does several things to ensure that the observation is helpful to the supervisee. Some supervisors meet with the supervisee prior to the observation to establish rapport. During this meeting, they discuss the supervisor's role during the observation. The purpose of this discussion is to help the supervisee see the supervision process as one that enhances his/her growth. After the meeting, supervisors position themselves in the room so they are able to observe and hear the dyad, yet not be a part of it, while at the same time providing a supportive presence if the need arises (Goldberg, Skaggs).

OBSERVATION. After preparing the supervisee for the supervision, and taking a position in the room, the supervisor begins the observation itself. The supervisor may use a variety of techniques for taking notes during an observation. Some supervisors write everything the traveler and supervisee say, as if they were guiding the session, and use an asterisk or star for points they want to revisit during the discussion after the traveler leaves. Others divide their paper into three parts, one for writing the client responses, one for what the supervisee is saying and the other for their comments (Goldberg, Kasayka, Keiser-Mardis, Skaggs). Because many things happen during a session, note taking provides an excellent reference for post-session discussion with the supervisee. After the supervisor has established rapport and completed his/her preparation, the observation begins.

The supervisor's focus during an observation can be divided into two parts: how the supervisee prepares for the session before the traveler arrives, and how the supervisee manages each stage of the session with the traveler. Before the traveler arrives, supervisors observe how the supervisee sets up the room, and how he/she manages the materials needed for the session. There should be a comfortable bed or mattress with blankets, pillows and tissues available should the need arise. The CD/tape recorder, additional music, and transcript papers should be close enough for adequate volume and reach without causing distraction (Clark, Keiser-Mardis). Also of importance is the physical position and proximity of the supervisee in relation to the traveler. The supervisee is expected to be close enough to the traveler to provide safety, yet physically distant enough for both to be comfortable. At the same time, the supervisee's seating level should be the same as that of the traveler. Thus, if the traveler is on the floor, the supervisee should be on the floor as well (Bruscia, Clark).

Once the spatial and logistical arrangements have been observed, and the session actually begins, the supervisor's focus moves to what the supervisee does during each segment of the session. During the preliminary conversation, the supervisor observes the supervisee's level and quality of presence (Borling, Kasayka). Presence may include the supervisee's ability to establish rapport with the traveler, the quality of the supervisee's voice in eliciting information from the traveler, and the amount of attention given to the traveler by the supervisee (Lewis). Supervisors look at the way the supervisee uses his/her voice in putting the traveler at ease, and how the voice is used to encourage the traveler to self-disclose. Once the traveler has begun talking, supervisors look at the amount of attention the supervisee pays to the traveler. That is, does the supervisee listen to what is being said, or is the supervisee anticipating his/her next question, and missing key information given by the traveler? Along these same lines, does the supervisee support the traveler in whatever he or she is saying, and seek clarification in such a way that it does not sound like interrogation? (Borling, Clark)

When the preliminary conversation ends, and the supervisee moves into the relaxation and induction, supervisors focus on the supervisee's presence, voice quality, and pacing. The amount of awareness the supervisee has of the traveler's level of relaxation and the supervisee's ability to adjust the pace of relaxation instruction is of central importance. The voice of the supervisee should easily help the traveler relax and enter the altered state of consciousness. Equally significant is the induction given to the traveler once he/she is relaxed. The induction has to be well-paced and appropriate to the traveler's needs, so that the traveler can enter an altered state.

Following the relaxation/induction, the music-listening section of the session becomes the focus. Here the supervisee's presence, ability to listen, pacing, type of intervention used, and awareness of the music are observed carefully. The supervisee's voice should be encouraging and supportive with interventions that allow the traveler to fully experience the emerging imagery. Supervisors also expect the supervisee to be familiar with what happens in the music so the intervention matches what is happening musically (Clark, Lewis, Toomey).

At the end of the music listening, as the post-session integration period begins, the supervisor's observations focus on the supervisee's ability to return the traveler to waking consciousness while also being sensitive to the vulnerability of the traveler at this time. The supervisee's verbal interactions with the traveler during this period should encourage response to and exploration of the imagery material and issues raised, while still allowing the traveler sufficient time to reflect on his/her experience. Of equal importance is the way the supervisee closes the session. Supervisors look for the ways the supervisee brings some kind of ending or resolution to the session that will give the traveler some support and encouragement, and invite continued work in the BMGIM process.

SUPERVISORY CONFERENCE. After the session has ended, and the traveler has departed, the supervisor and supervisee have a conference to discuss what both parties have observed. Here supervisors spend a considerable amount of time going through each stage of the session with the supervisee. Some supervisors begin the discussion in much the same way the observation was conducted—observations prior to, during and post session, going through each section of the session and discussing what went on at each stage (Bruscia, Keiser Mardis, Schulberg, Summer). Other supervisors let the supervisee chose the beginning topic of the discussion (Goldberg, Grocke, Kasayka, Schulberg, Skaggs, Summer, Toomey).

Trainers agree that supervisory discussions should always begin positively. A preferred method for initiating this positive discussion is to ask the supervisee to report on those aspects of the session that went well. When supervisors corroborate, the rapport established between supervisor and supervisee is further enhanced, and tensions regarding those aspects of the session that did not go as well are eased.

When supervisors discuss the less positive aspects of the supervisee's work, several approaches are employed. In one approach, the supervisee is asked to step back and become the observer of what had just occurred (Skaggs). This helps the supervisee more objectively see what the supervisor saw, and better understand the feedback given. Another approach is to ask leading questions of the supervisee (Kasayka). This is a nonjudgmental way of helping the supervisee look at the entire supervisory process as a helping one, rather than a critique. In either case, the amount of discussion given is dependent on the developmental level of the supervisee, and the purpose of the conference is to both educate and empower the supervisee.

## Video Observation Supervision

This form of supervision is very helpful for those supervisees who live in regions where there is no BMGIM supervisor, or when the supervisee requests additional guidance and a live observation is not possible. The major difference between the live on-site observation and the video-observation supervision is the physical presence of the supervisor during the session, and the timing of the feedback on the sessions. Another difference is that video-observation supervision conferences are generally conducted over the telephone.

A uniqueness of the video supervision is that it allows the supervisor several opportunities to re-review the tape prior to the supervision discussion. One supervisor also has the supervisee review the tape prior to it being sent to her (Goldberg). This provides an added dimension to the supervisory conference, both for the supervisee and the supervisor.

Procedurally, the supervisee who asks for video-observation supervision contacts the supervisor to arrange both approval for the supervision, and a timeframe for its completion. In most video-observation supervisions, the supervisee chooses a traveler with whom he/she has worked with in prior BMGIM sessions, and sends a full transcript and a summary of prior sessions along with the tape to the supervisor.

When the telephone conference occurs, the video observation follows the same format as the live observation. The emphasis is on the positive aspects of the session, with the supervisor offering guidance and suggestions on how the supervisee should proceed with further work.

## Consultation

Consultation is a form of supervision centered on the case material of a specific traveler. Consultation questions may be about the music, the client's imagery, theory questions, or questions about the direction of the series. Consultations may be carried out either with an individual supervisee or in small groups.

The purpose of the consultation is to provide guidance on how the supervisee may work more effectively with a traveler. In this vein, the supervisor serves as a resource to the supervisee (Borling, Toomey). It is expected that when a supervisee asks for a consultation, that that person has an understanding of the basics of guiding and is ready to move toward more in-depth issues related to the psychotherapeutic process of the traveler (Goldberg).

During a consultation, the supervisor has usually not seen the client, is working outside the therapy setting and is responding to what is being reported by the supervisee (Grocke, Summer). To more adequately assist the supervisee, some supervisors have them submit summaries of the traveler's previous sessions, while other supervisors insist on complete transcripts of the sessions.

Focus for a consultation is based on whatever is needed to help the supervisee both understand and work with the traveler's process, whether that be more technique-related or process-related. For example, when relevant to the traveler's work, and the supervisee's needs, the focus may be on psychodynamic issues such as transference and countertransference (Bruscia).

Supervisory techniques used in consultation are similar to those used in discussion of a live observation and video supervision. The supervisor encourages the supervisee to explore what the client has presented with the supervisee suggesting what might work more effectively.

## Transcript Supervision

The transcript plays several important roles in BMGIM. For the client, the transcript is an important reference for review after a session, and for an overall review of the work done in BMGIM. For the supervisee, the transcript provides a way to track the evolving imagery in a client's process, and can be used as a review prior to beginning subsequent sessions. For the supervisor, the transcript provides an ongoing record of the work done by the supervisee during sessions, and is an excellent supervision tool. As a supervision tool, transcript supervision is defined as "a method of analyzing the sessions guided by a supervisee with different clients" (Bruscia). It can be conducted in person or over the telephone.

The purpose of the transcript supervision is twofold. For the beginning supervisee, "the purpose is to identify patterns in the supervisee's guiding style that may need modification or improvement" (Bruscia). The transcript provides a concise way of looking at redundancies and/or weaknesses in guiding. For the advanced supervisees, the purpose may be to identify common countertransference issues across clients" (Bruscia).

In transcript supervision, supervisees are required to submit several documents. The first is a brief description of each client. The second is a concise summary of the prelude and postlude discussions. The third is a description of the induction and music programs used, and lastly, a concise, word-for-word transcription of the music-imaging portion of the session. This must include everything the client reported and everything the supervisee said and did while guiding the sessions.

Techniques used in transcript supervision follow the same pattern as techniques used in on-site, video, and consultation supervisions.

## Group Supervision

Group supervision can broadly be defined as a discussion forum that provides opportunities for supervisees to explore issues related to clients, music, guiding concerns, and other matters that are of concern to supervisees. In some cases, group supervisions are provided as training seminars (Goldberg, Keiser Mardis, Lewis, Toomey); in others, group supervision is a part of the training program, but separate from the seminar. Examples of the varied types of group supervision follow.

Grocke conducts group supervision as a part of her graduate training program that extends over a two-year period. In her program, supervisees present their cases to peers and different perspectives for viewing the case are shared with the supervisee. Borling conducts supervision weekends. These weekends provide opportunities for creative problem solving among supervisees with the supervisor serving as primary facilitator. For Ventre, group supervision is "supportive and constructive, and provides for different perspectives and therapeutic styles." Her group supervision includes cases, therapeutic techniques, personal issues, philosophical issues, ethical issues, professional issues, workshops, and referrals.

"Theme-oriented" group supervision is provided by Summer. In this approach, supervisees working in small groups present their cases. Summer then discerns commonalities across cases, and uses a theme-oriented approach to help the supervisees understand what might be happening in their traveler's process.

Another approach designed by Bruscia is called "psychodynamic group supervision." During the supervision session, the group engages in various projective activities aimed at uncovering unconscious feelings and conflicts that the supervisee may be experiencing in working with a traveler. These activities may include creating mandalas or music improvisations that portray the traveler, the supervisee and their relationship, and the "re-imaging" technique developed by Bruscia. Traveling to the same music, the group enters into an image that one of the supervisee's travelers created during a previous session. After exploring the image for a few minutes, the group returns to waking consciousness, and begins to compare the various ways that the image unfolded in their own imagination, thus revealing the multifaceted possibilities for how the fundamental image could have been guided.

What is clear is that whether group work is done within a training program or as something separate from the training programs, supervisors are interested in the positive growth and development of the supervisee and use similar feedback techniques found in on-site live observation, video observation, transcript supervision, and consultation.

## PROBLEMS IN SUPERVISION

When asked what kinds of problems the trainers have encountered with regard to supervision, several topics emerged. The main ones shared by the trainers were: the level of preparedness of the supervisee; differences in theoretical orientation between trainer; supervisor and supervisee; whether the supervisee used traditional or new music programs, and whose needs were met during the supervision.

### Supervisee Preparedness

A problem that supervisors sometimes encounter is when the supervisee does not have sufficient knowledge of the fundamentals of BMGIM to guide a session, and therefore benefit from supervision. A closely related problem is when the supervisee has not done enough practice sessions (Clark) and lacks sufficient guiding experience. Lack of basic knowledge and guiding experience can have negative effects on the supervisory process. Supervisors, in these cases, often find themselves instructing the supervisee more than offering feedback on guiding a session.

Another problem encountered by supervisors is when the supervisee is unable to deal with the feedback offered. When the student is not ready to hear, no matter how the supervisor presents material, or when the supervisee sees all feedback as a criticism of their personal or clinical skills (Bruscia, Toomey), it is very difficult to offer effective supervision.

The supervisee's failure to fully engage in the experience that is unfolding is another problem. The supervisee does not understand that the therapy is occurring as the session progresses (Borling, Keiser Mardis). This lack of understanding is two-fold: either the supervisee has little or no knowledge of psychotherapy, or the supervisee is fearful of the content of the traveler's work. This inability or fear of helping the client delve deeper into unfolding issues, is evident when the supervisee him/herself has not had enough personal work. The supervisee "can only take the traveler as far as he/she has gone himself" (Borling). When limited personal work and fear are present, the supervisee resorts to goal-oriented behaviors in their work with clients, which compromises the client and the integrity of the BMGIM process.

Along these same lines, the emotional issues of the supervisee impact supervision, and can cause problems. When emotional issues are present, supervisors are challenged to find the best way to treat the material, so that the essence of the session is covered, while maintaining awareness and sensitivity to the supervisee's issues (Clark, Summer).

## Theoretical Orientation

One of the first problem areas noted in supervision occurs when the supervisor does not know what the supervisee's training has been (Clark, Kasayka). Not knowing the theoretical framework poses a problem in terms of language as well as focus. When the supervisee does not understand the language used by the supervisor, rapport is affected and issues of fear and dominance emerge (Borling, Keiser-Mardis). Supervisors are then challenged to impart knowledge with caution because of their concern that they are teaching something the supervisee has not had in training.

Another problem is differences in what supervisors are looking for when observing the trainee. This leads to uncertainty surrounding the goals of supervision (Lewis). Some supervisors stress the psychological process while others stay at the skill level, yet both are needed. When supervision remains at the "nitty-gritty" procedural level without consideration of the larger issues, "the feedback of the supervisor can become an endless evaluation of every detail of the session, leading to a long list of largely forgettable do's and don'ts" (Bruscia).

## Traditional Versus New Music Programs

A problem can occur in teaching supervisees how to choose music programs when traditional programs do not fit the needs of the client. When BMGIM supervisors use programs other than the traditional programs that the trainee has been taught in his/her training program, there is a challenge in how to assist supervisees in selecting music in a way that does not compromise the training program, the supervisor, or the supervisee (Summer).

## Supervisor Versus Supervisee Needs

Possibly one of the most poignant points made by trainers was the need for supervisors to remain aware of client/supervisee needs over their own personal or professional needs (Bruscia, Goldberg). Supervisors must be sensitive to the unfolding scene, so that their own needs as supervisors—to intervene, to be helpful, or to be instructive—do not compromise the learning of the supervisee or the work of the traveler. It is also important that the supervisor's need for validation does not interfere with the work at hand. This occurs when a supervisor uses supervision as a platform to expound his or her personal ideas, techniques, beliefs, theories, or petpeeves. Getting on a soapbox during a supervisory conference is not only counterproductive, it also leads to gross misunderstandings about the nature of supervision. Additionally, supervisees are told things that the supervisor is never told, which further compromises the integrity of supervision and the training process.

## CRITERIA FOR EFFECTIVE SUPERVISION

When asked what defines an effective supervision, the trainers answered from three perspectives: the supervisee, the supervisor, and the traveler.

### For the Supervisee

For supervision to be effective, trainers agreed unanimously that the supervisee must come into the supervision with an open mind, ready for the learning that is about to take place, i.e., a "letting go of their ego, so that he/she is teachable" (Clark). Being teachable means (a) the supervisee views supervision as a growth experience rather than a critique of their clinical or personal skills, and (b) the supervisee willingly enters into relationship with the supervisor.

The trainers also agreed that an effective supervision occurs when the supervisee has gained some insight about his or her work as a guide, that is, when the supervisee is motivated to improve what they need to do better, and has some excitement about the challenge. An effective supervision has taken place when the supervisee gains greater awareness and understanding about what is good versus what is "subject to question" about his/her guiding, and then knows how to interpret "subject to question" as helpful feedback (Borling, Bruscia, Summer, Toomey). Most importantly, a sign of good supervision is when the skill level of the supervisee improves so that better services are offered to the client.

## For the Supervisor

The supervisor knows that he or she has done an effective supervision when, as a result, both supervisee and supervisor have learned something (Goldberg, Skaggs). Clark calls this dual learning "synergy." Keiser Mardis refers to it as "consonance" and Kasayka calls it "potential."

In an effective supervision, the supervisor brings nothing except his or experience into the session, and maintains clarity of focus. This enables the supervisor to address the supervisee's needs as presented at the time of the session, and helps avoid "canned" responses to each supervisee (Summer, Toomey). When maintaining a clarity of focus, supervisors are not only able to help the supervisee look at deeper issues that may be occurring between supervisee and client, i.e., transference and countertransference, but also help the supervisee look at his or her own process and how that might be affecting the work being done (Bruscia, Toomey).

## For the Traveler

An effective supervision has occurred when the supervision is client centered, and when the traveler has been able to deepen and go into the experience more as a result of the work done by the supervisee (Clark, Toomey).

# QUALIFICATIONS OF THE
# BMGIM SUPERVISOR

The effective supervisor is first and foremost a person who has a genuine interest in the development of the supervisee, has experience working with students, and is aware of his or her own theoretical views and motivations (Lewis). That person is willing to spend the time needed for supervision to be beneficial, and maintains awareness of dual roles, personal biases, and transference and/or countertransference issues that may arise in supervision. The supervisor is able to hear and see what the supervisee is presenting and works to empower the supervisee without prejudice. The effective supervisor approaches supervision with sensitivity, honesty, and frankness and is always ethical, while maintaining supportive rapport with the supervisee (Bruscia, Goldberg, Lewis, Summer).

The BMGIM supervisor has had a period of time where they can separate from being a trainee while at the same time, remembering what it was like to be a trainee (Grocke, Kasayka). All supervisors agree that the effective supervisor has fairly extensive experience working as a BMGIM practitioner with a variety of clients, knows the method, and has an excellent grasp on the issues that occur in BMGIM.

The supervisor is an informed person who is mature, flexible, and adaptable, with an eye for detail yet able to grasp the essence of the session. "The good supervisor has perspective, can step back and watch the figure/ground in a relationship, yet is not a part of it" (Clark). This implies a depth of understanding and experience that enables the supervisor to fully comprehend what is evolving, intervening at the right level and looking for potential in the supervisee. At the same time, the supervisor maintains sensitivity to the developmental level of the supervisee (Clark, Kasayka, Keiser-Mardis, Schulberg, Toomey). The supervisor is well versed in a variety of models, psychological techniques, and understands the psychodynamic, transpersonal, archetypal and mythological realms encountered in BMGIM (Borling). Additionally, the supervisor has had some training or mentorship in ways to increase effectiveness (Grocke, Lewis, Skaggs).

## SUMMARY

This chapter is the first survey of existing supervision practices in BMGIM. As evidenced by the material presented, supervision is of vital importance in the training of BMGIM clinicians. There are three levels of supervision provided for the student in BMGIM, where the focus is on the development of the supervisee. Within those levels of supervision, there are specific types of supervision offered to make the supervision effective. Whatever method used, supervisors agree that the aim is to develop good BMGIM practitioners who offer maximum services to the client.

Supervisors approach feedback from a positive perspective, enabling the student to hear and accept necessary comments on areas that still need work. The ultimate goal of supervision is to optimize the learning experience of the supervisee and to ensure that the traveler has a supportive and caring environment where he or she can safely experience BMGIM and its benefit.

*Chapter Twenty-Eight*

# INTERNATIONAL ADVANCES IN GUIDED IMAGERY AND MUSIC (GIM)

## Edited by Denise E. Grocke

While developing the method of Guided Imagery and Music, Helen Bonny made several overseas tours. The first was in 1974, when she visited Germany and met with Hans Carl Leuner, the founder of Guided Affective Imagery. During the second trip in 1977, she conducted workshops (with her son Eric) in several countries. These included Holland (for the Initiated Projective Analysis group); Dusseldorf, Germany; England (a three-day introductory workshop where Mary Priestley, one of the founders of British music therapy attended the evening lecture); Norway (where she met Even Ruud) and in Iceland. In 1986 Helen conducted further workshops in England, attended by Jill Carlisle, a key figure in the development of GIM in England.

The international development of GIM contributes an interesting aspect to the history of GIM and its current standing in various parts of the world. In this chapter the developments will be traced by documenting those GIM trainers who took GIM training to different parts of the world, and the pioneers of each country who nurtured and developed the BMGIM and enabled the method to find root.

Throughout this chapter key pioneers have written about their country's development. What seems to be a common phenomenon across all countries is that the initial seeds of GIM growth were not taken up immediately. Some years passed before pioneers undertook training themselves, or invited others to introduce training in the respective country. Subsequently each country developed its own training program.

This chapter documents the development of AMI-approved training programs and GIM organizations established in the following countries (in alphabetical order): Australia, Canada, Denmark, the European GIM Community, Germany, Mexico, New Zealand, Sweden, and the United Kingdom and Ireland.

# AUSTRALIA

## Florence Holligan

GIM in Australia began when Alison Short (an Australian music therapist) had the opportunity to undertake GIM training at New York University in the 1980s. In 1987, on one of her home visits, she fostered interest in GIM and consequently, in 1989, Linda Keiser Mardis, assisted by Alison Short (then a recently qualified AMI Fellow) offered a Level One GIM course in Melbourne. Eighteen music therapists took this course and continued to meet monthly, for support and to maintain interest.

In 1990, Madelaine Ventre, assisted by Alison Short conducted the first Level Two course in Australia, and subsequently an "Independent Study Programme" was devised for advanced level training between Madelaine Ventre at the Creative Therapies Institute in New York and Florence Holligan and Denise Grocke in Melbourne. Jessica Fleming, a GIM therapist in New Zealand, traveled to Melbourne three times a year to offer supervisions and personal sessions, and Ventre conducted further trainings in 1992 and 1993. By early 1993, Holligan and Grocke both gained Fellowship with AMI.

Helen Bonny made four visits to Australia (1992, 1994, 1996, and 1997.) Each of these visits was a highlight in the development of GIM in Australia, offering opportunities for workshops, supervisions, and leisure time with the founder of the method. On one of these visits, the Music and Imagery Association of Australia Incorporated (MIAA) was founded (in January 1994) and Helen Bonny graciously agreed to be its patroness.

Alison Short became a Primary Trainer in 1994, and this enabled GIM training to be offered in Australia with Australian trainers. In 1995, GIM training programs for all three levels were endorsed by AMI, and in 1996 Florence Holligan and Denise Grocke were both approved by AMI as Primary Trainers.

MIAA is active in promoting the Bonny Method of GIM in Australia, and organizes Level One and Level Two training courses in several states of Australia. MIAA also holds regular meetings with invited speakers, and publishes a quarterly Newsletter.

In July 2000, MIAA was accepted into membership of the Psychotherapy and Counseling Federation of Australia (PACFA), an umbrella organization that endorses qualified psychotherapists and counselors. Membership of PACFA paves the way for GIM therapists in Australia to be recognized as psychotherapists by being included on the PACFA National Register.

Advanced level training in GIM (Level Three) is offered as a two year Graduate Diploma in Guided Imagery and Music, through the University of Melbourne (Faculty of Music). It comprises eight intense seminars held four times each year. There are currently thirteen qualified GIM practitioners in Australia, and two advanced students.

Australian GIM therapists have contributed publications in journals and edited books, both national and international, encompassing a range of topics including medical applications, spiritual development, and pivotal moments in GIM. GIM therapists work within private practice, in directing spirituality retreats, and adapting GIM to home-based palliative care.

# CANADA

## Liz Moffitt

GIM had a slow beginning in Canada, even though for a time Helen Bonny was teaching GIM at the Institute for Consciousness and Music (ICM) just over the border in Port Townsend, Washington, USA. A few Canadians went for Level One training there, however they did not continue with the work. Despite that, they sowed the early seeds that were to later grow.

In 1980 Carolyn Sonnen presented on GIM at the Canadian Association for Music Therapy (CAMT) national conference in Regina, Saskatchewan, and in 1984 Helen Bonny was a keynote speaker at the CAMT conference in Vancouver. Another four years passed. The CAMT conference was again in Vancouver, and Ken Bruscia gave a very moving presentation with an enthusiastic response that was to lead to the beginning of GIM training in Canada.

The year 1988 was a period of transition. AMI, the professional association, was in its infancy. The Institute for Music and Imagery (IMI), the outgrowth of ICM as the training institute, had just closed and many primary trainers were forming their own training institutes. By 1989 the creative energy in the GIM community caused by the changes, spilled over the border into Canada. In May, two Level One courses were offered within two weeks of each other. The first was held in Ottawa after the annual CAMT conference at which Helen Bonny was again a keynote speaker. Helen Bonny, along with Lisa Summer and Carol Bush, taught ten participants. On the west coast at Capilano College in North Vancouver, Linda Keiser conducted a Level One training for twenty-five participants. This was the beginning of a continuing relationship between Linda Keiser assisted by Kirstie Lewis and Susan Hale, and Capilano College. Since that first pioneer training in May 1989, Linda Keiser has offered training at all three levels. To date this is the only Canadian training center that has conducted all levels of training.

In the early 1990s Madelaine Ventre taught two Level One training courses in Montreal in the east of Canada, and Helen Bonny taught two Level One courses and one Level Two training at Hollyhock Retreat Center on Cortes Island off the coast of British Columbia.

Between 1994 and 1998, Kirstie Lewis, under the auspices of her Northwest Music and Imagery Center, and assisted by Rosalie Lindquist, Liz Moffitt and Kay Thompson, came to Capilano College to offer three additional Level One courses.

At present the current Advanced Level training group of eleven students, taught by Mardis, Lewis, Moffitt, and Thompson, is fortunate enough to have a wide choice of trained facilitators within the region for their personal sessions and supervisions. There are ten Fellows in the Vancouver area. In other parts of the country, with only three Fellows, trainees have had to go to the U.S. for Advanced training.

Canadian Fellows of AMI have been, and continue to be, active in AMI on both the music and education committees. Kay Thompson and Liz Moffitt have served a term on the Circle. Thompson was conference chair for AMI's first international conference in 1996 in Vancouver, and Moffit was conference chair in 2001.

The majority of Canadian Fellows of AMI are using an adapted form of GIM in groups or individually. They work with the elderly, in palliative care units and cancer treatment centers, with church groups, and with emotionally disturbed children. A few have private practices that include working with high functioning adults using GIM. Canadian Fellows have also presented their work at a variety of conferences.

Liz Moffitt became the first Canadian Primary Trainer in 2001, making it possible for Canadian trainers to teach. In the near future it is hoped to offer Level One training as an elective part of the Capilano College music therapy program and this increased exposure to the method will likely expand its use. For everyone in Canada, the GIM work has served to profoundly enrich our lives, flowing out into our ways of being, into our relationships, and into all our various places of work.

# DENMARK

## Torben Moe

Working as a music therapist in psychiatry in Denmark and looking for all interesting events concerning music therapy, the author attended a Music Therapy conference at Lövenströmska Sjukhuset just north of Stockholm, in the mid 1980s. One of the keynote speakers was Fran Goldberg who talked about clinical issues concerning music therapy in psychiatry and GIM. At this time not many music therapists were working in psychiatry, and it was suggested that a Scandinavian supervision group for music therapists be formed. For some years the group met in Sweden and Denmark. The participants were Margareta Wärja, Anci Sandell, Steen Bunne, and Urban Yman from Sweden, Unni Johns from Norway and the author representing Denmark. The group quickly turned into an experimental group, and Fran Goldberg, who was invited as a supervisor introduced GIM. This had such a strong influence that the author traveled to Great Britain to participate in a training group led by Marilyn Clark. Being one man in a group with seven women was an extraordinary privilege, as was the experience of the power of GIM group work. Along with this training, the author assisted Fran Goldberg who was also establishing GIM training in Denmark and Sweden.

In 1993 the "Society of Guided Imagery and Music in Denmark" was formed, and the purpose was to spread information about GIM activities. Today the organization is lead by the present author, Lars Ole Bonde, Ellen Thomasen, Kirsten Toksvig, and Ilse Kjaer. Every year introductory workshops and other GIM related thematic workshops are organized, led by international guest speakers and ourselves.

In 1995 the first Level One training was held at the department of music, University of Oslo, Norway. Lisa Summer was the Primary Trainer, assisted by the author. Today GIM Level One training is an obligatory part of the music therapy training at the University of Aalborg, Denmark, and at the University of Oslo, Norway. Research in GIM is happening in Denmark, and the author has completed Ph.D, research on GIM in a modified version for psychiatric patients.

Lars Ole Bonde has been editor of *Accord*, the Newsletter of the European Community of the Bonny Method of Guided Imagery and Music, but this responsibility has been handed over to the north German GIM organization, host of the next European GIM conference in September 2002. Bonde is now building up a GIM database including writings, the GIM music programs, and music program analyses.

In January 2002 the author in cooperation with teachers from the "Society of GIM in Denmark" set up the first Level Three program in Denmark/Norway with twelve advanced trainees, comprising ten music therapists, one psychologist, and one musicologist.

## THE EUROPEAN GIM COMMUNITY

### Torben Moe

In 1996 the first European GIM Conference of GIM was held in Scotland at Findhorn with Helen Bonny as keynote speaker. There were about 30–40 people sharing the GIM experiences and enjoying the beautiful place and surroundings.

The 2nd European Conference in Skælskør, Denmark, was held in 1997. About the same amount of people gathered together and discussed GIM in Europe, research in GIM, case studies, and our personal experiences with GIM. A "working group" was organized to keep the contact through newsletters, and discussions about future events. At the conference it was decided that "GIM Europe" should be a free, unstructured organization, based on supporting interest in GIM in Europe.

The 3rd European conference was held in 1998 in Sweden, at a beautiful place in the Stockholm area, and the 4th conference was held in 2000 on the isle of Elba, Italy, organized by Gabriella Perilli, with Kenneth Bruscia and Helen Bonny as keynote speakers.

## GERMANY

### Carola Maack

In Germany, GIM was introduced from three independent directions. The first person to introduce GIM to Germany was Stephanie Merritt in 1990. She was invited by the Society for Suggestopedia in Germany, and gave weekend workshops for school teachers based on GIM. Stephanie Merritt directed her first Level One in 1994 in Austria together with Cecilia Schulberg, with a group of German and Austrian students. Her first Level Three training in this country started in 1996, and in addition to this work, Stephanie Merritt started a GIM group in Munich, for people who are the second-generation victims of the Nazi era.

Parallel to Stephanie Merritt's work in this country, Hildegard Kiel, a German music therapist who had studied music therapy in the United States, started organizing GIM introductory workshops and subsequently a Level One training program with Frances Goldberg. The first Advanced Training taught by Frances Goldberg started in 1995. It was a European group with students from Denmark, Sweden, Bulgaria and Germany. The training modules took place in the student's respective countries. Students in this group were mainly creative arts therapists, psychotherapists, and medical doctors.

In 1995, the German Association for Music Therapy asked Carola Maack to offer GIM introductory workshops as part of the continuing education program. She had just finished her M.A. in music therapy in the United States and was a Level Three student at the Mid-Atlantic GIM Training Institute. Since 1995, introductory workshops have taken place twice a year. In 1998, the first GIM training done in the German language (both Stephanie Merritt and Frances Goldberg do their trainings in English) took place near Hamburg. The training was offered by the Mid-Atlantic GIM Training Institute with Jim Borling as Primary Trainer and Carola Maack as assistant trainer and translator. Since then, two Level One and two Level Two courses have been offered. In December 2000, the first Level Three group started, with students who are mainly music therapists and psychotherapists.

As there are no German Primary Trainers yet, there has been no specifically German training programs developed till now. However, as many of the German Level Three students and Fellows work in the field of creative arts therapies, psychotherapy, and/or the medical field, GIM is used in general psychotherapy (both private practice and institutional settings), trauma therapy, women's and men's groups, and with cancer patients. Some of us have also introduced GIM in the form of lectures or workshops in music therapy and psychology programs at German universities.

# MEXICO

## Ginger Clarkson

GIM officially arrived in Mexico in 1995. Carol Bush and Jim Borling, Primary Trainers from the Mid-Atlantic Training Institute in Virginia Beach, and myself directed the initial Mexican GIM Level One training at La Universidad de las Americas (UDLA) in Puebla, Mexico. Debbie Addis, a GIM Fellow working in

Mexico City, assisted. Eighteen students and faculty members from UDLA participated, along with four psychotherapists from Mexico City. A portion of the training was conducted in Spanish (presented by Clarkson) and there was simultaneous translation of the material presented by Carol Bush and Jim Borling. The dyads were divided into Spanish- and English-speakers so that, on one side of the room, those who were guiding and traveling in Spanish were supervised by Clarkson, and the English speakers were supervised by Bush and Borling.

This historic GIM training was such a success that Bush and Borling met with Victor Munoz, the director of Mexico City's Instituto Mexicano de Musicoterapia Humanista. A medical doctor, fine musician, and psychotherapist trained in Gestalt and Core Energetic techniques, Munoz readily agreed to co-sponsor with Mid-Atlantic a complete series of GIM training modules to enable Mexican therapists and musicians to become AMI Fellows. The dream of graduating Mexican GIM trainees as Fellows came true in June 1998, when Helen Bonny congratulated Hilde Garcia and Kima Gomez at the AMI annual conference in Chicago.

A fourth generation of GIM training is scheduled to begin in 2002. In addition to AMI Fellow Alicia Picazo, both Munoz and his wife Angelines Ahrens are qualified to give GIM supervisions, lending Clarkson much-needed support. Ahrens serves as an excellent simultaneous translator for trainings. Of the dozen Mexican AMI Fellows most have had prior training in Gestalt, Core Energetic, and/or Music Therapy programs.

# NEW ZEALAND

## Lisabeth Toomey

The first person in New Zealand to be involved in GIM was Peggy Haworth, who attended a six-week training seminar with Helen Bonny in Maryland in 1977. Peggy was the first person outside of the United States to do this training, and on her return to New Zealand, she offered workshops and information to interested people including a group experience in a Maori setting.

In 1983, Peggy offered her resources to Lisabeth Toomey, a music therapy trainee with the New Zealand Society for Music Therapy (NZSMT). Adopting the GIM philosophy, Lisabeth began her GIM training with the Institute for Music and Imagery, in Maryland, in the fall of 1987. When this organization dissolved the following year, she was accepted into the newly created Bonny Foundation, where she completed her advanced training in December 1991.

In 1990 Jessica Fleming (who had given introductory workshops in New Zealand in 1982) returned to New Zealand and with Lisabeth co-founded the Auckland Center for Music and Imagery (ACMI). Here the clinical practice of GIM was offered to individuals and groups. In the same year Fleming was granted Primary Trainer status.

Training was initiated with Helen Bonny, assisted by Fleming and Toomey, leading the first Level One in 1990 and the first Level Two in January 1992. At this training Helen Bonny was also assisted by Rosalie Lindquist. Later in 1992, ACMI began the first Level Three training in New Zealand. Prior to its completion, Fleming withdrew from the role of Primary Trainer and Toomey continued to lead the training with the assistance of Madelaine Ventre and Helen Bonny. Four graduates completed this training. A second advanced training began in 1996 with Lisabeth Toomey assisted by Stella Clement as support trainer, and the other Fellows according to their areas of expertise. This group of trainees also included two Australians.

Out of the challenges experienced by this small group of committed people, the New Zealand Imagery and Music Association (NZIMA) was formed in 1995 as the new training body. This came at a time of burgeoning acceptance of a wide variety of alternative therapeutic interventions in New Zealand. NZIMA continues to offer regular group experiences and support to members and others. Visiting international Fellows are hosted and invited to participate as teachers, supervisors, personal therapists, colleagues, and friends. Helen Bonny has continued to visit New Zealand and has been an ongoing source of inspiration. These visiting GIM professionals enjoy the particular qualities of multicultural New Zealand whose people value their whanau (family), outdoor life-style, and natural environment. GIM practice embraces the practical synergy of these values. A published example is McIvor's case study (1998–1999) with a small group of Maori, the indigenous people.

New Zealand graduates continue to be affiliated with, and to support, the Association for Music and Imagery (AMI), USA, as committee members, conference presenters, and with journal articles and resources. Booth (1998–1999) has developed several new music programs, which are in use and taught in both the United States and New Zealand. Toomey has introduced GIM at university level through both counseling and creative arts courses, and Shaw, a New Zealand Fellow, presented a successful thesis on GIM and Spirituality toward his master's degree in Counseling at the University of Auckland.

GIM practitioners work in private practice often with medical referrals and in health and educational facilities. Links are maintained with other professional bodies through conference presentations, workshops, and journal articles, and by providing keynote speakers for the NZSMT. These have included Helen Bonny, Denise Grocke, and Kenneth Bruscia.

Although GIM has not had the rapid growth envisioned by its New Zealand pioneers, the trickle initiated by Peggy Haworth has become a steady current of interest. Creative modifications for both group and individual work continue to give fresh stimulus. New Zealand practitioners view GIM as a truly integrative modality for all aspects of human need and endeavor, ranging from the harshness often encountered in daily life to the sublime spiritual experience. With the upsurge of creative therapies as we move into this new millennium, the GIM Fellows of New Zealand will continue to develop Bonny's pioneering work in new and exciting ways in the service of their community.

# SWEDEN

## Margareta Wärja

Sweden is a country with the approximate size of California and a population of about eight million people. In the far north an old mythic mountain landscape stretches well above the Arctic Circle, and in the south an agricultural soft lush flatland serves as a gateway to continental Europe. Sweden provides a fertile "musical soil" for the growth and development of Guided Imagery and Music.

During music therapy studies in the early 1980s, Margareta Wärja was introduced to GIM by Frances Smith Goldberg. Some years later when Wärja returned to Sweden, she had the opportunity to develop music therapy at Löwenströmska Psychiatric Clinic outside Stockholm. She initiated a number of symposia on "Music Psychotherapy" and Fran Goldberg was invited twice to give keynote addresses and spoke of expressive music therapy and GIM.

These events created an enormous interest in the field of psychiatry and psychotherapy and became the beginning steps to develop training in GIM. What then took place is a manifestation of the power of synchronicity. Within months there was an educational structure in place and a large group of professionals came to take the first exploratory educational steps in GIM. In 1991 there were enough participants to start the first advanced training. This training was conducted by Fran Goldberg with Margareta Wärja assisting. Three other trainers came to participate in this pioneering event—Helen Bonny, Lisa Summer, and Linda Keiser Mardis. Since then two more training groups have started. These groups have included students from other European countries as well. Currently there is a meaningful discussion among the Fellows in Sweden on how to best structure a Swedish-based training conducted in Swedish.

As the Director of Music Therapy at the Royal College of Music in Stockholm, Ingrid Hammarlund has supported the development of GIM by making introductory seminars and group GIM seminars a required part of the curriculum. All students are also provided with three personal GIM sessions.

Two people who have been particularly instrumental in the initial development of GIM in Sweden are Björn Wrangsjö and Dag Körlin, who have initiated a longitudal study of the treatment effects of GIM therapy (Wrangsjö & Körlin, 1995; Körlin & Wrangsjö, 2000). Seven GIM therapists have participated and so far thirty individuals have been evaluated using the Symptom Check List (SCL 90), Inventory of Interpersonal Problems (IIP) and Sense of Coherence (SOC) scales. This study is an ongoing research project with a population growing in size. Körlin has also developed a specialized five-week day treatment program for anxiety and depressive disorders with a background of trauma where expressive arts therapy and Group GIM prove a vital and effective part of the treatment.

Today GIM has a broad application in Sweden. Therapists work in private practice, in psychiatric institutions, in oncology, in educational settings, and with various somatic and psychosomatic disorders. There is an active Swedish Society of GIM conducting public events as well as continuing education for GIM students and Fellows. In the fall of 1998 the society hosted the European Conference in GIM with Madelaine Ventre as a special guest.

## UNITED KINGDOM AND IRELAND

### Jill Carlisle

A birth, be it of a human or a creative project, needs a touch of magic, alongside the hard work. GIM came to the UK with those qualities and many more. The magic began on hearing Marilyn Clark's injunction to "Let the music take you wherever you want to go" when the author experienced GIM for the first time during a Level One training in Wheaton, Illinois in 1986. At the end of that training, Marilyn Clark and Linda Keiser asked what could be done to bring the GIM training to the UK. It seemed a timely synchronicity. Already there were ideas about bringing training and workshops to Canterbury. When, later that year, Helen Bonny came to Canterbury and gave a GIM workshop to about twenty people, it was the first organized by Jill Carlisle under the sponsorship of her newly created Pegasus Workshops. With Helen Bonny as presenter, it was nothing less than a magical beginning for GIM in this country.

From 1987 until 1990, Marilyn Clark and Linda Keiser, together and separately, gave several workshops to build up interest and student numbers. Jill Carlisle gave presentations to various groups of interested people, offered sessions to friends, and gave a talk on local radio. As a result, three Level One and one Level Two trainings took place. In 1991, Marilyn Clark began the first Fellow's training in this country. Although there were six of us, and we all completed in 1994, two were "imports" from elsewhere. Sara Hart returned to the United States, and Torben Moe to Denmark, leaving Celia Tudor-Evans, Catherine O'Leary, Georgette Zackey, and myself to form the nucleus of GIM Fellows in the UK. A further training, begun at Findhorn, Scotland, in 1996 and led by Marilyn Clark, yielded another Fellow, Sr. Mary Clavin who lives in Ireland. We have also been joined by two others, Carole Killick and Leslie Bunt, who have completed with other trainers. A grand total of seven Fellows now reside in the UK and Ireland.

We have adopted the name MAIA (Music and Imagery Association), and hosted the birthing of the new European Community for the Bonny Method of Guided Imagery and Music at a conference held in 1996 at Findhorn. We felt very honored that this meeting was attended not only by Helen Bonny, Marilyn Clark and Roseann Kasayka, but also by representatives from at least five other European countries. Subsequently, there have been further conferences held at regular intervals. This energy continues to blossom in Europe today.

Carole Killick, who was the first editor of *Accord*, the Newsletter of the European GIM Community, has written articles and given workshops on GIM and practices group and individual GIM within a hospice setting.

The future for the Bonny Method in this country could be very exciting. Through one of our Fellows, Professor Leslie Bunt, possible links with The Music Space Trust based at the University of the West of England in Bristol are being explored. This could provide us with supportive facilities for promoting the work in several areas, including not only teaching of the Bonny Method of Guided Imagery and Music by accredited trainers, but also clinical work, supervision, and research. The first Level One training program was based at The Music Space with Torben Moe as Primary Trainer, assisted by Leslie Bunt. Plans are in place to take the training through to Levels Two and Three.

# CHRONOLOGY OF INTERNATIONAL
# DEVELOPMENTS IN GIM

(Note: This table includes only the first Level One GIM Trainings offered in a country, organizations established, and publications initiated.)

1989    First training (Level One) in Canada: in Ottawa (Bonny, Summer, and Bush), and in North Vancouver (Keiser)
        First training (Level One) in Australia (Keiser and Short)

1990    The Auckland Society of Music and Imagery in New Zealand established (Fleming and Toomey)
        First training (Level One) in New Zealand (Bonny, Fleming, and Toomey)

1991    First training (Level One) in England (Clark and Carlisle)
        First training (Level One) in Sweden (Goldberg and Wärja)

1993    The Society of GIM in Denmark established (Moe)

1994    The Music and Imagery Association of Australia established (Grocke, Holligan, and Short).
        First training (Level One) in Austria (Merritt and Schulberg)

1995    First training (Level One) in Mexico (Bush, Borling, Clarkson, and Addis)
        First Advanced Level training in Europe (Goldberg)
        First training (Level One) in Norway (Summer and Moe)
        New Zealand Imagery and Music Association established (Toomey)

1996    First European GIM conference held at Findhorn, Scotland
        The Music and Imagery Association (UK) established (O'Leary et al)

1997    *Accord,* the Newsletter of the European GIM committee established (Editor: Carole Killick)
        Second European GIM conference held at Skælskor, Denmark
        First training (Level One) in Israel (Goldberg)

1998    First training (Level One) in Bulgaria (Clarkson)
        Third European GIM conference in Stockholm, Sweden

1999    Fourth European GIM conference held on the Isle of Elba, Italy
        (Perilli)

## CONCLUSION

In reviewing the developments of GIM in these countries it is evident that US trainers have played a crucial role in establishing GIM and assisting the pioneers to develop training courses. It is also evident that many countries early in their development created a structure for the organization of GIM activities, and that GIM Fellows carry on the work with commitment and enthusiasm. The future for the Bonny Method of Guided Imagery and Music internationally is assured.

## *References*

Booth, J. M. (1998–1999). The Paradise Program: A new music program for Guided Imagery and Music. *Journal of the Association for Music and Imagery*, 6, 15–35.

Körlin, D., & Wrangsjö, B. (2000). *Treatment Effects of GIM Therapy.* Manuscript submitted for publication.

McIvor, M. (1998–1999). Heroic journeys: Experiences of a Maori group with the Bonny Method. *Journal of the Association for Music and Imagery*, 6, 105-118.

Wrangsjö, B., & Körlin, D. (1995). Guided Imagery and Music (GIM) as a psychotherapeutic method in psychiatry. *Journal of the Association for Music and Imagery*, 4, 79–92.

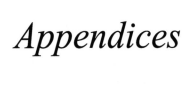

*Appendices*

*Appendix A*

# CODE OF ETHICS
# OF THE
# ASSOCIATION FOR MUSIC & IMAGERY

## (Revised 1992, 1995)

The Association for Music and Imagery (AMI) is an organization that has been created to maintain and uphold the integrity of the Bonny Method of Guided Imagery and Music (GIM) and to nurture and support all those who have trained in this method. Persons who have trained in the use of GIM understand the power that the method has to help individuals actualize their potential as human beings. Further, they understand that any application of the GIM Method has potential to reach the depths of an individual's psyche/personality and thereby warrants ethical considerations. Therefore, this Code of Ethics pertains to all individuals, professionals and laypersons, Members and non-members, who work with individuals to induce an altered state of consciousness and to introduce music as a powerful stimulus for the purpose of evoking internal response.

The Association recognizes that its collective membership represents individuals with diverse professional backgrounds, work experiences and academic qualifications. Regardless of these differences, Members of AMI are expected to adhere to this Code of Ethics in all matters pertaining to GIM and related techniques involving altered states of consciousness and music. Further, AMI strongly recommends that all non-members who use altered states of consciousness and music also consider this ethical code as a guideline for their responsible work in this field.

Any responsible work begins with personal integrity, which forms the basis for professional relationships with clients, peers, students, research subjects, and the public. The categories that follow reflect these relationships.

# PERSONAL INTEGRITY

Members who enter into working relationships with others for the purpose of healing, therapy, instruction, professional development, and research are expected to operate with a clear sense of personal integrity. The following are expectations set forth by AMI for its Members regarding the ethics of personal integrity.

The Members shall:

1) Demonstrate a continuing commitment to personal growth by engaging in therapy as needed for personal or professional reasons.
2) Demonstrate a continuing commitment to professional growth by engaging in continuing education in related fields.
3) Adhere to all official regulations and guidelines set forth by AMI.
4) Accurately represent their competency, education, training, and experience and not exceed the limits of these competencies.
5) Refer a client to another therapist or health care provider if unable to continue adequate services for any reason.
6) Seek referral or endorsement from other professionals involved in the case when accepting a client into private practice from the institutional setting.
7) Perform this work only in the context of a professional relationship and in a setting that ensures safety and protection for both client and Member.
8) Refuse to participate in activities that are illegal, immoral, or inhumane, or that result in discrimination or violate the civil rights of others.
9) Maintain all financial, business, and client records according to necessary legal record keeping requirements.
10) Respect all financial agreements entered into and shall not default payment for services rendered.
11) Be familiar with and adhere to existing copyright laws.
12) Be familiar with, adhere to, and have resources for all local, state, and federal laws pertaining to ethics principles/regulations.

# CLIENTS, STUDENTS, AND
# RESEARCH SUBJECTS

The Member is responsible for delivery of services to many people. The major categories considered here are clients, students, and research subjects. These ethical considerations apply to any direct working relationships engaged in by Members that have to do with GIM and related methods.
The Members shall:

1) Respect the dignity and worth of each individual with whom they work.
2) Not discriminate in professional relationships because of race, creed, color, sex, national origin, age, or sexual orientation.
3) Establish clear and voluntary agreements at onset of work with client, student, or research subject. Such agreements will include and not be limited to a description of the nature and scope of the therapy or study.
4) Keep all forms of professional records confidential and secure.
5) Waive confidentiality only when:
   a. Imminent danger to the person with whom they are working or others is present;
   b. Client, student, or research subject signs a waiver form to allow oral, written or taped publication or presentation of session material.
   c. Consultation or supervision is sought by a Member in order to assist the Member's work and the client, student, or research subject signs a waiver for such purposes.
   d. Subpoenaed by the judicial system.
6) Not make unrealistic promises regarding the GIM process or related methods or outcomes.
7) When doing research, present findings without distortion.
8) Not exploit clients, students, or research subjects physically, financially, or emotionally.
9) Not engage in sexual relationships with clients, students, or research subjects.
10) Be aware of and not exploit the vulnerability and suggestibility of persons in an altered state of consciousness.
11) Avoid dual relationships whenever possible. When a dual relationship cannot be avoided, the Member shall take appropriate precautions (such as obtaining supervision or consultation) to

ensure that professional judgment is not impaired and no exploitation occurs.

12) Make periodic evaluations of the client's progress and determine the need for: a) continued treatment, b) referral to adjunctive or alternative healthcare service or provider, and c) termination of therapeutic services.

## PEER RELATIONSHIPS

As Members of AMI we have a responsibility to relate to other Members and non-member peers in an ethical manner, respecting differences as well as furthering the spirit of professional cooperation. The following considerations are therefore put forth.

The Members shall:

1) Distinguish personal from professional views when acting on behalf of AMI and shall represent the Association only with appropriate authorization.

2) Refrain from the misuse of an official position within AMI.

3) Exercise integrity and confidentiality when carrying out their official duties in AMI.

4) Establish harmonious relations with Members from other professions and professional organizations.

5) Not damage the professional reputation or practice of others.

6) Not give or receive a commission, fee or privilege for making or receiving referrals (fee-splitting).

7) Not actively solicit nor initiate work with clients who are in therapy without expressed consent of client's therapist.

8) When publishing written or taped materials give credit to all who have contributed in proportion to their contribution. Acknowledgment shall be made for unpublished as well as published material that has directly influenced the publication.

# PUBLIC

In an AMI Member's ordinary professional work, contacts with the public will often occur. In order to accurately represent AMI, its Members, and the GIM method in the public arena, the following considerations are therefore put forth.

The Members shall:

1) Make every effort to ensure that public information materials are accurate and complete in reference to professional qualifications, services, programs, and fees.

2) Avoid the following in advertising services: misleading or deceptive advertising, misrepresentation of specialty, guarantees, or false expectations.

3) Keep up-to-date with the business and dealing of the AMI so as to provide correct and current information to the public.

*Appendix B*

# MUSIC FOR THE IMAGINATION: PLAY LIST

## IMAGINATIVE CD

### Imagery-M (39:47)

Cuts:

| | | |
|---|---|---|
| 1) | Ravel: *Introduction & Allegro* | 10:17 |
| 2) | Copland: *Appalachian Springs* | 8:13 |
| 3) | Tschaikovsky: *4th Symphony* (Scherzo) | 5:51 |
| 4) | Mendelssohn: *5th Symphony* (Andante) | 4:54 |
| 5) | Suk: *Serenade in E-flat Major* Op. 6 (Adagio) | 10:23 |

### Inner Odyssey (33:53)

Cuts:

| | | |
|---|---|---|
| 6) | Brahms: *3rd Symphony* (Allegro con brio) | 10:22 |
| 7) | Nielsen: *5th Symphony* (Excerpt of 1st movement) | 9:46 |
| 8) | Beethoven: *Violin Concerto* (Larghetto) | 10:13 |
| 9) | Corelli: *Concerto Grosso #8 in G minor* (Adagio) | 3:33 |

## SUPPORTIVE CD

### Caring (35:29)

Cuts:

| | | |
|---|---|---|
| 1) | Haydn: *Cello Concerto in C* (Adagio) | 8:36 |
| 2) | Puccini: *Madama Butterfly* (Humming Chorus) | 2:46 |
| 3) | Debussy: *String Quartet* (Andantino) | 7:56 |
| 4) | Bach: *Christmas Oratorio* (Shepherd's Song) | 5:55 |

| | | |
|---|---|---:|
| 5) | Dvorak: *Serenade in E Major* (Larghetto) | 6:49 |
| 6) | Warlock: *Capriol Suite* (Pieds en l'air) | 2:21 |

## Mournful (39:32)

Cuts:

| | | |
|---|---|---:|
| 7) | Sibelius: *Swan of Tuonela* | 8:50 |
| 8) | Goreczki: *3rd Symphony* (2nd Movement) | 10:13 |
| 9) | Boccherini: *Cello Concerto B-flat* (Adagio) | 5:53 |
| 10) | Russian Folk Song: *O the Steppes* | 4:09 |
| 11) | Russian Chant: *The Joy of Those Who Mourn* | 3:43 |
| 12) | Shostakovich: *2nd Piano Concerto* (Andante) | 6:37 |

## Solace (38:54)

Supportive Cuts: 1-7-9-10-11-12-5: Haydn, Sibelius, Boccherini, Russian Folk Song, Russian Chant, Shostakovich and Dvorak.

## Consoling (38:26)

Supportive Cuts: 7-3-5-9-12: Sibelius, Debussy, Dvorak, Boccherini, and Shostakovich.

## CREATIVE CD

Cuts:

| | | |
|---|---|---:|
| 1) | Debussy: *Prelude to Afternoon of Faun* | 10:30 |
| 2) | Liadov: *Enchanted Lake* | 7:58 |
| 3) | Holst: *The Planets* (Venus) | 8:07 |
| 4) | Holst: *The Planets* (Neptune) | 7:01 |
| 5) | Grieg: *Cradle Song* | 4:07 |
| 6) | Sibelius: *2nd Symphony* (1st Movement) | 10:07 |
| 7) | Vaughan-Williams: *2nd Symphony* (Lento) | 12:04 |
| 8) | Delius: *La Calinda* | 3:50 |
| 9) | Kallinikov: *2nd Symphony* (Andante) | 7:59 |
| 10) | Bizet: *Carmen* (Intermezzo) | 2:32 |

## Pastorale (30:42)

Creative Cuts: 1-2-3-5: Debussy, Liadov, Holst Venus, Grieg.

## Searching (39:17

Creative Cuts: 2-7-3-4-5: Liadov, Vaughan Williams, Holst Venus, Holst Neptune, Grieg.

## Creativity I (As modified by Bruscia) (36:32)

Creative Cuts: 6-7-8-9-10: Sibelius, Vaughan Williams, Delius, Kallinikov, Bizet.

## EMOTIVE CD

## Emotional Expression I (46:12)

Cuts:
| | | |
|---|---|---|
| 1) | Brahms: *2nd Piano Concerto* (Allegro non Troppo) | 17:19 |
| 2) | Brahms: *German Requiem* (Part I) | 9:13 |
| 3) | Brahms: *German Requiem* (Part V) | 7:07 |
| 4) | Brahms: *4th Symphony* (Andante Moderato) | 12:33 |

## Mostly Bach (End Only)

Cuts:
| | | |
|---|---|---|
| 5) | Brahms: *Violin Concerto* (Adagio) | 8:56 |
| 6) | JS Bach: *Concerto for Two Violins* (Largo) | 6:47 |

## Creativity II- First cut (As modified by Bruscia) (50:07)

Cuts:
| | | |
|---|---|---|
| 7) | D'Indy: *Symphony on French Mountain Air* (1st movement) | 11:40 |

## EXPLORATIVE CD

### Creativity II- Continued (As modified by Bruscia)

Cuts:

| | | |
|---|---|---|
| 1) | Elgar: *2nd Symphony* (Larghetto) | 14:53 |
| 2) | Mendelssohn: *3rd Symphony* (Vivace) | 4:32 |
| 3) | Faure: *Pavane* | 7:44 |
| 4) | Ravel: *Daphnis & Chloe Suite #2* (Play to end) | 11:38 |

### Explorations (As modified by Bruscia) (41:04)

| | | |
|---|---|---|
| 1) | Ravel: *Daphnis & Chloe (Suite #2)* Fade out to end at: | 7:15 |
| 2) | Brahms: *1st Symphony* (3rd Movement) | 5:02 |
| 3) | Respighi: *Pines of Rome* (Gianicola) | 6:20 |
| 4) | Debussy: *Nocturnes* (Sirenes) | 12:37 |
| 5) | Durufle: *In Paradisum* | 3:03 |
| 6) | Durufle: *Notre Pére* | 1:33 |
| 7) | Bach: *Suite #3* (Air) | 5:15 |

## POSITIVE CD

### Nurturing (As modified by Bruscia) (30:45)

Cuts:

| | | |
|---|---|---|
| 1) | Britten: *Simple Symphony* (Sentimental Sarabande) | 6:37 |
| 2) | Walton: *Touch her soft lips and part* | 1:51 |
| 3) | Faure: *Cantique de Jean Racine* | 6:23 |
| 4) | Faure: *Requiem* (Pie Jesu) | 3:28 |
| 5) | Puccini: *Madama Butterfly* (Humming Chorus) | 2:46 |
| 6) | Massenet: *Orchestral Suite #7* (Sous Les Tilleuls) | 4:57 |
| 7) | Schumann: *Funf Stücke im Volkston* Op. 102 | 4:44 |

### Positive Affect (As modified by Bruscia) (34:47 to 42:49)

Cuts:

| | | |
|---|---|---|
| 8) | Elgar: *Serenade for Strings* (Larghetto) | 5:49 |

| | | |
|---|---|---|
| 9) | Elgar: *Enigma Variations* (8 and 9) | 5:38 |
| 10) | Mozart: *Laudate Dominum* | 4:54 |
| 11) | Barber: *Adagio for Strings* | 7:47 |
| 12) | Brahms: *Requiem* (Part VI) | 10:34 |
| 13) | Strauss: *Death and Transfiguration* (Excerpt) | 8:04 |

Note: Open with both cuts 8 and 9 or only cut 9; end with cuts 12 and/or 13.

## PLAINTIVE CD

Cuts:

| | | |
|---|---|---|
| 1) | Albinoni: *Oboe Concerto in D Minor* | 5:23 |
| 2) | Rodrigo: *Concierto de Aranjuez* (Adagio) | 10:25 |
| 3) | Grieg: *Holberg Suite* (Air) | 5:44 |
| 4) | Arensky: *Piano Trio* (Elegia) | 7:01 |
| 5) | Vivaldi: *Violin Concerto in A Minor* (Largo) | 2:31 |
| 6) | Dvorak: *Czech Suite* (Romanze) | 4:32 |
| 7) | Bridge: *Lament* | 4:20 |
| 8) | Delius: *1st Aquarelle* | 2:28 |
| 9) | Chopin: *1st Piano Concerto* (Romance) | 9:19 |
| 10) | Rachmaninoff: *2nd Symphony* (Adagio) | 12:39 |
| 11) | Respighi: *Fountains of Rome* (Valle Guilia) | 4:28 |
| 12) | Respighi: *Fountains of Rome* (Villa Medici) | 5:45 |

## Grieving (As modified by Bruscia) (35:36)

Plaintive Cuts: 1-2-3-4-5-6: Albinoni, Rodrigo, Grieg, Arensky, Vivaldi, Dvorak.

## Grieving (As modified by Bruscia) (32:32)

Plaintive Cuts: 1-2-3-7-8-(6): Albinoni, Rodrigo, Grieg, Bridge, Delius, (Dvorak).

## Relationships (As modified by Bruscia) (32:11)

Plaintive Cuts: 9-10-11-12.: Chopin, Rachmaninoff, Respighi, Respighi.

# TRANSPORTIVE CD

## Peak Experience (As modified by Bruscia) (31:41)

Cuts:
| | | |
|---|---|---|
| 1) | Beethoven: *5th Piano Concerto* (2nd Movement) | 7:45 |
| 2) | Vivaldi: *Gloria* (Et in Terra Pax) | 5:19 |
| 3) | Bach: *Brandenburg Concerto #6* (Adagio) | 5:29 |
| 4) | Faure: *Requiem* (In Paradisum) | 3:17 |
| 5) | Wagner: *Lohengrin* (Prelude to Act I) | 9:57 |

## Transitions (As modified by Bruscia) (39:52)

Cuts:
| | | |
|---|---|---|
| 1) | Borodin: *1st Symphony* Andante | 6:12 |
| 2) | Brahms: *3rd Symphony* (Poco Allegretto) | 5:54 |
| 3) | Beethoven: *9th Symphony* (Adagio Molto) | 16:02 |
| 4) | Brahms: *2nd Piano Concerto* (Andante) | 11:45 |

# REGENERATIVE CD

## Emotional Expression II (End Only)

Cuts:
| | | |
|---|---|---|
| 1) | Shostakovitch: $5^{th}$ *Symphony* (Excerpts) | 18:38 |
| 2) | Mendelssohn: $3^{rd}$ *Symphony* (Adagio) | 11:07 |

## Death Rebirth (As modified by Bruscia) (44:54)

Cuts:
| | | |
|---|---|---|
| 3) | Wagner: *Siegfried's Funeral March* | 8:13 |
| 4) | Rachmaninoff: *Isle of the Dead* | 23:14 |
| 5) | Bach: *O Mein Jesu* | 5:08 |
| 6) | Mahler: *Der Abschied* (Excerpt) | 8:19 |

# ACTIVE CD

## Affect Release (27:40)

| | | |
|---|---|---|
| 1) | Holst: *The Planets* (Mars) | 7:43 |
| 2) | Bach: *Toccata and Fugue in D Minor for Organ* | 10:03 |
| 3) | Orff: *Carmina Burana* (Excerpts) | 5:24 |
| 4) | Orff: *Carmina Burana* (Excerpts) | 4:31 |

## Body Tape (49:09)

| | | |
|---|---|---|
| 5) | Shostakovitch: *3rd String Quartet* (Allegretto) | 6:52 |
| 6) | Shostakovitch: *8th String Quartet* (Allegretto) | 4:11 |
| 7) | Nielsen: *5th Symphony* (Excerpt) | 4:26 |
| 8) | Vierne: *Carillon de Westminster* | 7:12 |
| 9) | Beethoven: *3rd Piano Concerto* (Largo) | 9:56 |
| 10) | Prokofieff: *1st Symphony* (Larghetto) | 4:10 |

## Creativity III (End only)

| | | |
|---|---|---|
| 11) | Mahler: *5th Symphony* (Sehr Langsam) | 12:01 |

## QUICK GUIDE TO GIM PROGRAMS

| GIM Program | CD Title and Cuts | Timing |
|---|---|---|
| *Affect Release* | Active 1-2-3-4 | 27:40 |
| *Body Tape* | Active 5-6-7-8-9-10 | 49:09 |
| *Caring* | Supportive 1-2-3-4-5 | 35:29 |
| *Comforting* | See Mournful, Solace or Consoling | |
| *Consoling* | Supportive 7-3-5-9-12-6 | 38:26 |
| *Creativity I* | Creative 6-7 -8-9-10 | 36:32 |
| *Creativity II* | Emotive 7; Explorative 1-2-3-4 | 47:19 |
| *Death-Rebirth* | Regenerative 3-4-5-6 | 44:54 |
| *Emotional Expression I* | Emotive 1-2-3-4 (6) | 46:12 |
| *Explorations* | Explorative 4 (to 7:15)-5-6-7-8-9-10 | 41:04 |
| *Grieving* | Plaintive 1-2-3-4-5-6 or | 35:36 |
| | Plaintive 1-2-3-7-8-6 | 32:32 |
| *Imagery-M* | Imaginative 1-2-3-4-5  (9) | 39:47 |
| *Inner Odyssey* | Imaginative 6-7-8-9 | 33:53 |
| *Mournful* | Supportive 7-8-9-10-11-12 (6 or 2) | 39:32 |
| *Nurturing* | Positive (8)-1-2-3-4-5-6-7 | 30:45 |
| *Pastorale* | Creative 1-2-3-5 | 30:42 |
| *Peak Experience* | Transportive 1-2-3-4-5 | 31:41 |
| *Positive Affect* | Positive (8)-9-10-11-12-(13) | 34:47 - 42:49 |
| *Quiet Music* | See *Pastorale* or *Searching* | |
| *Relationships* | Plaintive 9-10-11-12 | 32:11 |
| *Searching* | Creative 2-7-3-4-5 (10) | 39:17 |
| *Solace* | Supportive 1-7-9-10-11-12-5 | 38:54 |
| *Transitions* | Transportive 6-7-8-9 | 39:52 |

* *As modified by Bruscia*

*Appendix C*

# MUSIC PROGRAMS
# FOR GUIDED IMAGERY AND MUSIC (GIM)

## Joanna Booth

### Affirmation and Joy (39:43)

| | |
|---|---|
| Vaughan Williams: *Romanza For Cello and Orchestra* | 5.03 |
| Finzi: *Introit for Violin and Orchestra* | 8.42 |
| Hovhaness: *Prayer of St. Gregory* (Trumpet Solo) | 4.45 |
| Hovhaness: *Symphony #53* (Star Dawn) | 5:08 |
| Moderato Sostenuto Con Molto Espressione (Saxophone Solo) | |
| Hovhaness: *Symphony #22* (City of Light and Angel of Light: Largo) | 3:49 |
| Hovhaness: *Symphony #29* (Trombone Concerto) | 2:00 |
| Vaughan Williams: *Symphony #5* (Passacaglia) | 10.16 |

### Bereft (39:00)

| | |
|---|---|
| Beethoven: *Coriolan Overture* | 7:20 |
| Shostakovich (arr. Barshai): *Chamber Symphony* Op. 110a (First Largo) | 5:13 |
| Tchaikovsky (arr. De Svert): *String Quartet #1* (Andante Cantabile) | 6.43 |
| Bruch: *Kol Nidrei.* | 10.29 |
| Brahms: *Symphony #1* | 9.12 |

### Doloroso (25:28)

| | |
|---|---|
| Tchaikowsky: *Song Without Words* | 3:15 |
| Canteloube: *The Forsaken Shepherdess* | 5:04 |
| Lotti: *Crucifixus* | 2:53 |
| Brahms: *Piano Quartet* (Andante) | 9.09 |
| Bizet: *Carmen Suite #2, Nocturne* (Michaela's Song, arr. Orchestra) | 5:07 |

## Lovers (29:41)

| | |
|---|---|
| Massenet: *Thais* (Meditation) | 6:01 |
| Bruch: *Concerto in E minor for Clarinet and Viola* (Allegro moderato) | 6:46 |
| Schumann: *Piano Quartet, Op. 47* (Andante cantabile) | 6:09 |
| Shostakovich: *Gadfly Suite* (Romance) | 6:30 |
| Brahms: *Piano Trio, Op. 101* (Andante grazioso) | 4:25 |

## Opening Out (25:28 or 30:00)

| | |
|---|---|
| Brahms: *Symphony #2* (3rd movement) | 5:12 |
| Dvorak: *Symphony, Op. 88* (3rd movement) | 5:48 |
| Copland: *Rodeo Suite* (Saturday Night Waltz) | 4:28 |
| Delius: *The Irmelin Prelude* | 5:00 |
| Grieg: *Peer Gynt Suite #1* (Morning) | 4:00 |
| and/or: Ravel: *Daphnis And Chloe Suite #2* (Daybreak) | 5:32 |

## Paradise (42:24)

| | |
|---|---|
| Mahler: *Symphony #1* (1st Movement) | 14:31 |
| Copland: *Rodeo Dance Suite* (Saturday Night Waltz) | 4:23 |
| Copland: *Rodeo Dance Suite* (Corral Nocturne) | 3:48 |
| Butterworth: *The Banks of Green Willow* (Idyll) | 6:02 |
| Delius (arr. Beecham): *The Walk to the Paradise Garden* | 8:39 |
| Delius (arr. Delius and Fenby): *The Irmelin Prelude* | 5:01 |

## Realm of Water (82:09)

| | |
|---|---|
| Binge: *The Watermill* | 3:53 |
| Liadov: *The Enchanted Lake* | 6:56 |
| Smetana: *The Moldau* [Excerpt] | 12:55 |
| Debussy: *En Bateau* | 4:25 |

## Tendresse (42:19)

| | |
|---|---|
| Elgar: *Sospiri* | 4:50 |
| Elgar: *Symphony #1* (Adagio) | 12:12 |
| Copland: *Clarinet Concerto* (1st movement) | 6:30 |
| Saint-Saens: *Symphony #3* (Poco Adagio) [Excerpt] | 9:45 |

Bruch: *Violin Concerto* (Adagio)      9:02

## Totally Brahms (37:00)

Brahms: *Symphony #2* (Allegretto Grazioso Quasi Andantino)      5:12

Brahms: *Symphony #2* (Adagio Non Troppo)      10:21
Brahms: *Double Concerto For Violin And Cello* (Andante)      7:19
Brahms: *Piano Concerto #2* (Andante)      14.07

## Yearning and Passion (27:12)

Elgar: *Dream Children #1* (Andante)      3:35
Villa-Lobos: *Bachianas Brasiliensis #5 for Soprano and Cellos*      6:41
     (Aria, Cantilena)
Rachmaninoff: *Piano Concerto #2* (Adagio Sostenuto)      11:53
Vaughan Williams: *Romanza for Cello and Orchestra*      5:03

*Appendix D*

# MUSIC PROGRAMS
# FOR GUIDED IMAGERY AND MUSIC (GIM)


# James Borling


## Melancholy (24:30 or 29:06)

| | |
|---|---|
| Bach: *Prelude in B Minor* | 4:11 |
| Bach: *Adagio in C* | 4:29 |
| Bach: *Mein Jesu* | 5:08 |
| Bach: *Chorale from Easter Cantata* | 3:51 |
| Bach: *Aria-Air on a G String* | 5:51 |

Possible Extender:
Bach: *Sheep May Safely Graze*                      5:36


## Deep Soul (32:04)

| | |
|---|---|
| Part: *Cantus in Memory of Benjamin Britten* | 6:04 |
| Part: *Fratres* (Version VI) | 9:57 |
| Barber: *Violin Concerto* (Adagio) | 9:28 |
| Picker: *Old and Lost Rivers* | 6:35 |

# Appendix E

# MUSIC PROGRAMS
# FOR GUIDED IMAGERY AND MUSIC (GIM)

## Kenneth E. Bruscia

### Childhood Experiences (27:04)

| | |
|---|---:|
| Ravel: *Mother Goose Suite* (Pavane, Petit Poucet) | 4:50 |
| | |
| Barber: *Capricorn Concerto* (Allegretto) | 3:16 |
| Tschaikovsky: *Album for Children* (The Old Nanny's Tale) | 2:54 |
| Mompou: *Scenas d'Enfants* (Jeu, Jeunes Filles au Jardin) | 5:35 |
| Saint-Saens: *Carnival of Animals* (Tortoises, Aquarium, Cuckoo) | 6:39 |
| Ravel: *Mother Goose Suite* (Le jardin feerique) | 3:50 |

### Consoling (38:26)

| | |
|---|---:|
| Sibelius: *Swan of Tuonela* | 8:50 |
| Debussy: *String Quartet* (Andantino) | 7:56 |
| Dvorak: *Serenade in E* (Larghetto) | 6:49 |
| Boccherini: *Cello Concerto in B-flat* (Adagio) | 5:53 |
| Shostakovich: *Piano Concerto #2* (Andantino) | 6:37 |
| Warlock: *Capriol Suite* (Pieds en l'air) | 2:21 |

### Elegy (38:33)

| | |
|---|---:|
| Grieg: *Ase's Death* | 5:43 |
| Cherubini: *Requiem in C Minor* (Introit & Kyrie) | 7:15 |
| JC Bach: *Cello Concerto in C minor* (Adagio molto espressivo) | 7:04 |
| Vivaldi: *Concerto in C Minor for 2 Cellos* (Largo) | 3:31 |
| Cherubini: *Requiem in C Minor* (Pie Jesu) | 3:49 |

Cherubini: *Requiem in C Minor* (Graduale)          1:43
Bridge: *Suite for String Orchestra* (Nocturne)     6:17
Bizet: *L'Arlesienne Suite* (Adagietto)             3:11

## Faith (33:11)

Part: *Cantus in Memory of Benjamin Britten*                 5:00
Ives: *Unanswered Question*                                  6:03
Alwyn: *Symphony #5* (4th movement)                          5:43
Saint-Saens: *Symphony #3* (2nd movement)                    9:10
Messiaen: *O Sacrum Convivium* (A Hymn for the World)        7:15

## Gaia (43:34)

Delius: *North Country Sketches* (Autumn)                    8:20
Part: *Fratres* (Version VI)                                 9:57
Elgar: *Sospiri*                                             5:17
Bach-Respighi: *Chorale Prelude, BWV62* (Come Redeemer)      5:33
Strauss: *Four Last Songs* (At Sunset)                       9:54
Handel: *Pastorale*                                          4:04

## Heroine's Journey (41:06)

Canteloube: *Songs of the Auvergne* (Bailero)                6:25
Glazunov: *Spring,* Opus 34                                  9:20
Schmidt: *Intermezzo from Notre Dame*                        6:12
Canteloube: *Songs of the Auvergne* (Deux Bourees)           5:25
Canteloube: *Songs of the Auvergne* (Antony)                 4:04
Mussorgsky: *Pictures at an Exhibition* (Great Gate)         6:28

## Lamentations (41:56)

Marcello: *Oboe Concerto in D Minor* (Adagio)                4:38
Albinoni: *Adagio in G Minor* (Adagio)                       11:46
Tschaikovsky: *Symphony #6* (Adagio Lamentoso)               9:36
Bach: *Adagio in C* (Stokowski Transcription)                4:03
Mahler: Symphony #5 (Adagietto: Sehr Langsam)                11:53

# Mournful (39:32)

| | |
|---|---|
| Sibelius: *Swan of Tuonela* | 8:50 |
| Goreczki: *Symphony #3* (2nd movement) | 10:13 |
| Boccherini: *Cello Concerto in B-flat* (Adagio) | 5:53 |
| Russian Folk Songs: *O the Steppes* | 4:09 |
| Russian Chant for Vespers: *The Joy of Those Who Mourn* | 3:43 |
| Shostakovich: *Piano Concerto #2* (Andantino) | 6:37 |

# Nostalgia (38:10)

| | |
|---|---|
| Alwyn: *Concerto Grosso #1* (Siciliano) | 4:15 |
| Barber: *Piano Concerto* (2nd movement) | 7:54 |
| Bach: *Siciliano* | 2:48 |
| Elgar: *Dream Children* | 3:25 |
| Elgar: *Dream Children* | 4:13 |
| Bach: *Piano Concerto in E* | 6:38 |
| Alwyn: *Sinfonietta* (Adagio) | 6:07 |
| Parry: *Minuet from Radnor* | 2:52 |

# Past Lives (44:52)

| | |
|---|---|
| Barber: *Fadograph of a Yestern Scene* | 6:53 |
| Bartok: *Piano Concerto #3* (Adagio Religioso) | 9:28 |
| Mathias: *Symphony #2* (2nd movement) | 7:27 |
| Sibelius: *Nocturne* | 5:05 |
| Debussy: *La Cathedrale Engloutie* | 8:34 |
| Respighi: *Three Botticelli Pictures* (The Birth of Venus) | 5:29 |
| Sibelius: *Pelleas et Melisande Suite* (Pastorale) | 1:56 |

# Pastorale (30:42)

| | |
|---|---|
| Debussy: *Prelude to Afternoon of a Faun* | 10:30 |
| Liadov: *Enchanted Lake* | 7:58 |
| Holst: *The Planets* (Neptune) | 8:07 |
| Grieg: *Cradle Song* | 4:07 |

## Searching (39:17)

| | |
|---|---:|
| Liadov: *Enchanted Lake* | 7:58 |
| Vaughan Williams: *Symphony #2* (Adagio) | 12:04 |
| Holst: *The Planets* (Venus) | 8:07 |
| Holst: *The Planets* (Neptune) | 7:01 |
| Grieg: *Cradle Song* | 4:07 |

## Solace (44:37)

| | |
|---|---:|
| Haydn: *Cello Concerto in C* (Adagio) | 8:36 |
| Sibelius: *Swan of Tuonela* | 8:50 |
| Boccherini: *Cello Concerto in B-flat* (Adagio) | 5:53 |
| Russian Folk Songs: *O the Steppes* | 4:09 |
| Russian Chant for Vespers: *The Joy of Those Who Mourn* | 3:43 |
| Shostakovich: *Piano Concerto #2* (Andantino) | 6:37 |
| Dvorak: *Serenade in E* (Larghetto) | 6:49 |

## Soliloquy For Men (31:55)

| | |
|---|---:|
| *Barber: *Hermit Songs* (The Crucifixion) | 2:13 |
| Mompou: *Los Improperios* (Ego te potavi) | 2:29 |
| Copland: *Clarinet Concerto* (2nd movement) | 7:03 |
| Schumann: *Alte Laute* | 2:29 |
| *Barber: *Hermit Songs* (The Desire for Hermitage) | 3:36 |
| Rachmaninoff: *Piano Concerto #1* (Lento) | 6:43 |
| Mahler: *Ruckertlieder* (Ich bin der Welt) | 7:22 |

Note: Only use the clarinet/piano transcription of the Barber Songs.

## Sublime I (35:07)

| | |
|---|---:|
| Chopin: *Piano Concerto #2 in F* (2nd movement) | 9:39 |
| Elgar: *Cello Concerto, Op. 85* (Adagio) | 4:55 |
| Mozart: *Clarinet Quintet in A* (Larghetto) | 7:28 |
| Mendelssohn: *String Symphony #7* (Andante) | 5:32 |
| Bach: *Piano Concerto in F, BWV 1056* (Largo) | 3:25 |
| Sibelius: *Scaramouche* | 4:08 |

## Sublime II  (37:14)

| | |
|---|---|
| Finzi: *Eclogue for Piano and Strings* | 9:56 |
| Bach: *Adagio in C* (Stokowski Transcription) | 4:29 |
| Mozart: *Ave Verum Corpus* K. 618 | 3:53 |
| Vaughan Williams: *Symphony #5* (Romanza - Lento) | 11:42 |
| Rachmaninoff: *Vespers* (Ave Maria) | 3:28 |
| Kedrov: *Our Father* | 3:47 |

## Warrior/King  (46:31)

| | |
|---|---|
| Rachmaninoff: *Russian Song for Chorus and Orchestra, Op. 41* | 3:17 |
| Alwyn: *Symphony #5* (1st movement) | 3:21 |
| Walton: *Symphony #1* (1st movement) | 13:14 |
| Rachmaninoff: *The Bells, Op.35* (4th movement) | 10:33 |
| Finzi: *Suite from Love's Labours Lost* (Introduction) | 4:15 |
| Durufle: *Messe Cum Jubilo* (Benedictus | 2:19 |
| Durufle: *Messe Cum Jubilo* (Sanctus) | 3:32 |
| Thomson: *Allelulia* (Male voices only) | 6:00 |

# MUSIC PROGRAMS
# FOR GUIDED IMAGERY AND MUSIC (GIM)

## Marilyn Clark

### Mythic Journey One: The Hero's Journey (40:58)

*The Call to Adventure:*
Williams: *Oboe Concerto* (Minuet and Musette)      3:30

*Crossing the Threshold of Adventure:*
Bartok: *Concerto for Orchestra* (Elegia)      6:00
Ennio Morricone: *Mission Soundtrack* (Gabriel's Oboe)      3:30

*Trials and Tasks:*
Hovhannes: *Meditation on Orpheus*      12:00

*Reaching the Nadir and Receiving the Boon:*
Mussorsky: *Pictures at an Exhibition*      8:15
     (The Hut on Fowl's Legs and The Great Gate of Kiev)
Durufle: *Requiem* (In Paradisum)      2:50

*The Return:*
Ennio Morricone: *Mission Soundtrack*
     (Gabriel's Oboe, Second rendition)      2:20

*Crossing the Return Threshold:*
Stravinsky: *Firebird Suite* (Finale)      3:00

## Mythic Journey Two: Persephone (39:51)

*Innocence lost:*
Albinoni: *Oboe Concerto*                                                    5:23

*The Descent:*
Arvo Part: *Tabla Rasa* (Canticle for Benjamin Britten)          4:50

*Exploring the Underworld:*
Shostakovich: *Piano Concerto #2*                                       6:37
Debussy: *String Quartet*                                                   7:56

*Making the Ascent:*
Bach: *Shepherd's Song*                                                     5:55
Dvorak: *Serenade*                                                           6:49
Warlock: *Pieds en l'air*                                                    2:21

*Appendix G*


# MUSIC PROGRAMS
# FOR GUIDED IMAGERY AND MUSIC (GIM)


## Denise E. Grocke


### The Magical Inner Child Program (19:00)

| | |
|---|---|
| Dohnanyi: *Variations on a Nursery Theme, Op. 25* | 14:04 |
| (Theme and variations 1-9, and finale) [excerpts] | |
| Tchaikovsky: *Nutcracker Suite* (Dance of the Sugar Plum Fairy) | 2:02 |
| Respighi: *Ancient Airs and Dances, Suite #2* (Laura soave) [excerpt] | 2:54 |


### The Adventurous Inner Child Program (11:33)

| | |
|---|---|
| Tchaikovsky: *Nutcracker Suite* (March) | 2:27 |
| Brahms: *Piano Concerto #2 in B-flat, Op. 83* (4th movement) [excerpt] | 4:51 |
| Tchaikovsky: *Nutcracker Suite* (Trepak) | 1:06 |
| Shostakovitch: *Ballet Suite #1* (Dance) | 1:39 |
| Brahms: *Waltz in Ab, Op. 39, No.20* | 1:30 |

# MUSIC PROGRAMS
# FOR GUIDED IMAGERY AND MUSIC (GIM)

## Linda Keiser Mardis

### Changing Patterns (45:06)

| | |
|---|---|
| Suk: *Under the Apple Tree, Op. 20* (A Dark Shade Fell) | 3:48 |
| Grieg: *Elegaic Melodies* (The Wounded Heart) | 2:55 |
| Rachmaninoff: *Vespers* (Simeon's Song) | 3:19 |
| Debussy: *La Cathedrale Engloutie* (Stokowski Transcription) | 6:43 |
| Glazunov: *Overture #1* (On Three Greek Themes) | 13:16 |
| Rachmaninoff: *Vespers* (Blessed is the Man) | 4:20 |
| Glazunov: *Spring* (Vesna) | 10:45 |

### Creativity I (44:42)

| | |
|---|---|
| Sibelius: *Symphony #2* (Allegretto) | 10:37 |
| Vaughan Williams: *In the Fen Country* | 17:40 |
| Delius: *Koanga* (La Calinda) | 4:05 |
| Kallinikov: *Symphony #2* (Andante) | 8:02 |
| Sibelius: *Scaramouche* (Flute Solo) | 4:08 |

### Creativity II (45:56)

| | |
|---|---|
| D'Indy: *Symphony on French Mountain Air* (1st movement) | 11:44 |
| Vaughan Williams: *Norfolk Rhapsody, No. 1* | 11:45 |
| Mendelssohn: *Symphony #3* (Vivace non troppo) | 4:09 |
| Faure: *Pavane, Op. 1* | 6:43 |
| Ravel: *Daphnis & Chloe* (Suite #2) | 11:41 |

## Creativity III (40:37)

| | |
|---|---:|
| Wagner: *Siegfried's Idyll* | 18:26 |
| Hanson: *Symphony #2* (2nd movement) | 7:21 |
| Elgar: *Sospiri* | 5:00 |
| Mahler: *Symphony #5* (4th movement) | 9:50 |

## Expanded Awareness (44:18)

| | |
|---|---:|
| Vaughan Williams: *Fantasia on a theme by Thomas Tallis* | 16:08 |
| Vaughan Williams: *Symphony #5* (1st Movement, Preludio: Moderato) | 12:40 |
| Vaughan Williams: *The Lark Ascending* | 15:30 |

## Grieving (38:45)

| | |
|---|---:|
| Marcello: *Oboe Concerto in C minor* (Adagio) | 4:28 |
| (or Albinoni: *Oboe Concerto in D minor* (Adagio) | 6:00 |
| Rodrigo: *Concierto de Aranjuez* (Adagio) | 10:27 |
| Grieg: *Holberg Suite* (Air) | 6:03 |
| Dvorak: *4 Romantic Pieces* (Larghetto) | 6:27 |
| Bach: *Prelude in E-flat minor* | 5:10 |
| Dvorak: *Czech Suite* (Romanze) | 4:38 |

## Mythic/Mystic (35:53)

| | |
|---|---:|
| Holst: *The Planets* (Neptune) | 7:56 |
| Bach: *Magnificat* (Suscepit) | 2:25 |
| Mozart: *Clarinet Quintet, K581* (Larghetto) | 6:26 |
| Vaughan Williams: *English Folksong Suite* (Intermezzo) | 3:17 |
| Stanford: *Piano Concerto #2, Op. 126* (Adagio molto) | 12:36 |
| Durufle: *Requiem, Op. 9* (In Paradisum) | 3:13 |

## Program 33 (41:46)

| | |
|---|---:|
| Bach: *Christmas Oratorio* (Sinfonia) | 6:40 |
| Bach: *Fantasia in C minor* (Elgar Transcription) | 5:46 |
| Bach: *Sicilian, BWV 1107* (Stokowski Transcription) | 2:43 |
| Bach: *Cantata #21* (Seufzer, Tranen, Kummer, Not) | 4:16 |
| Bach: *Cantata, BWV 82* (Schlummert ein) | 6:30 |
| Bach: *Geistliches Lied* (Mein Jesu) (Stokowski Transcription) | 5:27 |

Bach:  *Cantata, BWV 115* (Bete aber acuh dabei)                              7:07
Bach:  *Cantatas, BWV 147* (Herz und Mund und Tat and Leben)       3:17

## Program 34 (33:36)

Aubert:  *Feuilles d'Images* (Confidence)                                          3:41
Brahms:  *Clarinet Quintet in B minor, Op. 115* (Adagio)             10:26
Rachmaninoff:  *Vocalise* (Orchestral transcription)                    5:82
Faure:  *Pelleas et Melisande, Op. 80* (Prelude)                          7:14
Haydn:  *Symphony #13 in D* (Adagio cantabile)                          5:53

*Appendix I*

# MUSIC PROGRAMS
# FOR GUIDED IMAGERY AND MUSIC (GIM)

## Alison Short

### Reconciliation (40:58)

| | |
|---|---:|
| Handel: *Concerto Grosso, Op.3 No.2* (2nd movement) | 2:56 |
| Kreisler: *Concerto for Violin in the style of Vivaldi* | 4.05 |
| Purcell: *Dido and Aeneas* (Dido's Lament) | 4:06 |
| Purcell: *The Fairy Queen* (If love's a sweet passion) | 2:40 |
| Mozart: *Sinfonia Concertante, K.364* (Andante) | 11.56 |
| Ravel: *Piano Concerto in G minor* (Adagio assai) | 9:26 |
| Lili Boulanger: *Les Sirenes* | 5:49 |

*Appendix J*


# MUSIC PROGRAMS
# FOR GUIDED IMAGERY AND MUSIC (GIM)


## Ruth Skaggs


## All Bach (34:50)

| | |
|---|---|
| Bach: *Passacaglia and Fugue in C Minor* | 14:49 |
| Bach: *Prelude in B Minor, BWV 869* | 4:09 |
| Bach: *Nun Komm der Heiden Heiland, BWV 659* | 4:39 |
| Bach: *Piano Concerto in E Major, BWV 1053* (Siciliano) | 5:53 |
| Bach: *Air on a G String* | 5:51 |

## Centering (31:46)

| | |
|---|---|
| Bach: *Christmas Oratorio* (Sinfonia) | 6:30 |
| Vivaldi: *Trio in C, RV82* (Larghetto) | 2:22 |
| Vivaldi: *Guitar Concerto in D major, RV93* (Largo) | 6:05 |
| Boccherini: *Cello Concerto #7 in G major* (Adagio) | 4:06 |
| Haydn: *Cello Concerto in D major* (Adagio) | 6:07 |
| Bach: *Sonata in E-flat for flute and harpsichord, BWV 1031* (Siciliano) | 2:17 |
| Mendelssohn: *Song Without Words, Op. 30, No. 1* | 4:19 |

## Conversations (40:13)

| | |
|---|---|
| Elgar: *Cello Concerto, Op. 85* (Adagio) | 4:55 |
| Ravel: *Piano Concerto in G major* (Adagio) | 9:09 |
| Bizet: *Carmen Suite #1* (Entr'acte) | 2:49 |
| Mendelssohn: *Violin Concerto* (Andante) | 8:13 |
| Mozart: *Concerto for Two Pianos, No. 10* (Andante) | 7:09 |
| Schmidt: *Notre Dame* (Intermezzo) | 4:38 |

Stravinsky: *The Fairy's Kiss* (Adagio)     3:07

## Catharsis (25:23)

Saint-Saens: *Symphony #3* (Maestoso) [excerpt]     7:17
Beethoven: *Symphony #5* (Allegro) [excerpt]     4:57
Beethoven: *Symphony #9* (4th movement) [excerpt]     6:27
Bach: *Giant Fugue, BWV 680*     4:03

## The Crucible (42:28)

Bach: *Chaconne in D minor* (transcribed for 8 cellos)     14:15
Bach: *Prelude and Fugue No. 8* (transcribed for 8 cellos)     9:58
Elgar: *Symphony #2* (Larghetto)     15:15
Bizet: *L'Arlesienne Suite #1* (Adagietto)     3:00

## The Gathering (35:55)

Thuille: *Sextet for Wind Quintet and Klavier* (Larghetto)     8:39
Mozart: *Clarinet Quintet in A* (Larghetto)     7:08
Strauss, R: *Concerto for Oboe and Small Orchestra* (Andante)     8:13
Mozart: *Adagio in E for Guitar and Orchestra*     7:01
Danzi: *Wind quintet* (Andante con moto)     4:54

## Grief, Loss, Loneliness (30:43)

Sibelius: *Swan of Tuonela*     8:47
Alfven: *Gustavus Adolphus Suite, Op. 49* (Elegy)     5:19
Grieg: *Peer Gynt Suite #1* (Aase's Death)     4:34
Bach: *Mein Jesu, BWV 478*     5:07
Grieg: *Piano Concerto* (Adagio)     7:11

## Emotionally Evocative (35:24)

Barber: *Violin Concerto* (Andante)     8:49
Brahms: *Double Concerto* (Andante)     7:40
Bruch: *Concerto for Two Pianos* (Adagio ma non troppo)     8:14
Mahler: *Symphony #5* (Adagietto)     10:50

# Life Rhythms (33:29)

| | |
|---|---|
| Brahms: *Symphony #1* (Allegro) | 11:06 |
| Mahler: *Symphony # 2* (Andante Moderato) | 11:14 |
| Mahler: *Symphony #2* (5th movement) [excerpt] | 11:09 |

# Sanctuary (30:36)

| | |
|---|---|
| Satie: *Gymnopedie No. 3* | 2:42 |
| Debussy: *Reverie* | 4:35 |
| Faure: *Pelleas et Melisande* (Sicilienne) | 4:03 |
| Chopin: *Piano Concerto #1* (Larghetto) | 9:57 |
| Finzi: *Romanze for String Orchestra* | 7:01 |
| Humperdinck: *Hansel and Gretel* (Prayer)` | 2:58 |

# Serene Sketches (31:10)

| | |
|---|---|
| Mussorgsky: *Dawn on the Moscow River* | 4:55 |
| Respighi: *Suite in G Major* (Pastorale) | 5:25 |
| Delius: *A Song Before Sunrise* | 5:52 |
| Barber: *Canzone for Flute and Piano, Op. 38a* | 4:25 |
| Delius: *Fennimore and Gerda* (Intermezzo) | 5:13 |
| Barber: *Souvenir,Op. 28* (Pas de deux) | 4:52 |

# Soul Journey (32:40)

| | |
|---|---|
| Hovhaness: *Prayer of St. Gregory* | 4:45 |
| Durufle: *Requiem* (Lux Eterna) | 4:10 |
| Patterson: *Mass of the Sea* (Sanctus) | 6:21 |
| Hanson: *Symphony #4* (Largo) [excerpt] | 5:37 |
| Rachmaninoff: *Vespers* (Blessed Be The Man) | 6:12 |
| Rachmaninoff: *Praise Be The Name of the Lord* | 3:22 |
| Durufle: *Requiem* (In Paradisum) | 3:13 |

# Twentieth Century Psyche (30:52)

| | |
|---|---|
| Hovhaness: *Prelude & Quadruple Fugue* (Prelude) | 3:00 |
| Shostakovich: *Piano Concerto #1* (Lento) | 8:24 |
| Aaron Copland: *Tender Land Suite* (Introduction) | 9:32 |
| Shostakovich: *Piano Concerto #2* (Andante) | 6:37 |

William Walton: *See What His Love Can Do*                               4:18

## Vital Force (29:10)

Wagner: *Symphony in C major* (Andante)                               11:16
Franck: *Symphony in D Minor* (Allegro non troppo)            11:10
Beethoven: *Symphony #1* (Andante cantabile)                       6:54

*Appendix K*


# MUSIC PROGRAMS
# FOR GUIDED IMAGERY AND MUSIC (GIM)


## Sierra Stearns


### Abandonment to Bonding (30:00 or 32:25)

| | |
|---|---|
| Sibelius: *Swan of Tuonela* | 9:24 |
| Stravinsky: *The Firebird Suite* (Berceuse) | 3:39 |
| Chopin: *Prelude, Op.28, No. 4* | 2:07 |
| Bach: *Suite in D Major, BWV 1068* (Air) | 5:24 |
| Saint-Saens: *Carnival of the Animals* (The Swan) | 3:22 |
| Schumann: *Kinderszenen* (Dreaming) | 2:52 |
| Possible Extenders: (Either but not both) | |
| *Songs From a Secret Garden* (Serenade to Spring) | 3:12 |
| Joanne Shenandoah: *Lifeblood* (Path of Beauty) | 5:37 |

### Reflections (27:15)

| | |
|---|---|
| Respighi: *Pines of Rome* (Pines of the Janiculum Way) | 6:39 |
| Debussy: *La Cathedrale Engloutie* (Stokowski Transcription) | 6:36 |
| Holst: *The Planets* (Venus) | 8:20 |
| Mozart: *Serenade for Winds, K361* (Gran Partita – Adagio) | 5:40 |

### Paradox (Contemporary) (32:35 or 31:51)

| | |
|---|---|
| *Soundtrack from The Red Violin* (Red Violin Theme) | 2:50 |
| *Soundtrack from The Red Violin* (Red Violin) | 2:42 |
| Peter Kater: *Pagen Saints* (Dirge) | 5:47 |
| Peter Kater: *Pagan Saints* (Throes) | 4:27 |
| Jonathon Elias: *The Prayer Cycle* (Hope | 6:38 |

(or Jonathon Elias: *The Prayer Cycle* (Grace)                          5:54)
Michael Hoppe: *The Unforgetting Heart* (selection #1)                  4:51
Michael Hoppe: *The Unforgetting Heart* (selection #5)                  2:57
Michael Hoppe: *The Unforgetting Heart* (selection#9)                   2:23

**Transcendence (25:27)** (Developed with Carol Bush and James Borling)

Vaughan Williams: *Symphony #5* (I Preludio: Moderato)                 12:30
Vaughan Williams: *Symphony #5* (III Romanza: Lento)                   12:57

**For Addictions (27:10)** (Developed with Carol Bush and Jim Borling)

Phillip Glass: *Low Symphony* (2nd movement: Some Are)                 11:15
Phillip Glass: *Low Symphony* (3rd movement: Warszawa)                 15:55

**Loss (25:34)**

Albinoni: *Adagio in G minor for Strings and Organ*                    9:32
Bach: *Come Sweet Death* (Stokowski Transcription)                     5:04
Bach: *Mein Jesu*                                                      5:07
Bach: *Aria*                                                          5:51

**Sorrow (23:49)**

Marcello: *Oboe Concerto in D minor* (Adagio)                          5:00
Elgar: *Cello Concerto, Op. 85* (1st movement)                        7:51
Sviridov: *Three Choruses to "Tsar Feodor Ioannovich"* (Second Chorus) 3:49
Sviridov: *Three Choruses to "Tsar Feodor Ioannovich"* (Third Chorus)  3:16
Mozart: *Ave Verum Corpus, K.618*                                      3:53
                        Possible Extender:
Lloyd Webber: *Requiem* (Pie Jesu)                                     3:58

*Appendix L*

# MUSIC PROGRAMS
# FOR GUIDED IMAGERY AND MUSIC (GIM)


## Lisa and Joseph Summer


### Hero's Journey (31:44)

| | |
|---|---:|
| Dvorak: *Symphony #9* (2nd Movement) | 8:18 |
| Stravinsky: *4 Norwegian Moods* (Song) | 5:44 |
| Prokofiev: *Romeo and Juliet* (Morning Dance) | 4:16 |
| Mahler: *Symphony #1* (4th Movement) | 7:02 |
| Wagner: *Die Meistersinger* (Overture) | 6:24 |